SPIEGEL

THE INCREDIBLE LIFE AND TIMES OF HOLLYWOOD'S MOST ICONOCLASTIC PRODUCER, THE MIRACLE WORKER WHO WENT FROM PENNILESS REFUGEE TO SHOWBIZ LEGEND, AND MADE POSSIBLE *THE AFRICAN QUEEN, ON THE WATERFRONT, THE BRIDGE ON THE RIVER KWAI,* AND *LAWRENCE OF ARABIA*

Natasha Fraser-Cavassoni

timewarner
paperbacks

For Jean-Pierre–"Mon Ange"

A *Time Warner* Paperback

First published in Great Britain in 2003 by Little, Brown

This edition published by Time Warner Paperbacks in 2004

A CIP catalogue record for this book
is available from the British Library.

ISBN 0 7515 3555 9

Printed and bound in Great Britain by
Bookmarque Ltd, Croydon, Surrey

Time Warner Paperbacks
An imprint of
Time Warner Books UK
Brettenham House
Lancaster Place
London WC2E 7EN

www.TimeWarnerBooks.co.uk

Sam Spiegel was Natasha Fraser-Cavassoni's first employer. She worked as a 'company assistant' on *Betrayal* – his last picture. A journalist since 1988, Fraser-Cavassoni has respectively written and been a staff member for *Interview Magazine*, *Women's Wear Daily* and *W* magazine. She is currently the European Editor for *Harper's Bazaar*. Born in London in 1963, she has lived in Los Angeles, New York and Paris, where she presently resides with her husband and two daughters.

'Her book nails the most elusive guy since Sammy Glick, and, unlike most opuses about Hollywood types written nowadays, it reads like a dream. She sure got old S. P. Eagle – as he [Spiegel] was for a while – right' Taki, *Spectator*

'In devoting chapters to Spiegel's greatest hits, such as *On The Waterfront*, *The African Queen* and *Suddenly, Last Summer*, Fraser-Cavassoni is on well-trod terrain. Many accounts and memoirs already describe these projects – yet they are cast in a different light when the emphasis shifts to Spiegel . . . Memos exchanged by Lean and Spiegel – Spartan and Maharajah, respectively – reveal articulate, evenly matched combatants engaged in a creative tug of war' Janet Maslin, *New York Times*

'[Fraser-Cavassoni's] account is probably the fullest yet . . . She gives free rein to the gossip. Her book is thoroughly researched and entertaining' *The Economist*

'[Fraser-Cavassoni] chronicles the whole, wild ride in an engrossing biography that documents his professional achievements and vividly captures a personality as epic as any of his films. It's all here: the sleazy financial maneuvers and creepy taste for underage girls that makes Spiegel a decidedly flawed protagonist, as well as the wit, sophistication and Old World charm that make him a titanic fixture, the likes of which the movie industry will not see again' Wendy Smith, *Variety*

'This is an exhaustively researched, hugely entertaining biography. It is, to quote Billy Wilder, "S. P. Lendid." ' David Parkinson, *Empire*

'Fraser-Cavassoni's meticulously researched bio of the movie mogul behind Hollywood spectacles like *The African Queen* will inspire anyone who's ever fantasized about hitting it big in Tinseltown' *Marie Claire* US

'A conscientious chronicle of an extraordinary life' Gerald Kaufman, *Sunday Telegraph*

'After seven years of research and hundreds of interviews, Fraser-Cavassoni has turned out a delightful account of on-set intrigue and illicit affairs – in business as well as in love' Dana Thomas, *Newsweek*

'Fraser-Cavassoni offers illuminating insights into the making of his films and into his relationships with directors ... [a] generous, enjoyable and well-written biography' Michael Stern, *Jewish Chronicle*

'Natasha Fraser-Cavassoni writes a near-flawless account of Spiegel's many sides, and the cinematic legacy he leaves behind' *Los Angeles Confidential*

'Compelling anecdotes show a less-than-queenly side to Katharine Hepburn and a squeamish aspect to Humphrey Bogart. Also dished out are slices of skinny on Spiegel's onetime partner John Huston and not-very-pretty tales of Marlon Brando, Huston, Lean and others' Michael R. Farkash, *Hollywood Reporter*

'[Fraser-Cavassoni] presents an intriguing eye-opener on one of the most energetic and influential Hollywood producers' David Archibald, *Scotland on Sunday*

'A biography ... that's impressing all the right people (Harvey Weinstein)' Sebastian Shakespeare, *Tatler*

'Neatly captured ... engrossing ... clear-eyed but not ungenerous ... what made Spiegel unforgettable was the astonishing act of artistic self-creation that was his life. Fraser-Cavassoni interviewed scores of the producer's old friends and colleagues, and seemingly every one of them had a one-liner about him' John Powers, *US Vogue*

'The gripping tale of an enigma' Joshua Rich, *Entertainment Weekly*

'Meticulously researched, evenhanded, *Sam Spiegel* serves up the warts, the brilliant successes and many, many more warts ... Fraser-Cavassoni seems to have possessed both the social entrée and necessary doggedness for this, her now superb production'
Steven A. Alford, *Houston Chronicle*

'A Hollywood legend comes alive, flamboyantly ... [a] thorough, lively biography' Leah Rozen, *People Magazine*

'As portrayed in this compelling biography, Spiegel was, like his films, entirely larger-than-life: a domineering, manipulative character of gargantuan, globe-shagging appetites – in food, art, and especially women – who nonetheless possessed something of the taste and grace of an old-world aristocrat. He was a compulsive fabulist – a boon for someone in the movie industry' Andy Gill, *Word*

'As depicted affectionately but not uncritically by Natasha Fraser-Cavassoni in this compulsively readable biography, Spiegel was in a class by himself, even among his fellow moguls, as a charming scoundrel' Calev Ben-David, *Jerusalem Post*

'Natasha Fraser-Cavassoni gives a full and detailed picture, and reveals a great deal about the world in which Spiegel lived and flourished' Clive Donner, *Oldie*

'Meticulous research ... as [the] new biography of the legendary producer illustrates, Spiegel's own life would have made far more fascinating viewing than any of his films' Suzanne Harrington, *Irish Examiner*

'This is a rollicking account of the movie mogul who made *Lawrence of Arabia* and *The African Queen* – a liar, a cheat and a conman who makes great copy' Michelle Griffin, Australian *Business Review Weekly*

'[Spiegel] remains the only producer to win, by himself, the best picture Oscar three times ... Fraser-Cavassoni's biography gives a real sense of his character, both the smooth and the rough' Colin Waters, Irish *Sunday Tribune*

'Massively entertaining (and tall) tales about the golden age litter the pages – the two chapters covering *Lawrence* are worth the price alone' Simon Brennan, *Premiere Magazine*

SAM

Contents

Introduction   XI

PART I 1901–1939

CHAPTER ONE   **Childhood**   3

CHAPTER TWO   **Palestine**   13

CHAPTER THREE   **San Francisco**   19

CHAPTER FOUR   **Berlin**   25

CHAPTER FIVE   **Vienna**   33

CHAPTER SIX   **London**   39

CHAPTER SEVEN   **Paris/Mexico**   47

PART II 1939–1954

CHAPTER EIGHT   **Hollywood**   57

CHAPTER NINE   ***Tales of Manhattan***   67

CHAPTER TEN   **North Crescent Drive**   79

CHAPTER ELEVEN   ***The Stranger***   91

CHAPTER TWELVE   **The Second Mrs. Spiegel and Horizon Pictures**   101

CHAPTER THIRTEEN   ***The Prowler*** **and** ***When I Grow Up***   117

Contents

CHAPTER FOURTEEN   *The African Queen*   129

CHAPTER FIFTEEN   *Melba*   147

CHAPTER SIXTEEN   *On the Waterfront*   157

PART III 1955–1985

CHAPTER SEVENTEEN   The Third Mrs. Spiegel and
The Strange One   177

CHAPTER EIGHTEEN   *The Bridge on the River Kwai*   191

CHAPTER NINETEEN   *Suddenly, Last Summer*   217

CHAPTER TWENTY   *Lawrence of Arabia*–Part I   233

CHAPTER TWENTY-ONE   *Lawrence of Arabia*–Part II   259

CHAPTER TWENTY-TWO   The Spiegel Lifestyle   275

CHAPTER TWENTY-THREE   *The Chase, The Happening, The Night
of the Generals,* and *The Swimmer*   291

CHAPTER TWENTY-FOUR   *Nicholas and Alexandra*   317

CHAPTER TWENTY-FIVE   *The Last Tycoon*   335

CHAPTER TWENTY-SIX   *Betrayal*   361

CHAPTER TWENTY-SEVEN   The Final Years   375

Epilogue   383

Author's Note   387

A Condensed Filmography   395

Notes   405

Selected Bibliography   473

Photo Credits   481

Index   483

"Remember Churchill's line about Russia? A riddle wrapped in a mystery inside an enigma ... hmm, that was Sam."

—BETTY SPIEGEL

Introduction

The Academy Awards, March 26, 1958. There was a hush in the auditorium as Gary Cooper struggled with the envelope. Cooper paused, broke into one of his shy, charismatic smiles and announced: "Sam Spiegel for *The Bridge on the River Kwai*." A loud round of applause broke out in the RKO Pantages Theatre, while certain heads turned toward the film producer.

Once again, three years after gaining his first Oscar as the producer of *On the Waterfront*, Spiegel had won for best picture. A further five years on, he would repeat his Academy Award experience with *Lawrence of Arabia*. All three triumphs were financed by Columbia, and led to Spiegel becoming the studio's uncrowned prince. "Uncrowned because it would have been too expensive if he was crowned," said the producer Charles Schneer.

Spiegel had a face that stood out in a crowd. "In profile, he looked like a Roman emperor," said director Fred Zinnemann. His black hair was oiled and swept back behind large ears, showing a high forehead and a forceful, prominent nose. The eyebrows, more arched to the right than the left, indicated a mixture of wisdom and humor, while a sparse line of eyelashes, curled and pushed back to his heavy lids, betrayed a certain old-world vanity and charm. Yet his dark brown eyes, which usually twinkled, were still that night.

He knew better than to make an awkward rush for the stage. Like a portly eagle preparing for flight, Spiegel murmured something to his beautiful, much younger wife, and rose sedately. Immaculately dressed, with a white handkerchief in his tuxedo pocket, Spiegel's physique was hardly breathtaking; the fifty-seven-year-old stood at five foot nine, weighed over two hundred pounds, and was rotund with short, skinny legs, yet he was noted for his "nutty elegance."

As he walked to the stage, while the orchestra played the picture's

"Colonel Bogey" theme music, a friend in the crowd caught him unaware, and he smiled. He nervously licked his top lip. Spiegel was tense, but the moment Cooper presented him with the gilded statue, his face creased into its familiar dimples and smile. His joy–like a schoolboy being awarded the most important sports day prize–was overwhelming.

"The soundstages of Hollywood have been extended in recent years to the farthest corners of the world," Spiegel began. "No land is inviolate to the glare of our camera. Yet it is fitting and proper that people the world over are waiting for a decision which only you in this community are able to render . . ."

As his resonant voice continued, he pronounced every syllable, giving authority and pace to his words. The tradition in those days was that of one-line speeches during the awards ceremony, but, as always, Spiegel–a rogue elephant–set his own tone. Also, typically, the Eastern European producer was awash in intrigue, which that night concerned the authorship of his film's screenplay.

Pierre Boulle, who had written *The Bridge over the River Kwai,* the novel on which the picture had been based, was credited, and earlier in the ceremony, when the film won for best screenplay, Kim Novak collected Boulle's award. Breathy and mermaidlike in a tight sequined dress, the actress said that her boss, the late Harry Cohn, was "very proud" of the film.

In fact, the legendary studio head had not been. The picture was to put Columbia back in the black, but when first hearing of the project, Cohn had picked up the telephone and shouted, "How can you idiots in the New York office give a crook like Sam Spiegel two million dollars and let him go to some place like Ceylon?"

Nevertheless, the burning question in many people's minds that night was, "How the hell could a Frenchman write this script?" A month before the Oscars, gossip columnists such as Hedda Hopper had bandied about the names of two blacklisted writers–Carl Foreman and Michael Wilson. Was it just a coincidence that the theme music from *High Noon* was played at Cooper's entrance? *High Noon* happened to be the film that had earned the actor's last Oscar, but it was also Foreman's last credited film for Hollywood before becoming a victim of the McCarthy era. Or was it a nod from producer Jerry Wald, responsible for that evening's entertainment, to show that he was in the know about the film's dubious credit?

Backstage, speculation soared. When asked about the authorship of the screenplay, David Lean, who had directed the film, said: "That's the $64,000 question." He admitted that an American writer had worked on the screenplay, but he declined to mention his name "because none of his material was used." However, Spiegel was more of a hard-nosed businessman about the affair and continued to lie through his teeth, insisting to all the newspapers that "neither Michael Wilson nor anyone else worked on our version." Boulle had been credited, he said, "because it was taken directly from his contribution—the book."

His behavior may seem shocking, and has become one of the many black marks held against Spiegel by many, but he had his reasons for being careful. Columbia Studios, which had backed *The Bridge on the River Kwai* financially, refused to have anything to do with a blacklisted writer. They were nervous about the picture from the outset, thinking it was too "male-orientated" to do business. There had even been talk about whether or not it was to have an Oscar campaign. Clearly, any mention of Foreman or Wilson would have threatened the film's release.

Spiegel was well tuned to the ways of Hollywood. He personally loathed the town, dismissing it as "a factory in the sun," but he had spent twelve years living there, and he knew the studio system. It had taken time for Spiegel to prove himself professionally. He was a late, late bloomer, at least twenty years behind his fellow émigrés, who included Anatole Litvak, Otto Preminger, and Billy Wilder. According to Joseph L. Mankiewicz, he was the "perfect example of the producer who walked in without a penny and made himself into something . . . and made increasingly better films as he became wealthier."

Material success had come to Spiegel in his mid-fifties, by which time he had a reputation for being a hardened wheeler-dealer. In his opinion, there were no rules for his profession. "It's really a negative that makes you a success," he remarked. His maverick attitude allowed him to manage his one-time partner John Huston, as well as work with equally demanding but gifted directors such as Julien Duvivier, Orson Welles, Joseph Losey, Elia Kazan, David Lean, Joseph

Mankiewicz, and Arthur Penn. Not all their films were successes, but the best were to make up the pride of the Spiegel legacy: *The African Queen, On the Waterfront, The Bridge on the River Kwai, Suddenly, Last Summer,* and *Lawrence of Arabia.*

There was also Spiegel's Academy Award track record–he remains the only sole producer to win the best picture Oscar three times and, incredibly, he did it within a space of eight years. (It took the producer Saul Zaentz three decades to win his three best picture Academy Awards and he shared his first.) Spiegel is also the first to have had two films– *On the Waterfront* and *Lawrence of Arabia*–in the top ten of the American Film Institute's list of the 100 best films. In today's motion picture industry, it's impossible to think of Spiegel's equivalent. As Kevin Brownlow, the distinguished film historian, director, and editor, points out, "Nowadays, several producers are credited for the job that Spiegel did on his own. If you look at posters, you will often see six or seven."

Spiegel was driven. "You must feel that unless you make this picture you won't be able to sleep," he advised. There was also the producer's refusal to compromise. "Once you make . . . the slightest concession to demands by those lacking your devotion, you lose the purity of what you intended." Spiegel described each film as a love affair. "And if a love affair is going to work, there must be no consideration for the past or the future." It explained why emotions around his productions were so volatile. The feelings of directors and writers toward their producer swung like a pendulum from admiration to fury.

Like the best Dickensian characters, Spiegel was extreme. Although he could be accused of sharklike behavior and an appalling ruthlessness, he was also recognized for his exquisite manners and his *kleine Aufmerksamkeit,* a German expression meaning little gesture or courtesy. Honoring a financial agreement remained a problem, to such a point that Billy Wilder used to say that Spiegel was "a modern day Robin Hood, who steals from the rich and steals from the poor." Yet, there was always a certain panache to him, like being in the presence of a nobleman and a gangster.

"Why did I love Sam so much?" asked director Mike Nichols, who attempted to work with him on two pictures. "I suppose in the end it was his intelligence plus this gift of making you happy that he should have the advantage."

There was also the producer's courage. "Nothing fazed him," said Kazan. "When he went to Africa with John Huston, he was this fat Jewish fella who didn't have a gun. . . . He had a lot of guts."

It was Spiegel's choice of subject matter that made an impression on Mankiewicz–"conflicts between human beings, not between . . . supernatural forces, and Sam felt that very keenly." The director questioned whether the producer was a perfectionist, but recognized that he "was insistent on getting the best possible work out of people."

Occasionally, Spiegel's demonlike pursuit for quality pushed his employees over the edge, like Budd Schulberg, the screenwriter of *On the Waterfront,* who when asked why he was shaving at five in the morning, replied, "to kill Sam Spiegel."

There was also the stubbornness. David Geffen recalled the producer as having "his feet in concrete" when he wanted something. As a result, his methods could be staggeringly manipulative. During the making of *Lawrence of Arabia,* David Lean had had to contend with Spiegel's fake heart attacks. Afterward, there was even a new expression in the film community: to Spiegel–meaning to soothe, cajole, or con another; a talking-out-of, a sleight-of-mouth operation. Both Barry Diller and Mike Nichols recalled his "Jewish mother tactics," while it was Spiegel's quick wit that struck Harold Pinter. The producer was complaining about the American audience not being able to understand a certain line in *Betrayal,* the film of Pinter's play. "Fuck the Middle West!" cried the exasperated playwright. "Do you want to fuck the *whole* of the Middle West?" Spiegel shot back.

Sometimes, the tales concerning the producer were exaggerated, or just plain apocryphal, while he rarely corrected what he heard, because, as the last of the great showmen, he recognized the power of myth.

By the end of his life, Spiegel's pictures had collected thirty-five Oscars, he had personally made millions and acquired a priceless art collection, as well as having entertained some of the most glamorous people of the last century, including Gianni and Marella Agnelli, King Farouk, Greta Garbo, Sir James Goldsmith, Jackie Onassis, and Babe Paley. Yet who really knew Sam Spiegel and why did Arthur Miller call him "The Great Gatsby"?

The producer's personal life was deeply divided. The compartmentalizing was "obsessive." "His left-hand friends never knew what his right-hand friends were doing, or even who they were," said Kathleen Parrish, the wife of director Robert Parrish. "You never knew everything about Sam ever. You just knew little fragments that he wanted you to know."

Lord Weidenfeld, who published the autobiographies of many celebrities, once approached the producer about writing his memoirs, but Spiegel dismissed the idea as "maledictory." He refused to be a prisoner of his past. Let others dwell on their memories; the producer preferred to look forward, and hopefully upward. "He always struck me as a man with no native tongue who came from a cloudy place in the Balkans," said the writer James Goldman. Indeed, when asked about his birthplace by Annette Hohenlohe, an Austrian aristocrat, Spiegel replied, "I can't remember."

Of course, the film producer had a few stories that harked back to a different era, the set pieces he liked to bring out: his escape on the last train from Berlin when Hitler came to power, his escape from Vienna with Otto Preminger. The first was true, while the second was a bit exaggerated, though both stories gave credence to Spiegel's much repeated remark, "But for the grace of God, I would have been a lamp shade."

I heard all the differing versions of the escape stories, but I was personally more intrigued by the tales behind S. P. Eagle–Spiegel's professional nom de plume during the 1940s and 1950s. Whenever I tried to pinpoint him on the name change, the already hard-of-hearing eighty-year-old became very deaf indeed. Sam, or "Mr. Spieeegel," which was how Garbo pronounced his name, was my first employer. As a result, I have always felt a little blessed, since I thought he was fantastic–for all his faults.

I worked as a company assistant on *Betrayal,* his last film. It was at the beginning of the 1980s and he had lost his clout as a film producer, yet the mystery, the magic, and the mischief still remained. (But when had they ever left?) Sam, whose presence filled a room as soon as he entered it. Sam, with his rich mittel-European accent, curly eyelashes, and padded step, was the embodiment of his Dream Merchant lifestyle–the Mason blue Phantom Six Rolls-Royce with his chauffeur, Ken, at the wheel; his boat, *Malahne,* with her teak deck and Panama flag; Mas d'Horizon, his villa in the South of France, with the lingering al fresco lunches; the Park Avenue penthouse apartment; his table at the Connaught . . . There was also Sam in his Dover Street office, with Francis Bacon's painting–Pope no. 3–screaming behind his broad shoulders. Politically correct? He would have been appalled by the expression. "Sam had a gift for living–good food and very young girls," said the agent Robert Lantz. "But he was never embarrassing. He had great style and dignity."

Over lunch, Sam would tell me stories–though never about himself–tales such as the one when a Dutch aristocrat sought his advice about her elfinlike daughter Audrey. Naturally, it was Miss Hepburn. "She was wearing a silly black costume with little white feathers on her behind, but it was obvious that she was going to have a career. And I told her mother to let her continue." During such lunches, he was always respectful and never laid a hand on me.

Apparently, this was not the way he treated everyone, but my experience of being with Sam felt like sinking into the softest alpaca blanket–pleasure and protection. Armies of Young Turks could have tried the fortress's walls and all he had to do was turn his majestic head in their direction, cock an eyebrow, and the invaders would wither away. Sam used to tell people that he was my godfather; I was happy to back up the lie. Warren Beatty said that he "marked the end of an era." True, but how about another era, several hundred years ago! Was Sam a colorful pirate on the Seven Seas? A sultan with his harem? David Lean's Indian wife believed Sam had been a maharajah in a previous life, whereas Geoffrey M. Shurlock, from the Motion Picture Association of America, was reminded of the Roman emperor Vespasian, the founder of the Flavian Dynasty.

Nevertheless, when I stayed on *Malahne,* I was an ingrate. His boat was magnificent, the daiquiris arrived with lightning speed, the rich and the famous were everywhere on board, but having Sam as our "all controlling host" made my cousin and me feel restless and prisonerlike. We, on the other hand, drove him mad with our new discovery–Hollywood fruit-flavored gum. As we chewed, he fumed. "You look like cows in a field," he said with disdain. However, when Sophia Loren came on board, she too was chewing and then blew a bubble. Neither of us could wait. The next day, we were chewing so hard that our jaws were aching. Again Sam compared us to cows. "Well, Sophia Loren chews and she also blows bubbles," I replied–I had practiced the line all day long. "Yes, but you are little girls trying to be big girls, while she is a big girl trying to be a little one." The chewing stopped, as did the idea of outdoing Mr. Spieeegel.

The film producer was quick as a flash even in his later years. It was hard not to agree with Elia Kazan, who believed that were Spiegel "dropped, stark naked and without funds, into the heart of a capital city, by the next morning he'd be fashionably dressed and living at ease in a *grand luxe* hotel."

An extraordinary survivor, Spiegel faced adversity head-on during the first fifty-three years of his life, whether it meant fighting off anti-Semitic Polish hooligans, setting up camp in Palestine, fleeing from the Nazis and the Third Reich, or avoiding the United States immigration authorities, as well as any type of money collector. As a result, he had little time for such autobiographical details as being born in Galicia to a family of highly educated middle-class Jews who were Orthodox, but culturally well assimilated. He was Sam Spiegel–without any attachments or ties–who could adapt to any situation. "Baby, know your customer," he used to say, and baby, he meant it!

It was as if he had vowed to himself that by hook or by crook, he would discipline his emotions and be in control of his own destiny. He also became a perfect example of how living well is the best revenge. But what *were* his true origins and why was he so keen on hiding them?

"I think he popped out of his mother's womb full grown," said Betty Spiegel, his third wife. "He *never* talked about his childhood or his father."

Part I

1901–1939

Chapter One

CHILDHOOD

A vanished world–the Habsburg Empire, to which Samuel Spiegel belonged, was a place where languages were collected like stamps, and survival for people like him meant making "lightning-fast changes in protective skin coloring."

Samuel, or Mounik (his family nickname), was born November 11, 1901, in Jaroslav, a small town on the Krakow–Lemberg railway line where the level of anti-Semitism was moderate and almost a third of the population was Jewish. Lush green fields and the occasional windmill, evoking a Millet painting, surround the place, which is close to the San River. During his childhood, Jaroslav was in Western Galicia, a province in Austria-Hungary, but now it lies near the Ukraine border and is part of southeast Poland.

Spiegel, however, preferred to forget his place of origin. Sixty years later, when Edmund Hebenstreet, the head of the Jaroslav Society, wrote and addressed him as one of the town's more distinguished citizens, he never replied. "When he could, he used to say he came from Vienna," recalled Albert Heit, Spiegel's New York lawyer.

Mounik's childhood was supposedly spent at Mosergasse 9–a street in Vienna's Jewish quarter. "I remember sliding down the banisters very well at the house," he said, and showing his customary eye for detail, he described the interior perfectly.

Another boyhood memory was being sent out to buy bread, but sneaking into the famous Vienna opera house instead. He had seen Maria Jeritza, the Moravian soprano, perform in *Samson and Delilah*. Her curtain of glorious hair had made a lasting impression. "My first disillusionment with women was to find out it wasn't her own," he later remarked.

Both charming childhood reminiscences, but just a tad modified. First of all, Mounik only came to Vienna in 1920. True, he *did* live at Mosergasse–actually it was at number 6/7–but not until the autumn of that year–and surely eighteen was a little old to slide down the banisters? During the same period, he *might* have seen Frau Jeritza perform–she was a member of the Vienna State Opera from 1912 until 1935–but he was hardly seven years old!

Vienna was an obsession that stood the test of time with Sam Spiegel, which was of note since most of his other obsessions tended to fall by the wayside. *Survivors,* his final film project, was set in the Austrian capital.

Vienna was the city of dreams, and had the romance and escape that he so lusted after. The streets were certainly not paved with gold, but there was magic in its beauty. The Baroque buildings, the imperial parks, the fashionable Ringstrasse, the music of Brahms, Mahler, Strauss, and the paintings of Gustav Klimt, were all part of its splendor. There were also Jewish success stories in Vienna–the Rothschilds, intellectuals like Sigmund Freud and Ludwig Wittgenstein, the satirist Karl Kraus and his fortnightly periodical *Die Fackel,* the plays of Arthur Schnitzler. With its kaleidoscope of images and ideas, it was the perfect place for someone as curious as Mounik. In fact, many sensed that Spiegel's inquiring mind was, from the beginning, his real talent.

That he claimed Vienna as his birthplace also showed the inferiority complex of an assimilated Ashkenazi Jew, keener to be linked with the sophisticated West than with the old-fashioned, religious East. True to form, Spiegel was more attracted to the self-appointed elite, which among the Ashkenazi Jews were the German Jews from the West (the Westjuden): the Berliners, and the Viennese above all. He wanted little to do with the Jews from the East (the Ostjuden): the Poles, Russians, and Lithuanians.

For Spiegel, his birthplace was a shameful secret. He was a Galitzianer, as those born in Galicia were called. The name Galitzianer still causes certain eyebrows to rise, and during Spiegel's childhood, the term was derogatory. According to director Billy

Wilder, who also came from Galicia, the group was treated with "condescension with a touch of anti-Semitism." The Galitzianers were accused by other Jews as representing a side of Jewish life that was pre-emancipation. Many were dismissed for being both devout and peasantlike, resembling characters from an Isaac Bashevis Singer novel. There was also another side to the Galitzianer reputation. In the opinion of their neighbors, the Lithuanians (aka the Litvaks), they were charismatic schnorrers, not to be trusted in business. Robert Maxwell, the late press baron, no stranger to a fast deal or two, had Galitzianer origins. As did Harold Konigsberg, one of America's more intriguing criminal giants, who was a loan shark and a contract killer for the mob during the 1950s and 1960s.

But although Mounik later became renowned for his questionable business tactics, it has to be said that he was not raised in such an environment. He and his two brothers—Shalom, who was the eldest, and Leon (known in the family as Lonig), who was the youngest— were brought up in "a very learned household." Their father believed in a religious education as much as he believed in a secular one.

Mounik's education was to mark a difference between him and the Eastern European powerhouses who ruled Hollywood with such an iron fist—men like Samuel Goldwyn, Louis B. Mayer, Lewis J. Selznick (David Selznick's father), William Fox, Harry and Jack Warner, and Adolph Zukor, most of whom were born within a radius of a hundred miles or so from Lemberg, the capital of Galicia, which then became known as Lvov in 1918. (The city is now known as Lviv and is in the Ukraine.)

Thanks to his education—and natural intelligence—Mounik became articulate in nine languages, including Russian, French, Hungarian, and Spanish, as well as being able to write Hebrew and Sanskrit. His father, Simon Spiegel, a wholesale tobacco merchant by trade, was the representative of the Mizrachi movement in Jaroslav. Literally meaning "of the East," this was a group of religious Jews who worked toward establishing the State of Israel. As a result, Simon traveled extensively, attended Zionist conferences, and in 1934 became the vice chairman of the Jaroslav Community Executive and Council.

But despite having a father who was a pillar of the Zionist

community, in later life his second son rarely spoke of him. Was it because Simon was a peripheral figure in his life, at least by comparison to Regina, his mother? Photographs show him to be short and intense, with a good-looking, chiseled face.

Born in Zholkva, a town near Lemberg that was associated with the fur industry, Simon was the eldest of the three children of Abraham Solomon and Bruche Spiegel. The Germanization of the family name, which was done for tax purposes, occurred in the late eighteenth century during the Emperor Joseph II's reign. Since Spiegel means mirror, it suggests either that the family were in the looking glass business or were notably vain. (The former is the accepted explanation among most Spiegel family members.)

By comparison, Mechel and Eda Schwitz–Mounik's maternal grandparents–were of more earthy stock. They were tenant farmers from Unter Stanestie, Bukovina, then a duchy of Austria-Hungary, and now part of the Ukraine. In German, Schwitz means sweat, which indicated that the clerk giving out the names disliked the clan and was keen to emphasize either an unfortunate family habit or their reputation for making others sweat. (The latter might have amused those who worked for the future film producer.) Mounik's mother, however, who was the eldest of a brood of eight, had her own way of rising above her undignified surname. Although officially called Ruchel Regina, she only went by her middle name and, by most accounts, was "queenlike" in nature as well as in name.

She also lied about her age. Born in the same year as her husband, 1872, Regina used to knock a few years off, and in her final years became "sixty-eight forever." Like the rest of the Schwitzes, she had a big, bold face, high cheekbones, with a large nose. There was a no-nonsense expression in the eyes and a leonine authority to her bearing. It was the sort of face that thickened quickly in youth, but became dignified in maturity.

Physically, Mounik took after her, and even inherited her build: barrel-chested with thin, sinewy legs. He loved his *Mutter*. "My wife used to say, 'Do you think he loves his mother that much?' I mean he never stopped," said Jules Buck, who became a Spiegel Hollywood business associate. "I joked that it was out of superstition." Still, a large framed photograph of Regina had a prominent place in Spiegel's New

York apartment, while a smaller one was kept in his wallet with his money and credit cards. And whatever his financial state, he provided for Regina after she was widowed. (In fact, throughout his life, he tended to be kind to widows or "swans who were left," unless, of course, he was the culprit.)

If there was a key to Mounik's psyche, it was his mother. Several inches taller than her husband, Regina had a certain haughtiness in her carriage and was perceived to wear the pants in the household, since her scholarly husband was a quiet, bookish type. In short, she was *tonangebend*–a German word for someone who always has to be in charge.

Regina had her quirks, and was not averse to breaking certain Jewish traditions. "When her husband died, she refused to wear black and said it was only for old people," said Judge Raya Dreben, her granddaughter. Nor did she participate in her religion's ritual of visiting the ill. "It depressed her, she just wouldn't go to hospitals." Mounik inherited the same horror of disease and the institutions associated with such a state. "It was a mirror of vulnerability and he wanted to think of himself as invulnerable," said Dreben.

His mother also possessed the right mixture of energy and charm that attracted others to her. She was not worldly or sophisticated but neither was anyone else in her circle. She became thought of as "Tante [Aunt] Regina," the wise woman to whom relatives went for advice. Later, the same was said of Spiegel, but usually in cruder terms. As John Huston said, "If you had committed a murder, a totally unjustified act, of which you were guilty as hell, Sam would be one of the two or three friends you would turn to, certain that Sam would help."

In many ways, Regina controlled the family's image, and she passed her beliefs on to her son. He learned at her lap the importance of appearances and making a good first impression. Only German was spoken in her household–Yiddish was strictly banned. The goal was to give the impression that they were Austrian Jews with a German culture. Naturally, there was an academic target for the Spiegel sons, and that was for each of them to attend the University of Vienna.

In the Spiegel household, much was made of Shalom–the good sheep–finding his vocation in Judaic studies at an early age, whereas

Mounik–the black sheep–became renowned for his disappearing acts. Regina used to worry about her middle son. Was he dabbling in one of Jaroslav's chief attractions–the cinema? There were three picture houses in town. Or was Mounik just busy socializing?

Financially, Mounik's mother was particularly keen on showing her superiority in comparison to their relations. "I never knew if they were really as rich as Regina made out, but I often felt that she was hiding a lot behind the curtain," said Erna Shadwick, a Schwitz niece by marriage. As a tobacco merchant, Simon's fortunes must have ebbed and flowed, yet his wife could be counted on to make it seem that business had never been better. She always tried to put on a good show, just as her son later became the showman par excellence, renowned for living far beyond his means and keeping up a wealthy front. "There's a generation of Jewish mothers who have a lot to answer for, given the monsters of narcissism which they created, and Sam was certainly that," said director Mike Nichols.

One mystery that remains was how Regina and her family coped during the First World War, and why the experience never developed into one of her son's heroic tales. Sam Spiegel only ever made two remarks about the period. The first described his sadness at losing Emperor Franz Joseph in November 1916: "I was still a boy, but I felt the whole world around me had fallen to pieces." (Relative to the times, the emperor was associated with opening "the gates of the ghettos" and protecting his Jewish subjects.) His second remark about the period indicated the fall in his father's fortunes. "We had a fairly comfortable upbringing through my teens until the devaluation of the Austrian currency, after the First World War," he said.

Simon Spiegel, like all good patriotic Austrians, fought (on the Galician front), yet his wife and family stayed put, which was strange because most Jewish citizens fled west. Mounik's elder brother *did* move to Vienna in the autumn of 1917, but according to Austrian police records, he was the first Spiegel family member to do so, and three months previously he had been at Jaroslav's Obergymnasium (high school).

During the Great War, Jaroslav was in bitter need of food and supplies, as well as being dangerously close to the town of Przemysl, which being of strategic importance was always under attack. "Each time it fell into the hands of the Austrians, the Viennese [papers] came out with a special edition," recalled Billy Wilder, who was living in Vienna. Lajo Biro described the siege in his novel *Hotel Imperial.* In the hotel's reception area, there was a vast portrait of Franz Joseph, but as soon as the Russians arrived, the doorman turned the picture around, showing a portrait of Czar Nicholas II. When the Austrians returned, so did the emperor's portrait. Whether Mounik went through such Ernst Lubitsch-type experiences will never be known. He had a serious case of selective memory and later admitted to remembering details of his film productions better than certain names and unpleasant events, which he preferred to obliterate, "by some kind of providential gift of forgetting."

Nor did Sam Spiegel ever make reference to the 1918 pogroms in Galicia, which immediately followed the end of World War I. The Austro-Hungarian Empire had collapsed, and as pointed out by the historian Bruce F. Pauley in his book *From Prejudice to Persecution: A History of Austrian Anti-Semitism,* "Jewish survival depended on the protection of the Austrian rulers—whenever it was removed, expulsion or at least harsh social and legal discrimination was the likely result." Nor did the devastating effects of the war help. Again to quote Pauley, "Jewish-gentile relations were tolerable during periods of prosperity but rapidly deteriorated during social and economic crises brought on by bad harvests, plagues, wars or revolutions."

As a result, while other nationalities were celebrating the Armistice, which fell on Mounik's seventeenth birthday, the Galician Jews were put through a series of attacks and humiliations by Polish soldiers, which included torching synagogues with worshippers inside, pillaging their stores, and fining towns vast sums if they tried to defend themselves.

In comparison to Lvov, where the Polish brutality was compared to the infamous Saint Bartholomew's Day massacre, Mounik's birthplace was left relatively unscathed. However, on November 13, 1918, Jaroslav's Jewish community was disarmed by Polish forces, only to be attacked two days later by the same soldiers. And in the year that followed, like the rest of Western Galicia, the town would become part of Poland's Second Republic. Even before the peace treaty in Paris that led to the official carving up of the Austro-

Hungarian territories, the Polish Liquidation Commission had taken it upon themselves to claim Western Galicia from Austria.

In the meantime, Mounik had joined the Hashomer Hatzair, a Zionist youth movement, the goal of which was to live in Palestine. Most of its members were high school graduates. The philosopher Martin Buber was an influence on the group. They advocated his idea of taking ancient Jewish thoughts and reappraising them in modern terms.

Mounik became one of the youngest members of the movement's high command, which was no small feat since everyone took the movement extremely seriously—a case of "Brother this" and "Brother that." He even left Jaroslav in 1919 as a consequence of his new responsibilities and moved to Lodz—nicknamed the "Manchester of Poland"—a town that was known for its textile industry.

Although he lodged with a certain Dr. Eliezer Rieger, it marked Mounik's first experience of being away from *Mutter* and living in the "big city," where wearing the Hashomer uniform—a nod to Baden-Powell's Boy Scouts—led to vicious fights with anti-Semitic Polish youths. "Sam talked about some of his heroic deeds," said Isaac Stern. "And, at the time, I felt, and it should be stressed with great affection, that the stories were a little exaggerated." However, the violinist did not know Mounik when his broad face was slim, with high cheekbones, large eyes, and a wide, full mouth. There was no sign of the fleshiness that would eventually pad his cheeks, chin, and neck with such abundance. In his late teens, Mounik was broad-shouldered, muscular, and agile.

He used to juggle his day between attending his school, the männliches jüdisches gymnasium, and running the Hashomer Hatzair office, as the organization's local secretary. His duties led to his contacting other leaders of the organization in cities such as Warsaw, Vienna, Krakow, and Lvov, as well as being involved in *Haszomer,* the movement's monthly magazine that was sent all over Europe. "Beautiful language, but very little substance," he wrote, in regard to one book review. "Please be more accurate in your spelling," was another criticism. He also complained about the "bad Hebrew" in certain articles and poems that were being submitted. And Mounik showed his commercial sense, by being eager to sell more magazines.

"My beloved Krongolf," he wrote to the head of the Polish Hashomer Hatzair. "As you say, 'no one needs lectures,' but you have to persuade the local organization to order the periodical. You must make more of an effort." He also ran a tight ship. "Please send us the stamps which were ordered through Rosenberg when I was in Warsaw," was another request.

At the same time, he became the voice of reason regarding the hasty convoy of Hashomers who were leaving Vienna for Palestine. "This decision to hurry is causing us sorrow and weakening the spirit of the real volunteers," he wrote. The general lack of organization in regard to food and lodging annoyed him. " 'Everyone for themself and God will provide'—you cannot welcome thousands of guardians with this beautiful proverb." His suggestion to rent rooms in Vienna and adapt them into hostels was immediately accepted. He was also singled out as having the most practical attitude toward the members who were arriving in droves from Eastern Galicia due to the increased anti-Semitism and the inner fighting between the Poles, Ukrainians, and the Bolsheviks. (It was three years before the League of Nations would award the province to Poland.)

However, desperate as the Hashomers were to leave, most were unable to pay the fare to the Promised Land (five thousand Polish marks per head). "If they are not suitable, we have to instruct the high command in Galicia to stop allowing them to leave," he declared at one meeting. "They must realize that the Hashomer Hatzair will refuse to give them help." Mounik the pragmatist and *tonangebend* by nature, who even at eighteen was well versed in unit-manager functions.

As for his own departure, Spiegel left later than originally scheduled, no doubt because of his plans to attend the University of Vienna. Having acquired his *Abitur* (diploma), he had been accepted as a student of Staatswissenschaften (political sciences) by the Viennese law faculty. If he had left in the summer, he would not have been able to attend his first semester, beginning October 2, 1920. Was Spiegel planning to live in Palestine and become a student in Vienna at the same time?

It was an early example of Spiegel playing a double game. He planned to juggle a journey to Palestine with intellectual pursuits in

Vienna, like attending lectures by such prominent figures as the Marxist theoretician Max Adler and the right-wing sociologist Othmar Spann. Like all survivors, he was leaving his options open, because who knew what awaited him and his fellow members in the Middle East?

Spiegel's father was paying his tutorial fees. Somewhat affected by runaway inflation, the first year had cost 424 kronen (Austrian crowns), while the final year had come in at 534,000. Every semester of his so-called student period, the necessary enrollment form was meticulously filled out either by Samuel or his long-suffering elder brother. But why start a semester at university and then not complete it? In fact why go through the farce for three years with no intention of taking the final exams and no hope of writing his doctoral thesis? Because being his mother's son, Mounik recognized the importance of being linked to the University of Vienna. Throughout his career, he *never* stopped associating himself with the learned establishment.

Chapter Two

PALESTINE

Spiegel and his fellow Hashomers were part of the "Third Aliyah," the name given to the third wave of immigration to Palestine lasting from 1919 until 1924. They left on October 21, 1920. The journey lasted two and a half weeks, and on arriving at the port of Jaffa, they were immediately divided up and sent to different camps.

Spiegel was one of fifty to be chosen by the JCA–the Jewish Colonization Association. At first, it seemed like a decent place to land; the organization had a good reputation, having inherited all the settlements linked to Baron Edmond de Rothschild.

However, Spiegel was sent to Um-El-Alek, a farm meaning "mother of the leech" in Arabic, which was inhabited by Bedouins. It turned into a complete fiasco. Lying in the north of Palestine, near Zichron Yaakov, the camp's task was to dry out the farm's vast swamp area. Spiegel later described his activity there as "a drainage expert," which was an elaborate term, considering the primitive living conditions. Not only did Spiegel share a tent with strangers, the rats ate his clothes, malaria was rampant, and the food was minimal at best–pita bread and olives. There had also been a freak accident: a kerosene stove had exploded, killing one of the group.

Still, unlike most of his fellow camp members, he never fell ill with malaria–a sign of his "oxlike" constitution. As a result, Spiegel and the healthy few used to drain the land during the daytime, then return at nighttime to feed the sick, until he decided enough was enough. According to Yedidia Shohman, another member of the camp,

"Spiegel stood up and took it upon himself, along with [fellow kibbutz member] Kotzman, to be in charge. . . . They then declared that everyone had to leave the camp and look for other work because it was a kibbutz without assets."

Unless they were extremely vigilant and not averse to a little sand and swamp, Palestine could be a shock to the young Hashomer Hatzairs from Europe. Some were too ill or homesick to join in the enthusiasm. The writer Zeev Bloch described them as wandering "around the country like 'sheep without a shepherd.' "

Spiegel was too much of a survivor to have really suffered, but no doubt his spirits were dampened by his Um-El-Alek experience. Later, the camp went down in pioneer history as "the myth of disaster" in comparison to another settlement, Bitania, which was in the Jordan valley and acclaimed as "the dream." As it was described by Yonah Oren, one of the female members of Bitania, who cleared the land for planting olive trees, "our hands were full of calluses and blisters but this did not upset us, the singing never stopped and the hora dancing continued for hours despite our fatigue."

Bitania has since been romanticized in plays and films (three of the members included the painter Arye Allwail, the future political leader Meir Ya'ari, and David Horowitz, who became head of the Bank of Israel), but although Spiegel's name has been linked with the kibbutz, he was never there. However, he did work at the Yavne Umopseah settlement, near Rehovot. He and a certain Menachem Gelehrter shared a tent in the camp that was full of the "Mopsim," Communist spies who had come from the Soviet Union. They dug ditches on either side of the Lod–Kantara railway line. Spiegel and Gelehrter then boarded the same train for Europe in August 1921.

Exactly where Spiegel went was a mystery. He arrived in Vienna at the beginning of December, where he signed up for his third semester at the university and made a point of changing his native language from German to Yiddish on his *Nationalien* (the enrollment form). Nevertheless, by the following year, he was back in Palestine, living with the Bialik community, a group of Hashomers, including Meir Ya'ari and his wife, who had set up camp on a deserted sandy hill in Tel Aviv. The group was popular in town because of their work ethic and their high spirits–they were capable of starting impromptu parades in the streets of Tel Aviv while they danced and sang. Saturday nights at their camp became an informal event that attracted young writers and poets.

The group also caught the attention of Rachel "Ray" Agranovich. Romantic-looking, the twenty-year-old had the soft allure of a Burne-Jones painting. Her dark soulful eyes were set off by a translucent, pale complexion. Ray was not only beautiful, she also had excellent connections. Her father and stepmother–Eliezer and Susi Agranovich–were prominent figures in Tel Aviv.

Spiegel and his future wife either met on Herzl Street or Nahlout Benjamin. (Allenby Street had not even been paved yet.) Later on, Ray wanted to forget wherever it was. Indeed, she preferred not to discuss her first husband, calling him "one big zero," whom she had "erased" from her mind. Yet, according to Ray's half-niece, Sam was "her great love." "Her life was less eventful afterward," said Ilana Agron. "Sam was this dashing pioneer from Poland. It was terrible for her confidence to be walked out on."

Early photographs show a fetching couple. Spiegel looked ten years older than his wife, in spite of the fact that she was only three months his junior. In the Schwitz family tradition, his face had thickened. However, the new look, a shock of dark hair, a heavier jaw and neck, as well as an extra thirty pounds' body weight, made him look sultry and affluent. The lean look of the pioneer had disappeared; it was a new Mounik. Samuel Spiegel, entrepreneur extraordinaire, whom many liked, but few trusted, had replaced Brother Schmuel, the hero of the Hashomer Hatzair. Still, he found time to enroll for his final year at the University of Vienna and yet again altered his native language on the *Nationalien*–this time, from Yiddish to Hebrew.

As far as his relationship with Ray, it was to resemble those with all the other women in his life. Spiegel had a tendency to wax quickly and wane even faster. He was a better friend to ladies than a love interest. Was he genuinely smitten with Agranovich and desperate to marry her? No doubt several emotions were involved. Ray introduced him to a sophisticated world, and had turned his head as a result. Considering who Spiegel became, it is hard not to imagine that the marriage was his way of turning his back on the "poor pioneer" experience and left-wing idealism.

Ray's father, Eliezer Agranovich–who was known as Leon–had made his money in Winnipeg, Canada. An early pioneer of Palestine, he was one of the first to have a home in the center of Tel Aviv. When constructing the house, he had demonstrated his wealth by employing only Hebrew workmen, who charged considerably more than Arabs. However, it was Susi, Leon's second wife, who was to make a lasting impact on Spiegel.

In a few respects, she was not unlike his *Mutter*–being strong-willed and energetic–but there were two major differences: first, Susi was not religious, and second, so far as it was possible in a town of five thousand inhabitants, she was the social doyenne. It was Spiegel's first connection to a woman with society in her hands. Most of her guests spoke in English, German, French, or Russian. Despite coming from Russia, Susi mostly spoke German. "She thought it made her seem more aristocratic," said her granddaughter.

The second Mrs. Agranovich was not to everyone's liking. Ray described her stepmother as "mean, unkind, nasty, and always creating problems between people." Nor was Susi a beauty, but she was extremely chic and made the most of her assets. Admirers only remembered her sparkling eyes, her quick charm, and carefully groomed glamour. Mrs. Agranovich was also better equipped to deal with Mounik than her stepdaughter was.

Spiegel married Ray in Vienna on September 22, 1922. For most of their marriage–it lasted a brief five years–they lived in the German colony in Jerusalem. When his finances were on an upward surge, they resided in a fairly grand house called the Villa Gregorian that had been built by an Armenian merchant. One of Spiegel's early business endeavors was bringing cattle from Cyprus when Palestine had a severe meat crisis. Although an enterprising idea, it was not practical, since the city's refrigerators were too small to hold the carcasses.

Another of his schemes led to his visiting the Emir Abdullah, renowned for his Zionist connections, in Transjordan (now Jordan). Spiegel returned from Amman with his host's white Mercedes. "And he forgot to send it back–that was Sam," recalled Netty Gottlieb, a Spiegel associate. After a few weeks, the future king of Transjordan sent word that he wanted the luxurious automobile returned. "And Sam gave it to the police, who took it back for him."

Ray was not included in his travels. "He never took his wife, and she started to be fed up with him," said Gottlieb. The first Mrs. Spiegel was straightforward and had to deal with a husband who was consistent only in his inconsistency and something of a gonif to boot. A year after their marriage, Lonig, Spiegel's younger brother, died in Jaroslav–either of cancer or of a football injury that had become gangrenous. Three years later, on May 13, 1926, Alisa, their daughter, was born. Neither the death of his brother nor the recent paternal responsibility diminished Spiegel's wanderlust and schemes.

Spiegel was already leading a footloose, bachelorlike existence, and had started to entertain on a lavish scale. On one occasion, he gave a party for fifty people at the Warshawski Hotel in Jerusalem, but when it came to paying, his check bounced. The hotel owner summoned him and Spiegel delivered another check, which also promptly bounced. This particular method of payment continued well into the early 1950s. As Spiegel would admit, "All my life, I never believed in the permanent value of money. When people were saving, I was buying paintings that I could ill-afford."

The story that Spiegel represented an Egyptian lottery company, but was stopped when he was caught printing his own tickets, sounds too nickels and dimes to be true, since his money schemes were usually more ambitious. Nevertheless, the Egyptian connection sparks a tiny chord because apparently Spiegel stole someone else's Egyptian checkbook. As his in-laws were the wealthiest people he knew, it was probably theirs. Later, when Susi wrote to him, she reminded him of their last talk, when he promised to "arrive in Tel Aviv in the prettiest, most luxurious car and would then do many good deeds." Spiegel never replied, and she wrote another letter: "Do you bear a grudge? If anything I should. I forgive you and I rarely forgive those who have 'sinned against me.' You also left me in a very difficult situation."

She was not the only one in a "very difficult situation." Ray was left to cope with their daughter single-handedly. The alliance had abruptly ended on June 1, 1927, when Spiegel set off for the United States via Europe, never to return to Palestine. Some of his relatives have insinuated he was "deeply in debt," and that his business activities had become a little sinister.

As soon as the news reached the high command of the Polish

Hashomer Hatzair that Spiegel had deserted their organization for "capitalist America," they went into mourning for a year. They even placed their youth movement's insignia on a black funereal background instead of the habitual red one.

There was certainly a difference between Mounik, the hero of the Hashomer Hatzair movement who arrived in Palestine in 1920, and Samuel Spiegel, the wife-deserter and stealer-of-checks who left in disgrace in 1927. As a result, he was well prepared for his American challenge. He had told Susi, "I'll either become a very rich and famous man or I'll die like a dog in the gutter."

Chapter Three

SAN FRANCISCO

Regarding his Palestine experience, Spiegel would later portray himself as leading the life of a highly successful cotton broker until he caught malaria. This illness "forced" him back to Vienna where he managed to study dramatic literature, write "a few inferior plays," as well as start his own brokerage business. Impressive and resourceful, but every line was "Spiegelese"–an invented expression to describe the way he appropriated career details.

Spiegel did, however, arrive in the port of New York on November 4, 1927. Stating his profession as "economist," he was a second-class passenger on SS *Mauretania,* a ship belonging to the Cunard Line, which left from Cherbourg, France. A guest at New York's Penn Hotel for several weeks, he then went to Toronto, Canada. Exactly how Spiegel spent his time there remains a mystery. But, on his way back, he managed to slip past Immigration in both the towns of Niagara and Buffalo. Was it because he crossed the border with someone else's passport?

Because when he returned to New York City, Spiegel was suddenly treated as a guest of honor with special bands and welcoming committees. Flaunting "gilt-edged credentials," he introduced himself as a "confidential adviser" to both Britain and Egypt, touring America "to study" the country's economic and government conditions. The "confidential adviser" also went to smaller cities, such as Louisville, where he called on Ben Washer, who later became Mary Martin's press agent and business manager. They had met in Tel Aviv when Washer was on vacation, while attending the University of Michigan. Mounik had been his hospitable self and the young

American student promised to return the favor. However, when Spiegel appeared at his home, he was more interested in cash up front–about $150–than a tour of the sights.

Washer was given a bouncing Egyptian check for his pains, and although Washer's father tried to send people after their impertinent house guest, the bogus diplomat had already hot-footed it, "leaving a trail" of false documents through Illinois and other Midwestern states. Nevertheless, when Spiegel reached San Francisco in the month of June, it was "with a blare of civic trumpets."

What was the secret of Spiegel's success? It was simple–he looked respectable and had exquisite manners. His *kleine Aufmerksamkeit*– charming little gesture–stood him in good stead: flowers for the ladies, the pressed suit, the shined shoes, and the style. His portliness gave him a cherubic and affable air. The fluttering of the eyelashes, the dimples when he smiled, the joy of good food and the pleasure in a pretty face, made an impression. Yet, on closer inspection, beyond the mask of warmth, perhaps the hooded eyes did dart from side to side just as the quick lick of the top lip betrayed a certain deviousness. According to Elia Kazan, Spiegel was capable of lying "without a betraying tremor of his facial muscles." "He kept me intrigued just to see how he got away with everything."

Spiegel's budding diplomatic career, however, was cut short at seven months when Secret Service agents seized him on July 15, 1928. Tracked down to a prominent hotel on Wilshire Boulevard–possibly the Ambassador–he had been caught while literally in mid-negotiation for a $3,000-a-week contract with a top film studio– possibly with MGM's Paul Bern, who lived at the Ambassador. As a result of the chase and the circumstances, his arrest made the front-page headlines of the *San Francisco Examiner,* which hailed him as "the International 'mystery man' of the postwar [*sic*] decade."

"Possible deportation and immigration charges" were the suggested orders from Washington for the diplomatic fraud. But W. W. Ashe–the Secret Service *agent in charge*–was silent on the subject of any other details, especially some of the scandalous stories that "a number of film stars" had "lost thousands of dollars," or that various motion picture stars had entertained Spiegel on the strength of his passports and letters of recommendation.

Spiegel kept his calm. Despite being the focus of aggressive newshounds, he "refused to talk." With the customary one call, he telephoned his elder brother, who was living in New York, having become a professor at the Jewish Institute of Religion. It was the necessary note of respectability and since Shalom was "the defender of the world"—his wife's term for him—he tried to ease the plight of his younger brother, who was facing charges of entering the United States without inspection, falsifying checks, and being a fugitive from justice.

Spiegel received a nine-month sentence to the San Francisco County Jail. His time was spent in Jail No. 2, and he was grilled regularly about entering the United States "without inspection." During one interview, when asked if he could provide any evidence of his innocence or reason why he should not be deported, Spiegel replied, "No, but I would like to have it [the deportation] speeded up as much as possible."

When Spiegel's period in the County Jail expired on April 20, 1929, he was immediately turned over to the Immigration Department at Angel Island to await deportation. Angel Island was nicknamed "the Ellis Island of the West," but it was quite different from Ellis Island, where immigrants were usually welcomed and screened for medical reasons. Angel Island's objective was to exclude new arrivals. As one Chinese woman carved in the wall, "this mountain wilderness is a prison." Spiegel would be held there for four months.

Meanwhile, through Shalom's influence, Samuel G. Holcenberg, from the Jewish Committee for Personal Services in State Institutions, had taken an interest in his case. He even wrote to the secretary of state about Spiegel's expired passport, since the former diplomat (!) had been offered employment on a ship. Mounik—not one to rely totally on others—had also approached the deputy commissioner of immigration and had shown an elaborate, albeit groveling, grip of the English language: "which fortunate opportunity impels me to ask you, Sir, humbly that your kind attention be given to this application at your earliest convenience so as to enable me to leave on the above mentioned boat."

The ship—headed for South America—was never to be boarded by Spiegel. Thanks to Holcenberg, a prominent philanthropist paid

Spiegel's $500 bond, which led to his release at the end of August 1929, the idea being that he would work and make himself useful before being deported. Spiegel *did* work, but whatever he did made both Holcenberg and the benefactor, who insisted on anonymity, deeply regret their ever having helped him.

Having become Spiegel's protector, Holcenberg reported him as doing "many shady things" in San Francisco, as well as being "most unscrupulous" and lacking "a moral code." But he was soon horrified to discover that it was impossible to send Spiegel back to the Immigration authorities at Angel Island, since Spiegel could demand a writ of habeas corpus if he was detained longer than six months in custody. For once, Spiegel was protected by the law!

But what exactly were the "shady things" that Spiegel was doing? Was he gambling? Did he get mixed up in the illegal liquor business? Was he procuring women? Whatever he did during that time, it remained among the many secrets that he took to his grave.

As always, there were the conflicting circumstances. Just as Spiegel was awaiting deportation, he became the subject of a correspondence between Walter Morris Hart, the vice president and the dean of the University of California at Berkeley, and Elizabeth Ellis, the wife of Ralph Ellis, who donated annually to the university. For a brief moment, Spiegel was considered for employment at UC Berkeley, although it turned out that no position was available. However, his meeting with Mrs. Ellis may have led to his next bout of Spiegelese–his being discovered by MGM's Paul Bern while delivering one of his "brilliant lectures" on Pirandello at Berkeley's Greek Theatre.

Mrs. Ellis was a theater buff and had helped finance a lecture on "The Art of Theatre," delivered by Robert Edmond Jones in 1927. Did her enthusiasm about the lecture, the articulate manner of Jones, hit a chord in Spiegel? Was this like the imaginary sliding down the banisters in Vienna? It was an image that Spiegel liked, it was an image that he adopted, and suddenly, it became "his brilliant lecture."

During that period, UC Berkeley *did* have a Greek Theatre, but Spiegel's lecture appears to have been as bogus as his Egyptian credentials. Budd Schulberg–whose father was then running Paramount and went "way back with Sam"–sensed it was typical. "He was constantly reinventing himself, whether he had been a professor or this or that."

And according to the records, Spiegel's next job–working at Metro-Goldwyn-Mayer under Paul Bern–was just as questionable. Nevertheless, in February 1930, *Daily Variety* wrote about the studio establishing a foreign literature department, with a certain Harry Spiegel in charge, which would "read foreign magazines and current novels in search of material for foreign tongue talkers."

This was certainly the position that Spiegel claimed to have filled, even though the Turner Entertainment Group (the present owner of the MGM archives) insists that he was never employed by the studio. Was this because Spiegel was having problems with the immigration authorities and therefore being paid on the side (i.e., cash and no record)? His department certainly fitted in with the plans of MGM's production chief Irving G. Thalberg, after the talkie revolution began. "The competition for good stories is so keen," Thalberg had warned, "that the supply written in English was long ago insufficient." Meanwhile, working in Hollywood fitted in with Spiegel's agenda. "Early on, the film business was a quick way to get rich," said the writer Peter Viertel. It was also a "quick way" to meet beautiful women.

As for Spiegel's friendship with Bern, it was genuine, and to quote Schulberg, "showed Sam's knack of being there at the right time with the right people." However, a question mark remains whether Spiegel was actually with Bern when he was arrested in 1928. All evidence suggests that it was possible, since, as described by the newspapers, Bern lived at a "prominent" hotel on Wilshire Boulevard and also worked for "a top film studio." Indeed, the German-born Bern was one of Thalberg's five key people, and had written screenplays for such directors as Ernst Lubitsch and Josef von Sternberg, as well as directing stars like Pola Negri and Florence Vidor. At the height of her fame, Jean Harlow married Bern. As the platinum sex bomb said, "[He] doesn't talk fuck, fuck, fuck, all the time."

Spiegel's MGM experience did not last six months–at the very most, it was seven weeks. But being the spinner of Spiegelese, he embellished his moment in Culver City, saying that he was too "ambitious," and "got into trouble immediately by writing directly to publishers in other countries and closing deals with them–neglecting to consult the MGM story department." There was also Spiegel's other yarn, that the very man who fired him at the studio then approached him for a job many years later.

In reality, Spiegel had overstayed his visa and the United States government was keen to deport him. Had Samuel G. Holcenberg speeded up the process? Deeply vexed by Spiegel, Holcenberg fired off a letter to the chief of the visa office in Washington, who then sent Holcenberg's letter to the American minister in Warsaw, the Polish consulate in Buffalo, and anyone with weight regarding immigration. In his correspondence, Holcenberg delivered an impassioned message: Samuel Spiegel would neither "make a desirable citizen or a desirable resident in any community in this country."

A date was set, and Spiegel was supposed to be grouped with the "Klein party of deportees," but, typically, he had other plans. He sent a cable to the secretary of labor "humbly" asking his permission to sail to Europe at his own expense, to avoid forced deportation. Two days later, Bern and the Austrian ambassador sent similar wires making the same request.

Spiegel eventually left America aboard the SS *President Roosevelt* on April 2, 1930. Changing his name to Sam Spiegel, his sights were now set on Universal Studios in Berlin. The studio owner, fondly referred to as "Uncle Carl" Laemmle, was about to let him into his "very large faemmle."

Chapter Four

BERLIN

With its wealth of cafés, theaters, and nightclubs, Berlin suited Spiegel. There were those who described the town as "restless, feverish, wild." A walk down the fashionable Kurfürstendamm led to being "accosted and solicited by creatures of every description," the elegantly turned-out, the androgynous, and the streetwalkers in thigh-high boots.

Playwright Carl Zuckmayer, who won international acclaim for his masterpiece *The Captain of Koepenick,* and co-wrote screenplays such as von Sternberg's *The Blue Angel,* compared the Berlin of that time to a "highly desirable woman" who was criticized for being "proud, snobbish, nouveau riche, uncultured, crude." "Some saw her as hefty, full breasted, in lace underwear, others as a mere wisp of a thing, with boyish legs in black silk stockings," he wrote. "The daring saw both aspects, and her very reputation for cruelty made them the more aggressive. To conquer Berlin was to conquer the world." Spiegel's thoughts entirely.

No records exist to indicate how Spiegel talked his way into Universal's German office. In later years, he said that Carl Laemmle, Sr., employed him in Hollywood and then sent him to Berlin, "to produce for Universal's enterprises there." Considering that Spiegel was still at MGM before he was deported, this sounds like Spiegelese. Also, it seems highly unlikely that he arrived at the head office in Berlin (which he described as "a Nazi hotbed") "bearing the precious negative of *All Quiet on the Western Front.*" No doubt, it was a mixture of things, including Spiegel's uncanny "knack of being there at the right time" that led to him being employed by the studio, known as "the sausage factory of Hollywood." Universal had an important film to launch . . . Spiegel happened to arrive at exactly the moment that they were looking for an agent to do this. He appeared to have all the right credentials: he spoke perfect German, was persuasive as well as coming recommended by his former boss, Paul Bern, who had actually been involved with the casting of *All Quiet*.

It turned out to be a fortuitous appointment. Indeed, as Universal's agent, Spiegel was at the center of the historic storm of the film's release. At first, the promise of *All Quiet on the Western Front* was high. Not only had the film of Erich Maria Remarque's famous novel been an artistic and financial triumph in America, but it had also won the studio's first Oscar. As a result, Universal's plans for the German release were ambitious; the country had five thousand theaters to fill. Nevertheless, a few problems needed to be smoothed out. Remarque's antiwar best-seller was controversial, especially given Germany's recent wave of right-wing nationalism, but the studio had gone to great trouble to prepare the public, or so they thought. Such efforts included using German actors to dub the film to avoid the nation's dislike of subtitles, and also providing special screenings for tastemakers and officials.

Due to all the publicity, the premiere of *All Quiet* was a huge occasion. It was obvious that the guests arriving on the night of December 5, 1930, at the Mozart Hall–an ornate movie palace on Nollendorfplatz–had come not just to see a film, "but to participate in a major cultural and political event." They would not be disappointed. According to Lewis "Milly" Milestone, the film's director, Spiegel began the event by introducing him. But instead of receiving the expected thunder of applause, Milestone was greeted with a stony and embarrassing silence.

However, it was after the first reel finished, when Dr. Goebbels– the virulently anti-Semitic future minister of propaganda–headed for the exit, that his henchmen–the National Socialist SA Brownshirts– really started. Stink bombs were exploded, itching powder was thrown in the air, and hundreds of white mice were released, while the chants of "*Judenfilm, Judenfilm*" (Jewish film) echoed around the movie house. Spiegel was forced to stop the picture. Leni Riefenstahl– then the star of Arnold Fanck's mountain films–presumed a fire had started. "Panic broke out and girls and women were standing on their seats, shrieking," she recalled.

Later, Spiegel exaggerated the event. As well as describing thousands of white mice, he also mentioned three members of the audience being killed, which no other account confirms. However, the riots outside the cinema *were* violent. And, just six days after the premiere, the film was banned by the Supreme Film Censorship Board, the official explanation being that no German wanted to see their country defeated on screen.

For Universal, it was a huge financial disappointment. Two days later, Laemmle Senior sent a thousand-word cable to be used as an advertisement in Berlin newspapers. It was a waste of effort. In desperation, Universal's agent–presumably Spiegel–called on the American ambassador, Frederic F. Sackett, who was sympathetic, but refused to help until he heard back from the White House.

Despite Sackett's lack of commitment, Spiegel used the meeting as a trump card when dealing with the Austrian release of the film. As soon as he reached Vienna, he informed the American legation that the U.S. embassy had tried to lift the German ban and was expecting similar efforts to be made in the Austrian capital. Unfortunately, this piece of Spiegelese was exposed and the Americans refused to help. Spiegel then pursued more drastic methods. He sacked Universal's entire staff in Austria and closed the office. But it was a useless exercise. According to Andrew Kelly, the author of *Filming All Quiet on the Western Front*, "If he [Spiegel] felt that the Austrian Government would cave in to the threat of ending the distribution of Universal's films in Austria, he was mistaken." By mid-January 1931, *All Quiet on the Western Front* was officially banned in Austria as well.

With time, Spiegel's tales about *All Quiet* became more elaborate and, of course, cast him in the right heroic glow. He described showing the film to every member of the Reichstag, including Göring, and even showing it to Hitler. He said he went to Rome to arrange a private viewing for Mussolini. He also created a special law passed by the German parliament allowing *All Quiet* to be seen by private organizations. All of the above happened, and Spiegel was certainly *linked* to the events, but he may not have been at the center of them.

Nevertheless, how was it humanly possible for him to make "all the

European versions" of *All Quiet* for Germany, France, and Italy? And was his life really in such danger that he had to be assigned four bodyguards from the secret police? Perhaps the best Spiegelese was his claim that as soon as the ban on *All Quiet* was lifted in September 1931, the Nazis marched out of the Reichstag in military formation, singing the Horst Wessel song, and raising their clenched fists at him.

There is one slight problem with the latter event: Spiegel was no longer at Universal. He was working for producers Felix Pfitzner and Ilja Salkind (a member of the same clan who produced the Musketeer and Superman films) on their motion picture *Ehe m.b.H.,* the abbreviation of *Ehe mit beschränkter Haftung,* meaning *Marriage with Limited Liability.* (Later, Spiegel referred to the film as *Marriage Ltd.*)

It was his first experience on a film set, but contrary to his reports that he was the producer, he was merely the *künstlerische Oberleitung*– the artistic director. The picture, a musical comedy, was based on the play *Causa Kaiser* by Ludwig Sterk and Adolf Eisler.

Ehe m.b.H. was not without its interesting elements. It allowed Spiegel to work with Franz Wenzler, a director who was highly respected in European theatrical circles, while on the French version (*Mariage à Responsabilité Limitée*) he was in touch with Jean de Limur–a French aristocrat and a serious bon vivant–who had acted in Rex Ingram's *The Arab* and had been a technical advisor on Chaplin's *A Woman of Paris.*

However, from all accounts, Spiegel became closest to the musical team, Fritz Rotter, who wrote the lyrics for the composing partnership, Bronislaw Kaper and Walter Jurmann. "We had a big hit in it," Kaper recalled. *"Wer weint heut' aus Liebe Tränen?"*–"Who is shedding tears today because of love?" In the 1970s, Kaper played the song for Spiegel at a Hollywood party. "We had a kind of sentimental reunion."

And when *Ehe m.b.H.* came out, the *Film-Kurier* (Germany's *Variety*) gave the art director a favorable mention, though it dismissed the film for "trying too hard" to amuse the audience. Still, Spiegel insisted that the picture made a fortune, making him a "man of means." The official Spiegelese being that he bought himself a beautiful mansion, "acquired paintings by noted artists, and a wine cellar which was the envy of all Berlin."

All his claims are delightful, but lacking in reality. According to Paulette Dubost, his French girlfriend, he was "really poor," never had a "fixed address," and lived "with friends from one day to the next." "Perhaps Sam had servants the day that he was entertaining . . . there were lots of men like that. But it was hardly a steady income—just a lot of make-believe."

Nevertheless, even if "Sam was still building his pyramids," as one friend politely phrased it, he was to make enough contacts for a lifetime. One "die-hard" pal was Paul Kohner, a Czech who was also born Austro-Hungarian, and played an important role in Universal's European operation. "In some ways, my husband and Sam were like brothers," said Lupita Kohner. "They were so different, but there was an unspoken understanding. Paul accepted everything about Sam." Not everyone did. When Arthur Schnitzler met Spiegel in St. Moritz in the summer of 1930, the playwright wrote in his journal: "[He] inspires little confidence on my part."

Both Kohner and Spiegel shared a passion for gin rummy. Spanning from this passion came the close circle of fellow Europeans: William Wyler, Samuel "Billie" Wilder (changed to Billy when he arrived in the United States), and Anatole "Tola" Litvak. All five were card-crazy—as one female acquaintance pointed out, "It wasn't really for money, they would have played with buttons." They were also to form a bond that linked them for life—the "we escaped Hitler" one. However, in the early 1930s, Hitler was far from their thoughts. He was considered "a joke" for "sub-moronic people."

"At first, Berlin was fantastic," said Mrs. Kohner. Indeed, the town sparkled with vivacity. The Romanisches Café on the Kurfürstendamm, near the Gedächtniskirche, was the favorite rendezvous for intellectuals, critics, artists, and people in the movie business who often worked for Ufa, Germany's most important studio. It was a place where deals were made and information was passed. Spiegel and his other acquaintances—Oscar Homolka, Peter Lorre, Joe Pasternak, Walter Reisch, Robert Siodmak, and Robert Thoeren—used to meet there.

Spiegel also belonged to a "writer's club." He later compared the liberal-thinking group of German artists and politicians of that day to Americans who were against the Vietnam War in the early 1970s: "It was kind of a cult ... we frequently had lunch together, dinner together, and we pursued our careers."

Hotels such as the Majestic, the Adlon, and the Eden were where everyone who mattered stayed. In the Eden's hallway, there was a vast and sumptuous chandelier that one of Paulette Dubost's pals—a daredevil French actor—liked to swing from. "That was Roland Toutain, but then that was Berlin too!" she said. The newly married Lupita Kohner was introduced to Spiegel when staying at the same hotel. A few moments afterward, an exquisite orchid was delivered to her room. "I turned to Paul and said, 'My goodness, this is the most charming man. I just met him downstairs, and he sends me this.' My husband laughed and said, 'Yes, with my money.' Sam had borrowed the money to go to the florist, and that's how our friendship started."

He practiced his famous *kleine Aufmerksamkeit*, which never failed to flatter women. Paulette Dubost's mother adored him. "She was very keen on gifts, even a little venal ... and when Sam arrived in Paris, he bought champagne, caviar, foie gras and petits fours." According to the fresh-faced actress, who later appeared in Renoir's *La Règle du Jeu,* Ophuls's *La Ronde,* and Malle's *Viva Maria,* not all of Spiegel's friends were as generous. "Tola Litvak was nice but tight with his pennies. ... My girlfriend was his mistress and he went off with her and left me with the restaurant bill. I didn't have any money and was forced to leave my umbrella as a deposit."

Dubost was in the French version of her boyfriend's next film, *Ich will Dich Liebe lehren (I Will Teach You to Love)*. Made for Pax-Film, the first film that Spiegel actually produced was a musical comedy. This was less curious than it sounds because he was using the contacts from his previous production. Once again, Rotter wrote the words to the songs, while Kaper and Jurmann scored.

Based on *Herr Fünf (Mr. Five),* Alice Berend's best-selling novel, the story concerned the trials and tribulations of Hermann Schroeck (Willi Domgraf-Fassbaender), a musician who gave his lifelong opus— "Mr. Five"—to the opera house.

Although Domgraf-Fassbaender was a well-known tenor, he soon became a thorn in Spiegel's side. Divalike on the subject of his international reputation, he refused to be replaced in the French version *(L'homme qui ne sait pas dire non),* which loomed into a huge problem. "His accent was so thick that we couldn't understand a word that he said," Dubost said. Several scenes had to be reshot, which became complicated when the director, Heinz Hilpert, walked off the set in the middle of filming.

Meanwhile, the production's resources were limited. Spiegel and his cast managed to survive on vouchers–representing tokens of payment–rather than actual money. "Everything was paid for with these little pieces of paper–the taxis, boutiques, restaurants," Dubost recalled. But making the film had been "fun." At the weekend, Spiegel used to take the group to the Adriatic where they stayed in the seaside palaces and the extortionate bills were never settled. Dubost did not mind having a cad for a boyfriend. "We can't criticize Sam because he was on another level, he always thought big." She and Spiegel often dined with Lisette Lanvin, who was also in the film's French cast, and Henri Decoin, who had written the French screenplay. "Lisette wore jeans–she was one of the first–and Sam thought they were awful. He said, 'They're for gardeners.' He loved being seen with women who were beautifully dressed and very *coquette*. He hated ladies not making an enormous effort."

Despite all the dramas, Spiegel's film had a premiere at the Titania-Palast, a prominent cinema in Berlin, and was even respectfully reviewed by the *Film-Kurier*. By then, the producer had already left Germany.

"Autumn storms" was Remarque's description of the Nazi takeover. At the beginning of 1933, Remarque was drinking in a Berlin bar when someone passed over a note warning him to "get out of town fast." The Reichstag fire in late February sealed it for Billie Wilder. After having a farewell drink on the Café Wien's terrace, he and his girlfriend packed up all they could carry, and caught a train to France. Kaper also took the Berlin–Paris express. As soon as they crossed the Belgian frontier, everyone got up and kissed each other. "We were that happy that we were out of the madhouse."

Spiegel fled soon after, and his "escape from Berlin" story soon became legendary. Some confuse it with the tale that involved Otto Preminger–that one happened two months later, and took place on the Austrian-Swiss border.

Chapter Five

VIENNA

There were so many versions of Spiegel's escape from Berlin that choosing the most accurate would be nearly impossible. The story became grander with each decade–a kindly housekeeper and loyal butler were eventually added–but it was not entirely Spiegelese, because it *did* happen. And whatever the details, the producer became renowned for his remark, "These are the accidents of life that prevent you from becoming a lamp shade."

Spiegel's version from the 1940s appears to be the most credible. "I got up late that day, and went around the corner to my barber to get a shave. While he was shaving me, the barber whispered, 'Don't go home tonight.' That was sufficient warning. Without a hat, and with only a few marks in my pocket I walked out of the barbershop and went directly to the station, without returning home. The banks were closed that day, so I couldn't stop to get money."

The barber was a member of the SA who had been instructed to either beat up or kill Spiegel, as well as Peter Lorre and Oscar Homolka, the lead players in his next production. Lorre was already in Vienna, but Spiegel persuaded Homolka to catch the same train as he. Curiously enough, Josef von Sternberg and the violinist Jascha Heifetz were also on board, but it was "by accident," and no doubt prompted by the fact that the following day nobody would be able to leave Germany "without a special permit." "We arrived in Vienna without bags or anything because we had to pretend that we were going to the country for the weekend so as not to be molested on the train," Spiegel recalled. "The only thing I possessed was the script and several weeks later, we started shooting."

Did this explain why Spiegel wrote "film director" on his Austrian police form when he arrived? Still, whether he lacked a toothbrush or whether it was only four marks or six that he had in his pocket, he appeared at the Imperial Hotel on Sunday morning, March 5, 1933.

His Berlin escape story became a set piece, and with his "escape," Spiegel joined others who were to make up a new film community–the German Exile Cinema. Indeed, until his John Huston partnership, he was in the thick of the German Exile Cinema, which was fine when he was in Europe, but it was to hold him back when he reached Hollywood in 1939. Not that Spiegel thought clearly about his career in the 1930s. He was a luftmensch, living out of his suitcase and taking his life week by week.

Nevertheless, it was generally assumed that the production of *Unsichtbare Gegner (Invisible Opponents)* was "the one and only reason" for Spiegel's two-month stay in Vienna. No doubt, he sensed the possibility of trouble–the political climate in the city was a déjà-vu of all he had just experienced in Berlin. Most of Spiegel's friends had opted for France, but typically his reason for going to Austria was simply a question of finances. Pan-Film's Leopold Meissner–whose company was based in Prague, but worked out of Vienna–was funding his film, which cost between 400,000 and 450,000 Austrian schillings. (At the time, the average cost of a picture was 370,000, whereas an extravagant production such as Wilhelm Thiele's *Grossfürstin Alexandra* cost 880,000.)

When *Unsichtbare Gegner* was released, the *Kinematograph* reviewed it as a thriller with "all the right elements–fraud, betrayal, crime, fight, espionage, pursuit, hate and, of course, a little bit of love." The film, whose working title was *Öl ins Feuer (Oil in Fire)*, offered an inkling of Spiegel's future productions: the struggle of the protagonist–in this case the oil company's heroic engineer (Paul Hartmann)–against almost everyone else. It was a theme that was inherent in Spiegel and omnipresent in the legacy he was to leave behind.

As far as the casting, Spiegel (billed as the film's executive producer) was lucky to get Gerda Maurus to play Sybil Herford, the film's love interest. Thanks to director Fritz Lang, her mentor and lover, who shared her penchant for sadomasochism, she was a renowned femme fatale of the era. Having Lorre was also a plus, since he played in both the German and French productions of the film. At first, the owl-eyed Hungarian was unenthusiastic about playing Pless, one of the "Invisible Opponents." After his success as the child murderer in Lang's *M*, he was scared about being typecast. As a result, Spiegel had to use his legendary powers of persuasion.

The same powers were in full force when hiring Rudolf Katscher (who eventually changed his name to Rudolph Cartier), the director of the German version. Initially, he had come to Spiegel about another project, one that had Homolka attached as the star. But by the time their meeting ended, Katscher forgot about his previous film treatment *(Duel in the Dark)* and his former partners, and immediately signed up to do *Unsichtbare Gegner*, as well as persuading Homolka to join him. Such behavior became standard practice around Spiegel.

For the French version of the picture–*Les Requins du Pétrole*–Spiegel allowed Henri Decoin to direct (although the Frenchman had to share his directing credit with Katscher). It was the screenwriter's first break and he was to continue to have an interesting career, often directing his wife, Danielle Darrieux, and other major stars of the French cinema like Raimu and Jean Gabin.

Meanwhile, both Katscher and Decoin were to have a co-director in the shape of Spiegel. He was never out of Sievering Studios, which belonged to Sascha–the Austrian equivalent of Ufa–where most of the picture was shot. And proving himself to be truly *tonangebend,* the producer was either in elegant suit and tie pointing out some error on the set, or dressed in a long overcoat and hat, two steps behind the cameramen, Eugen Schüfftan (changed to Eugene Shuftan in the United States) and Georg Bruckbauer. In later years, it would be quite the contrary–Spiegel became renowned for his nonappearances and rare grand entrances, preferring to have his spies behind the scenes while he operated from his office. It was perhaps working on these early films that he learned an essential lesson: the director's power on the film set was infinitely greater than that of the producer.

In regards to payment, Spiegel was his usual unreliable self. "I was the only one who was paid promptly," said Phillis "Rudi" Fehr, who was a humble junior editor. "And it was only because Sam knew who my father was–the president of Deutsche Bank. He used to say, 'If your father ever wants to make a picture, you know who to send him to.' " Fehr, who later edited *Key Largo* and *Dial M for Murder,* found Spiegel's optimism to be "cute," especially since his father had no intention of joining the film business.

Nevertheless, he noticed a considerable change in Spiegel's lifestyle, which he attributed to a certain Konsul Rutgers. But despite considerable research, the well-heeled Austrian remains Harry Lime-like. Was Fehr referring to Robert Müller, the picture's Austrian distributor? Considered a big personality in the Viennese film world, he was an affluent man in his fifties who had that magic commodity—access.

Access was a currency that Spiegel tended to deal in more effectively than hard cash. Still, during his couple of months in Vienna, he "had the aura of a successful producer." Even if he did not make the film columns in either *Mein Film* or *Tonfilm-Theater-Tanz*–Spiegel was seen in all the right places. He became a regular on the terrace of the Imperial Hotel's café. He was spotted in Femina, a bar in the First District. He frequented the Döblinger Bad, an indoor pool in the Nineteenth District, as well as Café Filmhof on the Neubaugasse, which in atmosphere resembled the Romanisches.

Spiegel was also seen driving around with the likes of Otto Preminger and Hedwig Kiesler (later to become Hedy Lamarr) in his beautiful limousine. Indeed, there were rumors that Spiegel and the raven-haired beauty had a torrid affair on a train, several months before her marriage to Franz "Fritz" Mandl, the munitions magnate, that led to her conversion from Judaism to Catholicism.

Preminger was then running the Josephstadt-Theater, having taken over from "Herr Professor," as the director Max Reinhardt was called. Prematurely bald, Preminger had the height and Prussian looks that few could forget, and like Spiegel, the director had a reputation for being a ladies' man as well as a great charmer. Although there was a strange respect between the two, their relationship was mercurial. In later years, when Spiegel was annoyed with Preminger–and there were many such occasions–he made a point of telling their mutual friends that they had really never been close in Vienna, it was merely that everyone in the film and theater world mixed and knew one another. But being a gin rummy fiend, the director was a regular at the producer's inner-sanctum game in Hollywood. The famous Spiegel-

Preminger escape story was also to link them for life. As with the "flight from Berlin," there were many versions.

To begin with, Ingo Preminger dismissed the story as "a ridiculous myth." "Sam didn't escape with my brother because Otto didn't escape. . . . [He] never saw a Nazi in his life." The late director's autobiography stated the same facts.

Spiegel and Preminger left Vienna on May 10, 1933. Pertinent for two reasons, it was six months before *Unsichtbare Gegner* came out. Yet again, Spiegel was to miss his own film's premiere. But perhaps most significantly, it was five years before the Anschluss, therefore no Nazis were remotely involved in the adventure.

So what about the escape story? It did happen, but it was not so much an escape as Spiegel and Preminger breaking the rules–taking more money out of Austria than was legally permitted, and risking either imprisonment or paying a substantial fine–250,000 Austrian schillings (then equivalent to $43,691 or £10,593). According to a series of federal government decrees, released with the idea of protecting Austrian commerce, anyone leaving the country was only allowed to take a maximum of 200 Austrian schillings (then equivalent to $34.95 or £8.47–the average monthly wage being 234.55 Austrian schillings), while all foreign currency was supposed to have been reported to the National Bank of Austria. Since Spiegel and Preminger were traveling with hundreds of schillings as well as unaccounted for Swiss and French francs, they could have been arrested or fined on both accounts.

As far as what really happened, the true sequence of events, it remains a mystery since Spiegel's version of the story played in direct contrast with Preminger's. According to Spiegel, they were driving to Paris–presumably via Switzerland–in his car. Preminger had a thick wad of banknotes, amounting to more than the allowed quota. Both men knew that they would be searched at the border, and beforehand they had discussed what Preminger should do. The director had a very good-looking camel-hair coat from England and he proposed putting all the money in the lining. But Spiegel disagreed, insisting that since Preminger was a well-known figure in Austria, it would be the first place the guards would look. Despite their difference of opinion, Preminger stubbornly left the coat on the seat. However, when the

Customs official asked who the coat belonged to, he pointed to Spiegel, who was then hauled out and subjected to questioning. When alone in the car, Preminger broke out in a profuse sweat. Nervously, he reached into his jacket pockets and suddenly touched the bulk of cash, which Spiegel had craftily slipped back in.

However, when Preminger told his version, it was his car, he was the hero of the piece, and so forth. It was crazy, a duplicate story to the very last detail. As far as who turned in whom, both Spiegel and Preminger swore "on their children's head" that it was neither of them. Yet which one did?

After they were released, Spiegel drove in silence for several miles. He then abruptly stopped the car and, out of pure and utter relief that they had not been caught, he and Preminger laughed uproariously for several minutes. The rest of the journey went relatively smoothly until reaching Paris, where Spiegel's car was towed away due to an unpaid debt. Preminger was amazed, but Spiegel was very calm. "A car is a nuisance in Paris anyway," he said. "It's so much easier taking taxis."

Wheels or not, Spiegel stayed at the Hotel George V. Among all the other émigrés, only Fritz Lang was able to afford the most expensive establishment in Paris, but Spiegel was Spiegel. He then called on Paulette Dubost, who was filming *Le Roi des Champs-Elysées* with Buster Keaton (British title: *The Champ of the Champs Elysées*).

It was also a chance to freshen up his Berlin contacts, since Seymour Nebenzahl was producing, Max Nosseck was directing, and Robert Siodmak was supervising. Previously it has been written that Spiegel did errands for the producer, which has been hotly denied by Harold Nebenzal (family name changed in United States). "Sam was a social friend of my father's, a card-playing acquaintance." The writer-producer described Spiegel as "a unicorn" and someone with "this Napoleon-like personality." "How could he assist anyone? He was his own man."

Spiegel made full use of the production, since his meeting with Keaton led to the comedian starring in his next picture, *The Invader,* a curious title and perhaps more appropriate for Spiegel, who was about to arrive in London having just fled the Nazis in Berlin.

Or so he said.

Chapter Six

LONDON

When Spiegel arrived in England, Alexander Korda was reaping the rewards of a huge hit, *The Private Life of Henry VIII*. Released in the same year as *Unsichtbare Gegner*, it was the first British talkie to capture an international audience.

Korda was to make a lasting impression on Spiegel. Not only was he a European gentleman, swathed in the right stylish trappings, but he also aspired to greater heights than the film business. Korda's ultimate goal was to be an international statesman, having influence and socializing with politicians and important members of society. It was a goal that Spiegel thoroughly understood, and one he eventually aspired to.

In the early 1930s, Korda was the acceptable face of the British cinema while Spiegel was living off Joseph Jay "J.J." Bamberger, a film distributor. Naturally, a certain amount of Spiegelese was weaved to achieve this. He had appeared at Bamberger's West End office, having arrived "overnight from Berlin" and possessing only the clothes that he stood in. Such heroic details of fleeing the Nazis and so forth worked well with the "deeply Jewish" Bamberger, whose immediate reaction was to dress Spiegel and give him money, as well as an open invitation to his house in Elstree, Hertfordshire.

Spiegel then moved to Mount Royal, an apartment hotel in London's Marble Arch, where the other occupants included Robert Wyler, his friend's younger brother, the mouth organist Larry Adler, the comedian Will Hay, and Marcus Sieff, one of the heirs of Marks & Spencer, the British department store. Strangely enough, it was where David Lean and Spiegel first met, and the producer marked the occasion by trying to seduce Lean's girlfriend. Spiegel, who was fiercely competitive in the sexual arena, often did this, perhaps keen to prove that he was more exciting than other men, particularly the handsome ones, like Lean.

Spiegel also earned a reputation for being "dangerous in taxis." After sharing a cab with him, Angela Fox, mother of actors Edward and James Fox, announced that it was "the first and the last time." Around the same period, she lunched with a girlfriend whose knees were covered in bruises. "I asked if she had fallen down . . . well, Sam had offered to give her a lift."

Nevertheless, Spiegel could always be counted on to have a supply of the latest in American makeup–"particularly lipstick." Within a few months, he was squiring around Penelope "Pempy" Dudley Ward, one of London's most socially glamorous girls, whose mother was the acknowledged mistress of the Prince of Wales. "Pempy was patrician-looking, had beautiful manners, and laughed a lot," said Laurence Evans, the future agent. "Really, she had everything apart from acting talent"–a problem since she was eager to be in the movies.

Spiegel set up a screen test for Dudley Ward. He barreled into the Gaumont-British building, which was in Shepherd's Bush, found an empty office on one of the eight floors, and ordered a camera crew for his protégée. He supposedly had a "package deal" with her and the director Anthony "Puffin" Asquith, or so he told composer Bronislaw Kaper. As a result, the composer and Walter Jurmann, his partner, were summoned from Paris to give Pempy a singing test. "Everything was in grand style," said Kaper. While they were working, someone called her from the courtyard. It was the Prince of Wales. "I said, 'I can wait a little.' She said, 'No, no, let's go ahead.' I was impressed." But he was less impressed by Spiegel's financial schemes; Spiegel was "reluctant" to give Kaper and Jurmann a "five pounds advance." However, on his return to France, Spiegel arranged a tea for Kaper with the Polish ambassador. "He was unbelievable, if I would ask him to see Churchill . . . I bet you in five minutes I would have had an appointment with him."

It was unlikely that Spiegel had a romance with the charming and much admired Dudley Ward, who eventually married director Carol Reed, since he rarely let his libido get in the way of his social ambitions. Certainly, with Spiegel, there was always a significant division between women he was seen with and those who were reserved for the bedroom.

It was simple: Pempy looked good on his arm, she enjoyed his company, and both were mutually interested in the other's world. The relationship was relatively even-keeled, which was hardly the case with Dorothea "Dosia" Cook, another of London's social stars. Stagestruck, she was the third wife of a millionaire, and Spiegel was merciless with her. Not only did he sell her signed first editions of George Bernard Shaw, there was also a beautiful car, which he borrowed one afternoon and which then vanished, as well as a valuable walking stick. Once Spiegel became rich, the glamorous redhead, who had married director Terence Young, tried to tackle him about returning the items. "But it was no good," said Juliet Nissen, Dosia's daughter. "Sam gave my mother one of those witty, off-the-cuff answers, and she was so amused by his quickness that she let it go."

Others were less good-natured about his outrageous behavior. "Spiegel's stepping-stone was women," said Angela Fox. Spiegel's first wife and Susi Agranovich *had* paved his way in Tel Aviv, just as London's fashionable society girls launched his "bachelor-about-town" image, while his friendship with Kathleen, Countess of Drogheda, opened still other doors.

"Kathleen was a staunch supporter of Sam," recalled Laurence Evans. "In those days, society was so closed. Outsiders weren't really welcome, particularly German Jewish ones. It was before it became fashionable to invite everyone." The blue-eyed countess was an adventuress, while the soirées held at her Belgravia home were a meeting point for the intelligentsia, artists, and bohemian aristocrats. She also had a vital Eastern European connection—the love of her life was Chatin Sarachi, an Albanian artist. Close to King Zog, his country's monarch, one of his favorite expressions was "he's a bounder." Might he have applied this to Spiegel, who was a regular guest at his lover's home?

Nevertheless, as a result of his social energy and ability to "make things happen," Spiegel was welcomed everywhere. As Aileen Mehle, the society columnist (she writes as Suzy in *W* magazine), was to later notice, "It was hard to be bored in his company, and it was toujours '*la politesse continentale*.' " Spiegel treasured female company, particularly when it remained platonic. He loved to gossip and was the first to notice a new dress or different hairdo, another facet of his *kleine Aufmerksamkeit*.

Unless money was involved. "Sam just had this strange thing about money," said Evans, who became his partner when they formed British & Continental Productions Ltd. in 1934. Typically, the company was Spiegel's idea, but was financed with Evans's trust fund. "I was in my early twenties and rather bedazzled by him," Evans admitted. There were also the producer's nocturnal casting sessions. "One morning, I arrived to find that the glass panel had a terrible hole in it and there was a spattering of blood. When I asked what had happened, Sam replied that he had been holding auditions, had given a test and the lady in question wasn't right. 'Wasn't right'? I think there had been some ghastly running around the desk."

Such tactics, however, were put on hold when casting the female lead of their first production, *The Invader,* for which he chose Lupita Tovar, Paul Kohner's wife. Considered Mexico's Vivien Leigh because of her role in the epic film *Santa,* she had also starred in the Spanish version of Universal's *Dracula.* Physically, she was ideal to play Lupita Malez, the cantina beauty who feigns love for Leander Proudfoot (Buster Keaton), the rich American tourist in Spain.

Spiegel helped collaborate on the screenplay, but the picture, which cost around $120,000 and took less than a month to shoot, was a disaster. First of all, he and his director were at loggerheads. Adrian Brunel did not appreciate Spiegel's "creation out of conflict" theory. As Spiegel explained it, "films that ran smoothly were colourless—only those which were produced in strife had an outstanding merit." A mild type, who had made his name with *The Constant Nymph* and *The Vortex,* Brunel resented losing his temper, particularly when Spiegel congratulated him on doing so.

Another problem was Keaton, who spent most of his £12,000 salary on alcohol. It was tragic, taking into account that Keaton had been, with Charles Chaplin and Harold Lloyd, one of the greatest comedians of the silent era. On the first day of shooting, Spiegel's assistant had given a note to Mr. Brunel saying: DON'T LET HIM

DRINK. Officially, Keaton was paying Hank, a "big American football type," to keep him off the sauce, but unofficially the stone-faced comedian was also paying him to "let him booze."

There was also the noise of a pneumatic drill, which was spoiling the outside takes. Worse still, having Eugen Schüfftan as cameraman was entirely inappropriate. Although his dark and atmospheric effects had suited Spiegel's previous production, *The Invader* was billed as a comedy, not a thriller. And Spiegel's voracious sexual appetite got in the way—a series of showgirls were hired for the dance sequence but when it came time to shoot, it was evident that none of them knew how to dance a step! In Brunel's opinion, "much time and money had been wasted."

Spiegel was noticeably absent when it came to payday. Lupita Tovar never had a problem; she was always paid, roses were delivered daily to her Dorchester Hotel room, the Westmore brothers did her makeup, and Jo Strasser designed her costumes. Her list of benefits confounded Yves Mirande, who was co-writing the French version of the picture, *Un Baiser, s'il vous plaît*. "*Madame*," he dramatically declared, "will you please stand up so that we can see what you've got to make this man behave like that!"

There were also *The Invader*'s distribution problems. The film was rejected for its brevity, and as a result had to be completely reedited. Yet throughout, Spiegel was living in luxury. His friends recalled extravagant evenings at the Dorchester, although they all privately wondered who was actually picking up the tab.

Spiegel was probably surviving on borrowed credit, and what better place to get it from than a first-class establishment? The Dorchester's management knew all about high fliers and was more tolerant of a credit problem than a small hotel would be, whose livelihood depended on prompt payment. Besides, the producer's high-profile parties were good for the Dorchester's social image. As most hotel managers learned with Spiegel, there was always a new deal in the works, and a new deal meant new financing, some of which was then spent to pay off old debts.

In regards to Spiegel's methods of acquiring cash, the director John Berry offered the following: "Sam is staying at the Dorchester with no money at all. He is walking down the stairs and sees the banquet room is being prepared. The waiters tell him it's for Alexander Korda. And so he goes to the table, sees where Korda is sitting and removes the place card of the person who is sitting opposite him and puts his name down. Dinner ends and Korda asks for the bill and Sam insists that he is going to pay. There were about fifty guests and Korda says that he can't possibly do that. So Sam says, 'Well, at least, let me pay half,' and so Korda gives him a check on the understanding that Sam will settle the bill with the hotel." But afterward, Spiegel quickly cashed Korda's check–at last he had some money in his bank–and then took his own sweet time paying off the hotel. An amusing anecdote, but using Korda makes it apocryphal, since he was as unlikely to accept a change in the placement as he was to write out a check to Spiegel. However, the thrust of the story was not Spiegelese since the producer was capable of everything during the following twenty years, giving credence to Billy Wilder's quip about his being a modern day Robin Hood "who steals from the rich and steals from the poor."

Still, while Spiegel's techniques were notorious, they had a time limit; until the authorities were hot on his trail. He had a good three-year stay in London, making enough contacts there to last a lifetime, but by the beginning of 1936, most of Spiegel's misdemeanors had caught up with him. As usual, he was in hot water with the immigration authorities, while his other offenses included using "false pretenses" to pay his rent, as well as cashing bad checks at the Alexandre Gaudin, a Soho restaurant.

Spiegel's first arrest was for the nonpayment of the February bill of his apartment at Cumberland House. He traveled to Brixton Prison in a "taxi at his own expense." He was allowed his customary telephone call. "I always heard that his one call from prison was to Hollywood about a film deal," said director John Frankenheimer. But pitching ideas was perhaps on hold until Spiegel found someone to pay for his release, particularly as he only had two shillings in his bank account. It was a Wednesday evening, most of his pals were out on the town, but he managed to contact Budd Schulberg's mother.

Adelaide "Ad" Schulberg was living it up in London, the wife of a successful Hollywood producer. It was before she became an extremely powerful agent–the Sue Mengers of her time. "She had the house of some lord with all his staff," said her son. That night was significant because it marked her first English dinner party. "She was sort of showing off and in the middle of dinner, the butler came with a deadpan expression saying, 'Brixton Prison is calling. Madame, a Mr. Spiegel on the wire.' It did nothing for my mother's social standing." To her credit, she took the call, and immediately paid Spiegel's bail.

Afterward, Spiegel made several more appearances at the Marylebone Police Court. Ivan E. Snell was the adjudicating magistrate, and with each appearance, Spiegel's entrance in the registrar grew considerably longer. On his last visit, two entire pages of the book were devoted to his misconduct, while most other people took up only two lines.

But the real trouble began when Spiegel forged "a guarantee" to the prejudice of Edmund J. "Teddy Joyce" Curbertson–meaning he faked a document that allowed him to obtain funds by using Curbertson as a reference. Following this particular misdemeanor, Spiegel was tried at the Central Criminal Court at the Old Bailey on April 8, 1936. He pleaded not guilty and reserved his defense. "Sam stood in the dock looking very miserable, then we saw him sentenced," said his then partner, Evans. "I always thought he'd get away with it, but he didn't."

Less than a month later, there was another trial at Marylebone Police Court, which led to his third imprisonment and his deportation to France. But this time, New Scotland Yard were on Spiegel's tail as were British Immigration, who firmly insisted that on "no account" or "on anyone's authority" was he to return to the United Kingdom.

Needless to say, Spiegel was to continue his misconduct, this time with the French authorities.

Chapter Seven

PARIS/MEXICO

I have always believed in myself," Spiegel liked to say, "because, if I didn't, who would?" By his mid-thirties, he had been imprisoned in two different countries. Was he a changed man when he arrived that summer in France? Did the deportee who was banned from America and the United Kingdom plan to change his ways? The answer was no. "Sam was very sure of himself," recalled Irene Heymann, another member of the German Exile Cinema who became Paul Kohner's assistant. "He was completely above all feelings that he was not superior to everyone else."

In Paris, it was life as usual—another day, another deal. Spiegel's appearance was as sharp as ever, the twinkle in the eyes had hardly dulled, and once again he stayed at the Hotel George V. He was also a regular at Fouquet's, the café around the corner, where the entire film world met. "It was full of producers with wonderful names like Deutschmeister or Rabinowitsch, bringing to mind Russian literature," said Hélène Rochas, the sister-in-law of director Raymond Bernard. "They were adventurers . . . survivors, the last of a type. They lived out of a suitcase and could have been out of the country in a blink." As for their finances, there used to be a joke that went: "Monsieur, why do you have such a beautiful American car? Because, monsieur, I don't have the money for the Métro." Rochas sensed that even when Spiegel made it as a star producer, he would never lose the "gambler image." Nevertheless, there was a specific difference between Spiegel and his fellow producers. "Most of them didn't like the company of women, but Sam really did. In some ways, I think he preferred women to men."

During this period, Spiegel's inner circle included the novelist Joseph Kessel and Romain Pinès, a Russian producer whose name was really Rachmiel-Betsalel. He also joined the card-playing set, consisting of producers who traveled in the same circles, like Seymour Nebenzahl and Robert and Raymond Hakim–the latter being part of an Egyptian family who were establishment figures in Paris. Money was lost, won, and lost again, and the card games were constant. "They played whether it was in London, Venice, Cannes, or St. Moritz," said Harold Nebenzal.

The casino in Deauville was another place where the gamblers rallied. Run by Monsieur (François) André–a human computer–he was the only one to decide if gamblers could go over their limit or not. "There was never any exchange, he would just make a sign and continue sitting by the bar," recalled an associate. There were Dostoyevsky-like scenarios of entire family fortunes being squandered on the premises, which was hardly the case with Spiegel.

Still, when Simon Spiegel passed away in 1936, the producer received an inheritance. Somewhat meager, he supposedly referred to it as "a good start" for him and his brother. "When we cashed it in, I could buy a good dinner." Spiegel did not attend the funeral in Haifa, Palestine. To be fair, he was at a serious professional low point at the time. But later, showing his customary detachment from his family, he used to confuse the circumstances of his sixty-four-year-old father's death with that of his younger brother's.

Meanwhile, Paris was not going as well as anticipated. Despite the elaborate announcements about his partnership with Romuald Rappaport and their plans to produce a film called *Mircha,* it was a brief and fruitless period for Spiegel. No doubt it was frustrating, since most of his German Exile friends were doing admirably. Robert Siodmak had teamed up with the writer Henri Jeanson on *Mister Flow,* while Max Ophuls directed *La Tendre Ennemie* with Schüfftan on camera. Does this explain why Spiegel abruptly left for South America in 1936? It seemed unlikely that it was for a picture.

On his return he formed a film company with Yves Mirande in June 1937–the very same screenwriter who had complained about the lack of funds on Spiegel's previous production. A month later, Rappaport also joined, perhaps indicating that his former partner still owed him money. Their company, Mira-Films, was on the Champs-Elysées, which was the key area for the film business, as well as being conveniently near Spiegel's hotel and Fouquet's.

Mirande is now a forgotten figure in France. However, before the Second World War, he was as well known in his country as Sacha Guitry—the playwright and veritable *monstre sacré*. Mirande used to joke that he stopped being a simple lad from Brittany when the restaurant Maxim's made a sophisticated Parisian out of him. Although he played hard and prided himself on being *"mondain"* (social), he also worked hard and was extremely prolific. After a brief stint at MGM (*le garçon genie* was how he referred to Irving Thalberg), Mirande returned to France and became known as the champion of the *"cinéma de vaudeville sophistiqué,"* due to his gift for dialogue, humor, and lightness of touch. Terrible with money before Mira-Films, he spent it all on the horses, and during the Mira-Films period, on Spiegel. In his memoirs, Mirande described himself, the actor Raimu, and others as getting "as drunk as the Polish—that's to say when the Polish could still afford to drink." Was this a veiled reference to his partner?

Mira-Films's first and last project was *Derrière La Façade*. Paulette Dubost claimed it was her idea—the investigation of a murder in a Parisian apartment block leading to the exposure of the lives of all the neighbors. The picture was announced in the press, with Max Kolpé as the writer, Ophuls as the director, and a cast that included Raimu, Pierre Fresnay, and Jean-Pierre Aumont. But when the film was ready to start in 1937, the money failed to materialize. (Eventually, *Derrière La Façade* came out in 1939 with a different cast and Georges Lacombe as director.) Years later, Spiegel implied that a lady friend had withdrawn the funds at the last minute. This was Spiegelese, perhaps borrowing from fellow producer and émigré Alexander Granowsky's reputation of being supported by a female multimillionaire.

The truth was a little bleaker. Spiegel's normal business methods had caught the attention of the French police—things came to a head when one of his checks bounced and he received a fifty-franc fine in October of 1937. A popular Spiegel anecdote illustrated this. Spiegel was walking down the Champs-Elysées when he received a terrible kick in the pants. Without turning around or batting an eyelash, Spiegel immediately said, "The check is in the mail."

Around the same time he visited Seymour Nebenzahl, who was in Venice filming a remake of Raymond Bernard's *Tarakanova* (aka *Betrayal*). "Beforehand, Sam had gone to my father's Paris office demanding a ticket [to Venice], insisting that my father had promised him one," said Harold Nebenzal. This was Spiegelese, but the ticket was bought and, instead of being annoyed, Seymour Nebenzahl was amused by the entire episode. Nebenzahl also had his own code of behavior. "He said to [composer Franz] Waxman, 'Look, you're going to Hollywood anyway,' " recalled Bronislaw Kaper. " 'Instead of giving you the last payment, order yourself a nice white tropical suit and I'll pay for it.' " Nebenzahl's son sensed that allowances were made for "all these characters." "They had a different lifestyle."

But Spiegel's ways did not amuse the authorities and he was officially expelled from France on April 15, 1938. The French police force had been in touch with New Scotland Yard, which had confirmed their suspicion of his doubtful "conduct and morality." And as if his disgrace in a second European country was not enough, problems with the Italian and Swiss authorities were also reported.

Does this explain Spiegel's letter to Paul Kohner, his friend who had become a Hollywood agent? Officially, it was to introduce two dancers who, in his words, had "just absolved a very successful tour of South America." His postscript went on to say, "But beware, because I am due on your sunny shores shortly."

Unannounced, Spiegel arrived on the set of *Maria,* a film that Kohner's wife was making in Mexico City. Lupita Tovar was not surprised. "You expected everything with Sam. Then he starts speaking Spanish like a native and I was shocked." The picture went on longer than expected and she became pregnant. "I would say, 'I want some herring,' and Sam would come back with dry bread and some herring."

Spiegel was then living at the Hotel Reforma, a much-frequented establishment in the heart of Mexico City. "I don't think he had any friends at first," recalled Tovar. Nevertheless, he soon threw a dinner in her honor. A smart move—not only was she an important Mexican star, but she had also been in his last production. The French and

German ambassadors were invited, the evening was a success, but there was a slight problem: the next day Spiegel disappeared. In desperation, the nightclub owner contacted the actress. "He said, 'Naturally we couldn't bring the bill in front of the people . . . ' I replied that Sam would be back, and if not, then they should get in touch with me. Well, they never got in touch with me, so clearly, Sam took care of it." Given Spiegel's past, that seems unlikely.

By the beginning of 1939, however, he was recognized as an impresario who engaged artists for both the stage and screen, as well as looking for South American literary properties. Apparently, he had also struck up with fellow émigrés Jack Gehlmann and Oscar Danziger and had a project with Cantinflas–before he became Mexico's favorite comedian.

Spiegel had an office in the Aztlán building on Avenida Juárez, and employed a certain F. M. Sánchez to find material for him. One of the submitted books was *Historia de un Frac (Story of a Tailcoat)* by Francisco Rojas Gonzáles. Spiegel returned it, concluding that the subject matter was not of interest.

A few years later, he was accused of plagiarizing the same material for his first Hollywood production, *Tales of Manhattan*. And in typical style, he signed a statement saying that he had never seen the book, had never stayed at the Hotel Reforma, and had not been in Mexico since 1938. He even insisted on adding another clause to the document declaring that he did not speak Spanish. The Spiegelese was unnecessary since the producer was innocent of plagiarizing the book. But his innocence was irrelevant. Spiegel was only capable of conducting his affairs through misinformation. Telling the truth unnerved him. When confronted about his daily fibs, he was well prepared and armed with replies such as, "If I hadn't lied, I would now be a bar of soap . . . a lamp shade." But no, it was what made Spiegel, Spiegel. "He would prefer to climb a tree than tell the truth," his third wife said.

Before leaving Mexico, Spiegel had a brush with the authorities. Unfortunately, no records were kept, but whatever he did made him worried about applying for his American naturalization. Most evidence points to *Upa Yapa,* a stage musical, as being the source of Spiegel's problems with the law. Like the majority of his schemes, this cultural review—which he claimed to have written, directed, and produced (!)—started off at the summit of respectability, winning the approval of the Mexican minister of education, as well as the rest of the government. Spiegel then persuaded them to let him take the musical, which was renamed *Mexicana,* to New York. His selling point was that it would promote the country's art and folklore.

Despite his initial enthusiasm, Spiegel then distanced himself from *Mexicana*'s cast. He refused to travel with the performers and, at very short notice, left all the arrangements of their American arrival up to the Mexican embassy. Spiegel's behavior was curious, taking into account that the cast were non-English speaking and were also burdened "by a considerable amount of costumes and scenery." Fortunately, the embassy pulled a few strings. Consul Wormuth in Laredo, Texas, was contacted and the large troupe were allowed through border control, though it was a scramble, since their arrival coincided with Easter. In the meantime, "Mr. Sam Spiegel of New York"—as he was already referring to himself—was still in Mexico City.

Spiegel arrived in time for the opening of *Mexicana,* which took place at the Shubert 46th Street Theatre on Broadway, in May. He remembered the musical as an artistic success, which received a favorable review from the *New York Times,* but it was not a money-earner. "There were 126 people in the production," he recalled. Another problem was the World's Fair being in New York, which took away much of the business, plus there was a record-breaking heatwave. "So it won me prestige, but my share of profits was practically nil, for there were none." Actually, it earned him further problems, since he deserted the entire cast. The Mexican consul told Lupita Kohner about the mess. "It wasn't a success so most of the people were stranded there, which I understand," she said. "That does happen; some things don't work out."

All of Spiegel's family saw *Mexicana,* which included Shalom, his brother, who was teaching literature at the Jewish Institute of Religion in New York, Shalom's family, and also *Mutter.* "My grandmother had come over from Palestine to initially visit us and see the World's Fair," said Judge Raya Dreben, Shalom's daughter. "Then the war broke out . . . she stayed until 1945."

Meanwhile, Spiegel returned to Mexico City that month. He was staying at the St. Regis Hotel, and was existing on an expired passport. Judging from his correspondence with Mexican immigration, however, he was anxious to leave the country, even though his passport was invalid. Indeed, he had become of "indefinite nationality," with only a clutch of letters proving his identity. Did this explain the theory that Spiegel swam across the Rio Grande and was actually a "wetback" when he reentered America? Naturally, he insisted that he had entered the United States from Tijuana, Mexico, which was the respectable way to arrive. But, in the late summer of 1939, how did Spiegel–a former deportee–get through the American border control without a passport?

Gore Vidal offered the following anecdote on Spiegel's Mexican activities: "He and Otto [Preminger] meet for the first time in Hollywood and Ottsie just lets him have it. 'You are the greatest, most treacherous son of a bitch that ever lived. . . . You end up in Mexico where you get involved in selling dope. You get arrested also for a white slavery charge. You get thrown in prison. Somewhere or other you bribe yourself out of prison and you sneak illegally into the United States at Tijuana.' Otto said, 'Sam just looked at me sorrowfully and said "Baby, it wasn't Tijuana." ' That's pure Sam, the details are not right but that's the shape of the narrative."

Part II

1939–1954

Chapter Eight

HOLLYWOOD

Just as the war clouds were gathering in Europe and Hitler was preparing to invade Poland, Sam Spiegel reappeared in Hollywood. At the age of thirty-seven, the producer was starting again. He may have made films in Europe, but apart from *An Old Spanish Custom,* the American title for the Buster Keaton film disaster, none of his other efforts were known in the United States.

Yet, in another way, he was in a unique and liberating situation. In "the marketplace of lies," Bertolt Brecht's term for Hollywood, the stakes were high. Since he had nothing, Spiegel had plenty to gain and nothing to lose. It was the perfect situation for a bona fide gambler.

Creatively, Spiegel was still cutting his teeth. Some of his early films in Hollywood were to show merit, but they were many paces behind the peak that he was ultimately to reach. His contact with quality may have begun: besides working with directors such as Julien Duvivier, Orson Welles, John Huston, and Joe Losey, he also tried making films out of novels by Dostoyevsky, Gogol, Thomas Mann, and Zola, as well as Noël Coward's humorous play *Blithe Spirit.* But how he caught the film business's attention had more to do with his unique and outrageous personality than with his creative plans. "I don't think ever in the history of Hollywood, we have seen anyone like that," recalled the veteran director Frederick de Cordova.

Spiegel became famous in Hollywood for several reasons. He changed his name to S. P. Eagle and his New Year's Eve parties turned into *the* event to attend. "I remember Marilyn Monroe spellbinding the boys–just amazing," said one attendee. Spiegel's Beverly Hills home became known as "boys' town"–a kind of adult playpen, which became a bane to certain wives, while his business partnership with John Huston–Warner Bros.' wonder boy–confounded most of the film community. And, although it has never been acknowledged in print, Spiegel became the link between the owners of United Artists–Charlie Chaplin and Mary Pickford–and the lawyers Arthur Krim and Robert Benjamin. Indeed, he was the middleman in negotiations that were to change the entire face of independent picture making.

However, during his early years in Hollywood, Spiegel was coasting, professionally. Coasting because he was relying on his contacts with the European writers and technicians who formed Hollywood's German Exile Cinema. All very gemütlich, but it held him back from reaching the American audience. This led to there being two schools of thought about Spiegel: the rare few who believed that he would succeed –"we would have bet every cent that we owned," said Leonora Hornblow, the wife of Arthur Hornblow, Jr. (the producer of *Midnight, Hold Back the Dawn, The Asphalt Jungle*)–versus the many who dismissed any such notion. The skeptics shared Billy Wilder's opinion that Spiegel was an amiable "Mr. Fixit" with a veritable "genius" and "ingenuity" for absolutely everything except making pictures. For some, such as the writer L. P. Bachmann, the producer was "the slight butt of people's jokes" whose "stock in trade" was to amuse the people "with whom he courted favor." Jean Howard, who was a friend of all the wives of studio heads and who chronicled Hollywood's golden era, never took to Spiegel. "He was like Mike Todd," she said. "I called them 'those characters.' They were just fellows who appeared on the scene and wanted contact with the studios."

Howard was not alone in her opinion. "Sam had to swallow a lot," said Lupita Kohner. His reputation followed him. Spiegel's illegal status was not held against him. What were immigration lawyers for, after all? On the other hand, the tales of being imprisoned for debt in London was a different story: all three events had been covered in the trade papers.

Another factor that did not help Spiegel was that he loathed Los Angeles. Culturally, "the land of nod" was a shock. Spiegel had been spoiled by his life in Europe–the cafés, the theater, the opera and ballet. Such stimulation and sophistication were essential to him. In Hollywood, there were no distractions, the inhabitants lived and breathed the film business. And then there was the driving. Spiegel was a disaster at the wheel of a car, and to make matters worse—or more endearing—he had a poor sense of direction. Spiegel was too stoic to complain, and he played the game—where had he not? He became a regular at such restaurants as Lucy's, Ciro's, Chasen's, the Mocambo, Perino's, Romanoff's, and the Trocadero. His hooded eyes remained as impudent as ever, his suits were showier, while his tipping of *maître d*'s at fashionable spots went on as always. It was essential to show that he was a successful showman at all times.

Actress Evelyn Keyes compared Spiegel's behavior to that of his fellow producer Mike Todd. "If people were dumb enough to give to them, it was their dumb problem," she said. "The point is that those guys were generous. They were big people. Sam was the same having money or not having it—what was important is that he wanted to accomplish something."

Hollywood represented Spiegel's last chance in the motion picture industry. "Doing time" in Hollywood led to his being part of the community, and being "part of the community" paved the way to making pictures with the studios. Strangers were not greeted with open arms unless their talent had been sought out, which was hardly Spiegel's case. He was not greeted stepping off the *Super Chief,* nor had a purring limo been waiting, as it had been for fellow émigrés Anatole Litvak and Otto Preminger.

Fortunately, his loyal friends were at hand. Paul Kohner and William Wyler looked out for Spiegel and acted like his extended family, whereas friends such as Wilder, Litvak, and Huston teased him mercilessly, but always included him in their various bachelorlike pursuits.

Wyler moved Spiegel into 7655 Hollywood Boulevard, a brick apartment building owned by his mother, Melanie Wyler. Later, Spiegel recalled living in an attic—"Not even a picturesque attic," he complained. In fact, he lived in a cramped single-room apartment on the first floor in the back. He spent over a year there, creating the usual tension or excitement. According to Margaret "Talli" Wyler, the director's second wife, "Sam was always fleeing from someone."

No doubt Immigration was at the top of the list, since for the first time in his life, Spiegel was returning to a country from which he had been deported. But such fears did not restrain him from badgering producer Joe Pasternak and Billy Wilder to help him with one of his financial schemes. "Our signature allowed him to collect $80 a week from a Jewish relief fund in New York," recalled Wilder. Meanwhile, on his travels in search of more sponsors in the Goldwyn Studio building, Spiegel discovered an empty office, where he immediately settled.

Appropriating space was standard practice with the producer. In London, he had briefly done this at Gaumont-British, so why not at Goldwyn? However, his other little foible of gaining credit by using someone else as a reference—essentially piggybacking on their reputation—tried the patience of many, including Paul Kohner. "Dear Mr. Sam Spiegel," the agent's letter began, which was sent Special Delivery. "You have used my name at the Bank of America, with the Columbia Outfitting Company [nothing to do with the film studio] and probably others. Checks of yours are bouncing left and right." The agent threatened to take legal action. "I want no explanation of any sort," he warned. "I merely want you to digest this letter and believe every word of it."

Spiegel did not try such tricks with Wyler, or "90-take Wyler" as he was known in the industry. The brilliant director, who was born in Alsace-Lorraine when it belonged to Germany, had a tough approach to business. "He was the only one [of his generation] who got a really square deal from the studios," said the writer Peter Viertel. On the other hand, Wyler's mischievous side was amused by Spiegel. "He lived vicariously through Sam," recalled Melanie Wyler, his youngest daughter. "Before my mother, he had led a wild life, but Sam had never *not* had a wild life."

The director of such classic films as *Jezebel, Wuthering Heights,* and *The Best Years of Our Lives* also shared Spiegel's weakness for gin rummy. Both men were capable of giving their entire concentration to the game for hours and hours. The same applied to other members of their circle, which included Kohner, Huston, Litvak, Wilder, the actor Edward G. Robinson, and often Otto Preminger—indeed, their social life was intricately linked with arranging the next gin game.

For Spiegel and the other bachelors in the group, it was a footloose existence. As one acquaintance observed, "It was the three Cs: cocktails, cards, and c***." The occasional incident spiced up their existence, such as when Anatole Litvak's thick thatch of hair was said to have slipped down to Paulette Goddard's lap and beyond. ("Said" because Litvak fervently denied the incident, claiming that he "might have" kissed Goddard's breast when a strap on her dress fell down.) However, it was claimed that the director–who had been briefly married to film star Miriam Hopkins–had dared to do this publicly, in a booth at Ciro's, no less! Litvak's reputation was made and sent shock waves throughout Hollywood.

Although Spiegel and Huston and the rest were exciting to be around, they were not always chivalrous. "Billy [Wilder] said, 'Lupita, you must be the only woman with whom John [Huston] hasn't gone to bed because he always speaks so highly of you,'" said Lupita Kohner. "Sam was different, but I wondered why either he or John married, because they were unfaithful immediately." Did Spiegel belong to the same school of thought as Wilder, who insisted that if men were forced to choose between romantic company or playing a game of cards, 98 percent would choose the cards? Wilder's other misogynistic fantasy was inventing a mattress that, after making love, forced the woman to disappear, allowing a full-fledged card game– with three acquaintances–to appear instead. In his opinion, it was the perfect way to avoid the inevitable post-sex questions such as, "Do you really love me?" or "Is it still as it was?"

Certainly, sleeping with Spiegel was often at a woman's peril because once the conquest was over, he lost interest fast. However, like many Don Juans, he was adorable with the wives of his friends, because their relationship remained platonic. In Hollywood, Spiegel became close to Leonora Hornblow, Lupita Kohner, Talli Wyler, and eventually Irene Mayer Selznick. As a consequence, he had an open invitation to their homes, while becoming a sort of unclelike figure to their children. Of course, there were limits. "My sister and I used to hide under the piano to get away from Sam's wet kisses," admitted Catherine Wyler. According to Susan Kohner Weitz, the former actress (and mother of Chris and Paul Weitz, the writer/director team of *American Pie* and *About a Boy*), the producer liked to kiss on the mouth. "Somehow, it was not salacious . . . there was a big sweetness about Sam."

Most Sundays, Uncle Sam went to the Kohners' family home in Bel Air. "We would have a *kaffeeklatch*," said his hostess. Regulars included her husband's clients, such as Oscar Homolka, Marcel Pagnol, Luise Rainer, and other refugee Europeans. His successful talent agency aside, Kohner was a key figure in the European Film Fund, an organization that helped refugees to adjust to Hollywood, both financially and professionally.*

Kohner's household was European in feel. "As with my father, I never knew that all our guests had accents," said Susan Kohner Weitz. The dining table used to groan with the weight of coffee cake, pastries, and "marvelous chocolate goodies," which the agent made a point of buying himself. "After coffee and conversation, the men, such as my father and Sam, would slowly peel off to the breakfast room where the gin rummy game would go on and on." Sometimes the game lasted until seven the following morning. The room would be a disaster area. Thick with smoke, it would be covered with empty liquor bottles, dirty glasses, and overflowing ashtrays. As the help had long since been sent home, it was up to Mrs. Kohner to make the scrambled eggs and coffee for the ravenous gamblers. "At the time, it drove me mad," she admitted. However, she has now had a change of heart. "I must say that I miss that kind of man–they were bigger than life."

In the film community, cards were an accepted way of life. Studio heads Darryl F. Zanuck, Jack L. Warner, David O. Selznick, and Samuel Goldwyn were all keen players. "Zanuck used to suck on his cigar and be very quiet, he had all the respect," said John Aspinall, a fellow gambler, "while Warner came on very strong–he had this huge and warm personality."

Kitty Carlisle Hart–the actress wife of playwright Moss Hart–used to play with Goldwyn. "It was a friendly game–never for money–but

---

*Ron Meyer, the president and chief operating officer of Vivendi Universal Entertainment and one of the founders of C.A.A., started off his career as Kohner's office boy.

Frances, his wife, would sit on the sofa either doing needlepoint or knitting. Once in a while, she would look up and say, 'Watch him, he's cheating.' " As a rule, the Goldwyns were renowned for their "giant gin games" with serious stakes. "I once heard that Goldwyn lost $150,000 in one night and didn't speak to anyone for months!" said Yolande, the wife of Matthew Fox, a popular figure and a key executive at Universal Pictures and United Artists.

Selznick was involved in all the "big power" games but also liked to play at the Colony and Goldie's–the illegal gambling club on the Hollywood Strip. In time, the mogul joined Spiegel's game, which grew to include Spiegel's lawyer Morton Garbus, the actor Richard Conte, the agent Charles K. Feldman, Norman Greenthal–a power in advertising–and Matty Fox.

"It was Sam's favorite 'boys in the backroom' story," said Betty Spiegel. "Matty had a button under the table and when he pressed a certain code, Jack, his black butler, would open the door and announce, 'Mr. Fox has gin,' instead of Fox laying down his hand." According to Fox's widow, it only happened once, and "like the Paulette Goddard story, everyone was there that night!" Still, Spiegel was in attendance. As usual, his host and fellow gambler was playing in his underwear, eating licorice, popcorn, and chili.

Almost everyone in Spiegel's gin circle was superstitious–because so much was riding on each card. On one occasion, Mrs. Greenthal arrived when her husband had been dealt a poor hand. "Go away, you bring me bad luck," he cried. Obediently, she moved into another room, but it was still not enough. "I can still smell your perfume," he yelled.

Not everyone understood the card mania. "It was amazing for such intelligent fellows," said Peter Viertel. In the meantime, Viertel gained a reputation for looking "great in swimming trunks" and for always coaxing "everyone" to be "naughty." "Peter was a womanizer," said Joan Axelrod. "But a sweetheart with the best sense of humor." Salka, Viertel's mother, had the "intellectual" salon in Hollywood. Like Spiegel, she came from Galicia, although her childhood was grand and "Tolstoy-like." Married to the director Berthold Viertel, she was in the German version of *Anna Christie* with Greta Garbo, as well as collaborating on some of "the Swede's scripts." "Her Sundays were a

Hollywood institution," said Bronislaw Kaper. In the composer's estimation, "151 greatest people tried to get in," but with little success. "It was a snobbish group." Held at her home in Santa Monica, Viertel entertained the leading figures of the European colony, including Heinrich and Thomas Mann, Igor Stravinsky, Bertolt Brecht, Aldous Huxley, and Ernst Lubitsch. Her guests tended to be dismissive of anything American. In Billy Wilder's opinion, it was the "only place in Hollywood which had comfortable armchairs."

Spiegel used to go there, but only occasionally. "My mother always said, 'Sam has a very nice voice and nice eyes,' " said Viertel. It was at Salka's that Spiegel met "G," or "Miss G," as Garbo was known to her friends. Eventually, the actress and Mr. Spieeegel–her pronunciation of his name–became quite friendly. "The big bond between them was paintings," Viertel said. "She was interested because at the time she was acquiring. . . . Sam liked art and knew something about it."

When Spiegel worked at Universal Studios, he had a Monet on a wall of his office. No doubt, he was reticent about keeping the work of art at home because his creditors might have grabbed it. "Financially, Sam was always one step ahead of the sheriff," said Max Youngstein, an acquaintance and an executive at Fox, "and the one thing he always wanted to save were his paintings. It was funny, he didn't go for his suits."

Edward G. Robinson shared Spiegel's passion for paintings. However, in Leonora Hornblow's opinion, it was the actor and Wilder who were "the true collectors." "Others like Zanuck started buying art when it became fashionable." Robinson was the first to champion Paul Cézanne in Hollywood. ("Before people could even spell the name," she said.) A gentle soul, he was quite different in character from the bad-boy roles that had made him famous, like Rico Bandello in *Little Caesar*. Born in Bucharest, he came from a strict Orthodox Jewish background, and had even studied to be a rabbi. Spiegel and Robinson used to speak Yiddish together, and often played cards. "Figures speak louder than words," Spiegel wrote after a win, "and never have they been kinder than on this check!" There was also an "us Jews against them" camaraderie. "Once more–good for our side," the producer wrote, in regards to one of his friend's performances.

Fitting in with the Hollywood tradition, Spiegel took up tennis, but according to Samuel Goldwyn, Jr., "like most of that ilk, he cheated." When the character actor Norman Lloyd (Hitchcock's *Saboteur,* Renoir's *The Southerner,* and Chaplin's *Limelight*) sided with Spiegel in a doubles game against Wyler and Major General Carl A. Spaatz, he was terrified that they were going "to be court-martialed and shot because of some of the calls that Sam made."

There was a comic element to the producer's appearance. "He was a little heavy and he did sweat a lot," said producer Ray Stark. However, Spiegel surprised people with his speed. "Sam had that body and those very thin legs and, as a consequence, he could move very fast," Lloyd recalled.

Dancing was another of Spiegel's talents. His third wife compared him to "grass on the floor," while his fancy footwork so impressed Gene Kelly and his wife, Betsy Blair, that they wondered where he had learned to dance. "Maybe he danced as a kid," Blair said. "But I do remember because I was a dancer and married to 'The Great Dancer,' that there were only two other people who it was fun to ballroom-dance with in Hollywood—one was Danny Kaye, who was extremely gifted, and the other was Sam."

Chapter Nine

TALES OF
MANHATTAN

It was never clear where Spiegel met Boris Morros–his first Hollywood business partner. In the early 1940s, Spiegel had been doing the rounds, working at Goldwyn Studios under the guise of Lyric Films. He had projects with émigré pals, films such as *Ghost Music* with Billy Wilder and Jacques Thery, *The Barber of Seville* with Andrew Marton, and *Martha* with Jean Negulesco.

Perhaps the meeting was a result of pitching *Ghost Music* to Bing Crosby. The crooner worked at Paramount, the studio where Morros happened to be the musical director. Or it may have just been the Eastern European connection, since his partner was born in St. Petersburg in 1895. Boris the Bold (he would have deserved the name) turned to espionage and worked as a double agent to get his father–Mendel Moroz–out of Russia, and in time became the Soviet Union's longest-serving spy in America. Meanwhile, Morros's clandestine calls to Moscow did not prevent him from being a one-man hive of activity in Hollywood. After his attempt in the record business failed, he became the musical director on such films as Lubitsch's *Angel*, McCarey's *Make Way for Tomorrow,* and Ford's *Stagecoach*. He also produced *The Flying Deuces* with Laurel and Hardy, as well as *Second Chorus* with Fred Astaire and Paulette Goddard.

Bald, with slicked-back hair at both sides, Morros had merry black eyes and a curly, upturned mouth. Roly-poly, his physique resembled that of a toy clown—the type that when pushed down, bounces right up again. "He looked like Sam's jolly brother," recalled Ingo Preminger. Physically, the dynamic duo were easy to ridicule, resembling Lewis Carroll's Tweedle-dum and Tweedle-dee. Spiegel had taken to sporting loud flowery ties and a heavy camel hair coat. According to Max Youngstein, he was "a characterization of how Europeans conceive a Hollywood producer." He puffed on a pipe—his romance with Havana cigars had yet to materialize—while his partner occasionally wore a vast garnet crucifix over an Ascot sweater. The cross was a present from Rasputin, or so Morros said. The Mad Monk and he had a lot in common—"we are the spiritzel-type man." Although most thought him sweeter than Spiegel, he was just as much of a gonif, but with a difference—he stole from the Soviet Intelligence funds and did so for eighteen years!

A showman, Morros was seen escorting Igor Stravinsky when he was campaigning for Paramount to hire "contemporary composers for contemporary pictures." The mixture of chutzpah and impressive connections made him the perfect partner for Spiegel, who had come to him about making a sequence of films around an ill-fated tailcoat. Their idea was to use major Hollywood stars. Producers such as Alexander Korda scoffed at their ambitious scheme. "When I am breaking my neck, trying to get a single male star for this film *[Lydia]*, how do you suppose you can get a dozen—and without even a nickel to back you?" he had said. However, the producers proved the doubting Thomases wrong. Desperate and lacking in professional pride—Spiegel and Morros said or promised anything to get their way—they were also aware that one star led to another, and that in general a well-paid, short filming schedule appealed to actors.

Starting as *Tails of New York* at United Artists, their project became *Tales of Manhattan* when it reached Paramount. The partners then moved to Twentieth Century-Fox in August 1941. Morros's former studio was not pleased at losing out on a film that, in format, resembled their previous hit *If I Had a Million*. Paramount even held out the rights of the film's title until way past shooting. "We have no desire to destroy any investment of Fox," a studio executive wrote to Fox's president, Joe Schenck, "but you must know that further complications are going to develop and embarrassments take place."

Certainly, Spiegel's activities led to a few raised eyebrows, particularly when he was welcomed in New York as the guest of Fox Studios. "I proposed showing him places like the Metropolitan Museum and all he wanted to go and see was Polly Adler's—the best whorehouse in town," said Youngstein. "Sam spent the whole night there. I had to buy the place out . . . it was over $900."

There were also the endless yarns of the producer borrowing gas money for his pitch meetings at Fox. It was at this time that Spiegel changed his name. Like his infamous flight from Berlin, there were many versions of this event, all of which ended in the same outcome— henceforth, the producer became known as S. P. Eagle. (This professional nom de plume continued until the mid-1950s.) Some thought that the new name was meant to foil the immigration authorities. David Selznick, on the other hand, claimed that Spiegel wanted to sound mogul-like and was calling "himself S. P. Eagle for reasons of power and natural noblesse." He would have known, since he had added Oliver to his own name, turning it into David O. Selznick and thus emulating Louis B. Mayer, his future father-in-law, as well as other studio heads.

Then there were the producer's very own Spiegelese versions— either that he had seen the best fortune teller in Los Angeles, who had "predicted" that his career would "soar like an eagle" if he took the name of the bird that was America's national symbol, or that after the attack on Pearl Harbor, he was struck by a burst of patriotism. "My German name seemed positively profane in the circumstances, so I renounced it." However, the records show that Mr. S. P. Eagle was around many months before December 1941. According to England's New Scotland Yard, it was an alias that Spiegel had used in London in the mid-1930s.

The name change probably happened one late afternoon, in the Fox steam room. It was Darryl Zanuck who had set the plan into action by saying, "Look at everyone's name who is a producer, Selznick, Mayer—they all sound Jewish—even mine does [Zanuck was an Episcopalian], and we have got to find you a name which doesn't." Some dispute this theory and wonder whether it really was the tyrannical chief of production or the producer spinning Spiegelese. Yet it made sense for the time. Eleven months earlier, Joseph P. Kennedy—

America's ambassador to the Court of St. James–had given his "peace crusade" speech to fifty of Hollywood's heavyweights at Warner Bros. His message was simple: anti-Semitism was rising in Britain, and the Jews were being blamed for the war. "You're going to have to get those Jewish names off the screen," he advised. His words left his audience momentarily speechless, and according to Ben Hecht, resulted in Hollywood's most important Jewish executives going "around with their grief hidden like a Jewish fox under their gentile vests."

By changing his name, Spiegel was copying Edward G. Robinson and others who were born with Semitic or Central European-sounding surnames, including Kirk Douglas, Danny Kaye, and Judy Garland. During that period, it would have been impossible to be called Arnold Schwarzenegger and become a Hollywood star. In many ways, the name S. P. Eagle showed a certain S. T. Yle but, since it was Spiegel, it became the target of many jokes. Richard Condon, then the head of Fox's publicity department, used to send interoffice memos to the producer marked for the attention of E. A. Gull. (Wilder and Selznick also claimed to have invented the name.) One joker rang up and said, "Can I speak to Mr. S. P. Eagle . . . This is Mr. C. O. Hen." Zanuck, keen on a practical joke or two, was said to have joined in by signing himself Z. A. Nuck.

Spiegel's partner was equally audacious. Just when *Tales of Manhattan* was set at Fox, Morros was suddenly discovered to be trading off the studio's offer and renegotiating with Paramount! Such behavior was to try everyone's patience, particularly the great Charles Feldman, their agent behind the deal. Not only had he managed to square a budget for $860,000 with a 10 percent leeway, but he had given endless guidance to both producers, as well as having them around to his house on Coldwater Canyon.

Wisely, Spiegel was less meddlesome than his partner. Most associates recognized him as the intelligent partner in the team. To quote Youngstein, "Morros was legitimate as a musician, but what the hell was he doing making a movie?" Spiegel was keener to keep in with the Feldmans of the world than his reckless partner, whose agenda was anyone's guess. Being a power animal, Spiegel was impressed that the agent was close to all the studio heads, and that his

Famous Artists Agency had clients such as Claudette Colbert, Marlene Dietrich, and Irene Dunne. There was also Feldman's personal elegance. Well dressed, with a Cary Grant chic, he was courteous and kind. "He helped his clients, especially if they were down on their luck," said Fritz Lang. Charlie–as the agent was affectionately known–became a lifelong Spiegel intimate. He also provided Charles Boyer–the first star signed for *Tales of Manhattan*.

Initially, William Wyler was set to direct the Frenchman in a sequence that John Huston would write. However, the meetings between the three individuals and the producers came to nothing. Curiously, Wyler chose to forget this professional episode. "Daddy really loved Sam and he always said that the reason that they stayed such good friends is that they never worked together," said Melanie Wyler.

Morros and Spiegel had better luck with a Paul Kohner client–Julien Duvivier, a short, thin-lipped, dark-haired Frenchman, who inspired fear and dislike, but who was remarkably talented. *Lydia*, his previous Hollywood directing venture, had not been a success and the director's stock was considerably down. Had he been hot, it was unlikely that he would have agreed to make yet another picture that consisted of short films with a single subject matter. A contemporary of René Clair, Jean Renoir, and Marcel Carné, Duvivier caught Hollywood's eye with *Un Carnet de Bal,* which had been a major hit at the American box office and had led to invitations and the inevitable red-carpet treatment.

Among the *Tales of Manhattan* cast, Charles Boyer and Edward G. Robinson were the highest paid at $50,000 each. Just as Feldman had been instrumental in securing them, Leland Hayward had come up with two of his clients, Ginger Rogers and Henry Fonda. "Apparently, my father was very nice and took the money that Sam could give," said Bill Hayward. "As a result, Sam acted as if he owed his life to Leland." Yet, according to Ginger Rogers, Morros approached her personally about appearing in the film since he was "a friend from way back in the presentation theater days." Spiegel, however, was keen to keep in with "the Toscanini of the telephone"–Mr. Hayward's nickname–whose other clients included Greta Garbo, Fred Astaire, and Myrna Loy. He even went to Fleito, a fashionable Hollywood jeweler, and ordered a cigarette case engraved with Hayward's initials. His *kleine Aufmerksamkeit* was unnecessary in this case. "My father was fascinated by Sam."

Occasionally, the promise of gifts fell short. Spiegel had wanted to pay back Wilder and Walter Reisch for coming up with the theme of *Tales of Manhattan*–it was based on a screenplay they had written for Erich Pommer in Berlin in 1932–*Der Frack mit der Chrysantheme (History of a Tailcoat and Its Use)*. He asked how he could repay them. "We insisted that he didn't have to, he owed us nothing–with or without the Nazis," Wilder recalled. But Spiegel kept after both of them. So Wilder chose a pair of chairs that he had seen at the producer's house. "Not a problem, it was up to me to choose from the shop on Rodeo Drive. 'Make sure they're the most expensive,' he said." Reisch asked for speakers to go with his Capehart Gramophone. Ultimately, Spiegel failed to deliver on either of the items, and even had the nerve to ask the two men to pay for their own tickets for the charity performance of the film.

The question remains whether either Wilder or Reisch contributed to the writing of the sequences. Neither was credited, yet it was said that both did, although Wilder strictly forbade the use of his name. Like Wyler, he discovered that Spiegel was a better friend than a professional acquaintance.

There was a distinct German Exile Cinema feel to the picture, since the theme of the sequences was inspired by the plays of Ferenc Molnár, Laszlo Gorog, Ladislaus Fodor, and Laszlo Vadnai–mostly people whom Spiegel knew from Berlin. Meanwhile, the dialogue was presided over by the Academy Award-winning Ben Hecht (the former Chicago newspaperman was part of the Algonquin-to-Hollywood group, while his screen credits included Sternberg's *Underworld* and Wyler's *Wuthering Heights*), and his team of equally prolific screenwriters such as Samuel Hoffenstein, Donald Ogden Stewart, and Lamar Trotti. But despite the impressive mix of talent, the quality of the six tales was uneven.

The first episode was based on *The Marshall*, a one-act play by Molnár, and shows a love triangle between John Halloway, a big-game hunter (played by Thomas Mitchell), Ethel, his exquisite younger wife (Rita Hayworth), and her love, Paul Orman, a matinee idol (Boyer), who wears the tailcoat in question. According to Orson Welles (then Hayworth's husband), "They went a day over because every time Boyer gave [Rita] the *ooh ooh* look, she broke up. *Broke up!* The thing that all the women were panting for struck her as funny."

The second sequence was inspired by Fodor's play *Burberry* and was only of interest because of the actors. Diane (Rogers) looks in the tailcoat of her fiancé Harry Wilson (Cesar Romero) and discovers a letter from Squirrel, his pre-wedding romance. George, Harry's best friend (Fonda), is then called upon to smooth out the situation. Originally, Romero was to play the friend, but it had been the idea of the image-conscious Fonda to swap roles.

The third sequence was the director's favorite and, curiously, had shades of *Ich will Dich Liebe lehren,* Spiegel's first film as producer. Shot at Carnegie Hall, it concerns Charles Smith, an impoverished pianist (Charles Laughton) who gets his break to perform with Arturo Bellini (Victor Francen), the famous conductor at the New York Philharmonic. He wears the tailcoat that his wife (Elsa Lanchester) has found for him at a pawnshop. It is too small, and as Smith starts to wave his baton, he splits the tailcoat and the audience cruelly laughs. "My father was a perfectionist who had a horror of being embarrassed," said Christian Duvivier. "The idea that this could happen was his recurring nightmare."

The fourth sequence features Avery L. Browne (Robinson), formerly a prominent lawyer, who is living a hobo existence in Chinatown. Suddenly, he is invited to the twenty-fifth reunion with his old alma mater comrades at the Waldorf-Astoria. The dinner goes well until a wallet goes missing and Williams (George Sanders), his ex-partner from Chicago, tries to expose him as the culprit.

The fifth sequence starred W. C. Fields, and was co-written by the comedian, who was then on his last legs. He is his droll, stylish self, while Margaret Dumont plays her usual role as his gullible benefactress. Director Malcolm St. Clair, known for his comedies, worked with Duvivier on the sequence. But throughout the filming, Fields was always drunk. As a result, Duvivier–who was nicknamed "the professional of the professionals" by Jean-Luc Godard–refused to sign the sketch. "It was a huge scandal," said his son. The sequence was eventually denounced by Fox as being inappropriate, and there was even talk of replacing it with another sequence starring Tyrone Power or Jack Benny.

It was a pity that Fields's sketch was excluded from the other episodes (it can be seen on the released video) since it fit in better than the film's final, sixth sequence, which seems like something from another film entirely, enhanced by Richard Day's and Boris Leven's inspired, but totally inappropriate, sets. A hoodlum wears the tailcoat when robbing a fancy gambling club. Stuffed with $50,000 worth of notes, the coat is then thrown out of a burning plane. It falls in the fields worked by two black Southern sharecroppers, Luke (Paul Robeson) and Esther (Ethel Waters). Afterward, Robeson was "particularly despondent" about his role and announced that he was "through with Hollywood until movie magnates found some other way to portray the Negro besides the usual 'plantation Hallelujah shouters.' "

Tales of Manhattan was beautifully made and interesting to watch, but not one of Duvivier's better pictures, considering that he directed *Poil de Carotte, Pépé le Moko,* and *La Charrette Fantôme.* The cause may have been extreme homesickness. "There wasn't one day when my father didn't dream of coming back to France," said Duvivier. "He was too independent, and simply couldn't understand Hollywood and its rules." He was equally confused by Spiegel's games. Once he really insulted Spiegel, who merely gave him the warmest of smiles. "My father was absolutely staggered by his behavior and could not stop talking about it afterward." As was previously seen with Adrian Brunel, it fit in with Spiegel's "creation out of conflict" theory. There was also Spiegel's problem with time. He was "always late" for the punctilious Frenchman. But throughout his career he used to make his directors wait. Was the tardiness genuine, or was he playing a power game– showing who was boss?

Meanwhile, Spiegel and his partner were never far from Duvivier's set. Ecstatic about the roster of stars, one morning Morros would be escorting Carole Landis to meet Boyer and the next moment it would be S. P. Eagle with a journalist from *Variety.* Kings of self-promotion, the producers also took to writing about their experience. Presumably, Morros was behind the lines of wisdom captured by the following: "Because we believe that actors are people, we had no trouble with that thing called temperament."

Tales of Manhattan's premiere was held at Grauman's Chinese Theatre on August 5, 1942. A charity event, it was presided over by Walter Pidgeon. All the featured stars turned up, but due to wartime restrictions, the lobby and forecourt lights had had to be dimmed. That did not stop Spiegel, however, from making his grand entrance that Wednesday night. Looking every inch the affluent producer, he arrived with Hedy Lamarr on his arm.

Hedi, as he knew her, had just divorced Gene Markey and, between husbands, was on for a lighthearted romance. According to his third wife, Spiegel put Lamarr into the exquisite but "seriously" dumb category. "He and his friends would be playing gin rummy and she would sit in a chair flicking through piles and piles of magazines. Sam could play for hours, and I *mean* hours, but Lamarr would never leave; she just sat in the same chair." Perhaps Lamarr was playing dumb, because she was later credited and decorated by the U.S. government for thinking up the teleguided torpedo.

With the release of his first American film, life in Hollywood was looking up for Spiegel. Not only was he seen in the company of a screen goddess, but *Tales of Manhattan* was a critical, and moderate commercial, success. Murray Silverstone, a Fox executive, even enthused, "You boys will be able to lick your chops when dining at Romanoff's or Chasen's, with the knowledge that while the wolf may be at the door it won't get into your place, as far as this picture is concerned." Playing to packed audiences at Radio City Music Hall, according to the *New York Times,* it kept the audience "riveted by its variety of incident and mood." One of the main criticisms about the picture had been the "continental flavor," but this would give the film "a distinct asset" for foreign distribution, eventually.

Tales of Manhattan may have had legs (it also won the Box Office Blue Ribbon Award), but the Spiegel-Morros partnership had financial problems. Officially, it was dissolved in August 1943. "They came apart because they spoke the same language," said Jules Buck. The team realized that it made sense to get rid of their company and start afresh with new funds. Besides, Morros was yearning to make musicals again–he later produced *Carnegie Hall,* in 1947–while Spiegel was interested in more serious drama. It was not an acrimonious split. They divided their pending projects. Morros kept *The Snow Is Red,* and Spiegel held on to *The Grand Street Boys*. Neither continued with *The White Gown,* about two social harpies vying to wear the same dress at the same occasion. The associates kept in touch. Years later, after Spiegel's success with *On the Waterfront,* his former partner invited him to Vienna. "Please remember, when I say my guest I mean it fully! I would enjoy your enjoyment." Despite his work as a Soviet spy, Morros would remain unscathed during the McCarthy era. He was reported as traveling everywhere with the deeply right-wing Cardinal Spellman, even dining with President Truman.

Buck, who knew both men, felt that Spiegel was more at ease with the Boris Morroses of this world than the more genteel social crowd. "He had that side which liked distributors and delicatessens, lox and bagels." Among certain associates, there was a feeling that Spiegel was a social climber. He was, but Spiegel was also a unique personality whose "velvet octopus arms" reached out to so many different worlds. True, he was stimulated by success and by stars, but who in his business was not? More important, Spiegel was socially versatile. He could talk seriously with those who advised him about the moviegoing public, and just as easily gossip with the sophisticated Hollywood wives. Spiegel's brilliance lay in always recognizing his customer. "Sam always knew what the hot item was, and who the right people were," said Joan Axelrod, the wife of George Axelrod and the late interior designer of Lauren Bacall, Walter Matthau, Véronique and Gregory Peck. "That was part of his charm."

Through Morros, Spiegel met Sam Rheiner, who went on to become his chief henchman. "He [Rheiner] knew where all the bodies were buried," said one associate. A New Yorker, he had started at Paramount Studios, was assigned to their theaters, and ultimately ended up in the music department, where he met Morros. Born the same year as Spiegel, he worked with him until he died. "Sam used to beat Rheiner down to a jelly," said his lawyer. Small, dark, and nondescript, he favored ill-fitting suits, and in later years, used to keep the producer's New York office amused with stories about the old days. They tended to have the same theme: "Spiegel would be playing cards with a bunch of his old friends in California, the luminaries of the day . . . the sheriff would be at the door coming to serve a process, and his attitude was always 'Don't bother me, don't bother me.' "

Tales of Manhattan allowed Spiegel to move out of a rented apartment on Fountain Avenue and start living in his own house—or almost so. As with all his financial transactions, it was complicated. Fox helped with an advance of about $20,000, thanks to a certain amount of pressure from Morros. "I know that you are as eager to see Sam settled in his new home as I am," he wrote. Charles H. Medcraft, Spiegel's business manager, also forked out $30,000, in exchange for rights and interest in *Tales*. Indeed, throughout the following decade, the long-suffering Medcraft used to sign his name to all sorts of loans. "It's difficult to explain, but you always wanted to help Sam," admitted Buck, who would become an associate. It was also recognized that since S. P. Eagle was a con man—albeit polished, charming, and capable—the rules had to be bent.

"I warned him that he would be the talk of the town after *Tales*," said Youngstein. "Then people started to be jealous, and out came the knives. The old Spiegel stories resurfaced—London, Mexico City, New York . . . but Sam brushed it all aside."

Chapter Ten

NORTH CRESCENT DRIVE

Spiegel's early days at 702 North Crescent Drive did not go as smoothly as he had hoped. Just as he was enjoying his status as a Beverly Hills homeowner, driving around in a black Chrysler convertible with Devil, his German shepherd, his former wife and the immigration authorities suddenly darkened the horizon.

Nineteen forty-two may have been prosperous, but the following year was all about his old sins catching up with him. Ray Spiegel had heard about her husband's S. P. Eagle alias, then she read all the fanfare about *Tales of Manhattan*. Traveling from Philadelphia, she arrived in Los Angeles to sue him for maintenance.

The first hearing for the case was on May 10, 1943. Her request was not unreasonable–$1,500 a month for herself and Alisa. In the report, in which she accused her husband of cruelty, nonsupport, and desertion, she claimed that Spiegel's yearly income was $60,000. Ten days later, the case was resumed in court, and her husband was his usual duplicitous self. On the one hand, he told reporters that he had only $7 to his name, but then he was overheard saying "Don't worry dear, we'll settle this." They did. He even took his estranged wife's hand when they left the courtroom together. The following autumn, their seventeen-year-old daughter moved in with him in Los Angeles, where she attended UCLA.

Why the change of heart? Morton Garbus, Spiegel's business lawyer, had advised him that he had no alternative, as had his immigration lawyers at O'Connor, Gray & O'Connor. Threats about being deported to Mexico had developed into a strong possibility. Spiegel had been pushing his luck. It was the same old story–being fined $300 for failing to register his alien status, as well as being briefly arrested for a spree of invalid checks. Such details were not looking good for the pardon of Spiegel's criminal record–dating from 1928– and normally "no pardon" led to no naturalization and no U.S. citizenship. However, the appearance of his teenage daughter–an American citizen, since her mother had been naturalized in 1934– changed the circumstances. Alisa became an essential element in her father's quest for an American passport.

Meanwhile, Spiegel had made an excellent choice in his immigration lawyers–William V. and Edward J. O'Connor. Both brothers were vigilant, and with no apparent financial incentive. Two years after they succeeded in their quest, their bill for $3,384.79 had still not been settled. Six decades after the event, Edward O'Connor's son admitted, "The only thing that I can remember about Spiegel is that the guy didn't pay his bills." Both lawyers had great faith in their client, and if it had not been for their efforts and their obtaining a series of annual delays, Spiegel might well have been deported. Well connected, their uncle was J. F. T. "Jeftie" O'Connor, a federal judge, and they had important friends in Washington, including Harry Truman, Matthew Connolly, who would be Truman's secretary when he became president, and Tom Clark, Truman's attorney general.

William O'Connor was the first to approach the authorities about a pardon for Spiegel. At the beginning of 1943, he wrote to Earl Warren, then governor of California. His letter made all the necessary references to Spiegel's "character and principle," his having "written several plays and stories," and offered a whitewashed version of his career. Concerning his client's troubles on the West Coast, there was no mention of his having been arrested by Secret Service agents, or his spell on Angel Island; the only reference was to an invalid check for $10. (The offending sum was actually $9.) O'Connor's final paragraph captured the tone: "Since 1928 the applicant has completely rehabilitated himself and has lived in society with honor and distinction. He desires to obliterate this crime from his record by a pardon and I want to state unhesitatingly that in my opinion no man is more deserving of this relief." Was this the same Sam Spiegel whose questionable activities had brought him trouble in England, France, Italy, Switzerland, and Mexico?

Meanwhile, Edward O'Connor, the elder of the two lawyers, calmed people such as Ben Odell, a vice president of the California Bank, explaining that although Spiegel's first pardon had been refused, he was not about to be deported because such a decision lay with the United States government, not the state.

Spiegel was active too. He persuaded heavyweights such as Fox's Damon Runyon, RKO's Sol Lesser, and Joseph I. Breen of the Hays Office to send letters to the Advisory Pardon Board in Sacramento. "I know him to be a man of considerable integrity who is accepted on all sides as a truly worth-while man of honor," wrote Breen, who was renowned for his holier-than-thou attitude in regards to film censorship.

There was another problem, however, when Lieutenant Governor Fred Houser opposed Spiegel's second demand for pardon in December 1943. "I do not think the applicant has rehabilitated himself," he stated. This led to Spiegel's closest shave with deportation, but thanks to the O'Connor brothers, he was saved from such a fate. The court in San Francisco dismissed his charge of 1928 and, to quote Spiegel, "expunged my record." He had not been pardoned, but his misdemeanor was wiped off his record. The producer's crime and time in prison were no longer legally recognized. It was quite an achievement, but where there was a will as strong as Spiegel's and the O'Connors', there was a way–yet another case of Eastern European and Irish alchemy in Hollywood. Correspondence between the producer and Ugo Carusi, the U.S. attorney general's executive assistant, also suggested Washington's involvement. Paul Kohner had written to Attorney General Francis Biddle about Spiegel's association with *All Quiet on the Western Front* and how the film was eventually released through "his excellent connections with the democratic and Anti-Nazi circles in Germany."

It would be another four years until Spiegel was a full legal resident in the United States, but at least he was no longer in danger of deportation.

In many ways, the producer was more equipped to deal with the authorities than he was with his daughter, who arrived in September 1943. They had last lived together in Palestine, when Alisa was a thirteen-month-old baby. She had since matured into a voluptuous seventeen-year-old, who took after the Schwitz side of the family. Meanwhile, how could his daughter ever forget that Spiegel had walked out on her, and not even bothered to make contact? Sixteen years of abandonment was a high hurdle to cross, and as much as the teenager wanted to forgive her father, a certain amount of pent-up rage understandably stood in the way. A newfound trust with the deserter parent can lead to forgiveness, but it was never the case between this particular father and daughter. Spiegel had a tendency to let her down when she relied on him, and to help when it was least expected.

Extremely unpredictable, his course of action tended to be decided by one sole interest, himself, whereas his daughter was less narcissistic, and desperate for his approval. "To my best boyfriend, may your 41st birthday be the starting day of our future life together," she wrote in November 1943. "The past to be forgotten, the present and future with open minds and hearts." Strange that she called her father her "best boyfriend," and even more strange that she did not know his age—he was actually forty-two.

Owing to the war effort and soldiers taking over the UCLA dormitories, there had been a slight change of plans and Alisa had to live with her father rather than move straight into a sorority house or dorm. "Since this is the first time we have lived together," Spiegel wrote to his mother, "friction has been reduced to a reasonable minimum. In other words we are getting on all right."

Only close friends such as John Huston, Jules Buck, the Kohners, and the Wylers were introduced to Alisa. "She was rather shy," remembered Lupita Kohner. "It was quite a different world for her." Nor did Spiegel spend much time with her. Old acquaintances like Ad Schulberg were appalled, and dressed Spiegel down about how he treated his daughter. Others were taken aback by the producer's horror that Alisa wanted to wear lipstick. "Suddenly he was an old puritan," said Norman Lloyd.

Spiegel had his more mature moments when he recognized that he was fortunate to have a daughter who was good-natured and kind. "Please keep on growing as gracefully as you have till now and keep on loving your dad," read one birthday message. Yet, in general, he was too much of an egotist to have time for her. To catch his attention, Alisa had to either excel academically, or impress him socially, and she did neither. According to Raya Dreben, it was Spiegel's interference that spoiled her first cousin's education. "Alisa did magnificently in school, then Sam changed everything around," she said.

After six months, Alisa left UCLA and returned to the East Coast, where she planned to attend New York University, even though her father was against it. "The idea of going to Penn State was prompted by the consideration that this is a campus university away from the hustle and bustle of a big city. You will have ample opportunity to spend your vacations in New York and Los Angeles which will be your two departures in big cities," Spiegel argued in one letter. "I suggest you give up the idea of New York University and hope you mean to conform with my judgment and wishes on the subject. You didn't write me whether you have started working or whether you still loaf about New York. If you plan some vacation trip I would be much in favor of your spending it in the mountains and not on a crowded beach in Atlantic City."

Following the agreement with his wife, Alisa was meant to receive a monthly allowance of $180, but it seldom arrived. Nor were matters helped by her father's business manager continuing to misspell her name. "Haven't received my allowance in the past few weeks. Is there any trouble?" was the occasional postscript to some of her letters, as well as telegrams bearing a cryptic version of the same message. Alisa then became an eighteen-year-old war bride when she married Leonard Freedman in September 1944. Spiegel did not attend the wedding, but, twenty-one months later, he was ready with a check when she began to doubt her domestic situation. "If you're not happy . . . go away for a while and give the matter some calm and detached thought," he wrote. "Keep me posted where and when you want to go and again, don't worry."

However, by the time Alisa had given birth to her two children–Ellen and Michael–her relationship with Spiegel was distant and on a "dear dad, can I have," or "thanks for the check" basis. It was simple: he was there to provide on a strictly superficial level, whether it meant getting autographed publicity shots from his films, tickets for Broadway shows, or allowing her to use one of his charge accounts. Occasionally, they spent a few hours together in New York, but when Alisa proposed coming to California, her father ignored her letter.

Spiegel refused to make a commitment. "He couldn't bear having baggage," said his niece. Ellen Weisbord, Alisa's daughter, was more candid. "My grandfather was an emotional accountant. Everyone had his or her 3-by-5 card. Sometimes I stretched mine to 5-by-7. As far as he was concerned, my mother had had her time with him, in California." Weisbord remembered meeting her grandfather when she was a toddler. "I sat on his knee and then turned around and slapped him very hard on the face."

Spiegel always admitted that he was not father material. By his own admission, he was happier in the role of uncle. As Dreben said, "Sam was my favorite uncle and I was his favorite niece, but then he didn't have any other nieces." Maybe not blood nieces, but Spiegel had many surrogate ones, such as Susan Kohner Weitz and all the Wyler daughters. And unlike his blood relations, they were included in his day-to-day life. "Like many people, he didn't know how to integrate his family with his newfound friends," said Joan Axelrod.

Consequently, writers such as Arthur Miller were intrigued. "He was the Great Gatsby," said the playwright. Perhaps his sharp instincts and the haze of mystery made him similar to Fitzgerald's hero, but unfortunately in 1944, Spiegel lacked Gatsby's financial talent.

During this period, David Miller (who went on to direct *Lonely Are the Brave* with Kirk Douglas in 1962) was one of his house guests. "He sent his clothes to the laundry and was told 'they can't be delivered because the bill hasn't been paid,' " said Jules Buck. "Well, David said, 'Goddammit, I'm going to do it, I'm going to pay it.' The bill was for $1,600." Miller used to joke that it sent him straight back into uniform.

It was a rough moment in Spiegel's career; his contract had ended at Twentieth Century-Fox and he was back at Goldwyn Studios.

Nevertheless, his house was still christened "boy's town" because of always having an available card game, booze, and other delights.

The home, which previously belonged to Jackie Cooper, was not a mansion, but a compound, consisting of three buildings, with the main one facing North Crescent Drive and the other two being by the pool and backyard. A symphony in brown, it was obvious from the decoration that the owner was both male and gregarious, since there was no lack of chairs or ashtrays, and the tables were at the right height to place glasses on. When Arthur Hornblow first entered the house, he remarked, "Why is it the minute Sam moves in, it looks like the lounge of a men's club?"

In contrast, the living room, which overlooked North Crescent Drive, was quite formal–Empire-style sofas and Louis XV chairs. Regulars usually went straight to the den, which had bamboo card tables with chairs to match, wing chairs with ottomans, liquor bottles as lamp bases, and metal smoking stands. The area continued over several rooms and might have been nicknamed the "gambler's playpen." One morning, Buck arrived after there had been an all-night gin game. "The maid said, 'There's shit everywhere,' and Sam replied, 'There's shit all over the world.' "

There was also an expansive bar–the type to either sit at or serve from–a backgammon board, and several shelves filled with records for the Philco phonograph, which had a remote control box. Nothing was missing: an icebox loaded with smoked ham, turkey, and bacon from Forst's in Kingston, New York, fruit from the Bear Creek Orchards in Oregon, as well as goodies from Bottle and Spice and Everything Nice, on Beverly Drive. After playing tennis, Elia Kazan opened the refrigerator and was astonished to see champagne spritzers. "No Pepsis or Cokes for Sam. Only the best!" There were also an Ice-o-Mat cruncher, cigarette boxes filled to the brim, cocktail shakers, and a martini pitcher.

The Mason & Hamlin piano had a duet bench, and for the colder February months there was a cushioned hearth around the fireplace. In later, more prosperous years, paintings and drawings by Toulouse-Lautrec, Diego Rivera, Bernard Buffet, and George Grosz lined the walls.

Caroline Veiller, the daughter of Anthony Veiller (one of John

Huston's favorite writing partners as well as the co-screenwriter of *Stage Door* and *State of the Union*), recalled the library–sitting room where she had been "ushered in" to meet Orson Welles. He had briefly stayed at Spiegel's when his second wife–Rita Hayworth– threw him out. The room was "European" in atmosphere, and Welles was holding court among the bound books, leather chairs, and dark enameled wood.

The ground-floor powder room was in deliberate contrast. Short baby-blue satin curtains matched the corded skirt of the vanity table and the quilted dressing stool. The looking glass was tinted blue, while the lamp had a delicate figurine base, and the ashtray was made of cut crystal.

Of the house's three bedrooms, the smallest one was referred to as the maid's room even though Spiegel tended to have outside help such as Ed and Mae Laffin or Lily Mae Hendricks, whom he shared with Olivia de Havilland.

The other bedrooms, upstairs, were less modest in size. When unmarried, Spiegel slept in the front bedroom. After a fight with her second husband, Evelyn Keyes had thrown pebbles up at his window, late one night. "He wasn't surprised. I don't know what could have surprised Sam," she wrote. "He let me in, eyes at half-mast, explained that the bedrooms were full, led me to the living room couch, and went back to bed."

Following his second marriage, to Lynne Baggett in 1948, Spiegel lived in the master bedroom, which was at the back of the building. It had four windows that looked out onto the patio and pool. Nude drawings by artists such as Matisse, Schiele, Rodin, and Pascin covered the walls. Boudoirlike, the bedroom was decorated in various shades of pink and white. The dash of femininity was a concession to the taste of Lynne, since the rest of the house was strictly masculine.

In later years, much was made of the female company that was always found at North Crescent Drive. Welles referred to the prostitutes he met there. Marilyn Monroe was even labeled as one of the house "gals"–as a Fox contract player, there was a possibility that Harry Brand, in charge of the studio's publicity, introduced the starlet to Spiegel. In her memoirs, Keyes mentioned seeing Monroe at Spiegel's. "What I immediately noticed was her walk," said the actress.

Did Spiegel introduce the future screen goddess to Johnny Hyde, her mentor? Since the early 1940s, the William Morris agent had been a close friend, as well as acting as the second character witness in the producer's naturalization papers.

Spiegel was also friendly with all the studio talent scouts, and word soon circulated that a visit to his home was another way of meeting people in the business. "Sam really knew how to play on other people's weaknesses," said Budd Schulberg. "He was an inspired pimp. He could create those very high-class mosh pits. Women were looking for acting jobs and it was a knee up the ladder." The gamblers at his house, which included all his director friends as well as Preminger and occasionally Mervyn LeRoy, were quite a group for an aspiring actress to meet. There were also the agents: Charles Feldman, Kurt Frings, and Kohner.

According to Kazan, an upstairs bedroom was at his "disposal any afternoon when I had no other accommodation to take advantage of a sudden piece of social good fortune." It was merely a continuation of the pleasurable activities associated with the house. "I think it was made available to friends," offered one observer. "When Dana Andrews would send Sam a case of bourbon, I was surprised since the actor was not a poker player."

Inevitably, there were whispers that the producer was taking things further. "I was having breakfast with Sam," recalled another acquaintance. "He had served me some marvelous Canadian bacon– this was the time of rationing–and a couple of guys came in who I knew weren't part of Sam's circle. They kept on asking about a couple of girls and Sam kept on giving yes or no answers, and then one of the guys said, 'Well, you'll be getting a case of so and so.' "

No correspondence remains to suggest that Spiegel had entered this line of business, but certain people wondered about his New Year's Eve parties. "I don't know how he got the liquor," said Jules Buck. "There was always a *big* question about that." Schulberg recalled the "very silken, sexy atmosphere at those famous parties of his." "Ladies of the night" invariably used to appear when various wives left. "Sam knew about smoothing corners," said the writer. "He was the master of it, he was accomplished; few people have that."

Gradually, Spiegel's house became *the* place to be seen on

December 31. Although he had thrown two less formal parties, the first official New Year's Eve one was in 1944, and invitations were written in red ink on an ivory-colored card that was bordered in the same red as the italic handwriting.

"It was a good party, a great mixture of people, he asked everyone," recalled Leonora Hornblow. "Film studio heads, stars, starlets (which is a euphemism), and writers. Sam liked writers, and at the time writers were way down." The guests included Lucille Ball, Charles and Oona Chaplin, Zsa Zsa Gabor, Cary Grant, Danny Kaye, James Mason, Sir Charles and Lady Mendl, Judy Garland and Vincente Minnelli, George Sanders, Shirley Temple, Darryl and Virginia Zanuck, as well as rival columnists Hedda Hopper and Louella O. Parsons.

Spiegel's neighbors looked forward to the occasion, which led to ravishing creatures making a brief appearance, then sweeping into the house. It was the 1940s, Hollywood glamour was at its height, and the jewels glittered.

Charles Feldman took Lauren Bacall. "It was the first time that I saw Howard Hughes," she remembered. There was even a story about Hughes and the party. Apparently, Hughes had heard that Spiegel was too broke to pay for it, and he offered to help out. Supposedly, Spiegel turned him down, saying, "It just would not be the same." The story was unlikely on two accounts: Spiegel *never* had money when he threw a party, and since when had he ever refused financial aid?

The actress Betsy Blair recalled the evening's sophistication. "None of us had been in Europe unless we had been born there and it was the sort of party that we had read about in books. There was someone to take your wrap—a little maid in uniform." The food was different too. "It was an event . . . like Swifty Lazar's parties became after the Oscars . . . the whole town would be there or anyone who was important. . . . I am sure that Sam had that in mind, he was struggling and clinging on, but it was apparent that he was exceptional."

Ray and Fran Stark used to dine at Romanoff's. "Then, just before midnight, we would go to his party," said Ray Stark. "It was a circus." For some, such as the producer-writer Joan Harrison, it was the source of a square meal. She had been a Hitchcock collaborator and was about to be hired by Hughes until he sent a telegram saying that he only wanted pictures about two things—"fighting and fucking"—and she was out of a job. According to Eric Ambler, her husband, the parties always ended up the same way. "It would be the early hours of the morning and Abbey Rents—who Sam had rented the glasses and tables from—would turn up wanting all their stuff back as well as a check. The latter was always the difficulty." The writer heard that once when Spiegel was greeting a distinguished guest, his car was being towed away. "But I never knew whether to believe or dismiss that."

One year, S. P. Eagle's finances were *so* grim that the caterer had been able to bargain for an invitation. "I admire your ability to convey your reasons and on behalf of the Spiegel organization, the answer is yes," replied Jules Buck, who was then working with the producer.

Mike Todd took his son along in 1946. It was "the highlight" of Mike Jr.'s Christmas vacation. He had spent the first part of the night talking to James Stewart, who, "with the exception of my father and me, was the only bachelor at the party without a date." Hughes had then appeared solo wearing a "tuxedo and white tennis shoes." However, when the young man started to dance with a starlet, his father took him aside, insisting that he had seen "enough Hollywood high life." John Garfield then arrived in a Cadillac convertible with four girls. "Their fearful attention was focused on Garfield, who was blankly looking around at them, without even a glance where he was driving."

The same year, Shelley Winters and a miserable Rita Hayworth attended the party together. The estranged Mrs. Orson Welles was "so lonely and bored" that she dozed off and Ava Gardner—of all people—made a bed for her out of the pile of fur coats and wraps. But when Gardner proposed that they all "sneak off," Hayworth was having none of it. After flinging the furs aside, she fixed her face and hair, did a "Gilda" on the dance floor, and that night sped off with Tony Martin, the future husband of Cyd Charisse.

Another year, Humphrey Bogart was dancing with his wife when a sailor pinched her ass. Apoplectic with rage, the actor immediately seized on the offending pincher as well as two others from the navy and locked them in the lavatory while he reported them to the Shore

Patrol. "That was him, the hero of *Casablanca*!" recalled Billy Wilder.

The parties soon made Spiegel a Hollywood celebrity. "After his parties, he was then asked back," said Hornblow. "It was deliberate, but no one ever said that Sam wasn't smart. He was fluent, never at a loss for words. And he was a very good guest because he talked to everybody. . . . He liked to tell his stories, but he listened too. Some people didn't."

Nevertheless, Spiegel was not content to rest on his social laurels and graces. According to director Lewis Milestone, "Sam was always scared that he would *only* be remembered for his New Year's Eve parties."

Chapter Eleven

THE STRANGER

Tales *of Manhattan* had been an accomplishment, but it would be a further four years before S. P. Eagle's name loomed large on the screen again. His next film was *The Stranger*, or to quote Bronislaw Kaper—*The S. T. Ranger*. The former Berlin associate composed the music for the picture, the cast of which included Loretta Young, Edward G. Robinson, and Orson Welles, who was doubling as director.

Spiegel had projects in between, but they came to nothing. These included employing Daniel Fuchs and John Huston to adapt *The Russian People*, a Theatre Guild play, and acquiring *The Grand Street Boys,* a screenplay by Michael Kanin that was even hand-delivered to Fox's Joe Schenck on the *Super Chief* train, but alas, to no avail. Making a film of Gogol's *Inspector General* went further—Lewis Milestone was announced as the director. However, a fierce letter terminating the agreement suggested Spiegel's usual tricks. As well as neglecting to get Milestone's signature, Spiegel was accused of being "in default under the terms and conditions" of the agreement since he had not used the acquired funds—$5,059.81—"for paying writers or renting office space."

Furious correspondence aside, Eagle Productions—Spiegel's company—was taking shape.* In the mid-1940s, his portly figure was a familiar sight at Goldwyn Studios, and in spite of periods at

---

*As a result of the company's name, the producer has been erroneously linked with an Austrian film, *Geschichten aus der Steiermark* (1929), which was co-produced by Ottoton-Film and Eagle-Film but was not connected with Spiegel.

Universal and MGM, he always returned to the area, which is now where Paramount Studios stands. Gladys Hill ran his office, having done so since June 18, 1941.

Hill came from Williamson, West Virginia. And just as her brother Harry Hill was an attorney who became an "outstanding member" of the Mingo County bar, Gladys was equally "outstanding" at calming troubled waters. Regarding Spiegel's bad checks, her approach to irate creditors was invariably along the lines that she "was distressed to receive" their letter and that the mistake "was entirely the fault of the bank." She would then call the manager immediately, who would "settle this matter via long distance." As well as being the perfect foil for keeping the authorities at bay, Hill's other talents lay in recognizing the strength of a screenplay and being polite to the numerous lady friends.

"She was of medium height . . . blue eyes and very pale," recalled Irene Heymann, Paul Kohner's assistant. "In profile, without being beautiful, she looked like Grace Kelly somehow, but she never thought of herself or carried herself as pretty."

Described by Peter Viertel as "a kind of police dog," he sensed that "once Gladys was yours, she was prepared to bite everyone else." When Huston and Viertel were working on a script for Spiegel, Hill dismissed both of them "as a bunch of bums." "[She] thought that we were nasty to torture him and she knew all of Sam's high jinks." Viertel even wondered if her boss had, in his words, "taken her over the main fence." However, Huston quelled such a notion saying, "No, no, no, the lady is not like that." Yet decades later, when Hill worked for Huston in 1960, there was the same sort of rumor about her and the Oscar-winning director.

Hill, who stayed with Spiegel for twelve years, was the self-sacrificing type who put her needs well after those of her employer. On his second Hollywood production, she was the dialogue director, a position she held until their last film together. That the producer found her demonstrated his sharp instincts, because those who dismissed Spiegel for having a rhinolike hide were missing his innate shrewdness about human nature.

However, it was his "paternalistic stance" that Daniel Fuchs noticed. "We were pretty young in those days, Spiegel strangely too, only six and eight years ahead of us, but he was old in manner and looks," recalled the screenwriter, who became known for his work on suspense films such as Siodmak's *Criss Cross* and Kazan's *Panic in the Streets*. When they were adapting *The Russian People*, he and Huston used to meet at the producer's house after a late breakfast or lunch and then play gin rummy at the dining room table. "Spiegel would lecture us sternly, shaming us for being indoors all day when, he said, we should be out in the sun enjoying the bountiful spring weather, and then, after scolding us, would draw up a chair and kibitz, always at Huston's side of the table, giving him tips and telling which cards to play. I resented this and protested, no match for the two of them, and in the end lost heavily–well, $700. (Huston never saw a cent of it; he wasn't a good gin player either.) 'Make the check out to Toler (sic) [Litvak],' he said when we settled up, only partly reducing his gambling debt to the other fellow."

Meanwhile, Huston "delighted in tormenting" Spiegel. One afternoon, the producer was desperate to find him and Fuchs. "Huston got a girl to say she was calling from the county morgue that there had been a terrible accident, a car smash, two young men, and would Spiegel help identify them?" Afterward, they parked across from his house and watched the producer walk by while he was wiping the tears off his face. Then Spiegel caught sight of them. "He upbraided Huston right there out in the open on the street, shouting and threatening and actually crying. These people weren't as unfeeling as they have been depicted."

"The Monster," as Huston was nicknamed by Humphrey Bogart, also toiled on *The Stranger*, although he was never officially credited for his work. Later, he remembered his services being assigned to Warner Bros., hence the secrecy. However, in his contract with Anthony Veiller–his partner on the screenplay–Huston was an officer for the United States Army, and was therefore unable to take credit for civilian work.

But, undercover or not, it was to mark the first successful professional encounter between the wunderkind and S. P. Eagle. It was also the first time that the producer put *Stranger* in the title of his films, a word that he was particularly fond of and was to use several times.

Spiegel's plans for the picture had started in May 1944 when he acquired the rights to "The Trap," a story by Victor Trivas–an acquaintance from Berlin and Paris–who had taken the theme from material written by Decla Dunning and Philip MacDonald. Ten months later, two separate contracts were made with Veiller and Huston to write a screenplay for the project, which was called *Date with Destiny,* and became *The Stranger* in September 1945. And although it has been reported otherwise, none of the extensive correspondence ever mentioned Huston as directing the film.

Nevertheless, the financial dealings with the writing team on *The Stranger* had the usual telltale signs of S. P. Eagle. His first offer was generous–$30,000 in cash to be divided between the writing team, plus 10 percent of the profits upon delivery of the screenplay until they received a further $20,000, resulting in a halving of the previous percentage. However, as the weeks passed and the writing team became emotionally attached to their screenplay and therefore more prepared to make allowances, Spiegel went through his normal routine of pushing back the payment.

The first time was in May 1945. It happened during a meeting at Kohner's office, the agent of both Veiller and Huston. Suddenly the producer announced that the $30,000 would have to be paid in two installments. Spiegel's excuse was that it was a result of his agreement with International Studios. Originally, Veiller "flatly refused to concede," but then "as a favor to Sam" agreed to accept $15,000 upon delivery of the script and $15,000 upon completion of photography, prior to the end of 1945. An agreement was made and duly signed.

Two months later, Spiegel's finances took a serious nosedive. Indeed, when Robinson's agent received the screenplay, Hunt Stromberg was attached as producer and it was referred to as a property that was "originally owned by Sam." Then came William Goetz and Leo Spitz, who formed the Haig Corporation with the idea that the newly created corporation was to finance 70 percent of *The Stranger*'s negative cost. Goetz–Louis B. Mayer's son-in-law–was the president of International Pictures (a studio that was to merge with Universal Studios in August 1946).

This change of dynamics, which happened on August 9, 1945, resulted in the amendment of the previous contract and–surprise, surprise–pushed the writers' salary still further back. But adding insult to injury, there was yet another set of agreements, drawn up in late August, signifying how the second half of their payment was not to be paid until the negative cost was recouped. Veiller balked, describing the terms as "a direct flouting of the agreements previously made." The screenplay had been delivered on June 12, 1945, and he was keen to get all his monies due "for income tax purposes." "I'm a funny guy," he warned his lawyer from the Gladstone Hotel in New York, "and I will always give to the last extremity so long as I feel that I am getting a fair break. . . . However, once I think I'm getting pushed around, I'm through. And I'm through now."

Throughout Veiller's correspondence, a great deal of "friendship for Sam" was in evidence. In business, Spiegel tended to treat his friends even worse than his enemies, even if he often succeeded in making them feel that it was quite the opposite. It was the notorious guilt technique, used by a man who was incapable of feeling guilty. Of course, there was Spiegel's performance—"he was not afraid of being human," Barry Diller was to later remark—so that only the most cynical could doubt his sincerity. When S. P. Eagle was making promises, he almost always meant them—at the time. It was only afterward that he failed to keep his word.

During the 1940s, money was a game to Spiegel, because he rarely held on to it. Whatever he earned, he already owed, since he lived well beyond his means. Other people seldom had the same cavalier attitude to their personal finances, and it had the inevitable result—the friendliness between both parties soured. Did Spiegel care? Probably not. He lived for the moment—another day, another lunch, another project.

In regards to Veiller (who was also battling for Huston), Spiegel managed to negotiate the final $15,000 into five monthly installments, but it was still not forthcoming. "Let him have twenty-four hours of grace, but sue on Wednesday," the writer advised his lawyer, when the second installment failed to appear.

When it came to the final $3,000, Spiegel had the nerve to ask for it to be divided into weekly installments of $1,000! In spite of being granted permission to do this, his subsequent behavior prompted Mark M. Cohen, Veiller's lawyer, to send yet another letter in the early autumn. "As you know, Sam, we have been patient, and because of the estrangement between you and Tony, he has been pressing me to close the matter." Finally, everything was paid by September 26, 1946, by which time the film had been distributed by RKO for three months.

Orson Welles was also involved with the screenplay, but *he* was paid promptly. Like the rest of the talent, his salary came out of the Haig Corporation's pocket. *The Stranger,* which was filmed at the Goldwyn Studios and on the back lot of Universal, was a two-month shoot, which began in late September 1945. The picture's theme was somewhat melodramatic. In order to catch Franz Kindler (Welles), a Nazi war criminal, Detective Wilson (Robinson) persuades the American authorities to allow Konrad Meinike (Konstantin Shayne), a Nazi prisoner of war and Kindler's former assistant, to escape South America and be allowed entry into the United States. As expected, Meinike leads Wilson to the war criminal, who is living in Harper, a small town in Connecticut, where he is teaching history under the assumed name of Professor Rankin (Welles). The only key to his past is his interest in clocks. When Meinike arrives, his former mentor is about to marry Mary (Loretta Young), the daughter of the Supreme Court Justice Longstreet (Philip Merivale). However, as soon as he reveals that he has been followed, far from extending a wedding invitation, Rankin kills and promptly buries him. The only problem is that Meinike has left a suitcase at Mr. Potter's (Billy House) store in town. The evidence acts as a clue for Wilson, who already has his suspicions about Rankin. A talk about Karl Marx–"he was not a German, he was a Jew"–further convinces him. Meanwhile, Mary's dog discovers Meinike's grave, which forces her husband to confess to his dastardly deed. Horrified, she still promises never to reveal the secret. But when the professor tries to kill her in an accident which nearly kills her brother instead, Mary wakes up to the monster she has married. The climax of the film is at the town's clock tower. A fight ensues between the detective and criminal, and ends with Rankin being impaled by the clock face and plunging to his death.

The *Los Angeles Examiner* called *The Stranger* "a tense, suspenseful melodrama that is loaded with punch and gives something new to the standard chase formula." The picture was not without merit. European in atmosphere, Hitchcock was mentioned as an influence, but there was a touch of Robert Siodmak too. (In fact, the latter shot a scene for the film in January 1946, although it was eventually cut.) As far as performances, Shayne was good and Robinson fair. Yet according to Welles, it was House's picture.

True, the comedian added another dimension–the director took credit for all of his scenes–but his powerful presence, loaded with innuendos, actually stops the picture's flow and suggests another tale entirely. In general, *The Stranger* is uneven. The main problem is actually Welles himself, who is hindered by sporting wavy hair and a thick mustache. When he was part of the Mercury Theatre, there used to be a joke, "Tonight he thinks he's Herbert Marshall, or tonight he thinks he's Barrymore, or tonight he's being Ronald Colman," whereas in *The Stranger,* it is not apparent who Welles is–a charismatic monster or a dashing romantic lead? Later, he told Peter Bogdanovich that the ambiguity was "intentional" and that he thought "most heavies should be played for sympathy." However, it is hard not to agree with *The New Yorker*'s critic, who described the actor's features as "hovering between a cherubic smile and a ferocious scowl, which gives him a decidedly potty air."

Did that explain Loretta Young lacking her usual sparkle and spontaneity? She was under contract to Goetz at International Studios, and perhaps she had no choice in the matter, but in theory it should have been the perfect role for her. Although lacking credibility on screen–her vast eyes seem only mildly perturbed by her predicament–in reality, she had "a smashing crush on Orson." In her opinion, Welles, who was quoted as saying, "a star never goes to big parties or meets anyone by the swimming pool," was impossible "to surprise" and so many people in Hollywood–meaning "actor, writer, director"–were "jealous of him." "He was enormously sensitive to everyone, be it script girl or cameraman," she recalled. "Orson would come up behind me and then gently tell me what he felt. He was also funny. I wouldn't stop laughing and the cameraman said, 'Unless you stop laughing, you're going to have to redo your makeup.' He told me, 'Blow out your cheeks to stop the wrinkling.' Anyway Orson kept on passing by and finally on the third time he said, 'Of course, Loretta, I realize I'm gaining weight but I don't think you should make fun of me.' " She got on with Spiegel too, even if they had two tiny disagreements. "There was one scene where all the people were going to church and Sam said, 'I want all the people–women and children–dressed in black.' Well I am a fervent Roman Catholic and I replied, 'I cannot agree with you on that, Sam. I am someone who wants to get people into church not vice versa'–that wasn't his idea at all." There was also a problem about a line in the script. "I was meant to say, 'I have decided not to attend church,' and I said, 'Sam, I am not going to say that line of dialogue.' We laughed about it a lot. And all credit due to him, once he decided that I wouldn't [do it], he left me alone."

Welles always dismissed *The Stranger* as his worst picture. In his review, the *New York Times* critic Bosley Crowther was gratuitously cruel. "It is painful and sad to have to notice, in this fashion, the frailties of one who came to the screen so auspiciously and from that point took a fine and fancy dive." Yet, when the thriller came out in July 1946, it made money. In fact, it was the only one of Welles's pictures that made a profit on first release. Fifteen months later, the figures showed that against a negative cost of $1,034,000, the gross receipts were more than triple at $3,216,000. Trivas's story idea was also nominated for an Oscar.

Throughout the filming, Spiegel had written letters to his family to excuse his lack of communication, and then impress them with the people he was working with. He was clearly pleased to have his name linked with the creator of *Citizen Kane*. After the film, he and Welles continued to be friends. In 1947, Welles sent him his *Macbeth* screenplay to consider. But their relationship collapsed when the producer was making *The Bridge on the River Kwai* and refused to consider Welles for the starring role or the director. (Nor for the bridge, as one unkind person suggested, given Welles's size at the time.)

Did this feeling of betrayal explain his dismissal of Spiegel in *This Is Orson Welles,* his book-length interview with Bogdanovich? Regarding *The Stranger,* he claimed that the producer "was part of it much against Goetz's wishes," which seems utter nonsense, taking into account that the Haig Corporation had been specifically set up to help S. P. Eagle! Besides, the president of Universal-International was one of Spiegel's personal friends, who gave him a three-picture deal at his studio in 1946. After Walter Wanger, he was one of the highest paid producers on the lot.

The film also got "Spiegel's foot in the door as a producer," or so Welles reasoned. But Goetz had been the second-in-command at Fox when *Tales of Manhattan* was made, and according to Max Youngstein, "Bill was worried about letting him go because Sam had done one of the most extraordinary producer jobs in the business."

Nevertheless, Welles's artistic gripes on *The Stranger* were true. There had been an argument between Spiegel and him about the lack of a close-up on Loretta Young in a fight scene. "OK, but we need a close-up of Loretta," said Spiegel. Welles balked, brought Young and her agent into their dispute, and ultimately won. There were also the first reels of the picture, which were set in South America, and were cut, on the insistence of both Spiegel and Goetz. It was characteristic early Spiegel, because he still lacked the confidence that later marked him as a creative producer. However, at the time, he needed a hit, as did Welles, and a dreamlike sequence around South America did not necessarily smell like box office—especially in the mid-1940s. Nevertheless, it was unfortunate that both Spiegel and Goetz squashed Welles's suggestion of Agnes Moorehead for Robinson's part, the idea being that she would conduct her role like "a spinster lady on the heels" of the Nazis. Her features and beady-eyed presence might have strengthened the film.

Chapter Twelve

THE SECOND MRS. SPIEGEL AND HORIZON PICTURES

By the end of 1945, Spiegel had a new lady in his life, Lynne Ruth Baggett. Christened "Sam's Statue of Liberty" by Peter Viertel, her screen test on the *Stranger* set had not gone unnoticed. It was hard to miss the leggy, five-foot-eleven native of Wichita Falls, Texas.

Besides her showgirl figure, Lynne had fine hands and feet, which were of vital importance to Spiegel. A slight fetish with the producer, he was thrilled by the sight of pedicured feet and could admire a lady for her dainty hands just as he could chastise another for not taking enough care of them. It was hardly the case of Lynnie Ruth–as the starlet was nicknamed–who was always primping and used to arrive in a light cloud of White Shoulders perfume–her scent.

Like Spiegel, Lynne Baggett was gifted on the dance floor, while neck up, she had a face that could launch a thousand ships. Heavy-lashed, almond-shaped eyes, the creamiest of complexions, and a full and perfect-sized mouth–admirers described her as "otherworldly," since everything about her glowed.

No one disputed her physical allure, but as with many great beauties, not everyone was won over by her personality. Leonora Hornblow found the twenty-two-year-old to be "vain and affected." "And Sam used to say, 'Oh well, she's insecure' . . . I mean Lynne was gorgeous—how could she be? Really she was foolish, with no brains at all, she also drank and took dope—in those days it was cocaine." However, Joan Axelrod—a classmate of Lauren Bacall—viewed it differently, finding her "very dear in spirit." "Lynne had this wonderful laugh and a great kind of abandon about her," she said. "There was something so heartrending about it."

Born on May 10, 1923, Lynne Ruth was three years older than Spiegel's daughter. Her father, David Lynne Baggett, was in the oil business and her mother, Ruth Simmons, was a stenographer. Steven "Solly" Baiano, the head of the Warner Bros. talent department and something of a Hollywood tennis champion, discovered her in Dallas on July 25, 1942. There were rumors that Lynnie Ruth had been sighted selling cosmetics behind the counter, or that she had been seen in a beauty pageant, yet all the evidence confirms the official press release—she was on her way to the Harris department store when Baiano spotted her. Anxious to snap her up fast, he had handwritten Baggett's first contract on Baker Hotel stationery, then advanced her $25, with the agreement that she arrive at the studio around the beginning of August. At nineteen, she was a minor and her mother had to give her consent.

The contract with Warner Bros. only lasted three years. In spite of having small roles in such films as *The Adventures of Mark Twain, Mildred Pierce,* and *Night and Day,* none of the studio's top producers such as Hal B. Wallis, Mark Hellinger, and Jerry Wald had seen anything beyond Lynne's obvious attributes.

In fact, only Warner's publicity department was keen to use her, since she had the right look to either fill the magazines or make guest appearances. (In 1944, she was voted "The Serpentine Lady" by the boys at Kelly Field, as well as the "Triple-A-Girl" by the boys at Camp Haan—meaning adorable, amiable, and amorous.)

The problem was that although Lynne's fellow actors described her as "competent," on screen she lacked a "come hither quality." "There was no love affair going with her and the camera," said Peter

Viertel. "None of the alchemy happened that actresses such as Marilyn Monroe would be capable of sparking."

Pretty soon, Lynne joined the roster of starlets who were in demand at restaurants like Chasen's, Romanoff's, and Lucy's. Their duty was to look decorative and keep their opinions to themselves. The same also applied to the evenings at Spiegel's house on North Crescent Drive. "If you were a famous movie star, the studio system gave a tremendous sense of security," said Ivan Moffat, who worked closely with director George Stevens. "But if you weren't, it could be very cold out there. It was a very tough place for young women."

Either it was Lynne's role in Universal's *The Time of Their Lives*–both *Daily Variety* and the *Hollywood Reporter* mentioned her in the Abbott and Costello vehicle–or Spiegel's connection with Universal Studios, but she ended up getting a brief contract there at the end of 1946. For two and a half months, she was earning $300, and was alongside the likes of Ann Blyth, Yvonne De Carlo, Deanna Durbin, Edmond O'Brien, and the very young Natalie Wood.

As far as Spiegel's feelings toward Lynne were concerned, he reveled in having her on his arm, but looked to others for conversation. Leonora Hornblow recalled an occasion by the swimming pool. "After seeing her in a bathing suit, I said, 'Lynne, you have the longest, most glorious legs–did you have something added?' She replied, 'No, but can you do that?' She just didn't take my meaning and I could see murder in Sam's eyes. Sam was impatient, no patience whatsoever, but he couldn't resist beauty." Indeed, the producer became "sort of cross" if women were not attractive. "He'd say, 'What's the matter with her?' and I'd say, 'Sam, it's not her fault,' and he'd say, 'She's so nice, but so plain, couldn't you speak to her?' "

In Fred Zinnemann's opinion, looks were an obsession with Spiegel and reminded the director of why Edward G. Robinson had a magnificent art collection. "Eddie claimed he was unattractive and he needed beauty around him," he recalled. "I think it was the same with Sam. When surrounded by good-looking people, he felt better."

Meanwhile, the story circulating was that Lynne was with S. P. Eagle because she needed to have her teeth fixed and straightened. In reality, she had perfect teeth. However, if he did have one serious effect on her appearance, it was to encourage the natural auburn-haired bombshell to continue going blonder and blonder. In many ways, Spiegel acted like a missing father figure, since Lynne was firmly estranged from her own. Obviously, there was the age difference between the two, and Spiegel's easy access to a sophisticated, more mature world. There was also the fact that Lynne desperately needed looking after. (Scatterbrained, she was the type who forgot to inform Warner's—then her place of employment—that she had changed her address.) Besides putting her mother on a monthly allowance, Spiegel treated Lynne to perks such as jewels from M. Reingold in Beverly Hills, a mink stole, and a daily afternoon massage. He was also divorced from his first wife—another plus.

Still, when Spiegel proposed, his girlfriend sought the opinion of writer Edward Chodorov. Lynne had three options: return to Texas and marry an oil baron (which her Mama was pushing); struggle on with her acting career; or become the second Mrs. Spiegel. "My husband advised her not to marry, and to return home," said Rosemary Chodorov, "and Sam challenged him to a duel." The producer was furious, but clearly his writer friend was right. First of all, Lynne was hardly smitten, otherwise she would not have sought another man's opinion. And secondly, Spiegel's world was tough.

"Sam, Kazan, Huston, they were all hell on women," Lauren Bacall said. "They just used them and passed them around." When Spiegel used to lean forward to give Bacall one of his "big wet kisses," her husband would stand in the way. "He'd say, 'Get your cotton-picking hands off my wife,' and Sam would say, 'Bogie, daaarling.'" Before becoming Mrs. Bogart, Betty Bacall was capable of holding more than her own. Besides being beautiful and known as "The Look," her sharp tongue and intelligence made the guys stand back in respect.

This was not the case with Lynne, and soon Spiegel began to stray. One problem was that she was not curious, while he was an intense networker. "If you told Sam something twice, he got bored. He would say, 'I know that. I know that,'" said Kathleen Parrish. "Whether it was who was sleeping with who or who had signed a deal, Sam liked to be told." Dinners *chez lui* required a rapierlike wit—a case of who was "the smartest at the table"—in the meantime, Lynne, the gracious hostess, was described as "floating in and out, dressed to the nines."

To quote playwright Arthur Laurents, "She was very sweet, and very dumb."

Later, Spiegel blamed Huston and Evelyn Keyes for the mismatch. Despite being unhappily married themselves, it had not stopped them from convincing their friend to tie the knot. "Misery loves company," the producer later remarked. And to make sure that the Spiegels *did* take their vows, Mr. and Mrs. John Huston were witnesses at the wedding, which took place in Las Vegas on April 10, 1948. On hearing the news, Billy Wilder sent a telegram to the *Hollywood Reporter* saying: THE MARRIAGE OF S. P. EAGLE AND LYNNE BAGGETT HAS LEFT THE WHOLE TOWN S. P. EECHLESS. WHAT ELSE IS THERE TO SAY EXCEPT IT'S S. P. LENDID.

Although Spiegel always insisted that he "never ever wanted to marry anyone," perhaps there were other reasons for legalizing the love affair. Finally, after eighteen years of fleeing the immigration authorities, his future in the United States was secure, and perhaps that gave him a certain confidence. This had happened on September 11, 1947, when Spiegel and his lawyer Edward O'Connor drove to Tijuana, Mexico, where the American consul issued a certificate of admission. "I crossed the border," Spiegel wrote to Alisa, his daughter, "and re-entered this country as a fully-fledged immigrant on a permanent quota." Marriage to an American citizen could only help.

Professionally, Spiegel was also the envy of all his fellow producers when he and Huston announced their partnership. The papers for Horizon Pictures–their independent film corporation–were signed on December 8, 1947. "The name was taken from the saying, 'in the fond hope that one day they shall see the horizon,' " said Jules Buck, who became the company's associate producer. Buck was a "chummy, little, white-faced guy" with a shock of black hair who had been Huston's cameraman during World War II, when he made his documentary about *The Battle of San Pietro*. "At that time, it meant a lot to people that someone had been brave during the war," said Peter Viertel. Horizon Pictures was also referred to as "Shit Creek Productions" (since according to Buck, "That's where we always are"), as well as "Miracle Films" ("because it would be a miracle if one was made").

Huston was in demand. His latest film, *The Treasure of the Sierra*

Madre, was recognized as Oscar material. Yet, rather than stay with Warner Bros., the director wanted out after *Key Largo,* his next picture. But "out" with Sam Spiegel? The rumors started to fly that Spiegel had lent Huston $50,000 in cash—hence the agreement. Huston was renowned for his extravagant ways, such as buying race horses, having a set of Mark Cross luggage monogrammed on a whim, or just plain old gambling. "Sam smelt that here was a guy who had an Achilles heel," said Viertel. "Jesus, it was an Achilles heel that went all the way up John's legs!"

Spiegel had actually been helping Huston out for some time. In May 1947, he loaned him $25,000, as well as another $7,000 the following month, and a final $18,000 in August. Although the sums amounted to $50,000, it was hardly in cash, and meticulous letters between Mark Cohen, Huston's lawyer, and Spiegel's attorney, were exchanged. Spiegel had also been unusually prompt in his payments, needing no reminders. Since he had poor credit at the Bank of America, he acquired the funds from Charles Medcraft, his trusting business manager, but it was a watershed in Spiegel's life, since it marked the first time that he was thinking big creatively, and seizing the opportunity with financial resources.

The news of the collaboration sent shock waves throughout the community. "Huston was a genius, Sam was not," said Miss Bacall, echoing many people's sentiments of that time. What was the wunderkind son of the great actor Walter Huston doing with this charming but maverick producer? The decision was best explained by Huston's problems at the time. He was sick of the despotic studio executives. He had tried to direct Eugene O'Neill's *A Moon for the Misbegotten,* and Jack Warner barred him from making it. Business-wise, Horizon Pictures also appealed to him. At last, he would get a lion's share of the profits from his films, which the production company, in theory, promised to deliver. There was also "the rebel" element to the partnership. "John enjoyed shocking the established rulers of the industry," said Viertel. "I, among others, asked him why in the world he had signed with Sam, and he grinned and replied, 'Because it was the wrong thing to do, kid!'"

Nevertheless, he arrived well protected by his agent and lawyer. Ten months after his agreement with Horizon, Huston had a contract with MGM for his services as a director. Neither Paul Kohner nor Mark Cohen were allowing their brilliant client to put all his eggs in one basket. Cohen–a man who preferred to work at night and sleep during the day–was as familiar with Spiegel as Kohner was. Their paths had already crossed on *The Stranger*, while his other clients included Spiegel's old friends Anatole Litvak, William Wyler, and Billy Wilder. As a result, the lawyer was constantly after Huston–his term being "urgently advise and recommend"–not to sign any documents presented by S. P. Eagle that involved his personal affairs or those of Horizon unless he–Cohen–had initialed his okay. Such a warning insured Huston that his partnership with Sambo–his nickname for Spiegel–would rarely be dull–an ideal situation for an individual with a low boredom threshold.

Physically, the partners were in direct contrast. Huston was tall, lanky, and like a nineteenth-century dandy, capable of getting away with any look that took his fancy. "John used to say, 'I don't care about clothes,' but he'd immediately bring out four suits," said John Weitz, the former menswear designer, who was Kohner's son-in-law. " 'This one was made in Sicily,' and so on. He had hunting gear and capes." Spiegel, on the other hand, was limited in his choice of clothes, looking his best in well-cut, classic suits.

Yet both men were bon vivants to such a point that those steeped in film history, like Bayard Veiller, the son of Anthony Veiller, sense that there's a danger they will be largely remembered for "their life," that what will be forgotten is "the absolute skill and passion" that they brought to their films. "They would sit and tell stories to each other over drinks and over dinner and it was the love of that, that kept everything going. And then they were absolute masters at putting things together."

At the time, when questioned about the partnership, Spiegel declared that the business relationship with Huston was "unimportant." "It is the artistic relationship only which is important."

Before Horizon Pictures, Spiegel's career lacked focus, and that was simply not good enough for his new forty-one-year-old associate. Indeed, Huston could be credited with giving the final polish to S. P. Eagle, and allowing him to pass into his next phase–Sam Spiegel, the producer of daring and ambitious hits.

Huston's demands were high—he has been called everything from "Gentleman John" to "The Monster"—and he was the first to recognize that Spiegel was more than just a "Mr. Fixit," but that he needed to be pulled up—"or rather bullied"—to a higher level. Huston believed in Spiegel—he would not have stuck around him if he had not—and, as a result, he was insistent about getting the best out of him. However, the transformation of S. P. Eagle happened gradually. It would not be until their final project together—*The African Queen*—that Spiegel would show the full measure of his maturing talent.

Meanwhile, the charismatic director was hardly the nurturing type. Spending time around Huston was a nerve-racking experience—he was articulate, totally unpredictable, seductive, but absolutely merciless when he found a victim. One of his many skills lay in probing—gently and softly—until he found a person's vulnerable spot, which he would then attack. Some accused him of being sadistic, but Huston disagreed. "They put themselves on the block, kid, they put themselves on the block," he used to say. Others around him, such as his third wife, Evelyn Keyes, insisted that he was not a bully. "John just wanted you to stiffen your spine and be a mensch . . . if you really let him have it, he would be the first to come over and hug you. It embarrassed him when people were pitiful." The actress sensed that Spiegel was impervious to his partner's tricks: "He would tease Sam, but Sam knew what John was up to."

Not always. Spiegel had a horror of being the target of ridicule. In his early Hollywood years, this led to emotional outbursts, and uncontrolled feelings bothered Huston. Still, Huston recognized that with his back against the wall, Sambo "would suddenly cool down," and display an amazing gutsiness. There was also Spiegel's survival instinct. "Sam, somehow, who lived with this group who smoked too much, drank too much, drove fast cars, was always fairly disciplined," said Joan Axelrod. "I never saw him drunk. I never saw Sam wiped out."

Such resilience was a necessity around a director whose method was on a par with Nietzsche's comment that "the weak shall perish." Sometimes, the pranks were funny, such as when Huston put fake dog shit all over Spiegel's house. Or when Burt Lancaster was taking part in a local golf competition and Huston organized a low-flying plane to release two thousand Ping-Pong balls onto the course. Arthur

Miller, who collaborated with Huston on *The Misfits*, remembered when he gave a potion to a bald *Life* photographer with the specific instructions that if he took a teaspoon every day, his hair would grow back. "The photographer was in Africa and reported back that it was happening. Then Huston telegrammed him to say that he had suddenly learned that the medicine would make him impotent and he would keep him in touch with the other possible side effects." But on another occasion, Miller recalled a less "droll" incident. "His son had shot two pheasants and Huston insisted that he had shot them on the ground [an offense among game shooters]. It was so humiliating for the child that I had to leave the room."

Evelyn Keyes affirmed that "there were a lot of games." What was Huston trying to prove? The playwright sensed that the director's physique was the key. "Without his shirt, he resembled one of those skinny guys from the Gold Rush. He had a concave chest." Huston had been a sick child who was misdiagnosed as having an enlarged heart. This had led to a grueling diet that eventually made him as "bald as an onion." Back at school, the class bully had then picked on Huston until he had set him straight. Had being sick, then being made the subject of attacks left its trace? Was it a case of the victim becoming the victimizer?

Between Spiegel and Huston, many projects were discussed including short stories by the English writer John Collier, a screenplay called *For the Love of Mary* by Charles O'Neal and Fritz Rotter, and a remake of Duvivier's *La Fin du Jour*. However, *The Song of Norway*– one of Spiegel's ongoing projects for Universal–was "indefinitely postponed." Huston was an adventurer who saw films as a continuation of his own commitment to excitement, hence his interest in a Cuban project–*China Valdes*–an episode from Robert Sylvester's novel *Rough Sketch*.

Huston was to co-write the screenplay with Peter Viertel. "I used to go horseback riding with John, and when Sam said that they needed someone, John must have said, 'Let's try this kid, it can't cost us a lot of money.'" Viertel had a few credits to his name including Hitchcock's *Saboteur*. He had also collaborated with Irwin Shaw on *The Survivors*, a Broadway drama, and had written *The Canyon*, a well-received first novel.

In the meantime, Huston's behavior continued to unnerve Spiegel—such as his insistence on introducing Henry Wallace, the presidential candidate of the Progressive Party, at a rally in Gilmore Stadium. He felt it might thwart Horizon's chances of getting a deal with a major studio. "There was an undeniable logic to Spiegel's argument," wrote Viertel in *Dangerous Friends*. Huston was not a Wallace supporter, he was going to vote for Harry Truman, he was fully aware that a third-party ticket might split the liberal vote and allow Thomas Dewey, the Republican presidential candidate, to be elected. But it became an issue of honor, or so Huston convinced himself—Wallace had been the vice president of the United States—how could he not introduce him? The partners had a huge fight about it. "Sam felt this will kill whatever deal we have, you're going to antagonize everyone," Viertel said. The director then informed Spiegel that the writer Philip Dunne had persuaded him to come out for Wallace. Spiegel was enraged. He rang up Dunne yelling that he thought that he was his friend but that he had "ruined" him. "This is what John had told him, you see?" recalled Dunne. "That I had talked him into doing it." Actually, he had advised Huston that they should hold their noses "and be for Truman." "That was typical Huston, typical Spiegel, typical everyone," said Dunne. "You know John was a friend of mine, and we got along well for years, we were allies and everything else, but he was not a nice man."

By February 1948, the Horizon team had landed at MGM. Previously, there had been a legendary meeting with Louis B. Mayer and his top executives, Benny Thau and Eddie Mannix, at which Spiegel had pitched *Rough Sketch* as a film. Huston was sitting there, nursing a hangover, having spent the previous night partying with the Bogarts. However, at the end of the story, which was about anarchists blowing up a president, Spiegel suddenly described a United States destroyer pulling into the port. "The marines come on shore and everything is solved," he said. Huston had never heard this, and as soon as they left Mayer's office, he asked his partner where the idea came from. There was a brief pause and Spiegel replied, "Well, I could see that the story with the anarchists was beginning to bother Mayer, so I thought that I would put in that ending." In his memoirs, Huston described his performance as "one of the finest demonstrations of pure animal courage" that he had ever witnessed.

Once their deal was settled, Spiegel fired off a telegram to the despotic studio head that expressed his personal delight at their "new association." I HOPE THAT BOTH JOHN HUSTON AND I WILL JUSTIFY YOUR FAITH IN US FOR A LONG TIME TO COME. Clearly, not enough "faith," because Horizon Pictures's spell was extremely brief at the College of Cardinals–the nickname for the studio. Jules Buck had just arrived when Spiegel telephoned to say that their entire office had to be off the lot in an hour. Buck thought it must be a joke. "Baby, I kid you not," the producer replied.

Fortunately, Spiegel had continued to keep in touch with Columbia, which was where *Rough Sketch* finally landed. In the meantime, the film's screenplay was going at a snail's pace since the hours spent at Huston's ranch in Tarzana were more devoted to consulting the director's bookies or discussing topics of mutual interest, such as Spiegel, the war, and their wives, as opposed to compiling a screenplay about Cuban revolutionaries in the 1930s. "Whenever we listened to the races and John had lost money, I said, 'Let's talk about the black bird.' It came from *The Maltese Falcon* and it was our code word for getting back to work," said Viertel.

There were so few pages to read that as early as April, Spiegel had even agreed on a "recce" trip to Cuba, thinking that a little local color might inspire the writing team. He was still reeling from the time that his partner had handed him over the freshly typed eleven pages and Huston's pet monkey had grabbed them. Making matters worse, the beast had then reached for S. P. Eagle, who was thoroughly repelled by the animal. (There was even a story that Huston threw the pages in the pool and Spiegel had jumped in. This was purely apocryphal since Spiegel was not a swimmer.)

For the Havana trip, Spiegel trusted Viertel with the money, and chose to correspond with him. "Knowing that John is not the writing type, I rely on you to keep me posted on all and sundry," he wrote. "Keep your ear to the ground so that we can find out all that there is known about the touchy points of Cuban politics." Spiegel also attempted to use Viertel as a spy on his partner. "Most producers try to do that, but the basic rule of all good guys is not to peach on his fellow man–a rule which was broken during the Un-American Activities [Committee hearings]." The team returned and despite

Cuban activities such as fishing with Ernest Hemingway and betting heavily on public cock fights ("I remember thinking how was I going to justify a thousand dollars in petty cash?" admitted Viertel), neither of the men were wildly enthused. Huston later wrote that it was "pretty frail material."

Theme-wise, *Rough Sketch* was typical of a Spiegel production. "Stranger" eventually slipped into the title, as it was the recurrent idea that the belief of others can be destroyed by another's betrayal. In regards to the casting, Huston could not resist playing one of his practical jokes. It concerned Edward G. Robinson, who had been considered for a small role. "Sam had written a letter to Robinson and John had written, 'We appreciate that you want to be in the movie, but I don't think so,' and someone else had added, 'Your ugly mug isn't for this one,' " recalled Viertel. "John had not meant it, and Sam had added a Yiddish word afterward saying that it was a joke. They had sent a letter, but it was all part of a plot. Eddie was going to pretend to be offended and he wrote a terrible letter back. Everybody was in on it. . . . The joke was meant to torture Spiegel, and Sam really fell for it, hook, line, and sinker–he felt that Eddie had been upset by it. To top it all, we staged this scene, which I am afraid that I was part of–Sam was going to say one more thing and Eddie was going to get mad all over again."

The rest of the casting continued with less drama. John Garfield played the role of Tony Fenner, a Cuban revolutionary, who recruits a band of dedicated Cubans including China Valdes (Jennifer Jones) and Guillermo (Gilbert Roland) with the idea of overthrowing the government. They build a tunnel from China's house to a nearby cemetery. Fenner's plan is to blow up the Cuban dictator and his entire cabinet when they are in the middle of attending a senator's funeral. But then the site of the burial ground is changed, which completely destroys the rebels' plans. Instead, Armando Ariete (Pedro Armendáriz) and the rest of the police close in on the group. Fenner is fatally machine-gunned, but dies a happy man since he is in the arms of Valdes, the love of his life, and he also hears that the president has fled the country.

Rough Sketch was a difficult film to make. "We were always ten pages ahead of the camera, which is no fun," recalled Viertel. Huston was also in a foul mood. Not only did he loathe shooting in Cuba, but he was driven mad by Pedro Armendáriz, who kept forgetting his lines. And whenever Spiegel appeared, Huston did his best to ruffle his feathers, such as pretending to direct Charlie Granucci–the first prop assistant. "Sam had a seizure when he saw this," said Viertel. Pouring sweat, Spiegel grabbed his hand and said, "What's happening, baby? What's happening, baby?," which was Spiegel's standard code of behavior when amazed by Huston's antics. "Well, I replied, 'This is just a joke that we are playing out on Granucci,' and he said, 'A joke?' while wiping his brow with a handkerchief."

There was also the time that Spiegel arrived with Johnny Hyde and a "va-va-voom" blonde–the agent's girlfriend. Although he had agreed to a screen test, Spiegel gave specific instructions to his Horizon team that no extra time was to be spent on it. As a result, Huston asked Viertel to write a special scene for Garfield to play with the starlet, therefore taking many more hours–and many more dollars–than Spiegel envisaged. It was supposed to be a lesson to his partner "not to flaunt his power." Curiously, such behavior worked in Huston's favor, since he used the blonde in *The Asphalt Jungle,* his next film. Her name was Marilyn Monroe.

The stars of *Rough Sketch* were also made prey to Huston's sense of fun. When Jennifer Jones was digging in the tunnel scene, the director hid an extremely realistic hand in the earth that terrified the already highly strung star. But at least she had not been forced to cut her curls as had Gilbert Roland, a Latino star who was renowned for his hair. John Garfield, who was often included in the pranks, had been given expensive jewels to take care of with the strictest instructions that he was not to leave his Cuban hotel room. Huston then enticed the leading man out to dinner, having arranged for someone to burgle his room.

Although the practical jokes continued, the picture's ending was unresolved. It led to Spiegel going behind everyone's back and hiring the writer Lawrence Collier. Viertel was furious and wrote that the tone of the final scene was so different that he felt "foreign" to it. "Furthermore I don't think three guys can sit in a room and by a process of arguing resolve a piece of writing," he wrote to the producer. "You are a very persuasive guy ... and I know you think you can talk me into it . . . but you can't talk me into writing."

Subsequently, Billy Wilder was called upon. "Everyone likes to save the burning ship and Billy adored the role," recalled Viertel. "Sam thought that Billy was the best, which he was, but he couldn't come up with anything that helped us."

Eventually, the role of troubleshooter went to Ben Hecht. (Uncredited, he had worked on the screenplays of films like *Gone With the Wind, The Shop Around the Corner,* and *Gilda.*) Hecht was paid $5,000 for his services. But Spiegel was then horrified to see the writer having a long and winey lunch with another producer. "He was going crazy, because he was literally paying him on the hour," Kathleen Parrish said. "Those were the kind of events that made Sam miserably uncomfortable, and you had to laugh."

And as if he did not have enough difficulties with the picture, David Selznick had reared his ugly head—not only was Jennifer Jones on a loan-out from his studio, but she was also his mistress. As soon as *Rough Sketch* became *We Were Strangers* in January 1949, Selznick started to deluge Spiegel, Huston, and Harry Cohn, Columbia's studio head, with his notorious memos. Horrified by the new title, which he sensed had probably been thought up by the wife of Columbia's sales manager in Buffalo, he regarded it IN EXACTLY THE SAME LIGHT as if MR. DEEDS COMES TO TOWN WERE CALLED TWO IN A HAYSTACK OR THE RED SHOES WERE CALLED RIVIERA LOVERS. PICTURES OF DISTINCTION SHOULD HAVE TITLES OF DISTINCTION NOT THE SAME OLD CHEAP HANDLES THAT ARE USED ON ALL THE HOLLYWOOD BILGE THAT HAS LOST MILLIONS OF FANS FOR ALL MOTION PICTURES FROM COLUMBIA'S STANDPOINT. Huston had then suggested *Havana 33,* which won Selznick's approval, but the title was dismissed by a test audience as sounding too much like a musical.

Besides failing at the box office—Jones was hideously miscast and threw the entire picture off balance—*We Were Strangers* was seized upon by right-wing, "patriotic" Americans. "It is the heaviest dish of Red theory ever served to an audience outside the Soviet—and the repercussions will not end with this comment," declared the *Hollywood Reporter.* Afterward, Huston wrote a letter to Billy

Wilkerson, the magazine's owner and éminence grise. "To draw on Socrates addressing his accusers–I do not believe that you or your reviewer bore me any ill will, on the other hand you did not bear me any good will. I prefer to think Billy . . . that you did not even read it before publication, and that if you had, it would never have been published. . . . PS: It may amuse you to hear the only other paper that was unsympathetic to *We Were Strangers* was New York's *Daily Worker*."

The Red Scare was rampant and certain Americans were terrified by a possible Russian invasion of their country. In California, Anthony Veiller was once referred to as a Communist and he had jumped into his car, burst into the person's office, and told him "If you repeat that, I will sue you." "My father was absolutely serious, it would have destroyed his life," said Bayard Veiller.

Robert Parrish and others were being counseled by their agents to sign a loyalty oath for Columbia. The then film editor refused and called on the terrifying Harry Cohn, who was nicknamed "White Fang" by Hecht. "He said, 'Tell him to go fuck himself. It's none of his god dam business. Ask him if he's a Jew.' "

The negative cost of Spiegel's first Columbia picture was $1,496,900, and it only made a net income of $1,070,000. According to Lester M. Roth, one of the studio's executives, there was no reason "to believe that this picture will materially improve." Horizon Pictures also failed to come through with four other pictures for the studio, which included filming Frank Harris's novel *The Reminiscences of a Cowboy* with Walter Huston and Montgomery Clift, and a Garfield project referred to as *The Third Secret*. The company's neglect to respect the contract led to a court case with the studio.

However, Spiegel's next production with Columbia, *On the Waterfront*, would be quite a different matter, and would mark the start of a flourishing relationship that continued for eighteen years.

Chapter Thirteen

THE PROWLER AND WHEN I GROW UP

By the end of the 1940s, S. P. Eagle's life had expanded on all fronts. He was affiliated with an Oscar winner: Huston had won two Academy Awards, for the direction and screenplay of *The Treasure of the Sierra Madre*. Meanwhile his hopes were high on Horizon's next project, *The Cost of Living*. "A young man–very talented–named Joe Losey will direct," Spiegel informed his daughter. In fact, Losey was in his early forties, but he was a relative newcomer to Hollywood, having caught the town's attention with his 1947 stage production of Brecht's *Galileo*, starring Charles Laughton.

Moreover, Spiegel had a new passion–Israel. A few years before the dreamed of state was created in May 1948, he was involved in Ben Hecht's scheme to send a boat to rescue displaced persons from Europe to Palestine, even if, according to the writer, his solvency "could be said to be in question." With funds or without, Spiegel was enthusiastic. He and William Wyler sent a joint congratulatory telegram to the Israel Film Studio when it opened. "[WE] HOPE SOMEDAY WE WILL ALL BE MAKING FILMS THERE," they wrote. Spiegel also became a friend of the United Jewish Welfare Fund (Sam Goldwyn was the president) and was included in events such as welcoming Golda Myerson (Meir), Israel's minister of labor, to Hollywood.

"At the time, many Jews looked upon Israel as the homeland," said Peter Viertel. He recalled a conversation with Babe Paley when the social doyenne had announced that she and her husband, William Paley, the head of CBS, were going to Israel. "When I had said, 'really?' she had replied, 'Don't sound so surprised, that's probably where we're all going to wind up.' It was funny coming from her because she was such a WASPy lady." Even if Paley was not.

Meanwhile, Spiegel's New Year's Eve parties had become a Hollywood institution. *Life* magazine devoted two and a half pages to the 1948 (bringing in 1949) bash, where he had served champagne and hot dogs to 750 celebrities. Socially in demand, Spiegel and his wife were on the guest lists of Errol Flynn, Vi and Pandro Berman, Rosa and Joe Mankiewicz, Edie and Lew Wasserman, and when going to Palm Springs, Cary Grant was their first call. The producer also attended Truman's inauguration and was accepted for membership by the Beverly Hills Tennis Club. When Noël Coward and Henry Luce visited Hollywood, he was included in both of the welcoming committees. And the year that S. P. Eagle could not face another New Year's Eve celebration—"too many gatecrashers and it took the house several weeks to get rid of the smoke" being the chief of his complaints—one was given in his honor. Held at the exclusive Chanteclair restaurant, it was thrown by well-heeled social desirables such as Huntington Hartford III and Jay Gould.

Spiegel was always open to making new acquaintances. Once Peter and Virginia "Jigee" Viertel introduced him to a younger and attractive set—Irwin and Marion Shaw and the Parrishes—he was his hospitable self. "We ran in a pack and Sam took us in," said Kathleen Parrish. "Couples were couples. He saw us as BobandKathieParrish—all in one word." Spiegel had a rule about the wives of his friends—they were untouchable; he never made a pass. "A sixteen-year-old girl, but never a wife," said Parrish.

If the wife misbehaved, he was firmly on the side of the husband, as was demonstrated by his attitude toward Evelyn Keyes when she was still married to his partner. There was an incident at one of the many soirees given by the Milestones, which included all the usual suspects, as well as Jed Harris—the notorious Broadway director and producer—who was staying with the Hustons. The main portion of the party was held in the living room, which had French windows with floor-length drapes. But just as the three-piece band was playing, Norman Lloyd caught sight of the intriguing footwork of Harris and Mrs. Huston. "They started to dance and, as they did so, they worked their way in amongst the curtains and disappeared for a few beats," he recalled. "Then they'd work their way out." In the meantime, Huston was deep in conversation until Spiegel appeared behind the sofa, tapped his partner on the back, and whispered in his ear. "I thought, 'Oh my God, someone is about to get severely beaten,' " admitted Lloyd. "Anyway, John lumbered over and gullomped in. . . . He then reappeared out of the curtains dancing with Jed, Evelyn had been knocked out of the picture. . . . I remembered how it was Sam."

Despite the fact that top West Coast department stores were "demanding payment and threatening suit," and his checks to El Morocco, the 21 Club, and the Little 55th Street Club were merrily bouncing, Spiegel joined the art world. After buying Oscar Kokoschka's *Reclining Nude* from the Stendhal Art Gallery, he was contacted "about a flock of Picassos and other modern masterpieces" by the Sidney Janis Gallery in New York. The Bignou Gallery was also keen to do business with him, since Spiegel had been seen squiring around Mrs. Edward G. Robinson.

The affluent front was a farce. During the late 1940s, George Stevens went to discuss a project with him at his house. While Spiegel was spouting off his plans to the director, there was a terrible hammering at the door; it was the U.S. Marshals. When the situation got particularly out of hand—and it often did—Jules Buck used to receive the following call: "Baby, the sheriff is on the trail, will you take the car some place and get it hidden?" One person who was always game to lending out his garage was Clark Gable. "I like Spiegel," was the star's comment.

Ingo Preminger helped the producer escape in New York when he was unable to pay his St. Regis hotel bill. "That was Sam's beauty, he was great when he was in trouble," said the former agent.

Meanwhile, Horizon Pictures was in dire straits and still reeling from the failure of *We Were Strangers*. Yet it did not stop Walter E.

Heller's company from providing $452,199.75 for *The Cost of Living*. Wisely, the firm, which was the largest factoring company in the country, with headquarters in Chicago, insisted that "a corporation which had no debts" should be behind the production. As a result, Losey's film was made under the banner of Eagle Productions–not Horizon. Spiegel's following two pictures were also made under separate corporations.

Concerning the three productions, all three had "names" who agreed to take a deferred salary, which obviously minimized the initial raising of the funds for the film. This led to his independent pictures being made on a smaller budget, but with major talent. "Spiegel opened the doors to making pictures without too much money and resources," said Preminger. "It was almost more important than anything else that he did . . . salaries were paid out of the profits of the films."

Consequently, when working with Spiegel, those whose salaries were not deferred were liable to suffer, which was certainly the case of Robert Thoeren and Hans Wilhelm. Both writers knew the producer from Berlin, which, as already mentioned, was definitely a minus when dealing with Spiegel. To begin with, Spiegel's check to buy their story, "The Cost of Living," bounced twice. And ninety days later, when more money was due, the producer begged for an extension of three weeks. "You appealed to our old friendship," wrote Thoeren, who had worked at MGM. "At the same time, you were kind enough to inquire most solicitously after my health, the well-being of my daughter, my former wife, etc. My heart melted and I was filled with good will toward all mankind, including you." A couple of days later, Spiegel sent a long telegram announcing a letter to follow with a "most advantageous offer"–the letter never arrived. His behavior reminded Thoeren of the Eastern European folklore ("originating where Roumania borders on the believable") and the joke about a certain Mr. Levy returning home to find his wife in a highly compromising situation with one of his employees. " 'Sam,' he says (the name is a coincidence)," Thoeren wrote. " 'Three years ago you stole all the postage stamps from the office and I forgave you. Last year, you embezzled $32,740 and I forgave you. Now get off my wife and, I warn you Sam, if anything else happens, you're fired.' Feeling very much like Mr. Levy, I intend to fire you, Sam. If I don't hear from you by Thursday, January 12, 1950, and if you don't send me the story and screenplay I requested I will 1) inform the trade papers that the story 'The Cost of Living' does not belong to you in spite of all your publicity; 2) notify the Screenwriters Guild; 3) hand over the case to my lawyer; 4) do all this at the risk of not being invited to your 1951 New Year's party."

Dalton Trumbo, who wrote *The Cost of Living*'s screenplay, was equally annoyed by Spiegel's tactics. When driving with the producer, he allegedly said, "Listen, I have a gun and I will shoot you if I don't get my money today." Ingo Preminger affirms it was like his client, "a wild, unbelievable character," to say that. Trumbo was also a victim of the McCarthy era. One of the Hollywood Ten, he was sentenced to prison for refusing to "name names" or testify before the House of Un-American Activities Committee (HUAC) about his alleged membership of the Communist Party.

At the height of his MGM career, Trumbo had an extremely lucrative contract, but when he became a blacklisted writer in 1947, he was forced to work under an assumed name with a severely reduced salary. "There was no way Sam could have afforded Trumbo when he was the hottest writer in town," said his agent. "The blacklist opened the way for Sam to hire top writing talent for little money.... [It] also invited an adventurous kind of moviemaking–an undercover moviemaking–and Sam was in his element. He would rather live like that than under the traditional rules."

Although Spiegel was getting a bargain, he was also putting himself and the production at risk. Had it been known that a blacklisted writer was responsible for the script, the film would have been publicly ostracized. Hedda Hopper, Walter Winchell, and other powerful figures in the press were rabid red-baiters and hell-bent on exposing any "commie" associates. "Sam was wonderful, he was a big friend of all the blacklisted writers, but he *did* save a lot of money," said Preminger. "Nobody used blacklisted writers for the sake of giving them a chance, or for being interested in justice, everybody whether it was Kirk Douglas or my brother [Otto Preminger] who broke it with Trumbo with *Exodus*, they all did it for business reasons. These writers were bargains, you go to a bargain sale, and the blacklist was a bargain; that was the problem."

Throughout the production of *The Cost of Living,* great pains were taken by Spiegel's employees Gladys Hill and Sam Rheiner to keep a veil of mystery over the screenplay's authorship. "I only found out much later," admitted Evelyn Keyes, who co-starred in the picture. And although Huston was called upon to intensify the plot and help with the dialogue, another writer–Hugo Butler–was credited with the screenplay, which was essentially Trumbo's. Butler's services were paid to cover for the blacklisted writer, and to act as the writer on set.

The film's story begins with Susan Gilvray (Keyes) being frightened by a prowler and calling the police. Officers Webb Garwood (Van Heflin) and Budd Crocker (John Maxwell) arrive on the scene and Garwood falls for the blonde's slinky silhouette. He is a bitter, twisted individual, while she is lonesome since her husband, John Gilvray (Sherry Hall), is an all-night disc jockey. When searching for cigarettes, Garwood discovers a will, made by Gilvray, that leaves his wife $60,000. A love affair starts, and the police officer secretly plots to have both Susan and the bequest. Garwood succeeds in his machinations after staging a fake prowler call and killing Gilvray. There is a police investigation, but he is cleared, helped by Susan's claim that she has never seen him before. Afterward, Garwood resigns from the force and, amidst much public fanfare, Susan and he get married. However, later, she announces that she is five months pregnant, which is a problem, since it is known that her first husband was sterile. In order to avoid witnesses to the birth, they move to the ghost town of Calico, but, during labor, there are complications. Garwood seeks out the services of a certain Dr. James (Wheaton Chambers), whom he plans to kill immediately afterward. Suddenly, Susan realizes that her first husband's death was not an accident, and eventually the police arrive and her evil husband is killed.

In his preproduction notes, Losey was keen to build up the characters and intensify the atmosphere–two elements for which he later became famous. However, when the screenplay failed to reach the production code's standards because of its "extremely low moral tone with emphasis on almost animal-like instincts and passion," the director had to join Spiegel when he met with Joseph Breen's office. Considering how anti-establishment Losey was, the idea of that meeting remains somewhat of an amusing scenario. No doubt, Spiegel did all the talking, because with the promise of some rewrites–making the story one of love "rather than one of lust"–they were given the green light to continue.

The Cost of Living's shoot took three weeks, and was divided between General Service Studios and the Calico Mines, a ghost town that was nine miles outside Barstow. Robert Aldrich was the first assistant director, Boris Leven was the art director, and Arthur Miller– the recipient of three Academy Awards *(How Green Was My Valley, The Song of Bernadette, Anna and the King of Siam)*–was the director of photography. The technicians liked Spiegel. "He allowed them to do exactly what they wanted, while the studios were obnoxious," said Preminger, who also represented cameramen. "He didn't just do it to be charming, he did it in a very deliberate and shrewd way." Most of the filming was shot inside, although Losey was quoted as saying, "You always go bowling on location over dirt and rock roads. And dust such as you've never choked on before."

Keyes, who was borrowed from Columbia, considered her performance in the picture as the best of her career. Extremely attractive, she resembled Lana Turner–a slighter version–and had been in many films, including *Gone With the Wind, Here Comes Mr. Jordan,* and *The Jolson Story.* "Joe was the complete director as far as I'm concerned," she said. "He was so clever and subtle and he really went into the character." The actress, who later worked on *The Seven Year Itch,* had the same feelings for Billy Wilder. "But Joe was truly the artist–he knew all the parts and the essence of the actors maybe better than we did." She also admired Van Heflin, who had won a supporting actor Academy Award for *Johnny Eager,* and whose later films included *Shane* and *Patterns.* With time, Losey recalled getting very angry at Spiegel for hovering on the set. However, Keyes did not remember their producer putting on that "type of pressure" since "he had super instincts."

Nevertheless, Spiegel was in a bind about the thriller's title, which had gone from *The Cost of Living* to *The Cost of Loving,* leading to *Daily Variety*'s tease "Whatta difference." Eventually, Huston became involved. His suggestions, however, which were scribbled on the back of a gin rummy score–*The Fix, I'd Do It Again, No Second Chance,* and *Quick Kill*–lacked his usual flair. No doubt he was exhausted, since he had just finished with *The Asphalt Jungle,* and it was Spiegel who came up with *The Prowler.*

It was also the producer's idea that the picture, the negative cost of which was only $732,591.99, should have two publicists: Paul MacNamara, who ended up suing him for his salary, and William F. Blowitz, who was on all of his following productions until his untimely death in 1964. "He was always being asked to teach at universities," said Nina Blowitz, his wife. "But Bill's argument was you can't teach public relations, you have to feel it." His other clients included producer Albert "Cubby" Broccoli, Stanley Kramer, Danny Kaye, and producer Gottfried Reinhardt.

Born in the business, Blowitz's father was Charles Skouras's partner, and a close friend of Harry Warner. Starting at the *Pittsburgh Post Gazette,* he had gone on to work for MGM, Warner Bros., Paramount, and Enterprise Pictures—the ill-fated studio of Charlie Einfeld. It was likely Blowitz and Spiegel met at the latter since Horizon Pictures had their office on the same lot. It was also known as California Studios and had three different postal addresses, which, no doubt, S. P. Eagle used to optimal advantage. "Bill just adored Sam and while others laughed, he really believed in him and wanted to work for him," said his wife. "He used to sit in business meetings with Spiegel and he was mesmerized by how he operated. . . . At night, Bill used to come back and say 'He did it again, he did it again'—you see, Bill was a terrible businessman."

The wrap party for *The Prowler* was a perfect example of how Spiegel was conducting himself. Held at the restaurant Lucy's, it was more elaborate than the usual fare, since wives and family members were invited. As a result, the cast agreed to individually give money toward the event. But when someone asked to see the picture's budget, they noticed that the party had already been accounted for. Spiegel had pocketed the actors' contributions for himself! Such funds had definitely not gone toward the director's salary since his checks to Sam Jaffe—Losey's agent—continued to bounce to such a point that in the mid-1960s Spiegel still owed Losey the deferred $5,000, and bought him the rights to the novel *Accident* to make up for it.

Notwithstanding the lack of payment, Losey rated *The Prowler* higher than his other works in Hollywood, which included *The Boy with Green Hair, The Lawless,* and the remake of *M.* The *Los Angeles Times* called the thriller "an extraordinarily persuasive job of movie making, in writing, direction and performance."

While Huston was making *The Red Badge of Courage* for MGM, Spiegel had other irons in the fire, which included buying the rights for an original Michael Kanin screenplay and continuing to try and remake *La Fin du Jour.* Yet neither project could be compared to his role as the spark who fused two forces together—United Artists and two lawyers called Arthur Krim and Robert Benjamin.

"Without Spiegel, Krim and Benjamin would not have become United Artists," said Ingo Preminger. "And without United Artists, we wouldn't have had such a quick transition from big studio to independent production. . . . Sam not only benefited from it, but he did it." Nevertheless, the producer has never been credited for putting together two partners who refused to speak—Mary Pickford and Charlie Chaplin—with a couple of lawyers who were relative outsiders to Hollywood. Krim and Benjamin worked for Phillips & Nizer, a New York law firm "that specialized in the entertainment industry." "Sam was the first to mention to Krim and Benjamin that United Artists might be available," affirmed Max Youngstein, who became an executive at the studio.

Not that Spiegel's methods were entirely straightforward, especially when he took advantage of Mary Pickford's inebriated state. "One day Sam said, 'I think I have it locked up, I talked to Doug,' " recalled Jules Buck. "I said, 'But Doug isn't here' [Fairbanks Sr. died in 1939], and Sam said, 'Well, I pretended to talk to Doug.' He then told Pickford that her husband had always wanted to get rid of United Artists and use the money for something else."

When the negotiations were getting serious, Spiegel turned up at Chaplin's house while he was playing tennis with Norman Lloyd. "He sits there and I think to myself, 'Well, I'll never get a straight call from now on,' " Lloyd recalled. "Each time I served, it was out. Sam was ingratiating himself."

It was obvious that he "was dying to talk to Charlie alone" about Krim and Benjamin. "[They] were lawyers who were desperate to get into the picture business," said Albert Heit, Spiegel's New York attorney. "And they never paid off the moral debt to Sam, who had put it all together. They treated Sam worse than he was ever treated. For once, someone else got the better of him." Spiegel was so associated with the deal that when the widow of theater owner Max Kravetz sued United Artists, his name was included, alongside Chaplin's.

As described in Tino Balio's excellent book, *United Artists, The Company That Changed the Film Industry,* Krim and Benjamin revolutionized the state of independent filmmaking. Their selling point, "the producers are creators, we are the distributors," was an attractive one. "This was the plan," wrote Balio, "in return for distribution rights, UA would offer talent complete production financing, creative control over their work and a share of the profits. In essence, UA would go into partnership with its producers. The company and a producer had to agree on the basic ingredients–story, cast, director, and budget–but in the making of the picture, UA would give the producer complete autonomy including the final cut. Talent would have to defer much of their salary until the picture broke even, but UA would help keep production costs down by not charging any administrative overhead, which at another company could boost budgets by as much as 40 percent. Since UA owned no studio, a producer could make his picture anywhere in the world to suit the needs of the story or the economics of the venture. Moreover, . . . UA's brand of independent production gave ownership of the picture to the producer. . . . Contracts with UA were to be nonexclusive, which meant that a producer would not have to go forward with a project until he was satisfied with the terms and circumstances of the venture." All these terms dealt with the normal list of complaints that a producer had when working with the traditional studios such as Warners or Fox. Every single detail of the terms had been thought over umpteen times, Benjamin and Krim were meticulous and well versed in a creative person's needs. And with the government's decree that the studios could no longer control the theaters, it meant that theater managers, whose hands previously had been tied by studio ownership, were free to choose what films to show.

For a producer with individuality, United Artists offered the ideal situation, which was why Spiegel stalled *The Prowler* for over a year, in order to have the picture released by UA under Krim and

Benjamin, rather than their predecessors. After the film came out in May 1951, United Artists referred to it as "one of their most successful pictures."

When United Artists bought out Eagle-Lion Classics, they were behind the release of *When I Grow Up,* Spiegel's next project, which was written and directed by Michael Kanin. "It was a low-budget little movie," said his wife, Fay Kanin. "I don't know what it brought to Sam."

The film–christened *When I Throw Up* by Huston, who was paid to both rewrite and artistically supervise–was not typical of Horizon Pictures. It might have come about for either of two reasons: for old times' sake, since Spiegel was involved with Kanin in the early 1940s, or economy, since the production promised to be cheap and commercial. Taking less than a month to make, the child star Bobby Driscoll–whose credits included *The Window,* for which he won a special Academy Award, *So Dear to My Heart,* and *Treasure Island*–was borrowed from Walt Disney.

Danny Reed (Driscoll) is the problematic youth in both the modern and 1890 sequences. The eleven-year-old is convinced that his strict parents do not love him (Robert Preston and Martha Scott), while his live-in paternal grandfather, Josh Reed (Charley Grapewin), grates on his nerves. However, before running away, Danny finds his grandfather's diary, which was written when he was twelve, and suddenly the story goes back in time. It shows how Josh (Driscoll) had the same feeling about his own father (Preston) until he ran away to the circus and caught typhoid fever. It was while suffering from the illness that Josh realized that Pa, who fell victim to the fever and died, really did love him. This dramatic exit then leads to the diary entry, which sums up the moral of the picture: "When people love other people, why don't they show it . . . before it's too late."

(Clearly, Spiegel did not take great heed of the theme because, in spite of corresponding with Alisa, he had not seen her for fifteen months, nor had he remembered her birthday. "I'm quite proud to be your daughter," she wrote. "Let's try to be closer.")

The film was respectfully reviewed, although a chief complaint was that it was too long. Most critics praised Ernest Laszlo's photography, Jerome Moross's musical score, and the harmonica work of George Fields. Yet in spite of being recommended as the perfect child entertainment, it did not fare well at the box office. Unlike *The Prowler,* it lacked international appeal and ultimately legs. And whereas Losey's work became a cult classic, *When I Grow Up* disappeared without a trace.

Made under the banner of Horizon Pictures, the film, released in April 1951, only cost $459,932.16. But for the next two years, Kanin's lawyer, Pathé Laboratories, and others who were owed money from the supposedly modest production plagued the Horizon office.

In the meantime, Spiegel was far removed from such niggling issues. He was otherwise engaged on his next project–*The African Queen.*

Chapter Fourteen
THE AFRICAN QUEEN

Spiegel was so enthusiastic about *The African Queen* that he had even tempted fate by voicing his confidence. "It will give John the kind of commercial hit he had when he made *The Maltese Falcon* in 1941," he told Lillian Ross, the *New Yorker* writer. Moreover, Huston seemed equally convinced that the film would make money, and–if it did–he would then be able to make some pictures on his own that he felt strongly about. Both partners were seeking escape–Spiegel from financial ruin, Huston from commercial mediocrity.

Cecil Scott Forester's novel had made the rounds. Columbia purchased the rights for Charles Laughton and his wife, Elsa Lanchester, as had Warner Bros. for Bette Davis; then the British writer John Collier became involved. However, the project's past did not bother Horizon since their production promised to have top stars, and with Huston as the director, there would be no backdrop nonsense–the picture would be shot on location.

Regarding the cast, a story has since circulated that in order to get the movie made, Spiegel told Huston that he had Katharine Hepburn, then lied to Humphrey Bogart that he had Hepburn and Huston, and so forth. This was simply not the case. From the beginning, Huston– as both Spiegel's partner and a top-class director–was involved in pulling in the talent. It should also be added that the storyline appealed to both actors.

Set in Africa at the beginning of World War I, Rose Sayer, a proper English lady missionary (Hepburn), and Charlie Allnut (in Forester's novel he is Allnutt but in the film he is referred to as Allnut), a gin-soaked Canadian riverboat captain (Bogart), are thrown together when the Germans burn down the village where she and her brother (Robert Morley) have a mission station. The appalling event results in the Reverend Samuel Sayer dying of shock and his sister becoming determined to take her revenge and "do her bit" for Britain. She and Allnut plan to steer his boat down one of the roughest waterways in Africa and sink a German gunboat with homemade torpedoes. During the course of their adventures, the unlikely couple fall in love.

Hepburn was captivated with playing the opinionated spinster. Rose was a great role and she needed a hit. *Adam's Rib*, her last film, had done well, but the previous five had not. The actress had been labeled box office poison before, and she needed a project after touring the country with Shakespeare. A film in Africa with a talented director seemed intriguing. "Everything swings around him and his moods," she noted. It would be a unique experience, one for her memoirs, and perfect for the actress the critic Kenneth Tynan christened "the Garbo of the great outdoors." Despite being renowned for her high principles and no-nonsense attitude, she admitted to an inner thaw when receiving Spiegel's usual flowers and handwritten messages, such as "You are unique, Katie darling." There was also a flood of correspondence from him when her mother died.

As for Bogart, he and Huston went way back. Huston had co-written *High Sierra*, which allowed Bogart to play a gangster with soul. Then there was Huston's directorial debut, *The Maltese Falcon*, followed by *The Treasure of the Sierra Madre* and *Key Largo*. The actor had every confidence in his friend. "Before I met Huston my range was Beverly Hills to Palm Springs," he admitted. "Now the Monster wants me to fly 12,000 miles into the Congo. And the crazy thing is that I've agreed to go." And Spiegel? "Sam was able to woo people like my husband," said Lauren Bacall, "because although Bogie may not have trusted him, he respected the fact that he had the taste that he had and the people that he had."

Meanwhile, *The African Queen* was to be a major Spiegel production, even though he was sharing the costs with James and

John Woolf, the brothers behind Romulus Films, the British production company. Their previous film was *Pandora and the Flying Dutchman*, with Ava Gardner and James Mason. "British films were doing no good and the idea of making films with Hollywood actors greatly appealed," said John Woolf. Romulus was paying for the supporting actors, technicians, and the expenses involved with the *African Queen* location, while Horizon Pictures was responsible for the deferred salaries of the stars, director, and producer. Bogart was to receive $125,000 and 30 percent of the net profits, Hepburn $65,000 and 10 percent of the net profits, Huston $87,500, and Spiegel $50,000.

The African Queen screenplay was flawed and in need of an ending. Huston and James Agee—the novelist and film critic—had gone off to write at the San Ysidro ranch in Santa Barbara at the beginning of 1951. But a certain amount of boozing and playing tennis in the midday sun took place, which led to Agee having a heart attack. In spite of creating scenes and a certain ambience, his screenplay lacked dialogue. "Oh, Christ, Jim, tell me something I can understand," Huston had told his ailing co-writer. However, it was no good—even after being given guidelines, Agee's second attempt was unfit for the screen.

Then Spiegel's financing for the director and the leading players fell through. Initially, Walter E. Heller & Co. was supposed to provide for the deferred salaries, but when Spiegel was unable to provide a completion guarantee for the film, the Chicago firm refused to pay up. Moreover, as soon as Heller's funds vanished, so did the services of Hepburn. Despite being contracted to start in April 1951, she refused to budge until she was assured by Ann Rosenthal from the William Morris Agency, that monies were forthcoming. Spiegel immediately cabled her. I HAVE JUST RETURNED FROM AFRICA WHERE JOHN REMAINED WITH ENTIRE TECHNICAL STAFF BUSILY BUILDING BOATS FOR AFRICAN QUEEN. Claiming to be IN SHOCK THAT LAWYERS STILL HAGGLING OVER WORDING OF GUARANTEE BETWEEN LONDON AND LOS ANGELES, he urged her to sail the following day, AS DELAYS IN GUARANTEES PURELY OBSTINACY OF LAWYERS... WILL BE SETTLED LONG BEFORE YOU ARRIVE... PLEASE CABLE ME CLARIDGES.

In true Spiegel style, he wanted Hepburn to think that he was staying at one of London's most expensive hotels, when he was actually living in a rented apartment nearby, in Grosvenor Square. In the meantime, his partner had not been paid since mid-January and his faithful employees, including Gladys Hill and Sam Rheiner in California, were being threatened with eviction and the disconnection of the office telephone. But such news had never stopped Spiegel from sleeping at night. Indeed, he was eating hearty three-course meals, playing cards, and dancing the rumba, while girls were described as "coming in the front door and coming out of the back door." Relieved to be back in Europe, he was clearly also relieved to be a free man again, since he had left wife Lynne in Hollywood, along with his money problems. (Not that Lynne minded, since she was having an affair with the writer Irwin Shaw.) In fact, the sole issue nagging at Spiegel was Huston, who refused to concentrate on the screenplay.

"John was only interested in killing an elephant," said Viertel, who had been yanked from Klosters, Switzerland, to co-write the ending and add dialogue. There were also the demands of the Breen Office to deal with, who were concerned about the Rose-Allnut relationship, the "naked natives," and fear that the story's tone might offend the churchgoing public. As the days passed, it was apparent that Huston was more concerned about appointments with Tautz's, his sporting tailor, and Purdey's, the gun makers, than settling down to rewrites. "Poor old Sam, he believed in *The African Queen* much more than John did," said Viertel. Spiegel became increasingly convinced that if they did not get something down on paper soon, "the whole project might well be suspended."

Spiegel had also sensed a certain coldness in his partner. "He seems to hate me for some unknown reason," he admitted to Viertel. Was it the lack of payment for several weeks? The writer sympathized, because he was fond of Spiegel, particularly his "ability to appear as a father," and the fact that he was "a good listener." However, Viertel had not been paid his promised expense allowance, and when Spiegel offered to employ his wife, Viertel put his foot down, saying, "It would be too humiliating to have both of us *not* being paid by Sam Spiegel!"

In the interim, whenever Huston could disgrace his partner, he did. At one lunch with the Woolfs, he noticed that Spiegel had already started on his first course. The director stopped his speech mid-sentence and said, "I'll wait until my partner has finished going down on the asparagus and then proceed." John Woolf was also at a dinner when Huston made a reference to Spiegel's time in Brixton Prison. "It was very embarrassing for all concerned."

However, there was a truce when Huston confronted his partner on some piece of barefaced Spiegelese and Spiegel replied, "If I hadn't lied, I would now be a bar of soap." The director was amused, but when he left for Africa, he forgot to take a copy of the screenplay with him. "I'm hooked up with a madman," a penniless Spiegel declared as he and Viertel were being driven back from the airport in the comfort of the producer's chauffeur-driven Rolls-Royce.

When Huston returned to London–breaking the news that the picture was to be made in the Belgian Congo and Uganda–Hepburn was there to greet him. True to form, she was eager to discuss her role, but she was given a look at her director's hunting clothes instead. Concerned, she spoke to Bogart, who implied that it was standard practice for the Monster. Perhaps, but normally the financial situation was a little steadier. Although there was caviar and champagne in their hotel rooms and a chauffeur-driven car at their beck and call, the tab for the film star perks was being picked up by the Woolfs, not Spiegel. "When we got to England, there was no money," said Bacall. "Anyone else but Bogie or Hepburn would have walked." Wisely, Hepburn had prepared herself accordingly, having asked her father to credit an English bank with $10,000, so that she could "move out fast" if she had to.

Huston and Viertel then left to do screenplay revisions in Entebbe, Uganda. "We did make pretty good progress except for the end," said Viertel. "Willy Wyler once said, 'A lot of people come to me with great openings–I don't want a great opening–I want a great end, because with most stories you can't find a good end.' That stopped us and so we devised this ending–a comic scene . . . they had to be married by the German sea captain on the boat that they failed to torpedo."

Huston's attention was back on *The African Queen,* or so it seemed. He and Viertel flew to Stanleyville in the Belgian Congo to be there for Bogart and the company, who were arriving after hours of travel–a plane change in Rome and so forth. But suddenly the call of the wild was too much for Huston, and an hour before the group landed, he swept off in a private plane to the film's first location. Hepburn was irate, calling it an "utterly piggish thing to do," especially when she heard that he had chosen a selection of guns over the screenplay and was inquiring about an elephant permit. The Bogarts were calmer; they had each other, and were well used to Huston's lifestyle. "A lot of 'go fuck yourself' went on," recalled Bacall. "But, when you have that kind of talent, you have certain idiosyncrasies, and not everything goes as smooth as apple pie."

Spiegel arrived on May 20. In Bacall's opinion, he looked "quite a sight" with his "dead white skin in safari shirt, shorts and knee socks, with a regular hat." Yet, according to Viertel, he was fantastic. "Sam wanted to be in Africa as much as he wanted to be shot to the moon," he recalled. "He had absolutely no taste for that, but he really took charge. He was on death row and he had to function. Without him, we would never have made the movie."

Despite his high living circumstances in London, the last three months had been extremely difficult for Spiegel—reaching a hideous low at the end of April, with even his partner threatening to walk and return to making films for MGM. ACCORDING TO ALL AVAILABLE SOURCES NO MONEY IN SIGHT, Huston's agent had cabled. Then, in early May, ten days before the cameras were scheduled to roll, United Artists agreed to guarantee Hepburn's salary, while the contract with the studio satisfied Huston's representatives. In regard to the completion guarantee, John Woolf took care of it. "Lloyd's Bank put the money up," he said. "I had a million pounds in production with my personal guarantee and a million was a lot of money in those days." This had then led to Walter Heller & Co. paying up for the deferred salaries at the end of May. But it had been a narrow shave. Spiegel had been close to disaster, and would remain so throughout the making of the film.

To arrive at the first destination, the crew had to board a wooden train. "It would set itself alight every three or four yards," said Angela Allen, the film's "continuity lady." "You were bitten from ear to ankle by anything that happened to be flying around." Hepburn sat with Spiegel, who was pouring sweat. "He kept on mopping it up and taking showers," she recalled. When reaching the Ponthieville railway station, pontoons, trucks, and jeeps were then mounted to get to Biondo, nicknamed "Beyondo"—which was on the tar-colored Ruiki River. The blackness was due to the tannic acid from the vegetation. "It made a unique background," Bogart later said.

Aside from the presence of snakes, scorpions, crocodiles, tsetse flies, and huge biting black ants, clothes and most objects tended to collect mildew in the humid heat. "We felt it was only a question of days before we would be lying under the Congo earth with our name on fungoid crosses," recalled Jack Cardiff, the director of photography.

Only Hepburn took to the terrifying nature. "What divine natives! What divine morning glories!" she gushed, as her nimble figure slipped in and out of the lush undergrowth. However, she still insisted on having her own personal lavatory, which was nicknamed the "Queen's Throne" by the natives. "It used to drive everyone mad because it was yet another piece to add to the floating flotilla," said Allen.

One of Spiegel's first major tasks was trying to cajole Viertel into staying. The writer was desperate to leave, since he was disenchanted with the entire production, particularly Huston. "I can't handle the guy any more than you can," he told Spiegel. "He thinks I'm a coward because I wouldn't go elephant shooting with him." The subject of the screenplay's credit had come up. "I was really stupid," he admitted. "I was sick of everything and said, 'I don't care, goodbye and just give me that ticket.' " It was a mistake, because Viertel would miss out on an Oscar nomination as a result. But he wanted out. In his opinion, Huston's decision to shoot the picture in the Congo was solely based on the fact that "he thought that it was the best place to torture everybody." Huston certainly had that side to his nature, but he was also an original—"a real character," who could be counted on to do the unexpected. Perhaps he chose the most difficult locations in the world, but to quote Lauren Bacall, "He also made the most wonderful movies."

Africa agreed with Huston. He was his long-legged, seemingly relaxed self while his quick mind had completely assessed how to take on *The African Queen*. Since it was not in his nature to confide in others, his initial approach confounded Jack Cardiff and Guy Hamilton, his first assistant director. "At first, we felt that Huston was ruining the film–he was making it satirelike, and his setting of pace was wrong," Cardiff said. Such doubts disappeared when they realized that their director had "a complete grasp" of the situation. "He was just very casual and laid-back."

Off camera, Huston had recognized a certain comic chemistry between his two actors. Bogart had a very critical manner. Before shooting, he told the cameraman that he liked his lines and wrinkles. "So don't try and light them out and make me look like a god dam fag." And if someone made the mistake of saying "Good morning," he would quip, "What's so good about it?" In contrast, his co-star seemed like an irritating Girl Scout with a staggeringly high opinion of herself. Hepburn disapproved of her fellow star's drinking, and would make a point of sipping water throughout meals. While Bogart was annoyed by the jungle conditions–living in a bamboo hut and washing in water that was bright red–Hepburn was soaking up the experience and determined to find out the Latin names for all the flora and fauna that she came across. On one occasion, when she had a camera around her neck with one hand clasped on a tape recorder and the other on a butterfly net, she had the nerve to ask Bogie–the tough man of the movies–to carry her makeup kit for her! Another time, she requested that he help find a bamboo forest for her "to sit in and contemplate."

Nevertheless, it was all rather funny, allowing Huston to think that he could direct a comedy of sorts. His only problem was Hepburn, who, with her mannered ways, skinny face, and turned-down mouth– was too serious on camera. Being innovative, he found a solution. She should smile in the same way as Eleanor Roosevelt. The president's wife, he said, felt she was ugly, but recognized that she looked better when she was exuding cheerfulness. "It was indeed a FLASH of brilliance," Hepburn wrote in *Me,* her memoirs. (When Lauren Bacall wrote *By Myself,* she teased that she thought of *Me Too* as a title.) "In short, he had told me exactly how to play the part."

In the meantime, the location dramas continued. The sinking of *The African Queen* was the first disaster. On the night of June 6, the clapper boy had noticed that the boat was leaking. He warned the crew, but no one paid much notice. And far from being "all right in the morning," the boat was completely submerged. Huston broke the news to Spiegel, who was convinced that he must have misheard him. "I thought you'd said that *The African Queen* had sunk," he said over the telephone, somewhat merrily. "Yes, I did," replied the director. It then took three days for the crew and two hundred Congolese to pull the boat up on ropes.

Spiegel's infrequent visits were short and his partner did his best to make him feel out of place. "You know when producers decide to drop in, having not been there and then go back to the comfort of London? That was Sam," said Bacall. Regarding her attitude, it should be mentioned that the actress had a very "us who grinned and bared it" versus "those who didn't" approach. She had given Viertel hell for "deserting" the troops when he did.

In any event, once the unit moved to Butiaba, Uganda, their second location, Spiegel was there to greet them. He and his whipping boy, Edward Josephs (the location manager), had organized all the transport including *The African Queen's* which had had to chug through obscure rivers as well as being lifted onto trains before ending up at Lake Albert. It was quite an achievement, but Huston went off on a tirade that the organization was terrible. "While you've been sitting on your ass . . . ," he told his partner, in front of the somewhat embarrassed crew. A spider then bit Spiegel. Bacall had had to nurse him. "He had this enormous red boil on his neck," she said.

When shooting in Uganda, Spiegel arranged for the entire unit to live on board *Lugard II*, which was moored near the Murchison Falls on Lake Albert. The film crew of *King Solomon's Mines* had previously used the houseboat. Although the cabins were comfortable and pleasant in appearance, the water was being pumped through filters that were clogged and therefore of little use. As a result, the water drinkers of the group drank every microbe in the book of tropical diseases. To make matters worse, it was then discovered that all the bottled water from the East African Railway was contaminated as well.

Apart from Bogart and Huston, who had only drunk whiskey–it was joked that they shaved in the stuff–nearly all the crew came down with either malaria or dysentery. Hepburn was extremely ill, but being her stoic self, carried on courageously. When playing the church organ, a bucket had been installed to allow her to vomit in between takes. "I was concerned about her skin looking green in Technicolor," said Cardiff.

In spite of her insistence to the contrary, Hepburn was forced to take time off by the location's doctor, which led to a three-day shutdown on the film. Spiegel was sympathetic, but he had sent strict, strict instructions that "Katie" was to stay in bed for a minimum of seventy-two hours. He was concerned about his company claiming the time from the insurance. Any less and he would not have been able to. Needless to say, the award-winning actress got up before she was supposed to and returned to being "Katie the autocrat." "Tell him to learn the next scene," she used to say to Allen, who would then inform Bogart that he had to learn the next scene. And he would reply, "Well, if I learn the next one, I'll forget the first one and then she'll say that she wants the third one . . ."

Moreover, like all great autocrats, Hepburn refused to be contradicted. There was a young crewmember called von Kotze, but she insisted that it could not be his "proper name." The young man had politely replied that it was and explained where his parents came from. However, it was something that Hepburn was unable to accept. "She just had fixations on things," sensed Allen. The film star's personal life was also considered a little contradictory. "Here was this woman who had photos of Spencer Tracy all over her cabin and she was always talking about him. But *no one* was allowed to mention their relationship because he was married."

During the height of all the sickness, Spiegel flew in. "Huston started to foam at the mouth. 'If you don't get these people water, I'm going to shut down the movie,'" Bacall remembered him saying. "Then Sam looked at me and said, 'Why doesn't she take care of all of this.' And Huston yelled, 'Don't you dare talk to her like that; if she hadn't been here, there wouldn't be any food. We couldn't have had proper meals' . . . It was very tough and ugly, and John was ready to kill him."

At the time, David Lewin was writing about the picture for his *Daily Express* column. "Sam had never encountered a journalist on location before, and was fascinated that every five days I had to get my copy back." The trip consisted of taking a riverboat, switching to a jeep and driving several hours to Entebbe in order to send a cable to his London office. "When I had done this a couple of times, Sam took me aside, 'Baby' (they all addressed me as 'baby' or 'kid'), 'it's a bit of a schlepp, isn't it for you? But for you, baby, I've got something special. I'm building an airport at the bottom of the river and so all you've got to do is get down there and the plane will take you.' I kept on saying 'Thank you, Sam,' and then he said, 'But baby, if the plane crashes, the first thing you do is get my rushes out of the fire and into the safety of the jungle.' And I said, 'Sam, you're not doing this for me at all, you want your bloody rushes back.' And he said, 'But you want your copy back.' Sam had his priorities straight."

On the other hand, many of Spiegel's crewmembers were losing touch. Allen had been put in charge of the second unit and, by her own admittance, was getting "more and more stupid by the day." "One day, I led everyone up to the top of the Murchison Falls and there were all these crocodiles," she said. "None of our guns had bullets. The attitude was, 'Well we have come so far, no point in turning back now.' We could have been killed."

Meanwhile, Huston was obsessed about squeezing in two days of blood sport with an experienced white hunter. He had even tried to rope in Bacall. "You've got to come with me, honey, you've got to come with me," were his words, while her husband was firmly insisting that she was "going nowhere" with the Monster. "John was the worst shot, but very serious about it, which made it more endearing," she recalled. Nevertheless, the director's persuasiveness worked on Hepburn, and Spiegel was furious. The star of his picture was going to set off in a little plane and hunt for elephants. "You're a reasonable, decent human being . . . ," he tried by way of argument. The actress replied that normally she was "reasonable," but being around Huston made her crave adventure. Exasperated, Spiegel sent her to Bogart. "Listen Katie—have you ever shot a gun?" the actor asked. Naturally, she described herself as "a pretty good shot."

On set, as much as she admired her director, Hepburn was not averse to disagreeing with him. It was one of their last weeks in Africa. "In his usual way, John was sitting at the end of the boat and looking the other way," Allen recalled. According to Cardiff, Huston was actually fishing and he said, "Fine, print it." But it simply was not good enough for the actress, who narrowed her eyes and clenched her already pronounced jawline. "You weren't watching," she said. And Huston replied, "Nooo, but I'm listening, and I can hear it."

The director did have a reputation for losing interest. "He used to fall asleep on *The Misfits,*" said Arthur Miller later. The "continuity lady" used to wake him up and he would immediately suggest another scene. "Everyone would say, 'We've already done that.' " And without a flicker of embarrassment, Huston used to reply, "Well, on to the next."

In Bacall's opinion, Huston only started "thinking of the famous horses or the hunting" in the course of the last three weeks. "And that's when Bogie would say, 'Now, pay attention; now, pay attention.' "

Had Spiegel's whereabouts been known, he could have been accused of the same behavior. The stars and crew presumed that he was in Entebbe, and sent endless cables asking for more supplies of whiskey and chocolate, but since the telegrams remained unanswered, they were forwarded to Romulus in London. John Woolf was extremely surprised. Surely Spiegel's crew knew that he was in the South of France or Deauville or Rome or wherever he was? Bacall had her suspicions. "Sam was such a wheeler-dealer that you never knew where the hell he was," she said. Yet, as this was in the days of booking long-distance calls in advance or taking hours to find a good telephone connection, Spiegel had every excuse for not being in touch, which he would use to his full advantage.

He was also to take full advantage of the cast being away on location. Case in point—when Heller gave over $50,000, apart from a mere $7,000, the rest was owed to Huston. However, with the director in the depths of darkest Africa, Spiegel decided instead to put the sum toward his outstanding income tax bill. He owed $57,043.85, and the U.S. government was not to be reasoned with. It also demonstrated Spiegel's nerve—his partner was well protected by his agent and others—and his appalling selfishness, since Huston's young wife was expecting their second child in early July.

Stalling payment, then only giving 50 percent of the promised amount after considerable threats, typified Spiegel's behavior throughout the making of *The African Queen.* "Don't ask and don't tell, that was the way Sam operated," said Albert Heit, his New York lawyer. "If you didn't ask, you didn't get your money. In other words, if you forgot, he didn't tell you that you were entitled."

Spiegel's bad behavior was not just reserved for his business activities. That summer, he disgraced himself at Monsieur André's Casino in Deauville when he cashed two dud checks amounting to 692,400 francs. (Later, Spiegel promised that it had been "an oversight" on his part and pressing business on *The African Queen* had forced him to leave so suddenly–without due explanation.) Such behavior resulted in Spiegel being banned from playing in all the French gambling houses from February 28, 1952.

Joan Axelrod recalled one or two other Spiegel techniques that were practiced in Paris. She was then married to Arthur Stanton, who had made his fortune discovering "a little car called the Volkswagen," and belonged to the group of glamorous Americans living in Paris. "Marion [Mrs. Irwin Shaw] was a great anchor of that Parisian life– the Shaws had this huge apartment and she was a great hostess." The others included Art Buchwald, war photographer Robert Capa, playwright Arthur Laurents, the Parrishes, and the Viertels. "Bob [Capa] was the hero of the group," Axelrod said. "He and Sam used to speak in Hungarian." One night, the entire group had been invited by Spiegel to Korniloff's, the Russian restaurant. "There was tons and tons of caviar and champagne," said Axelrod. "But at around 1:30 in the morning, a policeman arrived who said that he just wanted to take Sam down to the station." Spiegel then explained to his throng of guests that someone in his office was having problems. "He told us to carry on and that he would be back in no time, he just had to sign something; but Sam never returned." Stanton was left to foot the bill. "When I told this story, everyone said this was an old ploy and he would do that quite often. He just wanted people to have a good time." Another Spiegel technique was being paged to the telephone when the bill needed to be settled. "My then husband was never mad at Sam for being left with the check. He just thought it was fun." Later, she teased the producer about it. "Sam used to laugh at the S. P. Eagle stories along with the rest of us. He had a great sense of humor about himself."

The humor, however, was severely lacking at Horizon Pictures in California. Gladys Hill and Sam Rheiner had continued to struggle, and in September 1951 had been evicted from their offices. "What irks me most is that people who are getting healthy slices of profits do very little, if anything toward keeping our ship afloat," Rheiner wrote. "We are all broke . . . and have exhausted every possible means of further borrowings. . . . I don't know of anybody else in the world who would have stuck to the foundering ship through all this storm as we have . . . living on less than baked beans. . . . You therefore must keep your promise to get us sufficient funds to exist on."

In desperation, Hill had telephoned United Artists's Robert Benjamin. In spite of being sympathetic, he was not forthcoming with funds, revealing that he had mortgaged his own house to help Spiegel's production. And when contacted, Arthur Krim also claimed that he was "personally strapped."

Finally, Spiegel sent $2,000. He also persuaded Lynne to come to Europe, which would allow his office to rent out their Beverly Hills home, which was costing $800 a month in overhead. Mrs. Spiegel did eventually leave, but three months later than planned. Ignoring the pleas of the Horizon employees, she demanded $1,000 for a five-day stopover in New York.

As soon as Lynne reached Paris, Spiegel left for his Grosvenor Square apartment. Perhaps it was a delayed reaction to her dalliance with Irwin Shaw, but Spiegel refused to have anything to do with her. It was unfair—throughout their sham of a marriage, he had hardly been a paragon of virtue—but she was his wife, and Spiegel was old-fashioned in that regard.

Whereas her husband was flighty and indifferent about his various lady friends, Lynne was deeply in love with Shaw, to the point of being suicidal. The writer was a rising star, his best-selling novel *The Young Lions* was highly praised, as were his short stories. Even if such literary standards were lost on Mrs. Spiegel, who referred to Shaw's best-seller as *The Youngest Lion,* Lynne was taken by the dark-haired novelist. He was very sexy, spontaneous, and exciting to be around. He was also a womanizer who was well protected by a beautiful and territorial wife, who naturally knew all about the affair. "It was in Paris," said Kathleen Parrish. "She just stuck her foot out and Lynne took a terrible tumble." Mrs. Spiegel broke her ankle. "And then Marion was struck with guilt afterward."

Meanwhile, Spiegel was storming in and out of Worton Hall Studios, where *The African Queen* was being finished. It was there that Bogart's famous leech scene was shot in which he emerged from the water, covered with the black suckers. Being squeamish, the actor insisted that rubber leeches be used. Typically, Huston refused to use fakes. A war started, the director, no doubt keen to dangle Bogart in his terror, pretended not to back down. A man who bred leeches arrived at the studio armed with a tank full of them. In the end, the close-up with the real leech was done on the breeder's chest, while the rubber ones were used on Bogart. However, it was a grueling episode for the actor.

Before the shoot ended on November 1, a certain amount of bad blood had built up between Spiegel and his partner. In his opinion, there had been too many instances when Huston was not paying attention. This had led to numerous shouting matches. Nor had Spiegel held back about certain rushes. "Some people were in awe of John—not Sam," said Angela Allen. "When he saw what he didn't like, he had the guts to argue with Huston." Much later, Huston admitted that despite their battles Spiegel was the best producer that he ever had. "He just had two big weaknesses: money and women."

Just as one of Huston's weaknesses was being incapable of resisting a practical joke. "The editors had made up a soundtrack of all the grunting, groaning, and double entendre phrases like 'Don't do that Mr. Allnut,' " said Jeanie Sims, his assistant. Bogart and Huston had then sent it to Hepburn claiming it was the film's soundtrack, with a note attached saying, "We don't just want your opinion, so it would be good if a few of you were around." They knew how proper she was. Luckily, just as she was ushering people into the theater to hear the music, the actress started to suspect something and decided to listen to the tape on her own beforehand. "She took it very well," said Sims. "And that was when Bogie and John concocted a letter saying, 'Dear Katie, neither of us can understand why you don't like the music.' "

In the meantime, Spiegel was determined to stir up United Artists's enthusiasm for the film. He was disappointed by how they had handled *When I Grow Up,* and this time he insisted on their undivided attention. Long letters were sent to the studio's executives including his pal Max Youngstein, who had joined the company. "Now my dear Max, I feel that either you or Mort Nathanson should make a flying trip to London to see the picture as there is no chance of getting a print to America before December."

Youngstein followed through. "I loved it, but the picture was a problem with the distributors—'We don't want Bogart looking unshaven and unkempt' was their chief complaint, and Hepburn, who everyone adored but no one would come and see." *The African Queen* was shown to Jean Picker, the president of Loew's, considered to have the best circuit of theaters in the States. "He said, 'Max, I can't place this film, it isn't for us.'" Youngstein then went for the independent theater route. "We rented New York's Capitol Theatre, which was about to be torn apart. It held three thousand seats and we did almost $90,000 the first week and then I get a call from Picker."

Spiegel also pulled in Bill Blowitz, who had just begun a public relations company with Maggy Maskel. For the promotion of *The African Queen,* his chief task was to convince Mike Romanoff to let them use his restaurant for the party. "Mike had said, 'I'm not giving Sam a party unless he gives cash, he has bounced so many checks,' " recalled Blowitz's wife. "He said, 'Bill, I'll give it, if you give me the check,' and my husband did."

Predictably, Spiegel's finances were in an appalling way, and as usual, he covered himself accordingly. Before his partner returned home, he sent an urgent telegram to his Hollywood office saying it was IMPERATIVE THAT HELLER'S ADVANCE TO RICKY [*sic*] [Huston's wife] BE MADE BEFORE HUSTON'S ARRIVAL. Spiegel had promised to pay his California office in time for Christmas, but Hill had had enough. BEGINNING TO TIRE OF STARVING WHILE YOU JOHN AND OTHERS LIVE LIKE KINGS she cabled Spiegel.

However, when the producer returned to Los Angeles, he was greeted like a hero. Not only did he personally deliver the picture, but he also arrived in time for that year's Oscar derby. Thanks to Blowitz, the trade papers had picked up on his mad rush. As a result, it became public knowledge that *The African Queen'*s cans of film had gone through a storm over the Atlantic and a Customs holdup in Boston before they hit Hollywood on Wednesday, December 19.

"Meanwhile, everyone here is proceeding calmly, as if the print had been in the vaults for months," *Daily Variety* quipped. Far from being a contender, the picture was viewed as a "true dark horse." Nevertheless, *The African Queen*–which cost Horizon $729,219.48 to make, and cost Romulus £248,000–struck gold at the box office.

Spiegel had proved his fellow producers wrong, particularly Sir Alexander Korda, who had said, "A story of two old people going up and down an African river. . . . Who's going to be interested in that? You'll be bankrupt."

Chapter Fifteen

MELBA

During the high tide of their success, Huston and Spiegel were on the best of terms. FIRST TEN REVIEWS HERE GREATEST I HAVE EVER READ, the director cabled from London. BELIEVE WE HAVE GREATEST FILM EVER MADE. He described *The African Queen* as causing a sensation in England, noting that EVERY PREVIOUS WARNER RECORD SMASHED DURING LAST FEW DAYS BY LARGE MARGIN.

They had a hit, and in show business lore there's nothing like a triumph to bring a director and producer close. The Oscar nominations helped too. Both actors, James Agee, and Huston were all nominated for Academy Awards. Spiegel was not included. Instead, productions such as *A Place in the Sun* and *A Streetcar Named Desire* were pushed forward for "best picture"–films of merit, but made under less strenuous circumstances.

The African Queen still remains a testament to Spiegel's relentlessness and tenacity, and in many ways, was one of his best achievements. As one friend remarked, "Sam made it with spit." When Heller's financing fell through and Hepburn threatened not to appear, other producers might have thrown in the towel–not Spiegel.

Regarding *The African Queen*'s distribution rights, Horizon received the Western Hemisphere, and Romulus the Eastern Hemisphere. Later, Sir John Woolf, who went on with his brother to produce important British films such as *Room at the Top, Alfie,* and *The Day of the Jackal,* referred to himself as the co-producer on the project. Perhaps their company had helped co-finance the film, but it was really Spiegel's picture because it was his risk from the start, whereas the Woolfs had arrived late at the party.

Much has been made of the fact that Huston was the artist and relished the African experience in comparison to his partner, who did not. Of course, Spiegel had barely been around the sick crew, the sunken boat, and the other dramas, nor did he wish to be. He was not the talent, he took *care* of the talent. "Sam told me that he preferred not being on the set to have an objective view," said the producer Richard Roth. "I don't believe that. Sam was a power animal and he recognized that the set was the director's domain. But as far as not being physically there, he always had his spies."

Spies or not, Horizon Pictures had a hit, and all was rosy until Huston's triumvirate of advisors—his agent, lawyer, and business manager—noticed that there was a discrepancy in the accounts. This caused a temporary break in communications and led to Huston refusing to see his partner in France. As a result, Spiegel wrote to Mark Cohen, Huston's lawyer. "On further reflection, I am not surprised at John, whose whims and caprices have alienated him from many friends before and will alienate him from many friends in the future. Personally, I feel far too cordial and affectionate towards him to be alienated by any such outburst, as I know only too well how easily he can be influenced by misinformation and prejudice."

Later in the letter, Spiegel argued, "It is ridiculous that, at this point, when there is almost a sure success on the cards, an issue of precedence in rank of payment of $5,000 should make as important a clash between you and me as to warrant any clouding of the amicable relationship of two partners, at the end of their partnership."

Once again, there was a truce between Spiegel and Huston, especially around Oscar time when Bogart won his first Academy Award. But then Huston's temper flared up when he heard that Spiegel and his wife had arrived at Les Ambassadeurs—a chic nightclub and gambling joint in London—and that she was dripping in mink and diamonds. Someone had admired Lynne's diamond necklace, which was blinking above her creamy décolletage, and Mrs. Spiegel replied, "Oh it's from *The African Queen,* you know, it's all from *The African Queen.*" Unfortunately, this happened at the precise moment that Spiegel was insisting that none of the film's profits had come through! Huston was fit to be tied. Sambo's woman flaunting jewels while *he*–the picture's director–was in need of funds? In some ways, he would take his revenge, since he subsequently had an affair with Lynne when Spiegel threw her out again. The ill-fated romance was short, and according to onlookers, was painful to watch. "John was very cruel to her," said Joan Axelrod. "He really knocked her socks off."

In regards to the missing funds, a meeting was set up with Spiegel at the Brown Derby in Los Angeles. "Sam had tried to make the picture pay for all of his New Year's Eve parties," recalled Jess Morgan, an employee at A. Morgan Maree's company–Huston and Bogart's business manager. "But we said, 'You can't do that,' and he replied, 'Okay, if you feel like that.' And then we noticed a bill from the 21 Club for about $25,000 and Sam said, 'Well, you didn't expect us to eat the food in England did you? We had steaks flown in every day from the restaurant!' "

Ultimately, the likes of Maree, Cohen, and Paul Kohner advised Huston to forget about his losses and settle. "We could see that John was never going to get a fair account–never ever," said Morgan. "We couldn't carry on chasing Spiegel, he was too tough." There was just one small contractual problem; the director still owed Horizon a picture–*Three Episodes,* which was based on three short stories by John Collier. "John was hot after *African Queen,* and we all figured his freedom was worth a hell of a lot more. It was no mystery that he had financial problems, and we needed him free so that he could make money." They then advised their client to live in Ireland, which was and still remains an artists' tax haven.

According to Huston, it was "the most best-intentioned, worst advice" that he ever accepted. "I got out of my contract with Horizon," he wrote in his memoirs. "No more partnership. No more share of the profits." *The African Queen* was one of his more successful pictures. On first release, United Artists predicted a gross of $3 million but it actually brought in $4.3 million.

The African Queen continued to make money and eventually became Spiegel's second biggest earning picture. The negative reverted to the producer in August 1960, and after a disastrous deal with Translux, he went on to collect from other deals such as his one with CBS. "It was called a color television network premiere," said his lawyer. "We got $250,000 for one showing and after three . . . we had $750,000. This was back in 1970, and those were supposedly lean years."

Huston sold his 250 shares in Horizon to Spiegel on May 1, 1953, for which he received $25,000. After countless reminders, it was only paid three years later. There was also the interest on the $3,000 that the director had lent for *The Prowler*, as well as the two notes that he had guaranteed amounting to $22,000 that were all to be paid on settlement of the agreement. Huston was also protected "against claims of any creditors of the corporations"–a protection that was worth its weight in gold considering Spiegel's financial state. The former partners were never to be close again.

The breakdown in their friendship may be explained by Huston's misjudgment of Spiegel. He presumed that he could always return and buy back the shares for the same price, but he had a shock when he tried to do so. It was in the mid-1950s, when *The African Queen* was rereleased with *Moulin Rouge*, another Huston film. Spiegel agreed to sell, but at a staggering price for each share. "The fact that John had used him as a patsy in the past had hardened Sam," sensed Viertel. "It was as if he had decided, 'This is never going to happen to me again.' " According to Irene Heymann, Huston felt "cheated," and held a substantial grudge. "John had certain dislikes and people became dead for him," she said. "He just turned off completely and didn't want to hear their name or anything."

No doubt, Huston must have been faintly amused by the trials of *Melba*, Spiegel's next production. Once again, it was to be made with United Artists, but it was to be collateralized with *The African Queen*, and was to result in Spiegel losing all the money that he had previously made.

The ill-fated picture was about the legendary opera singer Dame Nellie Melba, and Patrice Munsel–nicknamed "the baby of the Met"– was playing the title role. "When I accepted *Melba*, there was no script," the opera star admitted, "but, knowing what a marvelous bitch she was, I looked forward to playing her." Miss Munsel and her husband, the director Robert Schuler, had been warned about Spiegel. "At our wedding reception, the columnist Radie Harris said, 'Bob, the best wedding gift I can give you is this: If Sam Spiegel says it's going to be a sunny day tomorrow, reach for your umbrella and rubbers.' How true that proved to be."

Unfortunately, a few circumstances played against the project. Spiegel had presumed that Dame Nellie's kin would be delighted that the renowned producer of *The African Queen* was interested in her life. But, far from being "delighted," they refused to give him the rights of the true story. Unwilling to be discouraged, Spiegel employed his pal Harry Kurnitz (sometimes credited as Marco Page) to write the screenplay. Kurnitz was best-known for light-hearted romances such as *The Adventures of Don Juan* and *One Touch of Venus*. Their mutual friends were staggered. Surely Kurnitz had heard what had happened to Huston? But Kurnitz, who was quite a wag, had thought of that. Spiegel was paying him in handmade shirts from Paris, or so he claimed. In fact, like everyone else, Kurnitz was on a deferred salary, as well as receiving 3 percent of the film's profits.

Meanwhile, his screenplay failed to excite Munsel. Indeed, after reading it she wanted to get out of her contract, since what had emerged was a "very watered down version" of Dame Nellie's life, "a Janie Powell role," and definitely not the part that she had expected to play.

The plot of *Melba* was uncomplicated, tracing the diva's life along strictly Hollywood lines. Beginning with Dame Melba (Munsel) singing for Queen Victoria (Sybil Thorndike) at Windsor Castle, the story flashes back to Nellie Mitchell singing in the local church and herding her father's cattle in Australia. The young singer then arrives in France, where she persuades the great Marchesi (Martita Hunt) to come out of retirement in order to teach her. This allows her to make her debut at the Brussels Opera House as Nellie Melba–the Melba derived from Melbourne. Soon, she wins over Covent Garden and the rest of Europe and throughout her illustrious career manages to be pursued by an eager young dilettante (John Justin) and a wealthy hotel owner (Alec Clunes). Ignoring their advances, she marries her childhood sweetheart (John McCallum) instead. This arrangement, however, does not stop her from accepting an offer from Oscar Hammerstein (Robert Morley) to sing at his Manhattan Opera House.

Since all of *Melba*'s preproduction work was being set up from Paris, the opera singer and her husband had planned to have a second honeymoon and stay in a romantic little hotel on the Left Bank. But when Spiegel heard about their plans, he was appalled. "Bob, you are married to a star!" he exclaimed. "You must not stay in an obscure place like that." He then arranged for them to move into his suite at the George V. "With its marble columns and crystal chandeliers, it looked like a Balaban and Katz lobby in Chicago—just what we did not want," she said. Still, they stayed and, as the days passed, became used to seeing Spiegel with the film's director, Edmund Goulding, and Kurnitz.

Supposedly they were working on the screenplay. However, after a few hours of discussion, such sessions would lead into long, leisurely lunches, which—it turned out—were being put on the Schulers' bill. "Sam had charged everything to us," Munsel discovered. "I was incensed because I felt I had gotten us into a mess, so I sent Bob down to the barbershop, while I told Sam what I thought. He then agreed to pay HALF the bill. We were too naive to realize he should have been paying for everything, including the months we were delayed in Europe."

Adding to the drama, the film's director disappeared on a drunken spree and Spiegel hired Lewis Milestone to replace him. "I was appalled because Eddie Goulding was a fabulous women's director," Munsel said, making reference to his *Grand Hotel* with Garbo and Joan Crawford, *Dark Victory* with Bette Davis, as well as films with Joan Fontaine and with Dorothy McGuire. Whereas Milestone "had more the reputation of being a great men's director," due to his pictures *All Quiet on the Western Front, Of Mice and Men,* and *A Walk in the Sun.*

Of course, she was unaware that it suited Spiegel since he was already developing a project with Milestone called *The Hothouse,* with a screenplay by Walter Reisch. It was part of a four-picture deal with United Artists, which included the aforementioned *Three Episodes* as well as *The Witness,* which was supposed to star Ingrid Bergman and Marlon Brando, with a screenplay by Arthur Laurents.

In the meantime, *Melba* was labeled as a low-budget film in spite of all the exotic places that the screenplay had included. As a result,

Andrei Andreiev, the legendary art director, and his assistant, John Stoll, had to use their every effort to turn London's 45 Park Lane into the Ritz in Paris and the interior of a Monte Carlo casino, as well as reconstruct the likes of Berlin, Rome, and St. Petersburg at Nettlefold Studios.

The minimal production costs had not stopped Spiegel from celebrating the first night before filming. He and Sharman Douglas—the American ambassador's daughter—threw a party at Les Ambassadeurs. John Mills, a fellow-Pole who was one of his chums, ran the spacious and elegant club meticulously. The evening was a success until Munsel told Spiegel "the happy news"—that she was pregnant. White with rage, it caused Spiegel to leave his own party—a first!

Then, as luck would have it, Munsel started to miscarry (fortunately, she managed to keep the baby, who has made her a grandmother) at the very moment that Arthur Krim dropped by the film set. It was just when United Artists had put up *Melba*'s completion guarantee. So, while Krim was stepping out of his limousine, the opera singer was being carried out on a stretcher into an ambulance. "Sam, never at a loss for words, called Bob [her husband] over and said, 'Gentlemen, I want you to meet the bastard who is responsible for this goddamned fiasco!' " recalled Munsel.

Spiegel was right to be concerned, his personal finances were back to being bleak and he had been evicted from his Grosvenor Square apartment for nonpayment of rent. The British authorities had not forgotten his little stints at Brixton Prison. None of this, however, deterred Spiegel from throwing yet another party to celebrate Krim's decision.

Lady Edith Foxwell was in on the festivities. "Sam was a charming buccaneer who could have slit your throat and convinced you that it was necessary," said the socialite and ex-wife of film producer Ivan Foxwell. London had started to become glamorous again. Well-heeled ladies went out, wore big hair and big jewels. "Margaret, the Duchess of Argyll, then reigned as the hostess of high society," said Lady Edith. "She was terribly grand with white-gloved servants and all of that." There were also Hollywood moments. "Parties given where you had Ava Gardner, at her most beautiful, and Frank Sinatra who was either at her side or chasing her."

In the meantime, Inge Morath, *Melba*'s set photographer, was concerned about getting color film for her camera. "Sam used to keep it under his bed and he found it wildly funny that I didn't like going into his bedroom." They spoke in German and since he never tried to hide who he was, the distinguished late Magnum photographer took to him immediately. "We talked about his days as a pioneer in Palestine," she recalled. "He liked to give the sense that he was capable of doing the impossible." At the time, Spiegel favored baby-blue shirts and colored ties and had a certain iridescent shine about him. "You cannot imagine the amount of girls he slept with," she said. "He had all the dancers from the Covent Garden sequence. . . . I remember finding him with one dancer on his lap while he phoned another and the other girl didn't seem to mind."

On another occasion, Dana Wynter, who had a role in *Melba,* accompanied him, Milestone, and Kurnitz to a pub in the depths of the English countryside. "It was Sunday and Sam arrived in a loudly checked sports jacket which covered his broadness, and then banged his hand down on the counter and said, 'Champagne,' " the actress said. "Well, it closed the place down. Everyone looked at us and no one spoke."

Spiegel became quite the tyrant with his director. Throughout the shoot, which started at the beginning of September and continued until the end of November 1952, he never ceased to harass Milestone. "Sam used to come in and give Milly such hell," said Morath. "But then he had such warmth that you forgave him." Not always. As well as meddling in the editing, Spiegel was his cunning self in regards to settling outstanding salaries. "The game Spiegel is playing here is to pass the buck to Prinzmetal [Spiegel's West Coast lawyer]," Milestone fired off to Robert Kopp, his lawyer. "Ok Prinzmetal is your territory, nail him. . . . You have the picture! Bob, you know Sam, don't pull the punches." (I. H. Prinzmetal, known as Prinz, became Spiegel's lawyer when Spiegel and Morton Garbus came to blows in 1950 over unpaid bills and broken promises regarding *When I Grow Up.*)

Once again, Max Youngstein was assigned to the project. But just as the United Artists executive had been fired up by his friend's former picture, he was disappointed by the latest attempt, which cost £254,666.27. "The problem was that when *Melba* was shot, Sam did not have a picture. Then he cut out the best part, the whole ballet sequence. All that was left was Patrice singing."

The soprano performed "every aria known to man" from Mozart's *The Marriage of Figaro* to Bellini's *Norma*. Notwithstanding her hard work and her bouts of morning sickness, Munsel declined to do a publicity tour. "I had just had my baby and I wasn't really happy to do anything for Sam at that point," she admitted.

In spite of having a turkey on his hands, Spiegel went to considerable lengths to prove otherwise. As soon as he arrived on the West Coast—just a few weeks before the press preview—he converted *Melba* from straight photography and normal sound to a wide-screen stereophonic film. Instead of giving grandeur to his production, it actually had the reverse effect, since the theaters with wide screens lacked stereophonic sound projection.

When *Melba* opened at the Capitol in New York, the critics were harsh. *The Saturday Review of Literature* compared the experience to having one's head blasted off by "a high-fidelity addict in an attempt to show you the foolishness of paying eight dollars to hear a Metropolitan performance when you can hear it at home three times as loud." Nor did *The New Yorker* hold back: "I, for one, am determined to maintain friendly relations with Australia, and I shudder at what may happen when this affair goes into the Antipodes, where Dame Nellie was once a favorite singer."

Besides the rough reviews, there were other problems. "In those days, when you made two or three pictures, they were cross-collateralized," said Eric Pleskow, a United Artists executive. "In other words, the winnings of one picture would take care of the loss of another." The result of *Melba*'s failure led to United Artists holding on to $120,000 of Spiegel's earnings from *The African Queen*. The producer's "creative writing" had also caught up with him. All the financial discrepancies that had been overlooked during his previous triumph were suddenly seized upon when his operatic venture bombed.

"Krim told Sam where to get off when he saw *Melba*," Youngstein said. "He said something like 'You can jump out of a window for all I care.'" Although *The African Queen* had been a success, Krim had little time for Spiegel and his shenanigans. Krim—steely and brilliant–a new type of showman– refused to be charmed by S. P. Eagle. *Melba* rocked an already tenuous relationship, but it was eventually a fight over a missing $50,000 that led to Spiegel's ultimate split with the distribution company.

"I need not tell you that the association with United Artists was to me more than just a mere business arrangement," Spiegel wrote to Robert Benjamin. "Had it been a business arrangement I would have been left with considerably more than my present share of *African Queen*. I wouldn't have had the religious determination to salvage the picture for United Artists at the time when even you boys at United Artists felt that I should go elsewhere with it, owing to the difficulties with Heller. I had gone through hell for a long period rather than accept all the offers being waved at me by other distributing companies during March, April and early May of 1951. . . . How much work, tenacity and affection I gave to your project during the year of the negotiations with Chaplin and Pickford, you will remember as well as I do . . . you will realize how deeply saddened I must feel when suddenly a cloud, arising from an unfortunate picture, settles over it. When some of the fog has settled and some of the bitterness, I shall try to see you and talk over a few of the remaining projects."

Chapter Sixteen

ON THE WATERFRONT

Returning to Los Angeles was a risk. "Sam was always terrified that the authorities were going to grab him for unpaid debts," his New York lawyer recalled–a fear that continued until the late 1950s. Spiegel also had a problem with Lynne. In October 1952, he filed for divorce, charging that his wife "on divers days and times and at divers places committed adultery with various persons." However, there was a slight problem. "Sam never had enough money for the settlement, and so it continued."

For his divorce, Spiegel was using the New York firm of Irwin Margulies and Albert Heit, who were to become vital to his organization. The lawyers had been partners since the late 1940s. Margulies was the social one of the team, while his partner, by his own admission, "was the lawyer" and "all business."

Heit, at eighty-nine years old, was still in charge of Spiegel's affairs. Until his death in November 2001, he remained the type to believe that "you only get ripped off by your friends and people you trust." He was also suspicious of Hollywood bookkeeping. "Each time, I get a statement, I write a letter." Heit always sensed his client wanted to be a *Macher*, Yiddish for someone who has power. Yet only in spirit, because financially Spiegel was still a *Luftmensch* in July 1953. His house on North Crescent Drive was out of bounds for two reasons: first of all, he was scared of being arrested there, and it had also been royally messed up by Lynne. Armed with a pair of scissors, she had gone to work on his suits, his underpants, and even some of his paintings, which, according to Spiegel, included six Picassos. Every mirror and glass had also been smashed.

As a result, he checked into the nearby Beverly Hills Hotel, known locally as the Pink Palace—only the best for Spiegel. And who should be staying in the suite opposite but a certain director and screenwriter whose project *The Golden Warrior* had been refused by every studio? Elia Kazan and Budd Schulberg have both written about their shared experience on the project, which eventually became *On the Waterfront*.

"Sam kept on asking us to come to his party," said Schulberg. "And we knew that he was in bad trouble with *Melba* and big trouble with United Artists." This did not stop Spiegel from entertaining endlessly. Room service was at his beck and call while the noise of the laughter of his guests and the tinkling of their glasses could be heard drifting down the hallway. In contrast, neither Schulberg nor Kazan could move. "We were in our bathrobes because we were so demoralized from our rejection," said the writer. ("Who's going to care about a lot of sweaty longshoremen?" Darryl Zanuck had asked when presented with the project.) Spiegel then appeared at their doorway, "smart as paint" and smelling of crushed lilacs. "Are you boys in trouble?" he asked. Immediately, they told him about their project and described how not a single Hollywood studio was interested. Their admission to defeat marked the difference between their modus operandi and Spiegel's. The producer was in trouble and had every reason to be depressed, but by the way he was living it up, one might have thought that he was celebrating an Oscar winner. Spiegel was a showman, who could never afford to be down. He also had a nose for a good story. "He said, 'I'll do it,' and to my surprise, he did it right away," recalled Kazan. The next morning, Spiegel left for New York with the screenplay of *The Golden Warrior* in his briefcase.

"*On the Waterfront* wouldn't have been made without Sam and that's a pretty positive thing to say about someone," said the director. "Nothing fazed him. . . . That's what I liked about him most. He had a lot of guts. He had raw animal courage and he had courage in what he chose to do." Kazan was admired for his films such as *Gentleman's Agreement, A Streetcar Named Desire,* and *Viva Zapata!* Even though

Kazan's motion picture career was going through a shaky period–his last film *Man on a Tightrope* had bombed while his former film about Emilio Zapata "did not get back half of the negative cost"–he was still considered a major talent. Once Kazan's agent heard about Spiegel's involvement, he laughed. "Watch out for him!" he warned. "He has moves that you've never seen before."

In direct contrast to the blacklisted artists that Spiegel had worked with such as Arthur Laurents, Dalton Trumbo, and Lewis Milestone (who was graylisted), both Schulberg and Kazan had "named names" during the Un-American Activities Committee hearings. Being a friendly witness led to a shadow on both their lives. Not working represented death to Kazan and Schulberg just as it might have done to Spiegel, and as indeed it did to some of the blacklisted.

The day after his appearance in Congress on April 10, 1952, Kazan took out a full-page advertisement in the *New York Times* and criticized Communism for being "a dangerous and alien conspiracy," as well as urging liberals to speak out. In *A Life,* his autobiography, Kazan explains that he wanted "to name everybody and break open the secrecy" of the Communist Party. While writing this passage, Kazan admitted to coming down with shingles (herpes zoster)–a nervous condition that causes a painful, medieval-like rash across the middle of the body.

"When I was asked by the HUAC," Schulberg said, "I felt that I couldn't just take the Fifth and not say anything. . . . You don't know what it was like being a member of the Communist Party, each time you left the city, you had to inform them. They weren't this romantic bunch of people, but overcontrolling. . . . It was like the Moonies." The Party had tried to stop him from writing *What Makes Sammy Run?,* his novel about a blindly ambitious young man caught in the Hollywood system.

His project *The Golden Warrior* could not have been more different, but in the early summer of 1953, it had been around the block, as well as being snubbed by most of Hollywood. The property had originally belonged to Harry Cohn's nephew, Joe Curtis of Monticello Films, in 1951. The picture's story was based on a series of articles called *Crime on the Waterfront,* by Malcolm Johnson, who had won a Pulitzer Prize for his efforts. Robert Siodmak was set to direct (the project was called

A Stone on the River Hudson) and then Monticello had lost interest only to gain it again after hearing that Kazan was attached.

Originally, Spiegel had taken *The Golden Warrior* to United Artists, but Arthur Krim was to change the circumstances–dramatically. The former lawyer was apoplectic about the missing $50,000 from *Melba* and insisted that Spiegel pay all his outstanding loans, particularly on his pending project, now evolved into *On the Waterfront.* However, lady luck was on the producer's side. It turned out that Columbia had its offices in the same Fifth Avenue building as United Artists. Not wasting any time, Spiegel swept downstairs to meet with the rival executives. By the following Monday, Columbia had acquired the rights from United Artists. Their legal department worked throughout the weekend. Columbia's Leo Jaffe recalled the events as being freaklike. "We took *On the Waterfront,*" he said, "and in exchange gave United Artists a circus picture with Burt Lancaster [*Trapeze,* 1956.]"

But–and it's a big but–Harry Cohn was not involved. "The studio had nothing to do with the New York films," said Paul N. Lazarus, Jr., then the vice-president of publicity at Columbia. "It was a counter production unit which Harry Cohn didn't particularly like or approve of." Abe Schneider was the treasurer of the East Coast outfit, Jaffe was second in command, and Abe Montague was head of sales. Schneider, who subsequently became the president of Columbia Pictures, was unpretentious. "He made a point that he would never read the script," said Lazarus. "Abe would say, 'I handle the money, I don't know a good script from a bad one!' But when you are running a production company, there are some moments when you need to know, 'I am going to run with this.' " Jaffe was considered to be a warmer person and good with creative types. "Leo was Spiegel's buddy for the most part."

Jerry Tokofsky, who worked at Columbia in the mid-1960s, preferred Schneider to Jaffe. "He was very fluid, he understood the business. And I give a guy credit if he says, 'I can't read a script, I don't know about it.' . . . Abe was a stern taskmaster but what you saw was what you got." Yet Harry Cohn dismissed Schneider and Jaffe as mere accountants. "They were both New York University graduate accountants who rose in the ranks because they were the only ones who knew where the two or three books were," Tokofsky said. They were unpopular with the Hollywood studio head "because they set the budgets for the pictures and they were restrictive," said Lazarus. Cohn—who was famous for saying, "I kiss the feet of talent and kick the ass of those who don't have it" and for his foolproof device for judging a picture, "If my fanny squirms, it's bad, if my fanny doesn't squirm, it's good"—did not have time for Spiegel either. "In fact, he resented him," said Leo Jaffe.

With Spiegel's new production, his Horizon Pictures office moved to the East Coast. Their outfit, previously at California Studios, set up shop at 424 Madison Avenue. Only Sam Rheiner remained from the producer's previous team. "Sam used to make Rheiner sign *all* the business correspondence," recalled Albert Heit. "Sam [Spiegel] only signed one letter in a hundred. He was *always* nervous about signing anything." Meanwhile, Horizon-America—a subsidiary of Horizon Pictures—was the company behind *On the Waterfront*. However, it was Columbia—not Spiegel's office—that was responsible for sending out the six monthly statements and issuing the royalty checks. This was to be the case on all the films that Horizon made with the studio.

As the months went by, Schulberg became increasingly frustrated with Spiegel. Their screenplay conferences used to take place at the St. Regis Hotel. "I really wanted to murder him. I seriously considered it. I am not proud of it." Schulberg had mortgaged his farm in New Hope, Pennsylvania, in order to do the project. "I was literally losing everything." He was both emotionally and financially attached.

Although he credited Spiegel with a "very, very sharp story mind," it had, after all, been the producer's idea to change the film's theme, which was originally centered on the exposé of the waterfront by an undercover journalist. "It sounded pat and it was Sam's idea to make it more contained," recalled Betty Spiegel. "Instead of bringing in an outsider, they made one of their own turn after they killed his brother."

Set in the docks of Hoboken, Terry Malloy (Marlon Brando) is the errand boy for Johnny Friendly (Lee J. Cobb), the waterfront's crooked union boss. The film begins with Terry witnessing the murder of Joey Doyle, which has been orchestrated by Friendly's mob. The event comes back to haunt him when he falls in love with the victim's sister–Edie Doyle (Eva Marie Saint). Through her, he meets Father Barry (Karl Malden), who is encouraging all the offshore men to come clean and testify against union crime during the public hearings of the Waterfront Crime Commission. The theme of the film is about the change in Terry who starts off as a failed boxer with no self-respect and matures into "a contenda." First, he takes on his brother, Charley (Rod Steiger), Friendly's lawyer. Because of his change of attitude, Charley threatens to shoot him but then bows out, which leads to Friendly's gang killing *him* instead. But, in spite of his brother's death, Terry refuses to be scared. He testifies, is beaten up for his bravery, and defies the corrupt waterfront by showing up for work the following day.

Schulberg understood Spiegel's persistence on structure–his eternal "let's open it up again"–but it was the producer's "tricky ways" that pushed him to the end of his tether. "Instead of being open, he couldn't do that with you, he had to go sneaking around," the writer said. "It was just deep in his psyche to conspire and play one [person] against the other. I don't know where this all began, this cat and mouse game." Each time Schulberg went to the bathroom, he returned to find "Buddha"–the director's name for Spiegel–whispering in Kazan's ear. "Well, after about the eighth or ninth time, I blew up. I said, 'What the fuck are you two guys whispering about? What secret can you have that you don't want me to know about? This thing is part of me, I am starving with it, struggling with it . . . I can't conceive of any element that you could be keeping from me.' I was under a lot of strain and I said, 'I just can't do it anymore.' " After this outburst and a few that followed, Kazan used to take him around the block. "Gadg [the director's nickname created during his days as an assistant stage manager because of being handy like a gadget] apologized and said, 'It's absolutely true, every time you leave the room, Sam comes over and starts to whisper in my ear and almost all the time, it's nothing that can't be said in front of you.' But he'd say, 'You have to remember this, nobody in Hollywood would do our picture, he did bail us out.' "

Schulberg's fury with Spiegel nonetheless escalated into an event that has since become legendary and has been incorrectly attributed to Irwin Shaw. At 3:30 in the morning, the writer was discovered shaving by his wife. When questioned on what he was planning to do at that hour, Schulberg replied, "I'm driving to New York . . . to kill Sam Spiegel."

Ever since *The African Queen*–his first bout with international success–Spiegel had changed. Creatively, he had more confidence, which led to him becoming more focused in his role as a producer. However, a different type of ruthlessness appeared. Suddenly, dividing and conquering the director and writer, and occasionally the director and actor, became essential to how he conducted himself. Spiegel's attitude toward the film crew was also different. He now had little time for the film unit, whereas previously he had been known for respecting the craftsmen who worked on his productions.

On *Waterfront*, it was simple. Schulberg and Kazan had been through a lot. "The trouble we had bonded us for ever," said the writer. (Kazan joined the project when it was called *The Bottom of the River*.) Yet that involved them, not Spiegel, who was definitely the outsider in the trio. He had to change the dynamics, which was not too difficult with Kazan, who by his own admission was "two-faced." As a result, when Spiegel played his game of divide and conquer, he chose the director over the son of a former studio head who had worked with Selznick on *A Star Is Born*.

In many ways, Kazan's feisty character was better qualified to dealing with Spiegel's manipulative behavior. Like all the directors who delivered the producer's best films, he was born before World War I. And, in many respects, Kazan became the closest to Spiegel because each–in their curious ways–cared about the other. According to Kazan, their friendship depended on "a true understanding of our characters."

Huston had been essential to Spiegel's career, but the cruel jokes were too much. Nor had the producer been drawn by all the outdoors bravado and activity. Kazan did not play jokes. Being a Greek immigrant's son, that type of humiliation appalled him too. The immigrant issue was an important link–both were outsiders who had gone through life being on the defensive, even if Kazan wore his anger on his sleeve while Spiegel slyly hid his.

There was also the question of respect. "Sam is the best producer pre and post the film," Kazan told Warren Beatty in the early 1960s. The theatrical world held Spiegel's undying interest, and Kazan *was* the "boy genius of Broadway" who as director had an extraordinary track record, including *All My Sons, A Streetcar Named Desire, Death of a Salesman,* and had significant associations with Arthur Miller, Clifford Odets, John Steinbeck, and Tennessee Williams. "What made him a great director was that he had infinite understanding of people on an incredible level," said Tennessee Williams. Moreover, Kazan was the co-founder of the Actors Studio, an advocate of the Method, and had helped change the face of acting on screen with *A Streetcar Named Desire.* Like Spiegel, he was extremely intelligent, well informed, and ruthless about achieving his goal. Kazan was also a womanizer.

Similar to Spiegel, Kazan had extraordinary charisma but was not traditionally handsome. His appeal to women lay in his brash charm, vulnerability, and force of character. Short and wiry, Kazan was keen on taking off his shirt when he directed, a habit he continued until the mid-1970s.

Kazan and Spiegel had their fights, but they kept in touch. There was a camaraderie between them even when they were not working together. As was his way, Kazan badmouthed Spiegel, but Spiegel used to recall his period of collaboration with Kazan "as one of the happiest times of my life." He was not being disingenuous, because of all the directors he worked with, Gadg remained his favorite.

Spiegel made a lasting impression on both Schulberg and Kazan. "Gadg and I went on talking about Sam," admitted the writer. "In fact, we always talk about him even now. We have never stopped. He was an intriguing catalyst. He did fascinate the most intelligent and discriminating people."

Kazan later refused to admit "that he was fascinated." He preferred to dwell on being forced to keep his distance, which led him to understand the Spiegel-Huston falling out. "You couldn't stay in with Sam, really, because you would feel that you were being manipulated a lot of the time," he said. "I just got indifferent to him." The director sensed that just as Spiegel was "the king of commercial seduction," everything was practical. "If people hung out with him, you asked yourself what does he want?" Another technique was his "disarming vocabulary." "He never asked for a business conference, rather he suggested we might have 'a little chat.' "

Kazan recognized Spiegel's winning way with women. "My first wife, Molly, despised him. Then he came over for 'a little chat,' and all of a sudden, he had his arm around her waist." From France, Spiegel had sent Mrs. Kazan a bottle of perfume with an attached note saying: "Since you couldn't come to Paris, a bit of Paris is coming to you."

Just as his *k.a.–kleine Aufmerksamkeit*–was essential to Spiegel's modus operandi, so was the hidden agenda. "Like all good negotiators, Sam kept everything secret," Kazan noted in his memoirs. The producer's persuasive powers were another "essential quality." At first, Brando refused to do the film. "Marlon was going through a period when he felt very badly about Kazan testifying," said Jay Kanter, the actor's agent.

With articles such as Peter Biskind's "The Politics of Power in *On the Waterfront*" (which appeared in the fall 1975 issue of *Film Quarterly*), much has been made of the fact that the film was a personal apology for informing. Schulberg, however, has dismissed this idea as "insanity" and "unfair to the theme of the picture." "It would be hard to imagine Kazan coming up to me and saying, 'Budd, I would like to make a movie which justifies my testimony.' It simply didn't happen that way." Also, taking Spiegel's character into account– that he had to use rather than be used–it seems improbable that he would have allowed a writer-director team to use his production to apologize.

Schulberg and Spiegel were at Kazan's house when Brando turned down the picture. It was August 1953. There was a brief conference between the *Waterfront* team, then Frank Sinatra was contacted. "We had a handshake agreement," Schulberg recalled. Nowadays, Kazan claims that he was prepared to work with Sinatra, but correspondence dating back to that period suggests otherwise. The crooner was hot after winning an Oscar for his role in Zinnemann's *From Here to Eternity*, and he had other commitments. According to Sinatra's William Morris agents, he was only free in November, before he was due to start on another picture for Twentieth Century-Fox. "It is not worth the gamble that Sinatra might be taken away from us in the midst of our shooting," Kazan wrote to Spiegel. Two months later, when Sinatra appeared to be definite, Kazan reminded Spiegel of the "front office geniuses" who had tried to hurry him in the past and had not succeeded.

A copy of the screenplay was sent to Montgomery Clift, but Kazan seemed keener to work with Paul Newman. "He's a really wonderful prospect, handsome, rugged, sexy and somehow turbulent inside," he wrote to Spiegel. "He looks quite a lot like Brando." He was also part of the Actors Studio, which was of key importance to Kazan. Indeed, the entire cast of *Waterfront*–Lee J. Cobb, Karl Malden, Rod Steiger, and Eva Marie Saint–were followers of the Method.

Saint was cast at the last minute, "after Kazan decided against using Joanne Woodward." Beforehand, Spiegel had been shopping her role around. Clearly keen for another Hollywood name in the production, he had offered the Edie Doyle role to both Jennifer Jones and Grace Kelly. Fortunately, both actresses declined and *Waterfront* became Saint's first film.

In the meantime, Spiegel had not given up on Brando. "Marlon never liked to work to begin with," said Jay Kanter, his agent. "He was always looking for ways to avoid it." And while Sinatra was being measured for his costume, or so Schulberg remembered, Brando's father contacted Kanter. He was insistent that his son work. "He said, 'Isn't there anything that you feel that he should do?' Of course, at the time, people were chasing Marlon to do everything and anything. He was the top of the heap as far as the young stars of that period." Schulberg's screenplay was mentioned again. "Marlon said no, but asked if it had been cast." Kanter then rang Spiegel. "Sam asked why and he knew damn well." At the time, Brando was living at Room 867 at the Carnegie Hall apartment block, on West 57th Street. "We walked over to Spiegel's suite. I left the two of them together. Sam then got Marlon to meet with Kazan."

Legend has it that Spiegel was at the Stage Delicatessen on Seventh Avenue when Brando wandered in off the street at 3:00 A.M. Spiegel was then said to have called Kazan and persuaded him to join them. During the meeting he had turned to Brando and said, "Politics has nothing to do with this–it's about your talent, it's about your career." He may easily have said the latter, but Spiegel at a deli at 3:00

A.M.? True, he had a weakness for the pastrami served at the Stage Delicatessen, but at nighttime, Spiegel was a bon vivant, who ate in fancy Manhattan restaurants. Spiegel was also an eat and leave kind of guy, unless there was a card game in progress. Of course, if Brando suggested the delicatessen as a meeting place, Spiegel would have gone, but at that time in the morning, it was unlikely that Spiegel was sitting there as a mere coincidence.

In any case, Brando accepted. For his role as Terry Malloy, he received a flat sum of $150,000. Since it was a large fraction of the negative cost ($880,000), Spiegel's lawyer tried to negotiate a lower sum with a percentage. "But Jay Kanter wouldn't take less," he recalled. "He was like all those MCA agents dressed in black, emulating Lew Wasserman [the head of the agency]. And it was 'no we don't want profits.' It was a big mistake, I'm sure Brando regretted it later." (Clearly not, since the actor later refused to take profits against a higher salary on *The Godfather*.)

Spiegel had an expression—"he's an actor"—it was derogatory. "Sam had very little respect for actors," said Betty Spiegel. "He thought they were chattel—just get up there and say your lines." There were a few exceptions, including Kirk Douglas, Cary Grant, and Gregory Peck, while, among the post–World War II group of actors, Brando was his favorite. Later, Jack Nicholson was to have the same sort of father/uncle relationship with Spiegel. Both young men were unpredictable, and had a kind of trapped-animal magnetism. Moreover, Brando had something else, a nobility to his face, with a profile that might have been chiseled out of marble. Brando—the baby, the brute, and the beauty—who had a complex love and hate relationship with his ever growing public. Spiegel understood such idiosyncrasies and just as he forgave the beautiful, he had as much time for the talented. "Sam was very fond of Marlon," said his third wife. "He always thought that he was far more intelligent than people gave him credit for."

Spiegel also took an active role in the actor's appearance and was acutely aware of his audience appeal. "I feel that any intent to even slightly disfigure Marlon during the run of the picture until the final shot would be a grave mistake," he wrote to Kazan. "One of the most perfect things about Marlon is his nose and let's not deliberately go out of our way to mar it. . . . I would greatly appreciate if you would agree with me on this issue, as it may eliminate great regrets later."

On the set of *Waterfront,* Kazan was ready to punch Spiegel out, as were the rest of his film unit. "The crew used to refer to him as 'the Jew bastard.' I think if it hadn't been for me, some violence would have happened," he said. And to complete Kazan's conversation with Warren Beatty in the 1960s, which had begun with, "Sam is the best producer pre and post the film," just as Beatty was leaving his office, Kazan grabbed him and said, "Spiegel's heart is full of shit and, if you repeat that, I'll deny it."

During the filming, which lasted from mid-November until early January 1954, Kazan received word that Spiegel was upset about his being behind schedule. "Gadg went mad," said Schulberg. " 'That son of a bitch, I'm not going to let him near the set.' So I said, 'Just remember one thing, Sam Spiegel was the only one' . . . and Gadg said, 'Oh Christ, all right.' " Spiegel then started to call Schulberg at three or four in the morning, since Kazan was refusing to speak to him. "Sam would call to say, 'Budd this is serious, we only have $800,000 [*sic*], we have a little budget, we are going to run out of money, you have got to make Gadg go faster.' " The first assistant director had also been contacted. There were always veiled hints that if they did not speed up, the picture might be pulled away from Kazan.

It was a tough shoot. Nor was the time element helped by Brando's early departures. One of the terms of the actor's contract was to leave in the mid-afternoon to see his psychiatrist. Notwithstanding the conditions, Kazan was a trouper. He never left his crew, and braved the docks of Hoboken, which were extremely cold, made worse by a cruel, biting wind. His film unit also needed police protection since the real waterfront mob disapproved of the theme of the picture. "Some of the enforcers—three or four guys—got Gadg at the lunch break. They had shoved him up against the wall on the pier," said Schulberg. Luckily, Kazan's bodyguard had intervened.

Although Spiegel was constantly interfering, causing dissension and disruption, physically he kept his distance. "He was very aware that being on set was Gadg's call and he didn't like that," said Schulberg. The producer was remembered whooping it up at the 21

Club or the Stork Club and then making the occasional grand appearance with a blonde in tow. One night, the crew, who had been there all day, started to mutiny. "Charlie McGuire [Kazan's first assistant director] telephoned Sam, who had been at the 21 Club [Kazan said it was the Stork Club]," recalled the writer. "It was a marvelous scene, straight out of a movie, and he came out in his limo, in his camel-haired coat, his alligator shoes. These guys were freezing, exhausted and furious. He started to make a speech. 'I thought of you as professional and I cannot have anything happen on the set. You have got to fulfill your obligations. Am I making myself clear?' In that wonderful accent, but making this compassioned speech."

The exhausting shoot lasted thirty-five days. Neither Kazan nor Spiegel knew that it was going to be a classic. When he first saw the film, Brando was "so depressed" by his performance that he got up and left the screening room. "I thought I was a huge failure," he wrote. Kazan was deeply hurt. "Not a word, not even a goodbye," he recalled. Leonard Bernstein had been at the same screening, and it was hearing Spiegel's apologetic tone with the composer that caused Kazan to shout out: "This is a great picture!" Columbia, however, had other worries. Contractually, they could not prevent Spiegel from engaging Bernstein to score the music, but the studio was concerned about his being linked to so many left-wing organizations.

In the meantime, Kazan was not sure about Bernstein's score. "I am getting some very bad reactions to the music," he wrote. He was also convinced that S. P. Eagle should "put his right name on the picture" and return to being called Sam Spiegel. "I told Gadge [*sic*], Mr. Eagle had just died very happily," the producer told the *New York Times*.

Around the same time, Paul Lazarus, from Columbia's publicity department, received a call from Schneider. "He said, 'Sam is stony broke and I would like you to put him on the payroll to do public relations for the opening of the picture . . . work out a deal.'" Lazarus had offered $500 per week. But the former S. P. Eagle was outraged. "I tip more than that," he spluttered.

As soon as *On the Waterfront* opened at the Astor Theater in New York, Kazan flew to Los Angeles and began preparing *East of Eden* for Warner Bros. Work on his new picture, however, did not prevent him from keeping on top of Buddha. "Everyone says, 'for Chrissake I hope

Sam handles it right!'," he wrote. "I express my complete confidence but have said to a few, 'write him.' " *The Caine Mutiny,* Columbia's other successful picture at the time, starring Humphrey Bogart, stirred up Kazan's competitive nature. He was delighted to inform Spiegel that those "who have seen both," chose theirs "ten to one." "I've got a rib on poor Harry Cohn that will slowly drive him nuts," he continued. The studio head had originally passed on *The Golden Warrior,* saying "This is not an action picture."

Spiegel replied that he would do all he could "to protect our interests here. And make us both millionaires (in rubies or dollars—heaven knows which). . . . I prevailed on the Legion of Decency to forego all the cuts. . . . I am fighting now on the Maryland . . . and Chicago demands for cuts." True to form, Spiegel was at his best, postproduction.

"Sam hit the general public properly," said Leo Jaffe, the Columbia executive. "He was a rough man to do business with. Rough in the sense that he'd like to have control of everything. . . . And Sam was a tiger when he wanted something. Usually, his demands tended to make sense." As a Spiegel intimate, he was sometimes in a difficult position. "He was one of my three closest friends. We socialized a lot and played cards together. When we used to get into a fight, I'd say let's play a couple of hands of gin. That was always the way we straightened everything out." A childhood memory of producer Stanley R. Jaffe was dropping by his father's Columbia office and finding him and Spiegel. "The lights were turned low and there they were, at the end of the table, playing gin."

Amidst the fever of success, Schulberg was touched that Spiegel had arranged a screening for his father, B.P. "I know this will be the most exciting thing that has happened to him for a very long time," he wrote.

Yet notwithstanding all the goodwill between them, the honeymoon period quickly evaporated, as had happened with Huston. This time, the gripes were not about money, since that was being handled by Columbia—it concerned Spiegel's tendency to credit hog. "He did deserve credit, but just not all of it," said Schulberg. "David was like that too . . . David O. Selznick Presents—he didn't direct *Gone With the Wind,* but it was of that school."

Spiegel's behavior over the Venice Film Festival was a perfect example of how he was conducting himself. When *Waterfront* was entered in the festival, he flirted with taking Kazan and then made preparations to appear with Marlene Dietrich instead. "Kazan and I said to each other, 'How could this happen this way?' " the writer said. "Sam sailing in on a huge yacht with the idea that the Golden Lion [the name of the festival award] would be all his. . . . He just didn't want to share the praise." In fact, Venice was not the expected triumph. *Waterfront* lost out to Castellani's *Romeo and Juliet*. Spiegel was staggered. Aside, he complained, "How could a movie like that, beat mine?" Afterward, he said the festival had been rigged.

When Spiegel returned to New York in September 1954, he learned that both Kazan and Schulberg refused to promote *Waterfront* in Chicago. It was a joint protest against their billing. "It soured the sweet taste of all of this for me," Schulberg argued. "There is Sam Spiegel twice as big as life while the name of the writer (and in this case the originator of the project as well) is either left out entirely or reduced to almost ridiculous minuteness." He recognized that his name was not going to entice people into theaters the way Brando's would. "But I hardly think that an enlarged Sam Spiegel rushes them either." Ad Schulberg, who represented her son, also made contact. She *had* bailed out Spiegel in the mid-1930s, but Spiegel refused to budge on the issue, even for her.

Meanwhile, Kazan's lawyer contacted Lazarus. "Gadg continues to be unhappy and upset about his billing on *Waterfront*," the executive wrote to Spiegel. Nor was Kazan averse to telephoning Sam Rheiner and listing his numerous complaints.

Yet no wrath was as strong as Sinatra's. Notorious for his grudges, he never quite forgave Spiegel for welching and handing "his" role over to Brando. "I've never heard so much screaming from a pair of short, fat men," was how Kazan described the meeting between Spiegel and the legendary Abe Lastfogel, Sinatra's agent, who also happened to be his. The five-foot-two William Morris agent had "the Eagle flushing crimson, floundering and perspiring and flapping his wings. I was sure he'd have a heart attack."

On the other hand, during the same period, Lastfogel's agency welched with Horizon Pictures over Eva Marie Saint. "We did have another option at $7,500," said Albert Heit. "But they never signed the contract, they kept on stalling, that was William Morris again. So, when they were on the other side, they didn't honor the obligation . . . that's the business."

At first, Sinatra wanted $100,000 for the humiliation, but he finally settled for $18,000. "Out of the *Waterfront* profits, a screening room was built at Sinatra's house," said Spiegel's lawyer. The producer also delivered a crate of whiskey to the singer's house in 1955. "[This] is not a peace offering but an invitation for myself to come to your house and split a few of these bottles with you on my next visit," he wrote. Yet it was still not enough for Sinatra, whom "you didn't fool with." "He used to berate us," said Mrs. George Axelrod. "He'd say, 'I hear you saw Spiegel the other night.' "

There was an incident at Romanoff's, which happened a few years later. "Sinatra was in a particularly bad mood because he had broken up with Betty Bacall, whom he had decided that he wasn't going to marry," said Kathleen Parrish. Spiegel and his wife arrived with Billy Wilder and his wife, Audrey, and Rita Hayworth and her then husband, James Hill. "Sinatra was sitting in a booth with two men and when we passed them by, Sam said, 'Hey there,' " Betty recalled. Spiegel's party then went to the booth next door, sat down, and ordered martinis. Several times, Sinatra leaned around and congratulated Spiegel on the success of *The Bridge on the River Kwai.* Spiegel thanked him but continued talking to his guests. Sinatra then stood up and hit Spiegel on the shoulder. "Listen, when you speak to me, it's not 'hey there.' " Everyone at Spiegel's table froze, since the singer's violent temper was legendary. Sinatra then punched Spiegel on the shoulder a second time. Spiegel looked up at him and said, "You're lucky that I bother to speak to you at all." All of Spiegel's friends were shocked; the producer was not the confrontational type, especially with such a huge star. The Wilders started making "wooo, wooo" noises, while Rita Hayworth, who had just made *Pal Joey* with Sinatra, curled her fists and said, "Let me at him, let me at him!" ("Rita couldn't stand Sinatra," said Betty.) Sinatra sat down again and called out, "Hey, fat man." Spiegel grabbed the edge of the table until his knuckles went white. He then turned around and said, "Frank, if you would like to meet me outside, without your henchmen, it would be my pleasure." Sinatra did not take him up on the offer.

In the meantime, Spiegel had proved his critics wrong. He had survived without Huston. *Melba* was the fluke, not *The African Queen*. As an independent producer, Spiegel had shown Hollywood that it was possible to create masterpieces outside the town. S. P. Eagle had done the preparation work–fifteen years of schmoozing and giving the New Year's Eve parties–and now Sam Spiegel was to reap the rewards.

Nevertheless, certain scars had not healed. Betty Spiegel accompanied him on his first trip to Berlin since March 1933. It was for the German dubbing of *Waterfront*. "Just before we landed, Sam looked at me and said, 'I don't know why I'm going to this goddamned country–you know but for the grace of God, I would have been a bar of soap.' He was so nervous, I had never seen Sam so nervous. I guess it brought memories back of that train ride. . . . The plane landed and there was a red carpet on the tarmac and limousines on the runway. They threw red roses in my arms and the press was there. A great many people were coming up and greeting Sam in German and he was making asides to me like 'That man was in the Luftwaffe,' or 'He was the head of the Gestapo.' I said, 'Sam, some of them speak English. You had better stop that.' And he just said, 'I don't care.' "

Part III

1955–1985

Chapter Seventeen

THE THIRD MRS. SPIEGEL AND THE STRANGE ONE

On the evening of March 30, 1955, Spiegel collected his first Academy Award. By the time the award for best picture was announced, no one in the audience at the RKO Pantages Theatre seemed surprised. *On the Waterfront*–which was introduced as a New York production–had already won seven Oscars. Indeed, as the twenty-seventh awards ceremony progressed, a heavily pregnant Eva Marie Saint, as well as Brando, Schulberg, and Kazan, all had their turn.

The producer Buddy Adler, known as "the Silver Fox," presented Spiegel with his award. But, unlike Brando, who had cracked, "It's much heavier than I imagined" when taking his statuette, Spiegel took a pause before speaking. It was obvious that the showman was prepared. "I am very grateful to all of you," he began. "And in this year of great achievements in the motion picture industry, all of us who worked on *Waterfront* are deeply appreciative to all of you for the honor, the compliment, and the distinction."

Particular emphasis was put on "the honor, the compliment, and the distinction." Like most of the recipients, he disappeared backstage to be photographed, then teamed up with Brando. Both men were eager to call a number in Virginia where Josanne Mariani-Berenger, the actor's girlfriend, and a certain Betty Benson were staying. "I think Sam and Marlon wanted to make quite sure we weren't with anyone else," Betty said. Meanwhile, the press was camping out on her mother's lawn.

The following day, the congratulatory telegrams poured in from the likes of Grace Kelly, Anne and Kirk Douglas, Alma and Alfred Hitchcock, Irene Mayer Selznick, and Jack Warner. Friends and acquaintances were delighted that the former S. P. Eagle had finally made it. One cable was particularly long. It had four pages quoting from the Bible–the twenty-fourth chapter of Samuel–ending with YOU MAY NOT BE THE LORD'S ANOINTED BUT YOU HAVE RECEIVED YOUR SHARE OF HONOR AND I AM VERY GLAD FOR YOU. YOUR EX-DAVID LYNNE.

It showed the second Mrs. Spiegel's magnanimous nature because that very same morning, a marital settlement was made at the court of Santa Monica. Spiegel was absent, but it was agreed that Lynne would receive $25,000 immediately and then a further $60,000, which was to be paid out in the months that followed. It was not ungenerous, but considering she owed almost $40,000 in litigation fees, the settlement figure was not one to pop champagne corks about. Life had been pretty tough on the Texas beauty. On July 9, 1954, she had been arrested on the charges of manslaughter and a felony hit-and-run.

After coming back from a party given by Arthur Treacher (the British actor best known for playing butlers), she smashed into the rear of a station wagon, causing it to spin uncontrollably and throw its occupants out onto a nearby lawn–all apart from nine-year-old Joel Watnick, who landed on the concrete pavement and died instantly. Mrs. Spiegel failed to report the accident–resulting in a two-day police search–until she was brought in for questioning. On October 29, 1954, Superior Court Judge Mildred L. Lillie sentenced her to two months in the county jail and three years' probation. In spite of being cleared of manslaughter, the judge rejected her "blackout" story, pointing out that Mrs. Spiegel had "used every source at her command to get the car repaired [the car belonged to the actor George Tobias] and to conceal her identity." She was finally released on January 20, 1955.

When the accident happened, Spiegel was staying in splendor at the Connaught Hotel in London. However, he immediately made contact and arranged with Columbia to put up the $5,000 bail. He also made sure that he could not be incriminated, and was relieved to be informed by his lawyer that under the California law, he would "not be held liable in any way, shape, form or manner."

As a result of the West Hollywood tragedy, Lynne had to pay for a series of six civil suits that were eventually settled out of court. Unfortunately, she never recovered and her life continued to spiral down and down, just as her husband's began to surge.

Kathleen Parrish had seen the former starlet bicycling around at an ice cream parlor. "It was the saddest thing," she recalled. "Lynne was the loneliest lady and couldn't drive because she had had that accident." While certain Spiegel friends such as Walter Reisch and Bill Blowitz looked after his former wife, the producer was adamant that he had no financial or moral obligation. He was still smarting from her previous behavior. "She destroyed my Picassos, she destroyed the whole house," being his main complaints.

Besides, Spiegel was preoccupied. Just as he had a new girlfriend– "Beautiful Betty Benson," or Bet tee as the producer pronounced her name–he had a new sparring partner–David Lean. The forty-three-year-old English director was following in the footsteps of Duvivier, Welles, Huston, Milestone, and Kazan, and he was to crown the Spiegel legacy. Their first picture together was *The Bridge on the River Kwai*. "Sam could produce rabbits out of almost any hat," Lean later said. "And would get things that I wouldn't even dare make the first move towards getting."

However, before he could give his utmost to Lean, who, like himself, was a demanding fellow, Spiegel had to finish off his pending project with Columbia, New York. Called *End as a Man,* it was based on Calder Willingham's best-selling novel and hit play. As with most of Spiegel's projects, it had gone through various stages. At first, there was talk that Kazan would direct the picture, with James Dean in the starring role. Although, when that plan fell through, Spiegel decided to bill the project as a low-budget film–employ Jack Garfein as the director, and introduce Ben Gazzara to the filmgoing public. The young actor had become an overnight sensation in Kazan's stage production of *Cat on a Hot Tin Roof.* He was being hailed as the "New Brando."

In the beginning, all the details seemed perfect. Not only was Gazzara identified with *End as a Man*–he had starred in the stage production–but so was Garfein, who had directed him. A friend of Willingham's, it was Garfein who had originally introduced the play as "a class exercise" to the Actors Studio. A surprise hit, it had been performed at the Theatre de Lys in Greenwich Village and ended up on Broadway playing at both the Lyceum *and* Vanderbilt Theatres. Meanwhile, key to Spiegel's heart, the play's theme was absorbing and had the right dramatic flair for a film.

Set in a Southern military school, a sadistic bully, Jocko de Paris (Gazzara), plots to destroy the reputation of a fellow student (Geoffrey Horne) because he feels that his father, Major Avery (Larry Gates), who works at the college, has humiliated him. Machiavellian, Gazzara succeeds in involving in his schemes an assortment of cadets such as his foolish roommate (Pat Hingle), a dumb football player (James Olson), and a couple of freshmen (George Peppard and Arthur Storch). But eventually, de Paris's Iago-like schemes are discovered and he is dismissed from the school.

Whereas most of the actors had been in Garfein's production, nearly all of them were new to the screen. Initially, this had not bothered Spiegel, who had argued that the inexperience did "not lessen" their artistic and creative ability. "Rather, I feel, they contribute a freshness and excitement that cannot be duplicated." The followers of the Method were back in Spiegel's life, and the hopes were high. After all, *On the Waterfront* was a masterpiece. But alas, *End as a Man* was not to reach the producer's expectations.

"At first, we had a father-son relationship," recalled Garfein. Writing sessions used to take place either at the Horizon office, or the Lombardy Hotel where the producer was living. "I have to say that Sam's sense of story was really remarkable. He did not like the end of the original novel and play where the protagonist isn't punished and it was his idea to change that." However, just as the producer had picked on Schulberg during the writing of *On the Waterfront,* Calder Willingham became his victim. He was particularly annoyed by the long-winded ways of the novelist-playwright. "For vengeance, Calder used to steal the cigars off the desk, each time that Sam went to the bathroom," Garfein revealed. After their sessions, Willingham would proudly open his jacket to show how many he had stolen that day.

Having miraculously survived Auschwitz, Garfein was well educated in human cruelty, as described in Willingham's screenplay. The twenty-six-year-old was also one of the bright lights of the Actors Studio, as well as being married to Carroll Baker—an actress destined for the big time who would be the star of Kazan's next film, *Baby Doll.* They were a hip couple around New York—young, good-looking, talented—but so far as Spiegel was concerned, Garfein was a first-time film director. True, he had done television and had been on the sets of John Ford, George Stevens, and Kazan, but he lacked experience. Garfein felt that being around three such skilled and experienced directors had rubbed off on him. Consequently, he was not as modest as anticipated, and his "I've seen it all before" confidence grated on Spiegel's nerves. Spiegel had even written to Lean, "You know my thoughts and affections are with you and not with 'geniuses,' " which was a partial reference to Garfein.

End as a Man was made on location in central Florida. The law college of Stetson University in Gulfport served as the Southern Military Academy, while most of the interior scenes were shot in Shamrock Studios in Winter Park. The budget was tight and the location was as hot as Hades. Spiegel later referred to the film experience as "my banishment to Florida." "Poor Sam, he never could stand the heat, and every day he was battling it out with Garfein," Betty recalled. It was a tense set. "The first day of shooting, Garfein made George Peppard cry."

George Stevens, Jr., used to drop by. He was stationed with the air force at Orlando. "It was exciting, all these young actors who were destined to be big stars," he said. "Jack with his *big* stories, who formed an alliance with the actors—it was very 'us against him [Spiegel],' which I am afraid I was part of." The producer had tried the technique of "I'm known and you're not," but instead of shrinking, Garfein fought his corner. He was also irritated by Spiegel's appearances, as they were "disruptive" to his creative process. It reached such a point that he sought director George Stevens's advice, who simply said, "Throw him off." But since it sounded extreme, Garfein pressed Kazan for his opinion. "I repeated what Stevens had said and he replied, 'So, why don't you do it? Listen, Jack, he's been thrown off bigger and better sets than yours!' " And Garfein tried to do just that.

It did not help the already fraught relations. "Jack was very much under the influence of Lee Strasberg and showed absolutely no respect," said an intimate of both Spiegel and Garfein. "While many people couldn't handle Sam, Sam couldn't handle Jack."

Eventually, there was a huge fight over the ending. "Sam had had the idea that Jocko de Paris should be put on the milk train by his fellow cadets." However, his director wanted to take the idea further. "At night, I had seen a train of exhausted black cotton workers, and I had decided, This is the train that Jocko should be thrown on. Originally, Sam had said, 'Baby, that's brilliant.' But Columbia was horrified. There was still segregation in the South and they were terrified about how their distributors would react." Then Spiegel's dictates became firm, the milk train ceased to be an option, and all African-Americans were to be banned from the set. "But my second assistant suggested that one or two could always be hidden in the bushes." Isabella Leitner, Garfein's girl Friday, remembered "the king" saying no. "And Jack went out in the middle of the night, set up the train, and did the scene, without Sam's knowledge," she said.

Garfein was then summoned to an audience with Spiegel, in his limousine. Ever since hearing that there were "dangerously poisonous black snakes" in the vicinity, the producer preferred holding conferences in his chauffeur-driven car, which was a hearse, hired from the local funeral parlor. "Now listen, Jack, we can't have that scene," Spiegel said. But Garfein stood his ground. "Sam, why do you want to do this to me, I am an Auschwitz victim," he said. The battle continued, but Spiegel was not exhilarated as he often was from a fight, he was exasperated. "I never expected my Jewish director to give me such a terrible time," he had exclaimed. And eventually, he pulled the film from Garfein.

"I had nothing to do with the score or the edit," the director recalled. Initially, he had threatened to take his name off the film, but his William Morris agent advised him otherwise. " 'The basic work is yours,' he said, and so I kept my name on it."* Nevertheless, Spiegel was still steaming and had sent a stiff telegram from the set of *The Bridge on the River Kwai* with strict instructions that it was to be read out to Columbia's entire publicity department: I DON'T PROPOSE TO ENGAGE IN CONTROVERSY WITH GARFEIN. He wanted the director to be ignored in the studio's publicity campaign and did not want him jumping on THE BANDWAGON AFTER THE PREVIEW. Spiegel threatened that unless his directive was adhered to, I WILL INTERRUPT MY PRESENCE IN CEYLON AND FLY TO NEW YORK TO ENFORCE THIS DECISION.

Then the Motion Picture Code administrator insisted that the film had homosexual overtones. Since this threatened the likelihood of a national domestic release, Spiegel needed to take an emergency flight from Europe and meet with Hollywood's Motion Picture Association of America (MPAA).

Meanwhile, another unhappy individual was Willingham, Spiegel's other "genius"—who loathed the film's new title—*The Strange One*. He insisted that he WOULD NOT HAVE SOLD PROPERTY if he had known that the producer would change the title. Garfein claimed the name was chosen via a questionnaire that had been sent to Columbia employees, but perhaps he was forgetting Spiegel's past. "We always used to have a joke in the office that Sam liked the word Strange," said Albert Heit. "*The Stranger, We Were Strangers,* and then *End as a Man,* which ended up as *The Strange One.*"

In spite of the film's considerable merit and Columbia's enthusiasm, which labeled it the next *Marty,* it flopped at the box office. A few years later, Sam Rheiner suggested that the film be rereleased to coincide with Gazzara's success in Preminger's *Anatomy of a Murder,* but Spiegel was not interested. The final negative cost was $708,713.79, and by the late 1960s, the unrecouped loss of the film was $800,000, which was borne by both Horizon and Columbia.

---

*According to Albert Heit, "Garfein finished the picture, but they didn't have it, and so Bob Parrish, Sam's friend, was sent down to Florida to shoot some more scenes to get the film out to a full length." However, this has been denied by Kathleen Parrish.

In Garfein's opinion, the producer threw his picture away. He also wondered if Spiegel had ruined his Hollywood career as well. "George Stevens told me that I was on the Country Club Blacklist [a list of talent who were blackballed from working by Hollywood powers] and that Sam had put me there." But George Stevens, Jr., dismisses this claim. "My father would never say that."

Still, Spiegel did keep a framed photograph of Garfein and himself in his office. "It's the world's most outstanding photo," said Isabella Leitner. "Each are looking the other way–it was just before they were going to kill each other. The body language speaks volumes." The writer Edward Chodorov asked Spiegel why he kept the framed picture in his office. Considering the circumstances, it was a strange souvenir. "So I know never to work with a young director again," Spiegel snapped. Garfein was the first director born after the First World War to work with Spiegel. A few others were to follow, with films that were even more of a disappointment.

Betty, who had spent her time on location sipping martinis by the pool with Elaine Stritch, Gazzara's girlfriend, had hardly seen Garfein. "He'd come home and they [Garfein and a heavily pregnant Carroll Baker] kept totally to themselves," she said. "I am sure he thought that I was a dipshit." She was also otherwise engaged. "August '56, that was a period of time when I was seeing someone else."

Garfein remembered Betty and recalled Spiegel being "very cynical" about her. "It was 'there she goes,' it almost excited him. He sort of went for women he couldn't be certain about. There would always be pain." The director opined that Spiegel pushed himself further in his work than he did in his relationships with women. "On a certain level, she might be wearing diamonds that he had given her, but he wasn't sharing anything of himself. He was very like a lot of those powerhouses."

While Spiegel was prepared to fight it out with his directors and writers, he was less prepared to do this with the women he chose. "The secret of happiness is whores," he told Harold Pinter. "What Sam meant was no commitment, no emotion, no involvement. It didn't have to get mixed up," sensed the playwright. Yet if there was an exception, it was "Beautiful Betty Benson." "Sam enjoyed Betty," Rosemary Chodorov said. "They were chums . . . always whispering and conspiring. He never had an equal relationship after her."

Physically, Betty fit his tastes. Her feline features, green eyes, high cheekbones, small nose, and neat chin were enhanced by her dramatic brunette hair and a flawless magnolia complexion. "She was very 'naughty in Chanel,' which was a turn-on for Sam," said an acquaintance. Some compared Betty's looks to Rosalind Russell's but she also had an impish appeal. And being five foot seven and reed-thin, she was the perfect clotheshorse.

Spiegel spotted the model and NBC color girl at a party given in his honor by Luis Estevez, the fashion designer. "I asked Sam if there was anyone he wanted to meet," remembered Estevez. He did, and it was Benson. "I warned him, 'Well it so happens that girl has more suitors than she can handle.'" Regardless, Spiegel was still interested. "He charmed her like Sam could, but it was confrontation city because there was a chemistry," said Estevez. "Sam knew exactly what he wanted and so did Betty. Well, she thought she did."

When Spiegel took Benson to the Lido in Venice, the producer Mike Todd, one of her former suitors, spotted them. "'Hey, angel face,' Mike called out. 'You know where you were last year on this exact same day at this exact same time?' 'Never mind,' said Sam. But Mike bordered on. 'You were sitting right here, at this exact same table, with me, angel face.'" Spiegel may have had a past, but so did Betty. "I had a lot of charms on my charm bracelet, and I cannot deny that I was not a bit, how you say, promiscuous?"

As the saying goes, "A girl without a past is a girl without a future." Unlike Lynne, Betty Benson was extremely bright and eager to learn. "She used to carry a dictionary around with her, and if there was a word that she didn't understand, she'd look it up," recalled Betty Estevez, the former model and wife of Luis Estevez. Spiegel was interested in her opinion. "He used to toss me scripts and books to read." After reading a galley of *Dr. No*, Benson recommended it to Spiegel. "And Sam said, 'Baby, it's nonsense.' But I said, 'It's going to make a fabulous picture,' and he said, 'Baby, I don't make pictures like that.' Sam had to make a film that would give the world a message, or bring some kind of intelligence." Betty also made Spiegel laugh. "And he could never resist that," said Leonora Hornblow. In regards to the Spiegel-Lean relationship, she became the light relief. "I'd come in and say, 'Gee guys, I've lost my chewing gum and I can't find the heel of

my Ferragamo shoe,' or something equally ridiculous." Betty was the
needed antidote between the two individuals, who had an "incredible
love–hate relationship." "They would be screaming at each other and
then, an hour later, laughing and having lunch."

As the consequence of their age difference–Spiegel was twenty-
eight years older than his girlfriend–he played many roles in her life.
"Sam was my daddy, my protector, my companion, my friend, and
my lover," she said. While she was like the producer's mistress,
gangster's moll, wife, and moral conscience–all rolled into one. Betty
counted on Spiegel. "I always felt that if a tidal wave arrived, Sam
would hold out his hand and it would crash around me, but it would
never touch me. . . . He was my Rock of Gibraltar." He also gave her
the three rules by which to conduct her life: "Don't ever let anyone
bully you, always follow your heart, and never lend money."

Betty Lorraine Benson was born on October 11, 1930, in Daytona
Beach, Florida. When her parents separated, she and her mother moved
to Virginia. Benson was about six years old. A few months afterward,
Betty's father kidnapped her which–when his wife caught up with him–
led to a custody trial. "I was put up on a stand and asked with whom I
wanted to live. I said my mother not because I didn't love my father, but
she had been there when I had had the mumps, the measles, and
whatever." Once the young girl came out of the courtroom, her father
was crying hysterically. "He grabbed me and held me so tight that I
could barely breathe. He just sobbed and sobbed and I was in tears
because I didn't realize that it would hurt him the way that it did." The
next and final time that she saw her father was after he had remarried
and started a new family. "Sam and I were at the Racquet Club in Palm
Springs when I had got word that he had had a heart attack and died.
I didn't go back for his service because I didn't know him."

On the other hand, she was extremely close to her mother. "One
person who met her said, 'Well, Betty, you sure went to Central
Casting,' " she recalled. "When I think of Mother, I always think of
Lee Brodie's song 'Sweet and Lovely.' " Graceful and well mannered,
Mabel got on with her future son-in-law. "She thought Sam was an
angel, they adored each other."

The photographer Philip Stern discovered Betty when she was in
New York with a girlfriend. It was the old story, he had come up to

her and asked what modeling agency she was with. The meeting led to showroom work for designers such as Claire McCardell and Bonnie Cashin, as well as hats for Mr. John, but Betty was never tall enough for the catwalk. She then became a test color girl for NBC. It was in the early days of color television when a blonde, a brunette, and a redhead were used to test out the colors. "It was $100 an hour and the high-fashion models only got $75. I made a lot of money."

In the meantime, glamour boys such as Kenneth Jay Lane used to take her dancing at El Morocco and the Stork Club. The parties were endless, as were the cocktails and the romantic dalliances. "All I had on my head was my hat," she now admits. Her infectious laugh, quick wit, and spontaneity appealed to writers such as Truman Capote, Noël Coward, Gore Vidal, and Tennessee Williams, while Spiegel's female friends liked her too. "The first thing that Marlene [Dietrich] did was have my horoscope read." Slim Hayward, the stylish wife of Leland Hayward, discussed Betty's appeal with Irwin Shaw. "They had not been speaking about Sam or anything," Betty said. "And Irwin turned around and said, 'I wonder why he married her?' And Slim said, 'I don't know but I hear she's great in the feathers.' And I told her, 'Slim, you just keep spreading that rumor.' So later on in life . . . I guess Irwin had to find out for himself and we had a very sweet affair." Betty used to call him the VIW: "The Very Important Writer."

Naturally, there were those who disapproved of the wild child. "She was doing it all: women, drugs, drink," complained Spiegel's lawyer. "She had no aim in her life, no ability. She was only good at receiving people." Still, Betty was fairly accomplished at the latter. "Oh my God, her parties rivaled Charlie Feldman's," said Yolande Fox, Matty Fox's wife and former beauty queen.

The first time that Spiegel mentioned marriage, Betty caught him in bed with two women the following afternoon. "Well, I hope it was worth it, Sam," were her words, when storming out with a packed suitcase. "And, just as I was stepping into the elevator, he called out, 'Bet tee, it was worth it,' and slammed the door." He then hounded Bet tee Boo—Spiegel's favorite nickname for her—with telegrams such as YOU MIGHT AT LEAST HAVE A SENSE OF HUMOR ABOUT IT, daily deliveries of her favorite dark chocolate brownie to her apartment, as well as bringing her entire family to New York. "He was having dates with my mother," she recalled. "Finally, I said, 'Mother, you have got to stop accepting these invitations from Sam– I'm not with him, I'm with someone else' [Morris Levy, the record producer], and she said, 'But Betty, I love Sam.' "

Betty Estevez sensed that Betty, being "a free, free spirit," was "attractive to a control freak" like Spiegel. However, no one expected the couple to get married. "My husband liked Betty–everyone did," said Mrs. Fox, "but we were amazed by the relationship." Spiegel was nervous about marrying for the third time. "He asked everyone if he should marry her and everyone said no," said Paul Lazarus, the Columbia executive. His business associates were particularly against the idea. "The feeling was, 'You now have millions and why do you have to marry Betty, who you have this and that problem with?' " said Jules Buck.

There were even rumors that Betty had been in someone else's bed the morning of the nuptials. "Apparently she said, 'I have to get up early because I'm marrying Sam Spiegel.' Well, her companion was a little surprised," said an acquaintance. The story was not true, but it suggests the general feeling about Benson and Spiegel.

The couple married on November 26, 1957. It was three weeks before the American opening of *The Bridge on the River Kwai*. "He said, 'Baby, I'd just prefer to keep it secret for the time being–I can't concentrate on people congratulating me on being married, wanting to give us parties, I have to concentrate on the opening of *Bridge*.' I replied, 'That's perfectly fine with me, Sam, if no one *ever* knows.' "

Betty only invited her roommate to the hush-hush wedding ceremony. "She bought me daisies because daisies don't tell." The bride-to-be then rushed into Bergdorf-Goodman and bought a lavender dress, which had a satin bodice and chiffon skirt. "Halston was making hats at that time, it was a beautiful little satin hat with a big plume that rested under my chin." The Spiegels were married in the Savoy Plaza, which is now where the General Motors Building stands. "Sam called Columbia and said he needed the suite for a business meeting." Since two witnesses were needed, the judge brought his spouse and a male friend. Both added a comic element to the event. "The judge's wife kept on asking me, 'Where did you get that nose?'– she was convinced that I had had plastic surgery–while the male witness tried to sell us a house in Long Island . . . all night long."

The New York premiere of *The Bridge on the River Kwai* was going to be the occasion where Spiegel presented his new bride. Something of a society event, it took place on December 18, and was a gala benefit given on behalf of various charities. The chairperson for the evening was Slim Hayward, while others on the committee included Babe Paley, Doris Stein, and Leonora Hornblow. After the film's premiere, a lavish party was held on the roof garden of the St. Regis Hotel. "But I got caught in an elevator with Jerry Zipkin [the socialite and infamous 'walker']," Betty recalled. "We were stuck there for half an hour. . . . So Slim Hayward stood in for me." The producer was livid. "He said, 'Of all the times to be late when I wanted to announce our wedding. I wanted to introduce you as my wife and naturally everyone is here.'" Once the news leaked out, all the newspapers picked it up. But Louella Parsons was keen to get a quote from Spiegel himself. "And well, marriage, like murder, will out," were his words of wisdom. "I thought that was hilarious," Betty admitted.

Whereas Spiegel knew his wife's family and had a weakness for her mother, Betty never met his mother. "I sometimes wondered if Sam told her that he had remarried," she said. In a certain way, the two women were in communication, since Regina Spiegel was always asking for white kid gloves. "I used to send so many—in every length—that I was convinced that she must be selling them. I mean what was she doing with all those pairs . . . in Israel?" The third Mrs. Sam Spiegel would wrap up the parcel, containing Saks's best, with a little note inside. "But I never heard from her. She used to write and thank Sam."

Deeply unconventional, the couple would live apart within a few years of tying the knot, but they never did sever their marital ties. And throughout the late 1950s and early 1960s, their marriage continued to intrigue both friends and the gossip columnists. Would they or wouldn't they divorce? Was it an arrangement? "I think we were well suited, because neither of us should have married," Betty said.

However, in Lauren Bacall's opinion, Spiegel trusted and confided in her. "Betty was the closest to having a relationship with him," the actress said. "And they remained friends, which was odd for Sam."

Chapter Eighteen

THE BRIDGE ON THE RIVER KWAI

S am Spiegel used to say that he fell upon Pierre Boulle's *Le Pont de la Rivière Kwai* (English title: *The Bridge over the River Kwai*) when his flight had been delayed in Paris. He was so "gripped by the storyline" that he immediately made inquiries about the film rights. Henri-Georges Clouzot was the first to option the best-selling novel.

Yet when the renowned French director (*Le Salaire de la Peur/The Wages of Fear* and *Les Diaboliques/Diabolique*) had trouble finding a producer, Carl Foreman entered the scene. The American screenwriter had the backing of Sir Alexander Korda, on the understanding that his brother Zoltan was to direct. However, when Korda had financial setbacks and Zoltan Korda's health took a turn for the worse, Spiegel barged in. Columbia would fund the picture and since Foreman was blacklisted and the studio was nervous of artists with a former Communist connection, Spiegel kept on referring to him as "Zoltan's partner."

Initially, Spiegel tried to interest Elia Kazan in the project, but once Kazan declined, he approached other directors of his caliber, such as John Ford, Howard Hawks, Nicholas Ray, Carol Reed, William Wyler, and Fred Zinnemann.

Orson Welles also claimed to have been considered, but an incident at Freddie's—the Paris nightclub—suggested otherwise. Spiegel and Betty Benson were sitting at a table when Darryl Zanuck and Welles reeled toward them. "Zanuck looks at Sam and says, 'Sam, you're a son of a bitch,' and Sam asks, 'Why?' and then we started to laugh because they were both so drunk." The former studio head then verbally attacked Spiegel for ignoring Welles's talent and not employing him. The insults lasted a good half hour until Betty Benson interrupted the diatribe, demanding that he leave. The next morning, Zanuck wrote her an ill-spelled letter of apology, which was slipped under the door of Spiegel's suite at the George V. "It said, 'Of course it was wrong of me to come over and say those things. But, I do think, that at some point, Sam could have helped Orson.' "

Among Spiegel's choice of directors, Hawks was the most enthusiastic. Like Carol Reed, he had a problem with the book's ending, but as he traveled from Klosters to Rome and back to Klosters, he continued to keep in touch. Then Hawks lost interest. A two-hour discussion with Irwin Shaw in the Swiss ski resort hindered rather than helped. "Sam, the more I go into the yarn," he wrote, "the more I feel that this is not a big grossing picture." Hawks suggested using a British cast, an all-British crew, and doing it "for a limited budget."

Did this advice prompt Spiegel to send the book to David Lean? The British director was working on *Summertime* with Katharine Hepburn. Since the actress and Lean had become close, he sought her opinion. Hepburn had strongly recommended Spiegel, saying, "You'll learn a lot from him. And he'll learn a lot from you."

It is likely that Ilya Lopert—*Summertime*'s producer—alerted Spiegel to Lean's talent. He had done the same with John Huston, who had even dropped by the set to watch. "My father thought that Lean was a complete genius," said Tanya Lopert. The feeling was not reciprocated, since Lean dismissed Lopert as a dishonest vulgarian.

Nevertheless, Arthur Penn described Lopert as bringing "the pearls before the Philistines." As a distributor, Lopert was responsible for launching films such as *Hôtel du Nord* and *La Belle et La Bête* in the United States. Moreover, Lopert was the first to recognize Penn's film *The Miracle Worker*. "I found him terrifically smart and gracious," Penn said. Lean, on the other hand, had horror stories of Lopert tearing up the *Summertime* screenplay to keep on schedule. It did not matter that Lopert had given him his first chance to direct a major Hollywood star.

Previously, Lean had made such gems as *Brief Encounter, Great Expectations, Oliver Twist,* and *Hobson's Choice,* but only with English actors. He had reached a moment in his career when he had to go with a "major audience-orientated" producer with Hollywood funding. And Spiegel was perfect for the role. "He made the impossible possible and that was what was so exciting," said Kevin Brownlow, Lean's principal biographer. Director Anthony Perry sensed that Spiegel "saved" Lean "from a bleak, intellectually unrewarding future, and made him the brilliant landscaper we will remember." Perry had worked at Rank–the British studio–and knew Lean during his Cineguild days. He described Lean's films pre-Spiegel as being of "great quality," but in the final analysis, limited by an attitude of "I make films that I like and hope the public likes them too."

The picture that Spiegel was proposing, however, was quite different and promised to have international appeal. Set in a Japanese prisoner-of-war camp, deep in the Burmese jungle, the story concerns Colonel Nicholson (Alec Guinness), who at first is heroic in his initial stand against the camp's commander, Colonel Saito (Sessue Hayakawa), but then loses grip. To the irritation of his camp's doctor, Major Clipton (James Donald), Nicholson agrees to use his men–exhausted POWs–to build a railway bridge that will be a considerable help to the Japanese war effort. Meanwhile, Major Warden (Jack Hawkins), from the Allied headquarters, seeks to destroy the bridge using the help of Allied commandos Shears (William Holden) and his accomplice Joyce (Geoffrey Horne). When Shears and Joyce arrive to blow up the bridge, Nicholson tries to prevent their efforts and is killed in the attempt.

In regards to the Spiegel-Lean relationship, much has been made of Lean's playing the pukka gentleman to the producer's "Big cigar, baby, let's buy them out" approach. However, it should be emphasized that Lean lacked Spiegel's warmth, and was capable of being extremely steely. "There was a pattern in David's life," said

Norman Spencer, his associate producer. "People took enormously to him and he charmed them, but when he felt disappointed, he severed all contact and became quite glacial, and that was it."

Lean never quite did this to Spiegel. Between the two lone wolves, there was a mutual respect, although they did have endless battles. Lean–who knew his Dickens–was tickled by Spiegel, while Spiegel forgave Lean for his various foibles–Lean could be petty and paranoid–because Spiegel recognized that he was one of the great directors. In the meantime, there was a certain alchemy in their partnership because each was to give what the other was deficient in. Perhaps Spiegel lacked Lean's visual sense, but Lean lacked Spiegel's broad intellectual scope. Spiegel also had a sixth sense when it came to dealing with moneymen, and took care of such matters, which left Lean to concentrate on the picture.

"Could *Kwai* have been achieved without Spiegel?" asks Brownlow. "The answer is no because a film of this scale, however brilliant the director, depends on enormous financial support. The film could have been made in six days in an English studio like Merton Park using miniatures. It would have come and gone and everyone would have said 'he did the best he could,' but Lean resisted that sort of film." And so did Spiegel.

It had been Don Ashton's idea to shoot *The Bridge on the River Kwai* in Colombo, Ceylon (now Sri Lanka). The production designer knew the area because his wife's family came from there. Previously, Spiegel was more interested in Yugoslavia, since it was nearer London.

Ashton was one of the first of the crew to be hired. He had been on the set of *Charley Moon,* a film that was being shot at the Lyric Theatre, Hammersmith, when he was summoned to the telephone. "The great success at the time was *On the Waterfront*–it was a byword in successful filmmaking," he recalled. "And I said gaily, 'Oh that's Sam Spiegel wanting me in Hollywood,' and it was."

He had accompanied Spiegel on his initial visit to the island of Ceylon. "He was quite hairless and of course the leeches came at him in droves and my first job as production designer was to burn them off his legs." The producer had cabled Columbia's London office: AS FOR CEYLON, IN GENERAL, IT IS WONDERFUL . . . FOR

THE CEYLONESE–AND THEY CAN HAVE IT. In regards to the press: YOU CAN ANNOUNCE THAT IT IS PARADISE ON EARTH (FOR THE LEECHES).

Ashton, whose credits eventually included *A Countess from Hong Kong* and *Young Winston,* described Spiegel as "the most clever producer" he ever worked with. "He had a knack of decimating. He could break it all up, put it in slots, and pull out the ones that mattered." Spiegel used to spend his life on the telephone, either "chatting up the girls," or dialing a number in Hollywood and saying, "Hello, baby, how's that script going?" "Sam would keep tabs on everybody, he wouldn't let anyone escape, and he kept it all going."

However, if he had one major criticism, it was the producer's low regard for the crew. "There was a line for the director, the actors for whom he would do absolutely anything, but below that, he didn't treat the people very well. . . . He was of the attitude that you could always replace a technician, but you couldn't replace an actor." Nevertheless, Spiegel was known for his way with the secretaries. Each Christmas, White Shoulders and other scents were wrapped and delivered to their desks.

There was also his trick of smoothing troubled waters with a blink. "He made you beholden to him," said Kazan, who was not averse to accepting favors. But how cunning to bother to be personable, what Billy Wilder referred to as "Sam's velvet octopus arms" treatment. An opening night was never forgotten–the telegrams were delivered in abundance to writers, directors, and actors alike.

There was also the irresistible ceremony. The playwright George Axelrod had attended a pre-Christmas dinner at the Spiegels' house. "It was rather a dazzling group–people one had read about in the columns but had never seen–and fancy champagne. Sam got up and said, 'I have asked you all tonight because I am going away and I thought that, before I went, it would be nice to have my closest and dearest friends around for a little farewell dinner.' I had just met him but he was rather touching about friendship and departure. I said to Kazan, 'Where is he going?' 'To Klosters for Christmas.' There were neckties for men, perfume and compacts for the ladies. He would be back in ten days. I thought, this is my kind of guy."

Depending on the day, he could be Lean's kind of guy too. At their first meeting, Spiegel offered him an enormous cigar, which both the director and Norman Spencer declined. However, the producer poured on the charm and Lean was "thoroughly seduced" by his huge personality, as well as by his intelligence and enthusiasm for film. Spiegel then declared that he had "a magnificent script" by Carl Foreman. There was just a small snag, the writer was in New York, making a few final revisions, and Lean would have to join him. As Spencer wisely pointed out: "In matters like ensnaring people and getting his own way, Spiegel never hurried."

Still, Lean was thoroughly disappointed by the first draft of *Kwai*. Lean had liked Boulle's book, describing it as having "real size and style."* It reminded him "of a Shakespearean drama." "One feels almost at once that the stage is being set for a tremendous clash of wills, and that the situation can only be resolved by a mighty climax in which some of the leading characters are bound to die," he wrote to Spiegel. But after reading Foreman's screenplay, he sensed that the "whole spirit of the book" had been lost. "I said in my first notes that the writer and the book are like oil and water. I was too polite. The book and the characters in the book have completely escaped him."

Spiegel was taken aback by Lean's reaction. Indeed, when Lean first voiced his opinion about the screenplay, Spiegel supposedly turned white. If this was the case, it indicated that Spiegel had not read Foreman's screenplay, since his two last directors had credited him for his fine story mind.

In the six weeks that followed, Lean and Norman Spencer toiled on a film treatment at the Hotel Fourteen on East 60th Street. It was during this period that the director thought of the opening sequence–the soldiers whistling to the "Colonel Bogey March" when they arrive at the prisoner-of-war camp. "Sam kept on ringing up, he was a little scared of David because they hadn't formed a relationship yet," the associate producer said. "He would say, 'How's it going? How much longer is it going to be?' " Their treatment was finished on March 30, 1956. Throughout, they had script conferences with Spiegel, who, in Spencer's estimation, was "often brilliant." "Sam had this ability to put

---

*Boulle also wrote *Monkey Planet*, on which the *Planet of the Apes* films were based.

his finger on what was wrong . . . he was very focused and wouldn't forget the original intention."

Yet later on, Lean dismissed him as being useless in the creative process. He claimed that Spiegel had a batch of secret readers who used to give him ideas. There is certainly no evidence of these people in the producer's correspondence. It should also be taken into account that the aged Lean, whom one work associate referred to as "the most bitter man that I have ever known," painted an unkind, one-sided portrayal of Spiegel. A certain amount of selected memory and distorted facts built up over the years, perhaps stemming from Lean's deep paranoia about producers.

It was Spiegel's deviousness that got to the director, but then perhaps only a "devious" man could have made *Kwai*. Spencer compared Spiegel to "a corkscrew." "He was very effective but in order to do the job, he was somewhat twisted and bent." Spiegel's two maxims left a deep impression: "Always turn your liabilities into assets, and I'm not interested in your efforts, I am only interested in your results." Spencer was also amused by how Spiegel "never attended to his correspondence," Spiegel's theory being, "It's amazing how if you leave letters that they answer themselves."

Meanwhile, Harry Cohn was dead set against the project: "How can you idiots in the New York office give a crook like Sam Spiegel two million dollars and let him go to some place like Ceylon?" Moreover, it irritated the ailing studio head that Spiegel had been permitted final cut. "He was furious because he had never allowed an independent picture to have that," said Paul Lazarus. "Harry Cohn had nothing to do with it. . . . He hated the picture."

In regards to the budget, Spiegel had everyone foxed. During that period, M. J. "Mike" Frankovich was the head of Columbia's London office. "They would have meetings and lunches and the executives would come away with very little more knowledge than they came into the restaurant with, and that's the way Sam wanted it," Spencer recalled. "No one knew what the budgets were because they were never put down properly . . . Sam was a great finagler."

As seen on his past two films, the producer was also a master at dividing and conquering. Within a few months, he had managed to separate Spencer from Lean by offering him his own productions to work on. In Brownlow's opinion, "Like Korda, he wanted to be David's sole producer." No doubt, there was a touch of that, but also Spiegel refused to tolerate the idea of former relationships threatening his own. He was fully aware that Spencer had worked for and with Lean since the early 1940s.

Lean had followed his wishes and was working with Foreman in Ceylon–a curious combination considering the director's feelings about the writer's first draft. But what Spiegel wanted, he got. Then it transpired that the two men were incapable of getting on. "We began to have friendly arguments about whether a character would scratch his face or not," said the screenwriter. Typically, Lean remembered it differently. Foreman–best-known for collaborating with director Stanley Kramer and for receiving Academy Award nominations for *Champion, The Men,* and *High Noon*–accused Lean of being "an art house director." "You have only made small British films," he said. "You have no experience of the international market."

All true, but perhaps a little rough on Lean's ears, who described the experience to Spiegel in an eight-page letter. "This is not meant to be an attack," he wrote. "You see Sam, I don't think Carl did a good job on the script. When one gets into the scenes in detail, they are awfully rough and ready, and in many cases cheap and even derivative."

Calder Willingham was then sent over–one of the "geniuses" from Spiegel's last film. It was a perfect example of Spiegel's persuasive powers because, a month earlier, Willingham had been furious with him about changing the title of his work to *The Strange One.* Willingham arrived in Ceylon with instructions to strengthen Shears's character as well as introduce a love interest, since Columbia was concerned about the lack of women in the story. But within a few days, the writer fired off a furious telegram saying: I FEEL LEAN NOT VERY RESPONSIVE AND MEET CONSIDERABLE RESISTANCE STOP ADVISE WHEN YOU WISH ME TO LEAVE FOR LONDON OR NEW YORK.

Spiegel had immediately cabled back that Lean was VERY SENSITIVE AND HIS CONTRIBUTIONS ENORMOUS IF PROPERLY COOPERATED WITH.

In the meantime, Columbia's William Graf–who, on location, acted as Spiegel's spy–was keeping the producer abreast of the "ticklish affair." Yet again, it was a nebulous experience. "These American writers really frighten me," Lean wrote to Spiegel. "I don't mean to be offensive. . . . They talk so well, and write so badly. They are *so* touchy. I have now worked with five of them, and not one has come along with a big original idea. We need an original idea. Hence my fright." He promised that he had been fair with Willingham and had given him every chance. "He may be all very fine writing about the difficulties of the immature, but I think it will be many years, or a great experience, before he can cope with an adult love story–or even sex story." (Willingham was eventually involved with Mike Nichols's *The Graduate*.) Lean then insisted that the next writer of choice had to be "a yarn spinner." "We want someone who has written original stories. We don't want a script writer who has spent his time embroidering on other people's ideas." He recommended H. E. Bates, who had worked on *Summertime,* claiming that had the novelist been involved in the beginning, they would have had a finished screenplay.

Although Spiegel wrote about approaching Bates, he was not his forceful self about making contact. Perhaps he was wary about Lean's previous collaborator for two reasons: first, the novelist would be on the director's side, and second, he was British, which hardly fit in with his plans of having American input in the screenplay. Instead, Spiegel followed Foreman's advice and went for Michael Wilson, who in spite of being blacklisted and living in Paris, continued to write for Hollywood. His uncredited work on *Friendly Persuasion* was nominated for an Oscar in 1956, while prior to the McCarthy era he shared an Academy Award for Stevens's *A Place in the Sun* and had written Mankiewicz's *Five Fingers.* "Mike had the most integrity of any-one that I have ever met in my life," said director John Berry, who was also blacklisted. "I don't remember a moment when he was insincere. . . . He never came up with quick, casual answers."

Spiegel and Wilson arrived in Ceylon on September 9, 1956, to find that Lean was content. "It was really Mike's and my script," he later said. Wilson received $10,000 for his polish. As he was blacklisted, he was forced to write under a different name–John Michael. Concerning Wilson's employment, there was a strict rule in the Horizon offices in London and New York that "on no account" was his name to be mentioned "to Columbia or anyone else."

In the meantime, the bridge, which was being built in Kitulgala, an area near Colombo, was ready by January 1957. "Sam, who hadn't finished the casting or anything, asked me what would happen if the film didn't go," recalled Ashton. "And I replied, 'You'll be the unique and the only one with a bridge to sell.' He got over that pretty quickly." Afterward, the bridge was often quoted as costing a quarter of a million dollars; in fact it only cost £20,834 ($52,085). "Sam quoted that price to make the picture sound more important," said Ashton. "It was cheap because we used local labor, elephants, and the timber was cut nearby."

In regards to casting Nicholson, there had been many stages. Even before Lean's involvement, Boulle's novel was sent to Humphrey Bogart, Noël Coward, Cary Grant, Tyrone Power, and Spencer Tracy. Then, Foreman's screenplay was delivered to all four of the great British thespians—with little success. John Gielgud immediately declined, Alec Guinness was bound by his contract to Korda's London Films, Ralph Richardson was unavailable because of theatrical commitments, and Laurence Olivier was hard at work on his own project, *The Prince and the Showgirl* with Marilyn Monroe. Other actors whom Spiegel contacted included Douglas Fairbanks, Jr., James Mason, Ray Milland, and Anthony Quayle, but Lean had not been enthusiastic about any of the suggestions. The director had recommended Eric Portman, who was starring in London's West End, whom he described as an "almost ideal Nicholson." Spiegel, however, had his eye on a more international name.

"What do you think of approaching Guinness again, or do you think that he is as wrong as ever?" he wrote to Lean.

"I had been under the illusion that you were lining up Ronald Colman for Nicholson," the director replied. "As you know, I always thought Richardson was the next best to Charlie [Laughton]. Also Guinness I am still against in that I don't think he will give us the 'size' we need."

Nevertheless, Spiegel was keen to use Guinness. When he had first tried in 1955, Korda had stood in his way. It did not matter that Korda was extremely ill, not leaving his house and keeping his business meetings to the minimum, he simply did not want Spiegel to have Guinness. Was this a last competitive cry? If it was, the film mogul would die at the beginning of 1956, freeing Guinness. Or so Spiegel thought. But the actor refused. He was said to have turned down the role three times. Then, in the late autumn, Spiegel took Guinness out to dinner. "He was a very persuasive character," the actor recalled. "I started out maintaining that I wouldn't play the role and by the end of the evening, we were discussing what kind of wig I would wear."

Once again, Spiegel was vital to bringing in the talent as he had done on *Waterfront,* but whereas Kazan had been grateful to have an old collaborator back, Lean was not. The director was said to have welcomed Guinness with the following: "They sent me you and I wanted Charles Laughton." Lean later denied saying this but, to his dying day, Guinness assured everyone that it had been the case.

Laughton had, in fact, agreed to play Nicholson, but then he broke his word. The portly thespian blamed his decision on the health of his wife, Elsa Lanchester, claiming that a mysterious disease had struck her, which eventually proved less than serious. "Nevertheless, she is very scared and he feels that he must not leave her alone," Spiegel wrote to Lean. Of course, it sounded "very fishy." "I frankly feel that Laughton is unable to go through with a diet," he continued. Under normal circumstances, it was a state of mind that Spiegel could sympathize with, but, after spending a couple of hours and "listening to his maudlin protestations, regret and sorrow," Spiegel admitted that he was glad to get rid of him, both from the meeting and from their picture. "He looks like a big 'MOBY DICK,' weighing at least 10 pounds more than when you and I saw him last. It was actually sickening to listen to his tearful explanations."

In contrast to the difficulty of casting Nicholson, there was a scramble over the role of Shears. Cary Grant had accepted the role immediately. "Fortunately or unfortunately, by that time Holden had accepted it as well," the producer wrote to Lean. "I was in a most embarrassing position with Cary who was most eager to play it. . . . He was absolutely broken-hearted. He cried actual tears when notified." Grant then offered to play the role of Warden, which had already been assigned to Jack Hawkins. Afterward, Grant approached Holden directly, begging him to withdraw. Naturally, the circumstances thrilled Spiegel, who concluded, "All this, as sad as it is, because of Cary's hurt feelings, should be very cheering to us as indicating the effect that this script has on two intelligent actors."

Before taking on the venture, Holden had talked about taking a rest from films. His recent credits included his Oscar-winning performance in Wilder's *Stalag 17, Sabrina,* and Logan's *Picnic.* But the prospect of making *Kwai* had changed all of that. "I'm like the chorus girl who was offered an apartment, a diamond necklace and a mink coat," he enthused. A huge box office attraction, Holden was one of Hollywood's most dependable stars in the 1950s.

In Spiegel's opinion, the good-looking, all-American Holden had a unique gift: he could do no wrong with the audience. It became one of Spiegel's favorite analogies regarding the importance of casting–"If Holden wanted to kill his mother, you'd want him to get away with it. Whereas if Richard Widmark wanted to save his mother, you wouldn't give a damn." For *Kwai,* Holden received $250,000 for his services plus 10 percent of the gross over the guarantee of $2.5 million. However, his lawyer from Famous Artists (Charles Feldman's agency) put a special clause in his contract that whatever the profits, the star was to receive no more than $50,000 a year. Lazarus negotiated the deal. "He said we don't want all that money piling up in the same tax year."

In regards to the role of Joyce, Shears's accomplice, Montgomery Clift was approached with "the promise of beefing up his role." While Lean was in New York, he attended a disastrous dinner with Clift, Spiegel, and Betty. "Sam had a sixth sense about these things," Betty said. "And when we arrived at the steak house [Danny's Hideaway], he said, 'Put us some place away from everyone else.' " Their party was then put in a room that was even bigger than the main dining area. "Monty was taking pills and he was still vaguely coherent, although he would answer with non sequiturs like 'the sky is blue,' which had nothing to do with anything. David would look at Sam, who would say, 'All right, Monty; we are trying to get some information from you. First of all, do you want to do this part?' That he understood. Then a waiter arrived and took our cocktail orders, Monty ordered a martini, but Sam said, 'Bring him a cup of coffee and a glass of water.' " The actor ordered steak and lamb chops with instructions that both were to be rare. "Meanwhile, Monty was drinking my crème de menthe; I didn't want to draw attention to it. But by the time his food arrived, he picked up the steak and a chop and the juices were flying. David very carefully slipped out of the banquette and left. Sam said, 'For Christ sakes, Monty.' By this time, he was hanging on Sam and then he lay down in the booth and put his head in my lap. He could not move. It was as if he was numb." Ben Gazzara was then considered for the role. But finally Geoffrey Horne, who had also been in *The Strange One,* was cast as Joyce. "It was Betty's idea," recalled Horne. "She said, 'What about little Geoffrey for the part?' 'Little Geoffrey,' was only a bit younger than her! So, I got the role that Cliff Robertson was dying to do. I know this because we were both represented by the same agent."

On location, the actors stayed in the Galle Face Hotel, the villa on the tea plantation, while Lean preferred being hermitlike and residing at the Mount Lavinia Hotel, which was near the beach. Special barracks were set up for the crew. "It was christened the Mac Spiegel Hotel, and Sam didn't like that," Ashton said. "He wanted the banner torn down." In regards to catering, Phil Hobbs, considered the best in the business, used to serve all the food from a three-ton tea wagon. Although the meat was flown in from Australia, there was a great deal of canned food. Nevertheless, the standard was rated as exceptionally high.

During the first weeks of filming, which started in November 1956, Spiegel was very supportive. "Just saw the final walk off and the end of the rail sequence and both takes are absolutely beautiful," he wrote to Lean. "I am glad that you make such excellent use of the cinema scope [*sic*] proportions and please tell Jack [Hildyard, the cameraman] that the color is first rate."

The producer's *k.A.* was in full evidence. The finest Beluga caviar had been sent out as well as an expensive lighter, which Lean referred to as a "wonderful flame-thrower." "I have a great feeling about this film," he wrote to Spiegel. "Thanks to all your efforts I think we will pull something quite exceptional out of the bag."

Then the fights began. One bone of contention concerned Lean's personal life. At the time, he was separated from Ann Todd, his actress wife, and seeing Leila Matkar, a married Indian lady. The first time his mistress came to Ceylon, Lean sensed that Spiegel was trying to prevent her visit, but the producer sent one of his eloquent letters, assuring Lean that it was not the case. "As you well know, she [Leila] is highly strung; highly feminine; highly loyal and devoted to you;

consequently highly subjected to erroneous impressions." Leila
Matkar eventually joined Lean, but in general the producer tended to
be against the presence of wives or loved ones on location. Spiegel's
view was based on the information that Graf was feeding him, that
the filming in the jungle was extremely tough and the weather was
appallingly hot and humid. "There was a big battle over that," said
Ashton. "Jack [Hawkins] wouldn't go and Sam finally allowed Doreen
[Hawkins] to join us."

Lean was determined that his girlfriend should join him at
Christmastime. "I promise not to neglect my work," he wrote. This
was, it should be stressed, after Leila, who was psychologically fragile,
had been ill. She had just had electric shock treatment, which led to
her failing to recognize Lean's photograph. "Strangely enough, she
recognized Sam's," Betty Spiegel recalled.

Besides spending considerable time with Leila, Betty was one of
the few who understood her. "She talked very fast, as if she had just
jumped out of the Bible," she said. "I used to translate for Sam and
David. 'I have partaken of the sufficiency and I am quite replete,' was
her way of saying that she had had enough to eat." Although
extremely touching as a character, Leila was mentally troubled and
had needed the electric shock treatment twice. "I'll never forget the
top of her bureau in her hotel suite–there wasn't a place to put an
aspirin," Betty said. "It was covered in lipsticks which were not wound
back in their case, hairpins, brushes, combs, balls of hair, loose pills,
and other jumble . . . I really think there was a misconnection in her
head." Yet she had Lean's undying attention.

Leila then had a fateful meeting with Spiegel and the actor André
Morell, who had a role in *Kwai*, which led to her canceling her
December trip. As soon as Lean got wind of this, he fired off a cable
which told Leila to "cease contact" with Spiegel and rebook herself on
KLM. He then blasted the producer with a stinging four-page letter:
"You obviously believe that a film contract entitles you to complete
ownership of a human being. You are a dictator with no respect for
human dignity and individuality. You believe that the end always
justifies the means, and if the tragic recent story of your own noble
race has not made you question your methods and way of thinking,
how can my small voice hope to reach you?"

Spiegel cabled back and dismissed Lean's letter as "degradingly unconscionable": [I am] WASHING MY HANDS OF ENTIRE ISSUE AND HOPE YOU WILL LEARN TO APPRECIATE FRIENDSHIP IN FUTURE.

In regards to Leila, Spiegel and his office had, in the end, been more than helpful. They booked the hospital for her various treatments, as well as making frequent appointments with a certain Dr. Salmon. Moreover, Isabella Leitner, Garfein's previous assistant, was put in charge of baby-sitting her in New York. "Captive in her limousine, Leila told me everything," she said. "But when I called back to arrange dinner, she didn't know who I was." Yet in the weeks that followed, Leila was never out of Leitner's apartment. "She was always dressed in a sari and incessantly talking about Barbara Hutton and all these names. My husband, who is particularly compassionate to someone in trouble, was very patient. But I often wished that she went the hell back to India."

Another bone of contention between Spiegel and Lean was whether the rushes of the film should be sent to England directly, or kept in Ceylon. True to form, Lean demanded immediate access. Spiegel tried to reason otherwise and referred to his experiences on *The African Queen*. "We did not see rushes for eleven weeks until our return to London and the delight with which we waded through the stuff was encouraging and we were far removed from the scene of shooting. Of course we had constant reports from the cutter as to the quality . . . by cable." Fortunately, Lean won this particular battle. "I must see what I am getting on the screen," he argued. "I am far too used to seeing things under bad conditions for them to depress me. . . . I have never worked in this Cinemascope [*sic*] medium before, and although it doesn't alarm me in the least, I want to feel my way into the unusual and forceful. . . . If I am without this I will tend to overshoot out of fear of not being covered. . . . If I were at the North Pole with no airline I would have to do without it, but I'm not. I'm a cutter, Sam, first and foremost. Don't take that away from me."

The director and producer frequently corresponded about the actors. Initially, Spiegel took a great interest in James Donald, who was playing the doctor, whom he described as "the voice of sanity" in the picture and "almost the editorial of the author." In regards to the actor's appearance, he suggested that his "youthful honesty and enthusiasm" be emphasized. "I would try to keep his eyes youthful against slightly graying temples. I think by keeping him closely shaven throughout the picture, while many others display flamboyant moustaches and beards, he would endear himself to the audience by his looks as well." Lean, on the other hand, could not stand Donald. The actor had *not* endeared himself by saying that only George Cukor could handle his talent. He had also convinced the other English actors, such as Guinness, that the film, which was based on a satirical novel by a Frenchman, was bound to be anti-British.

The relationship between Guinness and his director was already difficult enough without the interference of others, and Spiegel was called upon to act as the necessary intermediary. Just as Spiegel was capable of infuriating people, he also had the force of character to be an effective peacemaker. "Guinness had an entirely different concept of the part than David and I," Spiegel recalled. The actor had a tongue-in-cheek approach and was trying to inject humor into his lines. "I totally agreed with David, that it would be disastrous." Both producer and director were keen to build up Nicholson as a tragic, misled character who had to be "made understandable" to an audience. As Lean wrote in his notes: "If they don't understand and admire him in spite of his misguided actions, his stature will diminish– and being the cornerstone of the film–the size of the film will diminish with him."

At first, a mild compromise had been reached between Lean and Guinness, allowing him to play Nicholson with a Scottish accent. But Spiegel was strongly against this. "I am sure I don't have to repeat what you and I have discussed quite frequently and that is the absolutely over-riding attempt to keep everybody's speech including Alec's to certain international norm and giving the picture the imprint of over Britishness that is inherent in this story," he wrote. Guinness eventually dropped the accent.

At one point, Lean was so frustrated by the actor that tears started to roll down his cheeks. "I tried to calm him," Spiegel said. "We had dinner together . . . and I went to Alec that same night . . . and I don't think that I've ever been so indignant with an actor. . . . I screamed, I really told him that what he was doing was destroying the director and the picture." The following day, Spiegel joined them on the bridge, where they were shooting the scene. "He [David] was still under the impact of the previous night, so I had to get on the set with him, and I kind of mediated between the two of them and referred David's instructions to Alec, and Alec's instructions to David for a good hour until they started communicating directly with each other."

No doubt, Spiegel's account of the event had a touch of Spiegelese, but between the two talented and deeply stubborn characters, a mediator was needed. Guinness's tempers tended to be particularly fraught after filming with Sessue Hayakawa. The basic problem was that the distinguished Japanese actor, who had had a career in Hollywood, was getting old and had lost his grasp of English. "He says 'yes' all the time," wrote Lean. Hayakawa, who would warm up after a few takes, was also of the "Hollywood starlet school of script reading"–he only read his own lines. Adding to the problems was the potion that Hayakawa used for his bloodshot eyes. "The liquid clears his eyes . . . but halfway through the scene, it comes streaming from his nose." Unfortunately, this tended to happen at the very moment that Guinness had found his pace.

Betty Spiegel remembered the British actor as keeping his distance. "Alec had a fly swatter . . . he would count the flies–one, two, three, four . . . he was obsessed, like something out of *Faust*." Hawkins and Holden made more of an effort to socialize with the crew. "It really was a godforsaken place," she said. "We didn't walk out at night because there were snakes and things."

And other dangers. "It used to have the highest murder rate in the world," said Ashton. "The locals would chop themselves up regularly." One night, after dining with Lean, Spiegel suggested a late-night stroll by the ocean. Out of nowhere, three youths appeared and the director was horrified to see that one of the gang was running his knife up and down Spiegel's back. "I said, 'Put that knife away,' and Sam said, 'What are you saying?' . . . I said, 'This man's got a knife at your back,' and it was as if ten feet of film had been cut out . . . I could hear Sam gulp even with the sea in the distance. And I turned round and I said, 'Look, just fuck off.'" Both men were terrified, but as soon as the gang member put the knife down, Spiegel began to roar and retaliate. "He stuck his hand in his trouser pocket, stuck a finger out and said, 'I'm now going to shoot you full of bullets, the shit will just pour out of you onto the grass,' and a whole string of obscenities, actually," Lean recalled. "And I said, 'Sam, will you shut your fucking mouth.' But he was in such a trembling state that he wouldn't and he kept on shouting." Eventually, the director guided him back to the Mount Lavinia Hotel. "Sam was up the flight of stairs like a rocket . . . jet-propelled . . . the next thing I knew he was yelling at the concierge over the desk and saying there were a gang of men, murderers out there with knives and guns and I don't know what they hadn't got by the time Sam had finished."

In the meantime, the four Thai actresses–Vilaiwan Seeboonreaung, Ngamta Suphaphongs, Javanart Punynchoti, and Kannikar Dowklee–were the film set's casual amusement. "Since no one could remember their names, they were nicknamed," said Betty. "Anna from *Anna and the King of Siam,* Gams because she had very long legs for a short girl, Rita because her black hair had a reddish hue. But the fourth–they were all friendly–shall we say–they liked to have fun, and since she didn't sleep with anyone for about a week, she was called Eadie because 'Eadie Was a Lady.' " One night when both the wives of Holden and Hawkins had gone off to Colombo, the Thai sirens approached her. " 'Miss Betty,' they said, 'okay you tell Mr. Bill Holden and Mr. Jack Hawkins that we sleep with them tonight. They no want? Okay, we sleep with Mr. David Lean and Mr. Alec Guinness.' " She delivered the message to the director and principal actor. "They looked at each other and David said, 'Well, Alec, I for one, won't bloody well take them up on their offer. We were, after all, second choice.' "

In the final months of the shoot, the fact of the film being $800,000 over budget and behind schedule did not make for happy relations between Spiegel and Lean. Yet, on a project this vast–the actual shoot was six months long–it was bound to be the case. Often, toward the end of filming, the producer and director tend to be at loggerheads–a case of a financial concern versus an artistic one. According to Lean, they had had to "skimp, skimp, skimp." "We used a lot of Singhalese with white faces as prisoners," he told his biographer. To be fair to Spiegel, what a waste of money had they flown anyone out (words bound to irk all filmmakers), and who remembers the extras?

"The day before the train was going over the bridge, Bill Holden said, 'I have a surprise,'" Betty recalled. He had covered a bamboo globe with *The Times* newspapers. It was about ten feet high and had a little burner underneath that was filled with rags dipped in oil. As soon as he lit the damp tatters, his creation rose from the smoke. Then the gentle breeze started blowing the fire balloon toward the direction of the wooden bridge. Spiegel was aghast. "He said, 'Bill, if that balloon lands on the bridge, you had better be on the next plane for England.' So everyone jumped in jeeps and on bicycles and raced down to the bridge. . . . Fortunately, it just floated straight on by."

The next day—the first attempt to blow up the bridge—was a complete fiasco. It had become a huge event, and viewing its destruction was Spiegel's thank-you to all the local dignitaries who had helped with the production. The prime minister of Ceylon, Solomon Bandaranaike, headed the band of a hundred invitees, which included ministers and important businessmen. Ashton compared it to the Ascot races. "We had built a big platform down the river. They were dressed up in their finery. Some had traveled overnight. And all they saw was a train cross the river."

In spite of endless rehearsals with the train driver, detailed discussions with three men from Britain's ICI (Imperial Chemical Industries) about the explosives, and an elaborate system of cameras being concealed in dugouts and trenches for the crew, it turned out to be a much awaited nonevent. Spiegel's every fear had been realized. The producer was so nervous that he was taking tranquilizers. "He took them out twice," recalled Ashton. "And when I asked, 'What are those?' he replied that he had a cold. . . . David was very nonchalant about it all."

Spiegel, Lean, and the explosives expert were down in the hut, which had a panel with lights that lit up when each of the five camera operators had switched on to film the bridge. The train started and, one by one, the lights went on until the last, which failed to come on. Lean had to make up his mind: allow the explosion to go off and risk the life of the cameraman, or abort the operation. "Don't blow up the bridge," he cried. The final cameraman—Freddy Ford—had forgotten to turn his camera on. In the meantime, the train continued and tore through the sand dragon—the pile of sand that had been put there as a precautionary measure—and went into the London transport bus that contained the generator.

"We rushed across, the train wasn't very damaged but it had gone off the tracks," Ashton said. "All we needed was a crane. . . . We were told that the only one in Colombo belonged to the Ministry of Works." The production designer called him up only to have his request denied. "He replied, 'My wife and I were the only people not to be asked to your party. I am very cross because I have looked after you since you have been here.' " Eventually, the train was jacked back into place. "We had to do it six inches at the time and by about 2:00 A.M., the following morning, we got the train back," Ashton recalled. Then the bridge caught fire from an oil lamp. "Sure enough there were fire extinguishers all along the bridge but they were empty, just these rather nice red cases. We started shoveling earth in hats, hands, you name it, we used it."

Meanwhile, Spiegel was infuriated by Lean's gallant gesture of giving dinner to the offending cameraman. "You can't take the biggest idiot to dinner to congratulate him for fucking up the scene," he reasoned.

Lean was never quite satisfied with the blowing-up sequence since he had wanted both the bridge and train to fall into the water. Another complaint concerned his use of a double for the final scene with Donald saying "madness, madness." Many decades later, he bitingly complained about both. Yet at the time, neither issue was mentioned in his correspondence with Spiegel. ". . . finished with Bill Holden by means of a hectic rush. I hope this does something to mitigate my 'criminal expenditure,' " he wrote. "You and I seem to leap in exaggeration when we put pen to paper. . . . I must say I can't wait to get through with the rest of it. I'm an exhausted wreck and nervy to boot. I am so longing to rest and sleep after this marathon which has been much stiffer than you realize." Later in the letter, Lean started to doubt the film's content. "These men have been marched to the camp to build the bridge and this is the first thing the audience will see of their work. It's just like a group of jolly boy scouts having pranks with the scoutmaster . . . sorry to go on like this but it has given me an awful hit below the belt. I didn't realize the thing could be so misinterpreted and it's nothing to do with me or my style of work–and yet it will be shown as my work. You would feel the same in my position."

The director was, in his own words, "an exhausted wreck" who was starting to doubt his work. William Graf had also reported back that he was "slowing down," and so Spiegel coped with the situation– he got him out of there. Yet it was held against Spiegel. He was not viewed as the voice of reason–instead he became the voice of treason. Lean's brilliance and scope as a filmmaker aside, emotionally, he could be unreasonable and immature. For whatever reason, he had an idée fixe about Spiegel–he was "a dictator with no respect for human dignity and individuality." As a result, whatever Spiegel did–good or bad–the die was cast. It did not matter that he enjoyed his company, appreciated his intelligence, and did two magnificent films with him. Instead, Lean always used to return to the same, rather sour conclusion that Spiegel was, after all, that "dictator." Was it his Quaker background that held him back from enjoying the rewards of working with Spiegel?

Spiegel, on the other hand, was magnanimous. "Nobody else could have shot that picture as well as he did, let's begin with that," he later said. "I remember the first screening of *Bridge on the River Kwai* was such a wonderful occasion for me that I hugged David."

But typically, Spiegel was parsimonious when dealing with his film crew. They were not sent first class, which was how the film unit usually traveled, but flown on a Flying Tiger–a freight plane. Graf had warned: "You're going to have a riot on your hands." However, the producer was spared such an event.

Due to Lean's complicated tax situation, the picture was cut in Paris. He was staying at the Queen Elizabeth, while Spiegel was at the George V. Of course, there were stories of Spiegel gallivanting around town and having endless parties, but he was also deeply involved in the editing. "I had quarrels with David in the cutting room because he wanted to cut too much," he recalled. There was an argument about the ending; it was at Spiegel's insistence that it remained ambiguous, with the idea "that the audience should make their own choice." Like David Selznick, he belonged to the school of showmen who believed in the importance of getting the spectators so involved that they wrote their own ending. Lean, on the other hand, wanted to make it clearer.

Since the dubbing sessions were held at Shepperton Studios in England, Lean's tax problems prevented him from attending. He had, however, left extensive instructions for Win Ryder–in charge of the film's sound–regarding the noise of the insects, the rustling of foliage, and so forth. Naturally, Spiegel had been involved.

Ryder admired Spiegel particularly for his instinctive knowledge, even if he had comic memories of the producer. ("He'd clutch me and I'd bounce off his fat tummy," he recalled.) Dorothy Morris Payne, the assistant of Malcolm Arnold, the composer who immortalized Kenneth J. Alford's "Colonel Bogey" tune, was both amused and a little exasperated by Spiegel. Their first meeting was at the Dorchester Hotel. "Malcolm said, 'You know he'll be in his dressing gown and will come rushing out, saying he was on the telephone all morning with America,'" said Morris Payne. "He did and his dressing gown was a beautiful silk one." However, during the sessions, he worked everyone "to death" because of "his enthusiasm." "It was the first time that I thought that the union was a good idea," Morris Payne admitted. Afterward, Spiegel used to give her a lift to the studio in his chauffeur-driven Rolls-Royce. "He treated everyone in the same expansive way."

The producer had promised to have *Kwai*'s print ready by September and–much to Lean's amazement–he delivered. Subsequently, Spiegel dealt with Columbia, New York. "The night that Sam brought in his picture, a funny coincidence happened," Leo Jaffe recalled. "Harry Cohn brought in one of his pictures–*Pal Joey* with Rita Hayworth–and we had screenings in the projection room two nights running on Saturday and Sunday and executives were asked to come with their wives to see both. It was so obvious that Harry had a good picture, while Sam had a masterpiece, and he never forgave Sam for that."

The film was an immediate hit in England. Jules Buck and his wife had attended the premiere on October 2, 1957. "Otto [Preminger] and Sam were talking. And Sam said, 'Otto, just think, baby, years ago–standing here with all the dukes and the tiaras and a picture which is British, British, British to the core–where would we be?' And Otto said, 'Well, you tell me, Sam, where would we be?' And he replied, 'Right here!' It had defiance. In other words, he would never compromise, he rose to heights that you had to admire."

Lean's tax problems prevented him from attending the opening. He and Leila were at the Grand Hotel, Venice. Spiegel's office had kept him abreast of all the action. "I have seen the advert in the *Sunday Times*. What a size! All the same, they've gone a bit far haven't they?" he wrote to the producer. "It's way over my head. My word, we film people don't half carry on when we think we've joined the arts!" A month after the film had come out, it was still playing at full capacity at the Plaza Theatre in London.

But after the excitement of the film's success, the director's letters and telegrams began to refer to the bogus screenplay credit—Pierre Boulle being named as the screenwriter—and the fact that "A Sam Spiegel Production" was looming above all the other titles. According to Brownlow, "Lean had never had worse billing, even in his early days." Both were to be major issues when Lean arrived in New York. Spiegel's need to have his name above the title was essential to his image as a producer. It was the emperor's stamp—showing that he was above the cast and crew. Kazan was the first of the directors to complain, and not the last. On their next production together, Lean would insist on having the same billing as Spiegel.

Even the studio was shocked by Spiegel's megalomania. Somewhat outrageously, he had tried to limit the Columbia credit to the trademark at the beginning and no other mention! Paul Lazarus and the other studio executives balked, and rectified the situation.

In regards to the bogus screenplay credit, the producer had legitimate reasons. Lazarus remembered a division of opinion about the picture at the studio. "They weren't sure whether the title was right. There were no women of substance in the picture and the sales department was very concerned." As the vice president of publicity at Columbia, Lazarus had to fight to enter the picture for the Oscars. "It meant opening the picture for one week in Los Angeles before the end of the year and opening it simultaneously in New York for a week—almost like a road show . . . and in January and February beginning to spread in major cities . . . gambling that we would win the Academy Awards. It made everyone very nervous."

Taking into account that *Kwai* was considered a risk, any hint of blacklisted writers might have been a disaster. It was three years before Otto Preminger cleared the way for blacklisted writers. When Spiegel confided to Lean that it will "ruin our chances, baby," making reference to Wilson and Foreman, he meant it. "It was a very difficult time," said Lazarus. "The blacklisted writers were all working incognito. . . . Sam would have risked the project if he put their names on."

As far as his decision to credit Boulle, Spiegel clearly sensed—and was no doubt advised—that it was the least incriminating way to handle the problem. But why was Lean so angry? "The script was written by two people—and I was one of them," he wrote to Columbia's Frankovich.

Curiously enough, during all of Michael Wilson's correspondence with Spiegel he was more concerned about their next project, which was called *Grand Tour*. His good-luck letter hardly showed sour grapes: "Accept my wishes for a successful opening of Kwai and long American run . . . [adding] to your fame and fortune." Indeed, the actress Betsy Blair—a close friend of Wilson's, who described her career as "definitely" suffering during the McCarthy era—remembered there being "a good feeling about Sam" and his treatment of those on the blacklist.

When there was a leak in the press about the screenplay's authorship, Carl Foreman immediately telegrammed George Seaton, the president of the Academy, in the producer's favor. I HAD NO FURTHER CONNECTION WITH THE PRODUCTION STOP . . . AND I HAVE NO INTENTION OR DESIRE TO CHALLENGE OR DISPUTE THE CREDITS STOP I UNDERSTAND THAT IT IS A FINE FILM THAT DOES CREDIT TO EVERYONE INVOLVED AND I CONGRATULATE SAM SPIEGEL ON HIS ACHIEVEMENT.

As predicted, the producer won his second Academy Award for *The Bridge on the River Kwai*, and Lean won his first. In total, their picture brought in seven Oscars, including best actor for Alec Guinness and best screenplay for Boulle. There was every reason to rejoice—the sparring partners had scored—but Lean could not resist irritating Spiegel.

When a journalist held a microphone under his nose and asked who really wrote the script, Lean replied, "You're asking the 64,000 dollar question, and as you have not got 64,000 dollars I'm not prepared to tell you." All the radio stations quickly picked up the provocative remark. "Sam went berserk," Lean recalled. "I remember standing outside the theatre after the Oscar ceremony with Sam holding his Oscar for best picture and shaking it at me in fury. I shouting back at him, brandishing mine. It was a ridiculous scene."

Mrs. Spiegel was unaware of the incident. "I was in a slight stupor from the boredom of the event, best picture was last on the bill," she recalled. "During the ceremony, I had been thinking three thousand things. How I would console Sam if he didn't win the Oscar, and how I would deal with him if he did. It was a double-edged sword."

Meanwhile, *Kwai* was a spectacular success in the States and launched Spiegel as Columbia's greatest asset—the producer who put the studio back in the black. Nevertheless, after receiving the first statement of the film's earnings, Spiegel and Albert Heit, his New York lawyer, were staggered to discover that his supposed 50-50 deal with the studio was not all that it seemed. "Because Columbia were taking so much off the top," explained Heit. Spiegel learned from the mistake and insisted on 60-40 in his favor on the next production. Such a percentage then allowed for distribution fees and other expenses that Columbia was charging before arriving at the net proceeds.

After his experience on *The Strange One,* which was cross-collateralized with *Kwai* and lost him $400,000, Spiegel made quite sure that it was the last time. Hence forward, cross-collateralization was out of the question. "Each film was to stand on its own," said his lawyer.

Kwai became Spiegel's highest earning picture. At the end of the last century, Heit recorded the picture as reaching a worldwide gross of $65 million in rental earnings (this does not include box office earnings). By 1980, it was ranked by *Variety* as twenty-third in the top-earning films. Yet Lean always claimed that he never received his share of the profits. "That is unfair and untrue," insisted Heit. "First of all, Sam did not handle the money, Columbia did." On the six monthly statements from the studio, Lean's name is there, right under Holden's.

Still, Lean never collected from the William Holden Fund. As previously explained, Holden was entitled to 10 percent of the gross of *Kwai*, but because of tax reasons, it had been arranged that "whatever the profits," the actor was *only* to be paid $50,000 each year and any money over that was to be held for him by Columbia in a special fund. However, *Kwai* had been an unexpected hit and Holden was making a great deal more than $50,000. By 1975, the money that had piled up in his fund was slightly in excess of $2,820,000. Holden tried to alter the situation, which led to various unsuccessful legal battles between himself, Spiegel, and the studio.

In the meantime, the yearly interest being made on Holden's fund was divided between Spiegel and Columbia. "Sometimes we were collecting as much as $100,000 per year," said Heit. Surely, it was unfair that Lean never collected from the fund? "That's the way the ball bounces," offered Spiegel's lawyer. Or to quote the Italians about luck: "Piove sempre sul bagnato [It only rains on the wet]."

Chapter Nineteen

SUDDENLY, LAST SUMMER

Hailed as the New Dream Merchant, Spiegel's next project, *Suddenly, Last Summer,* showed confidence and offered a change from his other pictures. It was based on a short work by Tennessee Williams, which had been the second play of *Garden District*–a double bill that had included *Something Outspoken,* and had first appeared at the York Playhouse Theatre in New York City on January 7, 1958.

The producer's attention was alerted to the play when flying to Europe. The air stewardess had refused to give him a sleeping pill. "I read an English newspaper instead, and saw that Patricia Neal was opening in *Suddenly, Last Summer.* I thought: 'Now what the hell makes her go to London to make that?' "

The theme of the story–an oedipal triangle of sorts–is set in New Orleans. Violet Venable (Katharine Hepburn), a rich benefactress, tries to bribe Dr. Cukrowicz (Montgomery Clift), a young neurosurgeon from Lion's View, the state asylum, to lobotomize her beautiful niece, Catherine Holly (Elizabeth Taylor). Violet wants the operation performed for several reasons. Mainly, because she's jealous of the relationship that Catherine had had with her late son, the poet Sebastian. And also, to prevent her niece from ruining Sebastian's reputation. Catherine has not stopped talking about her cousin's death the previous summer. The climax of the play occurs when Catherine has flashbacks of the events that had happened "suddenly, last summer."

Her homosexual cousin had taken her to Spain and had forced her to wear a tight white bathing suit—"a scandal to the jay birds"—in order to lure young men for him. It had turned horribly wrong and she had witnessed Sebastian being dismembered and partially devoured by street urchins, some of whom he had previously tried to pick up.

Tennessee Williams was "greatly surprised" that Spiegel saw his play as a film. "But I certainly wasn't inclined to discourage him in his madness," he said. Initially, Williams sold the rights to *Suddenly, Last Summer* "over the phone," without the use of Audrey Wood, his agent. Spiegel offered him $50,000 and 20 percent of the net profits, as well as $300,000 on completion of the film. "I thought that was a good deal so I said okay." Afterward, Spiegel told the *New York Times* that he and the playwright envisioned the film "as a Grand Guignol horror." It was not the first time that the producer was taken with Williams's work—he had been interested in *The Rose Tattoo,* but his attempt to buy it was turned down.

The contrarily choosy playwright was fond of Spiegel. "I think he rates next to Gadg in my list of normal male friends," Williams wrote to Maria St. Just (she was the executor of his estate until her death, and used to call Spiegel, "Spieglie Wieglie"), "and I think I like my normal male friends a bit more than the others." Williams was equally taken by Betty.

"Tennessee ratted on me once," she recalled. There had been an argument between Spiegel and Williams about whom she was accompanying that night. "Sam said, 'She's going with me,' and Tennessee said, 'She may not be going with either of us,' and named a guy who I was kind of seeing, and Sam said, 'Who's that?' and Tenn told him, hoping that Sam would be so angry that he wouldn't want to take me. I called Tenn and said, 'You Benedict Arnold.' He said, 'I had a few drinks and it kind of slipped out.' " Betty understood what he was aiming for. "But it worked the other way around. Sam became determined to take me."

It was Williams's idea that Gore Vidal should adapt his play into a film. The young writer received $35,000 for his services. "Yes, it was the Bird [Vidal's nickname for Williams], the glorious Bird," Vidal recalled. "Tennessee always tried a name on me, but none ever stuck, although he did come up with 'Fruit of Eden.' I had already had one successful play on Broadway called *Visit to a Small Planet,* and I had done three or four screenplays under my contract to MGM–one of them being *Ben-Hur,* to disputed credit."

Screenplay conferences between Williams, Vidal, and Spiegel took place at the Dupont Plaza Hotel in Miami in November 1958. "Tennessee was in a manic mood," Vidal said. "He was on something, but I knew so little about drugs in those days." Williams was taking downers, but he also seemed to be on something like speed.

It was then agreed that Vidal write the screenplay on his own and meet with Spiegel on a regular basis. These sessions were sweated out in either New York or Miami. After about three weeks, the thirty-three-year-old turned out his first draft. "Sam couldn't believe it, he wanted me to work for ever and ever, because he wanted his money's worth," he recalled. "I remember telling him, 'Yes, but what I do in the first draft is generally the best, and people usually end up going back to it,' but he said, 'No, baby, no, baby, we must work harder.' "

Around that period, he ran into Molly Kazan, the director's wife, who asked him how he found Spiegel as a taskmaster. "I replied, 'Well, he's boring but he's very bright. He's boring because he wants to talk about movies and he doesn't know much about them, but he has very sharp instincts and I think, that in a crazy way, he has feel for a story which not many producers have.' " Moreover, Vidal was impressed that Spiegel had chosen to make the film. "By himself, he had picked a minor play of Tennessee's that no one else had wanted."

During their screenplay conferences in Miami, Betty Spiegel was very much around. "Gore and I laughed more than I had in my life," she said. "Gore was *so* mean but then he was *so* pretty." Nevertheless, the giggling started to annoy her husband, who–no doubt feeling left out–accused Betty of being a distraction to Vidal. "It got to the point that he wouldn't let us go out to dinner alone." On one occasion, he even locked them in their hotel rooms. "We were treated like two bad children, but Sam had forgotten that the maid came in at night to turn down the beds," she said. "Well, we escaped. Bill Hamilton, George's brother, came to visit and we were out until 4:00 A.M. What did Sam care? He was downstairs playing gin rummy."

When Betty left, Vidal and Spiegel's relationship developed into "a bad marriage." "Sam would say, 'Why do you take the *New York Times* and put it out of order and fold it wrong?' and I replied, 'That's the way I read the *New York Times*.' 'Yes, but I haven't read it.' " Vidal sensed that "quarreling, complaining, and bitching at others" was the producer's technique of controlling them. "I learned quickly how to escalate with him because I knew all the steps by which he would go. How he would taunt, object, criticize until he got to a place where he felt he could dominate. I would skip all the steps and it would drive him crazy."

Vidal was to have more of a rapport with Spiegel than anyone else who worked on the project. True to character, Spiegel did the groundwork prior to production–he employed Joseph Mankiewicz to direct and was behind the casting–but in many respects he was more absent during this picture than was the case with his three earlier triumphs. A reason for this may have been that Mankiewicz was not a suitable sparring partner for Spiegel.

Unlike Huston, Kazan, and Lean, Mankiewicz had been an extremely successful producer before becoming a director. From the mid-1930s, Mankiewicz had made his name at MGM as Joan Crawford's producer, as well as being behind a variety of films such as *Fury*, *The Adventures of Huckleberry Finn*, and *The Keys of the Kingdom*–the latter being made for Twentieth Century-Fox. He knew all the tricks of the trade, and was too self-sufficient to ever be thoroughly wound up by the former S. P. Eagle. "Of course Joe got highly irritated," said Rosemary Mankiewicz, his widow. "But there was always a warmth between them."

The question remains whether Mankiewicz would have actually worked for Spiegel if his career had been soaring. At the end of the 1950s, the director's two Oscar-winning classics–*A Letter to Three Wives* and *All About Eve*–were distant memories. He had turned his back on Hollywood, dismissing the place as an "ivory ghetto" and "a cultural desert," and had moved to the East Coast with the idea of getting involved in the theater. But unlike Spiegel, his career post-Hollywood had diminished. Mankiewicz's film adaptation of Graham Greene's *The Quiet American* did quiet business at the box office in 1958. Previous to that, *The Barefoot Contessa* and *Guys and Dolls* fared better financially. However, considering Mankiewicz's reputation, both films had serious flaws.

In Vidal's opinion, the director was an example of Spiegel's cunning technique of getting first-rate people on their way down for nothing. He sensed that Spiegel had done this with Kazan, whose movie career had been going through a lull before *On the Waterfront*. "Sam had a truffle nose for this," he said. "Joe Mankiewicz had had three flops in a row, and he knew that Joe was due for a hit again."

Keen to show who was the boss, Spiegel flexed his muscles with Mankiewicz. "He was given the script and told 'this is what you make'–the old Hollywood way," Vidal recalled. During the first meeting between the writer, director, and producer, Spiegel insisted on showing off his recent proofs of success–paintings by Cézanne, Manet, and Soutine. "They were all in a big closet in his suite at the Lombardy Hotel," the writer remembered. "And as we were leaving, Mankiewicz said, 'You know those pictures . . . Every one will be in hock at the end of the picture.' He just knew that Sam was such a gambler that he could fuck it up. He didn't actually. But that was Joe's reading of him."

No doubt, it was difficult for Mankiewicz to shake off the Spiegel that he had first met in Hollywood in the early 1940s. S. P. Eagle–the man more famous for his New Year's Eve parties than his productions–while he, Mankiewicz, had been riding high. The director was also dismissive of the art collection. "Isn't it interesting that Sam has the worst picture by each of those famous painters?" he had remarked. "He has the name but not the game." It was an opinion that was also voiced by Lew Wasserman and John Huston. Their difference about art aside, Mankiewicz needed a hit just as Spiegel needed a woman's director.

Described by Richard Burton as "an Oxford don manqué," Mankiewicz was meticulous about research. Later, when preparing for *Cleopatra*, he would read Plutarch to get all the nuances right; during *Suddenly, Last Summer*, he was determined to find the right lunatic asylum. "When I speak with Tennessee, I will find out the exact location of the one to which he had referred to," he wrote to Spiegel. In regards to the prefrontal lobotomy, he became somewhat of an expert. "Enough to know it is essential that a neuro-surgeon be lined up with whom I can consult and who will be available as technical advisor both in regard to equipment and procedure during the actual shooting of the scene." Mankiewicz also spent time at the Manhattan State Hospital as well as getting permission to go through the photographic files of the National Association for Mental Health. "As soon as I acquire a practical amount of material, I will dispatch it to you," he advised. "It should be studied by the art, wardrobe and make-up departments asap."

Moreover, the director was obsessive about punctuation. "If Joe dictated anything to you, he would give you the commas, the full stops, the colons every time, and he knew," said Elaine Schreyeck, the "continuity lady" on *Suddenly, Last Summer.* "That's how he worked, and one appreciated it; he was a writer."

Mankiewicz's innate sense of casting, nonetheless, had not been called upon for the film. Instead, it was Showman Sam who had chosen the players. Originally, he had the idea of teaming Elizabeth Taylor with Vivien Leigh. Spiegel was on unfamiliar turf with the female-dominated project, which perhaps explained his eagerness to go with talent already associated with Tennessee Williams's work. Was he also trying to emulate Selznick and Korda, two producers who had been instrumental in Vivien Leigh's career? He was certainly serious about the British actress; she had even become a clause in Taylor's contract. An announcement had been released to the newspapers. "I think Vivien and Liz will be good together," Spiegel was quoted as saying. (Although privately he only ever referred to Taylor as Elizabeth, since the star abhors being called Liz.) "After all, Liz looks like a young version of Vivien Leigh."

It was, possibly, a combination of this statement—the idea of playing the "old" Liz—as well as being mentally fragile that caused Vivien Leigh to ultimately decline. Two years later, she would appear in the film version of Williams's novel *The Roman Spring of Mrs. Stone.*

Vidal also tried to get involved in the casting. He pushed Joanne Woodward forward to play Catherine Holly and Bette Davis to play Mrs. Venable. "But I lost on both pitches. Shrewd Sam, he said, 'Baby, Davis has played it, Hepburn hasn't.' In other words, you would know that Bette Davis would cut out the girl's brain, and you wouldn't think that Katharine Hepburn—such a healthy person—would."

In the meantime, the production had gone unusually fast for a Horizon picture. "Elizabeth had certain dates," Vidal recalled. "It had

Regina Schwitz, Samuel's mother, c. 1894. Queen-like, she wore the pants in the Spiegel household.

Simon Spiegel, Samuel's father, c. 1894. He was a pillar of the Zionist community in Jaroslav.

Samuel Spiegel standing outside his tent in Palestine in April 1921. At nineteen, he was lean, muscular, and a hero of the Hashomer Hatzair, a Zionist youth movement.

Jerusalem – Ray and Samuel Spiegel with daughter Alisa in 1927. Shortly afterwards, Spiegel walked out on his wife and child and left for America. Before the abrupt departure, he predicted: "I'll either become a very rich and famous man, or I'll die like a dog in the gutter."

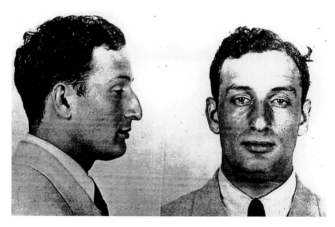

A mugshot of Samuel Spiegel, taken in San Francisco Prison, July 1928. He was arrested for avoiding the U.S. immigration authorities, falsifying checks, and being a fugitive from justice.

Boris Morros and S. P. Eagle (aka Spiegel) showing off their Box Office 'Blue Ribbon' award for Tales of Manhattan (1942). Morros was Spiegel's first Hollywood partner. "He looked like Sam's jolly brother," said Ingo Preminger.

From left: Orson Welles, Konstantin Shayne, Loretta Young, and feared gossip columnist Hedda Hopper on the set of The Stranger (1946). Although Welles dismissed the thriller, it was the only one of his pictures to make a profit on first release.

Lynne Ruth Baggett—a Warner Bros. starlet from Wichita Falls—who became the second Mrs. Spiegel on April 10, 1948. One of her many admirers described her as other-wordly since everything about her glowed.

In August 1947, Spiegel's brother and family came and stayed at his Beverly Hills home. It was a rare family get-together. From left: Rosa, Shalom's wife; Raya, Shalom's daughter (now Judge Raya Dreben); Sam and Shalom Spiegel.

Columbia Studios. From left: director John Huston, Walter Huston, Spiegel, and writer Peter Viertel on the set of We Were Strangers *(1949). It was Horizon Pictures's first production and a difficult film to make. "We were always ten pages ahead of the camera, which is no fun," said Viertel.*

Sam and Lynne Spiegel, snapped by Life *magazine, after ushering in 1949 with champagne, hot dogs, and 750 celebrities. "Sam usually acted as the host and the hostess," recalled Kathleen Parrish. From the mid-1940s, Spiegel's New Year's Eve parties were the Hollywood event. "Like Swifty Lazar's became after the Oscars," said Betsy Blair.*

The African Queen *starring Katharine Hepburn and Humphrey Bogart struck gold at the box office but led to the breakup of the Huston/Spiegel partnership. Huston admitted that Spiegel was "the best producer," but "he just had two big weaknesses: money and women."*

On the Waterfront *(1954): Terry Malloy (Marlon Brando) and Edie Doyle (Eva Marie Saint) watch the dancing couples on their first date. Spiegel was fond of Brando and was protective about the actor's appearance. "One of the most perfect things about Marlon is his nose," he wrote to Elia Kazan. "Let's not deliberately go out of our way to mar it."*

Colombo, Ceylon (now Sri Lanka): Alec Guinness (Colonel Nicholson) and Spiegel on location for The Bridge on the River Kwai *(1957). Guinness turned down the role three times until Spiegel took him out for dinner. "By the end of the evening we were discussing what kind of wig I would wear," the actor recalled.*

Palais de Chaillot for the Paris premiere of Kwai. *From left, French heartthrob Gérard Philipe entertains American heartthrob William Holden and fellow countryman, Pierre Boulle, the author of* Le Pont de la Rivière Kwai, *on which the film was based.*

Bagur, Spain – Elizabeth Taylor (Catherine Holly) flaunting her 39–23–35 hour-glass figure in Suddenly Last Summer *(1959) and wearing a white bathing suit that Tennessee Williams described as "a scandal to the jay birds." Thanks to Spiegel's efforts, the image became vital to the film's press campaign.*

Shepperton Studios: on Oliver Messel's set created for Suddenly, Last Summer *(1959). Spiegel and Katharine Hepburn (Violet Venable) have "a little chat." The friendly moment was short-lived. On her last day of filming, Hepburn spat at director Joseph L. Mankiewicz and called Spiegel "just a pig in a silk suit who sends flowers."*

to be made in England, not America, because of her tax situation."
Perhaps of note, the actress had taken up her British passport again.
But, contrary to her original demand–which led to Spiegel putting
down the telephone and hissing, "That bitch asked for a million
dollars!"–Taylor was paid half that figure. She also had two contracts:
the first, which named her as the artist and would pay her $125,000,
while the second cited her as the co-producer, under the name of
Camp Films–her Swiss company–and stated that she was to receive
$375,000 plus 10 percent of gross receipts in excess of $5 million.

The film was shot in England and on the Costa Brava in Spain. The
production designer, Oliver Messel–renowned for his opera sets and
elaborate costumes in films like *The Thief of Bagdad* and *The Queen of
Spades*–was paid £7,000 to convert Shepperton Studios into New
Orleans.* Five bales of vacuum-fumigated Spanish moss were shipped
over from Louisiana and since Venus flytraps were impossible to find
in England, several were sent over from Munich.

And while the premise of the film was dramatic enough, Taylor's
private life had thrown her fans into a complete flurry. In the early fall
of 1958, she had run off with Eddie Fisher; his wife, Debbie Reynolds,
had been abandoned, and Hedda Hopper–Madame Morality–was not
amused. The soap opera circumstances pushed hard news off the front
page. Taylor, the beautiful young widow of Michael Todd (her third
husband), had stolen the bobby sox troubadour from his fresh-as-
apple-pie wife. Even when they tied the knot in Las Vegas in May
1959, the press continued to hound the couple. Spiegel became
entangled in their honeymoon arrangements and persuaded
Columbia to rent *Olnico*–a luxurious boat–which awaited the "just
marrieds" in Barcelona. The producer and studio were taking care of
their princess, and ensuring that Elizabeth Taylor would arrive on time.

"I had told Sam, 'Don't let Liz fly into Heathrow,'" said Arthur
Canton, an associate for the Blowitz-Maskel Company, who was
handling all the film's publicity in London. "Well, you know how
great the English press is. I was standing in the back and the first

*Messel was also the uncle of Anthony Armstrong-Jones, the Queen of
England's future brother-in-law.

question was 'Were you and Eddie having an affair when Mike Todd was alive?' Remember he got killed in a plane crash." After escorting the couple to their rented home in Englefield Green, Surrey, Canton then called Spiegel. "You better get over here, I warned you about the press, but you have a greater problem–she's fat."

According to Jack Hildyard–the director of photography, who had worked on *The Bridge on the River Kwai*–Mankiewicz zeroed in on the extra weight. He described her upper arms as looking like "a bag of dead mice." Yet, waxing or waning, the twenty-seven-year-old actress looked sensational. This was her second Tennessee Williams film in less than two years; she had been nominated for an Academy Award for Maggie in *Cat on a Hot Tin Roof.* The star was in her prime and summed up the saying: "If you got it, flaunt it," whether it meant kissing Fisher in public, blinking from tits-to-toes in diamonds, or traveling en masse with her children; Miss Smith, the nurse; Richard Hanley–her secretary; and fifty-nine pieces of luggage. True, she was extravagant. "Her expense allowance for one day was greater than my salary for the entire year," said Spiegel's English business manager. She also swore like a sailor. "I would never have expected such foul language from such a beautiful face," Greta Garbo had remarked.

Katharine Hepburn, in comparison, shunned publicity and was low-key, particularly about her private life. When introduced on set to Hollis Alpert, the assigned journalist, she pointedly refused to acknowledge him, looking right past him and saying, "I had gathered that's what it was, and the less I see of him the better." However, her renowned unhappiness on *Suddenly, Last Summer* had more to do with other elements than her differences with Elizabeth Taylor. Most important, she had been a late second choice, which was reemphasized by Spiegel's lawyers, who had forgotten to erase Vivien Leigh's name from her contract. (Hepburn's first name also had been misspelled in the trade ad announcing her engagement on the film.) Spencer Tracy, the love of her life, was seriously ill. Adding to her vulnerable state was her age–she had reached her early fifties, always a strange moment for a great beauty, let alone an actress. "She didn't want her hands shown," said the director's wife. Moreover, Hepburn sensed that the director was favoring Taylor. "Of course he was," said Vidal. "She was the star, and also she needed the most help because she really wasn't up to playing it."

"Katie the autocrat" reacted by trying to take charge. She wanted to begin by being insane, whereas Mankiewicz was adamant that her descent into madness should be gradual and only appear with the film's climax and finale. "Kate and Joe would discuss things quite vehemently," said Schreyeck. "She would say, 'I don't know about this line,' and Joe would say 'Well, it's Tennessee Williams. I can't change it.' Then she would say, 'I don't feel like doing this,' and Joe would answer, 'We'll do it your way, and then my way,' but in the end he always won."

However, no problem was as bad as that of Montgomery Clift, who was described by Hildyard as being "a bog of tics and tremors." Although there is no correspondence to prove it, Elizabeth Taylor was held responsible for casting the actor in the production. She was devoted to Clift, whose career had collapsed after his car accident in May 1956. "It was tragic what happened," said Fred Zinnemann, the first to direct him on screen, in *The Search* (1948). "Monty broke his nose and it made his face just average instead of this very beautiful one. It really changed his personality. He could no longer play those kinds of parts when he was so marvelous."

Spiegel made sure to cover himself. He insisted on a supplementary letter of agreement being sent to Clift's lawyer and agent, which stated that "sobriety" was "essential during the shooting of the picture," (if there were delays because of Clift's inebriated state, the actor was "liable for all damages," and if Clift's speech was incoherent, "attributable to a lack of sobriety," he had to be available for post-synchronization). Spiegel had not forgotten his experience with Clift in Danny's Hideaway, the New York steak house—"I don't want to be near him, I never want to see him again," were his actual words. In the interim, Spiegel never quite gave up on William Holden, his original first choice. Bill Blowitz also contacted Henry Wilson, Rock Hudson's agent. Hudson liked the screenplay, but Universal Studios refused to loan him out.

Spiegel's spies kept him abreast about the problems with Clift, such as his arriving drunk for his first medical examination, but contrary to later reports, he never tried to have the actor replaced. In his opinion, it was Mankiewicz's job to handle the actor. The director was, after all, getting $300,000 for his services.

Nevertheless, when Norman Spencer arrived at Shepperton Studios, he recognized that Mankiewicz was being pushed to the end of his tether. As the result of his eczema, he was wearing white cotton gloves. (The skin ailment used to appear on the director's hands when he was agitated or nervous.) As soon as he saw Spencer, he would not stop asking, "Where's Sam?" or venting his frustration about Clift, who was staggering all over the set. "He said, 'I've taken about twenty takes and I can't go on.'" Usually, Elizabeth Taylor stood up for her fragile pal and kept him on balance, but she was not in this particular scene. "And Mankiewicz was probably a little cruel," the associate producer claimed. "David Lean, in my opinion, would have done the same. It's difficult for a director to become the mother and be soft, because he has the whole rest of the film, and has to worry about the other performances."

The news of the tense set, Taylor's weight problem, and Hepburn's unhappiness reached Louella Parsons, who dutifully reported all in her column. Mankiewicz was extremely annoyed, cabling that it was DISTURBING TO THE MORALE of his film, and his retaliation took two forms. As well as circulating photographs of a mock stage fight between the cast and himself, he sent a telegram saying: I HAVE JUST FINISHED TWO WEEKS OF EXTREMELY PLEASANT AND FRUITFUL SHOOTING WITH MONTGOMERY CLIFT AND ONE WITH ELIZABETH TAYLOR STOP WE STARTED AS SCHEDULED AND WE ARE EXACTLY ON SCHEDULE STOP SORRY TO DISAPPOINT YOUR INFORMANT BUT NOBODY IS MAD AT ANYBODY AND IF ELIZABETH TAYLOR IS OVERWEIGHT I FOR ONE AM AT A LOSS TO SUGGEST WHAT THERE SHOULD BE LESS OF.

In the meantime, where exactly was the film's producer? When he was not in the Mediterranean, on board *Olnico,* and searching for the right beach in Spain, Spiegel was back in contact with David Lean as well as juggling a few other projects such as Horton Foote's novel, *The Chase,* and William Golding's *Lord of the Flies,* which was to be directed by Peter Brook and written by Peter Shaffer. "Sam had many enterprises," said Shaffer. "The good side was that he left us alone. The bad side was that he would disappear and keep you dangling. Like Godot, he was always arriving."

In addition, there had been the strange experience when Shaffer was called at 2:00 in the morning. "Sam said, 'There's a crisis, you must come.' " The English playwright rushed over to the Connaught. "Sam opened the door and, sitting on the sofa, were two girls who looked completely bewildered and a doctor." The producer then left Shaffer and company in order to have a medical examination in his bedroom. "When Sam returned, I explained that I wanted to go, and asked what the crisis was. His reply was, 'Does there have to be a crisis to have a little fun?' It was in the middle of the night!"

Spiegel also had a new residence to contend with–475 Park Avenue. It became a fashionable address, and his other neighbors were to include Doris Duke–the notorious heiress–and C. Z. Guest–the society beauty and columnist. Originally bought as two separate apartments on the fourteenth and fifteenth floors, Spiegel chose Edward Durrell Stone to turn the space into a duplex. The architect had forged his reputation at the World's Fair in Brussels in 1958. Maria Stone, his wife, became Spiegel's appointed decorator.

"You know what Billy Wilder said? I loved it," said Betty. "He went into the red velvet room with all the Chagalls all around, stopped and said, 'Oh my, you have to be at least a cardinal to fuck in this room.' " The penthouse, which was ready by October 1959, did have a high church atmosphere. The walls were draped in platinum gold silk, the chandeliers were opulent, and there were fourteen Spanish Renaissance chairs, ordered from Antwerp, Belgium, which were upholstered in red velvet. But Spiegel was thrilled by his surroundings. Columbia's chief projectionist had advised him on his motion picture screening booth. (Films were shown in Spiegel's living room where two projectors hid behind paintings, which slid aside on a track when the feature commenced.) All of his art collection had been hung by the Metropolitan Museum's Joseph Carlin, Jr., and lit with special fixtures from the Kliegl Brothers. "It's designed especially for the paintings," Spiegel told the *Sunday Dispatch,* while he described himself as having "a small hole" to live in.

However, cozy it was not, since the apartment lacked closet space and was inconvenient for putting up family and friends. "That's why I took another apartment at East 77th Street," Betty said. Her husband was actually easy to live with. "But when he came home, he didn't want to be disturbed. He didn't like to talk to people; he needed his privacy." That they had two separate residences led tongues to wag that the Spiegels were living apart. "No, I lived there for about two years," she insisted. "When Sam died, my robe and makeup were still in the upstairs bathroom." Still, throughout that period, both were having extramarital affairs.

Without Betty in tow, Spiegel had returned to England for Montgomery Clift's and Katharine Hepburn's final scenes at Shepperton Studios. The actress's exit has since become legendary because after making quite sure that it was her last shot, she spat in Mankiewicz's face. Then she found Spiegel, denouncing him as "just a pig in a silk suit who sends flowers," and spat on the floor. Many have attributed the actress's behavior to the treatment of Clift, but years afterward, she claimed, "I didn't spit just for Monty Clift. I spat at them for the way they treated me." Hepburn felt particularly let down by the director and the producer because of their prior history together. She had been a huge name when she starred in Mankiewicz's productions *The Philadelphia Story* and *Woman of the Year,* and of course there was *The African Queen,* which was still making a great deal of money for the former S. P. Eagle.

But that was years ago and Hepburn was collecting on the film too, or so Spiegel might have reasoned. He chose to forget Hepburn's divalike conduct and divert his full attention to the film's true diva instead. Hollywood's Jean Louis had designed Elizabeth Taylor's entire look for the production, but the swimming costume he had sent over–in the producer's opinion–was hardly "a scandal to the jay birds." At Spiegel's suggestion, the infamous white suit was to be made of Helenca or nylon jersey, which would then stretch to Taylor's 39-23-35 hourglass figure. He was right to make such a fuss because the come hither look, which was ultimately cooked up by Joan Ellacott, the film's associate costume designer, became vital to the film's press campaign.

Moreover, Spiegel joined the actress for her final scenes in Bagur, Spain. He stayed on *Olnico,* while the rest of his team were at the luxurious Hostal de la Gavina. August on the Costa Brava had its dramatic moments. Such as the morning that Taylor–on the advice of her agent, Kurt Frings–refused to work. It turned out that Columbia and Spiegel had not signed her co-producer contract. Or when Eddie Fisher discovered that the location and rentals were not being hired via Camp Films–as agreed–and did not therefore show their Swiss Corporation's active participation in the picture–essential for tax purposes.

Yet, as usual, no complaints were as loud as over the looming "Sam Spiegel Presents" credit, and Vidal's lack of credit in the press campaign. It was a repeat of what had happened on *Waterfront*. Vidal's name was entirely left out of the advertisements in the *New York Times* and the *Herald Tribune*. This was adding insult to injury, considering that he had been forced to share the screenplay credit with Tennessee Williams. "Sam convinced Tennessee that it was going to win an Academy Award for writing and Tennessee loved awards," said Vidal. In fact, only Elizabeth Taylor, Katharine Hepburn, and Oliver Messel were nominated. "As it was, the film had the worst reviews in history," continued Vidal. "I said to the Bird, 'I wrote it, you didn't.' He said, 'Well, it's my play.' I said, 'The origin of my screenplay is indeed a forty-minute one-act play of yours'. . . . But he was a friend and I didn't give much of a damn."

Mankiewicz objected too. Columbia's advertisements included Spiegel and the cast, but had omitted to credit him. However, with the release of *Suddenly, Last Summer*, the director was back on top. Made for $2.5 million, the film would gross almost six times as much. As *Time* magazine wrote: "a practicing homosexual, a psychotic heroine, a procuress mother, a cannibalistic orgy and a sadistic nun. Showman Spiegel, who to Hollywood's amazement won a seal of approval for *Suddenly, Last Summer* from both the Production Code Administration and the Legion of Decency (separately classified), has shrewdly presented the whole mess as an 'adult horror picture.' Says Spiegel, 'Why, it's a theme the masses can identify themselves with.' "

Not everyone. Franco's Spain was appalled, particularly by the film's ending. The Spanish authorities banned the film as well as *all* of Columbia's other pictures. It was not a market that the studio could afford to lose and Spiegel was asked to intervene. He made immediate contact with Williams, who then wrote a public letter insisting that the country had "misunderstood the allegory, the symbolic meaning" of his work. "The hungry urchins, the desperately hungry urchins are all the used and abused young people of the world. They could be anywhere, in Africa, in China, in America, even." Williams ended his letter by claiming that he had promised to take his seventy-eight-year-old mother to Madrid that summer, "and I do hope that you will not exclude us." His plea worked and both bans were lifted.

Spiegel was well used to people being offended by his picture. When *Suddenly, Last Summer* was released in the United States, there was such an outcry from puritans such as John Wayne—who referred to it as a film "polluting the bloodstream of H'wood"—that he was forced to release a statement. "The shock values in this picture are used for their dramatic impact to strengthen the moral intent of the picture," Spiegel wrote. "At no point, is there a hint or suggestion that corruption could be pleasurable or that cruelty and immorality might be rewarded . . . enemies of life are destroyed, the good survive." Mankiewicz also insisted that, when directing, he had never thought about homosexuality or cannibalism—"only the basic humanity."

In the course of that period, Vidal was stopped for speeding. The policeman recognized his name. "He said, 'I just saw that picture of yours, was he queer?' I replied that he was. He then said, 'Me and the other boys were having an argument about it.' " (In England, the film was later nicknamed *Please Don't Eat the Pansies*. The gag title was based on an MGM comedy of 1960 called *Please Don't Eat the Daisies*.)

When Spiegel screened *Suddenly, Last Summer* in his new penthouse, Peter Brook and Peter Shaffer attended the party. All the white marble had impressed Shaffer. "I remember Joe Mankiewicz coming and saying 'touch wood, touch wood,' but there wasn't much wood to touch." The other guests included Diana Barrymore, Gypsy Rose Lee, and Tennessee Williams, who was drinking "what appeared to be a flower vase of whiskey." Williams had not liked the film. "He was wandering around saying, 'Who wrote this shit?' "

Even after Spiegel's interest waned in *Lord of the Flies,* he kept in contact with Shaffer. "He was always urging me to consider film as a proper medium," he said. Much later, the playwright won an Oscar for his adaptation of his play *Amadeus.* "Sam was like a cultivated pirate. I love that kind of man who seems fearless, but in the end you tend to feel used."

Feeling used was a frequent lament of those who worked with

Spiegel. Ten months after *Suddenly, Last Summer* opened, Betty went to a dinner given by Jessica Tandy and Hume Cronyn. The other guests included Laurence Olivier, Joan Plowright, Mankiewicz, and Kazan. "Gadg had gone back into analysis and evidently his shrink had told him that he had to speak out and tell everyone how he felt," Betty recalled. "He took off about Sam when they were shooting *On the Waterfront* and how Sam didn't pay anyone . . . how they all hated him and how they laughed at him because he looked so ridiculous. . . . I was becoming increasingly uncomfortable and increasingly nervous, and everybody including Molly–Gadg's wife–was trying to shut him up. Finally, I said, 'Sam is in Europe but when I get home, I'll call him and relay all this to him because he considers you his closest and dearest friend and I think he'll be surprised, to put it mildly, that you really have this very low opinion of him.' Mankiewicz then said, 'Look, Gadg, if you want to get a group together to knock Sam, I'll be happy to join it but I don't think this is the time or place to do it and Betty *is* his wife. I don't think this is appropriate.' But Kazan refused to stop. 'Well, that's her problem,' he replied, and continued to go on and on."

Afterward, Mrs. Spiegel called her husband. "I was crying, and Sam said, 'Oh, baby, he doesn't mean it, he's being analyzed.' And Sam always thought that anyone being analyzed was off their nut anyway and didn't know what they were saying." Clearly, he agreed with the Sam Goldwynism: "Any man who goes to a psychiatrist should have his head examined."

Chapter Twenty

LAWRENCE OF ARABIA — PART I

L awrence of Arabia, Spiegel's next production, surpassed all his other efforts. "He wanted to show that he was still the man to make the pictures," said Columbia's Leo Jaffe.

The producer was triumphant with a subject that had defeated others. Sir Alexander Korda had tried to make the film six times. Harry Cohn toyed with the idea in the early 1950s, while the producer Anatole de Grunwald had to give up on an attempt with Dirk Bogarde because of lack of funds in 1958.

The epic took twenty-three months to make, and was such an enormous directorial task that, unlike their previous triumph together, there was a crucial change in the billing: the director's name joined the producer's above the title. It marked the first time that Spiegel accepted this, but he was given no alternative. It was one of David Lean's conditions, as he was still smarting about *The Bridge on the River Kwai* billing. "I can still feel the chill when I was told that Sam Spiegel Productions was not Sam Spiegel personally–just the name of a company," he complained to his agent.

Without the brilliant director, it would have been an entirely different film. Yet without Spiegel, Lean might have made a film about

Gandhi. He proposed Alec Guinness as Gandhi, Cary Grant as a British policeman in the Indian force, William Holden as an American doctor, Yul Brynner as Nehru, Laurence Olivier as Lord Mountbatten, and John Gielgud as John Irwin. "There had been many times when I have fought—in my own mind—to keep you away from my next project," he admitted to Spiegel, "but the size of this film as it unfolds calls for the greatest producer of the industry—and in my opinion you are him. We have both reached our creative zenith together, and as you once said, we ought to have our brains tested if we don't join hands again."

Spiegel did join his sparring partner in Delhi, where he met Nehru and other Indian notables. He also went to Paris to see the novelist Albert Camus about the screenplay. However, in spite of Lean's hunch "that this will work out wonderfully," it did not. "It was Sam who persuaded David to forget Gandhi and do Lawrence," recalled Betty.

Referred to by Winston Churchill as "one of the greatest beings alive in our time," Thomas Edward Lawrence was a complex personality who played many roles, a man of action, a poet, a scholar, and leader of men.

Born in 1888 in North Wales, Lawrence's world was turned upside down when he discovered that he was illegitimate—the offspring of an Anglo-Irish landlord and a former governess. He was only ten years old, but henceforth he had to prove that he was superior to and different from everyone else. Not a hard task because in many ways he was. From an early age, he took a profound interest in the Scriptures, which led to a fascination for ancient history and medieval castles. However, it was when he attended Jesus College, Oxford, that he developed his passion for the Middle East.

Directly after university, he left to walk around Syria and Palestine on his own in 1909, and lived among the Arabs, learning their language and dialects. Lawrence became perfect fodder for British Intelligence, which recruited him in 1914. At the time, he was working on the excavation of Carchemish, on the banks of the Euphrates. The First World War had broken out, the enemy was Turkey; the Ottoman Empire ruled almost the entire Middle East and had aligned itself with Germany. Meanwhile, Lawrence was desperate to go into battle, win the confidence of the Arabs, and assist them in their fight against the Turks. By making himself extremely unpopular at headquarters, he succeeded in his aim and eventually became a crucial figure in the campaign of General Allenby, his commanding officer.

Lawrence was well aware that Britain and France were planning to carve up Arabia between them, but he was convinced that if the Arabs were victorious and demonstrated a united front, it would be difficult for the British to ignore their moral claims. Lawrence's adventures were countless. He formed an alliance with Auda abu Tayi, leader of the Howeitat tribe, and together they swept in and raided Turkish positions, dynamited sections of the Hejaz Railway, and seized the vital Red Sea port of Aqaba without firing a shot. He was caught by the Turks, who brutally tortured him. Yet perhaps his finest moment was leading the army of Prince Feisal, the son of Sherif Hussein, into Damascus in October 1918. Three years later, he assisted the enigmatic prince at the Paris Peace Conference.

Nevertheless, the adventure, triumph, and disillusionment became too much for him, and in 1922 he suffered a mental breakdown. To avoid the fame of his own legend, he enlisted in the Royal Air Force under the name of John Hume Ross. He then joined the Royal Tank Corps as T. E. Shaw, a name he adopted by deed poll in 1923. Two years later, Lawrence returned to the RAF, but after retiring in 1935, he died in a motorcycle accident near his home at Clouds Hill, Dorset.

The Spiegel-Lean production would only concentrate on the high points of Lawrence's life—his daring participation in the desert war. It was to be a vast project, and Spiegel's velvet octopus arms were indispensable. As Lean would later admit, "If you wanted the traffic stopped in Piccadilly for ten minutes from eleven o'clock on a certain day and have six tanks go down the middle of it, if anybody could get permission to do that, Sam would." Their production would even result in a new expression in the film community, "to Spiegel," meaning to soothe, cajole, or manipulate by sleight-of-mouth. Again, there was the startling contrast between the two men, Lean out in the midday sun in the furnacelike desert, and Spiegel lunching at the Connaught in London, or playing gin rummy on his boat, yet knowing exactly what was going on. But put the differences together and they were complementary, making it the ideal film partnership. There were bitter disputes, but with such an ambitious project and such diverse characters, how could there not be?

"Lean's world was all about film," said the late Freddie Young, *Lawrence*'s director of photography. "Other directors had another life but he had nothing else. . . . Sam had so many interests, he was very well educated, which David wasn't, and I think he always had a chip on his shoulder about that." Lean used to have "his list of complaints." "And Sam would be able to dance through all of that; he was incredibly articulate."

However, when asked by his wife if he had read *Seven Pillars of Wisdom*–Lawrence's own account of the Arab Revolt, as well as a considerable amount of background history–Spiegel's answer had been, "Of course not, baby, who could sit down and really read it?" "Sam skimmed it," Betty said. "I don't know if he revealed that to anyone else." Still, it had not stopped him from acquiring the invaluable 1926 version of the book, which lacked Chapter 11– removed at the suggestion of George Bernard Shaw. Yet it was unlike the producer not to do his homework, and this was one of the first signs that his success had made him a little dilettantish. Perhaps his argument was, why wade through such details when Lean will? Of course, the director had read the book, describing it as "boring and *very* fascinating in turns," and although he was on vacation in Venice at the time, he made elaborate notes.

Spiegel relied on Lean's notes, but on the other hand he knew how to solve every problem, and was a veritable maniac for detail. "Some guest would be arriving," said Norman Spencer, "and Sam would say to his secretary, 'Have you sent the car? Which car did you send? What time is the car arriving?' And I'd say, 'Sam, why do you get into that detail?' But he couldn't help it. He would suddenly get tense, 'Are you sure that the car is going to arrive?' "

Spiegel was also well versed in seducing the moneymen. Once again Columbia was backing the picture, which was to be shot in Super Panavision 70mm, which gives a superb picture on screen. "To us, it seemed like ages to shoot. It was also another male film," said Leo Jaffe. The negative cost of the picture amounted to $14 million, which was almost five times more than the scheduled budget. A steady two-year campaign had also been engineered to educate America to Lawrence–a very British hero. Bill Blowitz and his team were put on the case. Writers such as Alistair Maclean were commissioned to write books on Lawrence of Arabia. White terry cloth robes with hoods were manufactured for children. Lawrence's face was engraved on Bonbons Gilbert boiled sweets. And, when the production started, John Woolfenden–who had worked at the *Los Angeles Times* and MGM–was sent to the set in order to provide lengthy memos to the press.

"One of those qualities of working with Sam and his representatives was that you were hyped up," said Jonas Rosenfield, who had replaced Paul Lazarus as Columbia's vice president of advertising. "You felt that you were dealing with an important picture." He described Spiegel spinning "a web and a loop around everything." "He would talk you through it, show you a still, show you two minutes of the film. . . . It's not stupid, if you feel let in and the film delivers, well, it's fantastic."

However, before making the film, a few wrinkles had to be smoothed out. Professor Arnold Walter Lawrence, often referred to by his initials A.W., was dead against any film being made about his elder brother, T.E. That was a problem since he owned the rights to *Seven Pillars of Wisdom.*

Spiegel set the plans into motion to rectify this situation. He arranged a meeting with Lean and Robert Graves, who had been befriended by T.E. at Oxford. In turn, the ailing writer sent a letter to A.W. about the Horizon team. A preliminary screen treatment, prepared by Michael Wilson and illustrated with photographs, was then delivered to the professor, and within a day of receiving it, A.W. authorized his lawyers to negotiate a sale of rights. It was a feat, considering that other interested parties had failed for twenty-five years.

A meeting was arranged on February 8, 1960, which was followed by a special screening of *The Bridge on the River Kwai.* Three days later, Horizon Pictures owned the rights to *Seven Pillars of Wisdom.* Adding to the coup, Spiegel managed to get the rights "for a song"– he only paid £22,500. It was a lesson in negotiation, because while Professor Lawrence was desperate to preserve his brother's image, he was ignorant of Hollywood's extortionate prices, and too stubborn to accept advice from his companion, G. Wren Howard, the white-haired, pink-cheeked director of Jonathan Cape, his brother's publisher. Spiegel had asked if the professor had any sum in mind and since he did not, the producer threw out the figure. Lean later said, had he had a camera, "he would have lingered on a close-up reaction shot" of Wren Howard, who had attempted to press A.W. to bargain until reaching £100,000. One clause in the contract would end up as being relevant. Within a month of receiving the final screenplay, A.W. had the right to stop the film company from using the original title although it would cost him £5,000.

Nine days later, Columbia's Mike Frankovich hosted a gala reception. It was an invitation to meet Spiegel and Lean–the producer and the director of *Seven Pillars of Wisdom*, as the film project was then titled. Held at Claridge's on Wednesday, February 17, 1960, it began with the announcement that Horizon now owned the rights to the famous book, and then Spiegel took center stage. Wearing a scarlet velvet smoking jacket, he rapped on the table for silence, and all the guests–a mixture of newspapermen and society–stood to attention. The most astonishing piece of news in his speech was that Marlon Brando was to play the role of Lawrence.

Perhaps this is hard to believe, since Peter O'Toole is now so identified with the role of Lawrence of Arabia, but the American actor was a serious contender. "In a way, they [Lawrence and Brando] are very much alike," Spiegel declared. "Both have that mystic, tortured quality of doubting their own destiny." Lean had also seen Brando with blond hair–when he played a German officer in Edward Dmytryk's *The Young Lions*–and thought he had resembled "an absolute god" who "would look wonderful in the clothes."

Spiegel and Brando were in constant touch. When Spiegel's second wife–Lynne Baggett–committed suicide on March 22, 1960, the actor was one of the first to fire off a telegram: I WANT YOU TO KNOW THAT I AM THINKING OF YOU IN THESE MOMENTS AND IF I MAY I WOULD LIKE TO REMIND YOU THAT IN A TIME OF GREAT EMOTIONAL DISASTER WE ALL HAVE AN UNEXPLAINABLE TENDENCY TO BLAME OURSELVES FOR IT IN SOME WAY AND TO FEEL GUILTY. BUT IT IS

JUST PERHAPS THIS STRANGE PROCESS IN ITSELF THAT TENDS TO KEEP US TOGETHER IN LOVE AND SUPPORT OF ONE ANOTHER.

Just as a new chapter in Spiegel's life was opening with *Lawrence,* another had abruptly closed. Five weeks after Columbia's elaborate reception for her ex-husband, Lynne took her life with an overdose of sleeping pills–it was her second and final attempt. Her nurse found her, clad in a nightdress, with "orange stains on her lifeless palm" from the capsules she had swallowed.

Seven months earlier, the statuesque Texan had been trapped in a folding bed for three days. When she was found, she was unconscious and had no movement in her legs. However, once her condition improved and she started to walk, she killed herself. The second Mrs. Spiegel was three years short of her fortieth birthday. "It was bizarre, perfectly bizarre. I think she saw nothing in her future," Betty Spiegel said. "And Sam seemed to shrug it off and get on his merry way– planning evenings at the theater, reading scripts, and taking trips to Europe. He didn't like things that were unpleasant or depressing– illness or hospitals–and he didn't like Lynne."

Spiegel did not attend the funeral. There was even talk that he had refused to pay for the service, though, in fact, he did pick up the bill. Yet emotionally he had switched off. In his eyes, Miss Baggett had become an item with a price tag attached. "When Sam was through, he was through," his third wife said. In some respects, it was staggering, but indicative of a man refusing to be a prisoner of his past. Besides, Spiegel now had the wealth and contacts to behave as he pleased. Perhaps he was a loner, but he was an extremely surrounded loner, and that was how he planned to conduct his ivory-tower-like existence. Leo Jaffe sensed he was a friend, "But Sam never turned to me in any situation. He kept his cards close to his chest."

In Lean, Spiegel found another loner. "I don't think anyone could get very close to David," recalled director Nicolas Roeg, who ended up directing one of the second units on *Lawrence.* "He was a unique character. If somebody from Mars walked onto his set, they would walk straight up to his chair. There would be no doubt." Like Spiegel, Lean was ambiguous toward his family. He also had a habit of turning cold on each wife or loved one, then hastily beginning with someone else. Nevertheless, in the preliminary stages of *Seven Pillars of Wisdom,* both Leila and the third Mrs. Spiegel were in great evidence.

In the summer of 1960, the Spiegels had joined the newly married Leans and Michael Wilson at the Palace Hotel in Burgenstock, Switzerland. During the three-week stay, the screenwriter was put to work. "I barely knew Mike," Betty said. "But every time I saw him, he was very unhappy. I didn't realize the extent of the boycott in those days. Sam and David locked him up except when there were meetings." In the interim, the other guests, who included Mike Frankovich, Kurt Frings, Ilya Lopert, and Max Kettner–a major shareholder at Columbia–played gin and Lean, a nongambler, read.

During their European tour, there tended to be a mad rush for trains, further complicated by the fact that neither Mrs. Lean nor Mrs. Spiegel traveled light. "It was in the days of hardcovered books," Betty said. "And besides the books I was reading, I used to take a dictionary and an atlas with me." Leila, on the other hand, had her endless trail of little bags as well as her precious sitar, which–to the chagrin of her fellow travelers–she liked to play in the wee small hours.

On one occasion, Spiegel and several porters were struggling on the platform with the musical instrument, when his three companions had already climbed on board. "David, Leila, and I were in different compartments, but when we looked out of the window and caught sight of Sam, the perspiration going down his face and the sitar, which was bigger than he was . . . Well, we were hysterical." However, in spite of the laughs, it was to be Lean's and Spiegel's last holiday together.

As the autumn unfolded, the producer Herbert Wilcox announced that he too was making a film about Lawrence. His picture was to be based on Terence Rattigan's play *Ross.* A battle began, Spiegel threatened an injunction, and managed to stop his opponent. Wilcox wrote in his memoirs that he would have gone ahead and made *Ross,* "defying Spiegel." "However, the City wanted no part of litigation and so I had to let the whole subject drop since no distributor would finance me with an injunction hanging over my head."

Wilcox was infinitely more prepared than Horizon's team. He was basing his film on a hit play that was starring Alec Guinness; he had his Lawrence–Laurence Harvey; he had paid Rattigan £100,000 for his screenplay, and also had a start date for shooting. Other producers might not have dared to challenge him, but when the going got rough, so did Spiegel. To repeat Leo Jaffe's expression, "Sam was a tiger when he wanted something." Wilcox eventually sold his rights to Spiegel in March 1961. But beforehand, the rights to seven books were secured, including Lawrence's *Revolt in the Desert*, Robert Graves's *Goodbye to All That*, and Lowell Thomas's *With Lawrence in Arabia*. By buying up all the books concerning Lawrence, Spiegel was shrewdly covering his tracks and making it impossible for another producer to make a film about T.E.

Meanwhile, the hunt was back on for Lawrence. Brando had gone off to shoot *Mutiny on the Bounty* for Carol Reed (who was later replaced by Lewis Milestone). There had been an elaborate screen test with Albert Finney and Spiegel had immediately offered him a contract for several pictures. Yet, at that stage of the game, the lad from Salford, who first caught the film world's attention in Karel Reisz's *Saturday Night, Sunday Morning* and later caused a sensation in Tony Richardson's *Tom Jones,* was not seeking international stardom. Dubbed the Olivier of his generation, he insisted that he was "not a marketable property like a detergent." Spiegel never quite forgave him. "When I married Albert," Anouk Aimée said, "Sam was still angry that he hadn't played Lawrence. And that was ten years afterward!"

To find his Lawrence, Lean needed to see several films each day. Eventually, an actor portraying a feckless young man in a film called *The Day They Robbed the Bank of England* caught Lean's attention. It was the very same Peter O'Toole who had been tested for the hospital intern in *Suddenly, Last Summer*–not for Clift's role as previously reported–and had mischievously turned to the cameras and said, "It's all right, Mrs. Spiegel, but your son will never play the violin again." The producer was annoyed by the actor's impertinence, but since Lean was unaware of the screen test, he did not quite understand his partner's aversion to the twenty-seven-year-old Irishman, who was brought up in Leeds.

Even after O'Toole's participation was announced publicly on November 20, 1960, Spiegel remained concerned. His experience at Shepperton Studios aside, he had heard stories about how rowdy

O'Toole was. But prodded by Lean's enthusiasm and the reminder that they were desperate for a Lawrence, he was eventually persuaded that the newly married actor was ambitious for a future in motion pictures. Unlike Finney, he agreed to sign up for five further films. Nor did it hurt that O'Toole's manager–business partner was Jules Buck, Spiegel's former associate at Horizon Pictures. Moreover, O'Toole had had a nose job to improve his screen appearance. "Joyce, my wife, called it a Pinocchio nose and advised him to get it bobbed," Buck said. But it was ultimately director Nicholas Ray who convinced him to do it. "Listen, what are you going to do with this nose?" the director said. "You'll either be a big potential star or a big character actor—you can't be both."

Still, there was a slight problem—O'Toole's commitment to the Royal Shakespeare Company. Prior to his film offer, he was supposed to play the title role in Jean Anouilh's *Becket* at the Aldwych Theatre, London. A quarter of a million pounds' worth of tickets had already been sold. Understandably, Peter Hall, then the managing director, threatened to sue Horizon—a daring move, since he possessed nothing in writing committing O'Toole. The case then landed in court, where the judge turned to Hall and said, "Well, I'm sorry but you haven't got a piece of paper. Out!"

Anthony Nutting had been sent down to deal with the O'Toole RSC problem. A former member of Sir Anthony Eden's government, he was the needed note of respectability in the Horizon organization. Even if his official title on *Lawrence* was "Oriental Counselor," Spiegel and Blowitz took full advantage of this illustrious appointment. Nutting was then sent to Los Angeles to meet with the top brass at Columbia and fire up their enthusiasm about *Lawrence*— "chat the thing up"—and put their minds to rest about Spiegel using a blacklisted writer for the production. Although the first part of the exercise worked, the latter did not, since all the executives were convinced that working with Wilson was a catastrophe. "They said, 'This is a terrible mistake and Sam will rue the day, when he's hurt.'"

Strictly speaking, Nutting was only meant to deal with the Middle East. Having been a former minister of state for foreign affairs who resigned in 1956 over the Suez conflict, he was an inspired choice in regards to the Arab Problem. Indeed, in all the negotiations he became Spiegel's trump card. At the beginning of the 1960s, it was several decades before the words "peace talk" would be uttered, and the Middle East was in just as much of an unpredictable state as it remains today.

When applying to visit an Arab country, a certificate of religion was mandatory. Any Jewish connection and the applicant was liable to be refused, which put Spiegel in double trouble because, as well as his religion, he also had a mother living in Haifa, Israel. But, despite the hurdles, he still chose shooting in an Arab state in the Middle East over shooting in the North African Sahara or Israel. Moshe Pearlman, who worked for Israel's prime minister (David Ben-Gurion), had contacted him, writing, "for a producer like you, we offer a premium on the foreign exchange rate which enables your dollar to go further." But Spiegel refused to be tempted, his reasoning being, "Dunes, baby, I want dunes." (Although it took him about nine months to arrive at this decision.)

In the meantime, meetings were being organized by the British Foreign Office and the U.S. State Department concerning Spiegel's visa problems. The issue was so top secret that he had a special code name—"Betty's Husband"—yet somewhat perversely, the producer introduced himself as Jewish to various Middle Eastern diplomats. Spiegel's insistence was unlike him, and may have sprung from the fact that he was proud of his Jewish heritage, and concealing it was a hangover of his less respectable S. P. Eagle days. However, his behavior infuriated Nutting, who kept warning him, "You won't get into an Arab country like that."

By the end of 1960, King Hussein—the great-nephew of Prince Feisal and grandson of Spiegel's acquaintance the Emir Abdullah—had given his blessing to having the film shot in Jordan.* As a result, a joke started about Nutting's appointment among his pals David Niven and Harry Kurnitz. "David said, 'What's this about Nuttball getting involved with Hollywood?' Harry replied, 'It's very simple, he's the only man in the world who can persuade King Hussein that Sam Spiegel isn't Jewish.' In a sense, it summed up my job. Not that I persuaded the king . . . that didn't matter because Sam was going to

---

*King Hussein's second wife, Antoinette "Toni" Gardiner – and the mother of the present king – was working on *Lawrence* as Horizon Pictures's operator when he met her.

bring a lot of tourist trade with this fantastic movie which was going to be shot in places like Wadi Rumm."

The king also consented to loan out his army, essential for the picture's battle scenes, but it came at a price–£1 million. Spiegel had no alternative but to fly in and negotiate. Accompanied by Nutting and John Palmer, the production manager, he arrived in Amman for a lightning visit. In spite of being a canny operator, the producer was ill-prepared for dealing in such a closely knit country. Without consulting Nutting, Spiegel had already taken a loan from the bank of Amman for £1 million.

"Well, any child could have told you that the last place in the world that you take a loan out for a million pounds, when you are making a film in Jordan, is in Jordan itself," Nutting said. "For the very simple reason that they then know exactly how much you have got and they intend that you should spend it on them. But this was the way Sam did things. I simply could not believe it!" Nor did it help matters that the king's uncle–Sherif Nasser–happened to be the bank's director.

Fortunately, Nutting managed to sort out the situation with Gibran Hawa, the quartermaster general of the Jordanian army. They eventually arrived at the figure of £165,000. Afterward, they laughed about the original proposal. Hawa admitted that they had wanted to build a hospital. "I replied that I understood, but that they weren't going to get it from us," said Nutting. There had also been the business of negotiating for the Bedouins and their camels. Again, Nutting performed his magic. "I was promoted from 'baby' to 'sweetheart' for a few hours." Spiegel was so delighted that he wanted to show his gratitude to Hawa. "I have an account at Harrods, you must choose yourself a present," he said. "And what do you think he chose?" Nutting said. "A grand piano–Sam was flabbergasted."

Just as Nutting was equally "flabbergasted" to find that a wind machine had been ordered from California. "I said, 'Sam, how much are you paying me?' He replied, 'Oh I don't know, baby, much too much.' 'You're paying me, Sam, because I happen to know this area a bit better than you and you can depend . . . you can almost set your watch by it that there will be a wind every afternoon.' And he said, 'Oh those little dust devils.' " Nutting actually meant the dust storms that choked anyone in the vicinity. "The machine arrived in Aqaba and on being told it was 'to make wind' the locals fell apart," he recalled. "A few hours later, it became clogged and never worked again."

In the meantime, the casting for the production continued. Spiegel was adamant that not a single actor was to be above the title. Laurence Olivier was seriously considered for Allenby and was in Spiegel's words "champing at the bit" to play either Prince Feisal or Auda abu Tayi, but a theatrical commitment stopped him. David Niven was approached too, about a lesser role, but had declined.

"Kirk Douglas wanted to play the Lowell Thomas part (Jackson Bentley)," recalled Arthur Canton. "And Cary Grant was interested in the role of General Allenby. . . . But Sam was insistent, the star was Lawrence, not anyone else. Douglas and Grant below the title?" Regarding Grant, it was also a question of money. For tax reasons, or so his lawyer told Spiegel, he needed to make $300,000 plus 10 percent of the film's profits.

"Bugger and blast the star system," Lean wrote back on hearing the film star's demands. "I tell you, he [Jack Hawkins] would have a mighty good stab at the Allenby part." As a result, other actors of the caliber of Alec Guinness (Prince Feisal), Anthony Quinn (Auda abu Tayi), José Ferrer (Turkish Bey), Anthony Quayle (Colonel Brighton), Claude Rains (Mr. Dryden), Arthur Kennedy (Jackson Bentley) (he would replace Edmond O'Brien), and Donald Wolfit (General Murray) were to be chosen over more obvious film candidates.

In regards to playing Sherif Ali ibn el Kharish, Lawrence's Arab friend, Horst Buchholz was Lean's first choice; the young German had leapt to fame after *The Magnificent Seven*. But despite being represented by Paul Kohner, Spiegel's friend, it was impossible for him to get out of a film commitment with Billy Wilder. The producer was also interested in Alain Delon, but the brown contact lenses hurt Delon's eyes. Eventually, Maude Spector, the film's casting director–not Spiegel as Lean later reported–slipped Maurice Ronet into the role. As well as being put on a strict diet, the French actor was given diction classes to get rid of his accent.

Nevertheless, the screenplay–which started with Lawrence's untimely death and recounted his Arab adventures in flashbacks–was far from finished. Michael Wilson had walked off the picture at the end of 1960. "I felt I had gone about as far as I could go, that if I lived to be a hundred I could not fully satisfy David Lean," he wrote.

Indeed, the director described Wilson's work as being as "far off" as Carl Foreman's *Kwai* screenplay. "The character of Lawrence, which was what fascinated us in the first place, hardly peeps through at all," he wrote Spiegel, "and I don't think it ever can with the present way of telling the story." Lean sensed "the basic flaw" lay in their lacking a "margin for comment or kick-back off the main character." "He just keeps on doing things and the audience watches and draws their own conclusions."

Wilson was fairly peeved and Spiegel flew to Paris to massage his bruised feelings. Curiously, his partner was surprised that he had bothered to do so. "Sam, he's shot his bolt as far as this script's concerned," he wrote, "and whether he's bitter with you or me or both of us we've got to lump [it]. I only note him because I hope you are not proposing to give him the 2½ percent because, softy as I am, I would resent it very much under the circumstances." "Softy as I am"– was Spiegel the only monster?

In the interim, Robert Bolt was hired for seven weeks to write the dialogue that Wilson's script lacked. The British playwright was Baroness Budberg's suggestion, who from the start of the project had been employed to "dive into all the material and make herself a sort of information centre." Erudite and well-connected, Moura Budberg had previously been a script reader for Sir Alexander Korda and, in her youth, had been the mistress of Maxim Gorky, H. Bruce Lockhart (the famous British spy), and H. G. Wells. Nevertheless, the baroness's suggestion was not all that original, taking into account that Bolt's play *A Man for All Seasons* was then a considerable hit in the West End.

Bolt thought of himself as a playwright, not a screenwriter, and Margaret "Peggy" Ramsay, his agent, had to push him to meet Spiegel. However, as Spiegel discovered–left-wing or not–"Bob" had a price and was not averse to a little luxury. Perhaps the years of teaching English at Millfield, then the most expensive boarding school in England, had left their mark, or was it just the result of being paid pittance for plays that were broadcast on BBC radio?

With his golden ear for dialogue, Robert Bolt gave another element to the production. At the beginning, he stayed in England with Spiegel, which infuriated Lean. "As I told you in Burgenstock I have never been kept so far away from a script, and now it's happening all over again with Boult [sic]," he complained. The director was alone in Amman with a small production team, which included John Palmer, John Box, the production designer, and O'Toole, who was learning how to ride a camel. "I not only feel miles away in the cold, but the whole film is gradually drifting away from me. It's a very dangerous situation as I'm not a Michael Curtiz [legendary film director during the height of the Hollywood studio system] who can take over a script Saturday and start shooting Monday."

Spiegel replied that he understood his anguish concerning the script. He also made a point of writing, under the heading of "FINAL P.S.," that "in no way" did he underestimate Lean's contributions. "That is why Bolt is being brought in chains to Amman to join you. I assure you, you are not going to be 'kept out in the cold' beyond that date."

Lean then heard that Spiegel was hiring a crew with the instructions that filming was to start on February 28. The screenplay was still far from ready. "You have begged me to stop what you call 'playing the record' of the starting date, but the turn of events forces me to put it on once again, and in writing this time," Lean wrote.

"I wish I could get you to face up to reality instead of making accusations that I am putting the brake on your enthusiasm and undoubted gifts for pushing things through. I'm with you up to the hilt if only you would see it, and you are looseing [sic] me day by day both as a talent and a partner. I'm not angry as many people would be, I'm sad and can't understand you."

The following day, he received a letter from Spiegel and his tone became quite different. "I can't tell you what an impact your longest-ever letter has had on me!" he wrote. "I was feeling very wretched as there's so much to do and so much being done without my being able to do much in either direction, and now I feel part of the thing again. I'm so sorry you are so fatigued and plagued by all these problems, and hope very soon to start taking much of the burden off your back– at least at this end." Lean was also "madly impressed" by Bolt's notes and felt unable to "fault him." "At last someone is starting to bore some holes through the layers," he continued. "Thank god. You don't know how relieved I am. I wish I could talk to him before he gets too set on the rails, but I can't, so will have to risk all and put what I've been trying to unravel on this paper."

Typically, the producer was doing his own particular divide and conquer act in the shadows. Spiegel knew all about the rapport between the director and writer. On a minor level, he had experienced it with Huston and Viertel on *We Were Strangers,* and to a much greater extent with Kazan and Schulberg during *On the Waterfront.* Bolt would be allowed to arrive, but not until March, and he would never be far from the producer's side. Was Lean being Spiegeled? Hook, line, and sinker. But reacting immediately and not calmly assessing the situation was to Lean's disadvantage since he was missing Spiegel's strategy. As the producer used to say, "Baby, know your customer." With his uncanny nose for people, he knew "his David," but did Lean know or really understand *him*?

"All the arguments were filtered by Box and Palmer," recalled Phyllis Dalton, the film's costume designer. However, no one could filter their letters or their calls by radio.

"Obviously it is an unfortunate misunderstanding and an added reminder of thinking twice before sending messages of that kind," Spiegel once wrote to Lean, after he had attacked his lifestyle. "Under the circumstances I am neither in the mood nor am I capable of dictating a proper letter."

Lean then apologized, recognizing that their relationship had become "too personal with the result that you get hurt and I feel mean." But he criticized Spiegel for being such a tough taskmaster toward the film unit. "You hurt their pride, question their integrity of purpose and strip them of self-respect–if in their own estimation they haven't stood up to you. It creates awful resentments of which you seem quite unaware."

"With regards to my relations to the unit," Spiegel replied, "I quite understand that I unwittingly turn you into a valiant champion of the weak, while I try to drive them into a pace which you may deem too fast. Obviously, when you do this, I consider it disloyal to me and yet I can't help but understand your attitude. It is one of those inevitable conflicts into which you as a director–used to years of resentment against producers–must fall and it will take some time before you, as a director-partner of a producer, will begin to realize where the balance of loyalty lies . . . but you have yet to see me irritated as I may be, by your tensions, not side with you for the sake of a common front between two partners. I sincerely hope and wish that you may learn to do the same thing, no matter what the provocations. On the other hand, I promise to keep the provocations to a minimum."

The Jordan location had been Lean's idea. "I certainly advocated from the very start that we should find a much more comfortable location where both you and the unit could enjoy a less inclement climate and more suitable living conditions," Spiegel reminded him. "Consequently please don't, even in your most impetuous moments of grievance, reproach me for my air-conditioned yacht, which incidentally I offered to you as willingly as to myself." But Lean's frustrations continued. Spiegel was his partner, but on Spiegel's terms, not his.

In the meantime, the Jordanian desert had become Lean's kingdom. Immaculate in his uniform of a white cotton shirt and midnight blue pants, he cut a strikingly elegant figure and appeared to be entirely in his element. "You're like a bloody general out here," Anthony Quayle remarked. "You've got a huge army under your control. I'm madly impressed." The director also had his crew's undying loyalty. "I don't think he was as nice as Carol [Reed], who was lovable, but I was devoted to him," said Phyllis Dalton. "It was an extraordinary experience for all of us. David was ruthless, but I think he was a genius and one allows that sort of behavior."

In regards to the living conditions, all the tents had wooden floors and lighting. "We each had our own little fridge," said the costume designer. "Something we were never short of was water." Since Phil Hobbs was behind the catering, the food was first-rate.

Meanwhile, Spiegel created a kingdom in the bay at Aqaba. OLD PORT PERFECT WITH JAMAICAN BLUE SEA PALMS MASKING NEW BUILDING AND ANCHORAGE FOR YACHTING GENTLEMAN, was Lean's cabled description of the place. During the months of March and April, he lived in splendor on board *Malahne,* a 457-ton motor yacht. Every preparation had been taken to put the producer's floating palace in tiptop form, including endless sea trials and a handpicked crew from Southampton.

Spiegel was terrified of filming in an Arab country. According to

Nutting, for the first half of the filming, "he thought he was going to be poisoned intentionally," and during the second half, "he thought he was going to be poisoned accidentally." True to form, Spiegel turned the liability into an asset. He insisted that a boat be included in *Lawrence*'s production costs, his argument being that he would never have to sleep on Arab soil. The official reason given was that it was "perfect for script sessions, as well as entertaining."

Columbia chartered the boat from Spiegel during the months of *Lawrence* and picked up the expenses, which were in true pasha style– high to the point of being astronomical. (So astronomical that members of the boat community used to joke that Spiegel had actually charged the full purchase price of *Malahne* to the studio as a charter fee!) But contrary to all the rumors, Spiegel was the owner. True, the studio initially put $250,000 toward buying the yacht, but Academy Pictures–one of Spiegel's Swiss corporations–ultimately paid for her.

The general expense annoyed Lean, who sensed it was "stealing the stuffing from the turkey." But who was he in partnership with? Since Spiegel had achieved the impossible, he had to have his reward. It was the nature of the man, but Lean disapproved, and even complained that "on putting one's head to the pillow, the hum of the generator bored into one's ear like a dentist drill." He was one of the rare few to object.

Spiegel acquired *Malahne* in the autumn of 1960. Several months before, Robert Parrish and Billy Wilder went with him to see the 165-foot-long twin-screw motor yacht, which had been designed by Charles E. Nicholson and was built in Camper & Nicholson's boat yard in Gosport, England in 1937. While Spiegel and Parrish were inspecting the cabins, Wilder stayed on deck. Afterward, he took the producer aside. "I've been talking to the crew. They tell me it takes nine people to run the boat, and that's when it's in the harbor. When it's at sea, you'll need a crew of fourteen, day and night, twenty-four hours a day. Nobody can afford a boat this size anymore, Sam. You must be going crazy." After looking at him for a moment, Spiegel said, "Don't be so plebeian, Billy."

Gore Vidal was with Spiegel when he took possession of *Malahne*. "The captain [Hector Tourtel], who was like a retired British admiral, said, 'Mr. Spiegel, under what registry do we sail?' And Sam, knowing that I was standing there, gives me this tricky look. 'Panama,' he replied. I then looked at him and said, 'Sam, tell me, what is the national anthem of Panama?' 'Colonel Bogey's March,' was the reply. Sam could be quick, when cornered."

Although Spiegel bought *Malahne* off Maurice Solvay, the Belgian industrialist, the boat's original owner was William L. Stephenson, the head of the Woolworths chain in Britain. Stephenson was a passionate sailor and built *Malahne* as the tender to his racing boat, the J class *Velsheda*. Regarding the names of the boats, Stephenson had three daughters–Velma, Sheila, and Daphne–Velsheda was the combination of the first letters of their name, while Malahne was the combination of the last letters of their names. When *Malahne* was launched in June 1937, *Yachting World* magazine called her "a very graceful ship" with "proportions so good that she will never seem dull or unattractive."

The yacht was in Spiegel's possession for twenty-three years and, according to Faye Dunaway, was his "true love." "Sam became very English when he pronounced the word 'boat,' " said George Stevens, Jr. It reminded Louis Jourdan of Tony Curtis in *Some Like It Hot*.

His pride of being a yacht owner aside, Spiegel greatly preferred sleeping in his own berth than risking a night in Jordan. He was so petrified that when he stayed in the king's summer palace in Aqaba, he insisted that Lean share his bedroom. Before turning the lights out, Lean opened the French windows for a view of the bay. Spiegel, who was then in bed, asked where Israel was. "I'm not sure, Sam, but I think it's over there," he replied, pointing into the dead of night. "Don't point, they'll shoot!" the producer cried out.

Another incident took place in the king's presence. Spiegel and his team had been invited to the palace for dinner. Beforehand, the producer had rallied his troops and laid down the ground rules. "If you want to talk about politics or religion, I'm not taking you," he firmly stated. The crew promised to avoid both subjects. At that time, the king was living with his mother. At dinnertime, she used to sit at one end of the table and her son at the other. Suddenly, there was a silence and Spiegel heard one of his men ask, "What is Ramadan?" and the king replied, "It's the time of year that we fast." However, the crew member wanted to know what that meant, and the king was continuing to explain in the very soft manner that he had. But it became all too much for Spiegel. "You know what it's like," he boomed from the other side of the table. "It's exactly like our Lent."

In the meantime, the producer was very much around for the extensive *Lawrence* screenplay sessions, which took place on *Malahne*. Yet according to Lean, "the terrible thing was to get rid" of Spiegel. "Now honestly without trying to be funny or mean or anything, his work on the script was a disaster," he insisted. "He never knew, he used to make the most terrible suggestions and Robert [Bolt] and I would look at each other when one of these suggestions came out and that would mean that the rest of the day was occupied in weaning Sam away from his ideas." This was, of course, in contrast to Vidal, who had credited the producer for his sharp story mind.

During the sessions, Lean became terribly impressed by Bolt's mimicry. "After a while, it reached the point where I would ask Robert to read the script as he wrote it. And I would have it recorded." When the shooting began on May 15, Freddie Young used to join Lean for a daily routine of listening to the tapes before they began that day's work.

Omar Sharif was also privy to the tapes. The young Egyptian actor had replaced Maurice Ronet as Sherif Ali. The French actor had been a disaster for Lean, who complained, "When I put him in Arab dress it looked like me walking around in drag." Nor had Ronet's thick French accent helped, or his refusal to wear brown contact lenses because each time there was a gust of wind, the sand would get behind the lenses and sting his eyes.

None of these problems were to plague Shereif (the original spelling of his name), who looked gallant in his robes, had a passable accent, and possessed liquid brown eyes that were framed by thick lashes. When he had done his initial screen test, Ronet was still in the cast. "All the time, I didn't know what part I was being tested for, because there was another actor doing it there in the desert."

Sharif was then called to London where he signed a contract in Mike Frankovich's office to make seven motion pictures over a seven-year period. The contract also stated that Columbia and Horizon Pictures (Spiegel) were to have "equal rights to the use" of his services.

Sharif was informed that it was the standard agreement for beginners. "But it turned out that it was a kind of slave contract," he said. For *Lawrence,* the actor was officially paid 5,000 English pounds ($12,725), which was deposited in a Cairo bank. In spite of being a major film star in Egypt and having made twenty-three films, Sharif had never had an agent. "In Cairo, we just talked on the phone. 'How much do you want?' 'More than last time.' None of us had lawyers. Listen, it was 1961, television had just arrived." Even after realizing his mistake, he did not dare do anything about it. "I was terrified at being an Egyptian from Nasser's country, especially among Jewish people. There were lots of pressures."

Nevertheless, it was thanks to Spiegel that he was in the film at all. The producer had initially spotted him in an Arabic-Egyptian film with French subtitles. "He was really quite first rate," he wrote to Lean, "and while committed to half a dozen Egyptian pictures, some of which are being made by his own company, he is willing to chuck them all if we have a good part for him."

The director was not convinced. "I find it hard to believe that he hasn't got a bigger screen personality than Robert felt," he wrote after Sharif's screen test. "I think he could play an Ali, but it won't quite have the mocking aristocratic fine eyebrowed desert hawk quality that Robert has written into the script."

Spiegel disagreed, as did Bolt. "We both feel he is a wonderful choice and has a certain amount of native arrogance which I am sure you will gradually detect in him," the producer replied. "Bolt worded it 'quite a high opinion of himself' which I, personally, welcome very much as I think it will help in his performance."

When arriving on the set in June, Sharif quickly became friendly with O'Toole. "They were both young and a bit wild," Dalton said. The actors remain extremely close. " 'Omar Sharif. No one in the world is called Omar Sharif,' Peter said, at our first meeting. 'Your name must be Fred.' " After that, Michael Shalhoub, aka Omar Shereif aka Omar Sharif, was known as "Cairo Fred."

Throughout the filming, the cast and crew worked for twenty-one days straight and then would have three days off. "Some people went to Jerusalem . . . others Amman. We went to Beirut," said Sharif. At the time, the capital of Lebanon was a thriving, cosmopolitan city, known as "the sin city of the East." "The company gave Peter and I a little plane to visit the fleshpots. It was fun, except we were drunk from beginning to end—we would start on the plane and by the time we got there, we were out of it. We would take Dexedrine pills to keep awake. Neither of us wanted to waste time." O'Toole was taking Nutting's advice to heart, who had warned, "You can do what you like in Beirut and wherever outside, but if you don't stay sober in Jordan, you'll leave on your arse." As a result, he hit the bottle whenever possible.

Freddie Young was a witness to one of the binges. "We had a special dinner in Beirut organized by Sam, everyone was there except for Peter." Their host had inquired after the actor and Young had found him drinking in the bar. "I persuaded him to come, but the first course was French onion soup. So Peter, being drunk, took a spoonful of this red-hot soup and a piece of cheese stuck to his mouth, he swore blue murder and rushed out."

Roy Stevens, Lean's first assistant director, was included in Spiegel's entertaining. "He was a man's man," he recalled. "He used to say . . . who is going to get the accolade today because if Johnnie Box had done a very good job or if I had or John Palmer or whoever it was . . . he would give [him] one of these big Havana cigars. . . . I think he was one of the nicest, greatest personalities of film producers I've ever come across."

Phyllis Dalton, however, had a slightly different opinion of Spiegel. "Sam was an absolute monster, but he had an awful lot of charm." She recognized that he was "a great picker of teams." As far as entertaining . . . "He did have one or two parties on his boat, but when he'd had enough, he'd stand on the gangplank with a watch in his hand."

After seeing the first batch of rushes in Super Panavision, Spiegel immediately congratulated the director and his team. "I really felt that Peter sounded like a true Lawrence, who will be understood and appreciated both in England and America and I also thought that the photography of the night shot was absolutely the most beautiful thing I'd ever seen," he wrote. "For the first time, I felt I was not just seeing pretty scenery but began to realize a little of the heart of our story."

However, in between the praise, the telegrams began to pour out of Spiegel's Dover Street office that the production had to hurry up or else. Such threats increased when Bolt returned to England and was quoted by Atticus—the gossip columnist of the London *Sunday Times*—that life on location had been "a continuous clash of egomaniacal monsters wasting more energy than dinosaurs and pouring rivers of money into the sand."

Immediately after the article, Spiegel sent a cable in which he threatened to brush Lean out with a big broom. "That day I got hold of a big broom and I had myself photographed on 70mm," the director recalled. "I was sweeping up the desert. I said, 'You come out here, you bugger,' or words to that effect, 'and try having a go in my place. You wouldn't last an hour.' "

Nevertheless, Lean was equally upset by the *Sunday Times* piece, referring to it as Bolt's "boob." No doubt, it was the line: "Bolt worked a ten-hour day producing stuff for the director to alter: very laborious, but much easier than writing plays . . ." Bolt then apologized via a published letter in the newspaper.

It was early August and although Lean had his usual list of complaints with Spiegel, his wrath was diverted by the screenwriter. Each time he saw the rushes, Bolt fired off a letter taking "every delivery of every line to bits." "He hasn't yet finished his first film, and yet he seems to be under the impression that he has rocketed into a position where he can not only talk down to me, but be the guiding hand behind the direction of this film," Lean complained to Spiegel. He also accused the producer of appointing Bolt as his tutor. "Now he writes to the actors direct, enclosing a copy for me, and I ask you to stop this in the future," he continued. "He can write to me as much as he likes, but please allow me to pass on what I see fit to the actors."

"Bolt saw the rushes with me," Spiegel replied. "In all sincerity and honesty, he was deeply impressed. Under the circumstances I thought it wiser not to give him even a hint of any past resentment on your part and please remember he knows of no sour notes in his relationship with you. . . . Remember he continues sending you notes because he knows of no resentment on your part."

Bolt and Lean became a team, but it is interesting to note that when Spiegel could have poured gasoline on the fire, he did not. It was also curious that Lean had no memory of his fury toward the former teacher. In later years, he only recalled his problems with

Spiegel, such as his final visit to Jordan where he was photographed "stroking the camels, looking at me, stroking me and going around with the cast."

On another occasion, as they were posing to be photographed, the producer said, under his breath, "I don't know how I dare stand up like this." Lean asked him what he meant. "The way you look and the way I look," he replied. It was a rare moment of Spiegel letting his guard down—a rare cry of his inner doubts and fears. However, Lean refused to stand back and recognize that under Spiegel's bravado—the posing for cameras—the "Baby this and Baby that"—that he had many complexes, and had made a decision in life to overcome them. Or perhaps Lean was simply not interested in the vulnerable side of Spiegel.

Besides, at that point in time, Lean was furious that Spiegel wanted him out of Jordan. But in Phyllis Dalton's opinion, Lean needed Spiegel—"otherwise he would have died in the desert." Lean had fallen in love with Wadi Rumm, as had the rest of his crew. It was more grand and romantic than the other locations in Jordan, which included Jebel Tubeiq and El Jafr. Described by John Box as having "towering red cliffs rising two or three thousand feet from the pink sandy floor of the desert," Kevin Brownlow sensed that Lean used the place "like John Ford used Monument Valley which it vaguely resembles." It was difficult not to be awed by the Middle Eastern Grand Canyon. "The enormity of the rocks in comparison to the size of the people, it put your life into perspective," said Dalton.

When Nutting arrived on the set, there had just been a sandstorm. The first person he saw was Lean, who was caked in dust. "It looked as if he'd been with a make-up artist who'd really laid it on thick," he said. "So I said, 'Well, what do you think of my desert now?' I thought there was going to be an almighty explosion." But the director replied, "Anthony, everything you said was an understatement." In Nutting's opinion, it was yet "another Englishman going potty in the desert."

Taking this into account, Spiegel had good reason to be nervous. "I think it was more the sort of situation 'come on, baby, let's get on with the story,'" said Roy Stevens. "Spiegel was quite convinced that if he didn't pull the rug from under his [Lean's] feet, he would be there till now shooting pretty pictures."

Moreover, the producer had another problem, this one of a political kind. On September 17, 1961, Robert Bolt was arrested along with Bertrand Russell, Vanessa Redgrave, playwrights John Osborne, Arnold Wesker, and others in the Committee of 100 at an anti-nuclear demonstration in Trafalgar Square, which threatened to bring London to a standstill.

Two days later, Bolt sent a letter to Spiegel from prison. "I know you will think this gesture at best quixotic and at worse down right silly," he wrote, "but having made it I think I have a duty to carry it through if I possibly can."

Bolt's defiance made Spiegel very nervous indeed. "I don't feel at this point that I need to stress how anxious I am for the unit to return without inviting any further accidents or tribulations," he wrote to Lean. "I hope, dear David, that you will understand our [sic] reasoning."

The producer had tried to contact Bolt in prison. "I sent him a cable three days ago begging him to get himself released but have had no word from him," he continued. "I can only hope that when Jo [Bolt's wife] goes to visit him tomorrow, Saturday, she can persuade him to sign the necessary papers for his release."

On his last day in Wadi Rumm, Lean wrote two letters to Spiegel. The first poured out his feelings. "It's a sad day for me, because I've put all I've got into this venture of ours which started out as a partnership, and I now find myself way out on a limb not having the faintest idea of what you are proposing for the future." One of his major frustrations was the idea that both his partner and Bolt were trying to play down the magnificent background in order to emphasize the film's dialogue. "I don't disagree with you about the *great* importance of our real scenes, and if they are not top notch we haven't got a picture. *But,* listen to me, Sam. The thing that's going to make this a very exceptional picture in the world-beater class are the backgrounds, the camels, horses, and *uniqueness* of the strange atmosphere we are putting around our intimate story. . . . This is our great spectacle which will pull the crowd from university professor to newsboy."

However, the other letter, which was marked personal and was written on the same day, was quite different, and must have been personally typed by Lean. "It will be one of the big regrets of our association and friendship that I have to destroy your touching attempt at being a typist. [Spiegel's secretary had just had a baby and he was typing his own letters.] I have made MAny at5mpts tO imagine where/when & on whatmachine it was done–& every attempt brings on a new gaLE of laughter!!!!!!!!1 AM $till atit. Alas I can't add it to my list of affectionate anecdotes about you.

"Anyway, you are one up on me as you can always get a laugh out of my spelling."

After packing up his caravan, Lean was planning to bid farewell to the British and American ambassadors, the king, and "various other people who have done me kindnesses." "I don't know what the Syrian situation will be like by then, but rest assured I am not going to do a Robert Bolt on you and drive to Damascus Prison." He was tempted to go to Cairo and visit the museums. "I shall keep you informed in the innocent belief that you won't start ruining my rest by pressure phone calls to return and face the horrible music which is about to burst forth from the Horizon Symphony."

The first part of the epic had been filmed.

Chapter Twenty-one

LAWRENCE OF ARABIA— PART II

David Lean deeply resented leaving Jordan, and so yet another grudge was held against his partner. It was irrelevant that John Box advised the move. "There was no way we could have built Cairo or Damascus out there," the production designer said. The unit was exhausted and they were losing people.

Nevertheless, Lean remained convinced that it was a mistake to go to Spain and felt it was all to do with too many Jewish dollars going into enemy hands. "He [Spiegel] could have been accused of being a kind of traitor," he insisted. "And I have always guessed that he was forced with a gentle glove into the position, and we never returned to Jordan."

Lean was right–noises were being made about giving so much money to an Arab state. But perhaps more important, *Lawrence of Arabia* was over budget and "great spectacle" was getting to be an ugly expression in certain Hollywood studios. Ongoing disasters like MGM's *Mutiny on the Bounty* and Twentieth Century-Fox's *Cleopatra* were not helping the reputation of epic films.

Robert Bolt's imprisonment was another issue that added to the pressure. Spiegel was acquainted with how conservative the executives at Columbia were, and the fact that his picture's screenwriter was linked to a left-wing cause did not help. He did not want them to think that Horizon Pictures had hitched themselves to an English Michael Wilson.

Typically, Spiegel reacted in the only way he knew how, ruthlessly—but achieving the desired effect. "So have these people got to lose their jobs and lose thousands of dollars just so that you can go to heaven when you die?" he supposedly declared to Bolt, who was imprisoned at Drake Hall in Staffordshire. A fortnight later, the writer signed the necessary papers and was driven away from prison in Spiegel's Rolls-Royce, to a celebratory lunch at the Berkeley Hotel in Knightsbridge. Afterward, it became "the most shameful moment" in Bolt's life. For the following six months, he found it hard to look at his own reflection in the mirror, while he gave away the money he earned to Arnold Wesker's Center 42, an organization that took "theatre to real people by performing in factories and working men's clubs." Meanwhile, the playwright joined Lean in Madrid for extensive work on the second part of the screenplay.

Spiegel, on the other hand, was spending a lot of time at the George V hotel in Paris. He was smitten; Marie-Hélène Arnaud was the subject of his affections. A famous fashion model, the twenty-four-year-old was the public face of Chanel. "Marie-Hélène became Coco Chanel's muse and dream model," said fashion designer Gilles Dufour, "because she was chic and knew exactly how to wear Chanel's clothes."

Starting at Chanel in 1954, the seventeen-year-old had gone from strength to strength, eventually becoming the "directrice" of the studio. Ravishingly pretty, with auburn hair, huge almond-shaped, hazel eyes, and a wide mouth, she was so slight that the thickest Chanel tweed suit fell flawlessly on her. "Marie-Hélène was a trend setter," said Carlos Cambelopoulos, a hairdresser from Carita, the fashionable Paris salon of the 1960s. "She launched the look of the thick bangs with a layered bob."

Spiegel reveled in telling friends that Mademoiselle Arnaud had been Coco Chanel's girl. "So it made her, in Sam's eyes, practically a virgin because she was a lesbian," said Rosemary Chodorov. "And to show us what a wonderful woman she was, Sam would put his hand out to her at the table and she wouldn't take it. He thought that showed what a divine person she was."

There were those who thought that the bisexual beauty–who was also linked to André Malraux, Georges Pompidou, and other French politicians–had her own agenda. "She wanted to open a boutique in Paris and that's all she could talk about," said Nina Blowitz. "She seemed sure that Sam was going to back her. My husband knew otherwise. Bill said, 'There's no way that Sam is going to do that for her.' I think Marie-Hélène thought that Sam was richer than he was."

In the early part of 1962, whenever Spiegel was in Madrid and Seville, Arnaud was in attendance. In many ways, she became the needed distraction in the producer's life, because during the second part of the making of *Lawrence of Arabia*, his relations with Lean deteriorated dramatically.

Lean's chief complaint concerned Spiegel's lack of response about the footage. "You have given me no idea of the impact I am certain some of my work must have on the screen," he wrote. In fact, Spiegel had looked at every single take, but according to Blowitz, he was holding back his remarks because he had no power, at that stage, in the picture. "The biggest power is the power of withholding and that's what he is doing to you," he informed Lean. The production designer offered another viewpoint: "Sam wasn't going to tell them they were marvelous–David would have taken advantage of that."

Another dynamic to be taken into consideration was the role playing in the Spiegel-Lean relationship, the villain versus the hero. Spiegel was the perfect villain in the piece because he simply did not value other people's opinions over his own. In his view, there was only ever one way–his. If being the producer meant playing the bad guy, so be it, and so what? As Elia Kazan noted, the apologies came later. Besides, had he not squared the money, arranged the crew, and hired the people to organize the publicity campaign for *Lawrence*? Was that not enough? On the other side, Lean was convinced he was the hero of the piece–David of Arabia. There he was, toiling in the sun, completely unappreciated by his partner. He was going to show that "bugger Sam," which he certainly did. His rushes were astoundingly beautiful.

An additional difference between the two lay in the fact that Lean still struggled with his conscience, whereas Spiegel never had that problem. "He somehow had an absolute genius for making one feel guilty, you know, about what one was doing," Lean recalled. One of Spiegel's far-fetched methods was feigning heart attacks. Nutting considered them to be a set piece. "He was like [Mohammed] Musaddiq, who had kicked out the Shah [in the fifties]. Musaddiq was a very canny operator, because whenever he got himself in the position where he didn't know the answer and was really up a wall . . . he used to burst into tears. And Sam had his thing which was if he didn't like the way the conversation was going, he'd have a heart attack."

There is a much repeated story about Alec Guinness. Spiegel was said to have personally cast him as Prince Feisal. Depending on the version, which either happened preproduction or on the *Lawrence* set, Lean was so furious on hearing the news that Spiegel fell to the ground, the supposed victim of a heart attack. The story was apocryphal, but Spiegel's fake heart attacks were not.

Jokes about Spiegel's heart attacks were not callous. In all his health reports from Dr. David Sacks, Columbia's doctor in London and the brother of Oliver Sacks, the eminent neurologist and writer, there was no mention of potential cardiac problems in the 1960s and 1970s. Increasing girth aside—he weighed about 230 pounds—Spiegel had a remarkable constitution, with an allergy to aspirin his only ailment. As a result, the rare advice that his doctor ever offered was to cut back on the calories.

Spiegel rarely did; good restaurants and rich food were too much of a temptation. And while he continued his maharajah-like existence, it grated on his spartan partner's nerves. Indeed, so much passion was poured into Lean's fury that the relationship almost took on the form of Lean as the betrayed wife versus Spiegel, the betraying husband, who had ceased to listen and continued to rove. The director's complaints were falling upon deaf ears. The producer did not care. He wanted the picture finished.

On one occasion, Spiegel even appeared with the director William Wyler. There were those in Lean's entourage who sensed it was a veiled threat that Spiegel might replace him. But it was so veiled that it went right over Lean's head. Besides, Wyler was notorious for his endless takes, while his friendship with Spiegel depended on their never working together. "Working for Sam is for young people," he told Robert Parrish, "people with time to spare. It takes me a year to make a movie. Sometimes it takes Sam two years or more not to make a movie. That's because he knows how to live well and make a picture, or not make a picture, at the same time."

By late May, it was war between Spiegel and Lean. The producer, convinced that his partner was going too slowly, had fixed the New York and Los Angeles release dates as well as a scheduled royal premiere in London for the end of the year. In Peter O'Toole's opinion, it was a masterstroke. "David and I had begun to forget we were making a film," he admitted. "After two years it had become a way of life." But the director was furious and accused the producer of "sacrificing the quality of the picture."

Why was Spiegel in such a rush? Was he following the advice of Geoffrey Shurlock from the Motion Picture Association of America, who had written, "If you still love the picture business, you had better get *Lawrence* into circulation fast." Or was it just the Oscars? A later date would miss that year's Academy Awards entry. Or did Spiegel genuinely believe that his partner had lost his magic touch and had become "pedantic"?

They had had a pre-dinner meeting in Almeria, Spain, on May 21. At first, Spiegel tried the "Baby, you're overtired" routine. Moreover, he had claimed that he had not reported on the previous four rushes because there was "an alleged drop in quality and performance." It was all building up to the idea that Lean should hand over the "big action stuff" to the second units, which would save both time and money. But the director hated second units and was violently against Spiegel's idea that the second unit directors like Noël Howard, André Smagghe, and André de Toth would be "staging the big action scenes while I sit in the hotel." The disagreement continued until Spiegel realized that the argument was going nowhere. Suddenly, he started to shout, telling Lean that he–Spiegel–was a ruthless man and was going to be ruthless with him as regards the finishing of *Lawrence* and *his* method of doing it. The climax of Spiegel's rage was when he bent over Lean, red in the face, bawling "perfidious Albion." Afterward, Lean and Spiegel called John Box, who, according to Lean, "must have been standing by to call the doctor" (was this a snide reference to Spiegel's supposed heart attacks?) and had dinner with him. The next morning, Lean then informed the second unit directors "that under pressure of time and money" he was going against everything he had said and allowing them to shoot "a certain amount of film."

At that time, Nina Blowitz dined with the partners on Spiegel's boat. She was seated between them. "We had started with caviar and blinis," she recalled. "Sam says, 'Ask David if the wine is all right.' Then David replies, 'Tell him, it's all right.' This continued all night! They were like little kids."

The situation worsened when Spiegel left, but had a letter delivered to Lean stating that he expected the first unit shooting to be finished in Almeria by the weekend of June 22.

It was the final straw for Lean. "I have worked like the proverbial 'black' on this picture, Sam, and the harder I've worked and the more compromises I have made the more you have harassed me," he wrote. Later in his letter, he accused Spiegel of not having done "a good job," apart from "obtaining the rights to *Seven Pillars* and having Robert as a writer." He accused the producer of being involved in fits and starts. "You tell me you work a 15-hour day and have been doing so for weeks. You can't even get into the office until midday with luck. Up to a point that is your own business, but you cannot imagine how galling it is to have you nagging me to go faster and faster while you sail in on your yacht, have weekends in Paris, or show the results of my hard work in cut form which I haven't seen myself."

Was this the letter that was hand-delivered to Spiegel's boat by John Box? According to the production designer, it was both "vitriolic" and "terrifying." "So I take off for Monte Carlo, find Sam, I say it's a letter from David, it's very important, very urgent." But the producer was not in the mood to be rushed. "Sit, Johnnie, relax, you work much too hard . . . sleep on the yacht tonight and I'll give you an answer tomorrow before you go home." The next morning, Box awoke to find that they were in the middle of the Mediterranean. "Sam was up there with all these girls swimming around the yacht," he said. But Lean's letter had been left unopened on the writing bureau. Two days slipped by and Spiegel still refused to read it. However, on the third morning at breakfast, Box noticed that the letter had disappeared. "Sam came down, I said, 'The letter's gone–you must have read it.' " The producer then asked if Box had also read it. "I said, 'No, that's something between you and David . . . but it does need an answer.' " Spiegel looked at him and said that it would not be difficult. "Tell him to fuck himself."

Despite Lean's accusations to the contrary, Spiegel always knew exactly what was happening on *Lawrence* and what scene was being shot. This was proved by his conversation with Pedro Vidal, Lean's Spanish assistant director. "One day it was so windy [in Almeria], we really couldn't shoot because there was no way to hear the voices," said Vidal. "At the end of the day, I called Sam Spiegel on his yacht . . . [saying] 'nothing could be done, Sam, because it was a very windy day and the sun was impossible.' He said, 'How about the insert of the pistol?' Sam Spiegel had the script right there . . . Because the wind couldn't affect that–[the filming of] the insert of the pistol."

In the meantime, Spiegel continued to be busy. As well as buying the rights of fashionable novels like Edna O'Brien's *The Country Girls,* he was supervising another film called *Dangerous Silence,* which starred Jack Lemmon and Peter Sellers. Robert Parrish was going to direct the jewel robbery thriller-comedy, which was based on a book by Donald McKenzie, a former burglar. Scheduled to be filmed in London, writers such as Bill Bowers, Beverly Cross, and Daniel Fuchs had all toiled on the screenplay. Billy Wilder also contributed. His participation was surprising, considering that the Oscar-winning director felt about working for Spiegel as William Wyler did, but it was an indication of Spiegel's persuasive powers. Indeed, during his first screenplay conference with Parrish and Norman Spencer, Wilder had said, "Do you know what? I don't know what I'm doing with you guys. I'm here in Paris and on holiday with my wife and Spiegel comes up to me with his velvet octopus arms and I'm in a script conference and nobody is paying me anything."

Horizon Pictures had been expanded as an operation as a result of *Dangerous Silence.* Extra office space was found in Berkeley Street, an art director was hired, while Edward Chodorov was summoned from the States to oversee the production.

The picture was never to see the light of day. Chodorov had predicted as much. "It's not grand enough for Sam," he told Parrish.

"His mind's on *Lawrence of Arabia*. This is just a backup project to keep Columbia Pictures interested."

Another sign of Spiegel's diminishing enthusiasm was when he called upon the services of Norman Spencer, who was supposedly the project's associate producer. He needed him to clear the way for the filming of *Lawrence* in Ouarzazate, Morocco. "Sam didn't say, 'Would you?' Or 'Do you mind leaving *Dangerous Silence* behind?' " Spencer recalled. "He just said, 'You speak French' and I went out and was in charge."

Moving the film unit from Spain to Morocco was a huge operation, which Spiegel had nothing to do with. "Sam dismissed all that," said Spencer. "That's what you employ people for, was his attitude." All the equipment was put onto a coastal steamer and shipped across to Casablanca. A nine-hour drive, which included going down the Atlas Mountains, then followed from the port to the location in Ouarzazate. "We needed thirty of those British lorries that were called Queen Marys, those great big vehicles that used to take airplanes," said Spencer. Meanwhile, Spiegel, who had his boat stationed in Casablanca, refused to take the trip by car. Instead, a military plane was arranged, which he loathed, since he had to sit in a little tin seat with a buckle around him. Nor did he trust the Arab pilots.

While the Jordanian soldiers had been cooperative, the Moroccan ones were not. The negotiations had been elaborate. "Sam and I went to see King Hassan of Morocco, who said that he was going to put his brother Mulli Abdullah in charge," said Spencer. "The king was formal, like Queen Elizabeth, but his brother was like Princess Margaret–a complete playboy." Spiegel had also arranged with Paul Senouf, an American with Moroccan connections, to be their agent for the camels and troops. However, in spite of all the endless meetings and celebrations–Spiegel even threw a party for the prince, which resulted in thirty-two soufflés being made on *Malahne*–none of the military extras were actually paid. In Lean's opinion, the checks went to a bank account in Paris. As a result, the troops became fed up and started firing over everyone's head. "I had never heard a bullet whistling before," Lean admitted.

Nor did the Ouarzazate location help matters. "It was the arsehole of the world," Spencer said. "There were the most appalling conditions of heat and everybody went a bit mad out there." Lean had slowed down–his output was now down to a daily average of twenty-four seconds (when three minutes a day was then the average for feature films). The film crew were exhausted. It was a situation that might have continued until Spiegel flew in. "There was a full unit call so that Sam Spiegel could address us all in the patio of the hotel," recalled Nicolas Roeg, one of the second unit directors. According to Roeg, he was "brilliant." Like Napoleon, he had memorized everyone's names. After shaking various people's hands, Spiegel continued that he would never live to see a penny from the film. "I just want you to know that you've done a wonderful job and I'm proud of you. But boys, we've got to go faster!" Lean was noticeably absent.

The following day, the producer's plane appeared in the desert. Roeg recalled it circling and buzzing around the crew. "David looked at it and said, 'Bastard! Bastard! Last night he told me he'd had a heart attack and made me promise we were not going back to Spain. Made me promise. Bastard! I know he's going back to some girlfriend in the south of France. Heart attack! He's a better actor than I've got on the set.' "

Spiegel did return to the arms of Marie-Hélène and the comfort of the Riviera. His romance had also reached Walter Winchell, who warned his readers not to invite Mrs. Spiegel and Mademoiselle Arnaud to the same bash. "Sam's name has been linked to the French chic too often," he wrote. It was not the first time that a professional scandalmonger had linked the producer to another woman. Other girlfriends included models Cathy Andress and Dorian Leigh, Suzy Parker's sister. However, Betty admitted to crying more tears over Marie-Hélène. "I knew it was serious because Sam had taken her on the boat."

It all came to an embarrassing head in the late summer of 1962, when Mrs. Spiegel was staying in Rome with Denise and Vincente Minnelli. "A marquis was sitting next to me and he had a fabulous suntan and I said, 'Where did you get that?' he replied, 'I've just been on Sam Spiegel's yacht; I flew in tonight, just for this dinner. I left my wife on the boat with Sam and his girlfriend.' So I said, 'Oh, you just came from the boat?' Surely, the man must have seen my name card, but he hadn't. It blew my mind. I said, 'How is Mr. Spiegel?' He replied, 'Oh, he's very much in love with Marie-Hélène . . . they're like two little lovebirds in a nest.' I said, 'Really, well that's interesting and what is he planning on doing about all of this?' He said, 'It's all very unclear, it seems his wife is an alcoholic and a lesbian.' I said, 'I don't see what one thing has to do with the other. But who told you this?' And he said, 'Well, Sam told us.' " As they were leaving the restaurant to go to a nightclub, Betty was reintroduced to her dinner partner. "'You know Betty Spiegel don't you?' our host said. And the marquis looked at me for a moment. And I said, 'As in Mrs. Sam.' I thought that man would drop his teeth. I actually felt sorry for him, but boy was I on the phone with Sam."

"Get that bitch off the boat" were her exact words. She also confronted her husband about saying that she was both an alcoholic and a lesbian. "Maybe I had one martini too many," was his excuse. Betty replied that he never had one too many. "And you always know what you are saying." Spiegel promised never to say it again. "I didn't even give the incident much credence because why waste space in my head with that shit when I wanted to know whether my next lover was going to be wonderful and what I was going to wear to the party that night."

But Betty continued to have a reputation for preferring women. "After my record and all the men I was with during all those years?" she asks. "Let's put it this way, or to quote Tennessee [Williams]: 'I've covered the waterfront.' Someone once told me that if I ignored women, I was ignoring half the human race."

The complications of his personal life aside, Spiegel still found time for Maurice Jarre. The French composer had scored the music for Georges Franju's horror classic, *Les Yeux Sans Visage,* and had also scored Darryl Zanuck's production, *The Big Gamble.* However, it was Jarre's music on *Les Dimanches de Ville d'Avray,* a film that Columbia would distribute in the States under the name of *Sundays and Cybele,* that had caught Spiegel's attention.

"Sam informed me that *Lawrence of Arabia* was the biggest film ever to be made and he wanted three composers to do the music." Khachaturian for the Arab composition, Benjamin Britten for the English, while Jarre was meant to write the dramatic orchestration. But in spite of Spiegel's promises that he would be flown out to meet Lean, it never happened. "I was his discovery and Sam didn't want me to meet David until the last opportunity. He was terribly possessive." Spiegel then called to say that the two other composers were out of the picture and Jarre was shown assembled rushes in a private theater on South Audley Street. "It was magnificent and so exciting."

Lawrence's brother, however, who was shown a rough cut, was horrified. The picture was too sensational and not serious enough for his taste. Certainly, the professor was also unused to the film world and the print was incomplete, without music and all the effects. Immediately after the showing, he had stood up and shouted in Spiegel's direction that he should never have trusted him. "There was a horrendous row and he stormed out of that little theatre with his wife in pursuit, trying to placate him," Lean recalled. That was it; the professor withdrew the title *Seven Pillars of Wisdom*. Spiegel then retrieved his $5,000 and was left with *Lawrence of Arabia*, which, as Nutting wisely pointed out, "was a better title."

A few weeks later, the producer changed his mind about the film's music. Suddenly, Richard Rodgers, famous for his Broadway melodies, would be the main composer. "I found this very strange," admitted Jarre. "I asked, 'Did he see the film?' And Sam replied, 'He does not need to, he knows the story.' I was stupefied. . . . If I had known this before, I would have stayed in France. However, I tried to be positive, thinking, 'This is a way to meet Rodgers.' "

A meeting was then set up at Horizon Pictures's Dover Street offices in order to listen to Rodgers's various themes. As each piece was played on the piano, Lean became more and more annoyed. "Sam, what is all this rubbish?" he eventually said. "I am supposed to be editing, and you take up my time with this nonsense?" Spiegel then asked Jarre if he had written anything. The composer had. And once he finished playing his *Lawrence* theme, which was to haunt the entire epic, Lean walked over and put his hand on his shoulder. "He said, 'That's it, that's exactly what it should be.' " After explaining how he planned to continue, "David started to jump and so did Sam," and the Frenchman went back to composing the entire score. "It was to be a superman job, ready in six weeks." Everything had to be in time for the royal performance in the presence of Her Majesty Queen Elizabeth II, which had been set for December 10.

Spiegel was included in all the spotting sessions–the meetings to decide where the music would be. It was a tricky affair since he and his partner would not stop bickering. First of all, his tardiness drove the punctual Lean to distraction, then there was their difference of opinion. On one occasion, the director wanted subtle music, which would reach a crescendo, but Spiegel disagreed. "That night, at 10:00 P.M., Sam telephoned. 'Look, baby, I just want to tell you to completely ignore what David said, write something dramatic,' " Jarre recalled. "Well, I tried to call Lean, who was editing, and so I wrote two totally different pieces of music for that sequence."

Sir Adrian Boult–the musical director of the London Philharmonic–was employed as the conductor. "Sam understood that I liked to conduct my own music, but it didn't meet the quota subsidiary," said Jarre. Keeping in with the Eady Plan from the British government, Spiegel had to have a certain percentage of British people on the production. But during the first rehearsal, the musical director realized that he was incapable of synchronizing or adjusting the music to the scenes and he handed the work back to Jarre. "Boult did not do one note, but on the film, he was still credited," he said.

Concerning Jarre's pay, Spiegel took advantage as he had done with Sharif. "I didn't know what an agent was," Jarre admitted. "I signed a contract for $2,000. . . . In the end, my expenses turned out to be better than my salary." After ten years, Jarre received his first royalty check from the record. "It was $2.53, I wanted to frame it." Nevertheless, he recognized that *Lawrence of Arabia* was a turning point for him.

In the final days of editing, Spiegel and Lean had a terrible fight about the ending. "The terms of our contract was that if there was a dispute, my word would become final," Columbia's Leo Jaffe said. "The picture was supposed to have its first showing in eleven days and neither could agree. . . . When I arrived, they took me to a screening room. It was 11:30 at night, London time. . . . I then told them, 'If you want me to tell you how to finish this picture, I don't deserve to, I think you fellas have got to work it out.' " The executive left the projection room and the partners sat down. "They then called to say,

Sparring partners: director David Lean and Spiegel on location in Jordan for
Lawrence of Arabia *(1962). "It was the most incredible love–hate relationship,"
said Betty Spiegel. "They would be screaming at each other and then, an hour
later, laughing and having lunch."*

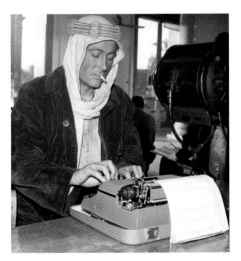

*Peter O'Toole (T. E. Lawrence)
writes home from the Horizon
Pictures' production office.
O'Toole, a renowned hell-raiser,
took Anthony Nutting's (the
film's Oriental Counselor)
advice to heart when he
warned, "You can do what you
like in Beirut and wherever
outside, but if you don't stay
sober in Jordan, you'll leave
on your arse."*

July 1962, while David Lean and crew were sweating it out in Morocco, Spiegel and the team from Dangerous Silence—*his other film production—cruised the Mediterranean. From left, Kathleen Parrish (the wife of director Robert Parrish), Marie-Hélène Arnaud (Coco Chanel's muse who was Spiegel's girlfriend), Spiegel, Edward and Rosemary Chodorov.*

Hollywood power at the Directors Guild Dinner in 1963: a white-haired Mike Frankovich stands behind Abe Schneider (Columbia's president) who is seated between Joan Cohn (left) and Betty Spiegel (right) who is talking to her husband, as über agent Kurt Frings rushes past.

Sam Spiegel and the Seven Dwarfs. After Lawrence of Arabia's *success at the Oscars, Spiegel was treated with even more respect in the film community. "Sam was the uncrowned prince of Columbia," said producer Charles Schneer. "Uncrowned because it would have been too expensive if he was crowned."*

Columbia Studios: on the set of The Chase *(1966). Marlon Brando (Sheriff Calder) and Spiegel. Brando was then a motorcycle enthusiast and Spiegel was worried that he might kill himself, as James Dean had. One of Spiegel's frequent questions to director Arthur Penn was, "Marlon didn't bring his motorcycle, did he?"*

Nicholas and Alexandra *(1971)*. *The Russian army salutes the czar, the czarina, and the members of their royal household. Since the epic was Spiegel's showpiece, everything was on an elaborate scale. Yet according to Pierre Sciclounoff, Spiegel's Swiss lawyer, there was a more personal element. "It was Sam's* Doctor Zhivago.*"*

London 1970: Adam Spiegel with his mother, Ann E. Pennington. Adam was to attend the right schools, know the right people— or so his father planned. "Many people were surprised by Sam having that side that adored Adam," said Pennington.

Paramount Studios: on the set of The Last Tycoon *(1976). Robert De Niro (Monroe Stahr), director Elia Kazan, and Spiegel. "When I first started seeing rushes, I thought this is dead," admitted Barry Diller, then Paramount's chairman and CEO. Later, the film was panned.*

Spiegel and Harold Pinter on location for Betrayal *(1983). "Sam and Harold had a father–son relationship," said director David Jones.*

London 1983: Spiegel, Jennifer Kent Attebery—the last Spiegelette—and Mark Littman, a Spiegel intimate.

Malahne—*Spiegel's motor yacht—was the place to be seen from the 1960s until the early 1980s. Stepping on to* Malahne *was like stepping into another era. "The bathtubs were perfect," said George Stevens, Jr. "And just as the sun was setting, James [Spiegel's Barbadian steward] would bring you a martini."*

The blue saloon on Malahne, c. 1979. Spiegel translates the French newspapers for Adam (right) and his schoolfriend (left). "Sam wanted to give a good life to the child," said Leonora Hornblow.

Pre-lunch cocktails on Malahne: *from left, Isaac Stern and Spiegel in casual form.
"Sam reveled in life," said Stern. "But he never reached a moment when he was
truly satisfied. Whatever he had was never enough."*

*Traveling on Warner Bros.' corporate jet, c. 1983, Ahmet Ertegun and Spiegel
share one of their many jokes. "Just as Sam was the sweetest of guys
and the most generous of hosts," said Ertegun, "on his boat, he changed.
He became a martinet."*

Spiegel in Barbados, a few years before his demise. "Sam had a great life," said David Geffen. "It wasn't as if he ever cut down on his cream. He ate what he wanted until the day he died."

'We've resolved it,' and the next day I flew back to New York and they put the ending on that Sam wanted."

Despite agreeing about the film, the partners were barely on speaking terms. "It was like a marriage that had run its course," Spencer sensed. "Even if Sam did something good, David wouldn't realize it at the time and there were daggers drawn." As a peace gesture, Spiegel invited Lean to dinner at the Berkeley, one of the director's favorite restaurants. But after a couple of drinks, Lean decided to let Spiegel have it—how it could have been "a very happy picture," but most of the time it was not because of the producer's cables, messages, and general behavior. "You were absolutely horrible," Lean said. "Why did you behave so badly to me?" Spiegel took "a great gulp," then replied, "Baby, artists work better under pressure."

It was staggering, it was infuriating, it was Spiegel. And yet in his happier moments, Lean was capable of declaring, "We were a jolly good partnership Sam and I, and it was a big regret of mine that we didn't go on together."

In John Box's opinion, Spiegel met his match in Lean. "But he was good for David, just as David was good for him," he said. "I didn't always agree with Sam but he was a brilliant producer. Listen, he kept *Lawrence* going and that wasn't easy."

As to *Lawrence*'s American promotion, Peter O'Toole was to be the focus of all the publicity, Spiegel's argument being, "He's the new star and the star of the film." Consequently, he refused to fly over Omar Sharif. But O'Toole balked when he heard the plan. "He said, 'bollocks,' and he meant it," Sharif recalled. " 'Omar is going and we're going together.' " It was fortunate that the Egyptian actor was included, since he was unbelievably helpful to the campaign, winning over all the journalists that he met, whereas O'Toole behaved disgracefully, leading to Spiegel's quip, "You make a star, you make a monster." The blond star was either drunk during his interviews, or demanding outrageous sums for appearing on television.

Wearing a white, floor-length mink, Betty Spiegel accompanied her husband to the New York premiere. "There was a blizzard," she said. Meanwhile, their driver was so short that she wondered how he could see the road. "I think he sat on books and things and lots of cushions."

Before arriving at the Criterion, Spiegel had given the driver strict instructions to be first in line. "Sam didn't want to greet people at the theater, he wanted to greet them at the party," said his wife.

The party was held on the roof garden of the St. Regis Hotel. *Women's Wear Daily,* which covered the event, called it "Great Film– Great Fashion." Alec Guinness and Margaret Leighton, Jean Simmons, Susan Strasberg, Babe Paley, and Jayne Wrightsman were a few who attended. There was also a Washington showing. "We had invited every congressman, as well as the president, who couldn't make the date," recalled Arthur Canton. "Sam used to say that he had had Jack [Kennedy] on his knee because he knew his father [Joseph P. Kennedy]." A special public relations person was hired for the town's protocol. "The picture starts, the Jarre music, the motorcycle goes down, the main title comes on, and the print breaks." Immediately, Lean appeared from one aisle and Spiegel from the other, both wondering what had happened. Canton went upstairs and the film was quickly laced up again. "But Sam did say something very funny, 'By the way, who's that lady over there, sitting on row x?'"

The most appreciative audience was in Los Angeles. "It was a sort of rave show and at the dinner afterward it was rather wonderful because I knew that everyone present thought we had done something very substantial for the film medium," Lean wrote to Robert Bolt.

A bout of unexpected publicity had come from Professor Lawrence. A.W. was determined to tell the public of his disapproval, but instead of hindering interest, the controversy incited the press's attention and was ultimately good for business. "I quite understand what the movie must mean to someone who has lived in the shadow of a legend of an older brother for some fifty years," Spiegel told the *New York Times.* "Professor Lawrence did not want family skeletons rattled. He wanted to preserve the Lawrence of Arabia legend in Victorian cleanliness." He revealed that in order to dramatize the British hero's life, his illegitimacy, homosexual tendencies, and pleasure from killing had to be revealed. "This was a man who became involved in all sorts of masochism as the result of the conflicts." Showman Spiegel had succeeded in revealing the spicier elements but also maintained the serious nature of the film. "We did not try to resolve the legend of Lawrence of Arabia. We tried to perpetuate it." Magic words from a producer promoting a three-hour-and-forty-minute film epic.

Adding to the excitement was the fact that the film was nominated for ten Academy Awards. One individual feeling left out of the celebrations was Michael Wilson. After reading the final draft of *Lawrence of Arabia,* he felt entitled to a credit, arguing that his blueprint had been used. "Why then is the screenplay attributed to Mr. Bolt so much like mine, to a degree that it virtually coincides with mine in terms of continuity?" he wrote to Spiegel. The producer replied in a businesslike fashion, but added a handwritten P.S.: "Forgive the brevity of this note which is prompted by my haste at this moment."

Spiegel was actually fond of Wilson, but he had dictated his terms about the screenplay credit. If he produced a statement denying any connection with the Communist Party, he would be entitled to the credit. Since Wilson refused, Spiegel refused to credit him. Although it was two years after Otto Preminger and Kirk Douglas had separately fought to have Dalton Trumbo's name on the screen, Spiegel was not going to get into that battle.

The Wilson matter had then been put in the hands of his solicitors. A few days later, they informed the writer that he was not "entitled to any credit whatsoever."

In desperation, the American writer approached Robert Bolt. He had shown, after all, that he had principles. But the British playwright described his letter as a bombshell. "I had no idea that there was any question of my sharing credit with anybody," Bolt replied. "I was under the impression that the script as shot was my own work utterly."

The British Writers' Guild thought otherwise. On December 18, 1963, Wilson was presented with an award for Best Screenplay of 1962. (It was exactly a year after Bolt had received his.) Nevertheless, the blacklisted writer was excluded from the 1963 Oscars ceremony.

A few hours before the event, Omar Sharif went to Spiegel's suite in the Beverly Hills Hotel. "The only sure thing, that year, was that I was going to get the Academy Award," he said. "David told me, 'Now Omar, when they call your name, I want you to walk slowly up the aisle, like you did in the film—don't rush, don't run'. . . . Sam said, 'Baby, walk slowly.' " The actor was so prepared that as soon as Rita Moreno started reading the nominees, he got off his chair. "I was walking slowly as David had told me. Then she said 'Ed Begley'."

Lean ended up winning, as did Spiegel. Olivia de Havilland presented the producer with the Oscar. A friend from his S. P. Eagle days, he kissed her warmly on both cheeks, and then began his speech, "Ladies and gentlemen, there is no magic formula for creating these pictures . . ."

That night, photographers snapped him greedily leaning into the tray of *Lawrence*'s winnings, which held seven Academy Awards. "Sam wanted them all for himself," sensed Jarre. The composer was nominated, and had been tempted to attend the ceremony. Spiegel discouraged him, saying, "No, baby, it's only for Americans, there's no point in your coming." Jarre followed his advice. In Spiegel's defense, the Oscars were not the international event that they have now become. However, it took Jarre several attempts to get his award away from Spiegel. He had to resort to saying, "Sam, that's *my* Oscar," several times until the statuette was delivered.

With his third Academy Award, Spiegel was treated with even more respect in the film community. The picture was a hit, and would eventually gross $70 million. "Sam was the uncrowned prince of Columbia," said the producer Charles Schneer. "Uncrowned because it would have been too expensive if he was crowned." But the uncrowned prince had changed. "After *Lawrence*, he became impossible, im-pos-si-ble—four syllables," Betty said. "I mean he just thought that there was no one that he couldn't get to, nothing that he couldn't do."

Lord Acton's aphorism, "Power tends to corrupt, and absolute power corrupts absolutely" might have been applied to Spiegel. "He changed after what may turn out to be one of the best movies of all time," said Mike Nichols. "Everything changed." Before that, Nichols sensed that Spiegel had been "the very soul of true ideas in a movie— the mystery and the contrast." Spiegel had the sort of "what if" mentality, with an artist's concerns, as well as supreme intelligence. "I think that's what made him unique, nobody combined those things. Put them all together and he was as close to an artist as a producer could get."

Chapter Twenty-two

THE SPIEGEL LIFESTYLE

After an extraordinary ten years of producing, Sam Spiegel floundered. There was a series of reasons for his creative downfall. First of all, he was a late bloomer–Spiegel was sixty-one when *Lawrence* was finished. Secondly, with so many triumphs, he started to confuse himself with the talent; he forgot the teamwork behind his extraordinary productions, and began to believe that he was the sole reason for their success. Edward Chodorov saw it happen during the second half of the making of *Lawrence*. "You don't listen anymore," the writer told Spiegel. It was a pity, because before that, four people could be arguing and the producer would know which one of them was right.

Was it that, or did Spiegel just never find a project that he was passionate about again? "It happens a lot in this business," said the producer Freddie Fields.

Spiegel's lawyer, however, put his lack of focus down to the producer's obsession with women. "It all stopped because it was women, women, and women," said Albert Heit. "There could be some dame outside, and Sam would say, 'You have to excuse me.' "

Or was it just the too sweet smell of success, as Barry Diller sensed. "People get corrupted. They don't lose their brains. God knows, they don't lose their talent. But part of the process of success and what it does, it corrupts in the way that it removes their objectivity, it removes their instinct."

"Objectivity" and "instinct"–two elements that had been fundamental to Spiegel's existence, were to disappear dramatically. "He should have stopped making films after *Lawrence*," was David Geffen's opinion. How could Spiegel do that? He may have lost interest, but he still wanted control. Once he was king, making pictures was his way of staying involved, mixing with the people he wanted to see, and getting the women he wanted to get. "He needed projects, it was my impression, in order to be able to do all that," said Mike Nichols.

Besides, as the Great Man of Film, Spiegel had a reputation to keep up. Hence his making a bid for British Lion, at the beginning of 1964. Fortunately, the attempt to take over Alexander Korda's former company failed. Spiegel–involved in the running of a studio? No doubt, the idea of filling the late mogul's shoes appealed to his ego, but he was an independent producer, not a manager. Day-to-day problems that related to other people (i.e., not Sam Spiegel) tended to bore him. And how could he have forgotten that British Lion had been a £3 million financial headache for Korda?

There were other projects, such as a film adaptation of Brendan Behan's *The Quare Fellow*. Spiegel was keen until he discovered that the Irish playwright had sold the rights of the play at every one of the London pubs that he had been boozing in.

He was also involved with Fred Zinnemann on a "Peace Project" film for the United Nations. For his research, the director had traveled all over Pakistan and India, as well as taking endless production notes. Although, when Zinnemann went to see Spiegel in his Park Avenue penthouse, he found him to be skittish. "We started to talk and then, in the middle, he picked up his telephone and started calling one of his girlfriends. And so I walked out." Spiegel did come running after him saying, "Baby, baby," but as far as Zinnemann was concerned, their collaboration was over. "In some ways, Sam was a tragic character that you laughed at. And yet, when you laughed, you felt sad, because he had a huge appreciation of things that were beautiful, and a great respect for good craftsmen–a real respect."

In the meantime, Spiegel was suffering a few professional problems.

Mike Frankovich–the head of Columbia's London office–had moved back to Los Angeles at the beginning of 1964. An important studio ally–some even argued henchman–was leaving the producer. "I heard Sam say, 'You've deserted me,' " said Jerry Tokofsky, who worked for the studio executive. Unlike Spiegel, Frankovich still lived with his wife, Binnie Barnes, the retired actress. However, the Columbia executive and Spiegel shared a few interests in common–gin rummy and nubile women. Peter Viertel had been with both men at the George V hotel. "After a huge lunch, Sam was then on the phone with Madame Claude [famous for providing the best-looking call girls in Paris]. He said, 'We'd like something really fresh and young,' like he was ordering something from the butcher's shop. I said that I admired their appetite and promptly left them to it." The call girls were charged to Frankovich's expense account.

While losing Frankovich to the West Coast was an inconvenience, losing Bill Blowitz was a tragedy. The producer's representative was run over by a taxi. "It was after rerunning *The Bridge on the River Kwai* for the Time-Life people," his wife said.

Blowitz, who died on March 14, 1964, was irreplaceable. He was renowned for being brilliant at laying down the groundwork, and was vital to Spiegel's ambitious schemes. During the late 1950s, it was Blowitz who approached the Academy of Motion Picture Arts and Sciences and started the campaign about Spiegel getting the Irving G. Thalberg Memorial Award–a prize given "for the most consistent high level of production achievement by an individual producer." (The recipient previous to Spiegel had been Stanley Kramer, in 1961.) And when they launched *Lawrence,* it was Blowitz's idea to make the ticket price $2 instead of the normal $1. After the film went "wide"–i.e., after New York and Los Angeles, when *Lawrence* was released in all the other major cities in America–he spent the whole period running between the theaters and checking on business. In an ideal world, Spiegel would have shown his appreciation for the sixteen years of unfailing devotion by sitting at Blowitz's bedside as he died. But since the producer had a horror of sickness and death, he never appeared at the hospital. "Sam called to make several appointments, but canceled them," recalled Nina Blowitz.

Perhaps of note, Bill Blowitz was not enthusiastic about either of

Spiegel's new projects, *The Chase* and *The Night of the Generals.* Ironically, he also died a few weeks before Spiegel was presented with the Irving G. Thalberg Memorial Award at the thirty-sixth Academy Awards, on April 13, 1964.

HOW RIGHT AND HOW GOOD read Irene Mayer Selznick's telegram. AND THE BETTER FOR BEING OVERDUE STOP. It was the cherry on the cake. From then on, Spiegel emerged as the authority on film—a sort of self-appointed industry statesman. Being articulate and original, he always gave good copy. "Spiegel Philosophizes on Superficiality of Films Including His Own, Too" had been the title of one *Daily Variety* article. "Movie Industry Could Sell the World on America, Says Spiegel" was another in the *Los Angeles Times.* As well as winning a David of Donatello, the Italian Academy Award, he met with the pope in the summer of 1964 to discuss censorship. Spiegel was reported as being "greatly moved by the interest and concern shown by His Holiness."

"Sam was more fun between *Waterfront* and *Bridge*," said his wife. "And then between *Bridge* and *Lawrence* is when he started to take on a pomposity that he had never had before." David Lean had also noted the change in the producer. He even remarked, "Betty, you know, we had Sam for his best years."

The Horizon Dover Street office remained an exciting address. Beautiful young actresses swanned in and out, but it was not the hive of activity it had once been. Nevertheless, the bills were paid. Evelyn Keyes teased, "Sam, you live now as you used to live when you didn't have any money." Yet in Ingo Preminger's opinion, his newfound wealth made him "less fascinating." "Sam was a guy who when he became rich became almost boring," he said. The former S. P. Eagle's endearing "gotta make it" gambler's edge *was* replaced by a certain amount of self-importance, but then his position had changed. According to Alan Silcocks, his English business manager, Spiegel "just paved his way" after *Lawrence.* "He lived off the proceeds; I don't think Sam minded, he kept on having new projects."

Minded? Spiegel had such a veritable genius for life that he reaped the rewards by creating a glamorous world that few found easy to resist. "He was a different person with different people because he spoke the jargon of so many worlds," said the publisher George

Weidenfeld. Knowing Spiegel became important, a sort of club for the elite. "I remember Jacqueline de Ribes thanking me for introducing him to her." Being with him, whether lunching at his table at the Connaught Hotel in London, or dining at his Park Avenue apartment surrounded by his Impressionist art collection, or staying on *Malahne,* became de rigueur in society.

Spiegel also branched out to the next generation of creative talent. Rudolf Nureyev and Harold Pinter became great friends. As did Warren Beatty and Mike Nichols, who altered the face of American film in 1967 with their pictures *Bonnie and Clyde* and *The Graduate.* Beatty had first seen Spiegel at El Morocco. "He took an interest in me after *Splendor in the Grass.* Sam was like that."

Nichols met the producer with Lillian Hellman, then at Mrs. Vincente Minnelli's house in Hollywood. "I sat next to Denise [Minnelli], who said, 'You know when I am here, I tell the chef to make what I like, it's how I am, I can't help myself. When I'm thirsty, I drink. When I'm hungry, I eat.' I was stunned by this, how it's her nature and how she follows her heart. . . . Anyway, I catch Sam's eye and he says, 'You wanted Hollywood? You got it.' . . . I always loved seeing him in Hollywood, because he was an antidote to all that bullshit."

Politics beckoned as well, ties were strengthened with the Smiths, the Shrivers, and extended acquaintances of the Kennedy family such as Arthur Schlesinger, Jr. Spiegel also befriended George Stevens, Jr., who was Founder of the American Film Institute (AFI), which the Kennedy Center launched in the late 1960s. As well as starting the AFI Life Achievement Award, Stevens Jr. would separately create the Kennedy Center Honors.

In the meantime, Spiegel's French girlfriend had been put aside. "Too many of Marie-Hélène's friends were pressing Sam to marry her," said one insider. No doubt because Mademoiselle Arnaud had been fired from Chanel as a result of her affair with the producer and her ambitious nature—she had designs on Coco Chanel's position.

Being compassionate, Betty Spiegel suggested that her husband set up the ex-model in some way. As was his way, he had completely lost interest in Marie-Hélène. "Sam said, 'She's a drunk . . . and she didn't have a business when I met her.' " Still, Betty felt that he should help in some way. "And he replied, 'I'm not responsible for her in any shape, way, or form.' I always thought he should be.... Sam could be very blasé about ruining people's lives."

It was not a situation that Spiegel's new escort–Jeannette Bishop–would ever find herself in. Exquisite, the blond British model, who was born in 1940, resembled Liv Ullmann, but without the Norwegian actress's sensual appeal. "Jeannette filled a very important role for Sam," said Simone Warner, a friend of both, "because she was very soignée, could mix well, and was even able to act as his hostess on occasion."

However, many wondered about the physical nature of the relationship, since Spiegel continued to see prostitutes during this period. Was he fulfilling his sensual needs, in ways that Bishop could not or would not do? It was a mystery and remained so, because just as Spiegel never discussed personal matters, neither did his girlfriend. "Jeannette hid her feelings," said Lady Warner, the wife of Sir Fred Warner, the late British diplomat. "You could only go so far and she'd withdraw. Emotionally, she was a female version of Sam." Clearly, Spiegel both respected and understood her discretion. Because even though Jeannette left him in order to marry Sir Evelyn de Rothschild in 1966, she briefly returned when her marriage was dissolved in the early 1970s.

Whether in New York or London, Spiegel was always immaculately dressed. James Higgins, his Irish butler, was in charge of his wardrobe in New York, while Charlie and Norman looked after him at the Grosvenor House Hotel, his London residence. In the hotel's hair salon, Spiegel could be spied having a manicure or having his hair straightened. His Sea Island cotton shirts came from Turnbull & Asser, his suits from Douglas Hayward on Mount Street, and his socks and cashmere from Simpson's of Piccadilly. Although content to use a limousine service in New York, Spiegel went all out in London. Until the early 1970s, he was driven around in his midnight blue Silver Cloud Rolls-Royce.

The pipes that Spiegel had previously smoked were replaced by the best cigars that Havana could offer–Monte Cristo II. But contrary to legend, Spiegel never "chomped" on a cigar. Robert Parrish insisted "it wasn't his style." "First of all, he was too much of a gentleman to be caught 'chomping' on anything, except maybe a script, a film director, an actor, a studio head, a critic, or a banker from time to time."

When Spiegel entered a restaurant, waiters hovered. There would be the bevy of beautiful young women around him, and when he sat down, he never looked to see if the chair was there, he presumed it would be and naturally it was. Although a big eater, the producer ate daintily while his never-ending enthusiasm for food continued. He was capable of flying back to London for a certain special that the Connaught Hotel would be serving. He could be contrary and was even known to order tinned sardines at the same place. On another occasion, when making a dinner reservation at the Hôtel de Paris in Monte Carlo, Spiegel told the maître d' that he wanted to eat pot au feu (beef stew). It was mid-August. "But Monsieur Spiegel, that's simply not possible," the maître d' said. "Your reservation is for tonight and pot au feu takes three days to make." However, Spiegel was adamant that he felt like pot au feu, had to have pot au feu and so forth. An exception was made and elaborate preparations were carried out by the hotel's kitchen. But when Spiegel arrived for dinner, he had already gone off the idea of eating hot stew and ordered something else!

Kenneth Jay Lane used to see Spiegel with the Paleys, the Whitneys, and all of "the intelligent New York society." "The other Hollywood moguls weren't part of the New York scene–maybe Selznick, but none of them were very bicoastal," he said. "Sam was also part of the European scene–Deborah Kerr, Peter Viertel, Yul Brynner. Sam was unique, totally unique." He also befriended European beauties such as Sally Crichton-Stuart, who became Salimah Aga Khan, Anouk Aimée, Afdera Franchetti Fonda, and Antonia Fraser.

"Sam had a foot fetish," recalled Sally Aga Khan. "I remember once going to his house for a dinner party and arriving before anyone else and he insisted on seeing my feet. Well, everyone arrived and there he was admiring one of my feet!" Spiegel had tried to get the former fashion model–renowned for her swanlike neck and bone structure– into films. "He was convinced that he could."

Anouk Aimée first met Spiegel when she was making *La Dolce Vita* in Rome. "We were alone in a restaurant and Sam said, 'Don't you think it's wonderful?' And I said, 'Yes, I think it's wonderful, but I would enjoy it much more if you would take your hand off my knee.' I could tell there was a split second of how he felt he should react and then he was fine. When he returned to Rome, he called and it cleared the air. There was no embarrassment."

Afdera Franchetti Fonda–Henry Fonda's fourth wife–also resisted his advances, and like the French actress, was stimulated by the producer's company. "You felt like scratching this ugly man," she said. "The power of this ugly man, I can't think of anything else–perhaps a dinosaur?"

According to Lady Antonia, Spiegel "invited" everyone to his bed. "He didn't mind the rejection at all," she said. "No meant nothing to him and, for all I know, yes meant little either." In regards to the night's entertainment, he had to "take two things in," in an evening. "He couldn't miss out on either event." It was something of a magical mystery tour, accompanying him. "One thing that it would never bring forward was an actual tête-à-tête, which was fine with me."

Spiegel's behavior reminded his third wife of the song from the TV sitcom *The Jeffersons,* "Movin' on Up." "Sam just became too busy for people who he did not think were important enough," she said. Those who had been dropped would complain to Betty. "They'd say, 'Sam doesn't bother to call any more, I'm not important enough.' I'd try to make an excuse. They knew it was an excuse. I knew it was an excuse. Then I stopped."

The Spiegels kept in touch, but they were well and truly separated by the early 1960s. There were many reasons for the final split. On the producer's side, his Betty Boo had grown up; she was almost thirty-two years old, and there was a side of him that did not want to deal with her increasing maturity–a case of the world being full of twenty-year-olds, and his having to pursue them. According to director John Frankenheimer, "At a party, you could always count on the most beautiful young woman in the room being next to Sam Spiegel." Betty, on the other hand, sensed that her husband's promiscuity was as famous as he was. "I thought, he is going to come home and give me genital herpes." However, they never divorced.

"I pleaded with Betty to leave Sam," said Denise Minnelli Hale.

"Because that kind of existence of being separated, but not being divorced, did not allow her to make another kind of life." However, Mrs. Spiegel preferred to hold on to her marital status. "I protected him and he protected me."

Yet according to Betty Estevez, the former S. P. Eagle did not come from the Mike Todd school of marriage and love. "Betty had no jewelry, well nothing important," she said. "And I used to give Sam hell about it. When men make money, they become nouveau riche, the biggest mink for their wife, the biggest diamond. But Sam wasn't like that—it was all for him."

By her own admission, Mrs. Spiegel was not materialistic, nor was she busy plotting out her future. "Everything fell along, it was unbelievable." Moreover, there was a fundamental difference between the two. "Sam cared about social acceptance," said Denise Hale. "Betty couldn't have cared less."

During the early years of their marriage, Spiegel pressed his wife to mix with society. "Sam encouraged me to call and have lunch with Babe [Paley] and Slim [Hayward]," Betty recalled. "I liked both ladies—they were chic and elegant, but we had nothing in common, and they were older. It was a world that just didn't interest me."

In many ways, she preferred the company of the Columbia wives—Mrs. Abe Schneider, Mrs. Leo Jaffe, and Mrs. Max Kettner—her fellow "gin widows." They used to meet regularly at the Monday night screenings, which were held at Columbia's New York office at 711 Fifth Avenue. Most films were shown at 8:00 P.M. sharp and it was wise to wrap up warm. "The rest of us would be there in our furs, scarves, and hats, and Ida Schneider would complain, 'It's too hot in here,' and try and turn the air conditioning on," Betty said. "It would be the dead of winter. . . . On one occasion Debbie Kettner turned around and said, 'Ida, if you don't go through the change of life soon, we'll all turn into Eskimos.' Seriously, it used to be cold enough to hang sides of beef in there."

Meanwhile, Mrs. Spiegel's love life was as charged as her husband's. This included having affairs with high-society brother-in-laws Bill Paley and John "Jock" Hay Whitney, as well as Omar Sharif. Not one to waste time, her liaison with the actor had surprised David Lean. "She must have got him into bed with her almost as soon as Sam had got on the plane for New York," he had written.

Nevertheless, Betty remained devoted to her husband. "Sam gave me and the Ryans the boat for ten days," Kenneth Jay Lane recalled. "Anyway, I told Betty, 'Sam has asked me on *Malahne* and if you don't want me to go, I won't.' And she said, 'Baby, if you don't go, I'll never speak to you again.'" She recognized the importance of the boat to her husband.

Indeed, until the early 1980s, it was the place to be seen. "There was a beautiful model who I had been after for years," said Nichols. "She didn't pay any attention to me until I asked her whether she wanted to come on Sam's boat, and she said, 'Yes, get me there instantly.'"

In many respects, *Malahne* became a never-ending Spiegel production. "Warren Beatty called Sam the 'unit manager' because he was always making arrangements," said George Stevens, Jr. "Whether he was telling the crew when to have lunch or calling ahead for the car to meet his guests, he was doing all the stuff that unit managers do. Using walkie-talkies, paying for the gas when the boat was filled up. The name was affectionate, but here he was organizing. When it was right, it was splendid. And, at its worst, it wasn't very bad." One time, when heading to see some ruins outside Rome, their car broke down on a small Italian highway. "It was one of the great sights of my life. Sam had this big leather wallet which he always carried and he was there trying to hitch a ride. Misfortune struck and you saw that he didn't always have boats."

Just as Spiegel's New Year's Eve parties in Hollywood were not to be missed, neither was an invitation on board *Malahne*. The boat was old-fashioned by today's standards. It lacked a helicopter or a swimming pool, but all that it lacked in modern equipment was insignificant when compared to its majestic charm. Stepping onto *Malahne* was like stepping into another era. "There was such comfort," said Stevens. "It was beautifully done–caviar, pâté, great wines, bullshots served in alabaster goblets." The service was flawless; James Jordan, the Barbadian steward, filled glasses without the sound of a footstep. "The bathtubs were perfect, and just as the sun was setting, James would bring you a martini."

The deck was teak, while the dining room, on the lower deck, was lined in walnut. During the day, most of the activity was on the upper deck. Before and after a drawn-out lunch, guests either soaked up the sun or stayed in the Blue Saloon–the lounge area–where the newspapers were delivered, gin rummy games were played, and screenplay conferences were conducted.

Spiegel occupied the main suite, which was under the bridge. It had an adjoining bathroom, as well as a connecting dressing room with a single bed and washroom. The latter was normally reserved for the producer's lady friend or future conquest.

In total, there were five cabins for Spiegel's other guests, but since they varied in size, there was always a mad rush for the first two suites, which had double beds and adjoining bathrooms in comparison to the other double cabin, which was much smaller, and the two single cabins–one with a bunk bed and wash basin and the other which only had a bunk. "People used to change their flight times to make sure they arrived before everyone else, and Sam used to get *so* angry about it," recalled Tessa Kennedy. "He would say, 'It's unbelievable. You would think Arthur Schlesinger is coming and she [his wife, Alexandra] is so tall and needs extra space, but I can't tell my guests this because it's always been 'first come, first served.' But I would assume that they would know how to behave."

The stories from *Malahne*–both true and apocryphal–became the staple of gossip and the stuff of stand-up comedians. Some tales were dark, leading to the ship being called the "floating ship of evil." "That was the place to have the video camera," said Arthur Canton. *Malahne* became synonymous with the Cannes Film Festival. The boat had even appeared on the cover of *Life* magazine under the heading "Luxury and Languor of Riviera Yachting."

It was where the stars rubbed shoulders with the aristocracy and the super-rich, which was not as obvious as it sounds. Being a social animal, Spiegel recognized how each elite was impressed by the other, and he became the catalyst. "Everyone wants to meet stars and no one more than the other stars," says Sue Mengers, the former agent, who was as famous for her clients–Warren Beatty, Gene Hackman, Ali MacGraw, and Barbra Streisand–as her parties. "Stars don't feel the need to reciprocate, they feel their presence is enough, and you know what, they're right." In her experience, legendary millionaires such as Malcolm Forbes and Stavros Niarchos were "the biggest groupies!" " 'You must come on my boat, stay in my château, etc.' There's nothing like a star to make people feel weak at the knees."

As a result of Spiegel's mix of worlds, there were the occasional odd incidents. Brigitte Bardot was introduced to Edward Heath, and the former British prime minister was clueless about who she was. But perhaps it was not as shocking as an Italian aristocrat who had never heard of his lunch partner–Greta Garbo.

Then there was a much less amusing occasion when the Manson murders happened in August 1969. As usual, the dinner party on board the boat was glittering; the guests were a mixture of the accomplished or the super-rich. However, no one was from Hollywood. Diana Phipps, the interior decorator, was there with Evangeline Bruce, the wife of the U.S. ambassador for Britain during the Camelot years. "Suddenly, Sam was called away from the table," she said. "When he returned, no one had really noticed until he tapped on his glass and said, 'Friends, I have the most terrible news, the most ghastly horrible tragedy has happened and I don't even know how to begin to tell you.' Well, the terror, each one thought our parents, our children were dead, that the war had started, and finally he said, 'Sharon Tate has been brutally murdered.' (I just happened to know who she was.) But there was such a relief that it wasn't our children, that the world was still intact, that everybody giggled."

When arriving at the St. Tropez port, *Malahne* was always moored on the left. "And everyone knew it was Sam," said Florence Grinda, a French socialite. The producer was a familiar figure at Chez Félix, a bar on the port, which was frequented by the hip and the famous. "People used to stand outside to see who was inside."

On board, guests were expected to dress up. "I couldn't believe it when Sophie Litvak [the model wife of Anatole Litvak] arrived with eleven pieces of luggage, and it was a short cruise," said Lilou Grumbach, the sister of Christian Marquand and Nadine Trintignant. "But there was such a rich state of mind." She described her generation as being that of *"je ne regarde jamais mes factures"* (I never look at my bills).

With Spiegel at the helm, it was not always smooth sailing. "He was like Captain Queeg," said Anne Douglas. The producer's word was law. "Now Sam and I had one thing in common—we loved to play cards." As a result, when the others went ashore, Mrs. Kirk Douglas was held hostage. "He used to shake his hands and say, 'Come on now, come on now.' "

Polly Bergen became a *Malahne* regular with her then husband, Freddie Fields. "I was extremely unsophisticated about Europe, I was seeing everything for the first time," the actress admitted. But just as they were pulling into an Italian port, Spiegel announced that he wanted his guests back in two hours. "I said, 'Sam, we've just got here and I've never seen Portofino.' And he says, 'No, Gaston [van Hanja, Spiegel's cook] is making a soufflé, you have to be back,' and I looked at him and said, 'Sam, I've had a soufflé, I have never been to Portofino. Don't be such a pain in the ass.' He was absolutely horrified that I was putting Portofino above his chef's soufflé."

In spite of being Spiegel the Sea Hawk, who was not afraid of sailing into a high wind and a cruel sea, he was always hesitant about water-skiing. Lauren Bacall remembered a terrible fight between Steve Smith, Sr. (Jean Kennedy Smith's husband), and the producer. "He said, 'Stop being Hitler.' Because Sam was saying, 'You have to do this, you have to do that,' and Steve said, 'Listen, we don't have to take orders for crissakes. We're all here to have a good time. Stop ordering us around like children.' "

Joan Juliet Buck, the daughter of Jules and the former editor-in-chief of French *Vogue,* had been on the boat with the Irwin Shaws and their son, Adam. Spiegel had two ladies on board—a blonde and a redhead—who spent their time sunbathing. "They had very little conversation," recalled Buck. " 'What do you do?' 'I'm a model.' 'Runway or photographic?' 'I'm a model.' " One night, the entire party of guests went over to Cala di Volpe in Sardinia. Afterward, no one could find Adam Shaw or Vereina Bloch, Spiegel's redheaded girlfriend. "There's all this talk. 'Have they gone dancing?' And I'm sitting there, not saying a word. I have a pretty good idea." The couple was then spotted, bobbing up and down, in the boat's Zodiac. That night, Adam's mother told him off for taking "someone else's girlfriend." While the next morning, Vereina was put in the tender with her black alligator luggage and left at the port of Ponza, among the cages of ducks, chickens, and other poultry. "Sam, see you in St.

Tropez," she cried out. In the meantime, Buck described Spiegel as, "standing implacable at the rail."

"There was a certain amount of thinness and meanness around the edges," said Mike Nichols. "Like the semi-hooker who dropped a cushion in the ocean by mistake and was made to get off the boat. She had to leave at the next port of call because of his cushion. But even then it was funny."

The hesitancy with gifts was another one of Spiegel's idiosyncrasies. Perhaps it fell into the department of a former con man being scared of being conned? Take the seventeenth birthday of Sophie Ouvrier, the daughter of Jacqueline de la Chaume, Yul Brynner's third wife. "Sam was very sweet and organized birthday cakes. He couldn't have been nicer." That afternoon, the boat was sailing to St. Tropez. "Sam said to Sophie, 'You and I will go to all those stores on the port and we will buy whatever you want.' " De la Chaume had instructed her daughter to either choose a T-shirt or a pair of espadrilles, but nothing expensive. However, they returned empty-handed. "He said, 'We couldn't find anything nice,' and I said to my daughter, 'Was there really nothing that you liked?' She replied, 'Oh yes, Mummy, but Sam was always saying it wasn't nice enough.' And I can't tell you how much I laughed. We were talking $5 or something like that."

Presents or not, Spiegel was capable of showing great empathy toward his lady friends such as Bettina Graziani, Kitty Carlisle Hart, Slim Hayward, and Leonora Hornblow. "He was very important to them when the worst things happened in their lives," Nichols sensed. "He had great sympathy with the swans who were left." When her husband publicly deserted Slim Hayward, Spiegel took the time and trouble to look after her. He also dared to tell her a few home truths, which no one else did. "Slim, everybody in the world knows Leland's going to marry Pam [Churchill]," he said. "She's told everybody, and he's told everybody."

Spiegel was also there for Lauren Bacall when Humphrey Bogart passed away. "He was always very generous about me coming to stay," she said.

He put his boat at Margot Fonteyn's disposal when she was dancing for the Monte Carlo ballet. "Tito Arias, Margot's husband, had been Ari Onassis's lawyer," revealed a mutual friend. "But when Tito had his accident [he was shot and paralyzed in South America], instead of making *Christina* available, which Onassis should have done, Sam came along and was marvelous."

On another occasion, Bettina Graziani, Givenchy's favorite model, was staying with him in Greece. "He took us to an ancient theater with an echo and he asked us all to go down, all the guests from the boat. Then Sam started to cry out, 'Bettina, I love you.' It was so incredible and the echo was so big. . . . Sam doing that, it was charming."

When Betty Spiegel's mother became ill, he flew out to see her in Virginia. "Sam, who had a horror of illness and hospitals, suddenly arrived," said his wife. He stayed for five days. "He said, 'Mabel, what do you want?' And she said, 'A red car.' Well, as soon as she got out, it was there. This big red car with a large ribbon around it."

In many ways, Spiegel continued to prefer female company to his male friends. Was it the lack of competition, which made him feel at ease, or was it the pleasure of being in their company? Daniel Selznick, David's son, recalled him flirting "outrageously with all women," including his mother. "Whether he actually acted on the seduction, we don't know, but there was that quality," he said. "Betty Bacall and any women of unique glamour would have stories about how he came on to them and part of it was the accent. You couldn't get away with what he was saying with an American accent. It was outrageous, but it was also part of the charm."

Spiegel tried to help Daniel's father with his pay TV idea. He arranged meetings with Columbia in the spring of 1964. It was the type of curious power switch that tends to happen in the motion picture industry, because although Selznick had once been dismissive of S. P. Eagle, now the tide had changed. Spiegel was riding high as a film giant, whereas the former studio mogul had lost his Midas touch. A year later, when Selznick died, Spiegel was an honorary pallbearer at the funeral, although he was unable to attend the event.

"Dad liked to feel you had modeled yourself after him," his youngest son wrote to Spiegel afterward. "I don't know whether such an arrogant thought would please or anger you—but you know, it was really because you are the only one in the last 10–15 years producing the kind of films he felt he could have been proud of. I think he sometimes wished they were his."

It was strange that Spiegel received this letter when he was making *The Chase,* his first Hollywood production in fourteen years. Based on Horton Foote's novel and play, as well as two of his television plays, *John Turner Davis* and *The Midnight Caller,* Marlon Brando, Lillian Hellman, and Arthur Penn were just a few of the illustrious names associated with the picture. Yet in spite of all the high expectations, it turned into a critical and financial disaster.

The first in years for Spiegel–but not the last.

Chapter Twenty-three

THE CHASE, THE HAPPENING, THE NIGHT OF THE GENERALS, AND THE SWIMMER

Sam was obsessed by his triumphant return," said Arthur Penn, who referred to the moment as "a fantasy time" for the producer. "It was the childhood dream of coming back and receiving the laurels that his heart desired. And there's no place in the world that admires power or riches more than Hollywood. Given Sam's previous history, those stories of his S. P. Eagle days and having no money, it was understandable."

The Chase was Spiegel's first film after *Lawrence of Arabia,* and his first Hollywood film since *When I Grow Up.* Moreover, it was Lillian Hellman's first screenplay since being blacklisted. "Sam viewed hiring Lillian as his ambassadorial mission to the screen," Penn recalled.

In Penn's opinion, a mutual admiration was going between two people who had known each other since the 1940s. "Lillian was two things, a major dramatist–perhaps overrated–but still very potent as a voice in the theater. She was also the queen of the intellectuals, and threw the best literary and political dinner parties in New York. The Styrons, the Mailers—all of that great crowd—she could attract them." Spiegel was the important producer with the rich, extravagant lifestyle—and power and money were always an aphrodisiac for Hellman.

Physically, she looked like Regina, Spiegel's mother. In character, there was also a resemblance. Both were capable of being imperious, with a need to be the center of attention. Each had personal elegance: shapeless flowery dresses, which might have looked frumpy on others, worked on both ladies. Hellman was more worldly and sophisticated, smoking like a chimney in one hand and a scotch in the other, with the customary two ice cubes. Richard Roth, the producer of *Julia,* which was based on a chapter from Hellman's *Pentimento,* labeled her a "man's woman." "Lillian was a handful: funny, tough, demanding," he said. The communication tended to be intense. "There was always lots of courtship, letters, and meetings."

For *The Chase,* the playwright received a fee of $125,000 from Lone Star Pictures Corporation—a production company created for the film. She was not the first writer on the project. Michael Wilson had been involved when Spiegel acquired the rights in 1956. Nevertheless, all his drafts were thrown away when Hellman took over in 1963. "You said that you wanted the picture to be 'large,'" she wrote to the producer. "So do I, but I always have trouble with the word large. (One can say that whatever is good is large, but that isn't what is usually meant.)"

The story was set in Texas. Bubber Reeves (Robert Redford) escapes prison with a fellow inmate. They stop a car and the inmate kills the driver and speeds off, leaving Reeves—who is innocent—to be accused of the crime. Reeves then returns to his hometown to see his wife, Anna (Jane Fonda). Adding to the plot's suspense is the fact that she is having an affair with his best friend, Jason "Jake" Rogers (James Fox). Meanwhile, the news of Reeves's breakout sends the town into pandemonium and leads to certain debauched citizens (including Richard Bradford) taking the law into their own hands and tracking him down. The town's sheriff, Calder (Marlon Brando), and his wife (Angie Dickinson) try to conceal the fugitive's whereabouts, but their efforts prove futile and Reeves is eventually killed.

Hellman agreed with Spiegel's idea that the film "should concern itself with a society that is not too distant from frontier life." "Such a society would carry with it violence, or the possibility of violence, because it must contain many displaced people who find that frontiers no longer exist," she wrote. The circumstances of John F. Kennedy's assassination were also to have an impact on the screenplay. "Texas, unlike most of the South, is rich and powerful, and often shows a kind of anger that its convictions do not govern the rest of America," she continued. "I would think that this is one of the reasons for the spitting at Adlai Stevenson and possibly one of the reasons of the *handling*–not the killing itself–of the Kennedy murder. It also accounts for Mr. Ruby." There were even those in the cast of *The Chase* who were told it was the story of Lee Harvey Oswald.

Brando was linked to the project from the start. (The actor was paid $750,000 for his services, and Pennebaker–his film company–received $130,000 as a production fee.) In the late 1950s, there was an idea that he would play Jason to Marilyn Monroe's Anna. But seven years later, he was considered too old. Initially, Brando was not eager to play Sheriff Calder. He had just been in Northeast India "where the Bihar famine was making headlines around the world, and he tried to make a documentary with his own money about UNICEF's emergency food programme." Brando was UTTERLY FATIGUED from traveling in a country he described as THE ANUS OF THE WORLD. When he returned to Los Angeles, Brando complained that his role only entailed "wandering around and doing nothing." He referred to himself as the old lamplighter.

Penn was more enthusiastic. He had been pushing his William Morris agent to get him the job for months. At first, Spiegel had ignored the forty-two-year-old's pleas, but he started to take an interest when Hellman started to plead for Penn too. Besides, *The Chase* had done the rounds. Elia Kazan, David Lean, Fred Zinnemann, and William Wyler had all passed. Joseph Mankiewicz had been a serious contender–he had urged Spiegel to make Bubber and his wife black–but ultimately he had also declined.

It appealed to Spiegel's commercial sense that Penn and Hellman had an excellent batting record. Penn's production of her play *Toys in the Attic* was a Broadway triumph. "We were very good friends," Penn said. "My wife and I had seen her through Dash's death [referring to her longtime companion, Dashiell Hammett]."

The producer, writer, and director had then joined forces on the East Coast and tinkered with the screenplay. Afterward, Spiegel wrote to Peter O'Toole: "I think that you and he [Penn] will have a great deal of fun together before, during, and after the picture." Penn also enjoyed Spiegel's company, finding him elegant and cultured. "I always liked Sam, that never changed." He admired the courage. "He had the guts of a blind burglar." Penn belonged to the Kazan school of thought: "I thought he was pretty good on construction." During the screenplay sessions, Penn actually got on better with Spiegel than with his former accomplice. "Lillian was pretty annoying and not really functioning very well."

Hellman could be thoughtless. For instance, when she agreed to meet with Richard Day, *The Chase*'s distinguished production designer, who had worked with Spiegel since *Tales of Manhattan* and had won an Oscar for *On the Waterfront,* she demanded that he join her at her house in Martha's Vineyard. No easy feat under any circumstances, it was the height of summer—always a difficult time to travel—and would mean changing planes several times. Once Day, a man in his late sixties, arrived, however, Hellman wanted him "to return the next day." Spiegel's New York secretary had to break the news to Day—with "your great tact," the playwright insisted. As with Spiegel, everything had to be on Hellman's terms.

In the meantime, Penn was tipped to be the next Kazan. He was a member of the Actors Studio; had a string of hits on Broadway including *Golden Boy,* starring Sammy Davis, Jr.; Paul Newman had starred in his first motion picture, *The Left-Handed Gun,* while his last released film, *The Miracle Worker,* had been nominated for an Oscar. But alas, another dynamic was afoot. The director was born after the First World War, and belonged to a generation that was very different from that of the directors behind Spiegel's triumphs.

Penn—like his peers—was less hard-nosed with actors, was open to the Nouvelle Vague (the New Wave of European cinema) and other influences, and had worked in a smaller medium—television. Old-timers like Burt Lancaster did not appreciate such ideas. Lancaster had had Penn taken off his film *The Train.* In the meantime, Columbia was a little distressed by *Mickey One,* the director's most recent effort. Penn recalled getting a "strangled call of congratulations" from Mike Frankovich and Leo Jaffe. "It was clear that they had seen *Mickey One* and had hated it." But it would be different with Spiegel, or so everyone presumed.

Spiegel left Penn and Hellman in order to lock up the casting on the West Coast. His attempts to have Peter O'Toole play Jason Rogers had failed. The actor dismissed *The Chase* as "one of those ghastly 'Lifts the Lid' subjects only it's not *PEYTON PLACE,* it's South West America." Moreover, O'Toole was furious that his contract with Spiegel prevented him from doing *Sherlock Holmes* with Billy Wilder, and *Doctor Zhivago* with Lean.

Spiegel was equally annoyed. "It might be interesting to reread your letter when *The Chase* has been completed and judged by our betters," he shot back.

James Fox was brought in to play Rogers. "Sam kept me waiting for weeks," the British actor recalled. "He wasn't sure if I could master the Texan accent." However, once Fox was cast, Spiegel "rather lost interest."

Regarding the other roles, Penn came up with the likes of Robert Duvall, E. G. Marshall, Janice Rule, and Richard Bradford for the town's citizens, while Spiegel suggested Jane Fonda and a certain young blond actor. "Robert Redford was totally his idea, I had never heard of him," the director admitted. "I have to say that as far as casting, Sam was fantastic. He certainly had a clear view of what the film should be like. At first, he certainly delivered."

Including one of his latest "Spiegelettes," Katherine Walsh, a pretty blonde from Covington, Kentucky, who played "the girl in the party scene." "She wasn't much of an actress but she had caught Sam's eye," Penn said. Introducing Walsh was an indication that Spiegel was using the casting couch. In his suite at the Beverly Wilshire, he had a secret bedroom with its own main door that allowed women to come and go without being seen.

"On the set, it was thought that most of the women in the party scene had gone down on their knees for Sam," said the actress Pat Quinn. "It was good old Hollywood." It was also a sign that Spiegel's personal life was overlapping with his professional life, and marked the beginning of his tempting actresses with the promise of furthering their careers, since he now had both the power and the projects. It was a distinct change in dynamics because although he had married Lynne Baggett, a beautiful starlet, he hardly helped her career. During the courting stages of their relationship, a screen test on the set of *The Stranger* was his only contribution.

With the end of his male-oriented projects, Spiegel's couch was much more in evidence. Not that he was handing out starring roles; it was more the case of tiny parts with a few lines. Spiegel certainly lacked the romantic flair of Selznick, who risked everything with the casting of Jennifer Jones, his lover, and then his wife. There were the exceptions–the untouchables whom Spiegel nurtured. He had noticed an all-American beauty–Candice Bergen–whom he had personally introduced to Columbia, which led to her being put under contract and being tested for several of his productions.

Meanwhile, *The Chase* screenplay remained in desperate need of work. Ivan Moffat was brought in to rewrite it. "Sam contacted me when I was working on *The Heroes of Telemark,* a film starring Kirk Douglas," he recalled. Previously linked with director George Stevens (he collaborated on *A Place in the Sun,* co-produced *Shane,* and co-wrote *Giant*), Moffat's other screenwriting credits included entertaining, albeit melodramatic star vehicles such as *Bhowani Junction* and *The Boy on a Dolphin.* The English writer was amused by his encounters with Spiegel. "He was crablike and all-controlling. Sam would hold on to everything." Moffat had taken a crumpled piece of paper from his desk. "He said 'What is this, Ivan? No, Pleeease.' And I had to put it back." Spiegel also liked to keep tabs on those in his employment. "On Saturday or Sunday, he would call up, saying 'Ivan, where are you going? Please leave a number. We might have to work.' There was never any question of our working." Nor could Spiegel be teased. "He, Marlon, and I were having dinner together, I said something flippant, and he said, 'Ivan, hold the humor.' "

Despite the countless script sessions as well as rewrites from Horton Foote, the screenplay still lacked originality and depth. "It was a bad version of *High Noon,*" said Moffat. In the interim, Lillian Hellman was horrified by the new draft and complained that "the bite and freshness and comment have been, in many places, lost altogether, and a rather well organized, old fashioned quality has crept in." During filming, Penn would be "troubled by a page that would arrive with new dialogue," which "all seemed to emanate from Sam's office," even if the producer himself was absent. "Once the film started shooting, there was no exchange between us," said Penn.

Spiegel did keep tabs on Penn, but since he was partying hard and meeting with Hollywood's power people, his calls were never before 11:00 A.M. "He'd say, 'Arthur, how is it going?' I started to feel that Big Brother was watching over me." Another question would be: "Marlon didn't bring his motorcycle did he?" Brando was then a motorcycle enthusiast. At the beginning of filming, he had lacerated his knee and Spiegel was worried that he might kill himself, as James Dean had.

Well aware of Spiegel's fears, Brando put his motorcycle in the back of a truck one day and had it delivered to the studio. "Marlon was very fond of Sam; jokes were part of his form of expression of that," said Penn. So the next time Spiegel called, the director admitted that he had seen the dreaded motorcycle, but that Brando was nowhere to be seen. "I'll be right there," Spiegel said, slamming down the telephone. Spiegel then arrived with a jacket over his pajamas. "When Sam found out it was a joke, he joined in and laughed, but he was clearly ill at ease."

Spiegel became genuinely angry with Brando when he missed a morning's filming because he was at home "trying to avoid being served by a Deputy Marshal [prosecution had asked him to be a material witness in Anna Kashfi's trial]." Brando also refused to be photographed, in spite of his contract, which gave him the right to approve all stills. Mistrusting the conditions, he argued, "someone might make duplicate negatives and a year later use a still that he had rejected." Moreover, his soft voice became a problem for the sound department. When asked to speak up, he refused. "I cannot sacrifice the mood of the scene for the sound track," had been his reply.

While there was a love fest going on in certain quarters—during the course of filming, Angie Dickinson and Jane Fonda married their respective boyfriends—Penn found *The Chase* to be a "hugely burdensome film to make." "It required a certain amount of baby-sitting. Miriam Hopkins, who played Bubber's mother, she needed a great deal of care. Now, I have nothing but compassion for a former movie legend playing an old lady, but it takes up time."

Penn was further weighed down by not getting the cameraman he wanted. Spiegel had hired Robert Surtees, a renowned and reliable Hollywood cameraman who had won three Academy Awards. Then Surtees got sick. Without consulting Penn, Spiegel replaced Surtees with another old-timer–Joseph LaShelle–who was highly respected, but not on Penn's wavelength. "It should be a close relationship, but I found him to be difficult and slow," said Penn. "For the night scenes, he would be lighting until midnight. And, in *The Chase*, we had a lot of night scenes."

Regarding the dailies, Spiegel occasionally saw them. "But not with great regularity." Such a lack of interest seemed a clear indication that Penn was to be left on his own to edit, but when the director was back on the East Coast and deep in rehearsals for the play *Wait Until Dark*, he received quite a different type of message. "Where do you want to edit, in Los Angeles or London?" Spiegel growled. Since neither place was possible for Penn, Spiegel's office arranged for all the cans of film to be sent to England, with specific instructions that the editor Gene Milford was to work there with the producer. "Sam wanted to be the author," stated the director.

When Penn finally arrived in England, he saw "eight reels of pretty well-finished film." "It was nothing that I would conspicuously differ with, but it lacked my sense of rhythm. I was shooting the film to be more nervous . . . and pop a little." It was the height of the Nouvelle Vague and both Truffaut and Godard were personal friends of Penn's. "That's what disturbed and drove me crazy," he said. "It was the beginning of that great shift–Sam and Gene were the other side of the cusp. I'm not saying that the film would have necessarily been better if I had edited it, but I just knew the rhythm that was in my gut and it was not on that screen. The tempos were not right and I pride myself on the tempo and on the accumulating velocity that is part of the volume." Nor was he involved with John Barry's score.

Spiegel was not to be reasoned with. "He said, 'This is the way it's going to be.'" Spiegel had kidnapped his baby and Penn was appalled.

At the end of the picture, Lillian Hellman was also furious with Spiegel. He had refused to show her a final cut. "She will see it in color–in black and white–in rough cut, with or without music," wrote Robert Lantz, her agent. "She wants to see the over-all work, and I urge you to make that possible for her here in New York as soon as it is practical."

Her ruffled feathers were soon smoothed by Spiegel. Professionally, they were ill-suited, but on a personal level, Spiegel and Hellman understood each other. (He later referred to her as being "a marvellous writer" with "more balls than two Arthur Penns and four Sam Spiegels.") "Sam had many of the same gifts as Lillian," said Mike Nichols. "They consisted of being so interesting and intelligent and having material that was so fresh. Neither of them repeated stories or anecdotes." Hellman continued to be a regular on *Malahne*. On one trip, she met a very beautiful Swedish movie actress. "Lillian told her that she reminded her of Marilyn Monroe and this Swedish actress said, 'Oh but that always makes me so sad.' And Lillian replied, 'Yes, it was a sad life.' And the actress said, 'Oh no, no, no, not that. It's not that. It's just that I am beautiful and she wasn't.' " Nichols described her telling the story "in rapture." "Lillian loved the people that she got to meet with Sam."

When *The Chase* hit the American screens in March 1966, it received a universal thumbs-down. "This is a picture to leave you cold," Bosley Crowther wrote in the *New York Times,* and compared it to "an obvious cross breeding of *High Noon* and *Peyton Place.*" *The New Yorker* described it as a "conventionally opulent melodrama" that had been "overproduced by Sam Spiegel, over plotted to the point of incoherence by the author of the screenplay, Lillian Hellman, and over directed."

Worldwide, the film received a mixed reaction. In Europe, it had quite a following, especially in France where it was released under the title *La Poursuite Impitoyable.* It is slow, but Brando's performance deserves patience, as do most of the cast, especially Richard Bradford. Favored by some as a kitsch classic, it contains pretty racy stuff for that period, such as wife swapping, and a hideously gory scene when the sheriff is beaten to a pulp.

The Chase died at the box office. The negative cost of the film was $5,660,166.16 and five years later it had lost almost $3 million. "There was an expectation that it would be newer and brighter," said Penn.

It was a very alive and electric time in the United States. The Watts riots in August 1965 took place while *The Chase* was being made; there was also the civil rights movement and the antiwar movement. "So many things were cooking, and perhaps people came to this film expecting it to speak for that moment." He admitted that he was both "dismayed" and "pretty angry" about his experience on the picture. "Fortunately, along came *Bonnie and Clyde*."

Doctor Zhivago, which had come out a few months earlier, was also panned by the critics. But there was an essential difference–business was booming and the lines to see Lean's epic went around the block and back. It had caught the public's imagination with its romantic story of ill-fated lovers.

Spiegel actually made $150,000 off the MGM production, since he and Columbia had loaned out Omar Sharif's services, but it was a tiny compensation for his future productions. *The Chase* was the first of a string of failures, yet with typical aplomb, he never looked back.

Spiegel continued with his plan to foster newcomers and make small productions, which were not to be cross-collateralized and interfere with his previous successes. Each picture was to stand on its own, and Jud Kinberg, who had just co-produced William Wyler's *The Collector,* was hired to oversee the operation. "Sam knew very little about me. The cachet was that I had worked with John Houseman, that's all that he had to hear." The job, which was based out of London, lasted two and a half years. Kinberg recalled the experience as "delightful." "Sam was a delicious dichotomy." The producer became a mentor.

Kinberg's projects for Horizon included co-producing *Fahrenheit 451,* the film of the Ray Bradbury novel which was to be directed by François Truffaut, and working on *The Curious Gentlemen,* a train robbery film idea with the team from *Beyond the Fringe,* the popular satirical revue–Alan Bennett, Jonathan Miller, Peter Cook, and Dudley Moore. Kinberg also optioned the rights of Nicholas Mosley's *Accident,* with Joe Losey in mind. Spiegel was anxious to do another film with Losey, and Kinberg soon discovered why. "He still owes me money on *The Prowler,*" Losey revealed. Harold Pinter–Losey's collaborator on *The Servant*–was paid £7,500 to write the screenplay.

As soon as Spiegel read the first draft of *Accident*, Losey and Pinter were summoned to his Dover Street office. He began his commentary by saying "You call this a screenplay?"

"Sam then said, 'I just don't understand what you're getting at.'" Pinter recalled. "'You can't make a movie out of this. Who are these people? I don't know anything about them. I don't know anything about their background. I don't know what they're doing. I don't understand what they're up to. I don't understand one thing. I think you have to seriously rethink the whole script.' So I said, 'No, I'm not rethinking it, that's it.' And Joe absolutely agreed, and [Spiegel] said, 'Well, I think that you are both crazy. . . . I don't want to do it, I'm not going to go on with this script.' He said something like 'It's all muscle, but there's no flesh. I can't understand the characters.' We sort of said, 'Sorry about that but we're not changing it.' It was quite a hard interview. Joe said that when we got out of there, I was sick on the pavement. It was not true. That's a false report."

Kinberg sensed it was a grave error not producing *Accident*. "It was the sort of picture we should have done." However, making small films in England did not appeal to Spiegel. "I think that bothered him a great deal in terms of the commerciality." (Meanwhile, entirely thanks to Spiegel, Columbia distributed Losey's *The Damned* in the United States. The film's title was changed to *These Are the Damned*.) Instead, Kinberg commuted between Los Angeles and Miami Beach and became the producer on *The Innocent*, a film that was based on a story by James D. Buchanan and Ronald Austin.

Although Spiegel was the film's executive producer, he became very involved in the preproduction aspect. It was his idea to use Elliot Silverstein and his writing partner Frank Pierson. The team had just made *Cat Ballou*–an unexpected hit for Columbia. Silverstein was impressed by Spiegel, particularly his "suave seduction of anybody," and the fact that he was "very conscious of it." However, despite being "very literate," "he [Sam] was not as hip as he thought he was." Spiegel's great line was, "I am surrounded by young life," but to the director's eyes, he was a little old-fashioned. (Still, the producer was more hip than Columbia's Leo Jaffe, who had flown into London to deal with the troubled set of *Casino Royale*. He had rushed up to one of the stars saying, "Woody, Woody, what are we going to do about this nut Peter Sellers?" The young man replied, "I don't know, I am Peter Sellers, what do you want me to do?")

Yet again, Spiegel was dealing with the younger generation, and a director who had cut his teeth in television. "Sam was interested in the story of the picture being told in a traditional way, it was more serious than how I saw it," said Silverstein. "I wanted to do a vaudeville kind of film, a mocking satire of certain social values." Their sessions were far from antagonistic, but just a case of two different attitudes. "Frank and I wanted to be tongue-in-cheek, and Sam was not comfortable with that."

The Innocent was about a group of hippies–Taurus (George Maharis), Sureshot (Michael Parks), Herby (Robert Walker, Jr.), and Sandy (Faye Dunaway)–who decide to kidnap Roc Delmonico (Anthony Quinn), a retired Mafia kingpin. But the plan takes a strange twist when his wife, Monica (Martha Hyer), and former associates refuse to pay the ransom and Delmonico teams up with his kidnappers instead.

Spiegel was concerned about the casting of Michael Parks. Maybe Silverstein had directed him for Universal Television and John Huston had cast him as Adam in *The Bible*, but Spiegel was looking for a Redford. "He wanted someone whom the camera loved, someone who could stay on the screen with Quinn, because Tony would gobble him up otherwise," Kinberg recalled.

On the other hand, Spiegel was thrilled with the film's newcomer, Faye Dunaway. The young actress was discovered in an off-Broadway production called *Hogan's Goat.* "The camera loves you," Spiegel told Dunaway. "As Sam spun his tale, I sat there barely believing what I was hearing, but willing my face not to give me away," she wrote in her memoirs. "I was star material, he said, the kind of actress who could expect a thirty-year career, which seemed like something close to forever."

In true Horizon Pictures style, Dunaway was signed up for a five-picture deal. She received $19,200 for *The Innocent,* which was more than double what the actress had earned previously in an entire year. "I called up my agency, CMA, and told them that they had better get down there," Elliot Silverstein recalled. "She was the only girl in a Sam Spiegel picture. Other agents tried to get hold of her. There was a lot of excitement, which is quite rare." Ultimately, Dunaway left her agency and signed up with David Begelman, then an agent at CMA.

Magazines such as *Harper's Bazaar, Esquire,* and others were also after Dunaway, who had bleached her dark brown hair for the part. As a result, there was a little tension in the Ivan Tors Studio in Florida. "Michael Parks was somewhat discomfited by all the press attention," Silverstein said. "It made it difficult for him to play love scenes with her and to continue his work in a normal manner."

The actor's unhappiness was soon referred to as the "Parks Emergency" and Carlo Fiore, Brando's former pal, was called in to baby-sit. On one occasion, Parks refused to work until Spiegel–hardly the film's official producer–personally telephoned him.

"Sam calls up and says, 'You have to go to Miami, it's chaos,' " said Jerry Tokofsky, who was working at Columbia. "And I said, 'I don't do those things, a guy who shows up yelling at people.' Half an hour later, it's Frankovich, and he's got Abe Schneider and Leo Jaffe on the phone." The executive had no choice. He promptly flew down, describing the atmosphere on the set as "terrible."

The director and producer were not seeing eye-to-eye. "I found communicating with Elliot difficult, he had a favorite phrase, 'Jud, this is a round conversation.' I wanted to kill him . . . it became a round experience." But in retrospect, Kinberg sensed that Spiegel's weight was needed. "We were acting out, 'Daddy, prove you love me.' And Daddy wasn't there."

Spiegel did advise on the film's rough cut. "He commented on the pace and what he felt was slow," said Silverstein. At first, the pre-buzz had been excellent. "Sam was elated as hell," Kinberg recalled. "When he had shown the film to all the Columbia offices around the world, he said that he had never gotten cables like that. . . . Things like 'Thank you so much,' and 'Most marvelous film–you've done it again.' And of course, it went out and died."

Released in March 1967, the picture's title had gone from *The Innocent* to *Mister Innocent* to *It's What's Happening* to *The Happening*. But despite the music by Frank De Vol, a hit song by the Supremes, the Kirk Douglases hosting an opening party, and an aggressive campaign by Columbia (leading one theater owner to remark, "I only wish it would gross what they spent on this promotion"), it was a disappointment.

The Happening remains an interesting and quirky film. "There are still things that I would not change," said the director. "The problem with the film was we went far too much in one direction to please, and we should have gone for our point or his [Sam's]. It should have been serious or satirical—not both."

Kinberg put their main problem down to both parties being off their first hit. "I frankly think we over-produced like hell, but this is what happens," he said. "You keep on wondering, 'Can I do it again?' And you try too hard. We should have relaxed on that film, instead of jiving it." He also wondered if Spiegel trusted the team too much. "I wish he hadn't, I think if he had been there, it would have been different."

Ultimately, Silverstein sensed that Spiegel was making a mistake dividing his time between his various productions. "Sam was a Tiffany producer, not a mass one." At exactly the same time as *The Happening*, he was also engaged on *The Night of the Generals*, which was being made in Europe. It was a pity, because if Spiegel had concentrated more on Silverstein's picture, it could have been a very good film as opposed to flawed, and Spiegel would have avoided two box office flops in a row. But it was a question of the locations—Miami versus Paris, with only a few weeks in Warsaw.

The Night of the Generals was based on Hans Hellmut Kirst's best-selling novel and also chapter 6 of James Hadley Chase's novel *The Wary Transgressor*. "Sam asked me who should direct," said Arthur Canton, in charge of the film's publicity. "I replied, 'A young Kazan with fire in his heart, he should do it,' and he said, 'Tola [Anatole Litvak] is going to.' I said, 'What, are you nuts?'" Even if Litvak had a European hit with *Aimez-vous Brahms?* (titled *Goodbye Again* in the United States) and came from Spiegel's generation, the director's greats—*Mayerling, Sorry, Wrong Number,* and *The Snake Pit*—were light-years back. "He had retired into Parisian society," Canton said. "He was kind of living a chocolate life. But Sam said, 'Well, he's the director,' and I said, 'Come on, Sam,' and then he said, 'He owns the book.'"

Peter Viertel described the film as Litvak's "last gasp." Friends and acquaintances were staggered that either of the characters wanted to work with each other, because the director was part of the band that included Wyler and Wilder, who had an unwritten pact that to be employed by Spiegel was to end the friendship. Nor could Litvak be described as the immovable object that Spiegel needed. "Sam was very good if he had a strong director," said Fred Zinnemann. "If he had a director who was rather scared of him, that was the end of it. Sam had a need to dominate."

But Litvak was to co-produce and it was to be a major picture with a glowing Franco-Anglo cast that included Peter O'Toole, Omar Sharif, Tom Courtenay, Donald Pleasence, Philippe Noiret, Charles Gray, Juliette Gréco, and Christopher Plummer. Alexandre Trauner, who was Marcel Carné's, Billy Wilder's, and Fred Zinnemann's art director of choice, was hired to whip up the right atmosphere. (He ended up reproducing the interior of Warsaw's Lazinekowski Palace in Paris's Boulogne-sur-Seine studios.)

The film's plot had the premise of a gripping whodunit. In 1942 a prostitute who is also a German agent is brutally murdered in Warsaw. Major Grau (Sharif) of German intelligence investigates three top-ranking Nazi generals: Kahlenberge (Pleasence), Seidlitz-Gabler (Gray), and Tanz (O'Toole). Two years later, the three generals and Grau are all present in Paris when another prostitute is killed. Grau is then murdered . . . A plot to kill Hitler fails . . . Twenty years thereafter, justice is served by Inspector Morand (Noiret) of the French police.

At last, in spite of their previous differences, Peter O'Toole was back with Spiegel. He was to play SS General Wilhelm Tanz–the murderer. The actor demonstrated his commitment by writing an eight-page analysis of the screenplay as well as ideas about his part. The thespian was concerned about "the pederast" content of the film. "I am sure that is, as they say, in hand," he wrote. "We are not going to fight, we are going to make a picture, so we will be peaceful. However, as someone once said, 'Peace comes not to sit but to brood.' Hence this plethora of brooding and concern." The olive branch was out and Spiegel's *k.A.* was in full form. When the actor's daughter went to hospital, Spiegel sent a parcel of goodies including clothes and a male mate for Kate O'Toole's Cindy doll (the English version of Barbie).

Concerning the French side of the production, Litvak and the novelist Joseph Kessel wrote the screenplay, while Jacques Prévert was pulled in to write a song for Juliette Gréco. In the meantime, Spiegel was having problems with the English side of the production. Both Robert Bolt and Harold Pinter declined his offer to write the screenplay. As did Peter Viertel. "Litvak mentioned enlisting my help," recalled Viertel. "But I had *had* working with Tola, and in spades for Spiegel." Then three different writers were separately tried out on the project: Robert Anderson, Paul Dehn, Gore Vidal.

"I was famous for being one of the few people who did two pictures for Sam Spiegel," Vidal said. "When asked why I returned, I would say, 'Well, I couldn't believe it the first time.' " Since the producer had said, "Just a couple of weeks," Vidal took advantage and instructed Alain Bernheim–his agent–to yank up his price. The writer, who referred to it as his "Paris period," had "a lovely time" and saw friends such as Jean Seberg and Romain Gary, and the Paul Newmans. He was not, however, referring to his sessions with Spiegel, whom he described as "getting more and more crazy and more megalomaniacal."

As they were working, the producer was approving the advertising campaign for *The Chase*. "The name Spiegel was everywhere," Vidal recalled. "Sam Spiegel who gave us *The African Queen, On the Waterfront* . . . now gives us *The Chase*. You didn't even know who was in the movie. I said, 'Sam, you are asking for it, you didn't give us these pictures, other people made them.' " Vidal also disputed Spiegel's idea that the audience bought tickets for a producer. "I wish I had known the famous Wyler-Goldwyn story at the time. Goldwyn had descended into utter megalomania and 'The Goldwyn Touch' became the selling point until Willy finally told him, 'Can you think of any picture with "The Goldwyn Touch" that William Wyler did not direct?' "

Whereas Vidal had given Spiegel top marks for his work on *Suddenly, Last Summer,* he sensed that "he was dragging" it out on *The Night of the Generals.* Their screenplay sessions eventually escalated into a dramatic scene in Spiegel's suite at the George V. Vidal arrived "a bit late one morning," and Spiegel, who was wearing a dressing gown, started in on him. " 'You say you come at nine o'clock and you are here at 9:45.' I said, 'Sam, I don't care what time it is, I am here when I am here, now we have a problem, let's straighten it out.' But he wanted to do six steps before the fight until I said . . . well, the sense of it was, 'Look, I am tired shitless of your complaints. You don't know what you're talking about. . . . You know marketing, you may know how to make deals, but you don't know how to make movies, and you intrude on other people who are talented and do.' Then he exploded. He had the fight he wanted. 'How can you say that to me?' he said. He was halfway across the room (we were on the second floor of the George V), 'I will, I will hit you.' He started to race toward me, this rhinoceros with his great nose out and the fists up in the air. Then I started toward him and said, 'Sam, I am going to throw you out of this window.' And I came at him, now we are about three feet apart and he's running toward me and he can't stop because he's got this great weight in front of him, velocity stuff. With that, he veers off to my right and runs into the wall, he can't stop. So the great nose cracks against the wall and I hear this great elephant cry, 'Where is your *esprit de corps*? People can hear in the next room.' . . . Then afterward, of course, it was 'Baby this' and 'Baby that.' He was pouring honey again."

In regards to the casting, Vidal had suggested Dirk Bogarde to play Major Grau–the film's central narrator. "Baby, he's a fairy, everybody knows that," Spiegel apparently replied. But Vidal argued that the role was not a romantic one. The producer then suggested that he ask Litvak. "So we all had lunch in the George V dining room and the two pigs ate away–I was very skinny in those days." The director had the same reaction as Spiegel. "So they get Omar Sharif, the first Egyptian Nazi officer, pure Aryan, to play the major."

It was Sharif's final film for Spiegel. At first, he resisted the role. His lawyer had written to Horizon Pictures that not only would it be "injurious to his career," but that playing a Nazi officer was going against his "political and moral beliefs." He finally agreed when he heard that O'Toole was part of the cast. However, there was a growing resentment from both men toward Spiegel. They had become major film stars, but were being paid ridiculously low salaries because of the "slave contracts" and the film option agreements that they signed when they made *Lawrence of Arabia*. Sharif was officially getting £7,500 ($19,086.75) and O'Toole was getting £15,000

($38,175). This was in comparison to Donald Pleasence, a well-known character actor, who was playing a lesser role in the film, but was being paid $80,000.

When asked about his agreement with O'Toole, Spiegel said, "I don't believe in any slavery contracts with actors. We made a deal with O'Toole going over several years. We have a kind of pre-emption right allowing us, say every year-and-a-half, to use him if we have something for him." Spiegel also added that he had "the same kind of deal" with Sharif.

Coming from Spiegel, the situation sounded relaxed and friendly. Of course, it was quite the opposite. Once again, Jerry Tokofsky was pulled in to calm the atmosphere, since "neither guy would talk" to Spiegel.

In Vidal's opinion, Spiegel was "outsmarting himself." "Sam should have been generous and said, 'Look, Peter, you're a big star, I don't owe you anything, but I will give you half your price and the same with Omar.'" Instead, he preferred getting a bargain price, which led to O'Toole sabotaging the film, or so Vidal believed. "When I saw the film I realized that he had killed it, absolutely, with a shot through the heart," he said. "He comes on insane, there's no development, and you know he's the murderer from the first moment that you see him. . . . He is so mad in his first scene that he has no place to go except stay insane all the way through the picture, and this was all resentment at Sam."

Throughout the filming, which started in Warsaw and ended in Paris, O'Toole was always in the company of three men—his makeup artist, his stuntman, and his assistant. "They were all tall, blond, and very striking looking," said Dzidzia Herman, who was involved in the Warsaw production.

She had been warned about Spiegel. "But he was always very elegant and nice," she insisted. "He asked if he could buy me a perfume from Paris that I liked. At the time it was *Dix*, by Balenciaga, and I really didn't think that a man who was so important would remember, but he did. He brought it for the other ladies too, and it made quite an impact." On his second visit in February, it had snowed. "He was very emotional and felt near to tears. He described his childhood memory of tobogganing on sleighs. The sight enchanted him and it was very touching."

Litvak, on the other hand, was a little too complex. "I knew that he was Russian Jewish," Herman said. "And I don't know why he did it but he would talk about his baptism and his holy communion. It was very strange."

The director also preferred hanging out with Nelly Rubenstein, the wife of Arthur Rubenstein, while Spiegel was keen to mix with the Polish intelligentsia, to such a point that when he went to Herman's home, he took up with Elzbieta "Elka" Czyzewska, who was then the wife of the writer-journalist David Halberstam. Considered Poland's Shirley MacLaine, she arrived "like a tigress," insisting that she had a very important message for Spiegel. As soon as they spoke, he left the party with the excuse that "Elka was going to show him something." She must have done, because the producer disappeared into the depths of Warsaw for the rest of his stay! "Litvak was furious, telling everyone that Spiegel was more taken with his new lady than the business side of the production."

Contrary to making it up to him in Paris, Spiegel's attitude toward Litvak became worse and worse. On one of the first days, he invited Sharif to lunch at the Plaza-Athenée. "He said, 'Do you know how Marlon Brando gave a great performance in *On the Waterfront*?' and I said, 'He's a great actor.' And he said, 'No, it's not only that, but he didn't do what the director told him to do, he did what he wanted to do.' He was implying, 'Don't listen to Tola.' . . . That was the purpose of the lunch."

Vidal was also witness to the treatment. "Sam was constantly insulting Tola," he said. " 'If you can't direct, you should quit, you know.' He would say stuff like that in front of the crew. It was unforgivable. And the way Tola would take it: he had a spray for his asthma and he would spray into his mouth." The director had a serious bronchial complaint as well as being plagued with diseases of the respiratory tract and sinuses. As a result of his illnesses, another $50,000 had been added to the picture's medical insurance.

In spite of his attachment to the production and his thousand-page screenplay, Vidal did not get a credit. Spiegel had a Franco-Anglo arrangement and, as an American, he did not fit in with the scheme. "In those days, you spent a lot of time taking your name off pictures," the writer recalled. "Meanwhile, Sam, unbeknownst to us [he and his agent], is trying to get my name off so that he can get Paul Dehn's name on. So we have our Dear John scene. Sam says, 'Baby, you know how much I love you and the great work you have done, and so on. But I think the script needs a little rewrite.' So I said, 'Look, I know you need the subsidiary.' He was rather surprised that I knew." Vidal had been willing to withdraw for $25,000. "Anyway, I got paid and so it worked out perfectly."

The film came out at the beginning of 1967 just before *The Happening*, and it was a total disaster. The negative cost of *The Night of the Generals* was $5,522,135.69. By 1972, the picture had lost more than $3 million. Many years later, Vidal chided the producer about his behavior. "Sam, you know for all your passion for meddling on the script, if ever there was a time when you as a producer were needed, it was during the shooting to watch the rushes. You should have done that every day and kept track of Tola. And Sam says, 'Oh, baby,' and you see the lazy side of Spiegel, because he's done his fun, the cheating, the lying, the getting picture on."

Afterward, the producer was at serious odds with Litvak, but this did not stop Burt Lancaster from accusing him of being too busy playing gin with the director to give his proper attention to *The Swimmer*. "Sam had personally promised me, *personally promised me*, to be there every single weekend to go over the film, because we had certain problems–the casting and so forth," Lancaster had complained to Judith Crist, the influential film critic and historian. "He never showed up one time. I could have killed him, I was so angry with him."

The Swimmer was the fourth picture to be made under the Horizon banner and it was to cause the most headaches. It was based on "The Swimmer," a John Cheever short story. Frank Perry was to direct, while he and his writer wife, Eleanor Perry, were to adapt the story, which had originally appeared in *The New Yorker* in 1964. At first, the couple were thoroughly Spiegeled. "I'm afraid that both of us seem now to require your direct stimulation before we embark or agree on truly significant changes, in short, we need you," they wrote to the producer.

It was the first time Cheever's work was being made into a motion picture, and it was a daring idea, which exemplified the style of a team who had had a phenomenal success with *David and Lisa*, their debut film. Like Arthur Penn, Frank Perry was involved with the Actors Studio, had worked in television, and was part of the new film world. However, until Spiegel appeared, he and his wife were having problems financing their venture. The terms of *The Swimmer* contract were to prove relevant. Horizon was to have final approval of the screenplay, the casting, the budget, and the final cut of the picture.

As with *The Happening*, Spiegel was only the executive producer, while Roger H. Lewis, a former United Artists publicist, who had worked on *The Chase*, was the producer. But this little detail had been vague when pursuing Lancaster, who referred to the project as "*Death of a Salesman* in swimming trunks." The actor was to play Ned Merrill—the film's protagonist—who decides to swim home via the pools of his friends in Connecticut. As he continues with the venture, it is apparent that he is a failure who has lost his wife, mistress, family, friends, and home. John Cheever told the *New York Times* that it was about "the irreversibility of human conduct."

"When Lancaster has to cross a six-lane highway in tight bathing trunks at the height of the afternoon, with people throwing empty beer cans at him, he realizes how completely committed he is to this adventurous—or ridiculous—pilgrimage. Similarly, he realizes, he cannot rectify his life."

As soon as Lancaster agreed to do the picture, Spiegel fired off an enthusiastic letter: "It is most heartening to know that there are people like yourself, in Hollywood, with perception and courage and with an interest in films that go beyond the obvious and ordinary." "The Build," as the actor was known, was accepting a role that William Holden, Paul Newman, George C. Scott, and Glenn Ford had all turned down. Demonstrating his commitment, the fifty-two-year-old actor spent several months in arduous training with Bob Horne, the head swim coach at UCLA. Lancaster had his reservations about Perry as director—would he be another Arthur Penn? But he took the role on the understanding that Spiegel would be "on the picture" and "convenient to the location." In other words, if *The Swimmer* was shot in Connecticut, the producer would be in New York, and if it was somewhere on the West Coast, he would be in Los Angeles.

Ted Ashley, Lancaster's agent, even wanted it stated in the

contract, which made everyone at the Horizon Neptune office–the company created for the picture–just a little nervous. The shooting was to start in the summer of 1966, and the very idea of Spiegel in Connecticut when *Malahne* and the Mediterranean beckoned seemed unlikely.

Although Lancaster later insisted that he "never showed up one time," this was not strictly true. Spiegel's poolside manner was once spied in Fairfield County. As far as the producer was concerned, he had worked on the screenplay with the Perrys, cast Lancaster, as well as appointing Roger Lewis to be in charge. The only problem was the choice. "Roger, alas, is not the best character to have around creative people," wrote Eleanor Perry. In all her correspondence to Spiegel, the writer never stopped criticizing the producer. Not only had Lewis forgotten to deliver the screenplay to Richard Day (*The Swimmer*'s production designer until he fell sick) but, on the set, he was more taken with cleaning his suede shoes or making sure that he, his children and nanny were first in line during the lunch-break than looking after the interest of the film crew.

Meanwhile, her husband perturbed Lancaster. "It was not Frank's nature to prepare," said a Perry associate. "He had done that lovely little film [*David and Lisa*], but it was a '*little* film' that was improvised. It had cost nickels and dimes. With Burt, not only was he an actor-star and a producer, but he was tough."

The fights were endless, with Perry trying to settle their differences privately and the film star insisting that the cast and crew be privy to their disputes. "And [Lancaster] said, 'I have balls. I do my fights in public,' " the director told Gary Fishgall. "So he made me do it in front of people. And his crowning blow was, 'Look, kid, do you know how much I'm making on this picture?' "

Lancaster was a well-seasoned performer. Up until the mid-1960s, he had made such films as *From Here to Eternity, Elmer Gantry,* and *The Leopard.* Besides being a producer (his production companies were Hecht-Norma, Hecht-Lancaster, and then Hecht-Hill-Lancaster), he also had worked with such directors as Robert Siodmak, Carol Reed, and John Huston.

Later, in the reviews of *The Swimmer,* much was made of the fact that Lancaster was miscast and that his background was hardly up to the Cheever character–a WASP, Ivy League type. However, this was a motion picture and it was inspired casting on the part of Spiegel. Perhaps the actor had been born on the wrong side of Italian East Harlem but he had a princely presence, which had certainly been shown with great effect by Visconti. "The Build" had one of the most extraordinary physiques in the movie business–broad shoulders, narrow hips, and long limbs. Moreover, he knew how to move. "He had an effortless grace," said John Frankenheimer, who directed him not only in *The Train* but also in *The Birdman of Alcatraz* and *Seven Days in May.* And he was capable of showing emotional pain on camera. In *The Swimmer,* as he continues to be rejected, it is hard not to feel pity.

However, as soon as Spiegel saw Perry's ninety-four-minute film, he recognized there were problems. Kazan was even called upon for his opinion, since his girlfriend, Barbara Loden, was playing Shirley Abbott, Merrill's mistress. The director agreed with Spiegel's analysis but wrote back that "simply to be negative" would not help. He proposed that they find "an attack, a creative key" that would bring "positive results." "Now you simply have two people in more or less static and un-life-like positions jawing at each other."

There were to be retakes. Initially, Lancaster had refused. "He feels Sam has fallen down miserably in his promise to adequately supervise the picture and to give it real time and attention and to be physically present for several weeks during the shooting," his lawyer stated. But six weeks later, he agreed. Sydney Pollack, who was part of Lancaster's production company, was to direct.

Originally, Barbara Loden wanted nothing to do with the retakes. She told Lewis that the picture was a "disaster" and likely "to be shelved." She even asked him to find her "a job to get out of it by not being available."

In the meantime, the Perrys had not given up on Spiegel and continued to flood his office with telephone calls and written correspondence. They admitted that the film was "in ill health," but had countless suggestions about how to correct the situation. "We feel we have accomplished two things in the picture: entertained the minds of the audience while at the same time, strongly involved their feelings." Their opinions were confirmed by Sidney Lumet, who was "going all over New York saying *The Swimmer* is a major work of art."

The couple was then horrified to hear Spiegel was replacing Barbara Loden with Janice Rule. Yet another letter was sent to Spiegel. "Janice Rule may be a dear, sweet girl and a lovely person, but she hasn't 1/10 the talent of Barbara," Eleanor Perry wrote from Rome. The writer was considered to be more brilliant than her husband. "It was really thanks to her that Frank had the career he had," said an acquaintance. Like Lillian Hellman, she was not afraid of taking on Spiegel.

But while the Perrys were upset at being "cut off" from a project that had been in their "guts and heart" for two years, Kazan was equally annoyed. "His [Spiegel's] behavior is hard concrete—and on the nose for that generation of producers...," Kazan wrote to Eleanor Perry. "Don't let the human interfere.... And let your sec'y tell the lies, get a hireling to drop the axe so that you never fog your aureole of culture and gentility. Notice Spiegel calls business meetings with artists chats?" The diatribe ended with Kazan saying that one reason he started to write novels was not to rely on producers. "Imagine hanging your life on Spiegel's favor!"

Janice Rule's scene with Lancaster was shot on February 8, 1967. "I took less than my normal fee," she recalled. "And Sam said, 'I'll leave you my Chagall in my will.' You know *Les Amants,* above his bed?" In fact, all of Spiegel's paintings were either sold at Sotheby's or given to The Israel Museum in Jerusalem. "I didn't mind. That was Sam and I loved him for it."

However, the reshoots of *The Swimmer* continued. (Since Lancaster had to get back into shape, the start dates kept on being pushed back.) Finally, by mid-October, with Slavomir "Ed" Vorkapich as the director (the son of Slavko Vorkapich), the picture's ending was completed. Like Pollack, Vorkapich was paid but not credited. In the meantime, Spiegel was not providing the star with his customary *k.A.* "Burt feels hurt" ... "Burt needs romancing" were part of the stream of messages, which were delivered to Spiegel. Still, he had discovered a new talent to write the picture's musical score—Marvin Hamlisch.

The Swimmer came out in May 1968 to reasonable reviews. Vincent Canby described it as staying "in the memory like an echo that never quite disappears." Financially it was yet another disaster. Seven years later, $2,538,340.78 remained unrecouped on the film, which was $200,000 less than the negative cost. It completed the fabulous four package. Spiegel was paid a handsome production fee for each project, but every single film had lost money for Columbia. It came to almost $10 million.

Flops or not, the producer Stanley Jaffe never felt that the pictures were "second rate division." "You didn't walk away saying, 'I don't understand why anyone wanted to make that picture'–there was always some value to something that he made," he said. "Some of Sam's failures were more interesting than a lot of the successes of the time."

Kinberg sensed that all four films lacked "categorical imperative." "If you look at each of Sam's triumphs, the protagonist has to go that extra mile and any time that was absent, such as in *The Chase,* the conflict that went on wasn't creative."

In spite of all Spiegel's failures, Columbia agreed to finance *Nicholas and Alexandra,* which was based on Robert K. Massie's book. It was to be Spiegel's next picture, and would be a return to the BIG picture, with only *his* name above the title.

Moreover, there was another production in the works of a different kind. Ann E. Pennington gave birth to Adam, Spiegel's first and only son, on June 2, 1968.

It was six months after Spiegel's mother had died in Haifa. Neither of the Spiegel brothers had gone over to Israel for Regina's funeral. Shalom, a professor of medieval Hebrew literature and one of the luminaries of the Jewish Theological Seminary, was afflicted with Parkinson's disease. "Your fame and achievement made her proud," he wrote to his younger brother afterward. Spiegel used to send his pictures to *Mutter* in Israel. She, in turn, would invite a list of friends and relations to see the first screening, where the distributor provided elaborate refreshments. "Life then was frugal," recalled a cousin. "The taste of those cakes remains in my wife's mouth." But Tante Regina was unfazed by the treatment. "This is the only way that I ever see films," she used to say.

Yet another rich, colorful chapter was about to be turned in Spiegel's life. "I had a sense of doom that it was going to happen, a sense of fate," Ann Pennington admitted. Blond, green-eyed, and extremely pretty, the petite twenty-two-year-old was noted for wearing "the most mini of mini skirts." (Anne and Kirk Douglas referred to her as "little Ann.") Spiegel had met her in Horizon's London office where she was Kinberg's secretary. "What happened was that I had to take a part for the boat and no one else was available." Then Pennington disappeared for six months. "That was the beginning of my affair with Sam, I arrived with a part."

Chapter Twenty-four

NICHOLAS AND ALEXANDRA

Sam Spiegel had had enough of having his name attached to small movies and delegating to others. His next–*Nicholas and Alexandra*–was to be an epic and he–Spiegel–was to be in charge. Besides, he was the last of the Dream Merchants and his public expected to see films of that type.

At first, he had shied away from paying for the rights to the book. "Sam said, 'The story belongs in public domain,' " recalled Robby Lantz, who was Robert Massie's agent, as well as Lillian Hellman's. "So, I said, 'See you in court.' " The deal was finalized at the beginning of 1968 and Massie was to get $150,000 as well as 5 percent of the producer's net share and profits.

The excitement about the project was high. Based on a best-selling book, it would tell the tragic story of the last czar and czarina, who were cursed with a hemophiliac son and were massacred with all their children during the Russian Revolution. In subject matter, it was being lauded as having the same echoes of romance and history that *Lawrence of Arabia* had. But did it?

From the start, Moura Budberg warned Spiegel that *Nicholas and Alexandra* was not up to that level. Instead, she advised a film about another czar, Alexander III, describing him as "the giant who held up the roof of the train when it crashed and frightened poor puny little Nicholas." Sadly, Spiegel ignored her advice. He was enchanted with the idea of the Russian palaces and exquisite jewels set against the rise of the revolution, and perhaps, most importantly, the young grand duchesses, Anastasia being the most famous of the four (played by Fiona Fullerton).

"The rumors were that Sam was after the young princesses, especially Lynne Frederick," said Jeffrey Lane, who was working at Columbia's publicity department in London. Wide-eyed and doll-like, she played the role of Grand Duchess Tatiana, and eventually wound up being the last Mrs. Peter Sellers.

During the production, Spiegel's desire for the sixteen-year-old met a formidable obstacle in the form of Maude Spector. The casting director was well versed in the producer's ways. With fondness, she referred to him as "an erudite guttersnipe," and she kept a sharp eye on Lynne Frederick, who, as a child performer, needed a court order to leave the country.

As with *Lawrence of Arabia,* a preproduction office was set up in Berkeley Street. Lew Thornburn was in charge, as he had been on Lean's epic. And despite her doubts, Baroness Budberg became an advisor of sorts. She had, after all, been dancing upstairs at the Yussopov Palace when Rasputin was being murdered down below. Hence, her being in frequent touch with Vincent Korda, the film's artistic production consultant.

The Hungarian, whose distinguished career included *The Private Life of Henry VIII* and *Catherine the Great,* was thorough about his research, whether he was interviewing a White Russian noble concerning the correct color of the imperial train, finding "exciting details of Rasputin's apartment," or searching for footage of the last czar in the *Cinémathèque Française.* He was also in frequent contact with Leon Barsacq, the Russian art director.

John Mollo, as military advisor, was in charge of medals and uniforms. There were two costume designers, Yvonne Blake, who dressed almost everyone, and Antonio Castillo, who was only in charge of the czarina and the Dowager Empress Marie. "Mink is for the coachmen," was his key phrase. (In czarist Russia, mink was for the lower classes. The royal family would not be seen in anything less than ermine.)

With regard to the location, Spiegel had looked into Russia, but the message from the Soviet Embassy's cultural counselor was loud and clear: Horizon's picture was "an American interpretation of events in Russia; the Soviet organization will not participate." Intricate plans to take *Malahne* to the Black Sea were dashed; Yugoslavia, Denmark, and Austria were explored, and Spain was finally decided on.

As always on a grand Spiegel production, everything was on an elaborate scale. Yet according to Pierre Sciclounoff, a more personal element was involved. "It was Sam's *Doctor Zhivago*," he said. Until his death, the Swiss lawyer claimed that it was to his client's lasting regret that Lean's film had not been his. (Curiously enough, Spiegel is often associated with the picture, whereas Carlo Ponti was actually in charge.) However, the filming of Pasternak's love story had been in the mid-1960s. Spiegel's epic Russian venture hit the screens at the end of 1971. Unfortunately, during the five-year gap, the public's taste had changed. There were also those in the motion picture industry who sensed that *Nicholas and Alexandra* was either too early or too late. "Besides, it wasn't as good as the others," said Stanley Jaffe.

Jaffe, the son of Leo Jaffe, had attended the *Lawrence* premiere in December 1962 and said that were he a critic, it would be a very short review: "I have just seen the best film picture ever made." But he questioned the fate of the film if it had been made in 1968. "I think it would have suffered."

At the end of the 1960s, he was the head of production at Paramount when the epic was starting to be "a little out of step" for the feeling of what was important. "It just wasn't what the public were going for," he said. At his studio, the important productions were *Darling Lili, Catch-22,* and *The Molly Maguires,* which were released in 1970. "And these big pictures didn't go where you thought they were going to." In the meantime, Twentieth Century-Fox had come up with *Hello, Dolly!*–another disaster–while James T. Aubrey (aka the "Smiling Cobra"), the new president of MGM, canceled Zinnemann's *Man's Fate,* three days before the cameras were about to roll. A year later, as part of the same economy drive, the studio was reduced to an end-of-era auction in which Judy Garland's ruby slippers from *The Wizard of Oz,* the *Ben-Hur* chariots, and other props and costumes emanating from its magnificent past, were sold to the highest bidder. "There was a great concern," said Jaffe. "Pictures were starting to cost [in 1941, the average cost per feature was $400,000, whereas in 1970, the average cost per production was estimated at $1,750,000.], even though they were a fraction of today's price." Cinema attendance was also at an all-time low. As reported by *Variety*, 1969 marked the beginning of an appalling three-year slump for the motion picture industry.

There was yet another piece of news for Spiegel to take in graciously—the power of the producer had been severely diminished. "In the late 1960s, the director was considered the filmmaker, 'the *auteur*,' " continued Jaffe. The golden era of the film business when the producers were dominant was essentially over. "It wound up with directors starting their own companies." Actors and actresses were jumping on the same bandwagon. "The star was going to choose the vehicle, develop, and be in the vehicle."

As captured by Peter Biskind's book, *Easy Riders, Raging Bulls: How the Sex-Drugs-and-Rock 'n' Roll Generation Saved Hollywood*, a sort of cinematic revolution was taking place. The moguls were panicking, the studios were in terrible financial shape and they were desperate for new blood. Nearly any young director with a hit (and a few without) could, in the words of Paul Schrader, "Just waltz in and have these meetings and propose whatever."

Spiegel was briefly caught in the eye of the storm when Luchino Visconti was the president of the 1969 Cannes Film Festival and he had been part of the jury. *Easy Rider*—which had been distributed by Columbia—was one of the entries, and he had invited the entire team on *Malahne*. Perhaps the smash hit biker movie was not of his taste— Spiegel was violently against drugs—but he had known most of the people involved since they were kids. Bert Schneider, Abe's boy, had co-produced the film, Bill Hayward, Leland's son, was the associate producer, and, of course, there was Peter Fonda—Hank's boy—who was both the star and co-director. "We [the party included Dennis Hopper and Jack Nicholson] looked pretty wild—fringe leather jackets, long hair; it was a funny day," said Hayward. "On the boat was all the Columbia brass who had pooh-poohed our picture when we first wanted to take it to Cannes." However, in a quiet moment, Leo Jaffe had taken him aside and said, "Now Bill, you make another movie like *Easy Rider* and we'll get you a boat."

The switching of power and taste was to affect Spiegel's epic, but he carried on with *Nicholas and Alexandra*–his future $8 million production–and turned lukewarm on his other project. Called *The Right Honourable Gentleman,* it was chiefly based on a play by Michael Dyne, but its budget was not to exceed $2 million, or so Columbia Studios insisted. George Cukor was attached to the project, as was Rex Harrison. Set in Victorian times, it concerned Sir Charles Dilke, whose brilliant political career was destroyed when he was named as the other party in a divorce case.

It was a pity that the project came to nothing. First of all there was the subject matter, which Spiegel could identify with, and second, both Cukor and Harrison belonged to the generation that he knew how to deal with. Esteemed writers such as John Osborne and John Mortimer–with and without his then wife, Penelope–had struggled on the screenplay. Yet, it was not to be. *Nicholas and Alexandra*'s budget was too much of a lure.

With everything that was happening in the world, was there room for an epic about a weak czar who let his country drift into ruin, and his hysterical wife who believed in Rasputin, a total charlatan? It was fine to read on paper, but who would want to see it on the screen? And did Spiegel himself really care?

His previous triumphs, *The African Queen, On the Waterfront, The Bridge on the River Kwai,* and *Lawrence of Arabia,* had carried important messages– protagonists who, like Spiegel, were stubborn about triumphing over great difficulties. The audience–thanks to the subject matter, the excellent direction, screenplay, and casting–cared. Alas, this element would be sorely lacking in *Nicholas and Alexandra.*

In theory, the picture was to show the fall of the last Russian empire. Yet, in many ways, the making of the epic was to demonstrate a tragedy of a different type–the decline of a great man who had been a giant in his field. Throughout the production, Spiegel was to defy everything that had made his glorious career possible. Each mistake was so serious that it was obvious he had lost touch.

James Goldman was employed to write the screenplay. He had just won an Academy Award for his screen adaptation of his play *The Lion in Winter.* Spiegel clearly liked Jim, which was how the older brother of William Goldman was then addressed. He had introduced him to food "which was to die for," fine wines, and had even talked about his own playwriting aspirations in Vienna during the 1920s.

Whereas Spiegel had driven many a writer to distraction in the past—who could forget Budd Schulberg shaving in the middle of the night in order to kill Sam Spiegel, or Gore Vidal having to pore over *Suddenly, Last Summer* again and again?—he was not to give the same vital input on *Nicholas and Alexandra*. Indeed, many, many months were spent on *Malahne* where "not a word was spoken of the screenplay." "It didn't seem a waste of time," Goldman said. "I was like Alice in Wonderland—Gregory Peck, David Niven, Anne and Kirk Douglas, and Yul Brynner. Sam entertained all the time."

Meanwhile, the production was to go through several directors, which was yet another bad sign for a Spiegel picture. The vast project needed a proper collaboration of the writer and director—as Schulberg had had with Kazan on *Waterfront*, Michael Wilson with Lean on *Kwai*, and Robert Bolt with Lean on *Lawrence*. Adapting Massie's biography to the screen was a difficult task, because with so many elements, the fall of the Romanov empire, the Russian Revolution, and the problems of having a hemophiliac son, it risked lacking intimacy on screen, and just becoming a sequence of events. Unfortunately, on *Nicholas and Alexandra*, Goldman was incapable of creating the right type of atmosphere with a director because each time he tried, the director ended up walking off the project.

Nor was Spiegel in the right state of mind to steer him. Massie's book had succeeded by rescuing the story from the realm of myth and propaganda and treating the story of Nicholas and Alexandra as a domestic tragedy, thus restoring it to a human scale. But Goldman would be working with a producer who encouraged pomp and ceremony, rather than getting to the heart of the matter. In fact, the same criticisms that were later applied to the film might have been applied to the producer's style of life. Spiegel's very center of life was "myth and propaganda." Intimacy was to be avoided, as was any hint of "domestic tragedy." Alas, the days of Spiegel being disciplined and making a firm distinction between his professional life and personal life had passed; everything had become intermingled. Consequently, Spiegel appeared to have only one aim throughout the entire production: *Nicholas and Alexandra* was to be his showpiece.

Spiegel's long memos and letters, which were so much part of his previous films, were almost entirely absent this time out. Moreover, he was impossible to reach. "I will threaten you with drilling a hole in the bottom of your boat, if you do not communicate with me," Massie's agent wrote. There was a distinct change in Spiegel, who had written to David Lean that producing a film "involves one's waking and sleeping hours; one's objective and subjective interest, it excludes nothing and it permits no sanctuary in which one can breathe on one's own."

Naturally, the producer was busy, but his focus was elsewhere, whether he was entertaining Adam, his baby son, attending the Scorpio party given by Grace of Monaco in November 1969, supervising the redecoration of *Malahne,* or scaring the hell out of the Columbia London office. According to Jeffrey Lane, Carl Foreman was just as terrifying. There was a great competition between the two producers, "with Carl insisting that more attention was being given to Spiegel."

George Stevens was the first director to be announced on *Nicholas and Alexandra.* The news was received with astonishment. Both Stevens and Spiegel were known for their "strongly held" opinions on filmmaking and their need to "be in charge," while the director's last film, *The Greatest Story Ever Told,* had been panned by the critics. Stevens was offered half a million dollars for his services, but three months later, he pulled out. His commitment to direct *The Only Game in Town* was the official excuse, a film that was to come out two years later.

"They started work in London," recalled George Stevens, Jr. "And my father says, 'Sam, we've got to scout some locations,' and Sam says, 'George, we'll do it on the boat.' My father replies, 'Sam, have you heard of the Learjet?' " Like Mankiewicz, the director had a hard time forgetting the S. P. Eagle days. His son had taken him to have a drink with the producer and Greta Garbo in the Park Avenue apartment. As they walked toward the elevator, the doorman stood in their way. "We said, 'We're going to meet Mr. Spiegel,' and he said, 'Who may I say is calling on Mr. Spiegel?' My father without missing a beat said, 'Tell him, it's Mr. S. T. Evens.' "

Then Anthony Harvey took over in December 1968. At first, it seemed a perfect fit. The Englishman had directed Goldman's *The Lion in Winter,* which had led to an Oscar for Katharine Hepburn and a nomination for Peter O'Toole. The relationship began well. After a few weeks, Harvey joined the writer and Spiegel in Austria. "For the right atmosphere, we went to the Imperial Hotel in Vienna," said Goldman. "Sam felt it was very Romanov in feel."

Spiegel was insistent that "the script had to be drastically rewritten." During the process, Goldman found him to be "very dogmatic and stubborn." The producer was also back to pulling his most infamous trick out of the bag. "He had a heart attack on me," he recalled. The event took place on the terrace of Spiegel's suite. "I suppose I gave in, I'm not a confrontational person," admitted Goldman. "Sam was very manipulative, but you can't be a producer and not be. Everyone is manipulating everyone on the film set, the actress is manipulating the director and so it continues." There was also the occasion when they arrived in an elegant Viennese restaurant and the band started to play Alford's "Colonel Bogey March." "His office had called the place to say that Mr. Spiegel would be lunching there. I cracked up laughing, but Sam was absolutely thrilled. He rose to the occasion. . . . The way he lived made me smile sometimes."

Spiegel's methods were too much for Harvey, who was off the project by early February. Other directors such as Ken Russell, Lindsay Anderson, and John Boorman were approached, but they all declined.

Then Joseph Mankiewicz showed a serious interest. Goldman was delighted. "I need your help to write this thing," he wrote, describing himself as "overwhelmed and egoless." "If this letter sounds prosy and dull, it's because I've been reading my script." There were endless battles. No doubt hardened from his last experience with Spiegel, Mankiewicz wanted the casting to be of mutual agreement and was also demanding a gross participation as well as a proper credit during the advertising campaign. "Joe didn't find it hard to disagree with Sam," Goldman recalled. "But it was the only time we worked on the boat." Despite Mankiewicz's endless notes and ideas, the collaboration did not work out.

After the second draft was completed, Charles Jarrott was introduced. "He had some charm but was of no talent," Goldman said. The English director had just come off *Anne of a Thousand Days*. "I kept on urging Sam to get rid of him, but he kept on working with him." Again, it was not to be. The writer suggested Franklin J. Schaffner, whose superb film on General Patton had just been released. A meeting at the Ritz in Madrid was arranged and after a crossfire of telegrams from Spiegel to his agent to Columbia Studios, the director was on *Malahne* in July 1970, and by August was hard at work on *Nicholas and Alexandra*. As stated in the director's contract, the picture was to be a Sam Spiegel–Franklin J. Schaffner Production.

Like Jack Garfein and Arthur Penn, Schaffner was from the generation of directors whom Spiegel tended to have problems with. He also arrived on the picture when almost everything was done. "As I recall it, he spent most of his time catching up," said Goldman. It was yet another mistake. Which of Spiegel's directors had ever done this before, and when had Schaffner? Renowned for handling large-scale productions such as *The War Lord, Planet of the Apes,* and *Patton,* he was an expert craftsman who mapped out every detail. On his most recent picture, which had a screenplay by Francis Ford Coppola, he had been passionate about the project. "When I started *Patton* everybody told me I was crazy. 'You're putting that son of a bitch on a pedestal,' they said," he had been delighted to recall.

On *Nicholas and Alexandra,* he only had a few months to prepare before shooting. Thanks to Spiegel, he had a strong film unit, which had previously worked on *Lawrence* and *Doctor Zhivago*. Freddie Young was the director of photography, Eddie Fowlie was in charge of props and special effects, and John Box, the production designer, was doubling as a second unit director. "Originally, I said no to Sam because I had already done my Russian film," said Box. "Besides, I was meant to be directing a film for Columbia, which then didn't happen. I have a strong suspicion that Sam was behind that." Although there is no correspondence to prove that Spiegel went behind Box's back and put an end to his first directing assignment, the producer *was* capable of doing this. At that point in time, Spiegel still had enough pull to convince Columbia's executives that he needed Box, that the production designer was essential for the success of his film, and so forth.

Initially, Spiegel asked Box to be the second unit director. "I would direct the crowd scenes," Box recalled. "Then, when I said yes, I discovered that Sam had fired Vincent Korda–his art director. That was Sam, he liked to get his money's worth."

Korda had been pushed out a few months previously. Yet despite Spiegel's shoddy behavior, Korda remained concerned about the picture, admitting that his one great worry was the costumes, while he "did not want to talk about the script." "I have a great feeling of responsibility, that I did not help you inoff [*sic*], and tell you stronger my opinion. I tried, but all that is not inoff good," he wrote to Lew Thornburn.

As far as the casting, Audrey Hepburn, Elizabeth Taylor, Vanessa Redgrave, and even Princess Grace of Monaco were bandied about in the press as playing the czarina, while Rex Harrison was hailed as a possible czar. In fact, the records show that only Redgrave and Katharine Hepburn were sent copies of the book, and Harrison was *only* offered a minor role, that of Prime Minister Witt. Somewhat miffed, Harrison had said to his agent, "Tell him [Spiegel] that I don't play bit parts."

Spiegel was interested in Redgrave for several reasons. Not only was she beautiful, aristocratic-looking, and a superb actress, but she had just been nominated for an Oscar for Karel Reisz's *Isadora*. "I remember going on Sam's boat during that period," said Natasha Richardson, her daughter. Yul Brynner documented the moment with his camera. Meanwhile, he–the best-looking bald man in the business–was desperate to play Rasputin. "He was terribly upset," recalled one of Spiegel's guests. "And when someone asked if it was about the film, he replied, 'Jesus, that's a civilian question.' " Meaning that only a nonactor could ask such an insensitive question.

But Spiegel was after Peter O'Toole. It did not matter that *The Night of the Generals* had been a failure; the actor had the right flair to play Rasputin. It was also a continuation of his contract. At first, O'Toole was committed. "Peter would want to meet with you and James Goldman about the dialogue and probably several other points he has in mind," wrote Jules Buck, his manager. "There will be no difficulty in agreeing to a revised credit to take into account his playing a 'guest star' type part." However, the option time ran out and O'Toole made Peter Medak's *The Ruling Class* instead.

So, why did Spiegel not go beyond that? Because Columbia was starting to cut back on the man who had once saved them in 1958. "The studio would only give him $8 million," said Albert Heit, his New York lawyer. "He needed $9 million to make *Nicholas and Alexandra* with the stars he wanted."

Spiegel was to go against everything that he knew about the necessary alchemy between the performer and screen. In his heyday, he was adamant about "screen presence" and had battled with his directors accordingly. He had been insistent on Marlon Brando for *Waterfront*. He had dug in his heels for Alec Guinness to star in *Kwai*. He had also recognized Omar Sharif's cinematic appeal as well as Robert Redford's and Faye Dunaway's.

But Spiegel's past four films had taken their toll, and box office flops were box office flops. There had also been a reshuffle at Columbia. Stanley Schneider, another of Abe's sons, was in charge, whereas the likes of Leo Jaffe and others from the *ancien régime* had been pushed aside. With a new generation in power, there was major pressure to rein in old-timers like Spiegel.

A strict eye was being kept on the "overheads accruing from the picture," and the heady days of paying for two Horizon offices were about to end. "We do not have a single producer who has an operation both in London and New York, particularly since the pictures are only being made abroad," Jaffe complained in a letter. "I believe it incumbent upon you to again review the situation to see how this dual operation can be reduced or possibly eliminated. We know it gives you certain conveniences in New York, but is the operation necessary based on the money involved?"

By contrast, the tone of Spiegel's letters to Jaffe were quite different: "The next two weeks are very rough for me, although I shall be on the boat. . . . But at least I will get some sun at the same time. . . . I wish you had a *Malahne* on which you could run Columbia, because it helps a great deal!"

The reminder that Spiegel the hedonist was at large on the Mediterranean while Jaffe et al. were hard at work on New York's Fifth Avenue was probably pushing it from a producer whose recent films had been failures. And since Spiegel's hands were financially tied on *Nicholas and Alexandra*, the leads had to be unknowns. Of course, he would give a different reason for his choice, and would even give interviews in the press about the subject. "When actors are still comparatively unknown, they are easygoing and amiable," he told the journalist Tom Hutchinson. "When they lose their sense of proportion, they become lionized and begin to believe their own publicity.

". . . I once had a dream of having a herd of stars, all of us being one big happy family, but experience of them has disabused me of that ideal."

In Goldman's opinion, the casting was "hellish." "Sam didn't want famous actors. His argument was that he wanted the audience to believe that the actors were Nicholas and Alexandra . . . if they were famous, they wouldn't."

Michael Jayston was cast as the czar and Janet Suzman as his wife. Both actors had distinguished themselves on the London stage–the Royal Shakespeare Company lent Suzman out–but *Nicholas and Alexandra* was Jayston's first starring role, while it was Suzman's second. (Previously, she had made *A Day in the Life of Joe Egg,* which was released after *Nicholas and Alexandra.*)

Although physically suited to their roles, they were drowned in the spectacle. Consequently, it was difficult for either of the actors to show their talent or their appeal. The winning element in Spiegel's top productions was moving the audience emotionally, whether it was Rosie and Allnut falling in love in *The African Queen,* Terry Malloy becoming "a contenda" in *Waterfront,* Shears destroying Colonel Nicholson's work in *Kwai,* or T. E. Lawrence leading the Arab Revolt in *Lawrence.*

All the actors involved in Spiegel's greats had inspired words to work with. "The great line from Sam was when people asked him when he was starting his movies he would reply, 'When the script will be ready,' " said the agent Alain Bernheim. "That was what made him a great producer, because he wasn't under the influence of the studios."

It was not to be on *Nicholas and Alexandra.* In spite of their months together and the endless rewrites, Goldman's screenplay did not have the right tone or depth. Attempts to humanize Lenin with lines such as, "Trotsky, you've been avoiding me," fell flat. Spiegel tried to rectify the matter. Once Goldman went back to the States, he hired playwright Edward Bond to write additional dialogue. However, the new lines did nothing to improve the quality of the screenplay.

Schaffner's skill with the cast on *Nicholas and Alexandra* was less apparent than it had been with George C. Scott and Karl Malden on *Patton.* As well as the leads, he had an endless line of distinguished actors to work with such as Irene Worth (Empress Marie), Eric Porter (Stolypin), Laurence Olivier (Count Witte), and Michael Redgrave (Sazonov). Yet, throughout the picture, most of the actors seem ill at ease. It was ironic because during filming, Schaffner received an Academy Award for *Patton,* which led to Leo Jaffe anticipating "a repeat performance next year." "Sam told me it looks great," the film executive wrote, "and I'm sure that when we will see the final picture, it will measure up to our expectations."

Spiegel had made his fleeting on-set visits. He was spotted at the Sevilla Studios in Madrid and at the Hostal de la Gavina for the Romanov family beach scenes. He even spent Christmas of 1970 in Marbella on board *Malahne,* as opposed to going to Klosters, Switzerland. Unfortunately, only his relationship with Schaffner measured up to expectations, and not of the right kind. The director did not take to the producer's imperious behavior, and toward the end of filming they were not on speaking terms. Spiegel fired off his "Please be good enough to come over to my office" letters, which Schaffner simply ignored.

The producer was worried about Tom Baker–the National Theatre actor recommended by Olivier–who was playing the evil monk. "Rasputin is our only figure that transcends the natural, the only figure that is much larger than life," he wrote to the director. "That accounts for the legend that far exceeded his actual responsibility for the course of events and the turns of history.

"It is incumbent upon us to dramatise the legend, I realise that in portraying a legendary almost super-human phenomenon we risk occasionally going over the top. Let's not. . . . [However,] unless we take some risks we will have a lack-lustre, dull and conventional Rasputin. Let's attempt some measure of risks to avoid it.

"Of course should you be in occasional doubt please cover yourself on both sides of the margin. I am putting this on paper as regrettably our channels of oral communication are so sadly cluttered. Heaven knows why. Hopefully they will clear when the shooting ends."

There had also been a fight in the editing room. Schaffner wanted to cut eighteen minutes, which Spiegel was against. Columbia then intervened, in favor of the director. A compromise was reached and only twelve minutes were taken out.

In true Spiegel style, *Nicholas and Alexandra* had several gala benefit premieres in Europe, including a Royal Command Performance in London. Columbia's top executives–Jaffe, Schneider, and Peter Guber (who was then the vice president of Columbia Pictures Corporation)– flew over for the latter, which was on Monday, November 29, 1971.

"The queen was meant to come," Goldman recalled. "But she had chicken pox." Instead, Princess Anne filled in for her, and was presented to the entire cast. Lord Mountbatten was also in attendance, which was of historical relevance, since the last czarina had been his aunt and her husband, his cousin. As he later wrote to Spiegel, "I suppose the shooting scene was so devastating to me because of my affection for the whole family who were murdered in this horrible way."

Jeannette de Rothschild escorted Spiegel to the Royal Command Performance as well as the supper party-dance, which was held in the ballroom at Claridge's hotel. But whereas she was well coiffed and exquisite in moiré taffeta, he was sporting long locks and wearing an ill-fitting velvet suit. Spiegel's hairstyle was particularly unbecoming. As one man wisely pointed out, "In the 1970s, we all resembled gorillas because we grew our hair over our ears." Spiegel looked different but worse–"like Golda Meir" was one comment.

Betty Spiegel accompanied her husband to the New York premiere on December 13, and, a few weeks later, Princess Grace of Monaco– wearing an ostrich-trimmed velvet cloak–attended the picture's first continental screening in Monte Carlo. While in Paris on April 13, 1972, Marie-Hélène de Rothschild arranged a gala at Maxim's, the proceeds of which went to L'Association des Hémophiles. Since Rothschild was the undisputed social queen of Paris, the occasion was glamorous. Andy Warhol, Gunter Sachs (Brigitte Bardot's millionaire ex-husband), and Spiegel mingled with the chic and stylish, including Cappy Badrutt, Marisa Berenson, and Gloria Guinness. Fashionwise, it was the height of Yves Saint Laurent and Marc Bohan (Bohan was then the designer at Christian Dior): ruffles and romance were rampant, the vodka flowed, and the spirits were high.

By that time, it was acknowledged that *Nicholas and Alexandra* was definitely not going to be one of Spiegel's smash hits. Apart from Judith Crist, who said that it stood out as "the spectacular film" of 1971, and managed "to paint human portraits and tell of events of world-upheaval in terms of flesh and blood and common experience," it was killed by the critics.

"All we do is watch the synoptic history of two silly people getting what, as justice goes in this world, they deserved," *The New Republic*'s Stanley Kauffmann wrote. "And all we can wish for, in this three-and-a-half-hour film, is that they might get it a bit sooner—both in history, so that thousands of lives could have been spared, and on film, so that we could get out sooner."

Nicholas and Alexandra remained too long at 187 minutes. Spiegel went against Columbia's suggestion of keeping it within two and a half hours and it remains a struggle to watch. The walks through the palace corridors are interminable. Under the title "Long Time a' Dying," Derek Malcolm, the critic from the *Guardian* newspaper in Britain, compared the film to having "as much intimacy" as the Charing Cross Railway Station during rush hour. "The film is seldom tasteless, but it is irredeemably dull, a traipse through one of the most extraordinary events the world has known with the gait of a brontosaurus."

Considering the richness of the subject, neither the sets nor the costumes were inspired either. The effect was well summed up by *Women's Wear Daily*, which wrote: "Flower arrangements look like Woolworth's best plastic, Alexandra's jewels look suspiciously like jellybeans and those obligatory panoramic ranks of Russian troops look like a lot of Spanish extras. [They are.]"

Nevertheless, the production designer and both costume designers were to win Oscars. Spiegel and Suzman were also nominated. And among the royals who were related to the Romanovs, the film won praise. Both Mountbatten and Constantine of Greece sent enthusiastic letters. But the Academy members and the royals were not the normal ticket-buying audience. By the end of the 1970s, the film, which went $537,025 over budget, had a loss of almost $3 million, with no hope of recouping the amount.

Nicholas and Alexandra was Spiegel's last production for Columbia. "They didn't want to finance him anymore," said his New York lawyer. Discounting *We Were Strangers,* which was made in 1949, it was the end of an era that had lasted eighteen years. Just as he had come in small with *Waterfront* and ultimately had scored, he was to sweep out big and trip. Spiegel was hardly thrown out; he continued to work at the studio's New York headquarters until 1982. Money was still to be made on his triumphs as it could be on his failures such as *The Chase,* which was sold to ABC television for $940,000 for two showings. Moreover, the introduction of videos provided another source of income.

Spiegel continued to keep after Columbia's executives. In 1972, Jaffe informed him of a two-run television deal with General Motors for *Lawrence* in Canada. But the producer took "exception, rather strongly," that no one had consulted him beforehand. "This highhanded kind of attitude was never exercised by the company when you ran it and I am rather upset—in the light of my recent observation about the management of the company—that such methods are employed now," he wrote.

Jaffe swiftly replied that he was "greatly disturbed" by the contents of his letter. "It is almost incomprehensible to me, Sam, that with your knowledge of the results of your pictures in recent years, that you would take an attitude that would be other than to encourage us to do everything possible to derive maximum revenues from all sources to enable us to reduce the size of the losses that have been sustained."

Harsh words indeed. Yet, the studio had problems of its own. "At the beginning of the 1970s, we were afraid Columbia was going under," said Heit. "And Sam saved Columbia by letting them hold on to some of the money they owed him. Then we thought the thing was going bankrupt." Spiegel was so worried about his money being "tied up in there" that he had hired Sidney Cohn—another lawyer—to make a financial settlement. Then Columbia paid off Spiegel. "They got prosperous again."

In the meantime, did Spiegel recognize the error of his ways? Several months after the release of *Nicholas and Alexandra,* he saw

Edward Chodorov, who had turned down his offer of doctoring Goldman's screenplay. "Sam was saying, 'You let me down, if you had done it, it would have been a different story,' " the writer's wife recalled. "And Eddie said, 'You had this very good screenwriter on the script for three years. Tell me truthfully, Sam, did you say, 'Mr. Goldman, you do the script and have it ready to be looked at and then I will discuss it?' Or did you sit him down and say, 'Mr. Goldman, this is what I want'?" The producer's face creased into its familiar dimples and smile. His response was irresistible. "Do you expect a leopard to change its stripes?"

Chapter Twenty-five

THE LAST TYCOON

Spiegel may have been out at Columbia, but he was in the thick of the 1970s. Included on Katherine Graham's exclusive guest list, he became a pal of Linda Ronstadt (Spiegel took the singer and her mother to the ballet), while *Malahne* would be just as associated with New Hollywood as it was with the old. After lending the yacht to Lew Wasserman, Wasserman's wife referred to it as "a dreamboat" in her thank-you note. And when Warren Beatty joined Irene Mayer Selznick on *Malahne,* he wrote the first draft of *Shampoo*–a film particularly associated with the Me Decade.

Spiegel also had a young son to contend with, even if his relationship with Ann Pennington became a combative affair. "Since he lied all the time, I assumed he was lying and sometimes he might be telling the truth," she said. In her opinion, Spiegel suffered from having "a crook's mentality." "He was always expecting to be discovered, which is what it is like when you are a crook. His whole mentality was bent around 'I don't want to be found out.'" Spiegel had not been there for Adam's birth; he was away on the boat. "And I never forgave him for it."

Once again, Spiegel was experiencing the difference of generations–there was a forty-four-year age gap between him and Adam's mother. "I was this grubby bohemian and quite different from anyone that he had ever been with," she said. "He used to say, 'You could be this great lady, you have it in you to be a great lady' . . . and he was always pushing that button." Having been at St. Andrew's University in Scotland, Pennington actually had aspirations to either act or direct, even though she had only been Jud Kinberg's assistant when they first met. "Sam had great curiosity and that's really what we shared," she said. "In many ways, his curiosity was his supreme feature because I think that's what drove everything else. . . . It kept him young. He was fascinated by the latest discovery or the latest gadget or the latest speedboat and how it worked." She recognized that he had "a genius for life." "Better than anybody," she said. "He got all the little things right. . . . In the South of France, he'd say, 'Now look at the wind crossing the tables in the restaurant, slightly fluttering the napkins.' That marvelous moment in the evening." Nevertheless, despite his "real appreciation" and "wonderful taste," Spiegel was "very alienated" and incapable of confiding in people. "I think money was the only thing that he trusted."

Whereas Spiegel had ignored his firstborn, their son was to be treated like a little prince. Adam was to attend the right schools, know the right people–or so Spiegel planned. Regarding Adam's Jewish education, it was nonexistent. More mention was made of his mother's religion, which was Church of England. Circumcision was Spiegel's only gesture toward his faith. And during that period, most London doctors, in any case, encouraged the practice.

"Sam didn't want to burden him with being Jewish," said Joan Axelrod. "But I believe he [Sam] really was burdened by it–very much so–even in his taste in women." The interior designer found it "understandable," considering his background. "I think it's impossible to have lived through those times and be where he was and not be affected." She also sensed that "Sam's need to be taken seriously" by the "right social people" was part of the same complex. Did this explain the dinner that Spiegel held on *Malahne* in honor of Herbert von Karajan–the conductor of the Berlin Philharmonic and the director of the Salzburg Festival–who had been an acknowledged member of the Nazi party? Spiegel was recalled as "wallowing in the importance of the occasion"–Karajan was famous, aristocratic and a fixture in certain social circles–but given Karajan's history, it was a little peculiar.

Isaac Stern had been on board and, according to Pierre Sciclounoff, the violinist had refused to shake Karajan's hand. "He said he was a Nazi," said the Swiss lawyer. "Arthur Rubinstein had done the same thing." Stern later denied this, but other guests claimed it was the case.

Meanwhile, from the late 1960s onward, a common sight was finding Adam either on Spiegel's knee on *Malahne*, or playing with an electric train set that covered the Grosvenor House apartment, or playing football with his father in Hyde Park on Sunday afternoon. "Many people were surprised by Sam having that side that absolutely adored Adam," said Pennington.

And some were just "surprised." "One day I arrived at my grandfather's apartment and saw a photo of Adam and I said, 'Who's that?' " Ellen Weisbord recalled. "And Sam told me it was his son. Basically, it was to tell my mother that she had a half-brother."

Betty, on the other hand, knew all about it. "I was delighted. Sam was absolutely thrilled to have a son." Adam was a particularly charming little boy. Good-looking with thick, nut-brown hair, large, blue eyes, and a winning smile, he resembled a child from a Frans Hals painting. It was still obvious who his father was. "When I saw him for the first time, I thought, 'My God, he's got the nose,' " said Gore Vidal. Others such as Leonora Hornblow were grateful that he was a boy. "Because if the baby had been ugly and a girl, I think Sam would have drowned it."

In many ways, Adam became the last great Spiegel production, except that it would last seventeen years—but since his upkeep could not be claimed against a film, every penny was accounted for. "He was stingy actually," said Pennington. Taking into account Spiegel's opulent lifestyle, she found it hard to deal with that side. "It was, 'For heaven's sake, I've done this all for you, and you could be decent.' " Marriage was never in the cards. "I think it sort of remained open and it was not something that we discussed," she said. Spiegel recognized his paternal limits. "I remember Sam saying that he wasn't really meant to be a father," his son recalled. "But that he would give it his best shot."

According to Mike Nichols, the producer was "like the head of the family." "Jack [Nicholson], Warren [Beatty], Anjelica [Huston], and me. That's spanning a lot of different kinds of people, careers and lives." Actresses Julie Christie and Diane Keaton—Beatty's former girlfriends—also "loved Sam." Spiegel could be demanding. "Once he got Warren to tell me that it was unforgivable that I had been in London for two weeks and not called him," remembered Nichols.

"And I called him up and said, 'Sam, you're angry that I didn't call you?' Then he yelled at me for a long time."

David Geffen—then a record producer—was also part of Spiegel's inner circle. "He used to refer to me as 'darling boy.' " Spiegel became "a kind of role model" for Geffen. Throughout their friendship, Spiegel never stopped trying to convert his "darling boy" to a suit and tie. "He always told me that if I wanted to be a big success that I had to dress like a big success." The lectures, however, came to an abrupt halt when Geffen informed Spiegel that he was wealthier than Spiegel was. "He couldn't understand how you could make more money with records than you could with movies."

After the early 1960s, Geffen felt that Spiegel should have stopped making movies. "Because the ones he aspired to make and the world in which he produced them, really didn't exist anymore." Yet, the idea of retiring was an impossibility for Spiegel. As already pointed out, he "needed projects"—it was his way of staying involved and mixing with the people he wanted.

In the summer of 1972, Spiegel agreed to produce Elia Kazan's and Budd Schulberg's project, which, in some respects, was a Puerto Rican version of *On the Waterfront*. It was based on two books: Piri Thomas's *Down These Mean Streets* and Oscar Lewis's *In the Streets*.

Despite Spiegel's initial enthusiasm, Schulberg and Kazan noticed a considerable change since their last collaboration. They invited him on a tour of Spanish Harlem and both "felt that he couldn't wait to get out of there." He seemed "very nervous and uncomfortable." "By that time, it was the sort of last place that Sam liked to be," Schulberg said.

At Christmas, Spiegel left for Klosters, Switzerland. "Meanwhile, he said, 'Keep on going with the screenplay, keep writing, because we should shoot by spring,' " the writer recalled. But when Spiegel returned, he did not call. He then backed out of the project unceremoniously. Schulberg wondered who had quenched his enthusiasm. "I don't know who he was talking to but you can imagine, 'Jesus, what do you want to do a film about Puerto Ricans for?' I think that when Sam got out of the atmosphere of Kazan and, to some extent me, it became a whole different world." In spite of being "shocked and stunned" by the outcome, in retrospect, he recognized that Spiegel was not up to it. "He had truly lost touch and if you are going to make real movies, you have to have some sense of where you are in the real life," he said. The producer's life "had become so cushioned" and, in many ways, he had taken on "the worst aspects of a con man becoming respectable."

Or was Spiegel just old? He was seventy when *Nicholas and Alexandra* was released. Quite a few people knew, although he chose not to celebrate the fact. Taking after his mother, his age remained sixty-eight for the next few years. Strangely enough, it was to his financial detriment, since in the fall of 1973, he became eligible for collecting Social Security, which was then a monthly $1,500 and completely tax-free. Albert Heit, his New York lawyer, had approached him about it. "But Sam says, 'Thanks for telling me but it's premature.'" This continued until Spiegel let his true age slip in a newspaper article in the mid-1970s. "I said to him, 'If you're admitting you're seventy-five, that's three years of Social Security and it's tax-exempt.'" Suddenly, Spiegel became interested and having avoided Social Security, it now became a monthly thrill. "Has the check come in?" he used to ask his secretary. "He was childish in a way," said Heit.

Was it childish or a genuine joy in discovering that growing old had its advantages? When reaching his seventies, there was a fifty-year age gap between him and most of his girlfriends. Spiegel had leaped again. Having started life with Ray Agranovich, who was his age, Lynne Baggett, who was twenty years younger, Betty Benson and Marie-Hélène Arnaud, who were thirty years his junior, Jeannette de Rothschild and Ann Pennington, who were forty years less, he was now pursuing women who were born in the mid-1950s and early 1960s.

After seeing a play in the West End, the Hornblows had joined the producer. He was with a pretty blond German girl who looked as if she was twelve years old. "She smiled very sweetly and said, 'Good evening,' and it soon became apparent that that was the end of her conversation. I tried to speak to her and Sam said, 'Give it up, she doesn't understand a word, she just wants to eat. We'll order a drink and she can eat. She's too young to drink, but she can eat.'"

Lauren Bacall had been on *Malahne* when Spiegel had "this little girl" who was "so intimidated" that she never knew how to behave. "Then she left and Sam had another little girl who arrived!"

A regular Spiegelette was Carrie Haddad, who was the producer's girlfriend from 1973 for almost six years, which, in "Spiegel years," was terribly long—to such a point that many of his friends never bothered to learn the first name of his girlfriends because they never saw them again.

It was not the case with Haddad, who met the producer shortly after her nineteenth birthday. She was then called Carrie Miller. The age difference was of little importance since she considered her boyfriend to be a strange dichotomy—part "little boy" and part "powerful, wonderful manipulator." "He'd flutter his eyelashes, and in some ways he thought of himself as twenty," Carrie recalled. "There he was with this huge stomach and he'd say I only need to lose five pounds . . . Five pounds!"

Her New York roommate—a runner-up to Miss America and the mistress of a film producer—had introduced them. "I was very naive. But she said, 'Sam is really nice, I think I'm going to get a piano out of him!' " After meeting Carrie, Spiegel's attention quickly switched to this trained dancer from San Francisco whose father was a doctor and who was one of nine children. As well as being a hit with his friends, Miller's parents were also "pleased."–"As compared to some of the other freaks that I had brought in," their daughter qualified.

Mischievously, she dared to make fun of Spiegel. On one occasion, they were waiting for Roman Polanski to arrive. It was just after the scandal that linked the director with an underaged teenager during a photographic shoot. "I put on a little pink shorts outfit, my hair in pigtails, and a camera in my arms and sat by the pool. He laughed but Sam was livid."

Carrie's appearance—pretty and tawny-skinned, with long limbs for her five-foot-seven height—became the type that the producer began to lust after. She was not sophisticated, but she had youth, which was a never-ending aphrodisiac for Spiegel. On the other hand, his charm and intelligence appealed to his girlfriend, as did his elegant lifestyle.

Ken Oakley, his chauffeur, used to collect her from her dancing classes in Covent Garden. "People on the street recognized the car," she said. Spiegel's Mason blue Phantom Six Rolls-Royce, built in the 1970s, was the same as the Queen of England's and the Lord Mayor of London's. Spiegel also introduced her to the Hotel Gritti in Venice and other top European hotels. "It was a fairy-tale existence, which was first-class all the way. I loved to eat and so did he. Would the romance have blossomed if we had eaten at McDonald's? I don't think so. It's rare to see an old man without money who is with a very young girl. And to young actresses he held up the ultimate carrot– maybe a part in his next movie."

To many men, Spiegel was living an ideal existence. "I have never seen so many scantily clad beautiful women in my life," said Michael Linnit. The agent and his client Richard Burton were invited on *Malahne* in the early 1970s. "You could hardly open a door without a floozy jumping out."

Not all the nubiles were ready for Spiegel's fun and games. When Janet Suzman arrived on *Malahne*, the actress was amazed to find a young beauty blocking the boat's entrance between the gangplank and teak deck. Since it was early in the morning, it was obvious that the young woman had spent the entire night there. However, she *was* blocking the entrance and Suzman *had* to step over her. But as she did so, the exquisite creature suddenly turned around, blinked, opened her eyes, looked up at Suzman and whispered, "Help!" What *had* happened?

Spiegel's deafness in his right ear was his only real sign of growing old. "He refused to wear a hearing aid," Adam's mother recalled. The producer did visit an audiologist, Dr. Wilbur J. Gould, who recommended a Starkey all-in-the-ear hearing aid. But the offending instrument was left untouched in its case.

In many ways, *Malahne* became Spiegel's Dorian Gray because just as he continued to court the young and hold on to a "bird of passage" existence, the boat was starting to show the wear and tear of the cruises. "It was like a very old car that every time you went to it, something had gone wrong," said Alan Silcocks, his English business manager. "Sam would fly down for the weekend and the captain would pick him up and say the tender wasn't right, or the launch wasn't working."

Yet this had not stopped *Malahne* from being considerably spruced up by Tessa Kennedy. The decorator's other clients included John Barry, Stanley Kubrick, and Stavros Niarchos. "I adored Sam, but he was the only client who reduced me to tears." When Spiegel first saw the result of her labors, he had been horrified. "What have you done with my boat? I hate this. How dare you?" She tried to remind him that he had seen all the presentation boards and every single fabric, but it was no good. "I didn't imagine that it was going to be like this," he replied, completely aghast. "I liked it the way it was. I want it all back again." (Meanwhile, Kennedy had auctioned off the previous contents for a paltry 500 francs–$130.) In retrospect, she wondered if it was the shock of the new. By the following morning, Spiegel apologized for his behavior. "His weekend party had just arrived and I suppose what had happened was that they came on board and said, 'Sam, this is fantastic, what have you done?' He lacked confidence about his taste."

Two years later, when Spiegel bought Mas d'Horizon, a villa in St. Raphael near St. Tropez, Kennedy was again his decorator of choice. "He used to say that the house in the South of France was for Adam," she said. Originally a farmhouse, it had a pool and adjoining tennis court. "It was more relaxed, and the nicest of Sam's houses," she said. His guest's children tended to stay there. Nevertheless, Spiegel never found the right couple to look after the villa.

"Sam had so many properties and the people weren't performing," Carrie recalled. "The cook on the boat [Gaston van Hanja] was always getting drunk. But Sam loved the power attached to having those places." The famous guests were also important. "Sam had to surround himself with celebrities, which I thought was a little gross." Certain people only telephoned during the summer months. "He'd never hear from them all year and then they'd start calling about the boat. Sam was definitely being used but he didn't mind." Besides, if they were famous, he was using them to continue his reputation as *the* host on the Côte d'Azur.

As a host, Spiegel was extremely possessive. "It wasn't as if you could really complain," said his son, "because you were presented with fantastic food, wine, and an amazing environment. But I do think that Sam felt that a deal was being done every time you accepted hospitality." Billy Wilder nicknamed him Captain Bligh, while Ahmet Ertegun accused the producer of being a martinet. (As a result, certain guests were amused by the modest words of the plaque in the Blue Saloon, which read: "Oh God, thy sea is so big, and my ship is so small.")

In many ways, Spiegel viewed his entertaining as another production. Michael White, the theatrical producer, remembered a dinner when there was something wrong with the placement. "And we were, after all, in St. Tropez on a casual holiday and Sam got into a terrific temper, way out of proportion. That sort of typified him." In Spiegel's defense, he wanted everything to be perfect. He would complain if the white wine was not cold enough or the red wine was not at room temperature. According to Mike Nichols, he was always "spontaneous," in the moment. "So that you had a very good time even while he was torturing the steward or the people who worked for him." The producer was obsessive. "He would say, 'Turn the fish; turn the fish before offering it to the princess. No, turn it all the way around.' And he would say, 'There used to be four screws in the doorknob, what happened to the fourth?' "

Certain rules had to be obeyed. Children were expected to eat separately. "Princess Caroline [of Monaco] and I were furious that we were considered as kids," admitted Melanie Wyler. (The princess was nineteen, while Wyler was in her mid-twenties.) "We would be served hamburgers and chips by a man in white gloves [James Jordan]," said Natasha Richardson, "while the grown-ups were at another table, eating lobster." No flirting with the crew. An unknown German actress broke this rule and slept with the captain. "Sam went wild," said Ahmet Ertegun, "and he wasn't in a good mood thereafter." Telephoning was also discouraged. Faye Dunaway royally disgraced herself in this area. "She had fallen in love with Marcello Mastroianni, who was making a film in Moscow and she never stopped calling him," said Pierre Sciclounoff. Nor did Spiegel encourage incoming calls, which became a sort of joke with Jack Nicholson. Each time the telephone rang, the actor used to look at his fellow guests and tease, "Please God, it's not for one of us."

There were those like Ertegun who delighted in setting Spiegel off. "It was late and I was having a chat in the salon of the boat with Barbara Howar, the TV personality. . . . Sam stayed a bit with us and then said, 'Well, I guess we should go in.' And I said, 'You go ahead. I am going to talk.' Sam then said, 'But you have to close the curtains.' And I said, 'We'll close the curtains,' and he said, 'Okay, but make sure the doors are closed and so forth.' And I said, 'Fine.' " Every half hour,

Spiegel came back to check on Ertegun and Howar until he finally fell asleep. "It was control, Sam wanted to control everything, except the events that were going on when he was having a good time." Ertegun and Howar stayed up talking until about three. But as a joke, no doubt in defiance of Spiegel's authoritative nature, they decided to rough things up before they left. "I took my shorts off and we had an empty whiskey bottle lying flat on the floor and the glasses knocked over and we rumpled all the cushions on the sofa and we went to bed. We left everything like that. The next morning, Sam said, 'Listen, I don't know what you did last night, but this place was a shambles–and how could you do it when your wife was only two rooms away?"

Michael White recalled that most male guests had their moment of being in disgrace with Spiegel. "But that was part of the fun–being treated like naughty schoolboys."

Spiegel was different with his female guests. " 'Darling, you sit there,' he used to say to Mica [Ertegun] and my wife," said George Stevens Jr. "But with Ahmet and I–it was, 'you here.' There was *such* a change of tone."

Ertegun kept after Spiegel about his deafness. "I used to say, 'Sam, I think you ought to get a hearing aid. And he would say, 'What?' " Ertegun would then repeat himself in a louder voice and would continue to do so until he was literally screaming, "SAM I THINK YOU OUGHT TO GET A HEARING AID." At which point, Spiegel would say, "Why? I hear perfectly well."

However, it was impossible for him to be deaf to Jack Nicholson's fans in the Mediterranean. "It would be a tiny port and there would be all these women screaming 'Fuck me Jack,' 'I love you,' 'I'm yours,' " recalled Carrie. "And I remember thinking what does that do to your head?" In fact, the actor remained even-keeled. "I enjoyed hearing him and Sam talk. They would discuss everything from books they were reading to politics, and the occasional film." Nicholson used to refer to Spiegel as "my main man." When ordering suits from John Pearse, his British tailor, he referred to the cut of Spiegel's jackets. "Nicholson liked the way that Spiegel's shoulders were always soft and sloping," recalled Pearse. "During fittings, he used to say, 'Gimme Sam's shoulders.' "

Spiegel, who did not seek the company of actors, had the same type of relationship with Nicholson as he had with Marlon Brando. Nor was he afraid of showing his disapproval, particularly when the film star mooned the paparazzi that were waiting for him on the St. Tropez pier. "Sam told Jack how undignified his behavior was," said the photographer Willy Rizzo, a regular on *Malahne*. "He scolded him like a son."

The producer was also angry with David Geffen when he told Irene Mayer Selznick "to fuck herself." First, Spiegel had called to check if his "darling boy" had really said this. Geffen admitted that he had. "She was driving me crazy," he reasoned. "And Sam said, 'Darling boy, she drives everyone crazy; you must apologize, you're on my boat and you must apologize.' I did and it was an unpleasant encounter with Irene for the entire cruise. We actually became quite good friends, but she was incredibly domineering—'Now we'll go water skiing at twelve and we'll eat lunch at one.' I was on vacation." Selznick wrote a letter to Spiegel insisting that she had done her "best not to be Mrs. Danvers," and all had worked out well, "despite David's distinct lack of charm."

The dramas were endless and a holiday shared with the producer was a series of social events. Still, Carrie was struck by how few of the guests enjoyed their wealth and position as much as her boyfriend did. "They were always suspicious of someone robbing or stealing from them." This was not the case with Spiegel. "He really knew how to live."

Although his position as a producer had taken a nosedive. Obviously, it was different from his S. P. Eagle days, since he was resting on well-deserved laurels and had a slew of assets, as well as several Swiss bank accounts, but he was on his own, as he had been prior to 1953.

His next film, *The Last Tycoon*, was based on F. Scott Fitzgerald's work, an unfinished novel that Scribner's published posthumously in 1941. Set in the 1930s, it was a Hollywood story, devoid of the usual tinsel, about Monroe Stahr (Robert De Niro), the top production executive at a studio, whose character was based on Irving G. Thalberg. Despite suffering from poor health, he is chained to his desk by the problems of his various productions, as well as being bullied by Pat Brady (Robert Mitchum), the studio head, who is an Irish version of Louis B. Mayer. He then falls in love with a young woman,

Kathleen Moore (Ingrid Boulting), who resembles his late actress wife, Minna Davis (Ingrid Boulting).

Many, including David Lean, thought that Spiegel saw himself as the Last Tycoon. The producer had been given the Irving G. Thalberg Memorial Award in 1964, but in every way the two men were quite different. Thalberg was a workaholic, who lived in a permanent state of ailing health, while his short life was limited to the confines of a Hollywood studio and a happy marriage. None of these elements would have appealed to Spiegel, who saw himself as an ebullient, international statesman, and was proud of his roving eye. However, if people made the comparison between him and *The Last Tycoon*, he was pleased. Spiegel was a showman, and the Thalberg link was good for newspaper copy and ultimately business.

As with *Lawrence of Arabia*, there had been previous attempts to adapt *The Last Tycoon*. Spiegel described it as being "frequently planned, frequently announced and frequently abandoned." In the early 1960s, Lester Cowan commissioned Irwin Shaw to write a screenplay, which had come to nothing. Then with the success of his film *The Story of G.I. Joe*, the producer attempted to make the movie again in 1967, either using Paul Newman or Warren Beatty as the Monroe Stahr character. It never happened and the rights had returned to Frances Scott Fitzgerald Smith, as the writer's daughter was then called.

It was Peter Viertel who had advised Spiegel to make the film in 1973. "Sam was the greatest brain picker, and when I was in London, he sat me down and then proceeded to tell me the worst fucking story I have ever heard in my life about the movie business," said Viertel. That night, the writer flew back to Paris. He had nothing to read and found a paperback of Fitzgerald's novel in the airport. "The next day I called Sam." Other intimates such as Leo Jaffe and David Geffen were against the project. "But there was no point talking Sam out of something, he had his feet in concrete," said Geffen. "When he was going to do something, nothing was going to stop him."

Spiegel had good intentions. "I am trying to do something that hasn't been done here in a long time," he told Charles Champlin from the *Los Angeles Times*–"a gentle picture." He sensed that his fellow producers were "trying to outdo each other in shock." "But it really is like electroshock therapy. The danger is that the treatment has to be stronger every time. You've got to keep scaring them more, and where's the limit? Violence makes the appetite for violence voracious." (It would be interesting to have Spiegel's feelings on the present state of the industry!) He insisted that it was "not sour grapes" on his part since his films had "done well." "It is sad that *Jaws* will outdo movies we all thought of as landmarks. It's like being brought up on humanist literature and then having to read schlock."

Spiegel was fully aware of his legacy and had great disdain for the new group of producers who, in his opinion, were just packagers. When speaking to *The Village Voice*, he had said, "They merely assemble the elements of a film and then let others take over. I prepare the script long before I know who is going to release it, even before I know who is going to direct it." It was not a put-on; Spiegel was horrified by what he described as a genuine falling of standards in the motion picture business. Where were the new David Selznicks who felt a responsibility to the audience? The behavior of the agents also perturbed him. ICM's Harry Ufland had used the F word with his secretary and Spiegel had been appalled. "He was very like Swifty Lazar in that way," recalled Michael White. "Rightly or wrongly, they said that class in Hollywood ended in the 1960s and that none of the stars of today knew how to hold a knife and fork or what to do with a bottle of wine. There was quite a lot of snobbery involved and Sam had that in full measure, that kind of European snobbery."

Spiegel's F. Scott Fitzgerald project had started at MGM. It made sense, since Thalberg–known as the Boy Wonder–had worked there until his death in 1936. There had also been Spiegel's brief spell at the studio with Paul Bern. At first, Mike Nichols was supposed to direct, with Buck Henry as the writer. But, on the quiet, Spiegel had approached two other directors. One was rumored to be Billy Wilder, while the second was Kazan. Spiegel then performed one of his *Waiting for Godot* tricks by sailing off to Europe and leaving both men to discover–via the *New York Times*–that Nichols was going to direct *The Last Tycoon*.

"This was a shock," Kazan wrote. "Not earth-shaking, but mild, gentle, still a shock. Not that I think you made a wrong move–I think Mike is a much better director for this."

In the meantime, Nichols was on the project, albeit warily so. "I realized that he adapted Jewish mother practices to business," he said. "Sam was not capable of guilt and he was not really capable of having his feelings hurt in those ways, but he did know how to use guilt with business and put you at a great disadvantage. He'd mix it all up so that whenever I said no to Sam, I felt that I was saying no to my uncle or someone in my family. He was a master of that."

When MGM backed out at the end of 1973, so did Buck Henry. The project quickly landed at Paramount, with Harold Pinter as the writer. At last, after several abortive efforts in the 1960s, Spiegel and the playwright were working together. In fact, Spiegel would be briefly ensconced with two of his favorite people. Just as Jack Nicholson was one of his boys, he had the same type of feeling toward Pinter and Nichols. Both were brilliant forces in the theater, which always had Spiegel's undying respect, while on a personal level, they were extremely charismatic, self-made, and Jewish, although non-practicing.

Although Nichols was an old hand in Hollywood, having directed Elizabeth Taylor and Richard Burton in *Who's Afraid of Virginia Woolf?*, and winning an Academy Award for *The Graduate*, it was Pinter's first taste of a grand-style Hollywood production. The playwright had an impressive list of European screenplays, including Michael Anderson's *The Quiller Memorandum* and Jack Clayton's *The Pumpkin Eater*, as well as his Losey collaborations–the latest being *The Go-Between*–but these were all relatively low-budget, independent films, and that was where his mind was set.

When handing in his first draft, Pinter had written to Spiegel: "As you'll immediately see, what I'm proposing is not a 'big film,' not in any sense an epic. I myself think this is right. I don't think the book's an epic and don't think the film should strive to be one. What I've been after is a sharp, dry, swift look at the facts. I've tried to show that the boundary between film and reality is not a hard and fast one. I've also tried to show that we're also making a film."

Spiegel, however, had other plans. *The Last Tycoon* had to be on a level with his prior picture, but better. As part of Pinter's Hollywood research, Spiegel took him around the old MGM lot where some of the sets for Thalberg's *The Good Earth* were still up, and pointed out the house where *The Philadelphia Story* was filmed.

Afterward, the screenplay sessions tended to take place in Spiegel's Grosvenor House apartment. "The three of us were talking and the doorbell rang," said Pinter. "And Sam said, 'My masseuse has come. You boys continue talking, and I'll see you in half an hour.' So we did continue. We made no comment. We got toward the end and Mike suddenly had a brilliant idea and I took it on board. You know you throw the ball and I suddenly went for it. We both became extremely excited. And I said, 'Jesus, I've got to tell Sam.' And Mike said, 'No, no, you can't tell Sam at the moment, he's having a massage.' And I said, 'I don't care what he's having, he's got to come out and hear this.' So I went down the corridor and knocked on the door. He said, 'What is it?' And I said, 'You must come out, now! We've . . . Mike and I have got something to tell you.' And he replied, 'Jeeesus Christ, can't it wait?' And I replied, 'No it can't wait, it absolutely can't wait, it's now or never, you've got to get this red-hot idea.' I could hear him grumbling. I left and went back and a few minutes later, I heard the front door. The masseuse had disappeared. Then Sam came into the front room in his dressing gown and he was furious. He said, 'Why did you interrupt my massage?' He wasn't at all happy. And I said, 'Look, Sam, Mike has this brilliant idea,' and he was standing up like a prizefighter. So I told him the end and his whole body started to relax. He had been quite tense and he sat down and said, 'You've made me so happy.' . . . At the end, his artistic judgment overrode his sensual needs."

While working on the second draft, the casting became an important issue. Kate Nelligan, who had burst onto the theatrical scene with David Hare's *Knuckle*, was considered for Kathleen, Stahr's love interest. "The porter called to say that she was on her way up and I can always remember Mike saying, 'I feel sorry for young actresses, can you imagine coming up to meet Sam Spiegel, Harold Pinter, and me—it must be terrifying for them.' And the next thing we knew, she walked into the room and took us to the cleaners. She was totally self-possessed, absolutely on top of everything, and made us feel that we didn't know what we were doing. She didn't get the part because of that, and I really regretted it because she was a very good actress and she could have played it, but nobody took to her wildly."

However, just as the project was coming together at last, Nichols asked for the meeting set for August to be put back two months. "Sam was so controlling that Harold's and my best work on the screenplay was when Sam was in the bathroom, literally," he recalled. "Finally, I said, 'I can't do this, I can't work, think, or live in his rhythm. In order to direct a movie, it has to be in my rhythm.' "

Spiegel did expect to be "in on every single discussion." Pinter had learned to accept it. "But Mike couldn't take it," he recalled. "Sam made him very nervous *indeed*." In the playwright's opinion, Spiegel was very good on construction. The only slight issue between them was about not working on Sundays. "Sam said, 'I thought you weren't religious?' And I said, 'I'm not, Sam, but I'm religious to cricket.' "

Nichols had had enough. After Al Pacino turned down the lead, he recommended Dustin Hoffman, then left. "I stepped away from it, but very carefully." Quite carefully–Spiegel was a little vexed to read a few weeks later that the ABC network had signed up the director-comedian to develop a half-hour sitcom for their 1975–1976 season. Naturally, he took his revenge. "Sam was paying me relatively modest amounts each six months [$25,000] and I took great care to tell him that I was going to withdraw before the payment was due," said Nichols. "Then he told a reporter that he had been very hurt because I had quit the picture just after a payment had been made and I was really mad. I didn't talk to him for maybe a year."

When Kazan took over, the pursuit for Dusty (Spiegel's name for Hoffman) continued. The actor came to London. "So Sam called and said, 'Dustin is in town and would like to meet you to talk about the script,' " Pinter recalled. "I said, 'What do you mean talk about the script?' And Sam said, 'Just to talk about the script.' So I said, 'All right, well ask him to give me a ring.' And then a couple of days later, I had a ring from a man called Jarvis Astaire, who was Dustin Hoffman's manager or something. And he said, 'Hello Mr. Pinter, Dustin would very much like to meet you to talk about your script. . . . So could you come over and see him at 5:30, he's at the Dorchester.' And I said, 'Well, why can't he come over here?' And Astaire said, 'Well, he's a very, very busy man.' " It was a red flag to a bull; Pinter became unavailable for all the suggested appointments. "He said, 'So, you can't make any of these?' And I said, 'No, I can't, but I tell you what, why don't you ask Dustin to give me a ring; we've met. I think that's the best thing to do and perhaps we can find a time for him to come over here to my place and have a cup of tea.' So he said, 'All right,' not liking it at all. I then sent a telegram to Dustin at the Dorchester saying something like, 'Sorry unable to accept royal command to visit you at your hotel. Ring, if you feel like it. Harold Pinter.' The next thing I had was Sam saying, 'I've just heard that you won't meet Dustin Hoffman. He's called me and he's very upset.' And I said, 'Sam, settle down, if he wants to meet me, he can meet me.' "

Meanwhile, Kazan was writing enthusiastic letters to Spiegel about cameramen. He was keen to see the work of "a few people who are from overseas who have both been in Hollywood films and at the same time brought something fresh to our screen." During that period, Jerry Tokofsky had seen a fair amount of the director and producer. The former Columbia executive was then teaching at USC. "One of the things I would say was 'go with your instincts, you're not old, you're not old.' They would get into this position where it was, 'Are we with it? Do we know what's going on?' "

Had Spiegel flirted with the idea of casting Jack Nicholson as Monroe Stahr? Kazan mentioned it in his memoirs. Was this why he had purchased an entire page of the *New York Times* Sunday edition to wish the star "best wishes" when he was making *One Flew Over the Cuckoo's Nest* in Salem, Oregon? In business, the producer was not spontaneously generous; an ulterior motive tended to loom behind such an act. Yet no correspondence suggests what it was. Nicholson eventually played a cameo role in *The Last Tycoon,* but surely Spiegel's grand gesture hinted at the "grand" part?

If he was up for the role of Stahr, the scheme was short-lived, because three months later De Niro was cast. The idea was Kazan's, and Spiegel was content. The actor was in demand, making films back to back, even though it led to Spiegel battling with De Niro's agency about the start dates of his prior film, *Taxi,* which ultimately became *Taxi Driver.*

Spiegel arranged for Pinter to see Scorsese's *Mean Streets.* He was impressed, describing the actor as being "on the brink," just as he was horrified by the choice of Ingrid Boulting as Kathleen. (Often referred to as Roy Boulting's daughter, she was actually the British producer-director's stepdaughter.) A favorite of Richard Avedon, she had been a successful fashion model. Her moonlike face and vast eyes had also set the tone of the Biba posters–the fashionable clothes and makeup line of the 1970s.

The Last Tycoon was the twenty-eight-year-old's fifth film but her first major role. Despite being ravishingly pretty in photographic stills, she was woefully wooden on camera. Nor were her five years of acting classes apparent, since she was at sea with Pinter. Afterward, she told journalists that reciting his words was equivalent to blowing air into yeast when making bread.

"I did meet her once, she was delightful," the playwright said. However, on screen, she simply "did not cut the mustard." He had tried to come up with alternatives, as had Peter Viertel, who had recommended Susan Sarandon. Other actresses, such as Anjelica Huston, were tested but it was no good. "Kazan was absolutely set on Ingrid Boulting and Kazan was the director," said Pinter. Yet according to the director, it was Spiegel who was gunning for the actress. "He kept saying, 'she's coltish.' " Indeed, the producer had a big crush. They were even those who felt that Boulting resembled Jeannette de Rothschild. Demonstrating his enthusiasm, Spiegel had put her under contract for three additional pictures, although this information was craftily withheld from Pinter. Thus he was in the middle. "With me as Ingrid's sponsor," said Kazan, who recognized that Spiegel was protecting himself from any blame "in case she didn't do well."

In the meantime, Kazan had problems with Theresa Russell, who was playing Cecilia, Brady's daughter. Spiegel had known Russell since 1973. It was before she had changed her name and was still called Theresa Lynn Paup. Spiegel had recommended the sixteen-year-old Californian to Nat Lefkowitz at the William Morris Agency. He wanted Russell to have the same star treatment as Boulting. Anthea Sylbert was called in to design her wardrobe and Jeanne Moreau's. While Anna "Johnny" Hill Johnstone, who had worked with Kazan since *On the Waterfront* and whose other credits included *The Godfather* and *The Stepford Wives,* was dressing everyone else.

Kazan was against the idea of Sylbert for several reasons. First, he considered her to be too Hollywood. Sylbert's recent credits included

Chinatown and *Shampoo*. (She had also been married to Paul Sylbert, the production designer of Milos Forman's *One Flew Over the Cuckoo's Nest*.) "Did you ever have a picture where the costumes or the special effects or the art direction or a song got an Oscar and the picture got nothing?" he wrote to Spiegel. "That kind of result sums up the costume people in California for me." (Kazan also referred to his experience on *The Sea of Grass,* where each time Katharine Hepburn "went to take a piss, she came out in a different dress.") Secondly, using a different costume designer for specific actresses reminded Kazan of his film *The Arrangement,* when Faye Dunaway had brought in her own fashion designer. "The result was embarrassing, dramatically unexpressive, somewhat false and–goddam expensive," he wrote.

But he succumbed, as he eventually did to Russell's charms. Moreover, while he gleefully described Spiegel as trying to "gentle her into his bed" (and, in his opinion, he had failed), the director hinted at having more success with young women.

A return to a Fitzgerald classic was just what the public needed, or so Spiegel argued. It did not matter that previous attempts at the novelist's work had not worked, such as Henry King's *Tender Is the Night* for Twentieth Century-Fox in 1962, or Clayton's *The Great Gatsby,* which was one of 1974's big flops. "Fitzgerald has never succeeded on the screen because he has been poorly interpreted," Spiegel told Bob Thomas of the *Los Angeles Times.* "Great works of literature can be converted into idiotic movies. That doesn't mean that you shouldn't try to make a good version of *The Brothers Karamazov* or any classic."

This time, his production was to be loaded with known film stars playing cameo roles such as Dana Andrews, Tony Curtis, Ray Milland, Jeanne Moreau, Donald Pleasence, and Jack Nicholson. "Jack was starting to get hot then and I said, 'Oh puh leese, Jack Nicholson is not going to do a cameo in this movie,' " recalled Sue Mengers, the former agent. "And Sam, who was much more experienced and knew much more than I did, said, 'Yes he will.' It became like this petulant game. Anyway, I was too unsophisticated to realize that Sam Spiegel was a great host and Nicholson went on his boat and that people in the industry *did* do favors for each other."

There were also a string of small female parts to cast. Just as Carrie Haddad was given a small role, Mengers had sent a few of her starting-out clients to meet the director. One of the hopefuls had been Mary Jennifer Selznick–the producer's daughter–who was to commit suicide on May 11, 1976. "Kazan had her back three or four or five times for a reading and it really looked like she was going to get it. . . . She was one of maybe twenty girls that horny old Kazan was trying out. It was horrible."

Meanwhile, the director was frustrated by the screenplay's love story. "Sam was so frightened of Harold's disapproval that it was disgusting," Kazan later said. "Sam was very snobbish, not for any real reason, but he liked playing up to a certain group of people." In his memoirs, Kazan cited the playwright's disruption in his personal life as being the cause for the "hole" and lack of romance in the *Last Tycoon* screenplay.

Pinter had left his actress wife, Vivien Merchant, for the writer Antonia Fraser. "I fell in love is what happened. And Sam was very kind not only to me but to Vivien too. He took great care." The producer lent him his London apartment, while the actress had an open invitation on *Malahne.* Suddenly, in his mid-forties, Pinter was homeless and "standing on my head." "Sam was great. He didn't make any judgments. He never said to me, 'What are you doing?' He was so experienced about life, he knew life was life and that happened."

The playwright was also pleased that the final draft of his screenplay was never tampered with. "The actors did my script as it was written. Kazan also made sure that this was the case. . . . It's very rare with a Hollywood film."

However, in Barry Diller's opinion–who was then the chairman and the CEO at Paramount–the screenplay lacked "a certain lushness." He also had problems with De Niro, whom he described as "miscast." "Irving Thalberg was Jewish." Yet in many ways, the actor's performance remains the one flawless detail throughout the film. Unlike Boulting, he could handle Pinter's lines. Thoroughly prepared, he dropped forty-two pounds for the role, read endless books on studio heads, as well as viewing all of Thalberg's greats, such as *Camille, Grand Hotel,* and *The Champ.* On his behalf, Spiegel contacted Norma Shearer, Thalberg's widow, and asked for photographs and other memorabilia. He was also in touch with Margaret Booth, MGM's legendary film editor.

Spiegel took particular care of De Niro. "Except that Sam was mad that Bobby really got drunk to prepare for the scene with Jack Nicholson," said Carrie Haddad. However, if Kazan's diaries are to be believed, Spiegel soon soured on De Niro. Was he just creating conflict on the set? He had not been able to do this with Franklin Schaffner on *Nicholas and Alexandra,* but he knew that his former sparring partner was always raw and ready to be wound up. If this was the case, it was a futile exercise, since Kazan was as much a shadow of his former self as Spiegel was. "Both their minds were elsewhere," said Carrie.

Nevertheless, throughout the production, which eventually cost $7.5 million and was either shot on the Paramount lot or around Los Angeles in places like the Biltmore Hotel, Spiegel was omnipresent and often spotted, sporting Ari Onassis-type sunglasses. Moreover, he liked to oversee the hairdos, makeup, and nail color of the actresses. When he attended Jeanne Moreau's fitting for a Balenciaga-styled gown, he lifted her skirt to check the shoes, and said, "Perfect dahling." "Most producers would ask why we were spending money on shoes that won't be seen on the screen anyway," said Anthea Sylbert.

Somewhat predictably, Kazan was not spared financial worries. Spiegel kept on telling him that he had five and a half million of his own money invested in the production. Kazan was right to dismiss this as Spiegelese.

"I worked with John Heyman on the budget," Albert Heit said.* "Creative bookkeeping. It worked out that he [Spiegel] got one million at the beginning before it was shot." Paramount had come forward with $2.6 million. There was also almost $2 million from Gelderse, the Swiss tax shelter group that Heyman had organized, while the rest was raised by selling the foreign distribution rights.

Spiegel was in constant touch with Diller, Paramount's moneyman. "When you were in the room with Sam, the willfulness and the power of the personality of being in his pull, his orbit, was very strong," he

*Father of David Heyman, the producer of all the Harry Potter movies – past and present.

said. They had their fights. "Sam always needed more money and he would con you around and play various games. I never got the heart attack treatment, but you got all forms–bravura stuff–wheedling and anger and threats of various kinds, but it was always fun. Sam was a great salesman. He knew that if he could get you in, he could get you out." However, in spite of his personal regard for the producer, Diller had his doubts about the picture. "In the middle, I was sorry I was in it. You do say to yourself in the movie business, on occasion, 'Who do I screw to get out? What do I do to get out of this mess?' I remember when I first started seeing the rushes, I thought this is dead."

The same could not be said for Spiegel's social life. Accounts were set up at such restaurants as the Brown Derby, Mr. Chow's, Chasen's, the Bistro, and La Scala. Hugh Hefner invited him to the Playboy Mansion. The producer also entertained. Old friends such as the Kirk Douglases, the Paul Kohners, the Irving Lazars, the Wilders, and the Wylers were invited to the Tara-styled mansion on 460 Martin Lane.

Sue Mengers threw a party in honor of Spiegel and Kazan. "I did give great parties because if you weren't a star, you didn't set a foot through that door. My mother could be standing outside trying to get in." Mengers was witness to a fight between the two old friends. "I was thinking, This is history, and I better remember it." During the argument, Spiegel apparently said, "What do you know? You only know about testifying on your friends." (He was referring to Kazan naming names.) "And it struck me how Kazan took it," she said. "He did nothing. I expected the Kazan I knew to say 'Fuck you.' But he just took it."

For old times' sake, Spiegel threw a party to usher in 1976. The guest list was extensive, with longtime acquaintances such as Joan Ambler, Rudi Fehr, Mike Frankovich, Kurt Frings, Walter Reisch, and Max Youngstein mixed in among the new generation, which included Jacqueline Bisset, Michael Douglas, Brian De Palma, Martin Scorsese, Robert Shaw, and Richard Zanuck.

Carrie was not sure about the soirée. "Sam was trying to produce the same sort of party that he had had before, but a lot of people were snorting cocaine. They were really edgy." Joan Juliet Buck recalled "stars at every table." "I was thrilled to be there and very conscious that this is Sam's New Year's Eve party."

The following day, Spiegel invited Tessa Kennedy and her brood for "brunch by the pool." (One of her sons is the actor Cary Elwes.) "I rang the doorbell and a member of the staff said, 'Is Mr. Spiegel expecting you?' And I said, 'Yes.' Anyway, I walked out to the terrace and there were these two naked girls and Sam in the middle of three different banquettes. I said, 'Oh Sam, you're here. You invited the children.' And he said, 'Are they here? Are they here? Don't let them in, don't let them in.' Of course, I wasn't going to."

In regards to his sex life, Carrie found him to be "puzzling" and a bit of a "kinky weirdo." "Sam was old," she said. "He wasn't some kind of virile stud, but I was fine with that. I was young and brought up in free love, hippie San Francisco. Nothing fazed me."

Maurice Jarre, however, was struck by their age difference. The Frenchman, who was composing the film's music, as well as a song for Jeanne Moreau, found it sad. "Sam was this really old guy with this very young girl." The sight of Kazan further depressed him. "He gave up totally to Sam. He was so tired that during one session, he was lying on the table."

But nothing beat the disastrous *Last Tycoon* New York premiere, held at Avery Fisher Hall. "The studio were determined to fill the theater," said Carrie. "And so they gave away the tickets to the Actors Studio." Unfortunately, the followers of the Method did not think much of the picture. "It was so embarrassing because as soon as Ingrid Boulting opened her mouth, people burst out laughing," said Antonia Fraser, who was sitting right behind the actress.

The picture was panned; some critics were even a little savage, perhaps stemming from a feeling of possessiveness toward Fitzgerald's work. In fact, the film still holds up, apart from the excruciatingly long love scene between Monroe and Kathleen in Malibu. Like a David Hamilton film, the camera lingers on Boulting's naked behind. Still, there are some extraordinary scenes: Kathleen's entrance on the gilded head of the goddess Shiva, the descent down the stairs after the premiere, as well as the table tennis match between Brimmer and Stahr. It remains a much more interesting film than *Nicholas and Alexandra*. Aside from De Niro, there are great performances by Jeanne Moreau as Didi, the aging actress (a role that was turned down by both Brigitte Bardot and Romy Schneider),

Donald Pleasence as Boxley, the frustrated screenwriter, Tony Curtis as Rodriguez, the swashbuckling actor, and Jack Nicholson as Brimmer, the Communist union organizer from the East Coast.

According to Arthur Abeles, who headed Cinema International Corporation, the distributors for Paramount in Europe, "It was a big disappointment." His first screening had been with the producer and director. "Gadg seemed very surly and very angry." The director later confessed that the whole story behind his making *The Last Tycoon* showed him in the worst light. "I did the film for no good reason except my mother was very sick and I wanted to get money."

A few months after the film's release, Spiegel was back harassing Diller and sending telegrams complaining about the lack of advertising in the university towns. Paramount's chairman immediately cabled him back, informing him that $855,000 had been spent on the advertising and that only a million had been agreed on. Meetings were held, telephone calls were exchanged, but Spiegel was still not satisfied. "I deeply regret that all I can offer at the moment is my good wishes," he fired back. "It is one of those cases where several years of my life and effort will have gone unrewarded. I wish I could have taken the major responsibility for it upon myself and absolve you and your company of any blame, but it would be untrue, unrealistic and insincere on my part to do so."

Despite his whining, Spiegel actually made money. "He was the only one who did," said his lawyer. "A peculiar deal" was made where the producer was supposed to pay off after $4 million was made at the box office in Europe. "They thought it was going to do minimum $4 million theatrical and it didn't," Heit said. "It dropped dead at the box office in Europe. So anything up to $4 million, we kept."

The New York office of Horizon Pictures–not a film studio–was responsible for supplying the royalty statements. Whereas David Lean had unjustly accused the producer of robbing him of money–unjustly because he *had* been paid–it was not the case on *The Last Tycoon* and *Betrayal,* Spiegel's final film. "Sam's bookkeeping and accountability were less than perfect," said John Heyman. "We tried to get statements for years." But having being involved on productions such as *The Go-Between* and *Marathon Man,* he stressed that accounting in the film business has never been perfect, nor does it ever tend "to favor the creative."

Spiegel's modus operandi resembled a more polished return to his behavior prior to *On the Waterfront*. "I used to say to Sam, 'How about those royalties?' " recalled Pinter. "And he would always manage to change the subject until I gave up asking."

Curiously, Nicholson employed more drastic measures. "Sam's attitude was 'Jack won't sue me,' but he did!" said Heit. The producer tried his old ploy of offering a share in his art collection, but the actor's manager rebuffed the idea. "Jack Nicholson does not want any painting, but wants a complete accounting of the gross for the movie *The Last Tycoon*, not a guestimate, but an official distribution statement as called for," wrote Sandy Bresler. In his estimation, the actor was owed $40,000. Eventually, it was settled. Proteus–Nicholson's company–was assigned a defined percentage of the producer's share of the gross derived from the domestic distribution. And throughout the entire proceedings, the film star continued to go on *Malahne*.

Between Kazan and Spiegel it was different, a case of two sparring partners, a gladiator recognizing another gladiator. Out of all the directors he worked with, he was closest to Gadg. When Barbara Loden, Kazan's second wife, died of cancer on September 5, 1980, Spiegel sent a telegram saying, I UNDERSTAND SO MUCH MORE NOW THAN I EVER DID AND I AM DEEPLY SORRY AND WISH YOU ALL THE BEST IN THE WORLD.

Kazan replied a few months later. He was working on another novel, which was keeping him from seeing people. "Writing, in case you don't know it, is much harder than directing films," he wrote. "Why, it may be the reason why I, perverse I, do it."

Twenty-six years after the event, Diller has fond memories of Spiegel and his tactics. "It's so missing today. The fact that it's a pleasurable process–that craziness, yelling and threats–it had a spirit underneath." One of Spiegel's many talents was that it was hard to be annoyed with him. "Part of it was that he wasn't angry, and part of it was that it was a game."

Chapter Twenty-six

BETRAYAL

In the late 1970s, Warren Beatty offered Spiegel a role in *Reds* as a Russian businessman. "I think Sam got a tuxedo made for the occasion, but it never happened," the actor said.

Rachel Chodorov (the daughter-in-law of Edward Chodorov), Spiegel's New York assistant, remembered it differently. The producer had asked for pages, which was impossible since the dialogue was being written three days ahead of shooting. "Beatty once called me and said, 'What should I do?' And I said, 'You know what Sam is like; you have to coddle and coax him. Why don't you have Diane [Keaton] send him a telegram? That might turn the tide.' And so she did, but Sam wasn't impressed by that, at all. I think the real reason was that he thought that he might make a fool of himself."

Extremely sensitive about his public image, Spiegel must have understood that his reputation had declined, but he still had his standards. In general, that meant not making cameo appearances, never stooping to the lowest common denominator, and stubbornly continuing to court writers. Regarding the latter, novelist J. P. Donleavy was at the top of his list.

Ever since *The Ginger Man,* the American writer had become somewhat of a celebrity. His reputation was that of a Joseph Conrad-like character living in Ireland. Spiegel was interested in the theme of the rich, solitary individual in *A Singular Man,* Donleavy's latest book.

Donleavy's screenplay of the novel was finished in September 1978, and Robert Redford was discussed with George Roy Hill as director. But once Redford refused to commit, Spiegel began to side-step. And by December 1979, the novelist, who was clearly exasperated by the lack of response to his registered letters, had terminated the project.

John Guare, whose plays included *The House of Blue Leaves* and *Rich and Famous* and who had co-written the screenplay of Forman's *Taking Off,* had less of a frustrating experience. Spiegel had taken an interest in his play *The Landscape of the Body,* which first appeared in 1977, with the idea that it could be transformed for the screen just as *Suddenly, Last Summer* had been.

The playwright used to join the producer at 475 Park Avenue for their sessions. "I was his day job," said Guare. However, despite the considerable rewrites, the meetings came to an end. "He said, 'You've done everything I wanted you to do, but the only place we could open this movie would be Jonestown'—then the site of a recent mass suicide!" It had been a learning experience for Guare. "Sam extended my narrative skills." Immediately afterward, Guare wrote the screenplay for Malle's *Atlantic City,* which was nominated for an Oscar.

No great confidences had been exchanged, apart from one Sunday night when they were watching tennis on television. Guare had asked Spiegel if there were any movies he wished that he had made. "He didn't look away from the screen and said, 'I've only made movies I wished I hadn't made.'" It was a rare example of Spiegel being off rather than on, because Guare was mostly struck by the producer's joie de vivre. "His days were filled, he was out every night, and he *loved* his address book."

Nevertheless, Spiegel's assistant sensed a profound loneliness. He used to inform her of every move from the moment he woke up. "He involved me because there was no one else to talk to." James Higgins—Spiegel's live-in butler of seventeen years—had been momentarily lured away by Kitty Miller, the widow of theatrical producer Gilbert Miller and one of New York's *grand dames.* "Sam trusted James," recalled Chodorov. "He [James] knew all the personal secrets but would never say a word because he was the perfect butler and he knew what it meant to be the perfect butler." A few years later, Higgins would return because he was "bored" and "missed" Spiegel. "People felt safe with Sam," said Chodorov. In the interim, Spiegel had

had to make do with a series of butlers who were either unprofessional or not nearly as dedicated as Higgins.

Working for Spiegel was hardly taxing for Chodorov. "The most exciting thing that happened was when Lean sent a telegram which said 'help' from Tahiti." From October 10, 1977, he and Robert Bolt had been working on their *Mutiny on the Bounty* project. Originally, Dino De Laurentiis was set to produce, until he withdrew on September 22, 1978. Six months later, Spiegel was in charge.

Seventeen years had passed since *Lawrence of Arabia,* but there was no great change in his relationship with Lean. "David would be exasperated, but it was all a game, and Sam knew how to get to him," said Chodorov. "He played with him like a mouse." Still, his former sparring partner sensed a sort of security around Spiegel. MY DEAR SAM HERE WE GO AGAIN AFTER ALL THESE YEARS AND VERY NICE TOO, had been his telegram, five months into the project.

. Spiegel, on the other hand, insisted that Lean write the screenplay in a place where the telephone worked. The director opted for the Dolder Grand Hotel in Zurich. Concerning the producer's grasp of the screenplay, Chodorov found him to be "brilliant," whereas Lean would get tied up in the details. "It was a beautiful script. It had long, long descriptions of how the prow of the boat would rise above the water and how the sun would hit the waves in the morning. But the thread of the story would get a little lost, and he needed Spiegel to pull it back together."

The collaboration collapsed in the middle of 1980 when De Laurentiis returned and Spiegel insisted on an equal division of artistic control between himself and Lean. There was a sigh of relief from his younger friends. "I remember sitting in Sam's apartment when he talked about making *Mutiny*," said David Geffen. "And I said, 'This will kill you, you cannot do this, you'll die.' I was screaming in his apartment that he must not do it, but he wanted to." For a brief moment, Spiegel had tried to rope producer George Stevens, Jr., into helping him with the epic. "And I had previously cemented in my head that my friendship with Sam was totally dependent on my *never* working with him," had been his attitude.

Between Lean and Spiegel, who would have drawn blood first?

Lean was not averse to needling Spiegel. Outside their projects, a subject of mutual interest was their investments–their stocks and shares. One day in Zurich, they were discussing gold, which had suddenly shot up in price. Spiegel admitted that he had not taken advantage of the previous slump in prices. With particular delight, Lean leaned back in his chair and informed Spiegel that *he* had, buying gold when it was down to $35–a bargain price. Spiegel, who at the best of times was competitive with Lean, was furious to be outwitted by him, especially in the field of finance. Spiegel called his stockbroker to try to correct his mistake, but it was too late. Afterward, he asked Warren Beatty's opinion about gold. "I don't think Sam knew too much about investments," said the actor. "I mean *me* knowing anything about gold?"

Albert Heit confirmed that Spiegel was lost in regards to financial dealings outside the film business. He preferred to put his money in socially prominent institutions that were not always the best choice. "Rothschild Bank and Lazard-Frères lost money for Sam," he noted.

When it came to the contrast of his social standing as the famous producer and his sensual needs, Spiegel's friends were either amused or turned a blind eye. He took his role as a godfather seriously, never forgetting a birthday or Christmas; he was photographed at the ballet with Jackie Onassis; he threw a high-society event for the Erteguns' twentieth wedding anniversary, as well as giving a speech at Harold Pinter's fiftieth birthday. But there remained the darker side of his nature.

"He used to go to some of those funny clubs in New York and I told him that he was too well known to do that," said Ahmet Ertegun. These were private sex clubs where it was possible to watch others indulge in their fantasies such as "golden showers" and *nostalgie de la boue.*

Sometimes, Spiegel's sexual preferences spilled out to his home. A chic Parisian couple was staying at his New York penthouse, and after a night at the theater they returned earlier than expected. However, they were a little taken aback to find three rough trade characters, wearing chains, leather, and rings in their noses, who were about to visit their host.

On another occasion, Anne and Kirk Douglas were invited to dine with the producer and two very "obvious ladies of the night." The film star was furious. There was also the African-American prostitute who stole several of Spiegel's treasured Oscars!

Fortunately, on the advice of "Katie the autocrat" Hepburn, Spiegel cut his hair. But after Carrie left in 1978, his life became a little out of control. "He liked little girls, what can I tell you," said David Geffen. In New York, many Spiegelettes came via Zoli–a liked and respected modeling agent of the 1970s, who had his own agency (Zoli Models) and whose clients included Veruschka, Lauren Hutton, and Pat Cleveland. Zoli was a fixture on the Studio 54 scene.

At a dinner following a David Hamilton exhibition–the photographer renowned for his soft-porn shots of nubile blondes–Spiegel was pretty honest about his pursuit of baby flesh. "Their skin is so smooth and they smell so good," he said. It was not just the freshness; they arrived without emotional baggage. Such an issue was particularly important to Spiegel, who had declared, "What a shame that they all get so crazy," after Hedy Lamarr telephoned him. Were his previous girlfriends and wives "crazy," or merely mature and beset with problems? Little girls growing up was not a transition that Spiegel believed in inflicting on himself.

George Weidenfeld was used to his friend's taste in women. "Sam had screenplayed himself an existence," he said. The producer had even recommended his choice in ladies as the only type to be involved with. "They're an insurance against heartache," he told Weidenfeld. Maybe, but surely no insurance against feeling lonesome? Indeed, was it all catching up on Spiegel, who had predicted that he would pay for living "a very footloose existence to live without a harness around my neck"? "I fully expect to spend my old age in solitary loneliness," he had said on various occasions. Yet obviously, there was a difference between voicing the prophecy and actually living it.

Financially, Spiegel could have continued without making any more films, but his pride as a producer made him go on. Finish with a failure? What about his reputation? Choosing to make a film of *Betrayal*–Harold Pinter's play–was a return to his previous idea with Guare.

Betrayal uncovers an extramarital affair–unveiled in a progression of scenes that recede chronologically—between Emma, an art dealer (Patricia Hodge), and Jerry, a literary agent (Jeremy Irons). The betrayal element of the liaison completes a full circle since Robert, Emma's publishing husband (Ben Kingsley), is the best friend of her lover.

Spiegel's production began to move in 1980. He had not been impressed by the National Theatre production, which he dismissed as "unelectric," or by the later Broadway production. "When Americans play Englishmen, they're more papal than the pope," he told *New York* magazine. Initially, he wanted to go with an unknown director. "I recommended David Jones," said Pinter. Spiegel then saw his acclaimed television film, *Langrishe Go Down,* which Pinter adapted for the BBC and which starred Judi Dench and Jeremy Irons.

But, somewhat typically, the producer changed his mind, deciding that *Betrayal* was perfect for Mike Nichols. "We were talking about the deal and Sam said to me, 'I want you to make a lot of money on this,' and I thought, 'Oh God, am I in a lot of trouble,'" recalled the American director, who was to be paid half a million dollars for his services. He was getting twice as much as Pinter, as well as being privy to a percentage of *Betrayal*'s profits. (The receipt of "profits" being an unlikelihood when dealing with Horizon Pictures.)

Irons was always set to play Jerry, and with Nichols on board, Meryl Streep was discussed as Emma. An added plus was that the actors had just worked together on *The French Lieutenant's Woman,* with a screenplay that was written by Pinter. However, it was over the British actor that Nichols found himself at odds with Spiegel. The producer was insistent that Nichols fly in to meet the actor. "Mike told me that he said, 'I don't want to do that, Sam, I'm exhausted. I want to go home and see my little girl,'" the playwright said. "But Sam really pressed him and did one of his, 'I really think that you should see him . . . How long is it going to take you?' and all of that. Finally Mike did, he shook Jeremy's hand. There was very little point in the meeting and he never forgave himself." Pinter then flew to New York in mid-June 1980, where he met "an ashen-faced Mike Nichols." "He kept on saying, 'I can't do it, I can't do it.' I thought he was going to have a nervous breakdown." Spiegel accepted his decision, but he did say, "Well, who are you going to get, Mike? You're going to have to help me."

Ever manipulative Spiegel used the Jewish mother practices that Nichols had previously encountered on *The Last Tycoon*. Yet, just as they affected the director, they fell flat with the playwright. "You see Mike didn't tell Sam why he couldn't do it, he just said he couldn't do it. He didn't say, 'Because I can't deal with *you*.' "

Spiegel's stalling on the project began to get to Pinter. In November 1980, he sent a letter, which began by saying it was "odd to write" since they "normally" talked, but he had to voice his thoughts on paper before the producer returned to Manhattan. "I am simply saying that I have to know before the end of the year whether we are doing this film or not. If not, no hard feelings, as they say, but let's realistically call it a day. I have to plan my working life for 1981 and I have to plan it now."

In fact, Spiegel's enthusiasm for the work had not been dulled. And it might have been, since Nichols had disappeared off the horizon as had Streep, who opted to make *Sophie's Choice* instead. The reason for his procrastinations was simple–he was weighing up the pros and cons of financing the film himself.

Pinter's letter was to have the desired effect. In the spring of 1981, Spiegel and he began a series of screenplay conferences in London and New York. It was an enjoyable experience. "After all, it was my own play and I could have been very defensive with him but we just explored other things that could be done." Spiegel became "a great source of energy and enthusiasm." "He allowed me to create," Pinter said. "He didn't inhibit me at any time. I could always say anything that I liked."

There was even talk of Pinter directing *Betrayal*. He did so, in 1973, for the film of Simon Gray's play *Butley,* which had starred Alan Bates and Jessica Tandy. If Pinter was directing, Nichols agreed to be the associate producer. Consequently, Julie Christie was approached, but since she could not make up her mind, nor did she want to create a situation where she was holding back the start date of *Betrayal,* she passed.

When that idea fell by the wayside, the director Louis Malle was considered, despite the fact that Spiegel had not enjoyed his latest film, *My Dinner with André.* ("Thank God, he spared us the dessert!" he quipped to the director's brother.) "He [Malle] was very sweet,"

Pinter recalled, "and said, 'Normally, I would love to do it, but I have just got married and I am in love with my wife [Candice Bergen], and I cannot do a film about adultery and betrayal. I just can't do it.' "

Then "right out of the blue," David Jones had a message to call Spiegel. "I thought it was a mistake!" the British director admitted. He had seen the play, but as he read the screenplay, he kept laughing. He called the playwright and said, "Listen, Harold, I've read the script but we really have to talk because I'm worried that I see it in quite a different way." That night, they had a drink together. "I said, 'My problem is that I think that the script is very funny, what do you think about that? And I didn't think the Broadway show was.' He said, 'Oh yes, yes, yes, some of it's quite amusing.' 'Even the worst scenes,' I said."

Professionally, they went way back. "I was in the third ever production of *The Birthday Party*," he said. In another production of the same play, he and the playwright had acted together. "So I learnt most of what I know about Harold Pinter verbally, from playing with him." Subsequently, Jones was at the Royal Shakespeare Company (RSC). He was also the artistic director at the Aldwych Theatre, the producer of the BBC Play of the Month drama series in the mid-1970s, as well as directing plays for the RSC. From 1979 to 1981, he was the artistic director for the Brooklyn Academy of Music.

However, despite his prolific career in theater and television, the forty-seven-year-old had never directed a motion picture before. "Sam spent the preproduction period relentlessly trying to tell me that I knew nothing about filming and that I had to be very careful. 'David, this is your first film.' I'd reply, 'Sam, I have made thirty-two films.' And he'd say, 'For TV, it doesn't count.' "

Pinter described Spiegel as being "really at his worst." "I mean half the time I was protecting David from the rampaging of Sam," he said. "He was getting on, I suppose, and he was at his worst in the way that he did have certain bullying tendencies. . . . Not even tendencies; he could be a bully." It was not a side that the playwright had seen before, but Spiegel was actually showing his true colors. In many ways, the producer's passion, which had lain dormant for so many years, was fired up again. Was it the subject matter, or was it the fact that he was using his own money?

Although Jones recognized that Spiegel was a stiff taskmaster, he sensed that he was "lucky" because he was "absolutely intensive in preproduction." "And I'm beginning to think that's where producers are their most useful." As far as the crew, Spiegel flatly refused to meet all the potential candidates. "Sam looked at me and said, 'David, when will you learn not to confuse yourself with choice?' I realize what he did. He had all the résumés, he would ring people endlessly about the guys, he would eventually decide who was top of the heap for him and that was the one." It was the modus operandi of an experienced producer.

Regarding the budget, Spiegel was "very tough." "Sam did it on a shoestring," the playwright said. "He would never disclose how much money was involved, but he did not break the bank." The film's negative cost was $4,212,000. It was not a vast amount, but it was still $4,212,000 more than Spiegel had ever spent.

The producer was also back to being the relentless perfectionist that he had been during *On the Waterfront*. "What he was almost doing was going back to the purity of the original," said the director. Once, there was a two-hour row about three lines. "Sam said, 'These are totally distracting, I don't care about these fucking workmen, I don't want to hear them.' Harold said, 'You know it just breaks it up a little.' And Sam said, 'Exactly, it just breaks it up a little.' . . . And at one moment, I put the script down and he [Spiegel] growled, 'Don't patronize me.' And I replied, 'Sam, I didn't say a fucking word, it's you and Harold who are having the row, I'm just sitting here.' And he replied, 'Yes, but you are looking.' "

Spiegel envisioned *Betrayal* as being like Lean's *Brief Encounter*. It was a comparison that he never stopped making. " 'David, this can be as important as *Brief Encounter*,' " he used to say, " 'I want it to have that sort of quality.' "

The casting continued. Charlotte Rampling was briefly thought of for Emma, then it was between Helen Mirren and Patricia Hodge. Spiegel was very taken with the latter. It was her first film and the thirty-five-year-old theatrical actress was to have special treatment. Jean Muir, the fashion designer, was to create her wardrobe.

At first, Jones had his reservations. "Patricia's public persona is very heavily made up. She came with the white makeup and the pillar box lips and I thought, 'Shit, this lady is very hard.' " However, he liked her. Moreover, she had read extremely well with Irons.

Initially, the director was keener to work with Mirren. They had met at Spiegel's office. "She sashayed past Sam's desk and said, 'Oh my God, Sam, is that a real Bacon?' And he replied, 'Helen, what do you think an unreal Bacon looks like?' " But, after lunch with the curvaceous and "very entertaining" actress, Spiegel declared that she was not right. "Her butt is too big for the part," were his exact words.

In the interim, the hunt was on for Robert. Both Tom Bell and Ian McKellen were in the running, but the director kept on rooting for Ben Kingsley, who had just finished making *Gandhi*, Richard Attenborough's yet-to-be-released epic. Jones had directed him twice for the Royal Shakespeare Company. But Spiegel refused to see him. "He looked at his photograph, said, 'He's too old,' and threw it in the waste paper bin." However, after a certain amount of coaxing from Pinter, a meeting was arranged. "Ben was brilliant," Jones recalled. "He was impish and funny and you could feel that Sam warmed to him."

Nevertheless, once the casting fell into place, Spiegel started in on the director again. "My mistake was that I was very cocky and self-reliant." Whenever the producer voiced concern about a scene or location, he never saw the problem. Then he got feedback from a mutual friend that Spiegel was "increasingly worried about him." "My friend asked, 'Why?' and Sam replied, 'Because he is never worried and that worries me a great deal.' "

It escalated to such a point that a week before shooting began, the producer threatened to pull the plug. Pinter–who acted "like a marvelous watchdog" between the director and Spiegel–had insisted that they meet. "He said, 'Sam doesn't see why at his age he should make a movie with someone he's not getting on with.' " Wisely, the director modified his tactics. "The family was in America, I was completely locked in with the movie, and I didn't resent having to go and stop Sam 'being lonely on Sundays.' "

As soon as the dailies came in, the producer's attitude changed entirely. "He did feel, within two days, that I was getting something remarkable." But the director had another problem–Irons, whom he had described as "lovely on *Langrishe*," had changed. With the success of *Brideshead Revisited*, the television series, he had become extremely famous in Britain. "Jeremy wouldn't really rehearse," Jones said. "He had had an epiphany on Jerzy Skolimowski's *Moonlighting* [his previous film] and he decided that what was great, was that you made up your own words and didn't know what the shot was until it happened." Difficult with Pinter who has a clause in his contracts that none of his original work can be altered. On one occasion, Irons even flung his screenplay dramatically on the kitchen table and cried, "Will no one help me with these words?" Only to hear the crisp voice of the author say, "Can I help?"

Meanwhile, Kingsley, wearing his specially created hairpiece for the film, continued to do a brilliant impersonation of Spiegel. It was quite a feat considering that all of his life the producer had been affectionately mimicked. The actor captured the rounding of his mouth, the expulsion of short breaths before speaking, the rich baritone voice, and the hand on the chest. It was so brilliant that when Spiegel made an unexpected visit to Twickenham Studios and began talking, all the crew immediately turned toward Kingsley, who was not moving his lips. The producer immediately understood the situation. Even at eighty-one, he was razor-sharp. And the next time he arrived, Edward Heath, the former prime minister, accompanied him. No doubt, he was keen to show that he was the man in charge, and someone with important friends.

The "creation out of conflict" skirmishes continued in the cutting room. Spiegel drove the editor "crazy." "John Bloom [the brother of Claire Bloom] would lie flat out on the floor and do a primal scream, 'If he comes in here again . . .' " said Jones. There had also been the "little brush" between Spiegel and Pinter. "He said, 'I can't understand the sentence that she is saying' and I said, 'What do you mean? It's perfectly clear, it's absolutely clear.' He said, 'They won't understand it in the Middle West,' and I said, 'Fuck the Middle West!' And he said, 'Do you want to fuck the *whole* of the Middle West?' He immediately changed the temperature."

Spiegel, on the other hand, was taken aback by Jean Muir's reaction to *Betrayal*. After seeing the film's first rough cut, the fashion designer said, "You know, the last scene will have to be shot again." Spiegel was amazed. "What do you mean? I don't understand," he said. "Did you see the pleats on her [Patricia Hodge's] skirt, they are crooked," Muir replied. "But no one will know," Spiegel insisted. "Seamstresses will," Muir answered. The scene was not reshot.

With regard to the score, *Betrayal* was shown to Simon & Garfunkel. However, Paul Simon—famous for his lyrics—was not interested, saying, "The problem is that this is a 'words movie,' and my big thing is 'words.' "

Betrayal was next screened for David Bowie. "He loved the movie, and the next day Sam and I had a big meeting with him and his manager," recalled David Jones. "It was going to be very tricky. . . . I was going to have to go to Switzerland to hear his basic ideas and then he was going to record it in New York as part of a recording session that he was doing there. It looked as if it was going to work. Bowie was very keen. . . . Then he was talking about how he would have to have an arranger and Sam said, 'Well, who arranges your stuff usually?' Bowie said, 'There's a terrific guy called Dominic Muldowney . . . ' Bowie leaves and I turn to Sam and say, 'Well, that's terrific.' And he says, 'He is not available. I don't want to work with him. Excuse me a minute, I am going to call Mr. Muldowney.' He picked up the phone immediately and offered Dominic the picture." Muldowney accepted.

A few weeks after the film was completed, the director saw Spiegel at his office. "I said, 'You look so happy today. What is up?' And he said, 'I have just got the final budget figures in and I don't have to sell the Cézanne.' He was very proud of this little Cézanne on the wall."

Unfortunately, in spite of all of Spiegel's efforts, he did a poor job on the film's release. It was further indication that he had lost touch. Samuel Goldwyn, Jr., was keen to distribute *Betrayal*. "I thought that he had a very specialized picture, but he visualized handling it like an action picture. I went through the whole process. I spent hours with him laying out a campaign, but it just didn't happen." It was a serious mistake for several reasons: Goldwyn could handle Spiegel, and, most important, he was passionate about the picture.

However, the producer was thinking "big" and *Betrayal* was shown to the important studios. It was a dismal exercise. Orion's Eric Pleskow was not interested, MGM's Freddie Fields fell asleep during a screening, while the head of Universal was said to have stormed out since the story's theme resembled his own life.

Finally, Spiegel went with Twentieth Century-Fox International Classics, which distributed the film in the States and Canada. It was a subsidiary of the same studio that had distributed *Tales of Manhattan,* his first Hollywood production. "We made the deal with Fox," said Arthur Canton, "because Sam was angry with Columbia Pictures." Frank Price, then the head of the studio, had not called him back. "The new regime wouldn't return his phone call. Sam Spiegel who put Columbia back in the black!"

Betrayal was a critical triumph. "I can't think of another recent film that is simultaneously so funny, so moving and so rigorously unsentimental," wrote Vincent Canby for the *New York Times.* Rex Reed, in the *New York Post,* noted the "articulate dialogue, sophisticated emotions and intelligent restraint." And just as *The New Republic*'s Stanley Kauffmann had rejected Spiegel's previous two productions, he wrote that *Betrayal* was "graceful, economical and strong." "It's a civilized entertainment, by which I mean that it's consistently engrossing, often funny, sometimes moving: and that it takes its being with exceptional directness from the civilization around it."

Elia Kazan admired the film, as did director Bob Rafelson, who wrote, "It's one of the most lucid interpretations of Pinter I've yet to see." In December 1983, *Betrayal* shared the National Board of Review's best picture award with James Brooks's *Terms of Endearment.* Yet notwithstanding all the praise and compliments, Twentieth Century-Fox refused to give the picture an Oscar campaign. Instead, the studio "noisily" promoted their other films such as *To Be or Not to Be* and *Reuben, Reuben.* Norman Levy, the head of Fox, was thought to be taking his revenge on Spiegel because of their disagreement about *Betrayal*'s cable TV rights.

The producer was miffed about the lack of an Academy Award campaign, which resulted in only Pinter being nominated. *Betrayal was* small. When first released, it only grossed $4 million in the United States and Canada. In Spiegel's opinion, the gross was irrelevant. "Films are honored for their quality and for the prestige they bestow on the motion picture art," he said. "We've spent years converting that art into an industry. And now comes a new generation of businessman who decides whether a picture deserves an award or not on the basis of its income."

Alas, the motion picture industry had changed, even if Spiegel had not. Once again, to quote Warren Beatty, "He marked the end of another era."

Chapter Twenty-seven

THE FINAL YEARS

During his final years, Sam Spiegel was obsessed with death and trying to avoid it. He started to have mini-strokes–frustrating moments when he was incapable of speaking or moving. Moreover, he was secretly confessing his final fears to a rabbi at the West End Synagogue in London.

Publicly, however, these things were brushed aside. "I believe in mortality but not inflicting it on myself" being one of Spiegel's better remarks. His official philosophy was that others died, he did not. "I think that Sam had almost persuaded himself that he was immortal," said his son.

The idea of his eventual demise remained a touchy issue, to such a point that when Spiegel was presented with a British Academy fellowship in 1984–the equivalent of a British Oscar–far from being flattered, he was peeved. In his opinion, it was a sign from his colleagues that they thought he was "about to die."

During his early years, he had successfully fled from the immigration authorities and debt collectors, and now he was attempting to play the same avoidance game with sickness and age. "I will give you eighty million dollars if you could take me back forty years," he used to tell his secretary, and he was not joking.

There was a masked desperation about his behavior. He could not face seeing his ailing brother; he even stopped telephoning him, offering his poor hearing as his excuse. Nevertheless, he paid for Eloise Battle, one of Shalom's nurses, and was also "a gracious and patient sounding board" when Judge Raya Dreben was upset about her father's condition.

Although, when Shalom slipped into a coma in May 1984, Spiegel—a regular on Concorde—immediately booked his passage on the QE2. He was accompanied by Jennifer Attebery, his twenty-three-year-old girlfriend. She was then called Jennifer Kent. The boat journey to Manhattan took five days, allowing him to miss out on both his brother's demise and the religious service that followed.

Spiegel did attend funerals such as those for Françoise de la Renta and Yul Brynner. However, they were deeply social affairs, which was hardly the case of Shalom's.

Thus, any letter asking him to leave his papers to a university or bestow his art collection to a museum remained unanswered. This led to many of them giving up in their quest—except for Teddy Kollek. The former mayor of Jerusalem and head of The Jerusalem Foundation never ceased inquiring after Spiegel's paintings, absolutely determined to get a written commitment that The Israel Museum would get a few of his "great masterpieces." "I cannot emphasize strongly enough the importance of this undertaking," Kollek wrote. After all, the producer had previously lent *The Kiss* by Rodin and *The Old Actress* by Chaim Soutine to the foundation. There had also been his promise of donating an Ingres painting. But when pushed on the subject, Spiegel refused to give his word.

Meanwhile, his amazing sexual appetite continued. "I think for him that sex meant more than one girl," said Mike Nichols. "Sam is not the only man who I've heard about—the guys who get into multiple women, hookers, and so forth and can never be anything but bored by what we would consider a regular relationship." Jennifer Attebery, who was fawnlike with green eyes and auburn hair, accepted that she "shared him with others." Describing herself as "a free thinker who was open to ideas," the former ballet dancer admitted to going further than she had ever gone. Many joined her. "It was the indulgent 1980s . . . and Sam could have charmed a nun into going to bed with him." She recognized that her boyfriend was emotionally stunted. "That's why he liked younger people; they weren't challenging for him." Moreover, there was another important factor. "Youth fueled him."

Youth was also a needed distraction from the various disappointments in Spiegel's life. It had hurt that the head of Columbia Studios had not returned his call about *Betrayal*. As a consequence, he had moved out of 711 Fifth Avenue, the Columbia building. "He used to say, 'Don't go in there,'" recalled Pat Rickey, his last secretary.

Spiegel sold *Malahne* to Sheikh (Adel) Al Mojil in the summer of 1983. "When James Jordan retired, Sam said, 'That's it,'" said Jennifer. But was his Barbadian steward really the cause? Or did Mrs. William Wyler, who had said, "Poor Sam, he has this expensive boat and half his life is spent searching for guests," sum up his decision best?

The yacht remained glamorous: the teak deck, the topless sunbathing, and the crewmembers at his command. "You never knew who you would meet there," said writer Larry Collins. But the casting had slipped a notch. "Sam did get very involved with the Euro Trash, which was very boring since they only seem to find themselves interesting," said Joan Axelrod. There were also the flood of little girls to contend with, who were either difficult to talk to, or were about to be fired for not performing. As one guest suggested, "Earlier, there was a sort of style, but this was getting a little sordid."

While Spiegel adjusted to working outside Columbia and continued his sumptuous existence at Mas d'Horizon, his villa in the South of France, he could never quite grasp the delinquent stage of his son. At the age of fourteen, Adam and two others were caught stealing a saxophone and other musical instruments from Westminster, their private London day school. Adam had done the deed to fuel "an addiction" to one-armed bandits, as well as "an addiction to cash." "I think I just liked having wads of money and it wasn't just Sam who I nicked money off, I would virtually nick money off anyone I could." The sums were not paltry, on occasion as much as £250 ($500). "It was really horrible," Adam recalled. "A regret of mine is that it wasn't solved before Sam died."

Adam's problem became a "specific disappointment" in Spiegel's life. He talked to his friends, who tended to take the liberal approach. "I would say, 'Lots of boys do that,'" said the producer Michael White. But Spiegel refused to take solace in such advice. He could not understand what had gone wrong. "Sam was the type of guy who thought, 'I fly Adam everywhere . . . he's got everything that he could possibly want in St. Tropez and he ought to be happy,'" said White. "And of course it doesn't work like that. What children want is intimacy."

Intimacy–the one commodity Spiegel was incapable of providing. From an early age, Adam had been caught in the crossfire between his parents. Surely his stealing was a cry for help? A way of saying, "I exist too"? The producer was too self-obsessed to give proper thought to the situation. "I remember him saying we have to think about institutionalizing you or something like that," said his son. Most of his circle was shocked by his attitude. "It was very extreme, considering Sam's past," said Antonia Fraser. Extreme indeed, but perhaps Spiegel's reasoning was that he could never afford to be honest, whereas his son could.

Keen to demonstrate his energy, he had an important film project at the beginning of 1985. After *Betrayal,* Spiegel had promised as much, declaring: "It's a good idea not to tie up all the little bows in the package." The picture–tentatively called *Survivors*–was set in Vienna after World War II and followed the life of a Jewish family until the Soviet withdrawal in 1955.

He had the idea while staying at the Hotel Sacher with Jennifer Attebery. "Sam felt that it would be his last film and very close to his heart," she said. Hugh Thomas, internationally known for his book on Cuba, was to write the story in the form of a novel, and Spiegel was to own the rights. Spiegel had only one director in mind, Billy Wilder.

Adam recalled the "reams and drafts" of Thomas's screenplay in front of his father. Yet just as he recognized the vastness of the venture, the teenager had "some sense that it was never going to happen," but it was giving him "something to live for." Did Spiegel think that his Vienna project was yet another recipe for prolonging his life? No doubt, he was entertaining the same logic as Irving Lazar who, toward the end of his life, used to make appointments years in advance, as if future plans would keep the Grim Reaper away.

During that period, a twenty-gram benign prostate growth was troubling Spiegel. At first, he was reluctant to remove it despite the fact that it was causing him considerable discomfort. Then Spiegel decided to go through with the procedure, but in London, not New York.

Physically, the eighty-four-year-old had declined. On his last trip to Zurich, he was described by Alan Silcocks, his business manager, as "walking like a zombie," and looking "so tired that he could hardly put one foot in front of the other." At the beginning of December 1985, there was even concern that Spiegel would not survive his operation. He spent longer recuperating at the Wellington Hospital than anticipated. However, his fragile condition had not stopped him from ordering plates of oysters from Scott's restaurant!

In an emotional moment, Spiegel telephoned Ruth Cheshin, who worked with Teddy Kollek. She described him as being "very excited" and "sort of crying." "He said, 'I would like to leave The Jerusalem Foundation everything that I have.' " His niece, however, dismissed the story. "Sam would never cry in front of a woman," she said. Nevertheless, as a result of the call, Cheshin visited Spiegel in London. "I don't recall it very vividly," she admitted. "Apparently, he was very weak already."

Harold Pinter "vividly" remembered his last dinner with Spiegel, which was at the Connaught. "We were there just before him and I saw him walk into the restaurant and he seemed to be floating. His face was almost translucent, very, very pale, you could almost see right through it. He was very gentle that evening. He talked about coming through his operation. And, in a way, he had floated away."

In the same week, Tessa Kennedy invited Spiegel to meet Queen Noor of Jordan. Looking frail, he had arrived using a walking stick. "Then at dinner he was just regaling." But he left early. Vexed by his condition, he had complained to his hostess, "How could I be like this? It's no fun getting old and why would I have to meet the Queen of Jordan with a walking stick? I wish that she had seen me when I was young and fun." When they kissed goodbye, he had held her very close. "I think we really both knew that it would be our last time."

At Spiegel's final meeting with Lord Thomas, they lunched at the writer's house in Ladbroke Grove. Spiegel came into the drawing room and remarked on the fireplace. "He said, 'I like the fire, it's a real home isn't it? A real fire, a real home.' I have never quite forgotten that."

Ignoring his doctor's advice, the producer left for New York in the middle of December. "He was told not to travel, and he flew six thousand miles," said Alan Silcocks. And on Christmas Eve, Spiegel signed his new will. It was drafted by David Bottoms, who had replaced Albert Heit as Spiegel's executor in August 1985. "Sam said to me, 'You know too much,' and he was always having problems with his taxes," Heit said. Each year, fairly incredible tax returns used to be sent in. "If I was an executor, I could be questioned, but as a lawyer, I couldn't be. So Sam said, 'We better get someone else.' " Bottoms was a partner of Lord, Day & Lord, a law firm that dealt with very respectable WASP wills. It was exactly the kind of firm that the IRS would not query. The other executor was Spiegel's niece, Raya Dreben. "Sam was very proud of Raya," said Adam's mother. Dreben was a partner at Palmer & Dodge, a prestigious Boston law firm, before being appointed a judge in the state appeals court in 1979. Dreben had been an executor of Spiegel's will since the mid-1970s.

Pat Rickey witnessed the signing of the testament. Heit was also present. "I kept on saying, 'What about Adam?' and Sam was shaking his hand down, saying, 'I've taken care of him,' " recalled Heit. Jennifer Attebery had been added to the will. "I looked at him and he said, 'Well, she does some nice things for me.' " Spiegel had always told Attebery that he would leave her money, which would let her go to university. "I was so focused on dance," she admitted. "Sam recognized that I needed to broaden my horizons, which I did when I went to college."

A few days later, an unaccompanied Spiegel left for St. Martin in the French West Indies. "He and Jennifer were at some kind of crossroads," said his secretary. The producer had tried to recruit Lord Thomas, who was invited under the guise of discussing his next chapters. "And I said, 'Sam, don't you think it's better that I write them?' "

Spiegel arrived on the island in a wheelchair. "He was fairly out of it and quite spacey," said William Rayner, a prominent New York socialite, then married to decorator Chessy Rayner, who had greeted him off the plane. Totally unprepared, Spiegel had arrived without any clothes. It was uncharacteristic behavior.

The producer had chosen to stay at La Samanna hotel, which was considered one of *the* places to stay in the Caribbean. A favorite with the Bouvier sisters—Jackie and Lee—it was the type of hotel where Gianni Agnelli and other boat owners used to drop by. It also had a touch of the Côte d'Azur, with its Mediterranean-style architecture and privately owned beach.

The hotel's name had a link to *Malahne*. Like his famous boat, La Samanna was created from the Christian names of the owner's three daughters—Samantha, Anouk, and Nathalie.

But despite the luxurious surroundings and the famous people—his fellow guests included Richard Avedon, Mary Tyler Moore, and Peter Ustinov—Spiegel was utterly miserable. He was never off the telephone with his secretary. "He was clinging to me and refusing to let me off the phone," she recalled. He had also contacted Betty, asking her to be in New York when he returned. "He wanted to talk to me about something." To this day, she does not know what it was about. "But he kept on telling Mrs. Rickey that he was going to change his will. That weighed very heavily on his mind."

Spiegel then cut his ten-day vacation short. He had had enough and would be leaving on New Year's Eve instead. On his final night, he declined to dine with the Rayners and the others from their elegant house party. "Sam had illusions of people coming to visit him," Rayner insisted. But did he? A lobster dinner for two had been set up in the intimacy of Spiegel's holiday cottage. And this was where the plot thickened. As usual, Spiegel made his regular evening call to Rickey. "We talked and talked, he was reaching out, and then he keeled over," she said. "I was the last person to speak to him." Or was she? Spiegel's $750 per night suite was on the beach. It was highly possible for someone to arrive late and leave early, unseen.

The next morning, a hotel guest who prefers to remain anonymous, recalled "a lot of noise and activity." "I went outside and found the manager, who was hysterical," he said. "The maids had arrived to clean Sam's cottage. He didn't answer the door and they got worried and called her." Peter Ustinov had then accompanied the manager inside the suite. Evelyn Veber, or Lyn as the manager was then known, suggested that the actor give the producer a kiss of life, which supposedly led to Ustinov saying, "Alive or dead, I would not kiss Sam Spiegel."

Fourteen years later, the manager claimed a different story. She was there alone with Dr. van de Waag. "Spiegel had a cerebral hemorrhage and died instantly." Nor was there any commotion. "We kept it very quiet and it was very quick." She had allowed Rayner to see the producer. "He was dead in the tub and lying there, looking blue," he said. In retrospect, Jennifer Attebery found the place of death to be "very strange" because throughout their four-year relationship, her boyfriend had only taken showers. "Unless there were four women in the tub, he wouldn't venture in."

The hotel's owner had tried to keep the news secret. "He thought Sam's death would ruin people's holidays," said Nancy Stoddart, a guest at La Samanna.

Afterward, Ustinov took on a real-life Hercule Poirot guise (a role he had played in two films, *Death on the Nile* and *Evil Under the Sun*). "There was a question of *if* a woman *had* been with Sam when he had the heart attack," another guest recalled. "She could have easily driven up outside and no one would have known." The actor's holiday quest was made: searching the beach for the lady who had sped away.

Many were devastated to hear the news of Spiegel's death. "I knew him for about sixty years," Billy Wilder told fellow revelers at a New Year's Eve party. Other intimates such as Ahmet Ertegun were sad that the producer had been alone. Joseph Mankiewicz recognized the irony of Spiegel dying "on the night that he was famous for, long before he was known as an excellent producer." Yet, all things considered, it was difficult not to agree with David Geffen that it was "exactly the right way." "Sam had a great life, it wasn't as if he ever cut down on his cream."

Epilogue

After Sam's wake, Elia Kazan returned to Spiegel's penthouse, where the event had been held. His visit was sudden and quite unexpected. "So, what did you get?" he hollered at Spiegel's daughter. In truth, not a lot. Alisa Freedman continued to get the same as when her father had been alive.

Although Kazan's behavior was a little brusque, he was asking the million-dollar question. Actually, make that the twenty-million-dollar question, and one that hounded me during my research. Throughout the interviews with Sam's friends and business acquaintances, almost everyone wanted to know what happened to the Dream Merchant status symbols: the art collection, the 475 Park Avenue apartment, Mas d'Horizon, the recently acquired Grosvenor Square apartment, and the $20 million that remained.

Briefly, all the residences were sold. Fourteen paintings from Sam's art collection–pictures particularly associated with him, such as Bacon's *Pope No. 3,* Cézanne's *Carrière de Bibemus,* and Rouault's *Clown*– were auctioned off by Sotheby's bringing $8.65 million, $2.3 million more than anticipated. It was a decision made by Spiegel's executors, who believed that his "holdings should be diversified" since his "estate was complicated and would take time to close." The rest of the paintings–eighty-one in total–were then donated to The Israel Museum on June 22, 1993. "Long before his death" Spiegel had told his niece that he wanted the collection to go there, "as it would mean more to them than to a large museum in the United States."

Such conditions were not actually written in Sam's testament. "He had left his will vague," said Albert Heit. "It was up to the discretion of the executors to give the money and his properties to charity. It could not go to an individual." So it was up to the discretion of Judge Raya Dreben and David Bottoms–who had only known Sam for four months–to choose the charities. (As Bottoms admits, "I was on the right street corner, at the right time.") Recognizing his "deep Zionist roots," Dreben and Bottoms decided to give Sam's art collection, plus the residuals from his films, to Israel. Besides that, Jerusalem also has the Sam Spiegel Film and Television School, which was created with the producer's millions, and again was the choice of the executors.

In retrospect, Sam's testament was curious and lacking in any personal touch. "You don't have to be venal to be surprised by it," said his son. "It's a very peculiar document, but then he was a very peculiar man." Of course, it disappointed his nearest and dearest, but when had Sam not? "The only thing I hold against Sam is that he didn't leave a picture to Adam," said Michael White. "He must have been in some kind of mad, angry state."

In fact, Adam's delinquent behavior had not influenced his father's will. Way back, since 1975, Spiegel had decided not to leave his son everything. This decision had been discussed "at great length" with his niece. "His view was that too much money may take away a youth's initiative and therefore he wanted to make sure that Adam had sufficient funds, but not enough to rob him of ambition," said Dreben. "I think Sam had a valid point." Now in his early thirties, Adam is happily married to the novelist Gay Longworth, and has become a successful theatrical producer. He produced the hit musical *The Mysteries*.

In regard to the rest of the will, quite a few ladies telephoned afterward. "It probably meant that Sam wasn't very generous when he was alive," offered Mike Nichols. "They probably felt that he must be planning something later." No doubt Sam had made many promises.

Only Betty Spiegel contested the will. "I sued the estate to not have Raya or David Bottoms in my life," she reasoned. Frank Sinatra's East Coast lawyer represented her and she won the case in 1987. It gave her more than the $750,000 and the properties that she had been previously bequeathed. The exact sum remains a mystery since part of the agreement was that it would never be disclosed. The *Daily News*'s Liz Smith indicated it was substantial, referring to her as one of the newest multimillionaires on Park Avenue.

Adam Spiegel disapproved of Betty's behavior. "I think people give their money to whomever they want," he said. However, she was with Sam when he produced most of his greats. Indeed, when *Lawrence of Arabia* was rereleased in 1989, David Lean was in contact with Mrs. Spiegel, not the executors of Sam's estate.

"He said, 'Betty darling—you're not angry with me are you?' And I said, 'What for?' 'For doing the restoration of *Lawrence of Arabia*?' I said, 'I could never be angry with you.' And David said, 'You know it was the first time that I was able to make any money, I never made any money.' " This was complete nonsense. But during the epic's relaunch, Lean told many, many lies.

First of all, Columbia Studios not Horizon Pictures was responsible for paying out the director's profit participations and he was to eventually receive over a million dollars, as well as his original fee.

Lean also told film journalists that Sam had hacked off thirty-five minutes from *Lawrence,* behind his back. "And so I, like loads of others, wrote what a cultural vandal Spiegel was and everybody took this line—Spielberg and Scorsese," Adrian Turner, the film historian and critic, admitted. In actual fact, the director knew about every single one of the cuts, since he had suggested all of them.

When *Lawrence* was shown at the Directors Guild in Los Angeles, Lean continued to vent his spleen. David Geffen was appalled. "I thought it was wrong because it was four years after Sam had died and he couldn't defend himself." Lean also entirely dismissed Spiegel's involvement. "He said that Sam had destroyed the movie. 'For a few more sheckels,' were his exact words. I felt that when he used the word 'sheckels,' it was anti-Semitic, and it was really disrespectful. I admired Sam and to this day, I still think of him as one of the great producers of all time, and one of the most elegant men. So much so that I was really disturbed by that screening. . . . Sam was big and Lean was bitter by the end, eaten up by little things."

Nevertheless, Spiegel was never far from Lean's thoughts. "I spoke to him three days before he died," Maurice Jarre recalled. Lean was excited about his new project. "David said 'Nostromo is the story of greed and power—greed like Sam Spiegel!' "

No doubt John Huston might have added a few words on the subject. Yet he had softened toward Sambo and invited him to participate in his American Film Institute lifetime achievement award in March 1983. Lauren Bacall introduced Sam, who, in his speech, had noted Huston's "insatiable curiosity" as his overriding quality.

The same might have been said of Spiegel. A further reminder about his legacy: *The African Queen, On the Waterfront, The Bridge on the River Kwai,* and *Lawrence of Arabia*–all were hits, both critical and financial, but as Spiegel said, "When a producer puts into each motion picture the amount of effort and dedication which I expend, he wants millions and millions of people to see and appreciate it. No producer can afford to be in the business of making pictures just for his friends." Taking this statement into account, did it allow the producer to be sorely disappointed with the state of the industry in the 1980s? When writing to Columbia's Pat Williamson, he referred to him as one of the "last Mohicans." "My recent experiences with the people who are running our business have driven me to the shocking conclusion that everybody seeks only one end: personal survival," he wrote. "I don't think there is any integrity, devotion, love for the medium or care left."

And Kazan, who–in spite of the "shipwreck of old age"– gets sparked up talking about Sam? "He didn't just become fat," he will complain. "He became fat and frail." Yet, he kept in touch with the former S. P. Eagle. A few months before Sam's demise, Kazan wrote to him about his contribution on *Waterfront.* " 'Let's open it up again!' you'd say to Budd and to me and Budd would become furious but since, at the time, I had not writer's pride, I would think 'Buddha thinks we can improve the script and maybe we can, so let's do it again, let's open it up again!' So we did and we did improve it." Kazan can still recall Spiegel on that film, how relaxed his body was sitting in an armchair but how tense and active his mind.

A few years after Sam's demise, Mike Nichols was having dinner with Jack Nicholson and Anjelica Huston. "It was in a place like Chasen's, and out of nowhere, Jack said, 'Let's drink a toast to Sam. I miss him so much.' Anjelica and I both cried. Jack just caught us because we also missed him so much. First of all, it's inconceivable to love a producer. I can't *think* of another producer, period. I don't *know* producers. And if I could think of some, I certainly wouldn't want to see them."

Author's Note

"Sam Spiegel! That's quite a subject."
–BILLY WILDER, APRIL 5, 1996.

It was while reading Gore Vidal's memoir *Palimpsest* that I decided to write about Sam. I knew the film producer. He was a treasured friend of my mother and stepfather–someone who came to our Christmas lunches with Adam, his delightful and much younger son.

In our household, Sam was associated with achieving the impossible. When *The King and I* was a sellout, he took my youngest brother and me to the musical, as well as introducing us to Yul Brynner. Another excursion with Sam was to see *The Cassandra Crossing* when the West End was rife with drunken football fans. The film wasn't good but the excitement of being shaken in his Rolls-Royce by the football hooligans was something else. (While nervous giggles were muffled, General Spiegel directed his terrified chauffeur into Leicester Square, a battlefield of smashed beer bottles.)

But I was intrigued. Vidal had described a different Sam–someone who was "spontaneously dishonest on every level." Frankly, I had never seen that side. Of course, there were the Sam stories. But aren't there always stories about the powerful, rich, and famous? I cold-called über agent Ed Victor. He was tremendously enthusiastic. If he hadn't been, I would never have started on this epic journey, a seven-year saga that took me to the Ukraine, Poland, Israel, Germany, and the United States.

I received so much help in compiling this book that it is hard to know where to start. The list that follows is absurdly long but everyone listed contributed something crucial. First and foremost, I am indebted to Adam Spiegel for introducing me to his first cousin, Judge Raya Dreben, and David Bottoms, the executors of his father's will. Dreben and Bottoms gave me access to Spiegel's private and professional papers, which were an indispensable source for this book. They did not, however, have approval of the manuscript and are not responsible for what I have written. Any errors are my own. During my research, Spiegel's professional papers were moved to The Jerusalem Foundation. Alan Freeman—the foundation's overseas coordinator—was both welcoming and extremely helpful. I am also grateful to Hanna Burak and Brida O'Callaghan for their work concerning the Spiegel archives.

A special mention to Betty Spiegel, Spiegel's third wife, who consented to many hours of interviews at her home in Virginia. Not all my questions were pleasant but she was always refreshingly candid as well as being extremely hospitable.

Ann E. Pennington, Adam Spiegel's mother, also offered insight, as did the late Ray Abrams, Spiegel's first wife, and Ellen Weisbord, Spiegel's granddaughter. Alisa Freedman—Spiegel's daughter—refused to be interviewed, although she gave me photographs of her parents.

Before leading into the list of interviewees, the following were staggering with their patience, help, and wisdom: The Israeli journalist Yitzhak Lev Tov, who wrote to kibbutzes on my behalf, went on the radio, and led me to all sorts of invaluable contacts regarding Spiegel's early years. Kevin Brownlow—the esteemed historian and filmmaker—who gave me carte blanche to his David Lean archives and endless contacts in the film world. Kevin became a mentor of sorts because he is a thorough talent and thoroughly generous. Like many others delving into the film world, I have joined the Ned Comstock fan club. Ned, the archivist at the Cinema-Television Library and Archives of Performing Arts at the University of Southern California, was a veritable godsend, especially for someone living in France. Not only is he wonderfully knowledgeable but also remarkably good-natured—whatever the request. Bob Morris—a *Lawrence of Arabia* expert—who was relentless with his advice. Peter Viertel, who was an invaluable source, having worked for S. P. Eagle on two occasions. Tony Reeves—the executor of the Sir David Lean Estate, Peter Hafer and Ryan Rudolph (the directors of Faraway Productions)—for their support of this book. Irene Heymann and Gary Salt from the Paul Kohner Agency for all their considerable time, knowledge, and effort. Robert Lantz–the first executor of Lillian Hellman's estate–who was unfailingly helpful. One of his many calls led to Rosemary Mankiewicz, who allowed me to go through her husband's professional archives.

From 1995 to 2002, I interviewed those who had worked with Spiegel on a professional level, including: Arthur Abeles, Angela Allen, Don Ashton, Jack Atlas, Alain Bernheim, John Box, the late Jules Buck, Arthur Canton, Jack Cardiff, Rachel Chodorov, Georges Cravenne, Phyllis Dalton, Barry Diller, Paulette Dubost, Laurence Evans, Rudi Fehr, Freddie Fields, John Flynn, James Fox, Jack Garfein, James Goldman, Sam Goldwyn, Jr., Desmond Gorge, John Guare, the late Albert Heit, Dzidzia Herman, John Heyman, Irene Heymann, Geoffrey Horne, the late Leo Jaffe, Maurice Jarre, David Jones, Jay Kanter, Elia Kazan, Tessa Kennedy, Evelyn Keyes, Jud Kinberg, Lupita Tovar Kohner, Teddy Kollek, Jeffrey Lane, the late Paul N. Lazarus, Jr., Isabella Leitner, Arthur Lemon, David Lewin, Michael Linnit, Mark Littman, Sue Mengers, Ivan Moffat, the late Inge Morath, Jess Morgan, Patrice Munsel, Mike Nichols, Jack Nicholson, the late Anthony Nutting, Ken Oakley, Dorothy Morris Payne, Arthur Penn, Diana Phipps, Eric Pleskow, Ingo Preminger, Pat Quinn, Pat Rickey, Jonas Rosenfeld, Mo Rothman, Janice Rule, Budd Schulberg, the late Pierre Sciclounoff, Elaine Schreyeck, Peter Shaffer, Omar Sharif, Alan Silcocks, Jeanie Sims, Elliot Silverstein, Rose Greb Sogge, Norman Spencer, Ray Stark, Hugh Thomas, Jerry Tokofsky, Kurt Unger, Gore Vidal, the late John Woolf, Dana Wynter, the late Freddie Young, the late Loretta Young, the late Max Youngstein, and the late Fred Zinnemann.

Many of the above were Spiegel's friends or associates. Others whom I interviewed included: Philip Adler, Sally Aga Khan, Ilana Agron, Anouk Aimée, Paul Albou, Eric Ambler, the late John Aspinall, Jennifer Kent Attebery, George Axelrod, the late Joan Axelrod, Lauren Bacall, L. P. Bachmann, David Bailey, Sue Barton, Warren Beatty, Polly Bergen, John Berry, Betsy Blair, Nina Blowitz, John Brabourne, Wendy Brigode, Joan Juliet Buck, Jacqueline de la Chaume, Ruth Cheshin, Rosemary Chodorov, Dr. William Collier, Joan Collins,

Larry Collins, the late Frederick de Cordova, Jules Dassin, Anne Douglas, Gilles Dufour, Christian Duvivier, Ahmet Ertegun, Betty Estevez, Luis Estevez, Afdera Franchetti Fonda, the late Angela Fox, Yolande Fox, the late Edith Foxwell, the late John Frankenheimer, David Geffen, Netty Gottlieb, Bettina Graziani, Florence Grinda, Lilou Grumbach, Richard Gully, Carrie Miller Haddad, Denise Hale, Kitty Carlisle Hart, Bill Hayward, Leonora Hornblow, Barbara Howar, the late Jean Howard, Stanley R. Jaffe, Louis Jourdan, Fay Kanin, John Kohn, Kenneth Jay Lane, Claude Leusse, Marguerite Littman, Norman Lloyd, Tanya Lopert, Frédéric Malle, Aileen Mehle, Sonia Melchett, Agathe Mengelle, David Metcalfe, Arthur Miller, Michael Mindlin, Jane Mitchell, Derry Moore, Stanley Myer, Harold Nebenzal, Juliette Nissen, William V. O'Connor, Kathleen Parrish, Anthony Perry, Hope Preminger, William Rayner, Jean-Marie Récamier, Régine, Maurice Rheims, Jacqueline de Ribes, Natasha Richardson, Dominique Rizzo, Willy Rizzo, Hélène Rochas, Linda Ronstadt, Richard Roth, Caroline Veiller Saltzman, Alexandra Schlesinger, Arthur Schlesinger, Jr., Charles Schneer, Daniel Selznick, Erna Shadwick, Curt Siodmak, the late Isaac Stern, George Stevens, Jr., Maureen Swanson Dudley, Evelyn Veber, Bayard Veiller, Simone Warner, George Weidenfeld, Susan Kohner Weitz, John Weitz, Michael White, Sandy Whitelaw, Catherine Wyler, Melanie Wyler, and Pat York.

Getting access to certain people can be difficult, leading to endless faxes, e-mails, and so forth. Fortunately, many of the previously mentioned were generous with their contacts, as were the following: Yehuda Avner, Harley Baldwin, Jessica Beer, Amnon Beeri, Doris Brynner, Rosalind Chatto, Yanou Collart, Michel Didisheim, Francis Dorleans, Gianpiero Dotti, Richard Edwards, Edward Jay Epstein, T. J. Erhardt, Peter Fiebleman, Charles Finch, Robert Fox, Paloma Fraser, Michael Gallagher, Robert Gottlieb, Caroline Graham, Sara Hatchuel, Mary Hayley, Joy Henderiks, India Hicks, Ellen Hooberman, Robin Hurlstone, Anjelica Huston, Beverley Jackson, Tracey Jacobs, Linda LeRoy Janklow, Nick Jeffrey, Charles Kidd, Lucca Lindner, Fiona Lewis Linson, Christian Louboutin, Lisa Love, Cristina Malgara, Michael Mindlin, Sheridan Morley, David Niven, Jr., Maggie Nolan, Gillian Osband, Manuela Papatakis, Pierre Passebon,

Véronique Perez, Lawrence Raskin, Ariel de Ravenel, Thaddaeus Ropac, Joe Rosenberg, the late Herbert Ross, Gil Shiva, Lois Sieff, Wendy Stark, Nona Summers, Konstantin Thoeren, Danny Unger, Connie Wald, Shelley Wanger, Rebecca Wilson, Jonathan Woolf, Selim Zilkha, and Andrzej L. Zoltowski.

With regard to primary research about Spiegel's early years, I am grateful to: Herbert Koch from the Magistrat der Stadt Wien, the Urzad Stanu Cywilnego (town hall) of Jaroslav, Professor Eli Tsur of the Givat Haviva of Advanced Studies for Youth Movements, Edmund Hebenstreet, the head of the Jaroslav Society, Rina Shaham of the Beth Hatefusoth (the Jewish Diaspora Museum), and Dr. Kurt Mühlberger and Thomas Maisel, the archivists of Vienna University.

Concerning Spiegel's Palestine years, a special mention to Muki Tsur, an authority on the Third Aliyah, Meita Hacohen from the Archives of Kibbutz Bet-Alfa, Zeev Bloch, Dan Havav, and Patrick Seale, an expert on Arab affairs.

In regard to Spiegel's first trip to America, I made a Freedom of Information request to the FBI, CIA, U.S. Department of Justice, and U.S. Secret Service. However, none of the organizations could shed light on his early years. As a result, I am extremely grateful to Sue Rosenfeld, a true connoisseur of the administrative maze, Bill Doty, from NARA's Pacific Region, Marian L. Smith, the INS historian, William Roberts, chief archivist from the Bancroft Library at UC Berkeley, and Rolinda W. Wittman, paralegal at the Turner Entertainment Company.

Concerning Spiegel's European years in the 1930s, the following were invaluable in their assistance: the late Claude Beylie; Lenny Borger, an expert on prewar European films; film historians Dr. Kevin Gough-Yates, Martin Koerber, Andrew Kelly, the author of *Filming All Quiet on the Western Front;* Universal's Jan Christopher Horak, the film émigré expert; Wolfgang Jacobsen, Gero Gandert, Werner Sudendorf, and Gerrit Thies of the Shiftung Deutsche Kinematek, Berlin; Malte Hagener, Hans-Michael Bock, and Jörg Schöning of the Cinegraph, Hamburg; Rüdiger Koschnitzki of the Deutsches Institut für Filmkunde, Frankfurt; Dr. Helmut Asper of the University of Bielefeld; Elizabeth Streit of the Austrian Film Archives; Julie Rene, Alberto Del Fabro of the Cinémathèque Française; and Walter Fritz and Peter

Konlech of the Österreichisches Filmarchiv. A special mention to Martina Stille, then a student at Bielefeld, who combed through the university's microfilms of *Film-Kurier, Kinematograph* and *Pems Bulletin* for Spiegel mentions.

Regarding Spiegel's brief period in Vienna, I am indebted to Wolfgang Astelbauer, who left no stone uncovered in his research. Since I do not speak German, this was of the utmost importance. I am also grateful to Stephen D. Youngkin, Peter Lorre's principal biographer, who gave me use of his unpublished interview with Spiegel, and also Dr. Werner Metz.

Many of the documents I looked at required translating. As a result, I am indebted to the translating skills of: Professor Eli Tsur for Polish documents, Dr. Shimon Bar Tzlil for Hebrew documents, John Crawley for Spanish documents, and Christa Michel for German documents. I am also grateful to Anne Dziubak, Mechtild Kalisky, and James Lieber.

Archivists, curators, and librarians who were of particular assistance included: Ed Carter, Scott Curtis, Barbara Hall, Faye Thompson of the Margaret Herrick Library, Academy of Motion Picture Arts and Sciences, Los Angeles; Caroline Sisneros of the Louis B. Mayer Library, the American Film Institute, Los Angeles; Markuu Salmi of the British Film Institute; Julie Cobb of the Newberry Library, Chicago; Brian Neve of the University of Bath; Julie Graham, Brigitte J. Kueppers, ARTS Library Special Collections of the University of California, Los Angeles; Michael Bott of the University of Reading; Dr. Charles Bell and Linda Ashton of the Harry Ransome Humanities Research Center, the University of Texas at Austin; Karen Pedersen, James R. Webb Memorial Library, Writers Guild of America, West; Jeanine Basinger and Leith G. Johnson of the Wesleyan Cinema Archives, Wesleyan University; and Marika Genty, Chanel Archives, Paris.

Many thanks to the following writers for their encouragement and/or guidance: J.G. Ballard, A. Scott Berg, Patricia Bosworth, Chip Brown, Kate Buford, Alicia Drake, James Fox, Julie Gilbert, Mel Gussow, André Leon Talley, Suzy Menkes, Kate Morris, Thom Mount, Joanna Rapf, Henri-Jean Servat, Kevin Sessums, Christopher Silvester, David Stenn, Tom Stoppard, Emma Tennant, and Adrian Turner, who read the manuscript.

Also thanks to: Rupert Everett, who initially had me to stay for two weeks in New York and was "Hyper-cool" when it turned into two months. Elinor Dee Pruder and Caroline Gruber Lewis–a mother-daughter team who were the first to introduce me to the joys of Hollywood films. Others for their unfailing hospitality: Matilde and Roberto Agostinelli, Abigail Asher and Douglas Schoninger, Annabel Brooks and James Dearden, Mary and Patrick Byrne, Lisa Fine, Louise Fletcher, Angela and Gerald Harrington, Kathryn Ireland, Carolina and Ian Irving, Henry and Tessa Keswick, Jean Pigozzi, Elizabeth Pollock, Nancy Stoddart, David Resnik, Pamela Hanson–a great hostess and a great photographer, and Diane Von Furstenburg–her royal kindness. A special mention to Anna Wintour–the fashion powerhouse–who helped me come to Paris in 1989. And Karl Lagerfeld–my first "patron" in Paris–a legend in any world that he chooses.

In regard to my employers during the writing of this book, many thanks to: John Fairchild–a class act; Patrick McCarthy–P.M.–an inspiring editor-in-chief; Kate Betts–the next generation who remains ahead of the game, and Glenda Bailey, another brilliant talent. Fellow colleagues who were encouraging: Alev Aktar, Spencer Beck, Ruth Benoit, Michel Botbol, Melissa Ceria, Anne Boas Christiansen, Mary Duenwald, James Fallon, Bridget Foley, Dennis Freedman, Mark Ganem, Chantal Goupil, Catherine Hong, Sasha Iglehart, Lorna Koski, Sarah Larenaudie, Hannah Lawrence, Cary Leitzes, Emilie Meinadier, William Middleton, Samira Nasr, Janet Ozzard, Daniel Peres, James Reginato, Elisa Rusconi, Sadie Ryan, Christine Shea, Mimi Shin, Richard Sinnott, Melanie Ward, Jennifer Weil, Katherine Weisman, Kevin West, Gwen Westley, Brana Wolf, and Kristina Zimbalist; with a special mention to Sarah E. Giles, James Scully, and Ron Wilson.

I was terribly fortunate to have had my book serialized in *Vanity Fair*'s magnificent Oscar issue (April 2003). As a result, my eternal gratitude to Graydon Carter and the following members of his "Dream Team": Aimée Bell, Michael Hogan, Mike Sacks and Robert Walsh.

My biography required a great deal of editing, patience, and editing. I was extremely fortunate to have worked with Philippa Harrison, Alan Samson and Catherine Hill at Little, Brown, London, and Chuck Adams and the great Michael Korda at Simon & Schuster, New York. Michael was *tireless*. I also thank Carol Bowie for shepherding the manuscript into print. Although I researched all the photographs, Natalie Goldstein went through the vast selection and chose the relevant order. A special mention to Ted Landry and Fred Chase for their copyediting skills.

I come from a family of writers who were terribly encouraging about my first venture. I refer to my beloved grandmother, Elizabeth Longford; my uncle, Thomas Pakenham; my aunt, Rachel Billington; and scholarly sisters, Rebecca Fraser and Flora Fraser. In particular, my first two readers: my stepfather, Harold Pinter–for his belief–and my mother, Antonia Fraser–"The Pro"–for her wisdom: "tips from the top."

Finally, in memory of my dear father, Sir Hugh Fraser, the British MP for Stafford and Stone (1918–1984). Like Sam, he was a passionate Zionist.

September 2, 2002

A Condensed Filmography

Film with Sam Spiegel as Art Director

1932 *Ehe mit beschränkter Haftung* (*Marriage with Limited Responsibility*–aka Ehe m.b.H)–b&w–75 min.

Tonfilm-Produktion G.m.b.H./Universal, Berlin. Producers: Felix Pfitzner and Ilja Salkind. Director: Franz Wenzler. Adaptation: Bobby E. Lüthge and Curt J. Braun. Based on the play *Causa Kaiser* by Ludwig Sterk and Adolf Eisler. Photography: Carl Drews. Music: Bronislaw Kaper and Walter Jurmann; Lyrics: Fritz Rotter. Set: Hans Sohnle and Otto Erdmann. Sound: Charles Metain. Cast: Charlotte Susa, Werner Fuetterer, Hans Moser, Georg Alexander, Paul Morgan. (Berlin opening: January 19, 1939.)
FRENCH VERSION: *Mariage à responsabilité limitée*
Vandor-Film, Paris. Director: Jean de Limur. Adaptation: Henri Jeanson. Photography: Léonce-Henri Burel. Set: Robert Guys and Marc Lauer. Cast: Odette Florelle, Pierre Larquey, Jean Wall, Marcelle Lucas, Simone Mareuil.

Films Produced by Sam Spiegel

1933 *Ich will Dich Liebe lehren* (*I Will Teach You to Love*)–b&w–75 min.

Pax-Film G.m.b.H., Berlin (Produktion/Vertrieb). Director: Heinz Hilpert (some scenes by assistant director Alfred Ibach). Based on the novel *Herr Fünf* by Alice Berend; Adaptation: Friedrich Raff and Julius Urgiss. Photography: Reimar Kuntze and Curt Courant. Music: Bronislaw Kaper and Walter Jurmann; Lyrics: Fritz Rotter. Set: Theo Ober and Erwin Scharf. Sound: Hans Grimm and Adolf Jansen. Sound editor: Conrad von Molo. Cast: Willi Domgraf-Fassbaender, Ery Bos, Kurt Strehlen, Eva Schmidt-Kaiser, Josef Danegger. (Berlin opening: March 24, 1933.)
FRENCH VERSION: *L'Homme que ne sait pas dire non*
Pax-Film G.m.b.H. and Societé des Films Osso, Paris; Co-Producer: Sam Spiegel (no other producer named). Dialogue: Henri Decoin. Cast: Willi Domgraf-Fassbaender, Lisette Lanvin, Paulette Dubost,

Raymond Galle, Raymond Cordy. (Never released in France because of Domgraf-Fassbaender's thick German accent.)

1933 *Unsichtbare Gegner (Invisible Opponents)*–b&w–90 min. (aka *Öl ins Feuer*)

Pan-Film K.G./Markische Film (for Germany); Robert Müller-Filmproduktion (for Austria). Executive Producer: Sam Spiegel (no other producer mentioned). Director: Rudolf Katscher. Screenplay: Philipp Lothar Mayring, Heinrich Oberländer, and Reinhart Steinbicker; from an idea by Ludwig von Wohl. Photography: Eugen Schüfftan and Georg Bruckbauer. Editor: Rudolf Schaad and Phillis Fehr. Set: Erwin Scharf. Cast: Gerda Maurus, Paul Hartmann, Oscar Homolka, Peter Lorre, Paul Kemp, Raoul Aslan. (Berlin opening: September 18, 1933; Vienna opening: November 24, 1933.)
FRENCH VERSION: *Les Requins du Pétrole*
Director: Rudolf Katscher and Henri Decoin. Dialogue director: Fred Ellis. Dialogue: Henri Decoin. Cast: Arlette Marchal, Jean Galland, Gabriel Gabrio, Peter Lorre, Raymond Cordy, Raoul Aslan.

1936 *The Invader* (U.S. title: *An Old Spanish Custom*)–b&w–61 min.

British & Continental Film Productions. Released in the United States by J. H. Hoffberg (MGM). Co-Producer: Harold Richman. Director: Adrian Brunel. Screenplay: Edwin Greenwood. Photography: Eugen Schüfftan. Editor: Dan Birt. Cast: Buster Keaton, Lupita Tovar, Esme Percy, Lyn Harding, Webster Booth. (U.S. release: January 2, 1936, although filming wrapped in late November 1934.)
FRENCH VERSION: *Un Baiser s'il Vous Plaît*
Dialogue: Yves Mirande and Robert Wyler.

Films Produced by Sam Spiegel as S. P. Eagle

1942 *Tales of Manhattan*–b&w–117/118 min. (without fifth sequence)

Twentieth Century-Fox. Co-Producer: Boris Morros. Associate Producer: Sam Rheiner. Director: Julien Duvivier. Original story and screenplay by Ben Hecht, Ferenc Molnár, Donald Ogden Stewart, Samuel Hoffenstein, Alan Campbell, Ladislas Fodor, L. Vadnai, L. Görög, Lamar Trotti, and Henry Blankfort. Photography: Joseph Walker. Editor: Robert Bischoff. Art directors: Richard Day and Boris Leven. Cast of first sequence: Charles Boyer, Rita Hayworth, Thomas Mitchell; second sequence: Ginger Rogers, Gail Patrick, Cesar Romero, Henry Fonda; third sequence: Elsa Lanchester, Charles Laughton,

Victor Francen; fourth sequence: James Gleason, Edward G. Robinson, George Sanders; fifth sequence (which did not appear in original film but now appears on video): W. C. Fields, Phil Silvers, Margaret Dumont; sixth sequence: Paul Robeson, Ethel Waters, Eddie "Rochester" Anderson. (World premiere: August 5, 1942; New York opening: September 24, 1942.)

1946 *The Stranger*–b&w–94/95 min.

International Pictures Inc./RKO. Director: Orson Welles. Assistant director: Jack Voglin. Screenplay: Anthony Veiller and John Huston (uncredited). Based on "The Trap," a story by Victor Trivas, taken from material by Decla Dunning and Philip MacDonald. Photography: Russell Metty. Production designer: Perry Ferguson. Editor: Ernest Nims. Music: Bronislaw Kaper. Dialogue director: Gladys Hill. Cast: Edward G. Robinson, Loretta Young, Orson Welles, Philip Merivale, Richard Long, Konstantin Shayne, Byron Keith, Billy House. (Los Angeles opening: July 3, 1946; New York opening: July 10, 1946.)

1949 *We Were Strangers*–b&w–105/106 min.

Horizon Pictures/Columbia. Associate Producer: Jules Buck. Director: John Huston. Screenplay: Peter Viertel and John Huston. Based on "China Valdes," an episode from Robert Sylvester's novel *Rough Sketch*. Photography: Russell Metty. Editor: Al Clark. Art director: Cary Odell. Dialogue director: Gladys Hill. Cast: Jennifer Jones (by arrangement with David O. Selznick), John Garfield, Pedro Armendáriz, Gilbert Roland, Ramon Novarro. (U.S. release: April 21, 1949.)

1951 *When I Grow Up*–b&w–91/92 min.

Horizon Pictures/Eagle-Lion Classics. Director: Michael Kanin. Screenplay: Michael Kanin and John Huston (uncredited). Photography: Ernest Laszlo. Editor: Bruce Schoengarth. Production designer: Nicolai Remisoff. Music: Jerome Moross. Production supervisor: Robert Aldrich. Cast: Bobby Driscoll, Robert Preston, Martha Scott, Charley Grapewin, and the world famous clown: Poodles Hanneford. (U.S. release: April 20, 1951.)

1951 *The Prowler*–b&w–91/92 min.

Horizon Pictures/United Artists. Director: Joseph Losey. Screenplay: Hugo Butler, Dalton Trumbo (uncredited). Based on a story by Robert Thoeren and Hans Wilhelm. Photography: Arthur Miller. Art director: Boris Leven. Editor: Paul Weatherwax. Assistant director: Robert

Aldrich. Dialogue director: Gladys Hill. Cast: Van Heflin, Evelyn Keyes, John Maxwell, Katharine Warren, Emerson Treacy. (U.S. release: May 25, 1951. Film wrapped on May 1, 1950, but Spiegel was waiting for United Artists to release the picture.)

1951 *The African Queen*–Technicolor–104/106 min.

Horizon/United Artists (Romulus had rights to the Eastern Hemisphere). Director: John Huston. Screenplay: James Agee, John Huston, Peter Viertel (uncredited). Based on C. S. Forester's novel. Photography: Jack Cardiff. Art director: Wilfred Shingleton. Editor: Ralph Kemplen. Cast: Humphrey Bogart, Katharine Hepburn, Robert Morley, Peter Bull, Theodore Bikel. (Los Angeles special premiere preview: December 23, 1951; U.S. release: March 21, 1952.)

1953 *Melba*–Technicolor–113/115 min.

Horizon Pictures/United Artists. Director: Lewis Milestone. Screenplay: Harry Kurnitz. Photography: Edward Scaife. Editor: Bill Lewthwaite. Production designer: André Andrejew. Operatic Advisor: Norman Feasey. Cast: Patrice Munsel, Robert Morley, John McCallum, John Justin, Martita Hunt, Alec Clunes, Sybil Thorndike. (U.S. release: August 7, 1953.)

Films Produced by Sam Spiegel

1954 *On the Waterfront*–b&w–108/109 min.

Horizon-America/Columbia. Director: Elia Kazan. Screenplay: Budd Schulberg. "Suggested" by the articles "Crime on the Waterfront" by Malcolm Johnson. Photography: Boris Kaufman. Editor: Gene Milford. Art director: Richard Day. Music: Leonard Bernstein. Cast: Marlon Brando, Lee J. Cobb, Rod Steiger, Eva Marie Saint, Karl Malden, Pat Henning, Leif Erickson, James Westerfield, Tony Galento, Tami Mauriello, John Hamilton, Rudy Bond, Martin Balsam, Fred Gwynne, Pat Hingle. (New York preview: June 29, 1954; New York opening: July 28, 1954; U.S. release: October 1954.)

1957 *The Strange One*–b&w–100 min.

Horizon Pictures/Columbia. Director: Jack Garfein. Screenplay: Calder Willingham. Based on his novel and play *End as a Man*. Photography: Burnett Guffey. Editor: Sidney Katz. Art director: Joseph C. Wright. Music: Kenyon Hopkins. Cast: Ben Gazzara, Pat Hingle, Peter Mark Richman, Arthur Storch, Paul Richards, Larry Gates, Clifton James, Geoffrey Horne, James Olson. Introducing:

Julie Wilson and George Peppard. (U.S. release: May 1957.)

1957 *The Bridge on the River Kwai*–Technicolor, CinemaScope–161 min.

Horizon Pictures/Columbia. Director: David Lean. Screenplay: credited to Pierre Boulle; Michael Wilson (1957 uncredited) and Carl Foreman (1957 uncredited). Based on Pierre Boulle's novel *Le Pont de la Rivière Kwai.* Photography: Jack Hildyard. Editor: Peter Taylor. Art director: Donald A. Ashton. Music: Malcolm Arnold. Cast: William Holden, Jack Hawkins, Alec Guinness, Sessue Hayakawa, James Donald. (London premiere: October 2, 1957; New York premiere: December 18, 1957.)

1959 *Suddenly, Last Summer*–b&w–112/114 min.

Horizon Pictures/Columbia. Director: Joseph L. Mankiewicz. Adaptation: Gore Vidal and Tennessee Williams. Based on Williams's play, the second from *Garden District.* Photography: Jack Hildyard. Editor: William Hornbeck. Art director: Oliver Messel. Art director: William Kellner. Set decoration: Scott Slimon. Costumes: Oliver Messel, Jean Louis (for Elizabeth Taylor), Norman Hartnell (for Katharine Hepburn). Cast: Elizabeth Taylor, Montgomery Clift, Katharine Hepburn, Mercedes McCambridge, Albert Dekker, Gary Raymond. (New York opening: December 22, 1959; U.S. release: January 1960.)

1962 *Lawrence of Arabia*–Technicolor, Super Panavision 70–222 min.

Horizon Pictures/Columbia. Director: David Lean. Adaptation: Robert Bolt and Michael Wilson (credit given posthumously). Based on T. E. Lawrence's *Seven Pillars of Wisdom.* Photography: F. A. Young. Editor: Anne V. Coates. Production designer: John Box. Art director: John Stoll. Set dresser: Dario Simoni. Costumes: Phyllis Dalton. Sound: John Cox. Music: Maurice Jarre. Cast: Peter O'Toole, Alec Guinness, Anthony Quinn, Omar Sharif, Jack Hawkins, Claude Rains, Arthur Kennedy, Anthony Quayle. (U.K. world premiere: December 10, 1962; New York premiere: December 16, 1962; Los Angeles premiere: December 21, 1962.)

1966 *The Chase*–Technicolor, Panavision–135 min.

Lone Star Pictures-Horizon Pictures/Columbia. Director: Arthur Penn. Adaptation: Lillian Hellman (uncredited: Horton Foote and Ivan

Moffat). Based on Horton Foote's novel and play of same name and two television plays: *John Turner Davis* and *The Midnight Caller.* Photography: Joseph LaShelle (replaced Robert Surtees). Editor: Gene Milford. Production designer: Richard Day. Music: John Barry. Cast: Marlon Brando, Jane Fonda, Robert Redford, E. G. Marshall, Angie Dickinson, Janice Rule, Miriam Hopkins, Martha Hyer, Richard Bradford, Robert Duvall, James Fox, Diana Hyland. (U.S. release: February 17, 1966.)

1967 *The Night of the Generals*–Technicolor, Panavision–148 min.

Horizon Pictures Filmsonor/Columbia. Director: Anatole Litvak. Adaptation: Joseph Kessel (for French screenplay: *La Nuit des Généraux*), Paul Dehn (uncredited Robert Anderson and Gore Vidal). Based on Hans Hellmut Kirst's *Die Nacht der Generale* and Chapter 6 of James Hadley Chase's *The Wary Transgressor.* Photography: Henri Decaë. Editor: Alan Osbiston. Production designer: Alexandre Trauner. Music: Maurice Jarre. Cast: Peter O'Toole, Omar Sharif, Tom Courtenay, Donald Pleasence, Joanna Pettet, Philippe Noiret. (U.S. release: February 2, 1967.)

1967 *The Happening*–Technicolor–101 min.

Horizon Dover/Columbia. Presented by Sam Spiegel. Producer: Jud Kinberg. Executive producer: Sam Spiegel. Director: Elliot Silverstein. Screenplay: Frank R. Pierson and James D. Buchanan and Ronald Austin. Based on *The Innocent*–a story by James D. Buchanan and Ronald Austin. Photography: Philip Lathrop. Editor: Philip Andersen. Production designer: Richard Day. Music: De Vol. Cast: Anthony Quinn, Michael Parks, George Maharis, Robert Walker, Jr., Martha Hyer, introducing Faye Dunaway. (U.S. release: March 22, 1967.)

1968 *The Swimmer*–Technicolor–94 min.

Horizon Dover/Columbia. Producer: Frank Perry, Roger Lewis. Executive producer: Sam Spiegel. Director: Frank Perry (uncredited: Sydney Pollack and Slavomir "Ed" Vorkapich). Adaptation: Eleanor Perry. Based on John Cheever's short story. Photography: David Quaid. Editors: Sidney Katz, Carl Lerner, Pat Somerset. Art director: Peter Dohanos. Music: Marvin Hamlisch. Costumes: Anna Hill Johnstone. Cast: Burt Lancaster, Janet Landgard, Janice Rule, Tony Bickley, Marge Champion, Nancy Cushman, Bill Fiore, John Garfield, Jr., Kim Hunter. (U.S. release: May 15, 1968.)

1971 *Nicholas and Alexandra*–Technicolor, Panavision–185/187 min.

Horizon Pictures/Columbia. Sam Spiegel Presents. Director: Franklin J. Schaffner. Adaptation: James Goldman, Edward Bond. Based on Robert K. Massie's *Nicholas and Alexandra*. Photography: Freddie Young. Editor: Ernest Walter. Production designer and second unit director: John Box. Art direction: Ernest Archer, Jack Maxsted, Gil Parrondo. Set dresser: Vernon Dixon. Costumes: Yvonne Blake, Antonio Castillo. Music: Richard Rodney Bennett. Cast: Michael Jayston, Janet Suzman, Harry Andrews, Irene Worth, Tom Baker, Jack Hawkins, Laurence Olivier, Eric Porter, Michael Redgrave, John McEnery, Michael Bryant. (U.K. world premiere: November 29, 1971; New York premiere: December 13, 1971; U.S. release: January 1972.)

1976 *The Last Tycoon*–Technicolor–122/123 min.

Tycoon Service Company (SS)/Paramount. Director: Elia Kazan. Screenplay: Harold Pinter. Based on the unfinished novel by F. Scott Fitzgerald. Photography: Victor Kemper. Editor: Richard Marks. Production designer: Gene Callahan. Art direction: Jack T. Collis. Set decoration: Jerry Wunderlich. Music: Maurice Jarre. Costumes: Anna Hill Johnstone. Additional costumes: Anthea Sylbert. Cast: Robert De Niro, Tony Curtis, Robert Mitchum, Jeanne Moreau, Jack Nicholson, Donald Pleasence, introducing Ingrid Boulting, Ray Milland, Dana Andrews, Theresa Russell, Peter Strauss, Tige Andrews, Morgan Farley, John Carradine, Jeff Corey. (Los Angeles press opening: November 9, 1976; New York world premiere: November 15, 1976; U.S. release: February 1977.)

1983 *Betrayal*–Technicolor–95 min.

Horizon Pictures/Twentieth Century-Fox International Classics. Director: David Jones. Screenplay: Harold Pinter, based on his play. Photography: Mike Fash. Editor: John Bloom. Art director: Eileen Diss. Music: Dominic Muldowney. Costumes: Jane Robinson. Additional costumes: Jean Muir. Cast: Jeremy Irons, Ben Kingsley, Patricia Hodge. (U.S. opening: February 19, 1983; London opening: October 6, 1983.)

Academy Awards

Nominations and Winners

Sam Spiegel won three Academy Awards for producing, on four nominations. His record as the sole producer to have his name, and his name only, associated with three best picture Oscars still stands—and he did it in eight years! His pictures won twenty-five Academy Awards, and in 1964 he won the Irving G. Thalberg Memorial Award. The nominations are listed below, with winners given in boldface.

1946 *The Stranger*
Writing, Original Story: Victor Trivas.

1952 *The African Queen*
Actor: Humphrey Bogart
Actress: Katharine Hepburn
Director: John Huston
Writing, Screenplay based on material from another medium: James Agee and John Huston.

1954 *On the Waterfront*
Picture: Sam Spiegel
Actor: Marlon Brando
Supporting Actor: Lee J. Cobb
Supporting Actor: Karl Malden
Supporting Actor: Rod Steiger
Supporting Actress: Eva Marie Saint
Director: Elia Kazan
Writing, Story, and Screenplay: Budd Schulberg
Cinematography—black and white: Boris Kaufman
Editing: Gene Milford
Art Direction/Set Direction—black and white: Richard Day
Music, Scoring: Leonard Bernstein.

1957 *The Bridge on the River Kwai*
Picture: Sam Spiegel
Actor: Alec Guinness
Supporting Actor: Sessue Hayakawa
Director: David Lean

Writing, Screenplay based on material from another medium: Pierre Boulle, Michael Wilson (presented posthumously), Carl Foreman (presented posthumously)
Cinematography: Jack Hildyard
Editing: Peter Taylor
Music, Scoring: Malcolm Arnold

1959 *Suddenly, Last Summer*
Actress: Elizabeth Taylor
Actress: Katharine Hepburn
Art Direction/Set Direction: Oliver Messel, William Kellner, Scott Slimon.

1962 *Lawrence of Arabia*
Picture: Sam Spiegel
Actor: Peter O'Toole
Supporting Actor: Omar Sharif
Director: David Lean
Writing, Screenplay based on material from another medium: Robert Bolt, Michael Wilson (nomination given posthumously)
Cinematography: F. A. Young
Editing: Anne V. Coates
Art Direction/Set Direction: John Box, John Stoll, Dario Simoni
Sound: John Cox and Shepperton Sound Department
Music, Scoring–substantially original: Maurice Jarre

1971 *Nicholas and Alexandra*
Picture: Sam Spiegel
Actress: Janet Suzman
Cinematography: Freddie Young
Art Direction/Set Direction: John Box, Ernest Archer, Jack Maxsted, Gil Parrondo, Vernon Dixon
Music, Scoring: Richard Rodney Bennett
Costume Design: Yvonne Blake, Antonio Castillo.

1976 *The Last Tycoon*
Art Direction/Set Direction: Gene Callahan, Jack T. Collis, Jerry Wunderlich

1983 *Betrayal*

Writing, Screenplay based on material from another medium: Harold Pinter

Notes

List of Abbreviations

AFI	American Film Institute, Louis B. Mayer Library, Los Angeles
AMPAS	Margaret Herrick Library, Academy of Motion Picture Arts and Sciences
NFC	Natasha Fraser-Cavassoni
MMC AMPAS	Mark M. Cohen Collection
CKF AFI	Charles K. Feldman Collection
GHI	Givat Haviva Institute, Israel
HH GHI	Hashomer Hatzair Central Archives
LH HRHRC	Lillian Hellman Collection
(I)	Interview
HRHRC	Harry Ransom Humanities Research Center, the University of Texas, Austin
JH AMPAS	John Huston Collection
JF	The Jerusalem Foundation, Israel
PK SDK	Paul Kohner Collection
DLE	Sir David Lean Estate
MPAA AMPAS	Motion Picture Association of America Files
NARA	National Archives and Records Administration
EP AMPAS	Eleanor Perry Collection
PCA AMPAS	Production Code Administration
EGR USC	Edward G. Robinson Collection
BBS	Betty Benson Spiegel Collection
SS	Sam Spiegel
SS JF	Sam Spiegel Collection
SSF	Sam Spiegel Foundation
SDK	Stiftung Deutsche Kinemathek, Berlin
U USC	Universal Collection
UCLA	Arts Library Special Collections, University of California at Los Angeles
USC	The Cinema-Television Library, University of Southern California
UoV	University of Vienna
WB USC	Warner Bros. Collection
MW UCLA	Michael Wilson Collection

All Sam Spiegel's professional papers are held at The Jerusalem Foundation, Israel. However, his personal papers are part of the Sam Spiegel Foundation and remain in the United States.

Please note that when I began my research, Spiegel's professional papers were still in New York and were being packed up for Jerusalem. (I subsequently continued my research there.) Meanwhile, Spiegel's personal papers were still being put into order by the Sam Spiegel Foundation. As a result, when I finished going through the majority of his personal documents, these were then filed away either into Box Series I (under the heading Personal,) or Box Series 2 (under the heading Miscellaneous), or Box Series 3 (under the heading Yacht *Malahne*). I was absent when this filing was done. When I am unfamiliar with the box series number, I simply put SSF.

Spiegel's archives contain countless clippings—many without sources, headlines and dates; this explains the omission of such data.

Regarding the dates of the interviews, unless the interview continued over a course of several days, the date only appears once in the chapter, indicating that all subsequent quotations are taken from that source. If the reference comes from a book, then the title of the book is given, sometimes in abbreviated form (full references can be found in the bibliography).

Introduction

Page xi Cooper paused: Details taken from footage of the Academy Awards ceremony in 1958, AMPAS.

"Uncrowned because": Charles Schneer to NFC (I), Mar. 1, 1999.

"In profile, he looked": Fred Zinnemann to NFC (I), Dec. 19, 1996.

"nutty elegance": Joan Axelrod to NFC (I), Nov. 16, 1996.

Page xii *"How can you idiots":* Paul N. Lazarus, Jr., to NFC (I), June 11, 1997.

Hedda Hopper: Letter from Ilse Kahn at Paul Kohner Agency to Michael Wilson, Feb. 8, 1958, MW UCLA.

Page xiii *"That's the $64,000 question":* Kevin Brownlow, *David Lean*, 388.

"neither Michael Wilson": SS to *Los Angeles Times*, Feb. 1958, MW UCLA.

They were nervous: Lazarus to NFC (I).

"a factory in the sun": SS to NFC (I), Feb. 1984.

"perfect example of the producer": Radio interview with Joseph L. Mankiewicz, Jan. 1. 1986.

"It's really a negative": William Wolf, "Doing It His Way," *New York* magazine, Feb. 21, 1983.

There was also Spiegel's Academy Award track record . . . letter from L. Robert Morris to NFC, Feb. 20, 2002.

Page xiv *"Nowadays, several producers":* Letter from Kevin Brownlow to NFC, Feb. 5, 2002.

"You must feel": Wolf, *New York* magazine, Feb. 21, 1983.

"And if a love affair": Spiegel quoted *Newsday*, "Spiegel Mourned as 'Last of the Giants'" January 4, 1986. BBS.

"a modern day Robin Hood": Peter Viertel to NFC (I), Apr. 26, 1997.

"Why did I love Sam so much?": Mike Nichols to NFC (I), Nov. 5, 1996.

Page xv *"Nothing fazed him":* Elia Kazan to NFC (I), Apr. 10, 1996.

"conflicts between human beings": Radio interview with Mankiewicz, Jan. 1, 1986.

"to kill Sam Spiegel": Budd Schulberg to NFC (I), Nov. 26, 1996.

"his feet in concrete": David Geffen to NFC (I), Nov. 20, 1996.
to Spiegel: Harlan Jacobson, *Film Comment*, Apr. 1983.
"Jewish mother tactics": Barry Diller to NFC (I), Oct. 12, 1996.
"Fuck the Middle West!": Harold Pinter to NFC (I), Jan. 13, 1998.
"The Great Gatsby": Arthur Miller to NFC (I), Nov. 6, 1996.
Page xvi *"His left-hand friends"*: Kathleen Parrish to NFC (I), Oct. 5, 1996.
Spiegel dismissed the idea: George Weidenfeld to NFC (I), Dec. 22, 1995.
"He always struck me": James Goldman to NFC (I), Oct. 18, 1996.
"I can't remember": Hugh Thomas to NFC (I), July 6, 1999.
"But for the grace of God": Parrish to NFC (I).
"Mr. Spieeegel": Betty Estevez to NFC (I), Apr. 10, 1999.
Mason blue Phantom Six Rolls-Royce: Ken Oakley, Spiegel's chauffeur, to NFC (I), Apr. 23, 1999.
Page xvii *"Sam had a gift"*: Robby Lantz to NFC (I), July 2, 1996.
"She was wearing": SS to NFC (I), Feb. 1984.
"marked the end of an era": Warren Beatty to NFC (I), Nov. 17, 1996.
Indeed, David Lean's Indian wife: Letter from David Lean to SS, Sep. 13, 1958, SSF.
Roman emperor Vespasian: Geoffrey M. Shurlock, Mar. 8, 1962, PCA AMPAS.
When I stayed: August 1980.
Page xviii *"dropped, stark naked"*: Elia Kazan, *A Life*, p. 513.
"Baby, know your customer.": Betty Spiegel to NFC (I), Oct. 10, 1996.
"I think he popped out": Betty Spiegel to NFC (I), July 24, 1998.

Chapter One: Childhood

For my research for this chapter, I went to Jaroslav, the town that Spiegel so passionately avoided. These days, little rests of Jaroslav's Jewish history. The last remaining synagogue is used for an overfill of schoolchildren during the summer examination period.

I also visited Zholkva, just outside of Lviv, where Spiegel's family originated. Concerning the history of the Spiegels, through *Le Cercle de Généalogie Juive* and using the *Jewishgen Family Finder,* I came in contact with different branches of the Spiegel family, originating from Poland and the Ukraine. Apparently, there was an element of romance about the tribe: tales of a Rothschild heiress marrying a Spiegel or certain members who escaped to America to avoid conscription since it was against their religious principles.

As far as Spiegel being a member of the Hashomer Hatzair, through Professor Eli Tsur I used the archives of Givat Haviva of Advanced Studies for Youth Movements, which includes the Yad Ya'ari Documentation Center and the Hashomer Hatzair Research Center.

Regarding Spiegel's time spent in Vienna, Stephen Youngkin, Peter Lorre's principal biographer, informed me of the Meldezettel–the Austrian police records–while Dr. Kurt Mühlberger and Thomas Maisel, the archivists of Vienna University, were a constant source regarding Spiegel's supposed student years.

Page 1 *"lightning-fast changes"*: Elia Kazan, *A Life,* p. 73.
Samuel, or Mounik: Erna Shadwick to NFC (I), June 22, 1998. (Her first mother-in-law was Regina Spiegel's sister.)

born November 11, 1901: Details from records in Przemysl, information sent via the Urzad Stanu Cywilnego (the Jaroslav Town Hall) to NFC, June 23, 1998. Translated from Polish by Dzidzia Herman.

    Jaroslav also spelt Jaroslaw, Yaroslau, and Yereslev.

    (Author's Note—Historically, Jaroslav was regarded as a Jewish spiritual center in the kingdom of Poland. From the seventeenth century, it was the meeting point for the Council of the Four Lands, which was known as the Vaad Arba Aratzoth and was considered to be the Polish Jewish parliament.

    In regards to the last Jewish population in Jaroslav, it was snatched from the community on September 28, 1939, when ten thousand people were assembled by German soldiers and deported across the San River to Soviet-occupied territory. Prior to this event, most of the major factories such as the Salik-Reif ribbons plant, the Gurgul's biscuit factory, the Glassberg and Korn flour mills, a meat processing plant, as well as a brickyard were Jewish-owned.)

level of anti-Semitism: Edmund Hebenstreet to Yitzhak Lev Tov (I), May 17, 1999. Translated from Hebrew by Yitzhak Lev Tov.

preferred to forget: Ibid.

"When he could": Albert Heit to NFC (I), Oct. 10, 1996.

Indeed, Mounik's childhood: Hugh Thomas to NFC (I), July 6, 1999.

"I remember sliding down": Ibid.

"My first disillusionment": Dana Wynter to NFC (I), Aug. 15, 1999.

Page 4 First of all: Meldezettel (police records) of Samuel Spiegel, July 16, 1920. Letter to NFC from Herbert Koch, Magistrat der Stadt Wien, Nov. 16, 1998. Translated from German by Christa Michel.

True he *did* live: Letter from Dr. Kurt Mühlberger, Archives, UoV, to NFC, March 17, 1998.

Survivors: Thomas to NFC (I).

Spiegel was more attracted: Raphael Patai, *The Jewish Mind,* pp. 266–70, 384–88.

    (Author's Note—How and why this snobbery happened between the Ostjuden and the Westjuden can be blamed on the birth of Haskalah, the Jewish enlightenment which occurred in the late eighteenth century. Suddenly, the Jewish religion was being questioned, assimilation, mixed marriages, and inevitably Jewish self-hatred came into being. At first, the philosophical movement sent the European Jewish community into an uproar—question their faith? mix with non-Jews? And then it was accepted by the German and West European Ashkenazi Jews and this was what really started the division. Generally speaking, it was the enlightened Jews who tended to be in the West versus the Hasidics, who tended to be in the East. The enlightened were those who embraced the idea of being assimilated and being detached about their faith, while the Hasidics were horrified at the idea of hiding their Jewishness and were passionate about keeping within their tight, religious circle. Of course there were exceptions in the East, the Spiegels for instance.)

According to director Billy Wilder: Billy Wilder and Helmut Karasek, *Et Tout le Reste Est Folie,* p. 23.

    (Author's Note—Other Galitzianers to hit Hollywood included art director Anton Grot, actors Elisabeth Bergner, Alexander Granach, Frederick Ledebur, Mike Mazurki, Paul Muni, Lionel Royce, the cameraman and director Rudolph Maté, and the actress-writer Salka Viertel. A question mark remains over Otto Preminger, who—like Billy Wilder—was always labeled as Viennese. One document states the director's birthplace as Wisniz Nowy in Galicia but two other equally official-looking documents state two other different places!)

Page 5 There was also another side: Leo Rosten, *The Joys of Yiddish*, pp. 124–25.

In the opinion of their neighbors: Ibid.

Robert Maxwell: Yehuda Avner to NFC (I), Nov. 24, 1996.

As did Harold Konigsberg: Eric Konigsberg, "Blood Relation," *The New Yorker*, Aug. 6, 2001.

But although Mounik: Judge Raya Dreben to NFC (I), June 27, 1996.

    (Author's Note–Until his mid-twenties, Shalom Spiegel also signed himself as Schulim Spiegel.)

"a very learned household": Dreben to NFC (I).

Eastern European powerhouses: A. Scott Berg, *Goldwyn,* p. 9.

Mounik became articulate: Jules Buck to NFC (I), June 13, 1997.

His father, Simon Spiegel: Dreben to NFC (I).

representative of the Mizrachi movement: *Jaroslav Book: A Memorial to the Jewish Community of Jaroslav,* p. 20.

Page 6 Simon was a peripheral figure: Ann E. Pennington to NFC (I), Jan. 13, 1998.

Born in Zholkva: Details from records in Przemysl, information received from Urzad Stanu Cywilnego (the Jaroslav Town Hall). Translated from Polish by Anne Dziubak.

    (Author's Note–Joseph II–an enlightened monarch–also introduced military conscription and banned bookkeeping from being done in Yiddish and Hebrew. Yet, in his aim to make his Jewish subjects "useful to the state," their horizons were broadened. Academic professions were encouraged and they could also create factories, employ Christian workers, and engage in manual labor and any of the arts.)

(The former is the accepted: Dreben to NFC (I). Also, Adam Spiegel to NFC (I), Dec. 22, 1996.

Mechel and Eda Schwitz: Details from Urzad Stanu Cywilnego (the Jaroslav Town Hall). Translated from Polish by Dzidzia Herman.

    (Author's Note–Regarding the Germanization of names, it was possible to bribe the clerk. According to Professor Eli Tsur, "When money was paid, you could have a lovely name like Goldenberg–a mountain of gold, Rosenberg–a mountain of roses." Other favorites included Kluger–wise–and Frohlich–happy.)

Mounik's mother: Yitzhak Lev Tov to NFC (I).

"queenlike": Yitzhak Lev Tov to NFC (I), Nov. 19, 1997. (Lev Tov's mother-in-law–Sally Loberbaum–was Spiegel's first cousin.)

Regina used to knock: Dreben to NFC (I).

"sixty-eight forever": Ibid.

"My wife used to say": Buck to NFC (I).

Page 7 Still, a large framed photograph: Heit to NFC (I).

while a smaller one: Jennifer Kent Attebery to NFC (I), June 3, 1999.

"swans who were left": Mike Nichols to NFC (I), Nov. 5, 1996.

"When her husband died": Dreben to NFC (I).

"Tante Regina": Erna Shadwick to NFC (I), June 22, 1998.

"If you had committed": Letter from Peter Viertel to NFC, March 15, 2002.

Only German was spoken: Dreben to NFC (I).

The goal was: Lev Tov to NFC (I).

In the Spiegel household: Dreben to NFC (I).

Page 8 There were three picture houses: Hebenstreet to Lev Tov (I).

Financially, Mounik's mother: Erna Shadwick to NFC (I).

"I never knew": Ibid.

"There's a generation": Mike Nichols to NFC (I), Nov. 5, 1996.

"I was still a boy": George Weidenfeld to NFC (I), Dec. 22, 1995.

the emperor was associated: Bruce F. Pauley, *From Prejudice to Persecution,* p. 23.

    (Author's Note–The history between the Jews and the Austrian royal family had not always been fortuitous. Empress Maria-Theresa of Austria (1740–1780), a staunch Catholic, was so violently anti-Semitic that she earned herself the distinction of being the last European ruler, before Hitler, to expel Jews. She was virulent about their wearing the yellow star badge, paying a special poll tax, as well as encouraging major trade restrictions. Her remark that she knew of "no worse plague for the state" became a popular Nazi slogan. Her son was Joseph II, who was the first to make genuine reforms, known as Judenreformen and Edicts of Toleration: Toleranzpatent. He ended the use of the yellow star badge and the poll tax, and lifted the ban on Jews going to university and stopped trade restrictions. Still, not all his methods were pleasing to his Jewish subjects.)

"We had a fairly comfortable upbringing": Harlan Jacobson, "Big Tusker," *Film Comment,* Apr. 1983.

Mounik's elder brother: Meldezettel (police records) of Shalom Spiegel, Oct. 16, 1917. Sent to NFC from Herbert Koch, Magistrat der Stadt Wien. Translated from German by Christa Michel.

Page 9 *"Each time it fell"*: Wilder and Karasek, *Et Tout le Reste Est Folie,* p. 26.

    (Author's Note–To quote film expert Kevin Brownlow, *"Hotel Imperial* was made into a film in 1927 by Garbo's director, Mauritz Stiller–the film starred Pola Negri– and producer Erich Pommer . . . Hotel Imperial was remade in 1939 and adapted by Billy Wilder as 'Five Graves to Cairo.')

"by some kind": SS to Jacobson, "Big Tusker," *Film Comment,* Apr. 1983.

1918 pogroms: From *Les Pogromes Anti-Juifs en Pologne et en Galicie en Novembre et en Décembre 1918,* facts and documents edited by L. Chasanowitch.

"Jewish Survival": Pauley, *From Prejudice to Persecution,* p. 11.

In comparison to Lvov: From *Les Pogromes Anti-Juifs,* p. 59.

However, on November 13, 1918: Ibid., p. 29.

Even before the peace treaty: Norman Davies, *Heart of Europe,* pp. 115–17.

Page 10 In the meantime: Professor Eli Tsur, Givat Haviva Institute, to NFC (I), Nov. 25, 1997.

    Hashomer Hatzair–also spelled Hashomer Hazair, Hashomer Ha-Zair, Hashomer Hatz' air and Ha-Shomer Hatzair.

    (Author's Note–Hashomer Hatzair was a sort of Zionist teen scouts that started in Vienna in 1911 and was a merger of two youth organizations that had originated in Galicia–the Hashomer–watchman in Hebrew–and the Ze'irei Zion–the youth of Zion.)

Most of its members: Tsur to NFC (I).

Mounik became one of the youngest members: Ibid.

"Brother this": Ibid.

He even left Jaroslav: Letter from Professor Eli Tsur to NFC, Oct. 19, 1999.

Although he lodged: Information taken from list from *Haszomer,* Sept. 1919, p. 24. Translated from Polish by Professor Eli Tsur.

"Sam talked about": Isaac Stern to NFC (I), July 3, 1998.

attending his school: Letter from Dr. Kurt Mühlberger, Archives, UoV, to NFC, Mar. 17, 1998.

His duties led to his: Tsur to NFC (I).

"Beautiful language": Letter from SS to High Command, Oct. 1, 1919. HH GHI (2) 118.1-2. Translated from Polish by Eli Tsur.

Page 11 *"My beloved Krongolf"*: Letter from SS to Krongolf, head of Polish Hashomer Hatzair, Oct. 1, 1919. HH GHI (2)118.1-2. Translated from Polish by Eli Tsur.

"Please send us the stamps": Ibid.

"This decision to hurry": SS quoted from the minutes, describing the Hashomer Hatzair's high command meeting, Nov. 3, 1919. HH GHI (3) 118. 1-2. Translated from Hebrew by Dr. Shimon Bar Tzlil.

unable to pay the fare: Ibid.

"If they are not suitable": Letter from Eliezer Rieger to the high command, June 14, 1920. HH GHI (3) 118.1-2. Translated from Hebrew by Dr. Shimon Bar Tzlil.

Having acquired his *Abitur*: In June 1920; letter from Thomas Maisel, Archives, UoV, to NFC, July 13, 1999.

he had been accepted: Letter from Dr. Kurt Mühlberger, Archives, UoV, to NFC, May 19, 1998.

first semester: Letter from Thomas Maisel, Archives, UoV, to NFC, Dec. 7, 1998.

Page 12 prominent figures: Letter from Dr. Kurt Mühlberger, UoV, to NFC, Mar. 17, 1998.

Spiegel's father was paying: Letter from Thomas Maisel, UoV, to NFC, Dec. 7, 1998.

had cost 424 kronen: Ibid.

his long-suffering elder brother: Ibid.

he *never* stopped: SS publicity biography for *Tales of Manhattan*, 1942, Box 2, SSF.

Chapter Two: Palestine

Through Yitzhak Lev Tov, I was put in touch with Muki Tsur, an authority on the Third Aliyah, as well as Netty Gottlieb, a Spiegel associate from the 1920s. He also found articles such as Zeev Bloch's "Centers of Hashomer Hatzair, 1920–21" and Dan Yahav's "Kibbutz C, Hashomer Hatzair, the Bialik Community."

Page 13 They left on: SS's Meldezettel (police records), July 16, 1920, sent to NFC, from Herbert Koch, Magistrat der Stadt Wien, Nov. 16, 1998. Translated from German by Christa Michel.

Spiegel was one of fifty: Letter from Muki Tsur, head of Kibbutz Ein Gev, and an authority on the Third Aliyah, to NFC, Sep. 7, 1998.

However, Spiegel was sent: Mattityahu Mintz, *Pangs of Youth*, pp. 416–17. Translated from Hebrew by Dr. Shimon Bar Tzlil.

Spiegel later described: SS publicity biography for *Tales of Manhattan*, 1942, SSF.

Not only did Spiegel: Letter from Muki Tsur to NFC, Oct. 9, 1998.

Page 14 *"Spiegel stood up"*: Mintz, *Pangs of Youth*, pp. 174–75. Translated from Hebrew by Dr. Shimon Bar Tzlil.

"around the country": Zeev Bloch, "Centers of Hashomer Hatzair, 1920–21," HH GHI. Translated from Hebrew by Dr. Shimon Bar Tzlil.

Later, the camp went down: Letter from Muki Tsur to NFC, Oct. 11, 1998.

"our hands were full": The Third Aliyah Book, pp. 417–18. Translated from Hebrew by Dr. Shimon Bar Tzlil.

However, he did work: Letter from Menachem Gelehrter to SS, Mar. 5, 1981, SSF.

They dug ditches: Ibid.

He arrived in Vienna: Letter from Thomas Maisel, UoV, to NFC, Dec. 7, 1998.

made a point: Letter from Dr. Kurt Mühlberger, UoV, to NFC, Mar. 17, 1998.

he was back in Palestine: Dan Yahav, "Kibbutz C, Hashomer Hatzair, the Bialik Community," *Al-Hamishmar,* July 14, 1993. Translated by Dr. Shimon Bar Tzlil.

Page 15 Her father and stepmother: Ellen Weisbord to NFC (I), Nov. 19, 1997.

"one big zero": Ray Agranovich Abrams to NFC (I), May 23, 1998.

"Her life was": Ilana Agron to NFC (I), Nov. 29, 1997.

yet again altered: Letter from Dr. Kurt Mühlberger, UoV, to NFC, Mar. 17, 1998.

Page 16 Ray's Father: Abrams to NFC (I).

Most of her guests: Agron to NFC (I).

"She thought it made her": Ibid.

"mean, unkind, nasty": Ray Abrams to NFC (I).

Spiegel married Ray: Ibid.

they lived in the German colony: Yitzhak Lev Tov to NFC (I), Nov. 19, 1997.

One of Spiegel's early business endeavors: Netty Gottlieb to NFC (I), July 7, 1998. (Gottlieb became the best friend of Rosa Spiegel, Shalom Spiegel's wife, when the Spiegels moved to Palestine.)

Another of his schemes: Ibid.

the Emir: Patrick Seale to NFC (I), Nov. 10, 2001.

"And he forgot": Gottlieb to NFC (I).

Page 17 *"He never took his wife":* Ibid.

A year after their marriage: Lonig died on Oct. 17, 1923. Details received from Urzad Stanu Cywilnego (the Jaroslav Town Hall), Poland, via Andrzej L. Zoltowski, June 23, 1998. Translated by Dzidzia Herman.

either of cancer: Gottlieb to NFC (I).

a football injury: Judge Raya Dreben to NFC (I), June 27, 1996. (Author's Note–Official Data does not reveal the cause of his death.)

Three years later: Weisbord to NFC (I).

On one occasion: Kurt Unger to NFC (I), Sep. 8, 1997.

"All my life": Harlan Jacobson, "Big Tusker," *Film Comment,* Apr. 1983.

Egyptian lottery company: Unger to NFC (I).

Spiegel stole someone else's Egyptian checkbook: Anshell Triber's memoirs from the Archives of Kibbutz Bet Alfa. (Triber was one of the kibbutz's founders.) Information provided by Meita Hacohen. Translated by Dr. Shimon Bar Tzlil.

"arrive in Tel Aviv": Letter from Susi Agranovich to SS, Jan. 18, 1954, SSF. Translated from German by Christa Michel.

"Do you bear a grudge?": Letter from Susi Agranovich to SS, June 21, 1954, SSF. Translated from German by Christa Michel.

The alliance had abruptly ended: *Los Angeles Examiner,* "Film Producer Sued by Wife," May 11, 1943, USC.

"deeply in debt": Judge Raya Dreben to NFC (I), June 27, 1996.

a little sinister: Ann E. Pennington to NFC (I), Jan. 13, 1998.

Page 18 went into mourning: Professor Eli Tsur to NFC (I), Nov. 25, 1997.

left in disgrace: SS's Meldezettel (police records), Oct. 6, 1927. Translated from German
    by Christa Michel.
"I'll either become": Letter from Tmima Rivlin, the daughter of Susi Agranovich, to SS,
    Oct. 2, 1955, SSF.

Chapter Three: San Francisco

Two vital files at the Textual Archives Services Division at NARA (National Archives
and Records Administration) at College Park, Maryland, proved essential for this
chapter and Chapter 7.
    I also contacted William Roberts from the Bancroft Library, University of California
at Berkeley, and Universal's Jan-Christopher Horak and Rolinda W. Wittman, paralegal,
at Turner Entertainment Company (TEC).

Page 19 Regarding his Palestine experience: SS publicity biography for *Tales of
    Manhattan,* 1942, Box 2, SS JF.
        (Author's Note–I checked with the University of Vienna's Dr. Kurt Mühlberger
        about the "dramatic literature" course. The university *did* have one during this
        period, but it was when SS was in Palestine.)
"a few inferior plays": SS quoted by Joyce Wadler, *Washington Post,* Nov. 20, 1983.
arrive in the port of New York: Details taken from SS interview with the Immigration
    and Naturalization Service, July 24, 1928. INS/Record Group 85, File No:
    12020/13921. Reproduced by NARA. SPIEGEL'S DEPORTATION NUMBER:
    55649/491.
Stating his profession: Ibid.
A guest at New York's Penn Hotel: Ibid.
went to Toronto: Details taken from SS interview with INS, San Francisco, Oct. 19,
    1928. INS/Record Group 85, File Number 12020/13921. Reproduced by NARA.
slip past Immigration: Ibid.
Spiegel was suddenly treated: Details taken from *Los Angeles Examiner,* July 16, 1928.
"gilt-edged credentials": Details taken from *San Francisco Examiner,* July 16, 1928.
"confidential adviser": Ibid.
        (Author's Note–Unfortunately, neither the American, British, or Egyptian
        governments have kept any documents regarding this event. The British Foreign
        Office mentioned a "Spiegel S.S." in the index of their 1928 correspondence but
        apart from stating "Arrest in U.S.A.: fraudulent activities"–the papers of the case
        were not kept. Nor was any evidence found at the Egyptian embassy in
        Washington. The American Department of Treasury came up with nothing, in spite
        of additional searches, prompted by a chain of aggressive letters. Their exact
        terminology being "the secret service is not maintaining any records pertaining to
        Sam Spiegel (aka Samuel Spiegel aka S P Eagle).")
"to study": *San Francisco Chronicle,* July 16, 1928.
also went to smaller cities: Details provided by Rosemary Chodorov to NFC (I), Oct.
    15, 1996.
They had met: Ibid.
attending the University of Michigan: Washer's obituary, Sep. 8, 1982, *Daily Variety.*
        (Washer was killed in San Francisco when a van crashed into the taxicab in which

he was riding with Mary Martin, Janet Gaynor, and Gaynor's husband, producer Paul Gregory.)

Mounik had been his hospitable self: Rosemary Chodorov to NFC (I).

Page 20 given a bouncing Egyptian check: Ibid.

although Washer's father: Ibid.

"leaving a trail": *Los Angeles Examiner*, July 16, 1928.

"with a blare": Ibid.

"without a betraying tremor": Elia Kazan, *A Life*; p. 73.

"He kept me intrigued": Elia Kazan to NFC (I), Apr. 10, 1996.

Secret Service agents: *Los Angeles Examiner*, July 16, 1928.

Tracked down: *San Francisco Chronicle*, July 16, 1928.

he had been caught: Ibid.

possibly with MGM's Paul Bern: Telegram from Paul Bern to Secretary of Labor, Washington, Mar. 17, 1930. INS/Record Group 85, File Number. SS's Deportation No. 55649/491. Reproduced by NARA.

the "International 'mystery man': *San Francisco Examiner*, July 16, 1928.

"Possible deportation": *Los Angeles Examiner*, July 16, 1928.

"a number of film stars": *San Francisco Examiner*, July 16, 1928.

Page 21 *"refused to talk"*: *Los Angeles Examiner*, July 16, 1928.

he telephoned his elder brother: Raya Dreben to NFC (I), June 27, 1996.

"the defender of the world": Ibid.

facing charges: Letter from P. J. Farrely, Immigrant Inspector, to Commissioner of Immigration, San Francisco, July 23, 1928. INS/Record Group 85, File Number 12020/13921. Reproduced by NARA.

Spiegel received: Details taken from SS interview with INS, San Francisco, Oct. 19, 1928. INS/Record Group 85, File Number 12020/13921. Reproduced by NARA.

Jail No. 2: Details taken from report of SS hearing, Nov. 9, 1928. INS/Record Group 85, File No: 12020/13921. Reproduced by NARA.

"No, but I": Ibid.

When Spiegel's period: Letter from Samuel G. Holcenberg to John Farr Simmons, Chief, Visa Office, Oct. 25, 1929. Visa Division Record Group 59, File Number 150.60C6. Reproduced by NARA.

"this mountain wilderness": From *Historical Guide of Angel Island State Park Immigration Station*, published by Angel Island Association.

Samuel G. Holcenberg: Letter from Holcenberg to Simmons, Oct. 25, 1929. Visa Division, Record Group 59, File Number 150.60C6. Reproduced by NARA.

He even wrote: Letter from Samuel G. Holcenberg to Secretary of State, June 18, 1929. Visa Division Record Group 59, File Number 150.60C6. Reproduced by NARA.

"which fortunate opportunity": Letter from SS to Edward L. Haff, Deputy Commissioner of Immigration, May 29, 1929. INS/Record Group 85, File Number 12020/13921. Reproduced by NARA.

Thanks to Holcenberg: Letter from Holcenberg to Simmons, Oct. 25, 1929. Visa Division Record Group 59, File Number 150.60C6. Reproduced by NARA.

Page 22 $500 bond: U.S. Department of Labor, Aug. 6, 1929. INS/Record Group 85, File Number 12020/13921. Reproduced by NARA.

Spiegel *did* work: Letter from Holcenberg to Simmons, Oct. 25, 1929. Visa Division Record Group 59, File Number 150.60C6. Reproduced by NARA.

"many shady things": Ibid.

since Spiegel could demand: Ibid.

subject of a correspondence: Letter from William M. Roberts, university archivist, Bancroft Library, University of California, Berkeley, to NFC, Mar. 19, 1998.

wife of Ralph Ellis: Letter from William M. Roberts to NFC, Apr. 11, 1998. Ralph Ellis was listed in the annual list of gifts to the university, giving almost annually during this period to the Museum of Vertebrate Zoology.

For a brief moment: Letter from William M. Roberts to NFC, Mar. 19, 1998.

discovered by MGM's Paul Bern: Harlan Jacobson, "Big Tusker," *Film Comment*, Apr. 83.

Mrs. Ellis was a theater buff: Letter from William M. Roberts to NFC, March 19, 1998.

as bogus: Letter from William M. Roberts to NFC, Apr. 11, 1998. (Roberts found no record of any lecture by Spiegel in Berkeley or for the University Extension in the Los Angeles area. He checked the thesis written on the Greek Theatre which has a chronology of events as an appendix. He also went through the following indexes: the Extension records, the campus calendar, and Berkeley's student newspaper.)

"He was constantly": Budd Schulberg to NFC (I), Nov. 26, 1996.

Page 23 just as questionable: Letter from Rolinda W. Wittman, paralegal, Turner Entertainment Co., to Adam Spiegel, June 10, 1999.

"read foreign magazines": *Daily Variety*, Feb. 12, 1930.

insists that he was never: Letter from Rolinda W. Wittman to Adam Spiegel, June 10, 1999.

"The competition": Thomas Schatz, *The Genius of the System*, p. 106.

"Early on, the film business": Peter Viertel to NFC (I), Apr. 25 1997.

"showed Sam's knack": Schulberg to NFC (I).

"[He] doesn't talk": Schatz, *The Genius of the System*, p. 141.

too "ambitious": SS interview with Norton Mockridge, *USA*, Nov. 27, 1954.

Page 24 Deeply vexed by Spiegel: Letter from Holcenberg to Simmons, Oct. 25, 1929. Visa Division, Record Group 59, File: 150.60oC6. Reproduced by NARA.

Spiegel was supposed: Telegram from SS to Secretary of Labor, Mar. 15, 1930. INS/Record Group 85, File Number 55649/491 (SS's Deportation No.). Reproduced by NARA.

Two days later: Telegram from Paul Bern to Secretary of Labor, Washington D.C., Mar. 17, 1930, and letter from Minister of Austria to Commissioner General of Immigration, Mar. 18, 1930. INS/Record Group 85, File Number 55649/491.

Spiegel eventually left: Letter from Harry E. Hull, Commissioner General to L. Fitzpatrick, July 26, 1930. INS/Record Group 85, 55649/491. Also reported by *Daily Variety*, Apr. 2, 1930.

"Uncle Carl Laemmle": Written by Ogden Nash.

"very large faemmle": Again, Nash, who wrote "Uncle Carl Laemmle has a very large faemmle." According to Kevin Brownlow, "It was a play on the way the name was pronounced in America. Laemmle was well known for being generous to his relatives–the trouble was, not all were talented and the studio was full of them."

Chapter Four: Berlin

I found no archival material to explain why Spiegel was put in charge of *All Quiet on the Western Front*, Universal's most important film, and despite scouring film newspapers of that period, did not fall on any articles offering reason for his appointment. The former actress Lupita Tovar, the wife of Paul Kohner, who worked at Universal from 1920 to 1936, felt that her husband had been "instrumental" in Spiegel's short career at Universal. However, when Spiegel arrived in Berlin, Kohner was living in the United States.

Jerold Simmons's article "Film and International Politics: The Banning of *All Quiet on the Western Front* in Germany and Austria, 1930–1931" was a tremendous source. I also quoted from Irene Kahn Atkins's interview with Bronislaw Kaper (July 14–Oct 14, 1975) for the Louis B. Mayer Foundation (AFI).

Page 25 *"restless, feverish, wild":* Joe Pasternak, *Easy the Hard Way,* p. 118.
"highly desirable woman": Otto Friedrich, *Before the Deluge,* p. 273.
In later years: SS publicity biography for *We Were Strangers,* 1949, Box 38, SS JF.
"knack of being there": Budd Schulberg to NFC (I), Nov. 26, 1996.
Page 26 *"the sausage factory of Hollywood":* Letter from Kevin Brownlow to NFC, Feb. 5, 2002.
antiwar best-seller was controversial: Julie Gilbert, *Opposite Attraction,* p. 92. (In 1929, over two hundred German essays and articles reflected the angry debate about *All Quiet.*)
great trouble: Simmons, "Film and International Politics," *Historian* 1989, Vol. 52, pp. 45–46.
December 5, 1930: Ibid., p. 40.
"but to participate": Ibid.
Spiegel began the event: Andrew Kelly, *Filming All Quiet on the Western Front,* p. 123.
headed for the exit: Simmons, "Film and International Politics," pp. 40–41.
"Judenfilm, Judenfilm": Ibid.
Page 27 *"Panic broke out":* Leni Riefenstahl, *The Sieve of Time,* p. 65.
Later, Spiegel exaggerated: SS publicity biography for *We Were Strangers,* 1949, Box 38, SS JF.
riots outside the cinema: Kelly, *Filming All Quiet,* p. 122.
six days after the premiere: Ibid., p. 123.
a thousand-word cable: Simmons, "Film and International Politics," p. 47.
called on the American ambassador: Ibid., p. 53.
he informed the American legation: Ibid., p. 55.
He sacked Universal's entire staff: Kelly, *Filming All Quiet,* p. 126.
"If he": Ibid.
By mid-January 1931: Ibid.
He described showing: SS publicity biography for *Tales of Manhattan,* 1942, Box 2, SSF.
every member of the Reichstag: Simmons, "Film and International Politics," pp. 57–58.
went to Rome: *Film-Kurier,* Sep. 16, 1931.
viewing for Mussolini: Kelly, *Filming All Quiet,* p. 131.
special law passed: Andrew Marton interviewed by Joanne D'Antonio, p. 73.
"all the European versions": SS publicity biography for *Tales of Manhattan,* 1942, Box 2, SSF.
Page 28 He was working: Ulrich J. Klaus, *Deutsche Tonfilme* Vol. 4, 1932, p. 32. Translated from German by Christa Michel.
"We had a big hit": Oral History with B. Kaper, AFI, p. 51.
"trying too hard": Film-Kritik, *Film-Kurier,* Jan. 20, 1932. Translated by Christa Michel.
"acquired paintings": SS publicity biography for *We Were Strangers,* 1949, Box 38, SS JF.
Page 29 *"really poor":* Paulette Dubost to NFC (I), Nov. 14, 1999.

"Sam was still building": George Weidenfeld to NFC (I), Dec. 22, 1995.

played an important role: from 1928–1929 Kohner was in charge of Universal's entire European production program. When he returned to Europe in 1932 until 1935, he produced twenty-six pictures for Universal including *The Rebel* and *The Prodigal Son*–both films starred Luis Trenker, a heartthrob of that period. Kohner's biography, Nov. 1, 1943, from PK SDK.

"In some ways": Lupita Kohner to NFC (I), Nov. 19, 1996.

"inspires little confidence": Arthur Schnitzler diary, entry dated July 24, 1930. Arthur Schnitzler: Tagebuch 1927–30.

"It wasn't really": Leonora Hornblow to NFC (I), July 29, 1996.

"a joke": Pasternak, *Easy the Hard Way,* p. 118.

"At first": Lupita Kohner to NFC (I), Nov. 19, 1996.

Romanisches Café: Billy Wilder and Hellmuth Karasek, *Et tout le reste est folie,* p. 54.

"writer's club": Spiegel to Stephen Youngkin (I), Feb. 1979.

"It was kind of a cult": Ibid.

Page 30 Hotels such as: Dubost to NFC (I).

"That was Roland Toutain": Ibid.

"I turned to Paul": Lupita Kohner to NFC (I).

"Tola Litvak": Dubost to NFC (I).

"She was very keen": Dubost to NFC (I).

Made for Pax-Film: Klaus, *Deutsche Tonfilme,* Vol. 4, 1933, pp. 79–80. Translated by Christa Michel.

Based on *Herr Fünf:* Ibid.

Page 31 *"His accent":* Dubost to NFC (I), Nov. 14, 1999.

Heinz Hilpert, walked off: Die Pax-Film erklärt, *Film-Kurier,* March 24, 1933.

"Everything was paid for": Dubost to NFC (I).

Lisette Lanvin and Henri Decoin: Klaus, *Deutsche Tonfilme,* Vol. 4, 1933, p. 80. Translated by Christa Michel.

"Lisette wore jeans": Dubost to NFC (I).

premiere: Klaus, *Deutsche Tonfilme,* Vol. 4, 1933, p. 79. Translated by Christa Michel.

respectfully reviewed: Film-Kritik, *Film-Kurier,* Mar. 25, 1933.

"Autumn storms": Julie Gilbert, *Opposite Attraction,* p. 121.

After having a farewell drink: Wilder and Karasek, *Et tout le reste est folie,* p. 80.

"We were that happy": Oral History with B. Kaper, AFI, pp. 53–54.

Chapter Five: Vienna

For the domestic cost of *Unsichtbare Gegner (Invisible Opponents)*–Spiegel's film in Vienna–Wolfgang Astelbauer went through the archives of Austria's Chamber of Commerce. Astelbauer also interviewed director Franz Antel (who worked as a voluntary helper on *Invisible Opponents* and introduced Spiegel to Hedwig Kiesler aka Hedy Lamarr) as well as finding information on Pan-Film.

Via The Austrian National Bank, Astelbauer provided essential information regarding a series of decrees released by the federal government of Austria. Concerning the average monthly wage, Astelbauer consulted Vienna's Arbeiterkammer.

Relevant articles included Jan-Christopher Horak's *German Exile Cinema for Film*

History (Vol. 8, No. 4, 1996,) *Mein Film*'s "Zu Schiff in Sievering" and *Mein Film*'s "Berühmte Filmmenschen im Hotel."

Page 33 *"These are the accidents":* Harlan Jacobson, "Big Tusker," *Film Comment* Apr. 1983.

"I got up late that day": SS publicity biography for *Tales of Manhattan,* 1942, Box 2, SSF. Peter Lorre and Oscar Homolka: Ibid.

Josef von Sternberg and Jascha Heifetz: SS to Stephen Youngkin (I), 1983.

"We arrived": Ibid.

Page 34 *"film director":* Meldezettel (police records), address given as Hotel Imperial, Mar. 5, 1933. (See Chapter 1's notes for full details on Meldezettel.)

he lacked a toothbrush: Harlan Jacobson, "Big Tusker," *Film Comment,* Apr. 1983.

Imperial Hotel: Meldezettel (police records), Mar. 5, 1933.

German Exile Cinema: Jan-Christopher Horak, "German Exile Cinema," *Film History,* Vol. 8, No. 4, 1996.

generally assumed: Director Franz Antel to Wolfgang Astelbauer (I), July 3, 1999.

Pan-Film's Leopold Meissner: Details from *Mein Film Buch,* Vienna, 1930.

400,000 and 450,000 Austrian schillings: Chamber of Commerce, Vienna. Under the title "B Austrian Export to Germany," Box 3.173/1, File 3.

the average cost of a picture: Armin Loacker, *Anschluss im 3/4-Takt,* p. 102.

"all the right elements": Kinematograph, Berlin, No. 181, Sep. 19, 1933.

Öl ins Feuer: Ulrich J. Klaus, *Deutsche Tonfilme,* Vol. 4, 1933, p. 200. Translated by Christa Michel.

who shared: Patrick McGilligan, *Fritz Lang,* p. 140.

Page 35 was unenthusiastic: Spiegel to Youngkin (I) 1983.

changed his name: Cargnelli/Omasta, Lexikon "Aufbruch."

Initially, he had come: Interview with Egon Eis, Cargnelli and Omasta's *Aufbruch ins Ungewisse–Österreichische Filmschaffende in der Emigration vor 1945,* pp. 68–69 (translated by Christa Michel).

For the French version: Klaus, *Deutsche Tonfilme,* p. 200. Translated by Christa Michel.

Sievering Studios: Ibid. and *Mein Film,* Nos. 371, 373, 376, 378.

was either in elegant suit: Set photographs, 1933.

"I was the only one": Rudi Fehr to NFC (I), June 10, 1997.

Page 36 Robert Müller: Armin Loacker, *Anschluss im 3/4-Takt,* p. 149.

(Author's Note–Müller (1877–1940) was one of the great personalities of the Austrian film world. He started in the export division of Pathé. From 1919, he was the director of Nationalfilm and was a member of the board of Sascha Filmindustrie as well as being the vice-president of the union of film financiers in Austria. In 1932, he created his own distribution company.)

"had the aura of a successful producer": Antel to Astelbauer (I).

spotted in Femina: Ibid.

the Döblinger Bad: Ibid.

seen driving around: Fehr to NFC (I).

affair on a train: Antel to Astelbauer (I).

several months before: Richard Brem, "Verletzte Diva," from *Hommage à Hedy Lamarr,* edited by Theo Lighart (published Vienna, 1999), p. 23.

conversion from Judaism to Catholicism: Ibid.

ladies' man: Leonora Hornblow to NFC (I), July 29, 1996.

made a point: Ibid.

Page 37 *"Sam didn't escape"*: Ingo Preminger to NFC (I), Nov. 21, 1996.
left Vienna: SS's Meldezettel, Mar. 5, 1933.
legally permitted: Decrees released by the federal government of Austria, Nov. 1931, Jan.
9, 1932, Mar. 24, 1933.
250,000 Austrian schillings: rate of Austrian schillings to pounds and dollars obtained
from the Österreichische Nationalbank Rechtsabteilung.
the average monthly wage: Rate obtained from the Austrian Arbeiterkammer.
According to Spiegel: Hornblow to NFC (I). (Author's Note–In regard to the Spiegel-
Preminger escape story, I heard many different versions from people such as Rudi
Fehr, Robert Lantz, Mike Nichols, as well as Spiegel himself. I have used Leonora
Hornblow's memory of the affair since her version was the most similar to
Spiegel's.)
Page 38 when Preminger told his version: Hope Preminger to NFC (I), Oct. 14, 1996.
Spiegel and Preminger swore: Hornblow to NFC (I).
abruptly stopped the car: Hope Preminger to NFC (I).
until reaching Paris: Ibid.
"A car is a nuisance": Letter from Peter Viertel to NFC, March 15, 2002.
stayed at the Hotel George V: Paulette Dubost to NFC (I), Nov. 14, 1999.
since Seymour Nebenzahl: All details of production from Jim Kline, *The Complete Films
of Buster Keaton,* pp. 150–51.
Spiegel did errands: Andrew Sinclair, *Spiegel,* p. 23.
"Sam was a social friend": Harold Nebenzal to NFC (I), May 12, 1998.
having just fled the Nazis: Laurence Evans to NFC (I), Mar. 24, 1996.

Chapter Six: London

Spiegel's early years in London are best documented by the London Metropolitan
Police files, held at the London Metropolitan Archives, and the files from the Ministère
de L'Intérieur, Paris. The Paul Kohner collection at the Stiftung Deutsche Kinemathek–
SDK, was another source. Other documents about *The Invader* are probably now
available via Adrian Brunel's Collection at the BFI (the British Film Institute). (When
I was researching this chapter, Brunel's papers had not been sorted.) Regarding *The
Invader,* Kevin Brownlow kindly gave me use of his yet unpublished biography of Buster
Keaton–his few pages provided invaluable information.

Important articles included the *Kinematograph*'s "Sam Spiegel Remanded" and "Sam
Spiegel for Trial."

Page 39 Joseph Jay "J.J." Bamberger: Laurence Evans to NFC (I), Mar. 24, 1996.
Mount Royal: Kevin Brownlow, *David Lean,* p. 108.
Page 40 *"dangerous in taxis"*: Angela Fox to NFC (I), Mar. 11, 1996.
"particularly lipstick": Ibid.
"Pempy was patrician-looking": Evans to NFC (I).
He barreled into: Details from letter to NFC from Curt Siodmak, Apr. 8, 1998.
"package deal": Oral History with B. Kaper, AFI, p. 67.
"He was unbelievable": Ibid.
Page 41 Not only did he sell her: Juliet Nissen to NFC (I), Oct. 10, 1998.
"But it was no good": Ibid.
"Spiegel's stepping-stone": Fox to NFC (I).

"Kathleen was a staunch supporter": Evans to NFC (I).

adventuress: Details provided by Derry Moore to NFC (I), Oct. 9, 1998. (Moore was the grandson of Kathleen, Countess of Drogheda).

meeting point: Evans to NFC (I).

love of her life: Moore to NFC (I).

"he's a bounder": Ibid.

"make things happen": Aileen Mehle to NFC (I), Oct. 7, 1996.

Page 42 *"Sam just had"*: Evans to NFC (I).

chose Lupita Tovar: Letter from A. E. Vere Barker Connies Ltd. to British and Continental Productions Ltd., Sep. 25, 1934, PK SDK.

cost around $120,000: Lupita Tovar Kohner to NFC (I), Nov. 19, 1996.

"films that ran smoothly": Adrian Brunel, *Nice Work*, p. 176.

£12,000 salary: Thomas A. Dardis, *The Man Who Wouldn't Lie Down*, p. 238.

DON'T LET HIM: Ibid. p. 238.

Page 43 Keaton was paying: Interview with camera operator Eric Cross from Kevin Brownlow's Keaton manuscript, p. 169A.

pneumatic drill: Brunel, *Nice Work*, p. 178.

"much time and money": Ibid., p. 177.

she was always paid: Lupita Tovar Kohner to NFC (I).

rejected for its brevity: Brunel, *Nice Work*, p. 177.

picking up the tab: Lupita Tovar Kohner to NFC (I).

John Berry offered: John Berry to NFC (I), Feb. 18, 1998.

Page 44 hot water: ps/mar/al/131, Register, Part 1 (Mar. 10 and 12, 1936), London Metropolitan Archives.

apartment at Cumberland House: Ibid.

"taxi at his own expense": *Kinematograph*, Mar. 4, 1936.

"I always heard": John Frankenheimer to NFC (I), Mar. 19, 1998.

two shillings: *Kinematograph*, Mar. 12, 1936.

"She had the house": Budd Schulberg to NFC (I), Nov. 26, 1996.

Page 45 Ivan E. Snell: Ps/mar/al/131, Register, Part 1 (Mar. 17, 1936), London Metropolitan Archives.

two entire pages: Ibid.

Edmund J. Curbertson: Ibid.

Central Criminal Court: *Kinematograph*, Apr. 9, 1936.

"Sam stood": Evans to NFC (I).

his third imprisonment: Letter from Laurent Buisson, Ministère de L'Intériéur, France, to NFC, Dec. 9, 1998.

New Scotland Yard: Ibid.

"no account": Ibid.

Chapter Seven: Paris/Mexico

Regarding Spiegel's professional life in Paris in the mid-1930s, the precious few documents that exist are held by the Ministère de L'Intérieur in Paris and are unavailable to the public. As a result, I am indebted to the ministry's Laurent Buisson for delving into this source and writing me an extremely detailed description of everything that he found. I also have to thank the late Claude Beylie, an expert on Yves

Mirande and Universal's Chris Horak for sharing his notes on Spiegel and introducing me to *Pems Persoenliche Berichte (Pem's Personal Bulletins),* which was a newsletter written for the entertainment industry by Paul Marcus (Pem).

Regarding documents, again Paul Kohner's collection at SDK was helpful, and also the three-page memorandum from the Textual Archives Services Division about the Mexican theatrical troupe working with Spiegel. I also went through UCLA's Twentieth Century-Fox archives for *Tales of Manhattan* that mentioned Spiegel's Mexican activities (TCF UCLA). Curiously, Spiegel kept two documents from this period, perhaps because they were written in Spanish! They were two letters from the Mexican government concerning his immigration problems.

A special mention to Eric Le Roy's "Romain Pinès ou L'Itinéraire d'un Producteur Racé," *Archives,* No. 73, Dec. 1997 (Institut Jean Vigo–Pempliman SP, Paris).

Page 47 "*I have always*": Said to Lilou Grumbach. Lilou Grumbach to NFC (I), June 2, 1998.

"*Sam was very sure of himself*": Irene Heymann to NFC (I), Nov. 12, 1996. (Although Heymann became Paul Kohner's trusted assistant in Hollywood, she first met Spiegel when she lived in London in the 1930s and was working for the producer Joe May.)

"*It was full*": Hélène Rochas to NFC (I), May 14, 1998.

Page 48 inner circle: Harold Nebenzal to NFC (I), May 12, 1998.

really Rachmiel-Betsalel: Eric Le Roy, "Romain Pinès ou L'Itinéraire d'un Producteur Racé," *Archives,* No. 73, Dec. 1997, p. 23.

"*They played*": Harold Nebenzal to NFC (I).

"*There was never*": Paul Albou to NFC (I), June 11, 1999.

"*When we cashed it in*": Andrew Sinclair, *Spiegel,* p. 27.

confuse the circumstances: Ann E. Pennington to NFC (I), Apr. 22, 1999.

elaborate announcements: *Pems,* Apr. 14, 1936.

left for South America: *Pems,* 24, Oct. 15, 1936. (Eight days later, on Oct. 23, *Pems* also announced that Spiegel was going to the U.S. In fact he only went to South America. Marking this event, he sent a South American doll to Paul Kohner's daughter–the future actress Susan Kohner–when she was born on Nov. 11, 1936. Details from SDK.)

film company with Yves Mirande: Letter from Laurent Buisson, Ministère de L'Intérieur to NFC, Dec. 9, 1998.

Page 49 he was as well known: Claude Beylie to NFC (I), July 23, 1999.

Terrible with money: Ibid.

"*as drunk as the Polish*": Yves Mirande, *Souvenirs,* p. 174.

Derrière La Façade: Pems 65, July 28, 1937.

Paulette Dubost claimed: To NFC (I).

Max Kolpé: All these film details from *Pems* 64, 67, 71, July 21, Aug. 11, Sep. 8, 1937.

withdrawn the funds: Norton Mockridge, USA, Nov. 11, 1954, SSF.

Alexander Granowsky's reputation: Oral history with B. Kaper, AFI, p. 60.

fifty-franc fine: Letter from Laurent Buisson, Ministère de L'Intérieur, to NFC, Dec. 9, 1998.

Page 50 "*Beforehand, Sam:* Nebenzal to NFC (I).

"*He said to*": Oral history with B. Kaper, AFI, p. 65.

"*all these characters*": Nebenzal to NFC (I).

April 15, 1938: Letter from Laurent Buisson, Ministère de L'Intérieur, to NFC, Dec. 9, 1998.

The French police: Ibid.

problems with the Italian: *Pems* 92, Feb. 3, 1938.

and Swiss authorities: Letter to SS from Louise Rosenthal, Apr. 4, 1949, SSF. (Rosenthal was the widow of Richard Rosenthal of Emelka Films, Zurich, who had lent Spiegel 400 Swiss francs as well as "doing other things that I don't want to mention." Spiegel was also reported by *Pems* as being helped by Mr. Weissman, a successful film distributor in Switzerland.)

letter to Paul Kohner: From SS to Kohner, Feb. 1, 1938, PK SDK.

"You expected": Lupita Tovar Kohner to NFC (I).

Page 51 impresario who engaged: Letter from Joe Mullen, Fox Film de México, to Murray Silverstone, Fox New York, June 24, 1943, TCF UCLA.

struck up with: Andrew Sinclair, *Spiegel*, p. 27.

had an office: Statement from J. M. Sánchez, June 19, 1943, TCF UCLA.

Spiegel returned it: Letter from E. Kilroe, Fox, to George Wasson, Fox, July 13, 1943, TCF UCLA.

he signed a statement: From SS to George Wasson, Aug. 10, 1943, TCF UCLA.

"If I hadn't": Peter Viertel to NFC, Apr. 26, 1997.

"lamp shade": Kathleen Parrish to NFC, Oct. 5, 1996.

"He would prefer": Betty Spiegel to NFC (I), Oct. 12, 1996.

American naturalization: Letter from Edward O'Connor to SS, Dec. 30, 1945, SSF.

Page 52 winning the approval: Letter from William V. O'Connor to His Excellency, Earl Warren, Governor of California, Feb. 18, 1943, SSF.

renamed *Mexicana:* SS publicity biography for *Tales of Manhattan*, 1942, Box 2, SSF.

selling point: Letter from William V. O'Connor to His Excellency, Earl Warren, Governor of California, Feb. 18, 1943, SSF.

left all the arrangements: Statement from Department of State, Division of the American Republics, Apr. 7, 1939, Textual Archives Services Visa Division, Record Group 59, Decimal file No. 811.4061/603.

"by a considerable amount": Ibid.

Consul Wormuth: Ibid.

"Mr. Sam Spiegel": Ibid.

still in Mexico City: Permit letter allowing SS to leave the country without a passport from Andrés Lana y Piña, Departamento de Migración, México, Apr. 29, 1939, SSF.

favorable review: SS publicity biography for *We Were Strangers*, 1949, Box 38, SS JF.

"There were": Ibid.

"It wasn't": Lupita Tovar Kohner to NFC (I).

"My grandmother": Judge Raya Dreben to NFC (I), June 27, 1996.

Page 53 St. Regis Hotel: Details from Sam Spiegel's statement, "(9. My last place of foreign residence)," when filing for a Petition for Naturalization, Nov. 2, 1949, SSF.

Mexican immigration: Letter giving three months extended validity of the previous letter dated April 2, 1929, from Francisco Trejo, Departamento de Migración, May 3, 1939 SSF.

"indefinite nationality": Ibid.

swam across the Rio Grande: Rudi Fehr to NFC (I), June 10, 1997, and *Los Angeles Citizen* newspaper, Dec. 8, 1943.

Naturally, he insisted: Details from Sam Spiegel's Statement, "(10. I emigrated to the United States from)" when filing for a Petition for Naturalization, Nov. 2, 1949, SSF.

Gore Vidal offered: To NFC (I), Dec. 29, 1996.

Chapter Eight: Hollywood

Regarding Spiegel's Hollywood period, Box 1 TT at the Sam Spiegel Foundation (SSF) was a vital source.

Page 57 *An Old Spanish Custom:* Jim Kline, *The Complete Films of Buster Keaton*, p. 153.

"I don't think": de Cordova to NFC (I), Apr. 3, 1996.

"I remember": Norman Lloyd to NFC (I), Nov. 18, 1996.

Page 58 *"we would have bet":* Leonora Hornblow to NFC (I), July 29, 1996.

Billy Wilder's opinion: Billy Wilder and Helmut Karasek, *Et Tout le Reste Est Folie*, p. 196.

"the slight butt": Letter from L. P. Bachmann to NFC, Oct. 9, 1998.

"He was like": Jean Howard to NFC (I), Apr. 3, 1996.

"Sam had to swallow": Lupita Tovar Kohner to NFC (I), Nov. 19, 1996.

"the land of nod": Expression used by Clifton Webb's mother, repeated by Richard Gully to NFC (I), Jan. 26, 1999. (Gully, a society columnist for the magazine *Beverly Hills 213*, had been Jack Warner's special assistant during Hollywood's golden era.)

Page 59 *"If people were":* Evelyn Keyes to NFC (I), Nov. 11, 1996.

7655 Hollywood Boulevard: Melanie Wyler to NFC (I), Apr. 10, 1996.

"Not even a picturesque attic": SS publicity biography for *We Were Strangers*, 1949, Box 38, SS JF.

"Sam was always": Melanie Wyler to NFC (I).

Page 60 *"Our signature":* Wilder and Karasek, *Et Tout le Reste Est Folie*, p. 196.

Meanwhile, on his travels: Ibid.

"Dear Mr. Sam Spiegel": Letter from Paul Kohner to SS, Oct. 14, 1939, PK SDK.

"He was the only one": Peter Viertel to NFC (I), Apr. 26, 1997.

Page 61 *"It was the three":* Name withheld.

"Said" because Litvak: Letter from Peter Viertel to NFC, Mar. 15, 2002.

a booth at Ciro's: Wilder and Karasek *Et Tout le Reste Est Folie*, pp. 201–2.

"Billy (Wilder) said": Lupita Kohner to NFC (I).

"Do you really": Wilder and Karasek's *Et Tout le Reste*, p. 369.

"Is it still": Ibid.

"My sister and I": Catherine Wyler to NFC (I), Apr. 7 1996.

Page 62 *"Somehow, it was":* Susan Kohner Weitz to NFC (I), July 23, 1996.

"We would have": Lupita Kohner to NFC (I).

"As with my father": Susan Kohner Weitz to NFC (I).

"Zanuck used to": John Aspinall to NFC (I), Oct. 30, 1997.

"It was a friendly": Kitty Carlisle Hart to NFC (I), July 1, 1996.

"I once heard": Yolande Fox to NFC (I), July 14, 1999.

Page 63 a popular figure: Matty Fox's obituary in *Variety,* June 3, 1964.

the Colony and Goldie's: Peter Viertel to NFC (I), Apr. 25, 1997.

Morton Garbus: Stanley Myer to NFC (I), July 14, 1999. (Myer's mother was Matty Fox's first cousin and the daughter of Nathan J. Blumberg, one of the presidents of Universal Studios.)

"It was Sam's": Betty Spiegel to NFC (I), July 24, 1998.

"like the Paulette Goddard story": Yolande Fox to NFC (I).

in his underwear: Myer to NFC (I).

Mrs. Greenthal arrived: Ibid.

"It was amazing": Viertel to NFC (I), Apr. 26, 1997.

"looking great in": Joan Axelrod to NFC (I), Nov. 16, 1996.

"everyone": Ibid.

"naughty": Ibid.

"Peter was a womanizer": Ibid.

"Tolstoy-like": Ibid.

"Her Sundays": B. Kaper, Oral History, AFI, p. 151.

Held at her home: Details from Isaac Stern to NFC (I), July 3, 1998.

dismissive of anything American: Viertel to NFC (I), Apr. 26, 1997.

Page 64 *"only place"*: Wilder and Karasek, *Et Tout le Reste Est Folie,* p. 118.

"My mother": Viertel to NFC (I), Apr. 27, 1997.

"G" or "Miss G": Betty Estevez to NFC (I), Apr. 9, 1999.

"The big bond": Viertel to NFC (I), Apr. 26, 1997.

Monet on a wall: Norman Lloyd to NFC (I), Nov. 18, 1996.

"Financially, Sam was": Max Youngstein to NFC (I), Nov. 15, 1996.

"Others like Zanuck": Leonora Hornblow to NFC (I).

    To finance his divorce with his first wife, Edward G. Robinson had to sell his much-treasured Cézannes. The paintings are now part of the acclaimed Stavros Niarchos art collection (the late Greek shipping owner).

"Figures speak": Letter from SS to Robinson, Sep. 10, 1946, Box 1, TT SSF.

"Once more": Letter from SS to Robinson, Aug. 12, 1965, SSF. (Written after SS saw *The Cincinnati Kid,* SSF.)

"like most of that ilk": Sam Goldwyn, Jr., to NFC (I), Nov. 13, 1996.

Page 65 *"to be court-martialed"*: Norman Lloyd to NFC (I).

"He was a little heavy": Ray Stark to NFC (I), Nov. 21, 1996.

"Maybe he danced": Betsy Blair to NFC (I), Oct. 28, 1997.

Chapter Nine: Tales of Manhattan

Spiegel only kept letters that referred to his first Hollywood film, from the 1950s and 1960s. (Most are in Box 2, headed "Miscellaneous," at the Sam Spiegel Foundation.) However, *Tales of Manhattan* is well documented in two collections–the late agent Charles K. Feldman's correspondence (File No. 1793) at the Louis B. Mayer Library, AFI (Feldman, who then owned Famous Artists Agency, represented Spiegel and his partner, Boris Morros), and the Twentieth Century-Fox collection at UCLA, Special Collections. USC also has articles concerning the film, since it holds Edward G. Robinson's collection as well as Boris Leven's–the film's co–art director. Unfortunately, the Newberry Library in Chicago, which houses Ben Hecht's collection, has no correspondence concerning this film.

    Relevant articles included Lenny Borger's "Genius is just a word"–his article about

Julien Duvivier for *Sight and Sound* (Sep. 1998), and Chris Horak's article "German Exile Cinema, 1933–1950" for *Film History* (Vol. 8, No. 4, 1996).

Page 67 under the guise: Letter from SS to Paul Kohner, Mar. 4, 1940, PK SDK.

Ghost Music: Letter from Paul Kohner to Billy Wilder, Jacques Thery, and SS, Oct. 23, 1939, PK SDK.

Barber of Seville: Letter from SS to Paul Kohner, Mar. 4, 1940, PK SDK.

Martha: Ibid.

to Bing Crosby: Letter from Paul Kohner to Wilder, Thery, and SS, Oct. 23, 1939, PK SDK.

St. Petersburg in 1895: Allen Weinstein and Alexander Vassiliev, *The Haunted Wood*, p. 110.

Soviet Union's longest-serving spy: Ibid., p. 112.

Page 68 *"He looked like":* Ingo Preminger to NFC (I), Nov. 21, 1996.

"a characterization of how Europeans": Max Youngstein to NFC (I), Nov. 15, 1996.

vast garnet crucifix: Ibid.

"we are the spiritzel-type man": Andrew Sinclair, *Spiegel*, p. 32.

for eighteen years: Weinstein and Vassiliev, *The Haunted Wood*, p. 112.

"contemporary composers": Ibid., p. 118.

"When I am breaking my neck": SS publicity biography for *Tales of Manhattan*, 1942, Box 2, SSF.

Tails of New York: Los Angeles Examiner, Jan. 20, 1941, USC.

August 1941: Interoffice Correspondence from Ned Marin to Charles K. Feldman, Aug. 26, 1941, CKF AFI.

"We have no desire": Letter from Paramount's Y. F. Freeman to Fox's Joe Schenck, Dec. 15, 1941, TCF UCLA.

Page 69 *"I proposed showing":* Max Youngstein to NFC (I).

borrowing gas money: Harlan Jacobson, "Big Tusker," *Film Comment,* Apr. 1983.

"himself S. P. Eagle": Louis Jourdan to NFC (I), Apr. 3, 1996.

had added Oliver: David Thomson, *Showman*, p. 41.

"predicted" that his career: Youngstein to NFC (I).

"My German name": Sinclair, *Spiegel*, p. 1.

it was an alias: Letter from Laurent Buisson, Ministère de L'Intérieur, to NFC, Dec. 9, 1998.

"Look at everyone's name": Leonora Hornblow to NFC (I), July 29, 1996.

Page 70 *"You're going to have":* Ben Hecht, *A Child of the Century*, p. 520.

"around with their grief": Ibid.

attention of E. A. Gull: Youngstein to NFC (I).

Wilder and Selznick: Ibid.

"Can I speak": Ahmet Ertegun to NFC (I), Feb. 6, 1999.

renegotiating with Paramount: Interoffice correspondence from Marin to Feldman, Aug. 27, 1941, CKF AFI.

$860,000: Finalized deal with Fox, approved by William Goetz, Sep. 5, 1941, CKF AFI.

"Morros was legitimate": Max Youngstein to NFC (I).

Page 71 clients such as: Feldman obituary, *Weekly Variety,* May 29, 1968. (Feldman died of cancer on May 25, 1968.)

"He helped his clients": Whitney Stine, *Stars and Star Handlers*, p. 189.

lifelong Spiegel intimate: In Feldman's will, as "a token of their friendship" he left Spiegel a Chinese terra cotta (Tang) of a horse with a long body and the figure of a girl on a horse, *Weekly Variety*, July 24, 1968.

Initially, William Wyler: Notes of meeting with CKF, Boyer, and SS, Aug. 8, 1941, CKF AFI.

"Daddy really loved Sam": Melanie Wyler to NFC (I), Apr. 10, 1996.

highest paid at $50,000: Fox's contract letter with SS and Morros, Sep. 5, 1941, TCF UCLA.

"Apparently, my father": Bill Hayward to NFC (I), Feb. 9, 1998.

"a friend from way back": Ginger Rogers, *Ginger*, p. 242.

"the Toscanini of the telephone": Hayward to NFC (I).

went to Fleito: Hornblow to NFC (I). (When Leland Hayward died, Hornblow was given the cigarette case by Pamela, his widow, who then became Mrs. W. Averell Harriman.)

Page 72 *"We insisted"*: Wilder and Karasek, *Et Tout le Reste Est Folie*, p. 197.

Wilder strictly forbade: Jan-Christopher Horak, "German Exile Cinema," *Film History*, Vol. 8, No. 4, 1996, p. 385.

Page 73 *"They went a day over"*: Barbara Leaming, *If This Was Happiness*, p. 68.

Originally, Romero: "Actors Are People" by Morros and SS, Twelfth Anniversary Edition, *Hollywood Reporter*, Vol. 70, No. 31, Section 2.

"My father was": Christian Duvivier to NFC (I), Nov. 1 1997.

Director Malcolm St. Clair: American Film Institute Catalogue volume 2, p. 2425.

Page 74 Tyrone Power: Interoffice correspondence from Marin to CKF, Mar. 14, 1942, CKF AFI.

"particularly despondent": *New York Times*, Sep. 23, 1942.

"There wasn't one day": Christian Duvivier to NFC (I).

escorting Carole Landis: Harry Crocker, "Behind the Makeup," Undated 1942, Box 40:6, USC.

"Because we believe": "Actors Are People" by Morros and SS.

Page 75 on August 5, 1942: American Film Institute Catalogue, Vol. 2, *Tales of Manhattan*.

"He and his friends": Betty Spiegel to NFC (I), Oct. 12, 1996.

teleguided torpedo: "Hedy Lamarr," *Stars and Stripes*, Nov. 19, 1946.

"You boys will be able": Fox's Murray Silverstone to SS and Morros, May 5, 1943, TCF UCLA.

"riveted by its variety": *New York Times*, Oct. 4, 1942.

"continental flavor": Letter from Morros and SS to Fox's Spyros Skouras, Feb. 27, 1943. TCF UCLA.

"a distinct asset": Ibid.

Officially, it was dissolved: Letter from Morros to Fox's W. J. Eadie, Sep. 7, 1943, TCF UCLA.

"They came apart": Jules Buck to NFC (I), June 13, 1997.

Morros kept: *The Snow Is Red*: Louella O. Parsons, *Los Angeles Examiner*, Aug. 27, 1943.

Page 76 Neither continued: *Los Angeles Examiner*, Apr. 1, 1942.

"Please remember": Letter from Morros to SS, Aug. 9, 1954, SSF.

unscathed during the McCarthy era: Weinstein and Vassiliev, *The Haunted Wood*, p. 125.

Cardinal Spellman: Ibid., p. 129.

"He had that side": Jules Buck to NFC (I), June 13, 1997.

"velvet octopus arms": Billy Wilder's term for SS. Norman Spencer to NFC (I), Oct. 29, 1997.

"Sam always knew": Joan Axelrod to NFC (I), Nov. 16, 1996.

"He [Rheiner] knew where": Rachel Chodorov to NFC (I), Oct. 15, 1996.

"Sam used to beat": Albert Heit to NFC (I), Oct. 10, 1996.

"Spiegel would be playing cards": Ibid.

Page 77 *"I know that you are"*: Letter from Morros to Fox's Skouras, Feb. 25, 1943, TCF UCLA.

"It's difficult to explain": Jules Buck to NFC (I).

"I warned him": Max Youngstein to NFC (I).

Chapter Ten: North Crescent Drive

Once again, BOX 1 TT at the Sam Spiegel Foundation (SSF) proved to be invaluable. *The Los Angeles Examiner* archives–from the USC Cinema and Television library–were also a relevant source.

Page 79 Devil: Details from Hollywood dog training school certificate, Feb. 17, 1943, Box 1, TT SSF.

$1,500 a month: Details from "Film Producer Sued by Wife," *Los Angeles Examiner,* May 11, 1943.

"Don't worry dear": *Los Angeles Examiner,* May 21, 1943.

took his estranged wife's hand: Ibid.

Page 80 had advised him: Letter from Morton Garbus at Simon & Garbus, to SS, Mar. 3, 1943, Box 1, TT SSF.

pushing his luck: "Houser Opposes Pardon for Film Producer Spiegel," *Los Angeles Times,* Dec. 8, 1943. (Spiegel was arrested on July 5, 1942.)

had still not been settled: Letter from Edward O'Connor to SS, Nov. 2, 1949, Box 1, TT SSF.

"The only thing": William V. O'Connor to NFC (I), Oct. 10, 1996.

Page 81 *"Since 1928 the applicant"*: Letter from E. O'Connor to Earl Warren, Feb. 18, 1943, Box 1, TT SSF.

calmed people: Letter from E. O'Connor to Ben Odell, Nov. 19, 1943, Box 1, TT SSF.

"I know him to be": Letter from J. Breen to Advisory Pardon Board, Dec. 2, 1943, Box 1, TT SSF.

"I do not think": "Houser Opposes Pardon for Film Producer Spiegel," *Los Angeles Times,* Dec. 8, 1943.

"expunged my record.": Letter from SS to Murray Chotiner, Jan. 21, 1944, Box 1, TT SSF.

"his excellent connections": Letter from Paul Kohner to Attorney General Biddle, May 26, 1942, PK SDK.

Page 82 *"To my best boyfriend"*: Letter from Alisa Spiegel to SS, Nov. 11, 1943, Box 1, TT SSF.

"Since this is": Letter from SS to Regina Spiegel, Dec. 22, 1943, Box 1, TT SSF.

"She was rather shy": Lupita Tovar Kohner to NFC (I), Nov. 19, 1996.

dressed Spiegel down: Budd Schulberg to NFC (I), Nov. 26, 1996.

Page 83 *"Suddenly, he was"*: Norman Lloyd to NFC (I), Nov. 18, 1996.

"Please keep on": Letter from SS to Alisa Spiegel, May 12, 1945, Box 1, TT SSF.

"The idea of going": Letter from SS to Alisa Spiegel, Aug. 2, 1944, Box 1, TT SSF.

"Haven't received": Letter from Alisa Spiegel to SS, Aug. 9, 1944, Box 1, TT SSF.

"If you're not happy": Letter from SS to Alisa Spiegel Freedman, Apr. 17, 1946, Box 1, TT, SSF.

Page 84 *"He couldn't bear":* Judge Raya Dreben to NFC (I), June 27, 1996.

"My grandfather": Ellen Weisbord to NFC (I), Nov. 19, 1997.

not father material: Adam Spiegel to NFC (I), Dec. 22, 1996.

"Sam was my favorite": Dreben to NFC (I).

"Like many people": Joan Axelrod to NFC (I), Nov. 16, 1996.

"He was the": Arthur Miller to NFC (I), Nov. 6, 1996.

"He sent his clothes": Jules Buck to NFC (I), June 13, 1997.

Page 85 "boy's town": Ibid.

belonged to Jackie Cooper: Ibid.

"Why is it": Leonora Hornblow to NFC (I), July 29, 1996.

"The maid said": Buck to NFC (I).

from Forst's: Letter from Forst's to SS, July 15, 1947, Box 1, TT SSF.

Bear Creek Orchards: Letter from Bear Creek Orchards to SS, Mar. 11, 1946, Box 1, TT SSF.

Bottle and Spice and Everything Nice: Bill, Sep. 30, 1947, Box 1, TT SSF.

"No Pepsis or Cokes": Kazan, *A Life,* p. 514.

Caroline Veiller: Caroline Veiller to NFC (I), June 12, 1997.

Page 86 Ed and Mae Laffin: Letter of recommendation by SS, June 17, 1949, Box 1, TT SSF.

Lily Mae Hendricks: Letter of recommendation by SS, Mar. 27, 1946, Box 1, TT SSF.

"He wasn't surprised": Evelyn Keyes, *Scarlett O'Hara's Younger Sister,* p. 144.

the prostitutes: Leaming, *If This Was Happiness,* p. 120.

"What I immediately noticed": Evelyn Keyes to NFC (I), Nov. 11, 1996.

Page 87 the second character witness: SS's application for petition for naturalization, Nov. 2, 1949, Box 1, TT SSF.

"Sam really knew": Schulberg to NFC (I).

"disposal any afternoon": Kazan, *A Life,* p. 514.

"I think it was": Name withheld.

"I was having": Name withheld.

"I don't know": Buck to NFC (I).

"very silken": Schulberg to NFC (I).

Page 88 the first official New Year's Eve: Invitation sent to Paul Kohner, PK SDK.

"It was a good party": Hornblow to NFC (I).

guests included: Names taken from *Life* magazine, Jan. 17, 1949.

"It was the first time": Lauren Bacall to NFC (I), June 25, 1996.

Supposedly, Spiegel turned him down: Jud Kinberg to NFC (I), Nov. 13, 1996.

"None of us had been": Betsy Blair to NFC (I), Oct. 28, 1997.

"Then, just before midnight": Ray Stark to NFC (I), Nov. 21, 1996.

Page 89 *"fighting and fucking":* Eric Ambler (Joan Harrison's husband) to NFC (I), Sep. 10, 1997.

"I admire your ability": Buck to NFC (I).

"with the exception": Mike Todd, Jr., *A Valuable Property,* p. 163.

"sneak off": Leaming, *If This Was Happiness,* p. 125.

Page 90 *"That was him":* Wilder and Karasek, *Et tout le reste est folie,* p. 363.

"After his parties": Hornblow to NFC (I).

"Sam was always": Repeated by Norman Lloyd to NFC (I).

Chapter Eleven: The Stranger

Regarding this film, Spiegel only kept a few letters (including a heated correspondence in the 1970s between his office and Mary Trivas, the widow of Victor Trivas), which are held at The Jerusalem Foundation in the Box Series No. 2 under the heading "Miscellaneous." However, he did keep *The Stranger*'s production notes, which served as an important source. I also went through the correspondence of Anthony Veiller (AV), a client at the Paul Kohner Agency (PKA). Other primary research sources included Edward G. Robinson's collection (EGR USC), Universal Pictures's contract talent reports from the Universal Collection (U USC), and John Huston's collection at the Margaret Herrick Library (JH AMPAS).

Page 91 The S. T. Ranger: B. Kaper, Oral History, AFI, p. 189.

Daniel Fuchs: Article by Daniel Fuchs, *Film Commentary,* July 1988.

The Grand Street Boys: Letter from SS to Joseph M. Schenck, delivered to the *Super Chief,* July 2, 1943, Box 2, SS JF.

"in default under the terms": Letter from Leon Kaplan to SS, Nov. 5, 1943, Box 2, SS JF.

Geschichten: Information taken from Armin Loacker's *Die Österreichische Filmwirtschaft von den Anfangen bis zur Einfuhrung des Tonfilms,* p. 88. (In: Maske +Kothurn, 39.Jg., Heft 4, Wien/Koln/Weimar 1998)

June 18, 1941: Letter from Gladys Hill to SS, June 18, 1947, Box 1, TT SSF.

Page 92 *"outstanding member":* Taken from Harry Hill's obituary, Oct. 11, 1968, Box 1, TT SSF.

"was distressed": Letter from G. Hill to J. D. Goodman, Arrowhead Springs Hotel, Sep. 3, 1946, Box 1, TT SSF.

"She was of medium height": Irene Heymann to NFC (I), Nov. 12, 1996.

"a kind of police dog": Peter Viertel to NFC (I), Apr. 25, 1997.

same sort of rumor: Joan Axelrod to NFC (I), Nov. 16, 1996.

"paternalistic stance": Article by Daniel Fuchs, *Film Commentary,* July 1988.

Page 93 hence the secrecy: John Huston, *Open Book,* p. 205.

unable to take credit: Letter contract between Veiller and Huston and SS, Mar. 1, 1945, AV PKA.

taken the theme: Details from Trivas contract, May 1, 1944, Box 2, SS JF.

Page 94 $30,000 in cash: Contract between Veiller and Huston and SS, Mar. 1, 1945, AV PKA.

further $20,000: Ibid.

was in May 1945: Letter from Anthony Veiller to Mark M. Cohen, Veiller's lawyer, Aug. 28, 1945, AV PKA.

"flatly refused to concede": Ibid.

"originally owned by Sam": Letter from Frank W. Vincent to Edward G. Robinson, July 25, 1945, Box 9:8, EGR USC.

happened on August 9, 1945: Letter from John Beck, Jr., Secretary of Haig Corporation, and SS, Aug. 9 1945, AV PKA.

Page 95 *"a direct flouting":* Letter from Veiller to Mark M. Cohen, Veiller's lawyer, Aug. 28, 1945, AV PKA.

"he was not afraid": Barry Diller to NFC (I), Nov. 12 1996.

"Let him have": Letter from Veiller to Cohen, Mar. 31, 1946; AV PKA.

"As you know": Letter from Mark M. Cohen to SS, Sep. 18, 1946, AV PKA.

Page 96 late September 1945: *The Stranger* production notes, Box 2, SS JF.
"a tense, suspenseful": *Los Angeles Examiner,* July 3, 1946, AMPAS.
the latter shot a scene: *The Stranger* production notes, Box 2, SS JF.
Page 97 *"Tonight he thinks"*: Norman Lloyd to NFC (I), Nov. 18, 1996. (Lloyd was a
member of the Mercury Theatre.)
"intentional": Orson Welles and Peter Bogdanovich, *This Is Orson Welles,* p. 189.
"hovering between": *The New Yorker,* June 29, 1946, AMPAS.
"a smashing crush": Loretta Young to NFC (I), Mar. 4, 1998.
"a star never goes": Peter Viertel to NFC (I), Apr. 27, 1997.
"to surprise": Young to NFC (I), Mar. 4, 1998.
Page 98 *"It is painful"*: *New York Times,* July 14, 1946, AMPAS.
only one of: David Thomson, *Rosebud,* p. 268.
Fifteen months later: Ibid.
"was part of it": Welles and Bogdanovich, *This Is Orson Welles,* p. 187
After Walter Wanger: Contract talent reports of Universal Pictures, U USC.
"Spiegel's foot in the door": Welles and Bogdanovich, *This Is Orson Welles,* p. 187.
Page 99 *"Bill was worried"*: Max Youngstein to NFC (I), Nov. 15, 1996.
"OK, but we need": Welles and Bogdanovich, *This is Orson Welles,* p. 188.
on the insistence: Ibid., p. 186.
"a spinster lady": Ibid., p. 187.

Chapter Twelve: The Second Mrs. Spiegel and Horizon Pictures

Concerning the professional life of Lynne Ruth Baggett—the second Mrs. Sam Spiegel—
the USC Cinema and Television Library provided essential material from the Warner
Bros. collection (WB USC) and also the Universal collection (U USC).

Regarding *We Were Strangers,* Spiegel only kept the production notes of the film and
a few letters. (Like his previous two films, again in Box 2 at the Jerusalem Foundation
as well as Box 1, TT at the Sam Spiegel Foundation in the U.S.) For the early years of
Horizon Pictures, I combed through correspondence at the Paul Kohner Agency, (HP
PKA). Other excellent primary research sources include the Mark M. Cohen collection
(MMC AMPAS) and Douglas Bell's interview with writer Philip Dunne, which is part
of the Margaret Herrick Library's oral history series.

Page 101 *"Sam's Statue of Liberty"*: Peter Viertel to NFC (I), Apr. 26, 1997.
her screen test: *The Stranger* production notes, Nov. 26, 1945, Box 2, SS JF.
"otherworldly": Alain Bernheim to NFC (I), Nov. 14, 1996.
Page 102 *"vain and affected"*: Leonora Hornblow to NFC (I), July 29, 1996.
"very dear in spirit": Joan Axelrod to NFC (I), Nov. 16, 1996.
Born on May 10, 1923: Details from birth certificate sent to NFC from Texas
Department of Health, Apr. 7, 1999.
Hollywood tennis champion: Peter Viertel to NFC (I), Apr. 26, 1997.
discovered her: Lynne Baggett file, WB USC.
Baker Hotel stationery: Ibid.
had to give her consent: Order approving contract of minor for dramatic services, filed
Oct. 15, 1942, WB USC.
lasted three years: Contract terminated Aug. 1, 1945, WB USC.
"The Serpentine Lady": Lynne Baggett file, WB USC.

"Triple-A-Girl": Ibid.

"competent": Norman Lloyd to NFC (I), Nov. 18, 1996. (Lloyd acted with Baggett in Jacques Tourneur's *The Flame and the Arrow.*)

"come hither quality": Peter Viertel to NFC (I), Apr. 26, 1997.

"There was no": Ibid.

Page 103 *"If you were"*: Ivan Moffat to NFC (I), Mar. 29, 1996.

Daily Variety: Aug. 12, 1946.

Hollywood Reporter: Aug. 12, 1946.

brief contract there: Contract talent reports, Universal Pictures, U USC.

"After seeing her": Hornblow to NFC (I).

"Eddie claimed": Fred Zinnemann to NFC (I), Dec. 19, 1996.

her teeth fixed: Lauren Bacall to NFC (I), June 25, 1996.

Page 104 firmly estranged: Letter from Warner's Roy J. Obringer to Robert H. Dietrich, Freston & Files, Aug. 14, 1942, WB USC.

changed her address: Memo about Baggett's new address, Oct. 30, 1944 (a letter from Warner Bros. to Baggett had been "returned to sender."), WB USC.

jewels: letter from M. Reingold to SS, Jan. 18, 1949, Box 1 TT SSF.

mink stole: Letter from SS to Mr. Rosenberg, Ben Cohen Fine Fur, New York, Sep. 20, 1946, Box 1 TT SSF.

"My husband advised": Rosemary Chodorov to NFC (I), Oct. 15, 1996.

"Sam, Kazan, Huston": Bacall to NFC (I).

"If you told Sam": Kathleen Parrish to NFC (I), Oct. 5, 1996.

"the smartest at the table": Jules Buck to NFC (I), June 13, 1997.

"floating in and out": Ibid.

Page 105 *"She was very sweet"*: Arthur Laurents interview, *Backstory* 2, p. 142.

"Misery loves company": Betty Spiegel to NFC (I), Jan. 29, 1999.

THE MARRIAGE: Billy Wilder and Helmut Karasek, *Et Tout le Reste Est Folie,* p. 199.

"never ever wanted": Hornblow to NFC (I).

"I crossed the border": Letter from SS to Alisa Freedman, Sep. 16, 1947, Box 1, TT SSF.

December 8, 1947: Articles of Incorporation, HP PKA.

"The name was taken": Jules Buck to NFC (I).

"chummy little": Peter Viertel to NFC, (I), Mar. 15, 2002.

"At that time": Ibid.

"Shit Creek Productions": Jules Buck to NFC (I).

"Miracle Films": Ibid.

Page 106 *"Sam smelt"*: Peter Viertel to NFC (I), Apr. 27, 1997.

In May 1947: Letter agreement from SS to J. Huston, Oct. 11, 1947, HP PKA.

acquired the funds: Letter from Charles Medcraft to Irwin Margulies (Spiegel's lawyer), Oct. 29, 1954. Box 12, SS JF.

"Huston was a genius": Lauren Bacall to NFC (I).

Jack Warner barred: John Huston, *Open Book,* p. 150.

"the rebel" element: Peter Viertel to NFC (I), Apr. 27, 1997.

"John enjoyed shocking": Ibid.

contract with MGM: Letter agreement from John Huston to Horizon Pictures, Feb. 13, 1950, HP PKA.

Page 107 had initialed his okay: Letter from Mark M. Cohen to John Huston, Jan. 26, 1950, MMC AMPAS.

"John used to say": John Weitz to NFC (I), July 23, 1996.

"their life": Bayard Veiller to NFC (I), Feb. 6, 1998.

"It is the artistic relationship": Box Office, Aug. 30, 1947.

Page 108 *"They put themselves":* Moffat to NFC (I).

"John just wanted you": Evelyn Keyes to NFC (I), Nov. 11, 1996.

"would suddenly cool down": Lawrence Grobel, *The Hustons,* p. 309

"Sam, somehow": Joan Axelrod to NFC (I), Nov. 16, 1996.

"Put fake dog shit": Letter from Joan Juliet Buck to NFC, Aug 27, 1999.

Or when Burt Lancaster: Grobel, *The Hustons,* p. 470.

Page 109 *"The photographer was in Africa":* Arthur Miller to NFC (I), Nov. 6, 1996.

"His son had shot": Ibid.

"there were a lot of games": Keyes to NFC (I).

"Without his shirt": Miller to NFC (I).

"bald as an onion": Huston, *Open Book,* p. 19.

La Fin du Jour: Letter from Paul Kohner to SS, Jan. 3, 1948, PK SDK.

"indefinitely postponed": Letter from SS to Abel Abrahamson, Sep. 11, 1947, Box 1, TT SSF.

"I used to go horseback riding": Peter Viertel to NFC (I), Apr. 27, 1997.

Page 110 *"There was an undeniable logic":* Peter Viertel, *Dangerous Friends,* p. 24.

"Sam felt this will kill": Peter Viertel to NFC (I), Apr. 27, 1997.

"This is what": Philip Dunne, oral history, AMPAS, p. 69.

"The marines come on shore": Peter Viertel to NFC (I), Apr. 27, 1997.

"one of the finest": Huston, *Open Book,* p. 164.

Page 111 *I HOPE THAT BOTH:* Telegram from SS to L. B. Mayer, Feb. 20, 1948, Box 1, TT SSF.

"Baby, I kid you not": Buck to NFC (I).

"Whenever we listened": Peter Viertel to NFC (I), Apr. 27, 1997.

Huston's pet monkey: Ibid.

There was even a story: Sam Goldwyn, Jr., to NFC (I), Nov. 13, 1996.

"Knowing that John": Letter from SS to Peter Viertel, Apr. 29, 1948, Box 2, SS JF.

"Most producers try": Peter Viertel to NFC (I), Apr. 27, 1997.

Page 112 *"pretty frail material":* Huston, *Open Book,* p. 165.

"Sam had written": Peter Viertel to NFC (I), Apr. 27, 1997.

"We were always": Ibid.

Page 113 *"not to flaunt his power":* Viertel, *Dangerous Friends,* p. 53.

realistic hand: Buck to NFC (I).

as had Gilbert Roland: Peter Viertel to NFC (I), Apr. 27, 1997.

had been given expensive jewels: Angela Allen to NFC (I), Feb. 27, 1998.

"foreign": Letter from Peter Viertel to SS, Aug. 12, 1948, Box 2, SSF.

Page 114 *"Everyone likes to save":* Peter Viertel to NFC (I), Apr. 27, 1997.

$5,000: Ben Hecht's contract, Dec. 23, 1948, Box 2, SS JF. Ray Stark, the future producer, was Hecht's agent.

"He was going crazy": Parrish to NFC (I).

which he sensed: Telegram from David O. Selznick to John Huston and SS, Jan. 29, 1949, JH AMPAS.

IN EXACTLY THE SAME LIGHT: Telegram from Selznick to Columbia's Lester Roth, forwarded to SS by Gladys Hill, Feb. 1, 1949, HP PKA. Courtesy of Daniel Selznick.

MR. DEEDS COMES TO TOWN: Ibid.

Havana 33: Telegram from Selznick to Columbia's Harry Cohn, SS, and JH, Feb. 1, 1949, JH AMPAS.

"It is the heaviest dish": Hollywood Reporter, Apr 22, 1949, JH AMPAS

Page 115 *"To draw on Socrates":* Letter from John Huston to Billy Wilkerson, May 10, 1949, JH AMPAS. Courtesy of Bermuda Trust Company Limited, as Trustee of the John Huston Trust.

"If you repeat": Bayard Veiller to NFC (I).

"He said, 'Tell him' ": Robert Parrish, *Growing Up in Hollywood,* p. 198.

$1,496,900: Letter from Columbia's Lester M. Roth to MMC, Oct. 25, 1950, HP PKA.

$1,070,000: Ibid.

"to believe that this picture": Ibid.

four other pictures: Letter from Horizon Pictures to Columbia, Apr. 29, 1949, HP PKA.

court case with the studio: *Columbia Pictures v. Horizon Pictures,* No. 601875, Nov. 13, 1953, HP PKA.

Chapter Thirteen: The Prowler *and* When I Grow Up

Spiegel's professional correspondence about this period is held at The Jerusalem Foundation (JF), Israel. *The Prowler* correspondence is in Box Series 22, while the *When I Grow Up* correspondence is in Box Series 24. In regards to *The Prowler,* other sources include Joseph Losey's Collection at the British Film Institute (JL BFI), the Production Code Administration files (PCA AMPAS), and Sam Jaffe's oral history with Barbara Hall in 1991–both being at the Margaret Herrick Library.

Page 117 *"A young man":* Letter from SS to Alisa Freedman, Feb. 14, 1950, Box 1, TT SSF.

Brecht's *Galileo:* Norman Lloyd, *Stages,* p. 117.

"could be said": Ben Hecht, *A Child of the Century,* p. 543.

sent a joint congratulatory telegram: From SS and Wyler, to Israel Film Studios, July 1, 1949, Box 1, TT SSF.

"[WE] HOPE SOMEDAY": Ibid.

Page 118 welcoming Golda Myerson: Letter from Sam Goldwyn to SS, June 7, 1948, Box 1, TT SSF.

"At the time": Peter Viertel to NFC (I), Apr. 26, 1997.

Hollywood institution: *Life* magazine, Jan. 17, 1949, UCLA.

Errol Flynn: Letter from Gladys Hill to SS, Feb. 9, 1949. Box 1, TT SSF.

Vi and Pandro Berman: Invitation, Dec. 13, 1948, Box 1, TT SSF.

Rosa and Joe Mankiewicz: Invitation, July 9, 1949, Box 1, TT SSF.

Edie and Lew Wasserman: Invitation, Feb. 9, 1950, Box 1, TT SSF.

Noël Coward: Invitation from Leonard Spigelgass for Feb. 13, 1948, Box 1, TT SSF.

Henry Luce: Invitation from James Parton, Time Life Fortune, Dec. 4, 1947, Box 1, TT SSF.

"too many gatecrashers": Los Angeles Examiner, Dec. 29, 1949.

Held at the exclusive: Louella O. Parsons, *Los Angeles Examiner,* Dec. 29, 1949.

"We ran in a pack": Kathleen Parrish to NFC (I), Oct. 5, 1996.

Page 119 *"They started to dance":* Norman Lloyd to NFC (I), Nov. 18, 1996.

"demanding payment": From Horizon Pictures's Jean Rigazzi to SS, Nov. 17, 1949. Box 1, TT SSF.

Oscar Kokoschka's: Bill from the Stendhal Gallery, Feb. 22, 1948, Box 1, TT SSF.

"about a flock": Letter from Sidney Janis Gallery, May 28, 1949, Box 1, TT SSF.

Mrs. Edward G. Robinson: Letter from George Keller, Bignou Gallery, to SS, Nov. 3, 1947. Box 1, TT SSF.

it was the U.S. Marshals: Ivan Moffat to NFC (I), Mar. 29, 1996.

"Baby, the sheriff": Jules Buck to NFC (I), June 13, 1997.

"I like Spiegel": Ibid.

"That was Sam's beauty": Ingo Preminger to NFC (I), Nov. 21, 1996.

Page 120 $452,199.75: Agreement between Eagle Productions and Beneficial Standard Life Insurance Company and I. H. Prinzmetal, July 24, 1950, HP PKA.

"which was the largest": Tino Balio, *United Artists: The Company that Changed the Film Industry*, p. 16.

"a corporation which": Memo from Mark M. Cohen, to Paul Kohner, Jan. 22, 1951, HP PKA.

"Spiegel opened the doors": Ingo Preminger to NFC (I).

"You appealed": Letter from Robert Thoeren to SS, Jan. 5, 1950, MMC AMPAS.

" 'Sam' he says": Ibid.

Page 121 *"Listen, I have a gun"*: Ingo Preminger to NFC (I).

"a wild, unbelievable": Ibid.

an assumed name: Chris Trumbo interview in Griffin Fariello, *Red Scare*, p. 64.

severely reduced salary: Preminger to NFC (I).

"Sam was wonderful": Ibid.

Page 122 *"I only found out"*: Evelyn Keyes to NFC (I), Nov. 11, 1996.

Butler's services: Interview with Jean Rouverol Butler, Butler's widow, from Patrick McGilligan, Paul Buhle and Alison Morley, *Tender Comrades*, p. 165.

preproduction notes: Written by Losey, Feb. 14, 1950, Box 22, SS JF.

build up the characters: Harold Pinter to NFC (I), Jan. 18, 1998. (Pinter wrote the screenplay for Losey's films *The Servant, Accident,* and *The Go-Between*.)

"extremely low moral tone": Letter from Joseph I. Breen to SS, Nov. 2 1949, PCA AMPAS.

Page 123 *"rather than one"*: Ibid.

green light: Letter from Breen to SS, Apr. 5, 1950, Box 22, SS JF.

"He allowed them": Ingo Preminger to NFC (I).

"You always go": *Daily Variety*, Apr. 5, 1950, JL BFI.

"Joe was the complete director": Keyes to NFC (I).

**"Whatta difference"*: *Daily Variety*, June 9, 1950, JL BFI.

Page 124 negative cost: Taken from statement, Feb. 28, 1951, Box 22, SS JF.

suing him: Newspaper clipping, "Publicist Wins $2000 Verdict in Suit Here," Apr. 6, 1953, Box 22, SS JF.

"He was always": Nina Blowitz to NFC (I), Jan. 23, 1999.

optimal advantage: 5360 Melrose Avenue, 650 North Bronson Avenue, and 5255 Clinton Street, Los Angeles, CA 90004, from Anthony Slide, *The New Historical Dictionary of the American Film Industry*.

"Bill just adored Sam": Nina Blowitz to NFC (I), Jan. 23, 1999.

As a result: Ivan Moffat to NFC (I), Mar. 29, 1996.

continued to bounce: Sam Jaffe, oral history, pp. 278–79, AMPAS.

still owed: Jud Kinberg to NFC (I), June 7, 1999. .

Page 125 *"an extraordinarily persuasive"*: *Los Angeles Times,* June 4, 1951, Box 22, SS JF.

"Without Spiegel": Ingo Preminger to NFC (I).

"that specialized in the": Tino Balio, *United Artists*, p. 16.

"Sam was the first": Max Youngstein to NFC (I), Nov. 15, 1996.

"One day Sam": Jules Buck to NFC (I), June 13, 1997.

"He sits there": Norman Lloyd to NFC (I), Nov. 18, 1996.

"was dying to talk": Ibid.

"[They] were lawyers": Albert Heit to NFC (I), Feb. 4, 1999.

Page 126 so associated: *Rina M. Kravetz v. United Artists (Arthur B. Krim, Robert S. Benjamin, Seymour M. Peyser, Matthew Fox, William Heinemann, Max Youngstein, Samuel Spiegel)* July 6, 1953. Also a letter from United Artists's Walter S. Beck to Heit, Apr. 24, 1957, Box 12, SS JF.

"the producers are creators": Youngstein to NFC (I).

"This was the plan": Balio, *United Artists*, p. 42.

stalled *The Prowler:* Letter from SS to Robert Benjamin, United Artists, Dec. 10, 1953, Box 6, SS JF.

Page 127 *"their most successful"*: Letter from John Huston to Mark Cohen and Paul Kohner, dated Jan. 6, 1951, but actually 1952, HP PKA.

bought out Eagle-Lion: Tino Balio, *United Artists*, p. 45.

"It was": Fay Kanin to NFC (I), Jan. 21, 1999.

When I Throw Up: Peter Viertel to NFC (I), Apr. 27, 1999.

rewrite and artistically supervise: Contract for Huston, Nov. 29, 1950, Box 24, SS JF.

"I'm quite proud": Letter from Alisa Freedman to SS, May 27, 1950, Box 1, TT SSF.

too long: *Motion Picture Daily,* Apr. 13, 1951, PCA AMPAS.

Page 128 only cost $459,932.16: Statement for cost of production, Mar. 24, 1951, Box 24, SS JF.

plagued the Horizon office: Letter from I. H. Prinzmetal to Mark M. Cohen, Nov. 3, 1952, HP PKA.

Chapter Fourteen: The African Queen

Most of Spiegel's correspondence about *The African Queen* can be found in Box Series 12 at The Jerusalem Foundation.

Page 129 *"It will give"*: Lillian Ross, *Picture,* p. 70.

Columbia purchased the rights: Peter Viertel to NFC (I), Apr. 26, 1997.

John Collier: Ibid.

Page 130 *"Everything swings"*: Katharine Hepburn, *The Making of The African Queen,* p. 16.

"'the Garbo": Dr. Kevin Gough Yates to NFC (I), Jan. 2 1999.

"You are unique": Hepburn, *The Making of The African Queen,* p. 7.

"Before I met Huston": Axel Madsen, "Bogey vs. Hepburn: Zaire's First Big Heavyweight Bout," *Los Angeles Magazine,* April 1978, AMPAS.

"Sam was able to woo": Lauren Bacall to NFC (I), June 25, 1996.

Page 131 *"British films were doing"*: John Woolf to NFC (I), Oct. 31, 1997.

Bogart was to receive: Agreement between Santana Productions (Bogart) and Horizon, Mar. 15, 1951, Box 12, SS JF.

30 percent: From Santana Productions to Horizon, Oct. 6, 1952, and "Spiegel Financial Deals on African Film Told," *Los Angeles Times,* Dec. 2, 1953, both Box 12, SS JF.

Hepburn $65,000: Agreement between William Morris (Hepburn) and Horizon, Dec. 26, 1950, Box 12, SS JF.

10 percent: "Spiegel Financial Deals on African Film Told," *Los Angeles Times,* Dec. 2, 1953, Box 12, SS JF.

Huston $87,500, and Spiegel $50,000: Statement, Horizon Enterprises Inc., *African Queen,* American dollar costs to date, Nov. 22, 1952, HP PKA.

"Oh, Christ, Jim": Laurence Bergreen, *James Agee,* p. 342.

I HAVE JUST: Cable from SS to Hepburn, Apr. 5, 1951, Box 12, SS JF.

Page 132 his partner had not been paid: Cable from Mark M. Cohen to SS, Feb. 2, 1951, HP PKA.

eviction: Cable from Gladys Hill to SS, Mar. 23, 1951, Box 12, SS JF.

disconnection of the office telephone: Ibid.

"coming in the front door": John Woolf to NFC (I), Oct. 31, 1997.

"John was only interested": Peter Viertel to NFC (I), Apr. 26, 1997.

"naked natives": Letter from Joseph Breen to SS, Apr. 2, 1951, HP PKA.

"Poor old Sam": Peter Viertel to NFC (I).

"the whole project": Ibid.

"He seems to hate me": Peter Viertel, *Dangerous Friends,* p. 126.

"ability to appear": Ibid., p. 127.

"a good listener": Ibid.

"It would be too humiliating": Joan Axelrod to NFC (I), Nov. 16, 1996.

Page 133 *"I'll wait until":* Viertel, *Dangerous Friends,* p. 125.

"It was very embarrassing": John Woolf to NFC (I).

"If I hadn't lied": Peter Viertel to NFC (I).

"I'm hooked up": Viertel, *Dangerous Friends,* p. 127.

"When we got": Bacall to NFC (I).

credit an English bank: Hepburn, *The Making of the African Queen,* p. 17.

"move out fast": Ibid.

"We did make": Peter Viertel to NFC (I).

Page 134 *"utterly piggish thing":* Hepburn, *The Making of the African Queen,* p. 23.

"A lot of": Bacall to NFC (I).

"quite a sight": Ibid.

"Sam wanted to be": Peter Viertel to NFC (I).

with even his partner threatening: Cable from Paul Kohner to SS, Apr. 26, 1951, PK SDK.

ACCORDING TO ALL: Ibid.

"Lloyd's Bank": John Woolf to NFC (I).

led to Walter Heller & Co.: Cable from Gladys Hill to SS, May 31, 1951, Box 12, SS JF.

"It would set itself": Angela Allen to NFC (I), Feb. 27, 1998.

"And he kept on": Hepburn, *The Making of the African Queen,* p. 65.

Page 135 *"It made":* Edwin Schallert, "Once Is Enough, Says Bogart on Filming of African Queen," *Los Angeles Times,* Nov. 11, 1951, AMPAS.

"We felt it was only": Jack Cardiff, *Magic Hour,* p. 150.

"What divine natives!": Axel Madsen, "Bogey vs. Hepburn: Zaire's First Big Heavyweight Bout," *Los Angeles Magazine,* April 1978, AMPAS.

"Queen's Throne": Allen to NFC (I).

"It used to drive": Ibid.

"I can't handle": Peter Viertel to NFC (I).

"a real character": Bacall to NFC (I).

"At first, we felt": Jack Cardiff to NFC (I), Jan. 15, 1998.

Page 136 *"So don't try":* Cardiff, *Magic Hour,* p. 148.

"What's so good": Cardiff to NFC (I).

"to sit in": Axel Madsen, "Bogey vs. Hepburn: Zaire's First Big Heavyweight Bout," *Los Angeles Magazine,* April 1978, AMPAS

"It was indeed": Katharine Hepburn, *Me,* p. 250.

Page 137 *"I thought you'd said":* Allen to NFC (I).

"You know when producers": Bacall to NFC (I).

"deserting": Peter Viertel to NFC (I).

"While you've been": Cardiff to NFC (I).

"He had this": Bacall to NFC (I).

drank every microbe: Cardiff, *Magic Hour,* p. 161.

shaved in the stuff: David Lewin to NFC (I), Oct. 31, 1997.

Page 138 *"I was concerned":* Cardiff to NFC (I).

"Tell him to learn": Allen to NFC (I).

"proper name": Ibid.

"She just had": Ibid.

"Huston started to foam": Bacall to NFC (I).

"Sam had never": Lewin to NFC (I).

Page 139 *"more and more stupid":* Allen to NFC (I).

"You've got to": Bacall to NFC (I).

"You're a reasonable": Hepburn, *The Making of the African Queen,* p. 92.

"Listen Katie": Ibid.

"In his usual way": Allen to NFC (I).

"Fine, print it": Cardiff to NFC (I).

Page 140 *"Nooo":* Allen to NFC (I).

"He used to fall asleep": Arthur Miller to NFC (I), Nov. 6, 1996.

"thinking of the": Bacall to NFC (I).

supplies of whiskey: Allen to NFC (I).

"Sam was such": Bacall to NFC (I).

when Heller gave: Cable from Gladys Hill to SS, Apr. 25, 1951, Box 12, SS JF.

owed $57,043.85: Letter from Charles A. Carter, Treasury Department, IRS, to SS, Mar. 6, 1951, Box 1, TT SSF.

second child: Anjelica Huston.

"Don't ask": Albert Heit to NFC (I), Oct. 10, 1996.

Page 141 he cashed two dud checks: Letter from Laurent Buisson, Ministère de L'Intérieur to NFC, Dec. 9, 1998.

"an oversight": Ibid.

from Feb 28, 1952: Ibid.

"a little car": Axelrod to NFC (I).

"Marion [Mrs. Irwin Shaw]": Ibid.

"There was tons": Ibid.

Page 142 *"What irks me":* Letter from Sam Rheiner to SS, July 10, 1951, Box 12, SS JF.

mortgaged his own house: Letter from Gladys Hill to SS, Aug. 13, 1951, Box 12, SS JF.

"personally strapped": Ibid.

$800 a month: Letter from Gladys Hill to SS, June 7, 1951, Box 1, TT SSF.

demanded $1,000: Ibid.

of being suicidal: Axelrod to NFC (I).

such literary standards: Kathleen Parrish to NFC (I), Oct. 5, 1996.

"It was in Paris": Ibid.

Page 143 famous leech scene: Lawrence Grobel, *The Hustons,* pp. 376–77.
"Some people were in awe": Allen to NFC (I).
"He just had": Jeanie Sims to NFC (I), Dec. 16, 1997.
"The editors had made up": Ibid.
Page 144 *"Now my dear Max":* Letter from SS to Youngstein, Oct. 24, 1951, Box 12, SS JF.
"I loved it": Youngstein to NFC (I).
"Mike had said": Nina Blowitz to NFC (I), Jan. 23, 1999.
IMPERATIVE THAT: Cable from SS to Horizon Pictures, Nov. 15, 1951; Box 12, SS JF.
BEGINNING TO TIRE: Cable from Gladys Hill to SS, Dec. 7, 1951, Box 12, SS JF.
"Meanwhile, everyone": Daily Variety, Dec. 19, 1951, Box 12, SS JF.
Page 145 cost Horizon $729,219.48: Statement from Horizon Enterprises (a subsidiary company of Horizon Pictures), Nov. 22, 1952, HP PKA.
£248,000: Letter from John Woolf to *London Times,* Aug. 23, 1990.
"A story of two old people": Ibid., speech given by John Woolf, titled "Sir John Woolf's Lunchtime Stories."

Chapter Fifteen: Melba

In regard to *Melba*–a film that the former S. P. Eagle preferred not to talk about–a small amount of correspondence as well as the production notes exist in Box Series 6 at The Jerusalem Foundation. There are also letters about *Melba* in Lewis Milestone's collection at the Margaret Herrick Library (LM AMPAS).

Page 147 *FIRST TEN REVIEWS:* John Huston to SS, Jan. 4, 1952, Box 12, SS JF.
EVERY PREVIOUS WARNER RECORD: John Huston to SS, Jan. 10, 1952, Box 12, SS JF.
"Sam made it": Joan Axelrod to NFC (I), Nov. 16, 1996.
Page 148 *"Sam told me":* Richard Roth to NFC (I), Nov. 17, 1996.
"On further reflection": Letter from SS to Mark M. Cohen, Feb. 5, 1952, HP PKA.
"Oh it's from": Jeanie Sims to NFC (I), Dec. 16, 1997.
Page 149 *"John was very cruel":* Axelrod to NFC (I).
"Sam had tried": Jess Morgan to NFC (I), June 10, 1997.
"We could see": Ibid.
"the most best-intentioned": John Huston, *Open Book,* p. 210.
brought in $4.3 million: Tino Balio, *United Artists,* p. 46.
reverted to the producer: Albert Heit to NFC (I), July 21, 1998.
disastrous deal: Letter from Albert Heit to SS, Jan. 8, 1970, Box 12, SS JF.
Page 150 *"It was called":* Albert Heit to NFC (I), Oct. 10, 1996.
May 1, 1953: Resolution adopted May 1, 1953, by the board of directors of Horizon Enterprises, Inc., HP PKA.
$3000: Letter from Mark M. Cohen to John Huston, May 18, 1953, HP PKA.
two notes: Ibid.
"against claims": Ibid.
"The fact that John": Peter Viertel to NFC (I), Apr. 26, 1997.
"cheated": Irene Heymann to NFC (I), Nov. 12, 1996.
"When I accepted": Letter from Patrice Munsel to NFC, May 3, 1998.

Page 151 paying him in handmade shirts: Leonora Hornblow to NFC (I), July 29, 1996.

3 percent of the film's profits: Letter from SS to United Artists, Sep. 19, 1952, Box 6, SS JF.

"very watered down version": Letter from Patrice Munsel to NFC, May 3, 1998.

Page 152 *"Bob, you are":* Ibid.

"Sam had charged": Ibid.

"I was appalled": Ibid.

called *The Hothouse:* Letter from Gladys Hill to SS, May 10, 1951, Box 1, TT SSF.

It was part: Letter from UA's Arthur Krim to UA's Bob Benjamin, Jan. 7, 1952, SSF.

to star Ingrid Bergman: Arthur Laurents, interview, *Backstory* 2, p. 147.

Page 153 London's 45 Park Lane: *Melba* production notes, Box 6, SS JF.

"the happy news": Letter from Patrice Munsel to NFC, May 3, 1998.

very moment that Arthur Krim: Ibid.

"Sam, never at a loss": Ibid.

"Sam was a charming": Edith Foxwell to NFC (I), Dec. 23, 1996.

Page 154 *"Sam used to":* Inge Morath to NFC (I), Nov. 6, 1996.

"It was Sunday": Dana Wynter to NFC (I), Aug. 15, 1999. (In *Melba*'s production notes, Wynter is referred to as Dagmar. It was Milestone's idea to change her name.)

"Sam used to come in": Morath to NFC (I).

"The game Spiegel": Lewis Milestone to Robert Kopp, Mar. 2, 1953, LM AMPAS. (The case Garbus vs Spiegel landed in court in March 1953)

Page 155 £254,666.27: Statement showing comparative balance sheet, Sep. 30, 1959, Box 6, SS JF.

"The problem was": Max Youngstein to NFC (I), Nov. 15, 1996.

"every aria": Patrice Munsel to NFC (I), June 20, 1998.

"I had just had": Ibid.

converted *Melba:* "Melba Finally Snares Theatre for Press Date," *Hollywood Reporter,* June 11, 1953, AMPAS.

"high-fidelity addict": "A Toast to Dame Nellie," *Saturday Review of Literature,* July 4, 1953, Box 6, SS JF.

"I, for one": "S. P. Eagle's Peachy Songfest," *The New Yorker,* July 13, 1953, Box 6, SS JF.

"In those days": Eric Pleskow to NFC (I), Oct. 14, 1996.

"Krim told Sam": Youngstein to NFC (I).

Page 156 missing $50,000: Ibid.

"I need not tell you": Letter from SS to Robert Benjamin, United Artists, Dec. 10, 1953, Box 38, SS JF.

Chapter Sixteen: On the Waterfront

Spiegel's correspondence for *On the Waterfront* can be found in Box Series 21 at The Jerusalem Foundation.

Page 157 *"Sam was always":* Albert Heit to NFC (I), Oct. 10, 1996.

"on divers days": Los Angeles Times, Oct. 8, 1952.

"Sam never had": Heit to NFC (I), Oct. 10, 1996.

"you only get ripped off": Heit to NFC (I), Feb. 9, 1998.

Page 158 Armed with: Betty Spiegel to NFC (I), Oct. 12, 1996.

The Golden Warrior: Letter from Sam Rheiner to Marlon Brando at MCA Agency, April 27, 1954, Box 21, SSF.

"Sam kept on": Budd Schulberg to NFC (I), Nov. 26, 1996.

"Who's going to care": Budd Schulberg, "The Inside Story of 'Waterfront,' " *New York Times Magazine,* Jan. 6, 1980, BBS.

"smart as paint": Ibid.

"He said, 'I'll do it' ": Elia Kazan to NFC (I), Apr. 10, 1996.

"On the Waterfront wouldn't": Ibid.

Page 159 *"did not get back"*: Letter from Darryl F. Zanuck, Fox to Kazan, July 15, 1954.

"Watch out": Kazan to NFC (I).

April 10, 1952: Bernard Weinraub, "Hollywood's Case Against Elia Kazan," *International Herald Tribune,* Apr. 1996.

"to name everybody": Kazan, *A Life,* p. 459.

coming down with shingles: Kazan, *A Life,* p. 486.

"When I was asked": Schulberg to NFC (I).

Joe Curtis of Monticello Films: Letter from Sam Rheiner to Irwin Margulies, May 26, 1954, Box 21, SS JF.

Robert Siodmak: Letter from Andrew J. Feinman (Robert Siodmak's attorney) to Horizon Pictures, July 17, 1953, Box 21, SS JF.

Page 160 *A Stone on the River Hudson:* Deborah Lazaroff Alpi, *Robert Siodmak,* p. 179.

pay all his outstanding loans: Max Youngstein to NFC (I), Nov. 15, 1996.

"We took": Leo Jaffe to NFC (I), Oct. 8, 1996.

"The studio had nothing": Paul N. Lazarus, Jr., to NFC (I), June 11, 1997.

"He made a point": Ibid.

"He was very fluid": Jerry Tokofsky to NFC (I), Jan. 22, 1999.

Page 161 *"because they set"*: Lazarus to NFC (I).

"I kiss the feet": Norman Spencer to NFC (I), Oct. 29, 1997.

"If my fanny": Fred Zinnemann to NFC (I), Nov. 19, 1996.

"In fact": Leo Jaffe to NFC (I).

"Sam used to make": Heit to NFC (I), Feb. 4, 1999.

"I really wanted": Schulberg to NFC (I).

"very, very, sharp": Ibid.

"It sounded pat": Betty Spiegel to NFC (I), July 24, 1998.

Page 162 *"let's open it"*: Schulberg to NFC (I).

Page 163 *"I'm driving to New York"*: Ibid.

"The trouble we had": Ibid.

The Bottom of the River: Kazan, *A Life,* p. 488.

"two-faced": Ibid., p. 530.

"a true understanding": Ibid., p. 766.

"Sam is the best producer": Warren Beatty to NFC (I), Nov. 17, 1996.

Page 164 *"boy genius of Broadway"*: Kazan, *A Life,* p. 242.

"What made him": Conversations with Tennessee Williams, ed. Albert J. Devlins, p. 335.

"as one of the happiest times": Telegram sent by SS when Kazan was honored at Williams College, Williamstown, Massachusetts, Aug, 1985, Box 2C, SSF.

"Gadg and I": Schulberg to NFC (I).

"that he was fascinated": Kazan to NFC (I).

"You couldn't stay": Ibid.

Page 165 *"disarming vocabulary":* Elia Kazan, *A Life,* p. 515.

"He never asked": Ibid.

"My first wife": Kazan to NFC (I).

"Since you couldn't come": Note from SS to Molly Kazan, Nov. 15, 1954, Box 21, SS JF.

"Like all good negotiators": Kazan, *A Life,* p. 514.

"essential quality": Ibid.

"Marlon was going": Kanter to NFC (I), Mar. 29, 1996.

"insanity": Schulberg to NFC (I).

"We had a handshake agreement": Ibid.

"It is not worth": Letter from Kazan to SS, Aug. 1953, Box 12, SS JF.

Page 166 *"front office geniuses":* Letter from Kazan to SS, Oct. 21, 1953, Box 12, SS JF.

sent to Montgomery Clift: Letter from SS to M. Clift, Oct. 7, 1953, Box 12, SS JF.

"He's a really": Letter from Kazan to SS, Aug. 1, 1953, Box 12, SS JF.

"after Kazan decided": Patricia Bosworth, *Marlon Brando,* p. 102.

Jennifer Jones: Letter from David O. Selznick to SS, Feb. 5, 1953, Box 21, SS JF.

Grace Kelly: SS to Joyce Wadler, *Washington Post,* Nov. 20, 1983.

"Marlon never liked": Kanter to NFC (I).

"He said, 'Isn't' ": Ibid.

Legend has it: Andrew Sinclair, *Spiegel,* p. 69.

"Politics has nothing": Patricia Bosworth, *Marlon Brando,* p. 99.

Page 167 weakness for the pastrami: Michael White to NFC, Sept. 9, 1997.

$150,000: Memo from Horizon Pictures to Kazan, July 15, 1953, Box 21, SS JF.

"But Jay Kanter": Heit to NFC (I), Oct. 10, 1996.

"he's an actor": John Weitz to NFC (I), July 23, 1996.

"Sam had very little respect": Betty Spiegel to NFC (I), July 24, 1998.

"Sam was very fond": Ibid.

"I feel that": Letter from SS to Kazan, Nov. 23, 1953, Box 21, SS JF.

Page 168 *"The crew used to":* Kazan to NFC (I).

"Spiegel's heart": Beatty to NFC (I).

"Gadg went mad": Schulberg to NFC (I).

"Sam would call": Ibid.

early departures: Kazan, *A Life,* p. 524.

"Some of the enforcers": Schulberg to NFC (I).

"He was very aware": Ibid.

Page 169 *"Charlie McGuire":* Ibid.

"so depressed": Marlon Brando, *Songs My Mother Taught Me,* p. 199.

"I thought I was": Ibid.

"Not a word": Kazan, *A Life,* p. 527.

"This is a great picture!": Ibid.

studio was concerned: Interoffice Columbia communication from B. B. Kahane to Leo Jaffe, Mar. 29, 1954, Box 21, SS JF.

"I am getting": Letter from Kazan to SS, May 19, 1954, Box 21, SS JF.

"put his right name": Obituary, *New York Times,* May 23, 1954, Box 21, SS JF.

"He said, 'Sam is' ": Lazarus to NFC (I).

"I tip": Ibid.

"Everyone says": Letter from Kazan to SS, May 20, 1954, Box 21, SS JF.

Page 170 *"who have seen both":* Ibid.
"to protect our": Letter from SS to Kazan, May 26, 1954, Box 21, SS JF.
"Sam hit": Leo Jaffe to NFC (I).
"The lights": Stanley R. Jaffe to NFC (I), Oct. 9, 1996.
"I know this": Letter from Budd Schulberg to SS, May 23, 1954, Box 21, SS JF.
"He did deserve": Schulberg to NFC (I).
Page 171 *"Kazan and I":* Ibid.
"How could a": Sandy Whitelaw to NFC (I), July 1, 2000.
festival had been rigged: Nicholas Beck, Budd Schulberg–*A Bio*–Bibliography, p. 54
"It soured": Letter from Budd Schulberg to SS, Sep. 14, 1954, Box 21, SS JF.
"Gadg continues": Letter from William Fitelson to Paul N. Lazarus, Nov. 17, 1954, Box 21, SS JF.
"I've never heard": Kazan, *A Life,* p. 516.
"We did have": Heit to NFC (I), Oct. 10, 1996.
Page 172 wanted $100,000: Letter from Irwin Margulies to SS, Jan. 7, 1955, Box 21, SS JF.
settled for $18,000: Letter from Sam Rheiner to Columbia, June 12, 1957, Box 21, SS JF.
"Out of the": Heit to NFC (I), Oct 10, 1996.
"[This] is not": Letter from SS to Frank Sinatra, Apr. 7, 1955, Box 21, SS JF.
"you didn't": Joan Axelrod to NFC (I), Nov. 16, 1996.
"He used to": Ibid.
"Sinatra was in": Kathleen Parrish to NFC (I), Oct. 5, 1996.
Spiegel and his wife: Betty Spiegel to NFC (I), Mar. 1, 2002.
"Sinatra was sitting": Ibid.
Page 173 *"Just before we landed":* Betty Spiegel to NFC (I), Oct. 13, 1996.

Chapter Seventeen: The Third Mrs. Spiegel and The Strange One

Spiegel's correspondence about *End as a Man,* which became *The Strange One,* can be found in Box Series 23 at The Jerusalem Foundation.

Page 177 *"the Silver Fox":* Fred Zinnemann, *An Autobiography,* p. 121.
"It's much heavier": details taken from footage of the Academy Awards ceremony in 1955, AMPAS.
Page 178 *"I think Sam":* Betty Spiegel to NFC (I), Oct. 12, 1996.
YOU MAY NOT BE: Cable from Lynne Spiegel to SS, Mar. 31, 1955, SSF.
court of Santa Monica: "Lynne Baggett Alimony Guarantee," *Los Angeles Examiner,* Apr. 1, 1955, USC.
On July 9, 1954: "Actress Charged with Hit-Run Death of Boy, 9," *Los Angeles Times,* July 10, 1954, AMPAS.
October 29, 1954: *Los Angeles Examiner,* Apr. 1, 1955, USC.
Judge Mildred L. Lillie: "Lynne Baggett on Trial in Boy's Death," *Los Angeles Herald Express,* Oct. 11, 1954, AMPAS.
Page 179 *"blackout"* story: *Hollywood Citizen* news, Oct. 19, 1954.
January 20, 1955: *Los Angeles Times,* Jan. 21, 1955, AMPAS.
"not be held liable": Letter from Sam Rheiner to SS, Sep. 16, 1954, SSF.
"It was the saddest thing": Kathleen Parrish to NFC (I), Oct. 5, 1996.

"She destroyed": Betty Spiegel to NFC (I), Oct. 12, 1996.

"Sam could produce": Kevin Brownlow to NFC (I), Jan. 13, 1998.

talk that Kazan: Jack Garfein to NFC (I), Feb. 15, 1999.

James Dean in the starring role: Letter from Calder Willingham to SS, Aug. 15, 1955, Box 23, SS JF.

Page 180 *"a class exercise"*: Garfein to NFC (I).

it had been performed: Columbia Studios, production notes for *End as a Man*, Box 23, SS JF.

"not lessen": Publicity notes from Blowitz-Maskel for *End as a Man*, Ho 2-2391, Box 23, SS JF.

"At first": Garfein to NFC (I).

Page 181 *"You know my thoughts"*: Letter from SS to David Lean, Aug. 6, 1956, Box 8, SS JF.

"my banishment": Ibid.

"Poor Sam": Betty Spiegel to NFC (I), July 25, 1997.

"The first day": Ibid.

"It was exciting": George Stevens, Jr., to NFC (I), Feb. 22, 1999.

"I'm known": Garfein to NFC (I).

Page 182 *"disruptive"*: Ibid.

"Jack was very much": Name withheld.

"Sam had had": Garfein to NFC (I).

"And Jack went out": Isabella Leitner to NFC (I), July 19, 1998.

"dangerously poisonous": Garfein to NFC (I).

"Now listen, Jack": Ibid.

"I never expected": Ibid.

"I had nothing": Ibid.

Page 183 *"Garfein finished"*: Albert Heit to NFC (I), Oct. 10, 1996.

I DON'T PROPOSE: Cable from SS to Horizon Pictures, Feb. 17, 1957, Box 23, SS JF.

homosexual overtones: *New York Times,* Mar. 10, 1957, AMPAS.

emergency flight: Memo from Geoffrey Shurlock of MPAA, Apr. 9, 1957, PCA AMPAS.

WOULD NOT HAVE: Cable from Calder Willingham to Spiegel's office, forwarded to SS by Anne Grossberg, Horizon, New York office, June 1, 1956, Box 23, SS JF.

"We always used": Albert Heit to NFC (I), Feb. 4, 1999.

the next *Marty:* Letter from Sam Rheiner to SS, Feb. 15, 1957, Box 23, SS JF.

Rheiner suggested that: Letter from Sam Rheiner to SS, July 9, 1959, Box 5, SS JF.

cost was $708,713.79: *The Strange One* balance sheet, Sep. 30, 1957, Box 23, SS JF.

borne by both: Letter from Rheiner to SS, May 9, 1968, Box 23, SS JF.

"George Stevens told me": Garfein to NFC (I).

Page 184 *"My father would never"*: Stevens Jr. to NFC (I).

"It's the world's": Isabella Leitner to NFC (I).

"So I know never": Rosemary Chodorov (Edward Chodorov's wife) to NFC (I), Oct. 15, 1996.

"He'd come home": Betty Spiegel to NFC (I), July 25, 1998.

"very cynical": Garfein to NFC (I).

"The secret": Harold Pinter to NFC (I), Dec. 23, 1995.

"Sam enjoyed Betty": Rosemary Chodorov to NFC (I).

Page 185 *"She was very 'naughty' "*: Name withheld.

"I asked Sam": Luis Estevez to NFC (I), June 11, 1997.

"Hey, angel face": Betty Spiegel to NFC, Oct. 12, 1996.
"I had a lot": Ibid.
"She used to carry": Betty Estevez to NFC (I), Apr. 9, 1999.
"He used to": Betty Spiegel to NFC (I), Oct. 12, 1996.
"And he could never": Leonora Hornblow to NFC (I), July 29, 1996.
"I'd come in": Betty Spiegel to NFC (I), Oct. 13, 1996.
"incredible love-hate": Betty Spiegel to NFC (I), July 24, 1998.
Page 186 *"They would be"*: Ibid.
"Sam was my daddy": Betty Spiegel to NFC (I), Oct. 12, 1996.
Page 187 *"All I had"*: Betty Spiegel to NFC (I), Jan. 30, 1999.
"She was doing": Albert Heit to NFC (I), Oct. 10, 1996.
"Oh my God": Yolande Fox to NFC (I), July 14, 1999.
"Well, I hope": Betty Spiegel to NFC (I), Oct. 12, 1996.
YOU MIGHT: Ibid.
Page 188 *"a free, free spirit"*: Betty Estevez to NFC (I).
"My husband liked": Yolande Fox to NFC (I).
"He asked everyone": Paul N. Lazarus to NFC (I), June 11, 1997.
"The feeling was": Jules Buck to NFC (I), June 13, 1997.
"Apparently she said": Name withheld.
November 26, 1957: Louella O. Parsons, "Sam Spiegel Ends Secret; Wed 3 Wks–Dec. 20, 1957," USC.
"And he said": Betty Spiegel to NFC (I), Oct. 12, 1996.
Page 189 *"But I got caught"*: Ibid.
"And well": Louella O. Parsons, "Sam Spiegel Ends Secret; Wed 3 Wks–Dec. 20, 1957," USC.
"I thought that": Betty Spiegel to NFC (I), Jan. 30, 1999.
"I sometimes wondered": Ibid.
"I think we": Ibid.
"Betty was the closest": Lauren Bacall to NFC (I), June 25, 1996.

Chapter Eighteen: The Bridge on the River Kwai

Most of Spiegel's correspondence about *The Bridge on the River Kwai* can be found in Box Series 8 at The Jerusalem Foundation. Other sources include letters from Sir David Lean's Estate (DLE) and the Michael Wilson collection at UCLA Arts Library Special Collections, Collection Number 52. (MW UCLA).

Concerning the abbreviation of the film's title, I have followed Brownlow's lead and used *Kwai*. However, those in Spiegel's camp such as his lawyer Albert Heit and Betty Spiegel used to refer to the film as *Bridge*. Spiegel, depending on his mood, referred to the film as both *Bridge* and *Kwai*.

Page 191 flight had been delayed: Lilou Grumbach to NFC (I), June 1, 1998.
"gripped by": Ibid.
Carl Foreman entered: Letter from SS to Sam Rheiner, Nov. 25, 1954, Box 8, SS JF.
"Zoltan's partner": Ibid.
Page 192 *"Zanuck looks at Sam"*: Betty Spiegel to NFC (I), Oct. 12, 1996.
"It said": Ibid.
Like Carol Reed: Telegram from Horizon London office to SS, Dec. 14, 1954.

"Sam, the more": Letter from Howard Hawks to SS, Mar. 28, 1955, Box 8, SS JF. (*Summertime*–the film version of Arthur Laurents's play *The Time of the Cuckoo*.)

"You'll learn a lot": Kevin Brownlow, *David Lean*, p. 347.

the same with John Huston: Michael Korda to NFC, Dec. 2, 1999.

"My father thought": Tanya Lopert to NFC (I), Oct. 26, 1996.

"the pearls before": Arthur Penn to NFC (I), Apr. 20, 1999.

"I found him": Ibid.

Page 193 *"major audience-orientated"*: Anthony Perry to NFC (I), Apr. 1, 1999.

"He made the impossible": Kevin Brownlow to NFC (I), Sep. 9, 1997.

"saved": Perry to NFC (I).

"There was a pattern": Norman Spencer to NFC (I), Oct. 29, 1997.

Page 194 *"Could* Kwai": Brownlow to NFC (I).

"The great success": Don Ashton to NFC (I), Jan. 14, 1998.

"He was quite hairless": Ibid.

AS FOR CEYLON: Cable from SS to Columbia's Mike Frankovich, June 23, 1956, Box 8, SS JF.

Page 195 *"the most clever producer"*: Ashton to NFC (I).

"He made you": Elia Kazan to NFC (I), Apr. 10, 1996.

"Sam's velvet": Spencer to NFC (I).

"It was rather": George Axelrod to NFC (I), Nov. 16, 1996.

Page 196 *"thoroughly seduced"*: Brownlow, *David Lean*, p. 348.

"a magnificent script": Spencer to NFC (I).

"In matters like": Brownlow, *David Lean*, p. 348.

"One feels almost at once": Notes from Lean to SS, Jan. 31, 1956, DLE.

"whole spirit": Notes from Lean to SS, continued, Feb. 1956, DLE.

"Sam kept on": Spencer to NFC (I).

Page 197 *"the most bitter man"*: Lord Brabourne to NFC (I), Mar. 12, 1996. (John Brabourne coproduced *A Passage to India*.)

"He was very effective": Spencer to NFC (I).

"How can you idiots": Paul N. Lazarus, Jr., to NFC (I), June 11, 1997.

"He was furious": Ibid.

"They would have": Spencer to NFC (I).

"Like Korda": Brownlow, *David Lean*, p. 353.

Page 198 *"We began"*: Ibid., p. 356.

"You have only": Ibid.

"This is not meant": Letter from Lean to SS, Aug. 10, 1956, DLE (also in Box 8, SS JF).

I FEEL LEAN: Telegram from Calder Willingham to SS, July 17, 1956, Box 8 SS, JF.

VERY SENSITIVE: Telegram from SS to Calder Willingham, July 17, 1956, Box 8, SS JF.

"ticklish affair": Letter from Bill Graf to SS, July 22, 1956, Box 8, SS JF.

"These American writers": Letter from Lean to SS, Aug. 10, 1956, DLE (also in Box 8, SS JF).

Page 199 *"We want someone"*: Ibid.

"Mike had": John Berry to NFC (I), Feb. 18, 1998.

"It was really": Brownlow, *David Lean*, p. 359.

"on no account": Gino Cattaneo, who ran Horizon's London office, sent an interoffice memo to the Horizon, New York, office, Sep. 7, 1956, Box 8, SS JF.

"Sam, who hadn't finished": Ashton to NFC (I).

Page 200 £20,834: Letter from Keith Best, Husband & Co., Consulting Engineers to SS, July 2, 1956, Box 8, SS JF.

"Sam quoted": Ashton to NFC (I).

"What do you think": Letter from SS to David Lean, Aug. 6, 1956, Box 8, SS JF.

"I had been": Letter from Lean to SS, Aug. 10, 1956, DLE (also in Box 8, SS JF).

Korda had stood: Letter from Gino Cattaneo to SS, Sep. 15, 1955, Box 8, SS JF.

turned down: Garry O'Connor, *Alec Guinness,* p. 160.

Page 201 *"He was"*: Brownlow, *David Lean,* p. 364.

"They sent me": Ibid.

"Nevertheless, she is": Letter from SS to Lean, July 6, 1956, Box 8, SS JF.

"Fortunately": Letter from SS to Lean, Nov. 8, 1956, Box 8, SS JF.

"All this": Ibid.

Page 202 *"I'm like"*: Untitled newspaper clipping in Box 8, SS JF.

"If Holden wanted": Jud Kinberg to NFC (I), Nov. 13, 1996.

For *Kwai*: Letter from Leo Jaffe to SS, Aug. 7, 1968, Box 8, SS JF.

no more than $50,000: Ibid.

"He said we": Lazarus to NFC (I).

"the promise of beefing up:" Betty Spiegel to NFC (I), May 8, 2002.

"Sam had": Betty Spiegel to NFC (I), Oct. 13, 1996.

Page 203 *"It was Betty's idea"*: Geoffrey Horne to NFC (I), July 28, 2002.

"She said": Ibid.

"It was christened": Ashton to NFC (I).

three-ton tea wagon: Notes from meeting between Columbia's Bill Graf and Phil Hobbs, Aug. 13, 1956, Box 8, SS JF.

"Just saw": Letter from SS to Lean, Nov. 12, 1956, Box 8, SS JF.

"I have a great": Letter from Lean to SS, Nov. 16, 1956, Box 8, SS JF.

"As you well know": Letter from SS to Lean, May 23, 1956, Box 8, SS JF.

Page 204 *"There was"*: Ashton to NFC (I).

"I promise": Letter from Lean to SS, marked personal, Nov. 16, 1956, Box 8, SS JF.

"Strangely enough": Betty Spiegel to NFC (I), Oct. 12, 1996.

"She talked": Ibid. (confirmed by letter from Betty Spiegel to SS, Nov. 14, 1956, Box 8 SS JF.)

"I'll never forget": Betty Spiegel to NFC (I), July 25, 1998.

"You obviously believe": Letter from Lean to SS, Nov. 22, 1956, DLE (also in Box 8, SS JF).

Page 205 *WASHING MY HANDS:* Cable from SS to Lean, Nov. 29, 1956, Box 8, SS JF.

"Captive in her limousine": Isabella Leitner to NFC (I), July 19, 1998.

"We did not": Letter from SS to Lean, Nov. 8, 1956, Box 8, SS JF.

"I must see": Letter from Lean to SS, Nov. 16, 1956, Box 8, SS JF.

"the voice of sanity": Letter from SS to Lean, Nov. 22, 1956, Box 8, SS JF.

Page 206 anti-British: Brownlow, *David Lean,* p. 365.

"Guinness had": SS to Melvyn Bragg, from transcript of his interview for South Bank Show (Kevin Brownlow).

"If they don't": Lean's notes for SS, Jan. 31, 1956, DLE.

"I am sure": Letter from SS to DL, Nov. 22, 1956, Box 8, SS JF.

"I tried to calm him": SS to Melvyn Bragg, from transcript of his interview for South Bank Show (Kevin Brownlow).

Page 207 *"He [David] was still"*: Ibid.

"He says, 'yes' ": Letter from Lean to SS, Dec. 7, 1956, Box 8, SS JF.

"The liquid clears": Ibid.

"Alec had": Betty Spiegel to NFC (I), Oct. 12, 1996.

"It really was": Ibid.

"It used to have": Ashton to NFC (I).

"I said 'Put' ": Unused transcript between Lean and Brownlow, p. 430.

Page 208 *"Since no one"*: Betty Spiegel to NFC (I), Oct. 12, 1996.

"skimp, skimp, skimp": Brownlow, *David Lean*, p. 375.

"We used a lot": Ibid.

Page 209 *"The day before"*: Betty Spiegel to NFC (I), Oct. 12, 1996.

thank-you: Ashton to NFC (I).

"We had built": Ibid.

Page 210 *"You can't take"*: Brownlow, *David Lean*, p. 378.

"finished with": Letter from Lean to SS, Apr. 14, 1957, Box 8, SS JF.

Page 211 *"slowing down"*: Letter from Bill Graf to SS, Apr. 5, 1957, Box 8, SS JF.

"Nobody else": SS to Melvyn Bragg, from transcript of his interview for South Bank Show (Kevin Brownlow).

"You're going": Letter from Bill Graf to SS, Apr. 5, 1957, Box 8, SS JF.

"I had quarrels": SS to Melvyn Bragg, from transcript of his interview for South Bank Show (Kevin Brownlow).

"that the audience": Ibid.

Page 212 *"He'd clutch"*: Unused transcript between Win Ryder and Kevin Brownlow, p. 13.

"You know he'll": Dorothy Morris Payne to NFC (I), Jan. 15, 1998.

"The night that": Leo Jaffe to NFC (I), Oct. 8, 1996.

"Otto [Preminger]": Jules Buck to NFC (I), June 13, 1997.

Page 213 *"I have seen"*: Letter from Lean to SS, Sep. 24, 1957, Box 8, SS JF.

"full capacity at the Plaza Theater": Letter from Jean Menz, SS's assistant in London, to Lean, Oct. 23, 1957, Box 8, SS JF.

"Lean had never": Brownlow, *David Lean*, p. 386.

Paul Lazarus: Letter from Paul N. Lazarus to SS, Aug. 13, 1957, Box 8, SS JF.

"They weren't sure": Lazarus to NFC (I).

"It meant opening": Ibid.

Page 214 *"ruin our chances, baby"*: Letter from Lean to Michael Wilson, Jan. 30, 1958, Box 46/Folder 13. MW UCLA.

"It was": Lazarus to NFC (I).

"The script was written": Brownlow, *David Lean*, p. 388.

accept my wishes: Letter from Michael Wilson to SS, Nov. 30, 1957, Box 46./Folder 13, MW UCLA.

"definitely" suffering: Hirschhorn, *Gene Kelly*, p. 159.

"a good feeling": Blair to NFC (I), Oct. 28, 1997.

I HAD NO FURTHER: Cable from Carl Foreman to George Seaton, Jan. 18, 1958, Box 8, SS JF.

Page 215 *"You're asking"*: Brownlow, *David Lean*, p. 388.

"Sam went berserk": Ibid.

"I was in a slight stupor": Betty Spiegel to NFC (I), Oct. 12, 1997.

"Because Columbia": Albert Heit to NFC (I), July 21, 1998.

60-40 in his favor: Ibid.

"Each film": Albert Heit to NFC (I), Oct. 10, 1996.

$65 million: Ibid.

"That is unfair": Albert Heit to NFC (I), July 21, 1998.
Page 216 $2,820,000: Interoffice memo from Sam Rheiner to SS, Nov. 25, 1975, Box
    8, SS JF.
unsuccessful legal battles: Letter from Mitchell, Silberburg & Knupp to Albert Heit, Feb.
    3, 1972. ("Bill Holden Lawsuit"–Superior Court No. 889,414. Box 8, SS JF.)
"Sometimes we were": Heit to NFC (I), July 21, 1998.
"That's the way": Ibid.

Chapter Nineteen: Suddenly, Last Summer

Spiegel's correspondence about *Suddenly, Last Summer* is in Box Series 5 at The
Jerusalem Foundation. Letters about Spiegel's apartment can be found in Box 1, UU at
the Sam Spiegel Foundation. Rosemary Mankiewicz, the second wife of Joseph
Mankiewicz, let me go through his notes about this film (JLM RM).

Concerning Tennessee Williams's papers at the Harry Ransom Humanities
Research Center (HRHRC), the University of Texas in Austin, I was given permission
to go through these by T. J. Erhardt, the director of Casarotto Ramsay Ltd., but there
remains little correspondence between Spiegel and the playwright. The same applies
to the estate of Audrey Wood (Williams's longtime agent), who also bequeathed her
papers to the University of Texas.

Page 217 on January 7, 1958: All details in letter from E. Fulton Brylawski (Tennessee
    Williams's lawyer) to Albert Heit, Oct. 15, 1958, Box 5, SS JF.
"I read": *Newsweek,* Dec. 28, 1959, Box 5, SS JF.
Page 218 *"But I certainly":* Blowitz-Maskel press release, Box 5, SS JF.
"over the phone": *Conversations with Tennessee Williams,* p. 275.
$50,000: Ibid.
$300,000: Contract of Thomas Lanier (Tennessee) Williams, Feb. 1, 1959, Box 5, SS
    JF.
"I thought that": *Conversations with Tennessee Williams,* p. 275.
"as a Grand Guignol": *New York Times,* Oct. 26, 1958, Box 5, SS JF.
turned down: Letter from Tennessee Williams to SS, Apr. 20, 1955, SSF.
"I think he rates": Maria St. Just, *Five O'Clock Angel,* p. 157.
"Tennessee ratted": Betty Spiegel to NFC (I), Oct. 12, 1996.
received $35,000: Letter from Sam Rheiner to Albert Heit, Dec. 1, 1958, Box 5, SS JF.
"Yes, it was": Gore Vidal to NFC (I), Dec. 28, 1996.
Page 219 *"Tennessee was in":* Ibid.
"Gore and I": Betty Spiegel to NFC (I).
"a bad marriage": Vidal to NFC (I).
"Sam would say": Ibid.
Page 220 *"Of course, Joe":* Rosemary Mankiewicz to NFC (I), Oct. 22, 1996.
"ivory ghetto": Kenneth Geist, *Pictures Will Talk,* p. 398.
"a cultural desert": Ibid, p. 7.
Page 221 *"Sam had a truffle nose":* Vidal to NFC (I).
"Isn't it interesting": Ibid.
"an Oxford don manqué": Geist, *Pictures Will Talk,* xii.
he would read Plutarch: Rosemary Mankiewicz to NFC (I).
"When I speak": Letter from Joseph Mankiewicz to SS, Apr. 2, 1959, JLM RM.

Page 222 *"If Joe dictated"*: Elaine Schreyeck to NFC (I), Jan. 12, 1998.

in Taylor's contract: Contract between Award Productions (SS's company for film) and Taylor as the artist, Apr. 25, 1959, Box 5, SS JF. There were two contracts.

"I think Vivien": *Sunday Express,* Feb. 15, 1959, Box 5, SS JF.

"But I lost": Vidal to NFC (I).

Page 223 *"That bitch"*: Betty Estevez to NFC (I), Apr. 9, 1999.

pay her $125,000: Contract between Award Productions and Taylor, Apr. 25, 1959, Box 5, SS JF.

under the name of Camp Films: Letter from Lee Toomey & Kent (Taylor's lawyers) to Irwin Margulies, Heit's partner, Feb. 16, 1959, Box 5, SS JF.

£7,000: Award Productions, list of salaries, Nov. 30, 1959, Box 5, SS JF.

Five bales: Letter from Walter B. Hoover Dire of Chamber of Commerce, New Orleans to Sam Rheiner, Horizon's New York office, phytosanitary export certificate, U.S. Dept of Agriculture No. 186885, June 29, 1959, Box 5, SS JF.

Olnico: Letter from Gino Cattaneo (SS's London office) to Sam Rheiner, May 15, 1959, Box 5, SS JF.

"I had told Sam": Arthur Canton to NFC (I), Nov. 18, 1996.

Page 224 *"a bag of dead mice"*: C. David Heyman, *Liz,* p. 201.

fifty-nine pieces: Letter from Gino Cattaneo to Sam Rheiner, Sep. 11, 1959 ($1,600 to be paid in duties), Box 5, SS JF.

"Her expense allowance": Alan Silcocks to NFC (I), Dec. 20, 1996.

"I would never": Betty Estevez to NFC (I). Garbo was asked to comfort Taylor when Michael Todd was killed.

"I had gathered": Interoffice memo from Harold J. Salemson (Blowitz's representative on set) to Arthur Canton, June 24, 1959, Box 5, SS JF.

forgotton to erase: Letter from Albert Heit to Martin Gang (Taylor's lawyer) at Gang, Tyre, Rudin & Brown, May 29, 1959, Box 5, SS JF.

Hepburn's first name: Letter from Irwin Margulies to SS, May 27, 1959, Box 5, SS JF.

"She didn't want": Rosemary Mankiewicz to NFC (I).

"Of course, he was": Vidal to NFC (I).

Page 225 *"Kate and Joe"*: Schreyeck to NFC (I).

"a bog of tics": Heyman, *Liz,* p. 202.

"It was tragic": Fred Zinnemann to NFC (I), Dec. 19, 1996.

"sobriety": Supplemental letter agreement between Horizon Pictures and Jack Clareman, at Polikoff & Clareman (Clift's lawyers), May 25, 1959, Box 5, SS JF.

"I don't want": Betty Spiegel to NFC (I), Oct. 12, 1996.

contacted Henry Wilson: Bill Blowitz to SS, Mar. 26, 1959, Box 5, SS JF.

arriving drunk: Letter from Sam Rheiner to Irwin Margulies, May 13, 1959, Box 5 SS JF.

$300,000: Mankiewicz's contract with Award Productions, Jan. 30, 1959, Box 5, SS JF.

Page 226 wearing white cotton gloves: Norman Spencer to NFC (I), Oct. 29, 1997.

"Where's Sam?": Ibid.

DISTURBING TO THE: Cable from Joseph Mankiewicz to Louella Parsons, June 6, 1959, JLM RM.

I HAVE JUST: Ibid.

"Sam had many enterprises": Peter Shaffer to NFC (I), Nov. 26, 1996.

Page 227 chose Edward Durrell Stone: agreement between SS and Stone, Sep. 17, 1958, Box 1, UU, SSF.

"You know what": Betty Spiegel to NFC (I), July 25, 1998.

ordered from Antwerp: Letter from Gino Cattaneo to Rheiner, Sep. 23, 1959, Box IUU, SSF

Columbia's chief projectionist: Letter from Rheiner to SS, Oct. 8, 1958, Box IUU, SSF.

the Metropolitan Museum's: Check sent to Joseph L. Carlin, Jr., Nov. 26, 1959, Box IUU, SSF.

"It's designed": *Sunday Dispatch,* May 31, 1959, SSF.

"That's why": Betty Spiegel to NFC (I), July 25, 1998.

Page 228 *"just a pig":* Barbara Leaming, *Katharine Hepburn,* pp. 481–82.

spat on the floor: Ibid.

"I didn't spit": Patricia Bosworth, *Montgomery Clift,* p. 342.

At Spiegel's suggestion: Press release from Jean Osborne, Horizon Pictures, London, Sep. 14, 1959, Box 5, SS JF.

Taylor's 39–23–35 hourglass figure: Ibid.

co-producer contract: Letter from Irwin Margulies to SS, Aug. 13, 1959, Box 5, SS JF.

Page 229 entirely left out: Interoffice memo from Arthur Canton to Sam Rheiner, Dec. 18, 1959 (Vidal's agent had complained to Canton), Box 5, SS JF.

"Sam convinced": Vidal to NFC (I).

omitted to credit him: Irwin Margulies (who was working in London) to his partner Albert Heit, Jan. 20, 1960, Box 5, SS JF.

"a practicing homosexual": *Time,* Jan. 11, 1960, PCA AMPAS.

"misunderstood the allegory": Letter from Tennessee Williams to editors of ABC, Mar. 28, 1960, Box 5, SS JF.

Page 230 *"polluting the bloodstream":* *The Hollywood Reporter,* Jan. 11, 1960.

"The shock values": statement from SS, Jan. 7, 1960, Box 5, SS JF.

"only the basic humanity": Statement from Joseph Mankiewicz, Dec. 28, 1959, Box 5, SS JF.

"He said, 'I just saw' ": Vidal to NFC (I).

"Please Don't Eat": Letter from Kevin Brownlow to NFC, Feb. 4, 2002.

"I remember": Shaffer to NFC (I).

"He was wandering": Ibid.

"He was always": Ibid.

Page 231 *"Gadg had gone":* Betty Spiegel to NFC (I), Oct. 13, 1996.

"Any man": *The Oxford Dictionary of Quotations,* p. 312.

Chapter Twenty: Lawrence of Arabia — Part I

Most of Spiegel's correspondence about *Lawrence of Arabia* is held in Box Series 14 at The Jerusalem Foundation.

Other invaluable sources included David Lean's letters–(DLE); Michael Wilson's Collection at UCLA's Special Collections, No. 52 (MW); and Barbara Cole's archives at The University of Reading (BC UoR). Cole worked as the "continuity lady" on *Lawrence*–(she is now called Barbara Beale).

Kevin Brownlow allowed me to go through his *Lawrence of Arabia* archives and

L. Robert Morris and his partner, Lawrence Raskin, gave me use of their Nutting transcript.

Regarding *Malahne,* I was in touch with Nick Jeffrey at Camper & Nicholsons and his colleagues: George Nicholson, Jean-Marie Récamier, and Jeremy Lines. However, it was Dr. William Collier, the yacht expert, who solved the mystery behind *Malahne's* name.

Page 233 *"He wanted to show":* Leo Jaffe to NFC (I), Oct. 8, 1996.

six times: L. Robert Morris and Lawrence Raskin, *Lawrence of Arabia,* p. 24.

Harry Cohn toyed: Kevin Brownlow, *David Lean,* p. 407.

with Dirk Bogarde: Ibid., p. 27.

"I can still feel": Letter from David Lean to Christopher Mann, Apr. 29, 1961, Box 14, SS JF.

Page 234 *"There had been":* Letter from Lean to SS, Sep. 13, 1958, SSF.

"that this will work out": Letter from Lean to SS, Mar. 4, 1959, SSF.

"It was Sam": Betty Spiegel to NFC (I), Oct. 13, 1996.

"one of the greatest": Morris and Raskin, *Lawrence of Arabia,* p. 21.

Page 235 *"If you wanted":* Kevin Brownlow to NFC (I), Sep. 9, 1997.

"to Spiegel": Harlan Jacobson, *Film Comment,* Apr. 1983.

Page 236 *"Lean's world":* Freddie Young to NFC (I), Dec. 15, 1997.

"Of course not, baby": Betty Spiegel to NFC (I), Oct. 13, 1996.

"boring and very *fascinating":* Letter from Lean to SS, June 15, 1959, DL TR (also Box 14).

"Some guest": Norman Spencer to NFC (I), Oct. 29, 1997.

"To us, it seemed": Leo Jaffe to NFC (I).

$14 million: Letter from Albert Heit to NFC, Apr. 16, 1999.

Page 237 Writers such as: Letter from Anthony Nutting to SS, June 21, 1960, Box 14, SS JF.

White terry cloth robes: All details Rose Greb Sogge to NFC (I), Jan. 24, 1999. (Greb Sogge was Bill Blowitz's secretary.)

"One of those qualities": Jonas Rosenfield to NFC (I), Nov. 21, 1999.

authorized his lawyers: Letter from A. W. Lawrence to SS, Jan. 13, 1960, Box 14, SS JF.

paid £22,500: Letter from Kennedy, Ponsonby & Prideaux (A. W. Lawrence's solicitors) to Horizon, Feb. 11, 1960, Box 14, SS JF.

Page 238 white-haired, pink-cheeked: Details from Caroline Brooks to NFC (I), Mar. 13, 2002. (Brooks was Jonathan Cape's assistant in the early 1950s.)

"he would have": Brownlow, *David Lean,* p. 409.

February 17, 1960: Morris and Raskin, *Lawrence of Arabia,* p. 33.

"In a way": Ibid.

"an absolute god": Brownlow, *David Lean,* p. 410.

I WANT YOU: Telegram from Marlon to SS, Mar. 24, 1960, SSF.

Page 240 *"orange stains":* Los Angeles Herald, Mar. 23, 1960, AMPAS.

"It was bizarre": Betty Spiegel to NFC (I), Oct. 13, 1996.

"When Sam was through": Betty Spiegel to NFC (I), July 26, 1998.

"But Sam never": Leo Jaffe to NFC (I).

"I don't think": Brownlow, *David Lean,* p. 263.

"I barely knew Mike": Betty Spiegel to NFC (I), Oct. 13, 1996.

"It was in the days": Ibid.

Page 241 *"defying Spiegel"*: Brownlow, *David Lean*, p. 409.

"Sam was a tiger": Leo Jaffe to NFC (I).

March 1961: Morris and Raskin, *Lawrence of Arabia*, p. 39.

rights to seven books: Letter from Columbia's Minerva Weisel to Twentieth Century-Fox's Harry J. MacIntyre, May 4, 1960, Box 14, SS JF.

Dubbed the Olivier: Edward Goring, *Daily Mail*, Sep. 15, 1960, Box 14, SS JF.

"not a marketable commodity": Morris and Raskin, *Lawrence of Arabia*, p. 39.

"When I married Albert": Anouk Aimée to NFC (I), June 28, 1999.

not for Clift's role: C. David Heyman, *Liz*, p. 202.

"It's all right": Brownlow, *David Lean*, p. 416.

Page 242 five further films: Agreement between Reten Establishment (O'Toole) and Horizon Pictures, June 20, 1962, Box 14, SS JF.

"Joyce, my wife": Jules Buck to NFC (I), June 13, 1997.

"Listen, what are": Ibid.

"Well, I'm sorry": Anthony Nutting to NFC (I), Oct. 31, 1997.

"top brass at Columbia": Anthony Nutting to L. Robert Morris and Lawrence Raskin (I).

Page 243 *"for a producer"*: Letter from Moshe Pearlman, the prime minister's office, to SS, Dec. 6, 1959, Box 14, SS JF.

"Dunes, baby": Nutting to NFC (I).

"Betty's Husband": Cable from Lean to SS, Apr. 1, 1960.

"You won't get": Nutting to NFC (I).

Antoinette *"Toni" Gardiner*: Howard Kent, *Single Bed for Three*, p. 50.

"David said": Nutting to NFC (I).

Page 244 *"Well, any child"*: Ibid.

"I have an account": Nutting to Morris and Raskin (I).

"I said, 'Sam' ": Ibid.

Page 245 *"champing at the bit"*: Letter from SS to Lean, May 2, 1961, Box 14, SS JF.

but had declined: Letter from David Niven (sent from his house in the South of France) to SS, no date, marked Sunday (presumably after Apr. 27, 1961, when Spiegel referred to Niven in a letter to Lean), Box 14, SS JF.

"Kirk Douglas wanted": Arthur Canton to NFC (I), Nov. 18, 1996.

"And Cary Grant": Ibid.

his lawyer told Spiegel: Interoffice correspondence from SS to Lean, Jan. 6, 1961.

$300,000 plus 10 percent: Ibid.

"Bugger and blast": Letter from Lean to SS, Jan. 7, 1961, DLE (also Box 14).

not Spiegel: Interoffice correspondence from SS to Lean, May 5, 1961.

"I felt I had gone": Letter from Michael Wilson to Robert Bolt, Nov. 29, 1962, Collection No. 52, Box 18, Folder 9 MW UCLA.

Page 246 *"far off"*: Letter from SS to Lean, Jan. 5, 1961, DLE.

"The character": Ibid.

"Sam, he's shot": Letter from Lean to SS, Jan. 7, 1961, DLE.

"dive into all": Letter from Lean to SS, Aug. 29, 1959, Box 14, SS JF.

"As I told you": Letter from Lean to SS, Jan. 5, 1961, Box 14, SS JF.

Page 247 *"in no way"*: Letter from SS to Lean, Jan. 6, 1961, Box 14, SS JF.

"You have begged": Letter from Lean to SS, Jan. 6, 1961, DLE.

"I can't tell you": Letter from Lean to SS, Jan. 7, 1961, DLE.

Page 248 *"All the arguments"*: Phyllis Dalton to NFC (I), Apr. 8, 1999.

"Obviously it is": Letter from SS to Lean, Apr. 26, 1961, Box 14, SS JF.

"too personal": Letter from Lean to SS, Apr. 28, 1961, DLE.
"With regards to": Interoffice correspondence from SS to Lean, May 5, 1961, Box 14, SS JF.
Page 249 *"I certainly advocated":* Ibid.
"You're like": Brownlow, *David Lean,* p. 443.
"I don't think": Dalton to NFC (I).
OLD PORT: Cable from Lean to SS, Apr. 8, 1960, Box 14, SS JF.
a 457-ton motor yacht: Ian Dear, *Camper & Nicholsons,* p. 100.
"he thought he": Nutting to Morris and Raskin (I).
Page 250 *"perfect for":* Jaffe to NFC (I).
initially put $250,000: Letter from Irwin Margulies to SS, Feb. 28, 1961, Box 14, SS JF.
Academy Pictures: Cable from Irwin Margulies to SS, Mar. 2, 1961, Box 14, SS JF.
"stealing the stuffing": Brownlow, *David Lean,* p. 429.
"on putting one's head": Ibid.
designed by: Dear, *Camper & Nicholsons,* p. 99.
in Gosport: Ibid., p. 250.
"I've been talking": Robert Parrish, *Hollywood Doesn't Live Here Anymore,* p. 12.
"The captain": Gore Vidal to NFC (I), Dec. 29, 1996.
Page 251 original owner: Dear, *Camper & Nicholsons,* p. 250.
Velsheda was a: Correspondence from Dr. William Collier to NFC, Feb. 5, 2002.
Malahne was the: Ibid.
launched in June 1937: Dear, *Camper & Nicholsons,* p. 100.
"a very graceful ship": Ibid.
"true love": Faye Dunaway, *Looking for Gatsby,* p. 92.
"Sam became": George Stevens, Jr., to NFC (I), Apr. 9, 1996.
"I'm not sure": Morris and Raskin, *Lawrence of Arabia,* p. 66.
"If you want": Tessa Kennedy to NFC (I), May 18, 1997. (Kennedy, an old friend of the Jordanian royal family, confirmed this entire story with both the late king and his mother.)
Page 252 *"the terrible thing":* Lean to Kevin Brownlow (I), pp. 112–13.
"After a while": Brownlow, *David Lean,* p. 444.
"When I put him": Ibid., p. 426.
"All the time": Omar Sharif to NFC (I), Jan. 9, 1998.
"equal rights": Omar Sharif's option agreement for seven motion pictures with Columbia and Horizon Pictures, Nov. 1, 1961, Box 14, SS JF.
Page 253 *"But it turned out":* Sharif to NFC (I).
£5000: Omar Sharif's option agreement, Nov.1, 1961. Box 14, SS JF.
"he was really": Interoffice correspondence from SS to Lean, May 2, 1961, Box 14, SS JF.
"I find it hard": Interoffice correspondence from Lean to SS, May 15, 1961, Box 14. SS JF.
"We both feel": Interoffice correspondence from SS to Lean, June 2, 1961, Box 14, SS JF.
"They were both": Dalton to NFC (I).
" 'Omar Sharif' ": Morris and Raskin, *Lawrence of Arabia,* p. 70.
"Some people went": Sharif to NFC (I).
Page 254 *"You can do":* Nutting to NFC (I).
"We had a special dinner": Young to NFC (I).

"He was": Roy Stevens to Brownlow (I), p. 32.

"Sam was an absolute": Dalton to NFC (I).

"I really felt": Interoffice correspondence from SS to Lean, June 2, 1961, Box 14, SS JF.

Page 255 *"a continuous clash"*: Atticus, *Sunday Times*, June 25, 1961, Box 14, SS JF.

"That day I got": Brownlow, *David Lean*, p. 438.

"Boob": Letter from David Lean to SS, Aug. 7, 1961, Box 14, SS JF.

"Bolt worked a ten-hour": Atticus, *Sunday Times*, June 25, 1961, Box 14, SS JF.

"every delivery": Letter from Lean to SS, Aug. 7, 1961, Box 14, SS JF.

"Bolt saw": Interoffice correspondence from SS to Lean, Aug. 29, 1961, Box 14, SS JF.

Page 256 *"stroking the camels"*: Brownlow, *David Lean*, p. 449.

"I don't know": Lean to Brownlow (I), p. 17.

"otherwise he would": Dalton to NFC (I).

"towering red cliffs": Brownlow, *David Lean*, p. 443.

"like John Ford": Ibid.

"The enormity": Dalton to NFC (I).

"It looked as if": Brownlow, *David Lean*, p. 438.

"I think it was": Ibid., p. 451.

Page 257 *"I know you will think"*: Letter from Robert Bolt to SS, Sep. 19, 1961, Box 14, SS JF.

"I don't feel": Interoffice correspondence from SS to Lean, Sep. 22, 1961, Box 14, SS JF.

"I sent him": Ibid.

"It's a sad day": Interoffice correspondence from Lean to SS, Sep. 29, 1961, DLE.

"It will be": Letter marked personal from Lean to SS, Sep. 29, 1961, Box 14, SS JF.

Chapter Twenty-one: Lawrence of Arabia — Part II

Again, most of Spiegel's correspondence about *Lawrence of Arabia* is held in Box Series 14 at The Jerusalem Foundation, while correspondence about *Dangerous Silence* is in Box Series 18, also at The Jerusalem Foundation.

Adrian Turner, Robert Bolt's principal biographer, gave me relevant letters between the playwright and David Lean as well as Bolt's letters to Michael Wilson (RB AT).

In regards to Marie-Hélène Arnaud's professional life, I went through the Chanel archives in Paris.

A special mention to Roy Frumkes's article "The Restoration of 'Lawrence of Arabia'" for *Films in Review*, Apr. 1989, Vol. 40, No. 4, and May 1989, Vol. 40, No. 5., and Gary Crowdus's "Lawrence of Arabia: The Cinematic (Re)writing of History" for *Cineaste*, Vol. 17, No. 2, 1989. Also, Robert Parrish's speech given during Edward Chodorov's memorial service.

Page 259 *"There was no way"*: Kevin Brownlow, *David Lean*, p. 456.

"He [Spiegel] could have been": Ibid.

Ongoing disasters: Letter from Geoffrey M. Shurlock to SS, Apr. 11, 1962, PCA AMPAS.

Page 260 *"So have these"*: Adrian Turner, *Robert Bolt*, p. 197.

"the most shameful moment": Ibid.

"theatre to real people": Adrian Turner, *Robert Bolt*, p. 519.

"Marie-Hélène became": Giles Dufour to NFC (I), May 20, 1999. (Dufour was Karl Lagerfeld's right-hand man at Chanel.)

"Marie-Hélène was": Carlos Cambelopoulos to NFC (I), Mar. 24, 1999.

"So it made her": Rosemary Chodorov to NFC (I), Oct. 15, 1996.

Page 261 *"She wanted to open"*: Nina Blowitz to NFC (I), Jan. 23, 1999.

"You have given me": Letter from David Lean to SS, Sep. 29, 1961, Box 14, SS JF.

"The biggest power": Brownlow, *David Lean,* p. 452.

"Sam wasn't going": John Box to Kevin Brownlow (I), p. 14.

Page 262 *"He somehow had"*: David Lean to Kevin Brownlow (I), p. 104.

"He was like": Anthony Nutting to NFC (I), Oct. 31, 1997.

Depending on the version: L. Robert Morris and Lawrence Raskin, *Lawrence of Arabia,* p. 55.

Spiegel fell to the ground: Andrew Sinclair, *Spiegel,* p. 99.

allergy to aspirin: Report from Dr. David Goldberg, Oct. 23, 1985, SSF.

Page 263 *"Working for Sam"*: Robert Parrish, *Hollywood Doesn't Live Here Anymore,* p. 9.

"David and I": Brownlow, *David Lean,* p. 469.

"sacrificing the quality": Letter from Lean to SS, May 22, 1962, Box 14, SS JF.

"If you still love": Letter from Geoffrey M. Shurlock to SS, Apr. 11, 1962, PCA AMPAS.

"pedantic": Letter from Lean to SS, May 22, 1962, Box 14, SS JF. (The entire account/episode was described in Lean's letter to SS.)

"an alleged drop": Ibid.

"staging the big": Ibid.

Page 264 *"that under pressure"*: Ibid.

"We had started": Nina Blowitz to NFC (I).

weekend of June 22: Letter from Lean to SS, May 22, 1962, Box 14, SS JF.

"I have worked": Ibid.

"vitriolic": Box to Brownlow (I), p. 13.

"So I take off": Ibid.

Page 265 *"One day it was so windy"*: Pedro Vidal to Kevin Brownlow (I), p. 3.

"Do you know what?": Norman Spencer to NFC (I), Oct. 29, 1997.

"It's not grand enough": Quoted from Robert Parrish's speech at Edward Chodorov's memorial, Jan. 7, 1990.

Page 266 *"Sam didn't say"*: Spencer to NFC (I).

thirty-two soufflés: Ibid.

"I had never heard": Brownlow, *David Lean,* p. 467.

"It was": Spencer to NFC (I).

Page 267 *"There was a full unit call"*: Brownlow, *David Lean,* p. 468.

"Sam's name": Walter Winchell, *New York Mirror,* Aug. 25, 1961.

"I knew it": Betty Spiegel to NFC (I), Jan. 30, 1999.

Page 268 *"Get that bitch"*: Ibid.

"Sam informed me": Maurice Jarre to NFC (I), Dec. 26, 1996.

Page 269 *"The picture was too sensational"*: Brownlow, David Lean, p. 476.

"There was a": Ibid., p. 475.

withdrew the title: Letter from SS to A. W. Lawrence, Aug. 22, 1962, Box 14, SS JF.

"was a better title": Nutting to NFC (I).

"I found this": Jarre to NFC (I).

"Sam, what is": Ibid.

Page 270 *"The terms"*: Leo Jaffe to NFC (I), Oct. 8, 1996.

Page 271 *"It was like"*: Spencer to NFC (I).

"a very happy picture": Lean to Brownlow (I), p. 100.
"We were": Ibid.
"But he was good": John Box to NFC (I), Nov. 23, 2000.
"He's the new star": Omar Sharif to NFC (I), Jan. 9, 1998.
"You make a star": Arthur Canton to NFC (I), Nov. 18, 1996.
outrageous sums: Letter from Columbia's Robert Ferguson to Irwin Margulies, May 17, 1963. Before appearing on the Ed Sullivan show, O'Toole had demanded $5,000.
"There was": Betty Spiegel to NFC (I), July 25, 1998.
Page 272 *"Great Film"*: *Women's Wear Daily,* Dec. 18, 1962.
"We had invited": Canton to NFC (I).
"It was a sort": Letter from David Lean to Robert Bolt, Dec. 23, 1962, BC UoR.
"I quite understand": *New York Times,* Jan. 26, 1963, Box 14, SS JF.
Page 273 *"Why then is"*: Letter from Michael Wilson to SS, Nov. 11, 1962, Collection No. 52, Box 46, Folder 9, MW UCLA.
"Forgive the brevity": Letter from SS to Michael Wilson, Nov. 19, 1962, MW UCLA.
"entitled to any": Letter from Cardew, Smith & Holland to Michael Wilson, Nov. 23, 1962, MW UCLA.
"I had no idea": Letter from Robert Bolt to Michael Wilson, Dec. 3, 1962, RB AT.
"The only sure thing": Sharif to NFC (I).
Page 274 *"Ladies and gentlemen"*: From footage of Academy Awards, Apr. 8, 1963, UCLA.
"Sam wanted them": Jarre to NFC (I).
"Sam was the": Charles Schneer to NFC (I), Mar. 1, 1999.
"After Lawrence": Betty Spiegel to NFC (I), July 25, 1998.
"He changed after": Mike Nichols to NFC (I), Nov. 5, 1996.

Chapter Twenty-two: The Spiegel Lifestyle

Much of the information gathered for this chapter was obtained from Sam Spiegel's personal files, which are in America and are now part of the Sam Spiegel Foundation (SSF). As already explained in the source notes to the Introduction, when I started researching, most of the papers were still being put in order by the Sam Spiegel Foundation and were either filed away under Box Series 1 (under the heading "Personal") or Box Series 2 (under the heading "Miscellaneous") or Box Series 3 (under the heading "Malahne"). When I am unfamiliar with the number of these boxes, I simply put SSF.

Regarding Spiegel's professional relationship with Fred Zinnemann, I went through the director's papers at the Margaret Herrick Library (FZ AMPAS).

Page 275 *"You don't listen"*: Rosemary Chodorov to NFC (I), Oct. 15, 1996.
"It happens a lot": Freddie Fields to NFC (I), Nov. 19, 1996.
"It all stopped": Albert Heit to NFC (I), Oct. 10, 1996.
"People get corrupted": Barry Diller to NFC (I), Nov. 12, 1996.
Page 276 *"He should have stopped"*: David Geffen to NFC (I), Nov. 11, 1996.
"He needed projects": Mike Nichols to NFC (I), Nov. 5, 1996.
British Lion: *Times* (London), Jan. 13, 1964, and Alexander Walker, "Will Sam Spiegel Bag British Lion," *Evening Standard,* SSF.
£3 million: "The Lion's Share in the Film Crisis," *Financial Times,* Jan. 1, 1964, SSF.

Pakistan and India: Letter from Fred Zinnemann to SS and Edgar Rosenberg, Oct. 20, 1964, FZ AMPAS.

"We started to talk": Fred Zinnemann to NFC (I), Dec. 19, 1996.

Page 277 *"I heard Sam say"*: Jerry Tokofsky to NFC (I), Jan. 22, 1999.

"After a huge lunch": Peter Viertel to NFC (I), Apr. 27, 1997.

"It was after": Nina Blowitz to NFC (I), Jan. 23, 1999.

it was Blowitz: Letter from Bill Blowitz to SS, Dec. 12, 1957, SSF.

"outstanding motion picture": *The Hollywood Reporter,* Apr. 6, 1964.

Stanley Kramer in 1961: Ibid.

"Sam called": Nina Blowitz to NFC (I).

Page 278 *HOW RIGHT:* Cable from Irene Selznick to SS, April (date smudged) 1964, SSF.

"Spiegel Philosophizes": *Daily Variety,* Feb. 6, 1963, SSF.

"Movie Industry": *Los Angeles Times,* Apr. 11, 1965, SSF.

"greatly moved": *Box Office,* Aug. 17, 1964, SSF.

"Sam was more fun": Betty Spiegel to NFC (I), Oct. 12, 1996.

"Betty, you know": Betty Spiegel to NFC (I), July 25, 1998.

swanned in and out: Ann E. Pennington to NFC (I), Apr. 22, 1999.

"Sam, you live now": Evelyn Keyes to NFC (I), Nov. 11, 1996.

"less fascinating": Ingo Preminger to NFC (I), Nov. 21, 1996.

"just paved his way": Alan Silcocks to NFC (I), Dec. 20, 1996.

"He was a different": George Weidenfeld to NFC (I), Dec. 22, 1995.

Page 279 *"He took an interest"*: Warren Beatty to NFC (I), Nov. 17, 1996.

"I sat next to": Mike Nichols to NFC (I), Nov. 5, 1996.

"Too many": Name withheld.

her ambitious nature: Claude Leusse to NFC (I), Sep. 9, 1998. (Leusse was a Chanel model and worked with Arnaud.)

"Sam said": Betty Spiegel to NFC (I), Oct. 13, 1996.

Page 280 *"Jeannette filled"*: Simone Warner to NFC (I), Apr. 28, 1999.

"Jeannette hid": Ibid.

immaculately dressed: Details from Ken Oakley, Spiegel's chauffeur, to NFC (I), Apr. 23, 1999.

"it wasn't his style": Robert Parrish, *Hollywood Doesn't Live Here Anymore,* p. 3.

Page 281 naturally it was: Simon Oakes to NFC (I), Apr. 23, 1999.

for a certain special: Jud Kinberg to NFC (I), Nov. 13, 1996.

order tinned sardines: Norman Spencer to NFC (I), Oct. 29, 1997.

"But Monsieur Spiegel": Ibid.

"the intelligent New York society": Kenneth Jay Lane to NFC (I), Oct. 21, 1996.

"Sam had": Sally Aga Khan to NFC (I), Jan. 20, 1998.

Page 282 *"We were alone"*: Anouk Aimée to NFC (I), June 28, 1999.

"You felt like": Afdera Franchetti Fonda to NFC (I), Jan. 13, 1998.

"He didn't mind": Antonia Fraser to NFC (I), Mar. 7, 1998.

"Sam just became": Betty Spiegel to NFC (I), July 25, 1998.

"At a party": John Frankenheimer to NFC (I), Mar. 19, 1998.

"I thought": Betty Spiegel to NFC (I), July 25, 1998.

"I pleaded with Betty": Denise Minnelli Hale to NFC (I), Feb. 7, 1998.

Page 283 *"I protected him"*: Betty Spiegel to NFC (I), Oct. 12, 1996.

"Betty had no jewelry": Betty Estevez to NFC (I), Apr. 9, 1999.

"Everything fell along": Betty Spiegel to NFC (I), July 25, 1998.
"Sam cared about": Hale to NFC (I).
"Sam encouraged me": Betty Spiegel to NFC (I), Oct. 12, 1996.
"The rest of us": Ibid.
high society brother-in-laws: Ibid.
"She must have": Letter from David Lean to Barbara Cole, Dec. 15, 1962, BC UoR.
Page 284 *"Sam gave me":* Kenneth Jay Lane to NFC (I).
"There was a beautiful model": Nichols to NFC (I).
"Warren Beatty called": George Stevens, Jr., to NFC (I), Apr. 9, 1996.
"There was such comfort": Ibid.
Page 285 *"People used to change":* Tessa Kennedy to NFC (I), May 18, 1997.
"floating ship of evil": Tokofsky to NFC (I).
"That was the place": Arthur Canton to NFC (I), Nov. 18, 1996.
"Luxury and Languor": *Life* magazine, July 9, 1965.
"Everyone wants": Sue Mengers to NFC (I), Apr. 2, 1996.
Page 286 Brigitte Bardot: Marguerite Littman to NFC (I), Jan. 14, 1998.
Italian aristocrat: Leo Jaffe to NFC (I), Oct. 8, 1996.
"Suddenly, Sam": Diana Phipps to NFC (I), Jan. 14, 1998.
"And everyone knew": Florence Grinda to NFC (I), Apr. 22, 1996.
"I couldn't believe it": Lilou Grumbach to NFC (I), June 1, 1998.
"He was like": Anne Douglas to NFC (I), Feb. 9, 1998.
Page 287 *"I was extremely":* Polly Bergen to NFC (I), Nov. 15, 1996.
"He said, 'Stop' ": Lauren Bacall to NFC (I), June 25, 1996.
"They had very little conversation": Joan Juliet Buck to NFC (I), Aug. 27, 1999.
Page 288 *"There was a certain amount":* Nichols to NFC (I).
"Sam was very sweet": Jacqueline de la Chaume to NFC (I), July 22, 1998.
"He was very important": Nichols to NFC (I).
"Slim, everybody": Slim Keith, *Slim,* p. 253.
"He was always": Bacall to NFC (I).
"Tito Arias, Margot's husband": David Metcalfe to NFC (I), Feb. 6, 1998.
Page 289 *"He took us":* Bettina Graziani to NFC (I), Mar. 20, 1996.
"Sam, who had": Betty Spiegel to NFC (I), Oct. 12, 1996.
"outrageously with all": Daniel Selznick to NFC (I), Apr. 10, 1996.
spring of 1964: Letter from David Selznick to SS, May 12, 1964, SSF.
Honorary Pallbearer: Letter from Daniel Selznick to NFC, June 26, 2002.
"Dad liked to feel": Letter from Daniel Selznick to SS, July 19, 1965, SSF. Courtesy of Daniel Selznick.
Page 290 novel and play: agreement between Horton Foote and Lone Star Pictures (Sam Spiegel's company) Oct. 24, 1964, Box 16, SS JF.
two television plays: Ibid.

Chapter Twenty-three: The Chase, The Happening, The Night of the Generals, *and* The Swimmer

Most of Spiegel's correspondence regarding these films can be found at The Jerusalem Foundation. *The Chase* archives are in Box Series 16, *The Happening* archives–Box Series 15 (titled *The Innocents*), *The Night of the Generals's* archives–Box Series 10, while *The*

Swimmer's archives are in Box Series 7. Regarding *Accident* and other films that Spiegel took an interest in but did not ultimately produce, most relevant documents are in Box Series 38 (titled "Miscellaneous"). Concerning the casting of the films, I went through the William Gordon Collection at the Margaret Herrick Library. During this period, Gordon was the head of casting at Columbia Studios.

For *The Chase,* I was given access to Lillian Hellman's archives, which are held at the Harry Ransom Humanities Research Center, the University of Texas (LH HRHRC). In regard to *The Swimmer,* I went through Eleanor Perry's collection at the Margaret Herrick Library (EP AMPAS).

Page 291 *"Sam was obsessed":* Arthur Penn to NFC (I), Apr. 20, 1999.
"Sam viewed": Ibid.
"Lillian was two things": Ibid.
Page 292 *"Lillian was a handful":* Richard Roth to NFC (I), Nov. 17, 1996.
fee of $125,000: Letter agreement between Lone Star Pictures Corporation and Lillian Hellman, Jan. 31, 1964, Box 16, SS JF.
rights in 1956: Agreement between Horton Foote and Horizon Pictures, Oct. 24, 1956, Box 16, SS JF.
"You said that": Undated notes from Lillian Hellman to SS (possibly end of 1963), LH HRHRC.
Page 293 *"Such a society":* Ibid.
Lee Harvey Oswald: Pat Quinn to NFC (I), July 29, 1999.
was paid $750,000: Agreement between Lone Star Pictures Corporation and Pennebaker Inc. (Marlon Brando), Feb. 3, 1965, Box 16, SS JF.
$130,000: Ibid.
play Jason to Marilyn Monroe's Anna: Letter from SS to Marvin Birdt (Monroe's agent), MCA, Mar. 31, 1959, Box 16, SS JF.
"where the Bihar famine": Patricia Bosworth, *Marlon Brando,* p. 146.
UTTERLY FATIGUED: Cable from Marlon Brando to SS, Apr. 3, 1965, Box 16, SS JF.
"wandering around": Ivan Moffat to NFC (I), Mar. 29, 1996.
Mankiewicz had been: Letter from Joseph Mankiewicz to SS, Nov. 16, 1963, JLM RM.
"We were very": Penn to NFC (I).
Page 294 *"I think that you":* Letter from SS to Peter O'Toole, Nov. 19, 1964, Box 16, SS JF.
"I always liked": Penn to NFC (I).
"to return the next day": Letter from Lillian Hellman to Anne Grossberg, SS's NY secretary, July 28, 1964, LH HRHRC.
Page 295 *"It was clear":* Penn to NFC (I).
"one of those ghastly": Letter from Peter O'Toole (dictated by O'Toole over the telephone) to SS, Jan. 12, 1965, Box 16, SS JF.
"It might be": Ibid.
"Sam kept me waiting": James Fox to NFC (I), May 4, 1999.
"Robert Redford was": Penn to NFC (I).
"She wasn't much": Ibid.
In his suite: Ivan Moffat to NFC (I).
"On the set": Quinn to NFC (I).
Page 296 tested for several: Letter from Irwin Margulies (SS's lawyer) to Columbia's Seymour P. Steinberg, Apr. 19, 1965, Box 16, SS JF.
"Sam contacted me": Moffat to NFC (I).

"He was crablike": Ibid.

rewrites from Horton Foote: Agreement between Lone Star Pictures Corporation and Horton Foote, May 14, 1965, Box 16, SS JF.

"It was a bad version": Moffat to NFC (I).

"the bite": Letter from Lillian Hellman to SS, May 11, 1965, Box 16, SS JF.

Page 297 *"troubled by a page":* Penn to NFC (I).

"trying to avoid": Letter from SS to Jay Kanter (Brando's agent), June 21, 1965, Box 16, SS JF.

"someone might make": Roger H. Lewis (the publicist on *The Chase*) to Irwin Margulies, Apr. 29, 1965, Box 16, SS JF.

"I cannot sacrifice": Letter from Charles Rice (sound supervisor for *The Chase*) to SS, June 17, 1965, Box 16, SS JF.

"hugely burdensome": Penn to NFC (I).

Page 298 *"It should be":* Ibid.

"But not with": Ibid.

"Where do you": Ibid.

"She will see it": Letter from Robert Lantz to SS, Dec. 7, 1965, LH HRHRC.

Page 299 *"a marvellous writer":* SS to Tom Hutchinson, "Last of the Tsars," 1971, *The Guardian,* Nov. 27, 1971. Box 13, SS JF.

"Sam had many": Mike Nichols to NFC (I), Nov. 5, 1996.

"This is": Bosley Crowther, *New York Times,* Mar. 19, 1966, PCA AMPAS.

"conventionally opulent melodrama": The New Yorker, Feb. 26, 1966, PCA AMPAS.

almost lost $3 million: Statement from Columbia, July 31, 1971, Box 16, SS JF.

"There was": Penn to NFC (I).

Page 300 made $150,000: Albert Heit (Speigel's lawyer) to NFC (I), Oct. 10, 1996.

foster newcomers: *The Hollywood Reporter,* Apr. 21, 1965, Box 19, SS JF.

"Sam knew very little": Jud Kinberg to NFC (I), Nov. 13, 1996.

"He still owes me": Ibid.

£7,500: Memo from Arthur Kananack (with Irwin Margulies) to Gino Cattaneo (SS's London office), Sep. 22, 1965, Box 38, SS JF.

Page 301 " 'You call this' ": Harold Pinter to NFC (I), Dec. 23, 1995.

"It was the sort": Kinberg to NFC (I).

entirely thanks to Spiegel: Letter from Joe Losey to SS, July 27, 1965, JL BFI.

"suave seduction": Elliot Silverstein to NFC (I), Mar. 31, 1999.

"Woody, Woody": Jerry Tokofsky to NFC (I), Jan. 22, 1999.

Page 302 *"Sam was interested":* Silverstein to NFC (I).

"He wanted someone": Kinberg to NFC (I).

"The camera loves you": Faye Dunaway, *Looking for Gatsby,* pp. 94–95.

$19,200: Agreement between Dunaway c/o Ashley Famous Agency and Horizon Dover (SS's company for the film), Jan. 10, 1966, Box 15, SS JF.

more than double: Dunaway, *Looking for Gatsby,* p. 95.

"I called up": Silverstein to NFC (I).

Page 303 *"Parks Emergency":* Report on Michael Parks's behavior by Jud Kinberg, May 25, 1966, Box 15, SS JF.

"Sam calls up": Tokofsky to NFC (I).

promptly flew down: Letter from Sam Rheiner (SS's New York office) to Columbia's Harvey Shaw, Aug. 2, 1966, Box 15, SS JF.

"I found communicating": Kinberg to NFC (I).

"He commented": Silverstein to NFC (I).

"Sam was elated": Kinberg to NFC (I).

"I only wish": Said by Earl Strebe, owner of the Village, Palm Springs, California, theater, *Film Daily,* Mar. 27, 1967, PCA AMPAS.

Page 304 *"There are still things":* Silverstein to NFC (I).

"I frankly think": Kinberg to NFC (I).

"Sam was": Silverstein to NFC (I).

"Sam asked me": Arthur Canton to NFC (I), Nov. 18, 1996.

Page 305 *"Sam was very good":* Fred Zinnemann to NFC (I), Dec. 19, 1996.

"I am sure": Letter from Peter O'Toole to SS, Feb. 17, 1966, Box 10, SS JF.

Page 306 *"Litvak mentioned":* Letter from Peter Viertel to NFC, Mar. 15, 2002.

"I was famous": Vidal to NFC (I), Dec. 29, 1996.

Page 307 *"injurious to his career":* Letter from Lee N. Steiner (Sharif's lawyer) to Irwin Margulies, Dec. 1, 1965, Box 10, SS JF.

£7,500: Letter from Horizon's Gino Cattaneo to Omar Sharif, Oct. 20, 1965, Box 10, SS JF.

£15,000: Agreement between Reten Establishment (Peter O'Toole's company) and Horizon, June 20, 1962, Box 14, SS JF.

Page 308 $80,000: Memo from Arthur Kananack to Irwin Margulies, Jan. 25, 1966, Box 10, SS JF.

"I don't believe": Robert B. Frederick, *Daily Variety,* Mar. 3, 1966, Box 10, SS JF.

"neither guy would talk: Tokofsky to NFC (I).

"Sam should have been": Vidal to NFC (I).

"They were all": Dzidzia Herman to NFC (I), Mar. 29, 1998.

Page 309 *"He said, 'Do you' ":* Sharif to NFC (I).

"Sam was constantly": Vidal to NFC (I).

another $50,000: Letter from Gino Cattaneo to Irwin Margulies, Sep. 27, 1965, Box 10, SS JF.

"In those days": Vidal to NFC (I).

Page 310 $5,522,135.69: Statement from Columbia, Oct. 27, 1973, Box 10, SS JF.

more than $3 million: Ibid.

"Sam, you know": Vidal to NFC (I).

"Sam had personally": Burt Lancaster to Judith Crist, *Take 22,* p. 75.

"I'm afraid": Letter from Frank Perry to SS, June 17, 1965, Box 7, SS JF.

Page 311 final approval: Memorandum of understanding between Horizon Pictures and Francis Productions (the Perrys), Mar. 12, 1965, Box 7, SS JF.

Death of a Salesman: Kate Buford, *Burt Lancaster,* p. 244.

"the irreversibility of human conduct": Joanne Stang, *New York Times,* Lancaster Swims in Deeper Waters, Aug. 14, 1966.

"It is most": Letter from SS to Burt Lancaster, July 1, 1965, Box 7, SS JF.

"The Build": John Frankenheimer to NFC (I), Mar. 19, 1998.

Demonstrating his commitment: Ibid.

"on the picture": Interoffice memo from Roger Lewis to Irwin Margulies, Oct. 7, 1965, Box 7, SS JF.

Page 312 *"Roger, alas":* Eleanor Perry to SS, July 6, 1966, EP AMPAS.

Not only had: details from letter Eleanor Perry to SS, Aug. 3, 1966, EP AMPAS.

"It was not": Name withheld.

"And [Lancaster] said": Gary Fishgall, *Against Type,* p. 248.

Page 313 *"He had":* John Frankenheimer to NFC (I).
"simply to be negative": Letter from Elia Kazan to SS, undated, Box 7, SS JF.
"He feels Sam": Letter from Leon Kaplan (Lancaster's lawyer) to Albert Heit, Aug. 12, 1966, Box 7, SS JF.
"disaster": minutes of telephone call between Roger Lewis and Barbara Loden, Nov. 11, 1966, Box 7, SS JF.
"She even asked": Ibid.
"We feel": Frank and Eleanor Perry to SS, Nov. 15, 1966, EP AMPAS.
Page 314 *"Janice Rule may":* Letter from Eleanor Perry to SS, Jan. 11, 1967, Box 7, SS JF.
"It was really": Name withheld.
"cut off": Eleanor Perry to SS, Jan. 11, 1967, Box 7, SS JF.
"[Spiegel's] behavior": Letter from Elia Kazan to Eleanor Perry, undated (possibly Jan.) 1967, EP AMPAS.
February 8, 1967: Interoffice memo from Marlene Scott to SS, Feb. 3, 1967.
"I took less": Janice Rule to NFC (I), May 31, 1999.
"Burt feels hurt": Minutes of telephone conversation between Horizon's Sam Rheiner and Pat Somerset (film editor), Aug. 21, 1967, Box 7, SS JF.
"in the memory": Vincent Canby, *New York Times*, May 16, 1968.
Page 315 $2,538,340.78: Columbia statement, Apr. 26, 1975, Box 7, SS JF.
"second rate division": Stanley Jaffe to NFC (I), Oct. 9, 1996.
"If you look": Kinberg to NFC (I).
"Your fame": Letter from Shalom Spiegel to SS, Nov. 24, 1967, SSF.
"Life then was frugal": Yitzhak Lev Tov to NFC (I), Nov. 19, 1997.
"I had a sense": Ann E. Pennington to NFC (I), Jan. 13, 1998.
Page 316 *"the most mini":* Kinberg to NFC (I).
"little Ann": Anne Douglas to NFC (I), Feb. 9, 1998.
"What happened was": Pennington to NFC (I).

Chapter Twenty-four: Nicholas and Alexandra

Most of Spiegel's correspondence about *Nicholas and Alexandra* is in Box Series 13 at The Jerusalem Foundation and Box 2F at the Sam Spiegel Foundation.

A special mention to Tom Hutchinson's article for *The Guardian,* "Last of the Tsars," Nov. 27, 1971.

(Author's note–During the 1970s the czar and czarina were referred to as the tsar and tsarina.)

In regard to *The Right Honourable Gentleman,* Spiegel's correspondence is in Box Series 17 at The Jerusalem Foundation. I also went through George Cukor's collection at the Margaret Herrick Library, which indicated how he and John Osborne really felt about Spiegel (GC AMPAS).

Page 317 *"Sam said":* Robert Lantz to NFC (I), July 2, 1996.
$150,000 as well as 5 percent: Letter from Robert Lantz to SS, Mar. 28, 1968, Box 13, SS JF.
"the giant who": Letter from Moura Budberg to SS, Nov. 8, 1967, Box 13, SS JF.
Page 318 *"The rumors were":* Jeffrey Lane to NFC (I), Feb. 7, 1998.
"an erudite guttersnipe": Maude Spector to Kevin Brownlow (I), Nov. 26, 1991. Taken from Brownlow's transcript.

"exciting details": Notes by Vincent Korda, March 1968, Box 13, SS JF.

"Mink is for the coachman": Emma Andrews, A chapter in "The Life of Janet Suzman," *Films Illustrated,* June 1972, Box 13, SS JF.

Page 319 *"an American interpretation"*: Letter from Jack Valenti to SS, Feb. 5, 1969, Box 13, SS JF.

"It was Sam's": Pierre Sciclounoff to NFC (I), Feb. 25, 1997.

"Besides, it wasn't": Stanley Jaffe to NFC (I), Oct 9, 1996.

Page 320 In 1941, the average cost: 1971 International Motion Picture Almanac, p. 36.

"even though": Jaffe to NFC (I).

"Just waltz in": Peter Biskind, *Easy Riders, Raging Bulls,* p. 22.

"We looked pretty wild": Bill Hayward to NFC (I), Feb. 9, 1998.

Page 321 not to exceed $2 million: Letter from Columbia's Leo Jaffe to SS, Mar. 11, 1968.

Page 322 *"which was to die for"*: James Goldman to NFC (I), Oct. 18, 1996.

Page 323 *"I will threaten"*: Letter from Robert Lantz to SS, June 21, 1968, Box 13, SS JF.

"involves one's waking": Letter from SS to Lean, May 23, 1956, Box 8, SS JF.

"with Carl insisting": Lane to NFC (I).

"strongly held": Daily Variety, May 22, 1968, Box 13, SS JF.

offered half a million dollars: Letter from Joe Schoenfeld (Stevens's lawyer) to Columbia's Seymour Steinberg, Mar. 1, 1968. Box 13, SS JF.

"They started work": George Stevens, Jr., to NFC (I), Apr. 9, 1996.

Anthony Harvey took over: Letter from John Redway (Harvey's lawyer) to Keith Turner (SS's lawyer), July 23, 1968, Box 13, SS JF.

Page 324 *"For the right atmosphere"*: Goldman to NFC (I).

by early February: Official announcement made by SS's London office, Feb. 2, 1969, Box 13, SS JF.

"I need your help": Letter from James Goldman to Joseph Mankiewicz, Aug. 16, 1969, JLM RM.

"Joe didn't find": Goldman to NFC (I).

Charles Jarrott: Letter from Anthony Williams, William Morris Agency, to Lew Thornburn (SS's London office), Dec. 17, 1969, Box 13, SS JF.

"He had some charm": Goldman to NFC (I).

Page 325 Ritz in Madrid: Cable from SS to Leo Jaffe, June 26, 1970, Box 13, SS JF.

"As I recall it": Goldman to NFC (I).

"When I started": Fred Robbins, "Nicholas and Alexandra," *Show Magazine,* Jan. 1972.

"Originally, I said no": John Box to NFC (I), Nov. 23, 2000.

"I would direct": Ibid.

Page 326 *"did not want"*: Letter from Vincent Korda to Lew Thornburn, July 2, 1970, Box 13, SS JF.

"Tell him": Letter from Laurence Evans to NFC (I), Dec. 24, 1996.

"I remember going": Natasha Richardson to NFC (I), Oct. 24, 1996.

"He was terribly upset": David Metcalfe to NFC (I), Feb. 6, 1998.

"Peter would want": Letter from Jules Buck to SS, July 29, 1970, Box 13, SS JF.

Page 327 *"The studio would"*: Albert Heit to NFC (I), Feb. 4, 1999.

"overheads accruing": Letter from Leo Jaffe to SS, Sep. 8, 1970, Box 13, SS JF.

"We do not have": Ibid.

"The next two weeks": Letter from SS to Leo Jaffe, July 25, 1969, Box 13, SS JF.

Page 328 *"When actors are"*: Tom Hutchinson, "The Last of the Tsars," *The Guardian*, Nov. 27, 1971, Box 13, SS JF.

"Sam didn't want": Goldman to NFC (I).

"The great line": Alain Bernheim to NFC (I), Nov. 14, 1996.

Page 329 hired playwright Edward Bond: Agreement between Margaret Ramsay (agent of Edward Bond) and Horizon Pictures, Mar. 12, 1971, Box 13, SS JF.

"Sam told me": Letter from Leo Jaffe to Franklin Schaffner, Apr. 20, 1971, Box 2F, SSF.

"please be good": Letter from SS to Schaffner, Mar. 18, 1971, Box 2F, SSF.

"Rasputin is our": Letter from SS to Franklin Schaffner, Mar. 19, 1971, Box 2F, SSF.

Page 330 twelve minutes: Erwin Kim, *Franklin J. Schaffner*, p. 282.

"The queen was": Goldman to NFC (I).

"I suppose the shooting scene": Letter from Lord Mountbatten to SS, Dec. 1, 1971, Box 13, SS JF.

"In the 1970s": Michael Linnit to NFC (I), Apr. 29, 1999.

"like Golda Meir": Joan Juliet Buck to NFC (I), Aug. 27, 1999.

first continental screening: *Evening Standard*, Dec. 30, 1971, Box 13, SS JF.

since de Rothschild was: *Women's Wear Daily*, "Marie-Hélène Scores Again," Apr. 17, 1972.

Page 331 *"the spectacular film"*: Judith Crist, "A Feast, and About Time," *New York* magazine, undated, Box 13, SS JF.

"All we do": Stanley Kauffmann, *The New Republic*, Jan. 22, 1972, Box 13, SS JF.

"The film is": Derek Malcolm, "Long Time a Dying," *The Guardian*, Dec. 2, 1971, Box 13, SS JF.

"Flower arrangements": *Women's Wear Daily*, Dec. 14, 1971, Box 13, SS JF.

Page 332 $537,025 over budget: Columbia statement, Sep. 30, 1977, Box 13, SS JF.

almost $3 million: Letter from Columbia's Jack Feigenbaum to Sam Rheiner (SS's New York office) Apr. 16, 1979, the unrecouped on the picture amounts to $2,980,256.77. Box 13, SS JF.

"They didn't want": Albert Heit to NFC (I), Oct. 10, 1996.

$940,000 for two showings: Letter from Sam Rheiner to SS, Feb. 17, 1969, Box 16, SS JF.

"exception rather strongly": Letter from SS to Leo Jaffe, Sep. 4, 1972, Box 2F, SSF.

"greatly disturbed": Letter from Leo Jaffe to SS, Sep. 11, 1972, Box 2F, SSF.

"At the beginning": Heit to NFC (I).

Page 333 *"Sam was saying"*: Rosemary Chodorov to NFC (I), Oct. 15, 1996.

Chapter Twenty-five: The Last Tycoon

Most of Spiegel's correspondence about *The Last Tycoon* can be found in Box Series 11 at The Jerusalem Foundation and Box 2F at the Sam Spiegel Foundation.

Concerning *Down These Mean Streets/In the Streets*–the project with Kazan and Schulberg–the correspondence is in Box 38, SS JF, and Box 1E, SSF.

Page 335 he took the singer: Linda Ronstadt to NFC (I), Jan. 28, 1999.

"a dreamboat": Letter from Edie Wasserman to SS, Sep. 26, 1972, SSF.

first draft of *Shampoo*: Warren Beatty to NFC (I), Nov. 17, 1996.

"Since he lied": Ann Pennington to NFC (I), Jan. 13, 1998.

Page 336 only gesture: Adam Spiegel to NFC (I), Nov. 22, 1995.

"Sam didn't want": Joan Axelrod to NFC (I), Nov. 16, 1996.

"wallowing in the importance": Adam Spiegel to NFC (I), Apr. 22, 1999.

"He said he was": Pierre Sciclounoff to NFC (I), Feb. 25, 1997.
other guests: Willy Rizzo to NFC (I), Apr. 9, 1999.
Page 337 *"Many people"*: were Pennington to NFC (I), Jan 13, 1998.
"One day I arrived": Ellen Weisbord to NFC (I), Nov. 19, 1997.
"I was delighted.": Betty Spiegel to NFC (I), Oct. 13, 1996.
"When I saw him": Gore Vidal to NFC (I), Dec. 29, 1996.
"Because if the baby": Leonora Hornblow to NFC (I), July 29, 1996.
"He was stingy actually": Pennington to NFC (I), Apr. 22, 1999.
"I remember Sam": Adam Spiegel to NFC (I), Apr. 22, 1999.
"Jack [Nicholson], Warren": Mike Nichols to NFC (I), Nov. 5, 1996.
"loved Sam": Warren Beatty to NFC (I), Nov. 17, 1996.
Page 338 *"He used to"*: David Geffen to NFC (I), Nov. 20, 1996.
"needed projects": Nichols to NFC (I).
"felt that he": Budd Schulberg to NFC (I), Nov. 26, 1996.
"very nervous": Elia Kazan to NFC (I), Apr. 10, 1996.
"By that time": Schulberg to NFC (I). Schulberg still harbors a grudge against Spiegel.
   "Listen, offering *The Last Tycoon* to Gadg was Sam's way of making it up to him but
   he didn't bother with me." A few years later, when both were invited by Jimmy Carter
   to the White House, Spiegel had been charm and warmth personified but Schulberg
   had been tempted to resist his effusiveness. "But I couldn't. There is something about
   the White House which makes you want to be friendly–even if you're very angry!"
Page 339 *"But Sam says"*: Heit to NFC (I), Oct. 10, 1996.
Has the check": Ibid.
""She smiled": Leonora Hornblow to NFC (I), July 29, 1996.
"this little girl": Lauren Bacall to NFC (I), June 25, 1996.
Page 340 never saw them again: Kathleen Parrish to NFC (I), Oct. 5, 1996.
"little boy": Carrie Haddad to NFC (I), June 2, 1999.
"As compared": repeated by Kathleen Parrish to NFC (I).
"I put on": Haddad to NFC (I).
"People on the street": Ibid.
same as the Queen: Ken Oakley to NFC (I), Apr. 23, 1999.
Page 341 *"It was a fairy-tale"*: Haddad to NFC (I).
"I have never seen": Michael Linnit to NFC (I), Sep. 22, 1999.
and whispered *"Help!"*: Tom Stoppard to NFC (I), Aug. 27, 2002.
"He refused to wear": Pennington to NFC (I), Jan. 13, 1998.
visit an audiologist: Bill from Carlyle Laboratories, Mar. 11, 1976, Box 1E, SSF.
"bird of passage": Alan Silcocks to NFC (I), Dec. 20, 1996.
"It was like": Ibid.
"I adored Sam": Tessa Kennedy to NFC (I), May 18, 1997.
Page 342 *"Sam had so many"*: Haddad to NFC (I).
"It wasn't as if": Adam Spiegel to NFC (I), Apr. 22, 1999.
"Oh God": Joan Juliet Buck to NFC (I), Aug. 27, 1999.
Page 343 *"And we were"*: Michael White to NFC (I), Sep. 9, 1997.
"spontaneous": Nichols to NFC (I).
"Princess Caroline": Melanie Wyler to NFC (I), April 10, 1996.
"We would be served": Natasha Richardson to NFC (I), Oct. 24, 1996.
"Sam went wild": Ahmet Ertegun to NFC, Feb. 6, 1999.
"She had fallen": Sciclounoff to NFC (I).

"Please God": White to NFC (I).

"It was late": Ahmet Ertegun to NFC (I).

Page 344   *"But that was"*: White to NFC (I).

" 'Darling, you sit there' ": George Stevens Jr., to NFC (I), Apr. 9, 1996.

"I used to say": Ertegun to NFC (I).

"It would be": Haddad to NFC (I).

"my main man": Jack Nicholson to NFC (I), Nov. 11, 1996.

"Nicholson liked": John Pearse to NFC (I), Aug. 25, 2002.

Page 345   *"Sam told Jack"*: Willy Rizzo to NFC (I), Apr. 9, 1999.

"fuck herself": Geffen to NFC (I).

"best not to be": Letter from Irene Mayer Selznick to SS, Aug. 24, 1975, SSF.

"They were always": Haddad to NFC (I).

Page 346   Spiegel saw himself: David Lean to Kevin Brownlow (I).

"frequently planned": *Village Voice*, "Scott and Spiegel: It Takes a Tycoon to Know One."
     Undated, Box 11, SS JF.

Paul Newman or Warren Beatty: *New York Post*, Sep. 22, 1967, Box 11, SS JF.

"Sam was": Peter Viertel to NFC (I), Mar. 13, 2002.

"But there was": Geffen to NFC (I).

"I am trying": Charles Champlin, "The Fruitful Decade: Play It Again, Sam," *Los Angeles
     Times*, Sep. 16, 1975, Box 11, SS JF.

Page 347   *"They merely assemble"*: "Scott and Spiegel: It Takes a Tycoon to Know One,"
     Village Voice, undated, Box 11, SS JF.

had been appalled: Letter from SS to George Chasin, from Chasin-Park-Citron Agency,
     Jan. 26, 1976, Box 11, SS JF.

"He was very like": White to NFC (I).

"This was a shock": Elia Kazan to SS, May 28, 1974, Box 11, SS JF.

Page 348   *"I realized"*: Nichols to NFC (I).

"As you'll immediately see": Letter from Harold Pinter to SS, Mar. 6, 1974, Box 11, SS JF.

Page 349   *"The three of us"*: Harold Pinter to NFC (I), Jan. 18, 1998.

"The porter called": Ibid.

Page 350   *"Sam was so controlling"*: Nichols to NFC (I).

"in on every": Pinter to NFC (I).

"I stepped away": Nichols to NFC (I).

1975–1976 season: *Daily Variety*, Dec. 4, 1974, Box 11, SS JF.

"Sam was paying": Nichols to NFC (I).

[$25,000]: Letter from Albert Heit to SS, Jan. 9, 1974, Box 11, SS JF.

Dusty (Spiegel's name . . .): Letter from SS to Dustin Hoffman, Dec. 23, 1974, Box 11,
     SS JF.

"So Sam called": Pinter to NFC (I).

Page 351   *"a few people"*: Letter from Elia Kazan to SS, Feb. 19, 1975, Box 11, SS JF.

"One of the things": Jerry Tokofsky to NFC (I), Jan. 22, 1999.

Kazan mentioned it: Elia Kazan, *A Life*, p. 765.

"best wishes": *New York Times*, Feb. 19, 1975, Box 11, SS JF.

battling with De Niro's agency: Letter from SS to Freddie Fields, ICM agency, May 16,
     1975, Box 11, SS JF.

"on the brink": Pinter to NFC (I).

Page 352   *"I did meet"*: Ibid.

"He kept saying": Kazan, *A Life*, p. 765.

three additional pictures: Agreement between Tycoon Service Company (SS) and Ingrid Boulting, Aug. 5, 1975, Box 11, SS JF.

"With me as": Kazan, *A Life*, p. 765.

recommended the sixteen-year-old: Interoffice correspondence between William Morris agents Leonard Hirshan and Nat Lefkowitz, July 24, 1973, Box 11, SS JF.

Page 353 *"Did you ever"*: Letter from Elia Kazan to SS, Aug. 12, 1975, Box 11, SS JF.

"went to take": Ibid.

"gentle her into his bed": Kazan, *A Life*, p. 765.

"Fitzgerald has never": Bob Thomas, "Tycoon Spiegel Dispels Myth," *Los Angeles Times*, Apr. 16, 1976, Feldman Library, AFI.

"Jack was starting": Sue Mengers to NFC (I), Apr. 2, 1996.

Page 354 *"Kazan had her"*: Ibid.

"Sam was so": Elia Kazan to NFC (I), Apr. 10, 1996.

"hole": Kazan, *A Life*, p. 767.

"I fell in love": Pinter to NFC (I).

"a certain lushness": Barry Diller to NFC (I), Nov. 12, 1996.

dropped forty-two pounds: John Parker, *De Niro*, p. 82.

all of Thalberg's greats: Notes from Lynn Horsford (SS's Los Angeles assistant) to SS, Oct. 3, 1975, Box 11, SS JF.

contacted Norma Shearer: Letter from SS to Norma Shearer, Oct. 20, 1975, Box 11, SS JF.

Page 355 *Margaret Booth:* Letter from Margaret Booth to SS, June 20, 1974, Box 11, SS JF.

"Except that Sam": Haddad to NFC (I).

"Both their minds": Ibid.

cost $7.5 million: Heit to NFC (I), Oct. 10, 1996. Also memo from Albert Heit to SS, Feb. 14, 1975, Box 11, SS JF.

"Perfect dahling": Karen Winner, *Washington Star*, Jan. 4, 1976, Box 11, SS JF.

"Most producers would ask": Ibid.

dismiss this as Spiegelese: Kazan, *A Life*, p. 770. Confirmed in a letter from Albert Heit to NFC, June 22, 1999.

"I worked with": Heit to NFC (I), Oct. 10, 1996.

come forward with $2.6 million: Memo from Albert Heit to SS, Feb. 14, 1975, Box 11, SS JF.

almost $2 million: Ibid.

"When you were": Diller to NFC (I).0

Page 356 *"I did give"*: Mengers to NFC (I).

"Sam was trying": Haddad to NFC (I).

"stars at every table": Joan Juliet Buck to NFC (I), Aug. 27, 1999.

Page 357 *"I rang the doorbell"*: Tessa Kennedy to NFC (I).

"puzzling": Haddad to NFC (I).

"Sam was this": Maurice Jarre to NFC (I), Dec. 26, 1996.

"The studio were determined": Haddad to NFC (I).

"It was so embarrassing": Antonia Fraser to NFC (I), Mar. 7, 1998.

Page 358 *"It was a big"*: Arthur Abeles to NFC (I), May 19, 1997.

"I did the film": Kazan to NFC (I).

$855,000 had been spent: Letter from Barry Diller, in answer to SS's cable of Jan. 28, 1977, Box 11, SS JF.

"I deeply regret": Letter from SS to Barry Diller, Feb. 17, 1977, Box 11, SS JF.
"He was the only one": Albert Heit to NFC (I), July 21, 1998.
"Sam's bookkeeping": John Heyman to NFC (I), May 5, 1999.
Page 359 *"I used to say":* Pinter to NFC (I).
"Sam's attitude": Heit to NFC (I).
"Jack Nicholson does not want": Letter from Sandy Bresler to Albert Heit, Nov. 7, 1978, Box 11, SS JF.
share of the gross: Letter from Albert Heit to NFC (I), June 22, 1999.
I UNDERSTAND SO MUCH: Telegram from SS to Kazan, Sep. 10, 1980, SSF.
"Writing, in case": Letter from Kazan to SS, Feb. 24, 1981, Box 11, SS JF.
"It's so missing today": Diller to NFC (I).

Chapter Twenty-six: Betrayal

Spiegel's correspondence about *Betrayal* is in Box Series 9, at The Jerusalem Foundation. Concerning *A Singular Man* and *Pandora's Box,* most of the correspondence is in Box Series 38, SS JF.

Regarding his personal life, Box Series 1B, 1E, 1K, 1L, and 1N, which belong to the Sam Spiegel Foundation, were an important source.

Page 361 *"I think Sam":* Warren Beatty to NFC (I), Nov. 17, 1996.
"Beatty once called": Rachel Chodorov to NFC (I), Nov. 6, 1996.
top on his list: Letter from George Weidenfeld's secretary to SS, Mar. 18, 1977, Box SSF.
George Roy Hill: Letter from Albert Heit to J. P. Donleavy, Mar. 12, 1979, Box 38, SS JF.
Page 362 terminated the project: Letter from J. P. Donleavy to SS, Dec. 6, 1979, Box 38, SS JF.
The House of Blue Leaves: Terry Curtis Fox, John Guare: "At Long Last, Landscape," *Village Voice,* August 15, 1977.
transformed for the screen: John Guare to NFC (I), May 7, 1999.
"I was his": Ibid.
"He involved me": Rachel Chodorov to NFC (I).
"Sam trusted James: Ibid.
Page 363 From October 10, 1977: Letter from David Lean to SS, June 9, 1979, Box 38, SS JF.
on September 22, 1978: Ibid.
Six months later: Letter from Robert Bolt to David Lean, Mar. 20, 1979, Box 38, SS JF.
"David would be": Rachel Chodorov to NFC (I).
MY DEAR SAM: Cable from David Lean to SS, Aug. 18, 1979, SSF.
"It was": Rachel Chodorov to NFC (I).
"I remember sitting": David Geffen to NFC (I), Nov. 20, 1996.
"And I had": George Stevens, Jr., to NFC (I), Apr. 9, 1996.
Page 364 were discussing gold: Alan Silcocks to NFC (I), Dec. 20, 1996.
"I don't think": Beatty to NFC (I).
"Rothschild Bank": Albert Heit to NFC (I), Oct. 10, 1996.
as a godfather: The following chose Spiegel to be a godfather for their children: Anne and Kirk Douglas, Patricia and Vere Harmsworth, Annabelle and Mike Nichols, Jayne and Max Rayne, Alexandra and Arthur Schlesinger, Janet Suzman and Trevor Nunn,

Gaby and Teddy van Zuylen. And judging from Spiegel's personal correspondence, he never missed a birthday and always gave Christmas presents. SSF.

with Jackie Onassis: *W* Magazine, "The Chic at Play," May 26–June 2, 1978.

twentieth wedding anniversary: Ahmet Ertegun to NFC (I), Feb. 6, 1999.

Pinter's fiftieth birthday: Oct. 10, 1980, NFC.

"He used to go": Ertegun to NFC (I).

such as "golden showers": Name withheld.

A chic Parisian couple: Ertegun to NFC (I).

Page 365 *"obvious ladies"*: Anne Douglas to NFC (I), Feb. 9, 1998.

prostitute who stole: Ertegun to NFC (I).

cut his hair: Letter from SS to Katharine Hepburn, Mar. 23, 1976, Box IE, SSF.

"He liked": David Geffen to NFC (I).

"All I knew": Rachel Chodorov to NFC (I).

"Their skin is": Betty Spiegel to NFC (I), Oct. 13, 1996.

"What a shame": Pat Rickey to NFC (I), July 24, 1998.

"Sam had screenplayed": George Weidenfeld to NFC (I), Dec. 22, 1995.

"a very footloose existence": International Herald Tribune, May 1, 1984.

extramarital affair: It has been written that *Betrayal* was based on Pinter's affair with Joan Bakewell, the British TV personality. Sep. 1, 2002, Pinter denied this.

Page 366 *"unelectric"*: William Wolf, *New York* magazine, Feb. 21, 1983, Box 9, SSF.

"When Americans play": Ibid.

"I recommended": Harold Pinter to NFC (I), Jan. 18, 1998.

"We were talking": Nichols to NFC (I).

half a million dollars: Letter from Albert Heit to Sam Cohn, ICM (Nichols's agent), June 3, 1980, Box 9, SSF.

twice as much: Ibid.

"Mike told me": Harold Pinter to NFC (I).

Page 367 *"odd to write"*: Letter from Harold Pinter to SS, Nov. 24, 1980.

"After all": Harold Pinter to NFC (I).

Pinter directing *Betrayal*: Letter from Jimmy Wax (Pinter's agent) to Albert Heit, Feb. 26, 1981, Box 9, SS JF.

associate producer: Ibid.

holding back the start date: Letter from Julie Christie to Harold Pinter, Mar. 3, 1981, Box 9, SS JF.

"Thank God": Frédéric Malle to NFC (I), Nov. 8, 2001.

"He [Malle] was": Pinter to NFC (I).

Page 368 *"right out of the blue"*: David Jones to NFC (I), Oct. 25, 1996.

"I thought it was": Ibid.

Page 369 negative cost was $4,212,000: *Betrayal*'s production budget, Box 9, SS JF.

"What he was": Jones to NFC (I).

Page 371 *"Will no one"*: NFC was present when this happened, she was company assistant on *Betrayal*.

when Spiegel made: Ibid.

"John Bloom": David Jones to NFC (I).

"He said, 'I can't understand' ": Harold Pinter to NFC (I).

Jean Muir's reaction: Pinter to NFC (I).

Page 372 *"The problem is"*: Jones to NFC (I).

"I thought that": Samuel Goldwyn, Jr., to NFC (I), Nov. 13, 1996.

the important studios: Arthur Canton to NFC (I), Nov. 18, 1996.

Page 373 *"We made the deal":* Ibid.

"I can't think": Vincent Canby, "Film: Pinter's 'Betrayal,' Directed by David Jones," *New York Times,* Feb. 20, 1983, Box 9, SS JF.

"articulate dialogue": Rex Reed, "Betrayal Is More Satisfying on Screen," *New York Post,* Feb. 21, 1983, Box 9, SS JF.

"graceful, economical": Stanley Kauffmann, "Unbetrayed," *The New Republic,* Feb. 28, 1983, Box 9, SS JF.

Kazan admired the film: Letter from Elia Kazan to SS, Feb. 24, 1983, SSF.

"It's one of": Letter from Bob Rafelson to SS, undated (possibly February 1983), SSF.

"noisily" promoted: Michael London, "Betrayal: Showdown in the Commerce Corral," *Los Angeles Times,* Jan. 25, 1984.

"Films are honored": Ibid.

Page 374 *"He marked the end":* Warren Beatty to NFC (I).

Chapter Twenty-seven: The Final Years

Regarding *Survivors,* Spiegel's Viennese project, most of the correspondence is in Box 2C at the Sam Spiegel Foundation.

Page 375 incapable of speaking: Jennifer Attebery to NFC (I), Apr. 29, 1999.

confessing his final fears: Alan Silcocks to NFC (I), Dec. 20, 1996.

"I believe in": Victor Davis, *Daily Express,* May 6, 1982, Box 9, SS JF.

"I think that Sam": Adam Spiegel to NFC (I), Dec. 22, 1995.

"about to die": Ibid.

"I will give": Pat Rickey to NFC (I), July 24, 1998.

poor hearing as his excuse: Letter from SS to Shalom Spiegel, Sep. 14, 1983, SSF.

paid for Eloise Battle: Bill from Eloise Battle, Apr. 6, 1982, Box IL, SSF.

"a gracious and patient sounding board": Letter from Raya Dreben to NFC (I), Feb. 25, 2002.

Page 376 The boat journey: Cable from Betty Spiegel to SS on *QE2,* May 24, 1984, BBS.

to miss out: Cable from Leo and Anita Jaffe to SS on *QE2,* May 25, 1984, SSF.

any letter asking him: In his later years, SS was contacted by Boston University, Brandeis University, New York University, and Syracuse University, SSF.

Brandeis deserved a consideration since Spiegel had been a fellow of the University since May 22, 1967.

his *"great masterpieces":* Letter from Teddy Kollek to SS, May 22, 1984, SSF.

donating an Ingres: Letter from Teddy Kollek to SS, June 27, 1980, SSF.

"I think for him": Mike Nichols to NFC (I), Nov. 5, 1996.

"shared him with others": Jennifer Attebery to NFC (I), June 3, 1999.

Page 377 *"He used to say":* Rickey to NFC (I).

the summer of 1983: Jean-Marie Récamier, Camper & Nicholsons, to NFC (I), Feb. 5, 2002. Récamier was Spiegel's broker and sold the boat for him.

"when James Jordan": Jennifer Kent Attebery to NFC (I).

Page 341 *"Poor Sam":* Melanie Wyler to NFC (I), Apr. 10, 1996. (Mrs. William Wyler was her mother).

"You never knew": Larry Collins to NFC (I), June 29, 1999.

"Sam did get": Joan Axelrod to NFC (I), Nov. 16, 1996.

"Earlier, there was": Antonia Fraser to NFC (I), Mar. 7, 1998.

"I think I just liked": Adam Spiegel to NFC (I), Apr. 22, 1999.

"I would say": Michael White to NFC (I), Sep. 9, 1997.

Page 378 *"I remember him"*: Adam Spiegel to NFC (I), Apr. 22, 1999.

"It was very extreme": Antonia Fraser to NFC (I), Mar. 7, 1998.

"It's a good idea": Dale Pollock, "Betrayal: The Spiegel Has Landed," *Los Angeles Times,* Mar. 28, 1983.

"Sam felt": Attebery to NFC (I).

only one director in mind: Hugh Thomas to NFC (I), July 6, 1999.

"reams and drafts": Adam Spiegel to NFC (I), Apr. 22, 1999.

same logic as Irving Lazar: John Frankenheimer to NFC (I), Mar. 19, 1998.

benign prostate growth: David Goldberg, medical report, Oct. 23, 1985, SSF.

"walking like a zombie": Alan Silcocks to NFC (I), Dec. 20, 1996.

Page 379 would not survive: Pennington to NFC (I), Jan. 13, 1998.

plates of oysters: Ken Oakley to NFC (I), Apr. 23, 1999.

"He said, 'I would like' ": Ruth Cheshin to NFC (I), Nov. 27, 1999.

"Sam would never cry": Raya Dreben to NFC (I), Feb. 5, 1999.

"I don't recall": Cheshin to NFC (I).

"We were there": Harold Pinter to NFC (I), Jan. 18, 1998.

"Then at dinner": Tessa Kennedy to NFC (I), May 18, 1997.

"He said, 'I like' ": Hugh Thomas to NFC (I).

"He was told": Ibid.

in August 1985: Letter from Raya Dreben to NFC, Feb. 25, 2002.

"Sam said to me": Heit to NFC (I), Oct. 10, 1996.

Page 380 respectable WASP wills: Pennington to NFC (I), Apr. 22, 1999.

"Sam was very proud": Ibid.

Dreben was a partner: Letter from Raya Dreben to NFC, Feb. 25, 2002.

since the mid-1970s: SS's will, dated Jan. 7, 1975, SSF.

"I kept on saying": Heit to NFC (I).

"I was so focused": Attebery to NFC (I).

"He and Jennifer": Rickey to NFC (I).

"And I said": Hugh Thomas to NFC (I).

"He was fairly": William Rayner to NFC (I), May 27, 1997.

Page 381 fellow guests included: Rickey to NFC (I).

"He was clinging": Ibid.

"He wanted to talk": Betty Spiegel to NFC (I), Oct. 13, 1996.

"Sam had illusions": William Rayner to NFC (I).

A lobster dinner: Ibid.

"We talked and talked": Rickey to NFC (I).

"a lot of noise": Name withheld.

"Alive or dead": Andrew Sinclair, *Spiegel,* p. 139.

"Spiegel had": Evelyn Veber to NFC (I), Aug. 19, 1999.

"He was dead": Rayner to NFC (I).

Page 382 *"very strange"*: Attebery to NFC (I).

"They thought": Stoddart to NFC (I).

"There was a question": Name withheld.

actor's holiday quest: Ibid.

"I knew him": Anonymous source.
"on the night": Joseph L. Mankiewicz on public radio, Jan. 1, 1986.
"Sam had a great life": David Geffen to NFC (I), Nov. 20, 1996.

Epilogue

Regarding this chapter, I went through Spiegel's personal archives, particularly Box Series 1B, 1E, 1K, 1KK, 1L, and 1N.

Page 383   *"So, what did you get?"*: Ellen Weisbord to NFC (I), Nov. 19, 1997.
$20 million: Letter from John F. Loflin, Lord, Day & Lord, to Kenneth E. Warner (Betty Spiegel's lawyer), Nov. 26, 1986, BBS.
auctioned off by Sotheby's: May 11, 1987.
"holdings should be diversified": Letter from Raya Dreben to NFC, Feb. 25, 2002.
"He had left": Heit to NFC (I), July 21, 1998.
Page 384   *"I was on"*: David Bottoms to NFC (I), Feb. 27, 2002.
"deep Zionist roots": Letter from Raya Dreben to NFC, Feb. 25, 2002.
"You don't have": Adam Spiegel to NFC (I), Apr. 22, 1999.
"The only thing": Michael White to NFC (I), Sep. 9, 1997.
"at great length": Letter from Raya Dreben to NFC, Feb. 25, 2002.
"It probably meant": Mike Nichols to NFC (I) Nov. 5, 1996.
"I sued the estate": Betty Spiegel to NFC (I), Jan. 30, 1999.
more than the $750,000: Testament signed by SS on Dec. 24, 1985, BBS.
newest multimillionaires: Liz Smith, *New York Daily News,* Sep. 6, 1997, BBS.
"I think people": Adam Spiegel to NFC (I).
Page 385   *"He said, 'Betty darling' "*: Betty Spiegel to NFC (I), Oct. 13, 1996.
"And so I": Adrian Turner to NFC (I), Sep. 11, 1997.
suggested all of them: Letter from David Lean to Lew Thornburn (SS's London office), Jan. 11, 1968, Box 14, SS JF.
"I thought it was wrong": Geffen to NFC (I), Nov. 20, 1996.
"I spoke to him": Maurice Jarre to NFC (I), Dec. 26, 1996.
American Film Institute: Letter from George Stevens, Jr., to SS, Nov. 16, 1982, Box 1KK, SSF.
Page 386   *"insatiable curiosity"*: Minutes from SS's speech, Mar. 3, 1983, sent to NFC by George Stevens, Jr.
"When a producer": SS quoted from press release for *Suddenly, Last Summer,* 1959, Box 5, SS JF.
"last Mohicans": Letter from SS to Columbia's Pat Williamson, May 26, 1983, SSF.
"He didn't just become fat": Elia Kazan to NFC (I), Apr. 10, 1996.
"Let's open it up again!": Letter from Elia Kazan to SS, Aug. 21, 1985, SSF.
"It was in a place": Mike Nichols to NFC (I).

Selected Bibliography

Alpi, Deborah Lazaroff. *Robert Siodmak: A Biography, with Critical Analysis of His Films Noirs and a Filmography of All His Works.* Jefferson, NC: McFarland, 1998.

Ambler, Eric. *Here Lies Eric Ambler.* London: Weidenfeld & Nicolson, 1985.

American Film Institute Catalogue of Motion Pictures Produced in the United States: Feature Films, 1941–1950, indexes. Patricia King Hanson, executive editor. Berkeley, Los Angeles, and London: University of California Press, 1999.

The American Film Institute Catalogue of Motion Pictures: Feature Films, 1961–1970. Richard P. Krafsur, executive editor. New York and London: Bowker, 1976.

Bacall, Lauren. *By Myself.* New York: Alfred A. Knopf, 1978.

Bach, Steven. *Final Cut.* London: Faber & Faber, 1985.

Balio, Tino. *United Artists: The Company That Changed the Film Industry.* Madison: University of Wisconsin Press, 1987.

Barrow, Andrew. *Gossip: A History of High Society from 1920–1970.* London: Hamish Hamilton, 1978.

Baxter, John. *The Hollywood Exiles.* London: MacDonald and Jane's, 1976.

Beck, Nicholas. *Budd Schulberg: A Bio-Bibliography.* Lanham, MD, and London: Scarecrow Press, 2001.

Berg, A. Scott. *Goldwyn.* Lanham, MD, and London: Sphere, 1990.

Bergreen, Laurence. *James Agee: A Life.* New York: Dutton, 1986.

Billington, Michael. *The Life and Work of Harold Pinter.* London: Faber & Faber, 1996.

Biskind, Peter. *Easy Riders, Raging Bulls: How the Sex-Drugs-and-Rock 'n' Roll Generation Saved Hollywood.* New York: Simon & Schuster, 1998.

Block, Alex Ben. *Outfoxed: Marvin Davis, Barry Diller, Rupert Murdoch, and the Inside Story of America's Fourth Television Network.* New York: St. Martin's, 1990.

Bosworth, Patricia. *Marlon Brando.* London: Weidenfeld & Nicolson, 2001.

——. *Montgomery Clift.* New York: Limelight, 1996.

Boulle, Pierre. *The Bridge over the River Kwai.* New York: Bantam, 1957.

Brando, Marlon, and Robert Lindsay. *Brando: Songs My Mother Taught Me.* New York: Random House, 1994.

Brassai. *The Secret Paris of the 30's.* London: Thames & Hudson, 1976.

Brook, Peter. *The Shifting Point: 1946–1987.* New York: A Cornelia & Michael Bessie Book, Harper & Row, 1987.

Brook-Shepherd, Gordon. *The Austrians*. London: HarperCollins, 1996.

Brownlow, Kevin. *David Lean*. New York: Wyatt/St. Martin's, 1996.

Brunel, Adrian. *Nice Work: The Story of Thirty Years in British Film Production*. London: Forbes Robertson, 1949.

Buford, Kate. *Burt Lancaster: An American Life*. New York: Da Capo, 2000.

Cardiff, Jack. *Magic Hour*. London: Faber & Faber, 1997.

Cargnelli, Christian, and Michael Omasta. *Aufbruch ins Ungewiss: österreichische Filmschaffende in der Emigration vor 1945*. Vienna: 1993.

Cassini, Oleg. *In My Own Fashion: An Autobiography*. New York: Pocket Books, 1990.

Caute, David. *Joseph Losey: A Revenge on Life*. New York: Oxford University Press, 1994.

Chambers, Colin. *Peggy: The Life of Margaret Ramsay, Play Agent*. London: Nick Hern Books, 1997.

Charles-Roux, Edmonde. *L'Irrégulière ou mon itinéraire Chanel*. Paris: Grasset, 1974.

Chasanowitch, L., ed. *Les Pogromes Anti-Juifs en Pologne et en Galicie en Novembre et Décembre 1918–Faits et Documents*. Stockholm: Bokförlaget Judaea A.-B., 1919.

Cheever, John. *The Stories of John Cheever*. London: Vintage, 1990.

Churchill, Mary C. *King Abdullah, Britain and the Making of Jordan*. Cambridge: Cambridge University Press, 1987.

Crist, Judith. *Take 22: Moviemakers on Moviemaking*. New York: Viking Press, 1984.

Crowe, Cameron. *Conversations with Wilder*. New York: Alfred A. Knopf, 1999.

Curtis, Tony, with Barry Paris. *The Autobiography*. New York: William Morrow, 1993.

Custen, George F. *Twentieth Century's Fox: Darryl F. Zanuck and the Culture of Hollywood*. New York: Basic Books, 1997.

Dardis, Thomas A. *Keaton: The Man Who Wouldn't Lie Down*. New York: Charles Scribner's Sons, 1979.

Davies, Norman. *Heart of Europe: A Short History of Poland*. Oxford: Oxford University Press, 1986.

Dear, Ian (consultant editor, Jeremy Lines). *Camper & Nicholsons: Two Centuries of Yacht Building*. London: Quiller Press, 2001.

Devlin, Albert J., ed. *Conversations with Tennessee Williams*. Jackson and London: University Press of Mississippi, 1986.

Dick, Bernard F., ed. *Columbia Pictures: Portrait of a Studio*. Lexington: University Press of Lexington, Kentucky, 1992.

Dubost, Paulette. *C'est court, la Vie*. Paris: Flammarion, 1992.

Dunaway, Faye, with Betsy Sharkey. *Looking for Gatsby*. New York: Simon & Schuster, 1995.

Dyne, Michael. *The Right Honourable Gentleman*. New York: Dramatists Play Service, 1965.

Erez Yehuda, ed. *The Third Aliyah Book*. Israel: Am-Oved, 1964.

Evans, Robert. *The Kid Stays in the Picture*. London: HarperCollins, 1995.

Everson, William K. *The Art of W. C. Fields.* New York: Random House, 1967.

Eyman, Scott. *Print the Legend: The Life and Times of John Ford.* New York: Simon & Schuster, 1999.

Fariello, Griffin. *Red Scare: Memories of the American Inquisition.* New York: Norton, 1995.

Felleman, Susan. *Botticelli in Hollywood: The Films of Albert Lewin.* New York: Twayne, 1997.

Finler, Joel W., ed. *The Hollywood Story.* New York: Crown, 1988.

Fiore, Carlo. *Bud: The Brando I Knew.* New York: Delacorte, 1974.

Fishgall, Gary. *Against Type: The Biography of Burt Lancaster.* New York: Scribner, 1995.

Fitzgerald, F. Scott. *The Last Tycoon.* London: Penguin, 1965.

Flynn, Errol. *My Wicked, Wicked Ways.* New York: G. P. Putnam's Sons, 1959.

Fontaine, Joan. *No Bed of Roses.* New York: William Morrow, 1978.

Foote, Horton. *The Chase.* New York: Dramatists Play Service, 1998.

Fraenkel, Joseph, ed. *The Jews of Austria: Essays on Their Life, History and Destruction.* London: Vallentine, Mitchell, 1967.

Friedrich, Otto. *Before the Deluge: A Portrait of Berlin in the 1920s.* New York: HarperCollins, 1995.

——. *City of Nets: A Portrait of Hollywood in the 1940s.* New York: Harper & Row, 1986.

Frister, Roman. *The Cap, or the Price of a Life.* London: Phoenix, 2000.

Fritz, Walter. *Die österreichischen Spielfilme der Tonfilmzeit (1929–1938) mit dem Anhang Die Spielfilmproduktion in den Jahren der Annektion (1938–1944).* Wien, österreichisches Filmarchiv, 1968.

Gabler, Neil. *An Empire of Their Own: How the Jews Invented Hollywood.* New York: Anchor, 1988.

Geist, Kenneth L. *Pictures Will Talk: The Life and Films of Joseph L. Mankiewicz.* New York: Da Capo, 1978.

Gilbert, Julie. *Opposite Attraction: Erich Maria Remarque and Paulette Goddard.* New York: Pantheon, 1995.

Gilbert, Martin. *Israel.* London: Weidenfeld & Nicolson, 1998.

Gottlieb, Sidney, ed. *Hitchcock on Hitchcock: Selected Writings and Interviews.* Berkeley, Los Angeles, and London: University of California Press, 1995.

Grobel, Lawrence. *The Hustons: The Life and Times of a Hollywood Dynasty.* New York: Cooper Square Press, 2000.

Guinness, Alec. *Blessings in Disguise.* London: Hamish Hamilton, 1985.

Halberstam, David. *The Fifties.* New York: Fawcett Columbine, 1993.

Haver, Ronald. *David O. Selznick's Hollywood.* London: Secker & Warburg, 1980.

Hawkins, Jack. *Anything for a Quiet Life.* London: Elm Tree Books, 1973.

Hayward, Brooke. *Haywire.* New York: Alfred A. Knopf, 1977.

Hecht, Ben. *A Child of the Century.* New York: Simon & Schuster, 1954.

Hepburn, Katharine. *The Making of the African Queen, or How I Went to Africa with Bogart, Bacall and Huston and Almost Lost My Mind.* New York: Alfred A. Knopf, 1987.

——. *Me: Stories of My Life.* New York: Alfred A. Knopf, 1991.

Herman, Jan. *A Talent for Trouble: The Life of Hollywood's Most Acclaimed Director–William Wyler.* New York: Da Capo, 1995.

Heyman, C. David. *Liz: An Intimate Biography of Elizabeth Taylor.* London: William Heinemann, 1995.

Hirschhorn, Clive. *Gene Kelly: A Biography.* London: W. H. Allen, 1974.

Horak, Jan-Christopher. *Fluchtpunkt Hollywood: Die deutschsprachige Filmemigration von Hollywood, 1933–1950.* Muenster, 1986.

Howard, Jean, with James Watters. *Jean Howard's Hollywood: A Photo Memoir.* New York: Abrams, 1989.

Huston, John. *An Open Book: The Autobiography.* London: Virgin, 1994.

International Motion Picture Almanac: 1971. Richard Gertner, ed.

Isherwood, Christopher. *The Berlin Novels.* London: Minerva, 1992.

——. *Diaries, Volume One, 1939–1960.* London: Vintage, 1997.

Jaroslav Book: A Memorial to the Jewish Community of Jaroslav. Tel Aviv: Jaroslav Societies, 1978.

Johnson, Paul. *A History of the Jews.* London: Phoenix, 1995.

Katz, Ephraim. *The Macmillan International Film Encyclopedia.* London: Macmillan, 1994.

Kazan, Elia. *A Life.* New York: Da Capo, 1997.

Keith, Slim, and Annette Tapert. *Slim–Memoirs of a Rich and Imperfect Life.* New York: Simon & Schuster, 1990.

Kelly, Andrew. *Filming All Quiet on the Western Front.* London: I. B. Tauris, 1998.

Kelly, Andrew, Jeffrey Richards, and Pepper James. *Filming T. E. Lawrence: Korda's Lost Epics.* London: I. B. Tauris, 1997.

Kent, Howard. *Single Bed for Three: A "Lawrence of Arabia" Notebook.* London: Hutchinson, 1963.

Keyes, Evelyn. *Scarlett O'Hara's Younger Sister: My Lively Life in and out of Hollywood.* Secaucus: Lyle Stuart, 1977.

Kim, Erwin. *Franklin J. Schaffner.* Lanham, MD, and London: Scarecrow Press, 1985.

Klaus, Ulrich J. *Deutsche Tonfilme,* Vols. 3 and 4. Berlin and Berchtesgaden: Klaus-Archiv, 1990, 1992.

Kline, Jim. *The Complete Films of Buster Keaton.* New York: Citadel, 1993.

Kohner, Frederick. *The Magician of Sunset Boulevard: The Improbable Life of Paul Kohner, Hollywood Agent.* California: Morgan Press, 1977.

Korda, Michael. *Charmed Lives: A Family Romance.* New York: Random House, 1979.

Lally, Kevin. *Wilder Times: The Life of Billy Wilder.* New York: Henry Holt, 1996.

Lamarr, Hedy. *Ecstasy and Me: Hedy Lamarr: My Life As a Woman.* New York: Fawcett Crest, 1967.

Lawrence, T. E. *Seven Pillars of Wisdom.* London: Jonathan Cape, 1940.

Leaming, Barbara. *If This Was Happiness.* New York: Viking Penguin, 1989.

——. *Katharine Hepburn.* New York: Crown, 1995.

——. *Orson Welles*. New York: Limelight, 1995.

Lloyd, Norman. *Stages of Life in Theatre, Film and Television*. New York: Limelight, 1993.

Loacker, Armin. *Anschluss im 3/4-Takt–Filmproduktion und Filmpolitik in Österreich, 1930–1938*. Wissenschaftlicher Verlag Trier, 1999.

Loos, Anita. *Kiss Hollywood Good-By*. New York: Ballantine, 1974.

McBride, Joseph. *Orson Welles: Actor and Director*. New York: Harvest, 1977.

McCann, Graham. *Cary Grant: A Class Apart*. London: Fourth Estate, 1997.

McCarthy, Todd. *Howard Hawks: The Grey Fox of Hollywood*. New York: Grove, 1997.

McClintick, David. *Indecent Exposure: A True Story of Hollywood and Wall Street*. London: Columbus, 1982.

McDougal, Dennis. *The Last Mogul: Lew Wasserman, MCA and the Hidden History of Hollywood*. New York: Crown, 1998.

McGilligan, Patrick. *Fritz Lang: The Nature of the Beast*. London: Faber & Faber, 1997.

McGilligan, Patrick, ed. *Backstory 2: Interviews with Screenwriters of the 1940s and 1950s*. Berkeley: University of California Press, 1991.

McGilligan, Patrick, Paul Buhle, and Alison Morley. *Tender Comrades: A Backstory of the Hollywood Blacklist*. New York: St. Martin's, 1997.

Madsen, Axel. *John Huston*. New York: Doubleday, 1978.

Manso, Peter. *Brando*. London: Orion, 1995.

Marnham, Patrick. *Dreaming with His Eyes Open*. London: Bloomsbury, 1998.

Martin, Len D. *The Columbia Checklist: The Feature Films, Serials, Cartoons, and Short Subjects of Columbia Pictures Corporation, 1922–1988*. Jefferson, NC, and London: McFarland, 1991.

Marton, Andrew. Interviewed by Joanne D'Antonio. Metuchen, NJ, and London: Directors Guild of America and Scarecrow Press, 1991.

Massie, Robert. *Nicholas and Alexandra*. New York: Ballantine, 2000.

Meir, Golda. *My Life*. London: Weidenfeld & Nicolson, 1975.

Mintz, Mattityahu. *Pangs of Youth: The Hashomer Hazair, 1911–1921*. Israel: Hassifria Haziyonit, 1995.

Mirande, Yves. *Souvenirs*. Paris: Librairie Arthème Fayard, 1952.

Morand, Paul. *L'Allure de Chanel*. Hermann, 1996.

Morley, Sheridan, and Graham Payn, eds. *The Noël Coward Diaries*. London: Weidenfeld & Nicolson, 1982.

Morris, L. Robert, and Lawrence Raskin. *Lawrence of Arabia: The 30th Anniversary Pictorial History*. New York: Doubleday, 1992.

Morros, Boris, as told to Charles Samuels. *My Ten Years as a Counter-Spy*. New York: Viking, 1959.

Muir's Historical Atlas: Ancient Medieval and Modern. London: George Philip and Son, 1976.

Naremore, James. *The Magic World of Orson Welles*. Dallas: Southern Methodist University Press, 1989.

Navasky, Victor S. *Naming Names*. New York: Viking, 1980.

O'Connor, Garry. *Alec Guinness: Master of Disguise*. London: Sceptre, 1995.

Ogden, Christopher. *Life of the Party: The Biography of Pamela Digby Churchill Hayward Harriman.* Boston: Little, Brown, 1994.

Oldham, Gabriella. *First Cut: Conversations with Film Editors.* Berkeley, Los Angeles, and Oxford: University of California Press, 1992.

O'Toole, Peter. *Loitering with Intent.* London: Macmillan, 1992.

Parker, John. *De Niro.* London: Victor Gollancz, 1995.

Parrish, Robert. *Growing Up in Hollywood.* Boston: Little, Brown, 1976.

——. *Hollywood Doesn't Live Here Anymore.* Boston: Little, Brown, 1988.

Pasternak, Joe, as told to David Chandler. *Easy the Hard Way.* New York: G. P. Putnam's Sons, 1956.

Patai, Raphael. *The Jewish Mind.* Detroit: Wayne State University Press, 1996.

——. *The Vanished World of Jewry.* London: Weidenfeld & Nicolson, 1981.

Pauley, Bruce F. *From Prejudice to Persecution: A History of Austrian Anti-Semitism.* Chapel Hill and London: University of North Carolina Press, 1992.

Pinter, Harold. *Betrayal.* London: Faber & Faber, 1978.

Preminger, Otto. *Preminger: An Autobiography.* New York: Doubleday, 1977.

Rachum, Stephanie. *The Sam Spiegel Collection.* Jerusalem: The Israel Museum, 1993.

Remarque, Erich Maria. *All Quiet on the Western Front.* London: Jonathan Cape, 1994.

von Rezzori, Gregor. *Memoirs of an Anti-Semite.* London: Vintage, 1991.

Riefenstahl, Leni. *The Sieve of Time.* London: Quartet, 1992.

Riva, Maria. *Marlene Dietrich.* London: Bloomsbury, 1992.

Robinson, Edward G., as told to Leonard Spigelgass. *Edward G. Robinson: An Autobiography: All My Yesterdays.* New York: Hawthorn, 1973.

Ross, Lillian. *Picture.* London: Faber & Faber, 1998.

Rosten, Leo. *The Joys of Yiddish.* London: Penguin, 1971.

St. Just, Maria, and Kit Harvey. *Five O'Clock Angel: Letters of Tennessee Williams to Maria St. Just, 1948–1982.* New York: Alfred A. Knopf, 1990.

Sanders, George. *Memoirs of a Professional Cad.* New York: Dutton, 1960.

Schatz, Thomas. *The Genius of the System: Hollywood Film-making in the Studio Era.* London: Faber & Faber, 1998.

Schnitzler, Arthur. *Tagebuch 1927–30.* editors: Peter Michael Braunwarth, Suzanne Pertlik and Reinhard Urbach, Wien, Österreichische Akademie der Wissenschaften, 1997.

Schulberg, Budd. *Moving Pictures: Memoirs of a Hollywood Prince.* New York: Stein & Day, 1981.

——. *On the Waterfront: The Final Shooting Script.* New York: Samuel French, 1980.

——. *What Makes Sammy Run?* New York: Random House, 1941.

Schulz, Bruno. *The Collected Works of Bruno Schulz.* London: Picador, 1998.

Selznick, Irene Mayer. *A Private View.* New York: Alfred A. Knopf, 1983.

Silvain, Gérard, and Henri Minczeles. *Yiddishland.* Paris: Editions Hazan, 1999.

Sinclair, Andrew. *Spiegel: The Man Behind the Pictures.* London: Weidenfeld & Nicolson, 1987.

Slide, Anthony. *The New Historical Dictionary of the American Film Industry.* Lanham, MD, London: Scarecrow Press, 1998.

Spoto, Donald. *Notorious: The Life of Ingrid Bergman.* New York: HarperCollins, 1997.

Stadiem, William. *Too Rich: The High Life and Tragic Death of King Farouk.* New York: Carroll & Graf, 1991.

von Sternberg, Josef. *Fun in a Chinese Laundry.* London: Macmillan, 1965.

Stine, Whitney. *Stars and Star Handlers: The Business of Show.* Santa Monica: Roundtable, 1985.

Summers, Anthony. *Goddess: The Secret Lives of Marilyn Monroe.* London: Vista, 1996.

Swindell, Larry. *The Reluctant Lover: Charles Boyer.* New York: Doubleday, 1983.

Taylor, A. J. P. *The Habsburg Monarchy, 1809–1918: A History of the Austrian Empire and Austria-Hungary.* London: Hamish Hamilton, 1948.

Telushkin, Dvorah. *Master of Dreams: A Memoir of Isaac Bashevis Singer.* New York: William Morrow, 1997.

Thomas, Bob. *King Cohn: Life and Times of Harry Cohn.* New York: G. P. Putnam's Sons, 1967.

Thomson, David. *Rosebud: The Story of Orson Welles.* London: Abacus, 1996.

——. *Showman: The Life of David O. Selznick.* London: Abacus, 1993.

Todd, Mike, Jr., as told to Susan McCarthy. *A Valuable Property: The Life Story of Michael Todd.* New York: Arbor House, 1983.

Turner, Adrian. *Robert Bolt: Scenes from Two Lives.* London: Hutchinson, Random House, 1998.

——. *The Making of David Lean's Lawrence of Arabia.* London: Dragon's World, 1994.

Vardi, Don. *Against the Stream: Seven Decades of Hashomer Hatzair in North America.* Yad Ya'ari, Givat Haviva, 1994.

Vidal, Gore. *Myra Breckenridge and Myron.* London: Abacus, 1993.

——. *Palimpsest: A Memoir.* New York: Random House, 1995.

Viertel, Peter. *Dangerous Friends: At Large with Hemingway and Huston in the Fifties.* New York: Doubleday, 1992.

——. *White Hunter, Black Heart.* Garden City: Doubleday, 1953.

Viertel, Salka. *The Kindness of Strangers.* New York: Holt, Rinehart & Winston, 1967.

Weidenfeld, George. *Remembering My Good Friends: An Autobiography.* London: HarperCollins, 1995.

Weinstein, Allen, and Alexander Vassiliev. *The Haunted Wood: Soviet Espionage in America–The Stalin Era.* New York: Random House, 1999.

Welles, Orson, and Peter Bogdanovich. *This Is Orson Welles.* New York: HarperCollins, 1994.

West, Nathanael. *Complete Works.* London: Picador, 1988.

Whelan, Richard. *Robert Capa: A Biography.* New York: Bison, 1994.

Wilder, Billy, and Helmut Karasek. *Et Tout le Reste Est Folie.* Paris: Robert Laffont, 1993.

Wilkerson, Tichi, and Marcia Borie. *Hollywood Legends: The Golden Years of the Hollywood Reporter*. West Hollywood: Tale Weaver Publishing, 1988.

Willingham, Calder. *End as a Man*. New York: Donald I. Fine, 1986.

Wilson, Derek. *Rothschild: A Story of Wealth and Power*. London: Mandarin, 1992.

Zinnemann, Fred. *An Autobiography*. London: Bloomsbury, 1992.

Photo Credits

Index

Abbott and Costello, 103

Abdullah, Emir (of Transjordan), 16, 243

Abeles, Arthur, 358

Abrams, Ray, *see* Spiegel, Rachel "Ray" Agranovich

Academy Awards, 26, 88, 123, 198, 263, 324, 348
  SS's films and, 177–8, 214, 215, 274–5, 402–4

Accident, 125, 300–1

Actors Studio, 164, 166, 180, 181, 294, 357

Adam's Rib, 130

Adler, Buddy, 177

Adler, Larry, 39

Adler, Polly, whorehouse of, 69

African Queen, The, 108, 173, 205, 321, 386, 398
  Academy Awards and, 134, 147, 148, 402
  cast and crew of, 129–30, 131, 134, 136–8, 140
  Columbia and, 129
  crew accommodations for, 137, 138
  director of, 129–44, 147, 148
  distributors and, 144, 147
  financing of, 130–1, 134, 140
  grosses of, 149–50
  Hays office and, 132
  as hit, 144, 145, 147, 148
  Horizon Pictures and, 131–44, 147–8
  Huston-SS tensions over, 132–3, 137, 138, 143, 148
  leech scene in, 143
  locations of, 130, 131, 133, 134, 135, 136, 137, 143
  physical dangers in shooting of, 134–5, 137–8, 139, 148
  plot of, 130
  promotion for, 144–5
  salaries for, 131, 140
  screenplay of, 131, 132, 133, 135, 147
  SS as producer of, 129–45, 147, 148, 149, 150, 155
  TV deal for, 150
  UA and, 143–4, 149, 156

Aga Khan, Salimah "Sally," 281

Agee, James, 131, 147

Agranovich, Eliezer "Leon," 16

Agranovich, Susi, 16, 17, 41

Agron, Ilana, 16

Aimée, Anouk, 241, 281–2

Aldrich, Robert, 123

Alford, Kenneth J., 212, 324

Allen, Angela, 134, 138, 139, 143

All Quiet on the Western Front, 152
  German release of, 26–8, 81
  U.S. success of, 26

Alpert, Hollis, 224

Amadeus, 230

Ambassador Hotel (Los Angeles), 20, 24

Ambler, Eric, 89

Ambler, Joan Harrison, 88–9, 357

American Film Institute (AFI), 279, 385

André, François, 48, 141

Andreiev, Andrei, 153

Andrews, Dana, 87, 353

Angel Island, 21, 22, 80

anti-Semitism, 3, 9–10, 11, 26, 70, 385

Aqaba, 249, 251

Arias, Tito, 288

Armendáriz, Pedro, 112–13

Arnaud, Marie-Hélène, 260–1, 267–8, 279, 339

Arnold, Malcolm, 212

Ashe, W. W., 20

Ashley, Ted, 311–12

Ashton, Don, 194–5, 200, 203, 207, 209, 210

Asquith, Anthony "Puffin," 40
Atlantic City, 362
Attebery, Jennifer (Jennifer Kent), 376, 378, 380, 382
Aubrey, James T., 319
Auschwitz, 181, 182
Austria, 27, 37
Austro-Hungarian Empire, 3, 6, 9
Axelrod, George, 76, 195
Axelrod, Joan, 63, 76, 84, 102, 108, 141, 149, 172, 336, 377

Bacall, Lauren, 88, 102, 104, 106, 172, 189, 287, 288–9, 339, 385
  on *African Queen* location, 130, 133, 134, 136, 137, 140–1
Bachmann, L. P., 58
Baggett, Lynne, *see* Spiegel, Lynne
Baiano, Steven "Solly," 102
Baiser, s'il vous plaît, Un, 43
Baker, Carroll, 181, 184
Baker, Tom, 329
Bamberger, Joseph Jay "J.J.", 39
Bandaranaike, Solomon, prime minister of Ceylon, 209
Barber of Seville, The, 67
Bardot, Brigitte, 286
Barry, John, 298, 341
Barsacq, Leon, 318
Bates, H. E., 199
Battle of San Pietro, The, 105
Beatty, Warren, 164, 168
  SS's relationship with, 279, 284, 335, 337, 361, 364, 374
Becket (Anouilh), 242
Behan, Brendan, 276
Beirut, 253–4
Belgian Congo, *African Queen* locations in, 133, 134, 136
Benjamin, Robert, 142, 156
  in UA acquisition, 58, 125–6
Benny, Jack, 74
Benson, Betty, *see* Betty Spiegel
Bergen, Candice, 296, 368
Bergen, Polly, 287
Bergman, Ingrid, 152
Berlin, 25
  artistic and intellectual life of, 29–30
  SS's escape from, 31, 33–4, 37, 38, 39, 173
  SS's return to, 173

Bern, Paul, 20, 22, 23, 24, 26
Bernard, Raymond, 47, 50
Bernheim, Alain, 328
Bernstein, Leonard, 169
Berry, John, 43–4, 199
Betrayal, 401
  Academy Awards and, 373, 404
  acclaim for, 373
  cast and crew of, 366, 369–72
  director of, 365–70, 371–3
  distribution of, 373
  editing and scoring of, 371–2
  financing of, 369
  Horizon and, 366, 369
  screenplay of, 366, 368, 369, 370–1, 373
  SS as producer of, 365–74
Beverly Hills Hotel, 158
Bishop, Jeannette, 280
  see also Rothschild, Jeannette de
Bitania (kibbutz), 14
Blair, Betsy, 65, 88, 214
Blake, Yvonne, 318
Bloch, Vereina, 287
Bloch, Zeev, 14
Bloom, John, 371
Blowitz, Nina, 124, 144, 261, 264, 277
Blowitz, William F., 124, 179, 225
  African Queen publicity and, 144
  death of, 277–8
  Lawrence publicity and, 237, 242, 261, 255
Bogarde, Dirk, 233, 307
Bogart, Humphrey, 89–90, 93, 104, 110, 170, 200, 288
  in *African Queen,* 129, 130, 131, 133, 135, 136, 137, 138, 139, 140, 143, 144, 148, 402
Bogdanovich, Peter, 97, 98
Bolt, Robert, 306
  in anti-nuclear demonstration, 257, 259–60
  Lawrence screenplay and, 246–8, 252, 253, 255, 260, 264, 273
  Mutiny project and, 363
Bond, Edward, 329
Bonnie and Clyde, 300
Bottoms, David, 379, 384
Boulle, Pierre, 191, 196, 213, 214
Boult, Adrian, 270
Boulting, Ingrid, in *Last Tycoon,* 346, 351–2, 354, 357, 358

Bowie, David, 372
Box, John:
   Lawrence and, 247 256, 259, 263–5, 271
   Nicholas and, 325–6
Boyer, Charles, 71, 73, 75
Bradford, Richard, 292, 295, 299
Brand, Harry, 86
Brando, Marlon, 152, 238, 241
   in *Chase,* 292, 293, 297–8, 299
   SS's relationship with, 167–8, 178, 238, 297, 345
   in *Waterfront,* 161, 165–8, 169, 177, 309, 327
Brecht, Bertolt, 57, 63, 117
Breen, Joseph I., 81, 122
Bridge on the River Kwai, The, 172, 17, 183, 188–9, 191–3, 237, 277, 321, 386, 399
   Academy Awards for, 214, 402–3
   billing for, 213–14, 233
   bogus screenplay credit of, 199, 213–14
   bridge in, 199–200, 209–10
   budget of, 197, 208
   cast and crew of, 193, 194–5, 200–2, 205–7, 208, 209, 211, 224
   Columbia and, 191, 197, 198, 212, 213, 215, 216
   crew accommodations for, 203, 208
   editing and dubbing of, 211–12
   first SS and Lean meeting on, 195–6
   grosses of, 215
   Horizon Pictures and, 199
   Lean-SS tensions over, 203–5, 208, 215
   locations of, 194–5, 199–200, 207
   plot of, 193
   premieres of, 189, 212
   promotions for, 213
   rushes of, 205
   salaries for, 202
   screenplay of, 191, 196–7, 198–9, 213–15, 246
   SS as producer of, 191–216
   success of, 212–13, 215
   theme music of, 196, 212, 251, 324
Bridge over the River Kwai, The (Le Pont de la Rivière Kwai) (Boulle), 191, 196
Brief Encounter, 193, 369

British & Continental Productions Ltd., 42
British Lion, 276
Brook, Peter, 226, 230
Brownlow, Kevin, 193, 194, 197, 213, 256
Bruce, Evangeline, 286
Bruckbauer, Georg, 35
Brunel, Adrian, 42
Brynner, Yul, 234, 281, 288, 322, 326, 376, 387
Buchholz, Horst, 245
Buck, Joan Juliet, 287, 356
Buck, Jules, 6, 75, 76, 82, 84, 85, 87, 89, 105, 111, 125, 212, 212, 242, 287, 326
Budberg, Moura, 246, 317, 318
Burton, Richard, 221, 341, 348
Butler, Hugo, 122

Caine Mutiny, The, 170
Camper & Nicholson, 250
Camp Films, 223, 229
Camus, Albert, 234
Canby, Vincent, 314
Cannes Film Festival, 285, 320
Canton, Arthur, 223, 245, 272, 285, 304, 373
Capa, Robert, 141
Cardiff, Jack, 135–6, 138, 139
Carnegie Hall, 75
Carnet de Bal, Un, 71
Cartier, Rudolph, *see* Katscher, Rudolf
Carusi, Ugo, 81
Casino Royale, 301
Castillo, Antonio, 318
Cat on a Hot Tin Roof (Williams), 180, 224
CBS, 150
censorship, film, 81, 122, 132, 278
Ceylon, *Kwai* locations in, 194–5, 199–200, 207, 208
Chambers, Wheaton, 122
Champlin, Charles, 346
Chanel, Coco, 260, 279
Chaplin, Charles, 28, 42, 88
   UA sale negotiations and, 58, 125, 126, 156
Chase, The, 278, 290, 311, 315, 399–400
   cast and crew of, 292, 293, 295, 297–8, 299

Chase, The – *cont*
 Columbia and, 315, 332
 director of, 290, 293–5, 297–8
 editing of, 298
 plot of, 292–3
 publicity for, 306
 reception of, 299
 salaries for, 293
 scoring of, 298
 screenplay of, 290, 291, 292–4, 296–7
 SS as producer of, 291–300
 TV rights sold for, 332
Chase, The (Foote), 226, 290
Chaume, Jacqueline de la, 288
Cheever, John, 310
Cheshin, Ruth, 379
Chodorov, Edward, 104, 184, 265–6,
 275, 333
Chodorov, Rachel, 361, 362–3
Chodorov, Rosemary, 184, 260–1, 333
Christie, Julie, 337, 368
Churchill, Winston, 234
Ciro's, 59, 61
Cleopatra, 221, 259
Clift, Montgomery, 115, 166, 202–3
 in *Suddenly,* 217, 225–6, 228
Clouzot, Henri-Georges, 191
Clunes, Alec, 151
CMA, 302
Cobb, Lee J., 161, 166
Cohen, Mark M., 95, 106, 107, 148
Cohn, Harry, 114–15, 159, 233
 Columbia's East Coast office and, 160
 SS and, 160, 170, 197, 212
Cohn, Sydney, 332
Collier, John, 109, 129, 149
Collier, Lawrence, 113
Collins, Larry, 377
Colman, Ronald, 200
"Colonel Bogey" march, 196, 212, 251,
 324
Columbia:
 films financed by, *see specific films*
 New York unit of, 160, 180, 212
 Red Scare and, 115, 191
 SS as savior of, 215, 332, 373
 SS snubbed by, 373, 376
Communist Party, 115, 121, 159
 see also Red Scare
Condon, Richard, 70
Cook, Dorothea "Dosia," 41

Cooper, Jackie, 85
Cost of Living, The, see Prowler, The
Courtenay, Tom, 305
Coward, Noël, 57, 118, 187, 200
Crime on the Waterfront (Johnson),
 159
Crist, Judith, 310, 331
Cronyn, Hume, 231
Crosby, Bing, 67
Crowther, Bosley, 98, 299
Cuba, 110, 111–12
Curbetson, Edmund J. "Teddy Joyce," 45
Curious Gentlemen, The, 300
Curtis, Joe, 159
Curtis, Tony, 251, 253, 357
Czyzewska, Elzbieta "Elka," 309

Daily Express (London), 138–9
Daily Variety, 23, 103, 123, 145, 278
Daily Worker, 115
Dalton, Phyllis, *Lawrence* and, 248, 249,
 254, 256
Dangerous Friends (P. Viertel), 110
Dangerous Silence, 265–6
Davis, Bette, 129, 152, 222
Day, Richard, 74, 294, 312
Dean, James, 179–80, 27
Decoin, Henri, 31, 35
de Cordova, Frederick, 57
Dehn, Paul, 306, 310
De Laurentiis, Dino, 363
De Niro, Robert, *Last Tycoon* and, 345,
 354–5, 357
Derrière La Façade, 49
Dewey, Thomas, 110
Dickinson, Angie, 292, 297
Dietrich, Marlene, 71, 171, 187
Diller, Barry, 95, 275–6
 Last Tycoon and, 254, 255, 257, 258
Doctor Zhivago, 295, 300, 319
Domgraf-Fassbaender, Willi, 30–1
Donald, James, 193, 205–6, 210
Donleavy, J. P., 361
Dorchester Hotel (London), 43, 44
Douglas, Anne, 178, 286–7, 316, 322,
 356, 364
Douglas, Kirk, 70, 84, 121, 167, 178, 245,
 273, 296, 322, 356, 364
Douglas, Sharman, 153
Dover Street (SS's London office), 278,
 300

Dreben, Judge Raya (SS's niece), 7, 52, 83, 84, 375, 380, 383–4
Driscoll, Bobby, 127
Dr. No, 185
Drogheda, Kathleen, Countess of, 41
Dubost, Paulette, 29, 30–1, 38, 49
Dudley Ward, Penelope "Pempy," 40–1
Dumont, Margaret, 73
Dunaway, Faye, 251, 343
    in *Happening*, 302, 327
Dunne, Irene, 71
Dunne, Philip, 110
Duvivier, Christian, 73, 74
Duvivier, Julien, 3, 57, 109, 179
    Tales of Manhattan directed by, 71, 73, 74

Eagle, S. P., *see* Spiegel, Sam
Eagle-Lion Classics, 127
Eagle Productions, 91
Easy Rider, 320
Easy Riders, Raging Bulls: How the Sex-Drugs-and-Rock 'n' Roll Generation Saved Hollywood (Biskind), 320
Ehe mit beschränkter Haftung (Marriage with Limited Responsibility) (Ehe m.b.H), 28, 395
Ellacott, Joan, 228
Ellis, Elizabeth, 22
Ellis, Ralph, 22
Ellis Island, 21
End as a Man, see Strange One, The
End as a Man (Willingham), 180
Enterprise Pictures, 124
epic films, 259, 319
Ertegun, Ahmet, 342–4, 364, 382
Estevez, Betty, 185, 188, 283
Estevez, Luis, 185
European colony, in Hollywood, 58, 59, 62, 63–4
European Film Fund, 62
Evans, Laurence, 40, 41, 42, 45
Exodus, 121

Fahrenheit 451, 300
Fairbanks, Douglas, Jr., 200
Fairbanks, Douglas, Sr., 125
Famous Artists Agency, 71, 202
Fehr, Phillis "Rudi," 35, 356
Feisal, Prince, 235, 243

Feldman, Charles K., 63, 87, 88, 187, 202
    Tales of Manhattan and, 70, 71
Ferrer, José, 245
Fields, Freddie, 275, 287, 372–3
Fields, George, 128
Fields, W. C., 73–4
Filming All Quiet on the Western Front (Kelly), 27
Film-Kurier, 28, 31
Film Quarterly, 165
Fin du Jour, La, 109, 125
Finney, Albert, 241
Fiore, Carlo, 303
Fisher, Eddie, 223, 228
Fishgall, Garry, 312
Fitzgerald, F. Scott, 345, 353
Fonda, Afdera Franchetti, 282
Fonda, Henry, 71, 73, 320
Fonda, Jane, 292, 295, 297
Fonda, Peter, 320
Fonteyn, Margot, 288
Foote, Horton, 226, 290, 296
Ford, Freddy, 209
Ford, John, 67, 181, 191, 256
Foreman, Carl, 323
    Kwai screenplay and, 191, 196, 198, 214, 246
475 Park Avenue (SS's N.Y. apartment), 227, 323, 362
Fouquet's (Paris), 47, 48
Fowlie, Eddie, 325
Fox, Angela, 40, 41
Fox, Edward, 40
Fox, James, 40
    in *Chase*, 292, 295
    Fox, Matthew, 63, 187–8
Fox, William, 5
Fox, Yolande, 63, 187
Foxwell, Lady Edith, 153–4
Frack mit der Chrysantheme, Der (History of a Tailcoat and Its Use), 72
Francen, Victor, 73
Frankenheimer, John, 44, 282, 313
Frankovich, M. J. "Mike," 197, 214, 238, 240, 252, 277–8, 295, 303, 356
Franz Joseph, Emperor of Austria, 8
Fraser, Lady Antonia, 282, 354, 378
Frederick, Lynne, 318
Freedman, Alisa (SS's daughter), 105, 117, 337
    education of, 80, 83

Freedman, Alisa – *cont*
  SS's relationship with, 79–80, 82–4,
    127, 336, 383
Freedman, Leonard, 83
Freedman, Michael, 84
Frings, Kurt, 228, 240, 356
From Here to Eternity, 165
*From Prejudice to Persecution: A History of
  Austrian Anti-Semitism* (Pauley), 9
Fuchs, Daniel, 91, 92–3, 265
Fullerton, Fiona, 318

Gable, Clark, 119
Galicia, Galitzianers, 3, 4–5, 9–10
Galileo (Brecht), 117
Gandhi, 370
Garbo, Greta, 64, 152, 224, 286, 323
Garbus, Morton, 63, 80, 154
Garden District (Williams), 217
Gardner, Ava, 89, 131, 153
Garfein, Jack, 180, 181–3, 183–4, 205
Garfield, John, 89, 112, 113, 115
Garland, Judy, 70, 88
Gates, Larry, 180
Gazzara, Ben, 180, 184, 203
Geffen, David, 276, 363, 364, 382, 385
  SS's relationship with, 338, 345, 346
Gelehrter, Menachem, 14
George V hotel (Paris), 38, 47, 152, 192,
    211, 260, 277, 306, 307
German Exile Cinema, 34, 47, 58, 72
Ghost Music, 67
Gielgud, John, 200, 234
Godard, Jean-Luc, 73
Goddard, Paulette, 61, 63, 67
Goebbels, Dr. Joseph, 26
Goetz, William, 94, 97, 98–9
Golden Warrior, The see On the Waterfront
Golding, William, 226
Goldman, James
  Nicholas screenplay of, 321–2, 324–5,
    328–9, 330, 333
Goldman, William, 321
Goldwyn, Frances, 62
Goldwyn, Samuel, 5, 62–3, 117, 306
Goldwyn, Samuel, Jr., 64, 372
Goldwyn Studios, 60, 67, 84, 91
Goodbye to All That (Graves), 241
Göring, Hermann, 27
Gottlieb, Netty, 16
Gould, Jay, 118

Goulding, Edmund, 152
Graduate, The, 199, 279, 348
Graf, William, 198, 204, 211, 212
Grand Street Boys, The, 76, 91
Grant, Cary, 118, 167, 234, 245
  Kwai and, 200, 201
Granucci, Charlie, 113
Grapewin, Charley, 127
Grauman's Chinese Theatre, 75
Graves, Robert, 237, 241
Gray, Charles, 305
Graziani, Bettina, 288, 289
Gréco, Juliette, 305, 306
Greenthal, Norman, 63
Grosvenor House Hotel (SS's London
    apartment), 280, 337, 399
Grunwald, Anatole de, 233
Guare, John, 362
Guber, Peter, 330
Guinness, Alec
  in *Lawrence,* 245, 262
  and Lean's Gandhi project, 234
  in *Kwai,* 193, 200–1, 206–7, 208, 214,
    327
Guitry, Sacha, 48

Haddad, Carrie, 340, 342, 344, 345, 354,
    355, 365
Haig Corporation, 94, 96, 98
Hakim, Raymond, 48
Hakim, Robert, 48
Hale, Denise Minnelli, 279, 282–3
Hall, Peter, 242
Hall, Sherry, 122
Hamilton, Guy, 135
Hamlisch, Marvin, 314
Happening, The, 400
  as box office flop, 304
  begun as *The Innocent,* 301
  cast and crew of, 302–3
  Columbia and, 301–3
  director of, 301, 302, 304
  location of, 301, 303, 304
  plot of, 302
  SS as executive producer of, 301–4
  trouble on set of, 303
Harlow, Jean, 23
Harris, Frank, 115
Harris, Jed, 119
Harris, Radie, 150–1
Harrison, Rex, 321, 326

Hart, Kitty Carlisle, 62, 288
Hart, Walter Morris, 22
Hartmann, Paul, 34
Harvey, Anthony, 323–4
Harvey, Laurence, 240
Hashomer Hatzair, 10–11, 13–18
    SS and, 10–12, 13–15, 17
Hassan II, King of Morocco, 266
Hawa, Gibran, 244
Hawkins, Jack:
    in *Lawrence*, 245
    in *Kwai*, 193, 201, 204, 207, 208
Hawks, Howard, 191, 192
Hayakawa, Sessue, 193, 207
Hays Office, 81, 122, 132
Hayward, Bill, 71, 320
Hayward, Leland, 71, 187, 288, 320
Hayward, Slim, 187, 189, 283, 288
Hayworth, Rita, 72, 86, 89, 172, 212
Heath, Edward, 286, 371
Hecht, Ben, 70, 72, 114, 117
    as *We Were Strangers* script doctor, 114
Heflin, Van, 122, 123
Heifetz, Jascha, 33
Heit, Albert, 3, 125–6, 140, 157, 161,
    172, 184, 215, 216, 275, 327, 332,
    339, 355, 364,380, 383,
Hellinger, Mark, 102
Hellman, Lillian, 279
    Chase and, 290, 291–4, 296–7, 298–9
    SS's relationship with, 291–2, 298–9,
    314
Hemingway, Ernest, 112
Hendricks, Lily Mae, 86
Henry, Buck, 348
Hepburn, Katharine, 192, 324, 353, 365
    in *African Queen*, 129, 130, 131, 133,
    134, 135, 136, 137–8, 139–40,
    143, 144
    in *Suddenly*, 217, 222, 224–5, 226, 228,
    229
Herald Tribune, 229
Herman, Dzidzia, 308
Heyman, John, 355, 358
Heymann, Irene, 47, 92, 150
Higgins, James, 280, 358
Hildyard, Jack, 203, 224, 225
Hill, Gladys, 91–2, 122, 132, 141–2
Hill, James, 172
Hilpert, Heinz, 31
Hingle, Pat, 180

Historia de un Frac (Story of a Tailcoat)
    (Rojas Gonzáles), 51
Hitchcock, Alfred, 88, 96, 110, 178
Hitler, Adolf, 27, 29, 57
Hobbs, Phil, 203, 249
Hodge, Patricia, 336, 369, 372
Hoffman, Dustin, 350–1
Holcenberg, Samuel G., 21–2, 24
Holden, William, 225, 234
    in *Kwai*, 193, 201–2, 207, 208, 209,
    210, 215–16
Hollywood:
    card playing in, 60–1, 62–3, 64, 75, 76,
    85, 87, 93
    European and Jewish refugee colony
    in, 58, 59, 61, 64
    Jewish names in, 70–1
    Red Scare in, *see* Red Scare
    SS's attitude toward, 59, 279, 347
    support for Israel in, 117
Hollywood Reporter, 103, 114
Homolka, Oscar, 29, 33, 35, 62
homosexuality, in films, 183, 229,
    230
Hopkins, Miriam, 61, 297–8
Hopper, Dennis, 320
Hopper, Hedda, 88, 121, 223
Horizon-America, 161
Horizon Pictures, 131–44, 147–8, 171,
    184, 199, 237, 242, 243, 252, 260,
    265, 366, 385
    East Coast move of, 161
    finances of, 119–20, 128, 129, 131,
    134, 142, 144, 145, 148, 149
    Huston bought out of, 150
    incorporation of, 105
    meaning of, to SS and Huston, 106,
    107, 129
    productions of, *see specific films*
    reactions on founding of, 106
Hornblow, Arthur, Jr., 58, 85, 337
Hornblow, Leonora, 58, 61, 64, 88, 90,
    102, 103, 185, 189, 288, 337
Horne, Geoffrey:
    in *Kwai*, 193, 203
    in *Strange One*, 180
Hotel Imperial (Biro), 9
Hotel Reforma (Mexico City), 50,
    51
Hothouse, The, 152
House, Billy, 96, 97

Houser, Fred, 81
House Un-American Activities
    Committee (HUAC), 121, 159
Howar, Barbara, 343–4
Howard, G. Wren, 238
Howard, Jean, 58
Howard, Noël, 263
Hudson, Rock, 225
Hughes, Howard, 88, 89
Hunt, Martita, 151
Hussein, King of Jordan, 243–4, 251–2,
    258
Huston, Anjelica, 337, 386
Huston, John, 82, 86, 87, 106–8, 123–4,
    192, 312
    adventurousness of, 109
    AFI lifetime achievement award and,
        385–6
    as *African Queen* director, 129–44,
        147, 148
    as hunter, 132, 134, 135, 139–40
    as philanderer, 61, 149
    practical jokes of, 93, 108–9, 112–13,
        143, 163
    as screenwriter, 91, 92–3, 109,
        111–12, 117, 127, 131, 133
    SS's personal relationship with, 59,
        60, 105, 107–8, 132–3, 150
    SS's professional relationship with,
        58, 93, 105–50, 173, 385
    wives of, 119, 140
Huston, Walter, 107, 115
Hutchinson, Tom, 328
Hyde, Johnny, 87, 113
Hyer, Martha, 302

*Ich will Dich Liebe lehren (I Will Teach
    You to Love)*, 30–1, 73, 395–6
Immigration and Naturalization Service
    (INS), 20, 21, 22, 23
independent films, 58, 120, 125–6,
    173
Innocent, The, see Happening, The
International Studios, 94, 97, 98
Invader, The (An Old Spanish Custom),
    42–3, 396
    cast and crew of, 38, 42–3
    distribution of, 43
    money problems on, 43–4
    production company for, 42
Ireland, 149

Irons, Jeremy, in *Betrayal,* 366, 371
Irving G. Thalberg Memorial Award,
    277, 346
Israel, 5, 251, 315
    American Jewish support for, 117–18
    offered as *Lawrence* location, 243
    SS's bequests to, 376, 378, 383–4
Israel Film Studio, 117
Israel Museum, The, 376, 383

Jaffe, Leo, 160, 170, 212, 233, 236, 239,
    241, 270, 295, 301–2, 303, 319, 320,
    327, 329, 330, 332, 346
Jaffe, Mrs. Leo, 283
Jaffe, Sam, 124
Jaffe, Stanley R., 170, 315, 319, 320
Jaroslav (Galicia), 3, 5, 8, 9
Jaroslav Society, 13
Jarre, Maurice, 357, 385
    Lawrence score and, 268–9, 270, 274
Jarrott, Charles, 325
Javanart Punynchoti, 208
Jayston, Michael, 328
Jeritza, Maria, 3–4
Jerusalem, 16
Jerusalem Foundation, The, bequest for
    SS's art collection sought by, 376,
    378
Jewish Colonization Association (JCA),
    13
Jewish Committee for Personal Services
    in State Institutions, 21
Jewish Institute of Religion, 21, 52
Jews, Judaism, 3, 7, 36, 60, 64, 70, 115,
    182, 336
    Ashkenazi, 4
    as refugees in Hollywood film
        community, 58, 59, 62, 63–4
    support for Israel by, 118–19
    as targets of Galician pogroms, 9
    in Vienna intellectual and cultural life,
        4–5
    and visas to Arab countries, 243
    see also anti-Semitism
Johnstone, Anna "Johnny" Hill, 352
Jones, David, as *Betrayal* director,
    366–70, 372
Jones, Jennifer, 166, 296
    in *We Were Strangers,* 112, 113,
        114
Jones, Robert Edmond, 22

Jordan, 249–50, 251–2
  Lawrence locations in, 243–4, 249, 256, 257
Jordan, James, 284, 343, 377
Josephs, Edward, 137
Julia, 292
Jurmann, Walter, 28, 30, 40
Justin, John, 151

Kanin, Fay, 127
Kanin, Michael, 91
  as *When I Grow Up* director, 125, 126, 127, 128
Kannikar Dowklee, 208
Kanter, Jay, 165, 166, 167
Kaper, Bronislaw, 28, 30, 31, 40, 51, 63, 91
Karajan, Herbert von, 336
Kashfi, Anna, 297
Katscher, Rudolf, 35
Kauffmann, Stanley, 331, 373
Kaye, Danny, 65, 70, 88, 124
Kazan, Elia, 20, 92, 179, 180, 181, 191, 201, 218, 220, 294, 338, 373
  as HUAC friendly witness, 159, 356
  as *Last Tycoon* director, 347, 351, 352, 354, 355, 357, 358, 359
  as philanderer, 87, 104, 164, 354
  on SS as producer, 158, 163–4, 168, 195, 231, 261, 314, 386
  SS's relationship with, 85, 163–4, 195, 231, 313, 359, 383, 386
  as *Waterfront* director, 158–9, 162–72, 177, 221, 231, 386
Kazan, Molly, 165, 219, 231
Keaton, Buster, 38, 42–3, 57
Keaton, Diane, 337, 361
Kelly, Gene, 65
Kelly, Grace (later, Grace of Monaco), 166, 178, 323, 326
Kennedy, Arthur, 245
Kennedy, John F., 272, 293
Kennedy, Joseph P., 69–70, 272
Kennedy, Tessa, 285, 341–2, 356–7, 379
Kennedy Center Honors, 279
Kent, Jennifer, *see* Attebery, Jennifer
Kessel, Joseph, 48, 306
Kettner, Debbie, 283
Kettner, Max, 240
Keyes, Evelyn, 59, 86–7, 108, 109, 278
  Huston and, 105, 118–19

in *Prowler,* 122, 123
Key Largo, 36, 106, 130
Kinberg, Jud, 300, 315
  as producer of *The Happening,* 301, 303, 304
Kinematograph, 34
Kingsley, Ben:
  in *Betrayal,* 366, 370, 371
  in *Gandhi,* 370
Kohner, Lupita (Tovar), 29, 30, 50, 52, 58, 61–2, 356
  in The Invader, 43, 43
Kohner, Paul, 42, 47, 82, 92, 149
  as agent, 50, 62, 71, 87, 107, 245
  SS's relationship with, 29, 30, 59, 60, 81, 82, 356
Kolleck, Teddy, 376, 379
Korda, Alexander, 39, 44, 68, 145, 222, 233, 246, 276
  Kwai and, 191, 197, 200
Korda, Vincent, *Nicholas* and, 318, 326
Korda, Zoltan, 191
Korniloff's (restaurant), 141
Kramer, Stanley, 124, 198, 277
Kravetz, Max, 126
Krim, Arthur, 142, 153
  missing *Melba* funds and, 155–6, 160
  in UA acquisition, 58, 125–6
Kurnitz, Harry, 243
  as *Melba* screenwriter, 151, 152, 154

Lacombe, Georges, 49
Laemmle, Carl, Sr., 35, 27, 29
Laffin, Ed and Mae, 96
Lamarr, Hedy, 36, 75, 365
Lancaster, Burt, 108, 160, 294, 312
  in *Swimmer,* 310–13, 314
Lanchester, Elsa, 73, 129, 201
Landscape of the Body, The (Guare), 362
Lane, Jeffrey, 318, 323
Lane, Kenneth Jay, 187, 281, 284
Lang, Fritz, 34, 38, 71
Lantz, Robert, 299, 317
Lanvin, Lisette, 31
La Samanna hotel, 381
LaShelle, Joseph, 298
Lastfogel, Abe, 171
Last Tycoon, The, 401
  Academy Awards and, 403
  cast and crew of, 345–6, 349–53, 355, 357

Last Tycoon – cont
director of, 347, 349–50, 351, 352, 354, 355, 357, 358, 359
earlier attempts at making of, 346
finances of, 355, 358
location of, 355
Horizon and, 358
Paramount and, 348, 354, 355, 358
plot of, 345–6
premiere of, 357
reviews of, 357
screenplay of, 346, 348–9, 350–1, 352, 354, 359
SS as producer of, 345–59
Laszlo, Ernest, 127
Laughton, Charles, 73, 117, 129, 200, 201
Laurents, Arthur, 105, 141, 152, 159
Lawrence, Arnold Walter "A.W.," 237–8, 269, 272
Lawrence, Thomas Edward "T.E.": 234–5
books and plays by and about, 237, 240–1
others' attempts at filming story of, 233, 240–1
Lawrence of Arabia, 317, 318, 319, 321, 385, 399
Academy Awards and, 263, 273–4, 403
background material for, 234–6
billing for, 233, 273
cast and crew of, 236, 238, 241–2, 245, 247, 248–9, 252–4, 256, 257, 258, 259, 262, 264, 267
Columbia and, 233, 236, 238, 242, 250, 252, 260, 262, 274, 332, 385
cost and financing of, 236, 259
crew accommodations for, 249–51
days off from, 253–4
director of, 233–74
grosses of, 274
Horizon and, 237, 238, 240, 242, 243, 252, 260, 385
Jordanian army in, 244
locations in, 243–4, 249, 256, 257, 259, 261, 263, 264, 265, 266–7
plot of, 235
premieres of, 271–2
publicity for, 237, 242, 271–3, 277
rerelease of, 385

royal performance of, 270
rushes of, 254–5, 261, 263, 269
salaries for, 253, 270, 385
scoring of, 268–70
screenplay of, 237–8, 240, 242, 245–8, 252, 255, 260, 264, 273
shooting duration of, 233, 263
SS as producer of, 233–74, 275, 276, 291, 385
SS-Lean clashes over, 235–6, 247–9, 255–6, 259, 261–2, 263–5, 267, 270–1
TV deal for, 332
Lazar, Irving "Swifty," 88, 347, 378
Lazarus, Paul N., Jr., 169, 188, 197, 202, 213, 237
Lean, David, 226, 293, 295, 346, 359
early films of, 193
first meeting of SS and, 39–40
Gandhi film envisioned by, 234
as *Lawrence* director, 233–74
Lawrence rerelease and, 385
Mutiny on the Bounty project of, 363
personality of, 193–4, 235, 239–40
Kwai and, 192–216
SS as catalyst in career of, 193
on SS as producer, 179, 234
SS's personal relationship with, 181, 185–6, 235, 240, 255–6, 257–8, 363
SS's professional relationship with, 185–6, 193–4, 196–7, 198, 212, 235, 25, 255–6, 257–8, 259, 261–2, 262–5, 267, 270–1, 363, 385
Lean, Leila Matkar, 203–5, 212, 239–40
Legion of Decency, 229
Leigh, Vivien, 222, 224
Leitner, Isabella, 182, 184, 205
Lemberg, 5
Lemmon, Jack, 265
LeRoy, Mervyn, 87
Lesser, Sol, 81
Leven, Boris, 74, 123
Levy, Norman, 373
Lewin, David, 138–9
Lewis, Roger H., 311, 312, 313
Life, 104, 109, 118, 285
Life, A (Kazan), 159
Lillie, Mildred L., 178
Lion in Winter, The, 321–2, 324
Lion in Winter, The (Goldman), 321–2

Litvak, Anatole "Tola," 29, 30, 59, 61, 93, 107, 286, 309
   as *Night of* director, 304–5, 307, 309–10
Litvak, Sophie, 286
Lloyd, Harold, 42
Lloyd, Norman, 64, 83, 119, 125
Loden, Barbara, 313, 314
Lodz (Poland), 10
London, 1950's social scene in, 153
Longworth, Gay, 384
Lopert, Ilya, 192, 240
Lopert, Tanya, 192
Lord of the Flies (Golding), 226, 230
Lorre, Peter, 29, 33, 34–5
Los Angeles Examiner, 96
Los Angeles Times, 125, 237, 278
Losey, Joseph, 57
   Accident and, 125, 3001
   as *Prowler* director, 117, 120, 122–5, 128, 300
Lubitsch, Ernst, 23, 64, 67
Lucey's, 124
Lvov (Lviv), 5, 9
Lydia, 68, 71
Lyric Films, 67

M, 35
Macbeth (Welles), 98
McCallum, John, 151
McGuire, Charlie, 169
Maclean, Alistair, 237
MacNamara, Paul, 124
Maharis, George, 302
Malahne (yacht), 249–51, 264, 266–7, 312, 320, 329, 359
   sale of, 377
   social scene on, 266, 279, 284–8, 299, 322, 335, 336, 341–4
Malden, Karl, 162, 166
Malle, Louis, 30, 362, 368
Maltese Falcon, The, 111, 129, 130
Man for All Seasons, A (Bolt), 246
Mankiewicz, Joseph L., 118, 199, 230, 293, 382
   Nicholas and, 324
   as producer, 220
   as *Suddenly* director, 220–2, 224–5, 225–6, 228, 229, 230
Mankiewicz, Rosemary, 118, 220
Mann, Thomas, 57, 63

Mannix, Eddie, 110
Manson murders, 286
Maree, A. Morgan, 149
Margulies, Irwin, 157
Maria, 50
Mariage à Responsabilité Limitée, 28
Mariani-Berenger, Josanne, 178
Markey, Gene, 75
Martin, Tony, 89
Marton, Andrew, 67
Mas d'Horizon (house), 342, 377
Maskel, Maggy, 144
Mason, James, 88, 131, 200
Mauretania, 19
Maurus, Gerda, 34
Maxwell, John, 122
Maxwell, Robert, 5
Mayer, Louis B., 5, 69, 94, 110
MCA, 167
Me (Hepburn), 136
Medcraft, Charles H., 77, 106
Mehle, Aileen, 41–2
Mein Film, 36
Meir, Golda, 118, 330
Meissner, Leopold, 34
Melba, 173, 398
   cast and crew of, 150, 151, 153, 154, 155
   director of, 152, 154
   financing and costs of, 150, 152, 153, 155, 160
   plot of, 151, 154
   reviews of, 155
   screenplay of, 151, 152
   SS as producer of, 150–6
   UA and, 153, 154–6, 160
Melba, Dame Nellie, 150–5
Mengers, Sue, 285, 353, 356
Merchant, Vivien, 354
Merivale, Philip, 96
Messel, Oliver, 223, 229
Metro-Goldwyn-Mayer (MGM), 20, 23–4, 25, 49, 91, 107, 110, 120, 125, 347, 348, 372
Mexicana, 51–2
Mexico, 42
Mexico City, 50–3
Mickey One, 295
Milestone, Lewis "Milly," 26, 90, 91, 118, 159, 179, 241
   as *Melba* director, 152, 154

Milford, Gene, 298
Milland, Ray, 200, 353
Miller, Arthur (cinematographer), 123
Miller, Arthur (playwright), 84, 108–9,
    140, 164
Miller, Carrie, *see* Haddad, Carrie
Miller, David, 84
Mills, John, 153
Mira-Films, 49
Mirande, Yves, 43, 48–9
Mircha, 48
Mirren, Helen, 369, 370
Misfits, The, 109, 140
Mitchell, Thomas, 72
Mitchum, Robert, 345
Mizrachi movement, 5
Moffat, Ivan, 103, 296
Mollo, John, 318
Monaco, Princess Caroline of, 343
Monaco, Grace of, *see* Kelly, Grace
Monroe, Marilyn, 57, 86–7, 103, 113,
    200, 293, 299
Montague, Abe, 160
Moon for the Misbegotten, A (O'Neill),
    106
Moorehead, Agnes, 99
Morath, Inge, 154
Moreau, Jeanne, 353, 355, 357, 358
Morgan, Jess, 149
Morley, Robert, 130, 151
Morocco, *Lawrence* locations in, 266–7
Moross, Jerome, 127
Morrell, André, 204
Morris Payne, Dorothy, 212
Morros, Boris, 67–77
    early credits of, 67
    as Soviet spy, 67, 68, 76
    Tales of and, 67–75
Motion Picture Association of America
    (MPAA), 183, 263
Moulin Rouge, 150
Mountbatten, Louis, Lord, 330, 331
Muir, Jean, 369, 371
Muldowney, Dominic, 372
Mulli Abdullah, prince of Morocco, 266
Müller, Robert, 36
Munsel, Patrice, in *Melba,* 150–1, 152,
    153, 155
Musaddiq, Mohammed, 262
Mussolini, Benito, 27
Mutiny on the Bounty, 241

Mutiny on the Bounty (Lean-Spiegel
    project), 363

NBC, 187
Nebenzahl, Seymour, 38, 48, 50
Nebenzal, Harold, 38, 48, 50
Negulesco, Jean, 67
Nelligan, Kate, 349
Newman, Paul, 166, 294
New Republic, 331, 373
New Scotland Yard, 45, 50, 69
New York magazine, 366
New York Daily News, 384
New Yorker, 97, 129, 155, 299
New York Post, 373
New York Times, 52, 75, 98, 159, 169,
    218, 219–20, 229, 272, 299, 311,
    351, 373
Ngamta Suphaphongs, 208
Nicholas and Alexandra, 357, 401
    Academy Awards and, 331, 403
    art design and costumes of, 318, 326,
        331
    budget of, 321, 327, 332
    cast and crew of, 318, 325–6, 328–9
    Columbia and, 323, 325–7, 330, 331,
        332
    directors of, 322, 323–5, 329–30, 355
    locations for, 318–19, 329
    as outdated from its inception, 319,
        321, 333
    plot of, 317, 321, 322
    premieres of, 330–1
    reviews of, 331
    Schaffner-SS tensions over, 330
    screenplay of, 321–3, 324–5, 327,
        328–9, 333
    SS as producer of, 315, 317–33
Nicholas and Alexandra (Massie), 317,
    318
Nichols, Mike, 4, 5, 8, 199, 274, 276, 284,
    288, 289, 299, 376, 384, 386
    Betrayal and, 366
    Last Tycoon and, 347–8, 349–50, 366
    SS's realtionship with, 279, 337
Nicholson, Charles E., 250
Nicholson, Jack, 320
    in *Last Tycoon,* 351, 353, 354, 358
    SS's relationship with, 167, 337, 343,
        344–5, 348, 359, 386
Night of the Generals, The, 278, 304, 400

as box office flop, 304, 310
cast and crew of, 305, 307, 308, 310, 326
Columbia and, 304, 315
credits of, 309–10
director of, 304–5, 307, 309–10
Litvak-SS tensions over, 309–10
locations of, 304, 305, 308, 309
plot of, 305
publicity for, 304
salaries for, 307–8
screenplay of, 306–7, 309
SS as producer of, 304–10
Nissen, Juliet, 41
Niven, David, 243, 245, 322
Noiret, Philippe, 305
Noor, Queen of Jordan, 379
Nosseck, Max, 38
Nouvelle Vague (New Wave), 294, 298
Nureyev, Rudolf, 279
Nutting, Anthony, *Lawrence* and, 242–4, 250, 254, 256, 262, 269

Oakley, Ken, 340
O'Brien, Edmond, 103, 245
O'Connor, Edward J., 80, 105
O'Connor, William V., 80–1
Olivier, Laurence, 200, 231, 234, 245, 329
Olson, James, 180
Onassis, Aristotle, 289
Onassis, Jacqueline Kennedy, 5, 364
On the Waterfront, 76, 194, 294, 386, 398
  Academy Awards won by, 1, 177–8, 402
  billing for, 171, 229
  cast of, 161–2, 165–8, 201, 309
  Columbia and, 115, 160–1, 169–70, 332
  director of, 158, 162–72, 221, 231, 386
  financing of, 160–1, 168, 171
  German dubbing of, 174
  Horizon-America and, 161
  initial rejected pitches of, 158, 159
  plot of, 1612
  promotion for, 170–1
  score of, 169
  screenplay of, 158, 162, 168, 170–1, 177, 180, 321, 386
  shooting conditions of, 168
  SS as producer of, 158–73, 231, 248, 386

tensions between SS and crew on, 168–9, 231
  UA and, 160
Ostjuden, 4
O'Toole, Peter, 253, 271, 294, 324
  Chase and, 294, 295
  under contract to Spiegel, 294, 308
  in *Night of,* 305, 307, 308, 326
  in *Lawrence,* 238, 241–2, 247, 253, 254, 263, 271
  Nicholas and, 326
  Suddenly screen test of, 241
Ouarzazate, Morocco, 266
Ouvrier, Sophie, 288

Palestine, 117
  Hashomer Hatzair and, 10, 11, 13–18
  kibbutzim in, 13–14
Paley, Babe, 118, 189, 283
Paley, William, 118, 283
Palimpsest (Vidal), 387
Pal Joey, 172, 212
Palmer, John, 247, 248
Pan-Film, 34
Paramount Studios, 22, 67, 68, 70, 91
Parks, Michael, 302, 303
Parrish, Kathleen, 104, 115, 118, 142, 143, 172, 179, 183
Parrish, Robert, 115, 118, 141, 183, 250, 263, 280
  as director of *Dangerous Silence,* 265
Parsons, Louella O., 88, 189, 226
Pasternak, Joe, 29, 60
Patton, 325, 329
Pearlman, Moshe, 243
Pearse, John, 344
Peck, Gregory, 167, 322
Penn, Arthur, 192–3, 291–2, 312
  as director of *Chase* and, 290, 293–5, 297–8, 299–300
Pennington, Ann E., 315–16, 335–6, 337, 339, 377
Peppard, George, 180, 181
Perry, Anthony, 193
Perry, Eleanor, *Swimmer* screenplay and, 310–14
Perry, Frank, *Swimmer* director and, 310–14
Pfitzner, Felix, 28
Phipps, Diana, 286
Picker, Jean, 144

Pickford, Mary, 58, 125, 156
Pidgeon, Walter, 75
Pierson, Frank, 301
Pinès, Romain, 48
Pinter, Harold, 184, 279, 306, 379, 387
  Accident screenplay and, 301
  Betrayal screenplay and, 365–6, 368,
    369, 370–1, 373
  Last Tycoon screenplay and, 348–9,
    350–1, 352, 354, 359
Place in the Sun, A, 147
Pleasence, Donald, 305, 307, 353, 357
Pleskow, Eric, 155
Plowright, Joan, 231
Plummer, Christopher, 305
Polanski, Roman, 340
Poles, Poland, 9–10, 11, 57, 304, 305,
  309
"Politics of Power in *On the Waterfront,*
  The" (Biskind), 165
Pollack, Sydney, 313, 314
Pommer, Erich, 72
Porter, Eric, 329
Portman, Eric, 200
Power, Tyrone, 74, 200
Preminger, Ingo, 37, 68, 119–20, 121,
  123, 125, 278
Preminger, Otto, 53, 59, 60, 87, 183, 212
  blacklisted writers and, 121, 214
  escape story of, 31, 368
Preston, Robert, 127
Prinzmetal, I. H., 154
Private Life of Henry VIII, The, 39, 318
producers:
  decline of, 320, 373
  megalomania of, 306
  as packagers, 347
  of violent movies, 347
Production Code Administration, 183,
  229
Progressive Party, 110
Prowler, The, 117, 128, 150, 397–8
  cast and crew of, 122, 123
  as critical success, 125
  director of, 117, 120, 122–5, 128, 300
  financing for, 120, 124
  Hays office and, 122–3
  locations and shooting of, 123
  plot of, 122
  release of, 126–7
  screenplay of, 121–2

SS as producer of, 120–6

Quare Fellow, The (Behan), 276
Quayle, Anthony, 200, 245, 249
Quinn, Anthony, 245, 302
Quinn, Pat, 295

Rafelson, Bob, 373
Raimu, 35, 49
Rains, Claude, 245
Ramsay, Margaret "Peggy," 246
Rappaport, Romuald, 48–9
Ray, Nicholas, 191, 242
Rayner, William and Chessy, 380, 382
Redford, Robert, 361
  in *Chase,* 292, 295, 327
Redgrave, Michael, 329
Redgrave, Vanessa, 257, 326
Reds, 361
Red Scare:
  blacklisted artists and, 121, 159, 196,
    198–9, 214, 238, 240, 242, 246,
    273, 291
  loyalty oaths and, 115
Reed, Carol, 40, 191, 192, 241, 249, 312
Reed, Rex, 373
Reisch, Walter, 29, 72, 152, 179, 356
Remarque, Erich Maria, 26, 31
Renoir, Jean, 30, 71
Requins du Pétrole, Les, 35
Revolt in the Desert (Lawrence), 241
Reynolds, Debbie, 223, 224
Rheiner, Sam, 76, 122, 132, 141–2, 161,
  183
Ribes, Jacqueline de, 279
Richardson, Natasha, 326, 343
Richardson, Ralph, 200
Rickey, Pat, 376, 380, 381
Riefenstahl, Leni, 26–7
Rieger, Eliezer, 10
Right Honourable Gentleman, The, 321
Rizzo, Willy, 344
RKO, 81, 95
Robertson, Cliff, 203
Robeson, Paul, 74
Robinson, Edward G.:
  art collection of, 64, 103
  SS's relationship with, 60, 64, 70, 112
  in *Stranger,* 91, 94, 96, 99
  in *Tales,* 71, 73
  We Were Strangers and, 112

Rochas, Hélène, 47
Rodgers, Richard, 269
Roeg, Nicolas, 239, 267
Rogers, Ginger, 71, 72
Roi des Champs-Elysées, Le (The Champ of the Champs Elysées), 38
Rojas Gonzáles, Francisco, 52
Roland, Gilbert, 112, 113
Romanoff, Mike, 144
Romanoff's, 59, 88, 103, 144, 172
Romero, Cesar, 73
Romulus Films, *African Queen* and, 131, 134, 144, 147
Ronet, Maurice, 245, 252
Ronstadt, Linda, 335
Rosenfield, Jonas, 237
Rosenthal, Ann, 131
Rose Tattoo, The (Williams), 218
Ross (Rattigan), 240
Ross, Lillian, 129
Roth, Lester M., 115
Roth, Richard, 148, 292
Rothschild, Edmond de, 13
Rothschild, Evelyn de, 280
Rothschild, Jeannette de, 330, 339, 352
    see also Bishop, Jeannette
Rothschild, Marie-Hélène de, 330
Rotter, Fritz, 28, 30, 109
Rough Sketch, see We Were Strangers
Rough Sketch (Sylvester), 109
Royal Shakespeare Company (RSC), 242, 328
Rubenstein, Nelly, 309
Rule, Janice, 295, 314
Runyon, Damon, 81
Russell, Theresa, 353
Russian People, The, 91, 92–3
Ryder, Win, 212

Sacks, David, 262
Saint, Eva Marie in *Waterfront*, 166, 171, 177
Salkind, Ilja, 28
Sam Spiegel Film and Television School (Jerusalem), 384
Sánchez, F. M., 51
Sanders, George, 73, 88
San Francisco County Jail No. 2, 21
San Francisco Examiner, 20
Sascha (Austria's film corporation), 35
Saturday Review of Literature, 155

Schaffner, Franklin J., as *Nicholas* director, 325, 329–30, 355
Schenck, Joe, 68, 91
Schlesinger, Alexandra, 285
Schlesinger, Arthur, Jr., 279, 285
Schneer, Charles, 274
Schneider, Abe, 160, 169, 303, 327
Schneider, Bert, 320
Schneider, Ida, 283
Schneider, Stanley, 327
Schnitzler, Arthur, 4, 29
Schrader, Paul, 320
Schreyeck, Elaine, 222, 225
Schulberg, Adelaide "Ad," 44–5, 82, 171
Schulberg, B. P., 22, 44–5, 170
Schulberg, Budd, 22, 23, 44, 87, 338
    infuriated by SS, 4, 161, 162–3, 322
    Waterfront screenplay and, 158, 162–3, 168, 170–1, 177, 180, 321, 386
Schuler, Robert, 150–1, 152
Schwitz, Mechel and Eda, 6
Sciclounoff, Pierre, 319, 336, 343
Scott, Martha, 127
screenwriters, blacklisted, 121, 159, 196, 198–9, 214, 238, 240, 242, 246, 273, 291
Seaton, George, 214
Sellers, Peter, 302, 318
Selznick, Daniel, 289–90
Selznick, David O., 5, 62, 69, 114, 170, 211, 222, 289–90, 296
Selznick, Irene Mayer, 61, 178, 278, 335, 345
Selznick, Lewis J., 5
Selznick, Mary Jennifer, 354
Senouf, Paul, 266
702 North Crescent Drive (SS's Hollywood home), 79, 85–90, 103, 157–8
    bar in, 85
    as "boy's town," 57–8, 85, 76–7
    decoration of, 85–6
    financing for, 77
Seven Pillars of Wisdom (T. E. Lawrence), 236, 237
    rights acquired to, 237–8, 264
Shadwick, Erna, 8
Shaffer, Peter, *Lord of the Flies* and, 226–7, 230

Sharif, Omar, 283–4
    under contract to Spiegel, 252, 300,
        307–8
    in *Doctor Zhivago*, 300
    in *Night of*, 305, 307, 309
    in *Lawrence*, 252–3, 271, 273–4, 327
Shaw, Adam, 287
Shaw, Irwin, 110, 118, 132, 142, 163,
    187, 192, 288
Shaw, Marion, 118, 141, 142, 288
Shayne, Konstantin, 96, 97
Shepperton Studios, 223, 225
Shohman, Yedidia, 13–14
Shuftan, Eugene (Eugen Schüfftan), 35,
    43, 48
Shurlock, Geoffrey M., 263
Sievering Studios, 35
Silcocks, Alan (English business
    manager), 224, 278, 341, 378–9
Silverstein, Elliot, as *Happening* director,
    301, 302, 304
Silverstone, Murray, 75
Simon, Paul, 372
Sims, Jeanie, 143
Sinatra, Frank, 153–4, 172–3
    Waterfront role and, 165–6, 171–2
Singular Man, A (Donleavy), 361
Siodmak, Robert, 29, 38, 48, 92, 96,
    159–60, 312
Smagghe, André, 263
Smith, Jean Kennedy, 287
Smith, Liz, 384
Smith, Steve, Jr., 279, 287
Something Outspoken (Williams), 217
Song of Norway, The, 109
Spaatz, Carl A., 64
Spain, 229–30, 263–5
    Lawrence locations in, 260, 325
    Nicholas locations in, 318, 319
    Suddenly locations in, 221, 223, 228
Spector, Maude, 245, 318
Spencer, Norman, 194, 196–7, 225–6,
    236, 265, 266–7
Spiegel, Abraham Solomon and Bruche,
    6
Spiegel, Adam, 337, 378, 387
    birth of, 315, 335
    delinquent behavior of, 377–8, 384
    Jewish identity of, 336
    SS's relationship with, 323,
        336–7,342, 377

    SS's will and, 380, 384
    success as theatrical producer, 384
Spiegel, Betty Benson, 63, 65, 161, 167,
    172, 173, 179, 181, 231, 239, 240,
    271, 274, 278, 279–80, 282, 330,
    337, 385
    affairs of, 185, 187, 283–4
    age difference between SS and, 186,
        339
    birth and childhood of, 186
    career of, 185, 186–7
    intelligence and quick wit of, 185, 187
    Lean-SS relationship and, 185–6
    parents of, 186, 187–8, 189, 289
    Regina Spiegel and, 189
    on *Kwai*, 192, 202, 204, 207, 208, 209,
        215
    SS's relationship with, 185–6, 187–8,
        189, 227–8, 267–8, 282–3, 284
    on *Suddenly*, 219
    wedding of, 188–9
Spiegel, Leon (Lonig), 5, 17, 48
Spiegel, Lynne Ruth Baggett, 86, 101–5,
    185, 296
    affairs of, 132, 142, 149
    age difference between SS and, 102,
        104, 339
    death and funeral of, 238–9
    decline of, 179
    divorce of SS and, 157, 178
    film contracts of, 102, 103
    in hit-and-run accident, 178–9
    SS's possessions destroyed by, 158,
        179
    SS's relationship with, 103–4, 132,
        142, 239
    talent of, 102–3
    wedding of, 105
Spiegel, Rachel "Ray" Agranovich,
    15–17, 80, 339
    abandonment by SS of, 17
    SS's relationship with, 15, 17
    SS sued for alimony by, 79–80
Spiegel, Regina Schwitz, 6–10, 52, 82,
    292
    Betty Spiegel and, 189
    death of, 315
    parents and background of, 6
    personality of, 7
    SS's relationship with, 6–7, 189,
        315

Spiegel, Sam:
actors as regarded by, 167, 195
aging and, 339–40, 340–1, 357, 375, 378
art collection of, 64, 86, 119, 158, 179, 221, 227, 359, 370, 372, 376, 383
awards received by, 177–8, 214, 215, 274–5, 277–8, 346, 375, 402–3
in Berlin (1930–1933), 25–31
birthplace of, 3–5
blacklisted screenwriters and, 2–3, 121, 159, 196, 198–9, 214, 238, 240, 242, 246, 291
as bogus diplomat and economist, 19–21
as butt of Huston's practical jokes, 93, 108–9, 112–13, 163
card-playing of, 29, 36, 38, 48, 60–1, 62–3, 64, 75, 76, 85, 87, 93, 170, 219, 240, 276, 286, 310
childhood and adolescence of, 3–12
children of, see Freedman, Alisa; Spiegel, Adam
courage of, 108, 158, 294
criminal record and incarceration of, 21–2, 44–5, 47, 58, 80–1, 133, 153
as dancer, 65, 101
deafness of, 341, 344
death and illness feared by, 7, 239, 277, 375–6
death of, 381–2
decline in reputation of, 274, 275–6, 338, 345, 361
as deliberately obscure about his origins, 3–4
deportations of, 24, 44, 45, 50, 53, 60, 80, 81–2
education of, 5, 11–12, 14, 15, 235
as emotionally detached, 15, 48, 82, 83, 184, 239, 280
escape stories of, 31, 33–4, 36–7, 38, 39, 69, 173
exaggerations and lies of, 19, 20, 22, 23, 25, 27–8, 39, 49, 51, 133, 335
family background of, 3–7
financial problems and schemes of, 16–17, 20, 22,3, 31, 35, 40, 41–4, 45, 49–50, 51, 60, 77, 80, 85, 89, 91, 3, 93–6, 119, 120, 124, 132, 140–2, 144, 148, 149, 152, 153,
154, 157, 197, 355–6, 358–9, 364, 385
first Hollywood visit of, 22–3, 25
flirting and womanizing of, 30, 40–2, 43, 47, 57, 61–2, 75, 86–7, 92, 101, 104, 132, 142, 154, 164, 165, 184, 187, 195, 260–1, 267–8, 275, 276, 277, 279, 281–3, 289–90, 295–6, 309, 315–16, 318, 335, 339–41, 352, 353, 356–7, 365, 378, 380, 382
formally admitted to U.S., 105
in friendships with women, 15, 41, 47, 61, 84, 118–19, 165, 281
glamorous lifestyle of, 31, 36, 38, 41, 43, 47, 59, 85–6, 131, 133, 152, 153–4, 158, 226, 230, 250, 262, 266, 279, 280–1, 284–8, 299, 335, 336, 340–4, 377
health of, 262, 375, 379, 381
Hollywood return of, 57–65
immigration authorities and, 19, 20–2, 24, 44, 50, 53, 58, 60, 80–1, 105
independent filmmaking and, 58, 120, 125–6, 173
Jewish identity of, 10–12, 13–14, 18, 64, 117, 336
languages known by, 5, 11, 14, 15, 50
in London (1933–1936), 39–45
manipulative and controlling behavior of, 92–3, 163, 164–5, 196, 197, 198, 201, 231, 235–6, 262, 267, 306, 324, 342–4, 348, 350, 355, 367
manners and charming gestures of, 20, 30, 42, 59, 72, 108, 130, 131, 153, 165, 171, 195, 196, 212, 254, 288–9, 306, 308, 347
as maverick and wheeler-dealer, 38, 40, 41, 47, 57, 60, 76, 179, 193, 194, 237, 240–1
in Mexico City (1938–1939), 50–3
in Palestine, 13–18, 19, 41, 154
pardon sought for, 80–2
parents of, see Spiegel, Regina Schwitz; Spiegel, Simon
in Paris (1933 and 1936–1938), 37–8, 47–50
production philosophy and style of, 35, 42, 148, 195, 197, 211 254, 267, 271, 347, 359, 369, 386

Spiegel, Sam – *cont*
  in return to Berlin, 173
  ridicule feared by, 108, 151, 164, 341,
      361, 371
  in San Francisco (1928–1930), 19–24
  self-importance of, 278
  siblings of, *see* Spiegel, Leon (Lonig);
      Spiegel, Shalom
  social ambitions and skills of, 15, 39,
      40–1, 76, 90, 98, 118, 158, 196,
      279, 281, 283, 285–7, 336, 353,
      356, 365, 377
  as tennis player, 64–5
  in UA-Krim-Benjamin negotiations,
      58, 125–7, 156
  in Vienna, 11–12, 14, 15, 33–7
  will of, 380, 381, 383–4
  wit and intelligence of, 42, 104, 141,
      274, 336, 371
  wives of, *see* Spiegel, Betty Benson;
      Spiegel, Lynne Ruth Baggett;
      Spiegel, Rachel "Ray"
      Agranovich
  Zionism of, 10–11, 14, 15, 16, 117,
      383–4
Spiegel, Sam, films of:
  cross-collateralization of, 155
  as outdated, 275–6, 319, 321, 333, 338
  quality of, 57, 315
  themes of, 34, 185, 315, 320, 321
  see also Horizon Pictures; *specific films*
Spiegel, Shalom, 5, 8, 9, 12, 52, 315
  death of, 375–6
  and SS's INS problems, 21
Spiegel, Simon,
  death of, 7, 48
  parents of, 6
  SS's relationship with, 6
  in World War I, 8
  Zionist activism of, 5
Spitz, Leo, 94
Stanton, Arthur, 141
Stark, Fran, 88
Stark, Ray, 65, 88
St. Clair, Malcolm, 73
Steiger, Rod, 162, 166
Stein, Doris, 189
Stephenson, William L., 251
Stern, Isaac, 10, 336
Stern, Philip, 186–7
Sternberg, Josef von, 23, 25, 33, 181, 182

Stevens, George, 103, 119, 183–4, 199,
      296
  Nicholas and, 323
Stevens, George, Jr., 181, 183–4, 251,
      279, 284, 323, 344
Stevens, Roy, 254, 256
St. Just, Maria, 218
Stoll, John, 153
Stone, Edward Durrell, 227
Stone, Maria, 227
Storch, Arthur, 180
Strange One, The, 198, 398–9
  as box office flop, 183
  cast of, 179–80, 181
  Columbia and, 179, 182, 183
  director of, 179–80, 181–3, 183–4
  ending of, 182
  Horizon Pictures and, 183
  locations of, 181
  plot of, 180
  producer-director on, 181–2, 183–4
  screenplay of, 180–1
  SS as producer of, 179–84
Stranger, The, 91–9, 101, 107, 397
  cast of, 91, 96, 97, 8, 99
  director of, 91, 97, 99
  financing of, 94–5
  plot of, 96
  profitability of, 98
  reviews of, 96, 98
  screenplay of, 93–6
  SS as producer of, 93–9
  Welles-SS differences over, 99
Strasberg, Lee, 182
Stravinsky, Igor, 63, 68
Streep, Meryl, 366
Streetcar Named Desire, A, 147, 158, 164
Stritch, Elaine, 184
Stromberg, Hunt, 94
Suddenly, Last Summer, 306, 399
  Academy Awards and, 229, 403
  cast and crew of, 217, 220, 222–6, 228
  Columbia and, 223, 228, 229
  credits on, 229
  director of, 220–2, 224–5, 225–6, 228,
      229, 230
  gag title of, 230
  grosses of, 229
  locations of, 221, 223, 226, 228, 229
  publicity for, 223, 228, 229
  salaries for, 223, 225

screenplay of, 218–20, 229, 230, 322
SS as producer of, 217–31
Taylor's swim suit in, 228
theme of, 217–18
Summertime, 192, 199
Sunday Times (London), 255
Supreme Film Censorship Board
(Germany), 27
Surtees, Robert, 298
Survivors, 4, 378
Suzman, Janet, 341
in *Nicholas*, 328
Swimmer, The, 400
cast of, 310–13, 314
Columbia and, 315
directors of, 310, 311, 313, 314
locations of, 311
plot of, 311
reviews of, 312–13, 314
screenplay of, 311–15
SS as executive producer of, 311–15
Sylbert, Anthea, 353, 356

Tales of Manhattan, 79, 91, 294, 373,
396–7
budget for, 70
cast of, 68, 71, 72–3, 74
director of, 71
Fox and, 68–77, 9
German Exile Cinema feel to, 72, 75
plagiarism accusations against, 51
premiere of, 75
producers of, 67–77
screenplay of, 72
success of, 75
theme of, 72
Tandy, Jessica, 231, 367
Tate, Sharon, 286
Taylor, Elizabeth, 223, 348
in *Suddenly*, 217, 222–4, 225, 226, 228,
229
Tel Aviv, 15, 16, 19
Thalberg, Irving G., 23, 49, 345, 347, 354
Thau, Benny, 110
This Is Orson Welles (Welles and
Bogdanovich), 98
Thoeren, Robert, 29, 120
Thomas, Hugh, Lord, 378, 379, 380
Thornburn, Lew, 318, 326
Thorndike, Sybil, 151
Three Episodes, 149, 152

Tijuana, Mexico, 53
Time, 229
Time of Their Lives, The, 103
Todd, Mike, 58, 59, 89, 185, 223
Todd, Mike, Jr., 89
Tokofsky, Jerry, 160–1, 277, 303, 308, 351
Tonfilm-Theater-Tanz, 36
Toth, André de, 263
Tracy, Spencer, 138, 200, 224
Transjordan, 16
Trapeze, 160
Trauner, Alexandre, 305
Treasure of the Sierra Madre, The, 105–6,
117, 130
Trivas, Victor, 93, 98
Truman, Harry S., 76, 80, 110
Trumbo, Dalton:
as blacklisted, 121. 159
as *Prowler* screenwriter, 121
Turner, Adrian, 385
Turner, Lana, 123
Turner Entertainment Group, 23
Twentieth Century-Fox, 68–77, 81, 84,
85, 99, 373
Twentieth Century-Fox International
Classics, 373

Ufa, 29, 35
Ufland, Harry, 347
Uganda, *African Queen* locations in, 133,
134
Um-El-Alek (kibbutz), 13–14
United Artists (UA), 63, 68, 143–4, 149,
153, 154–6, 160
independent filmmaking and, 58,
125–7
SS's split with, 156
*United Artists, The Company That Changed
the Film Industry* (Balio), 126
United Jewish Welfare Fund, 117–18
Universal Studios (Berlin), 24, 25–7, 63
Universal Studios (Hollywood), 24, 25–6,
58, 91, 94, 96, 98, 103, 109, 225
Unsichtbare Gegner (Invisible Opponents),
34–6, 39, 396
casting of, 34–5
French version of, 35
funding for, 34
salaries for, 35–6
SS as producer of, 35
Ustinov, Peter, 381

Variety, 215, 320
Veiller, Anthony, 85–6, 107, 115
    and *Stranger* screenplay, 93–5
Veiller, Bayard, 107, 115
Veiller, Caroline, 85–6
Velsheda (boat), 251
Venice Film Festival, 171
Vidal, Gore, 53, 187, 250–1, 337, 387
    Night of screenplay and, 306–7,
        309–10
    Suddenly screenplay and, 218–21, 229,
        230, 252, 322
Vidal, Pedro, 265
Vienna:
    claimed as SS's birthplace, 3–4
    SS's "escape" from, 5, 37–8
Vienna, University of, SS and, 11–12, 14,
    15
Viertel, Berthold, 63
Viertel, Peter, 23, 60, 63, 64, 92, 102–3,
    105, 106, 111–13, 118, 277, 281,
    204–5, 306, 346
    African Queen and, 132, 133, 134–5,
        137
    We Were Strangers screenplay and, 109
Viertel, Salka, 63
Viertel, Virginia "Jigee," 118, 132
Vilaiwan Seeboonreaung, 208
Village Voice, 347
Visconti, Luchino, 313, 320
Vorkapich, Slavko, 314
Vorkapich, Slavomir "Ed," 314

Wald, Jerry, 102
Walker, Robert, Jr., 302
Wallace, Henry, 110
Wallis, Hal B., 102
Walsh, Katherine, 295
Walter E. Heller & Co., 119
    African Queen and, 131, 135, 140, 147
Wanger, Walter, 98
Warner, Harry, 5, 124
Warner, Jack L., 5, 62, 106, 178
Warner, Sir Fred, 280
Warner, Simone, Lady, 280
Warner Bros., 58, 70, 93, 102, 104, 106,
    129, 169
Warren, Earl, 80
Washer, Ben, 19–20
Wasserman, Edie, 118, 335
Wasserman, Lew, 118, 167, 221, 335

Waters, Ethel, 74
Watnick, Joel, 178
Waxman, Franz, 50
Wayne, John, 230
Weidenfeld, George, Lord, 278–9, 365
Weisbord, Ellen, 84, 337
Weitz, Chris, 61
Weitz, John, 107
Weitz, Paul, 61
Weitz, Susan Kohner, 61–2, 84
Welles, Orson, 57, 73, 86, 8, 98, 179
    Kwai and, 98, 192
    SS's relationship with, 98, 192
    Stranger and, 91, 96, 97–9
Wenzler, Franz, 28
Wesker, Arnold, 257, 260
Westjuden, 4
We Were Strangers, 397
    anti-Communist backlash and,
        114–15
    as box office failure, 114, 115, 119
    cast of, 112, 113, 114
    Columbia and, 111–15, 332
    difficulties in making of, 112–13
    Huston's practical jokes during
        making of, 112–13
    location shooting of, 111–12
    other names for, 114
    pitched to MGM, 110
    screenwriters on, 109, 111–12, 113–14
    SS as producer of, 110–15, 248
    theme of, 112
What Makes Sammy Run? (Schulberg), 159
    United Arists acquires, 127
When I Grow Up, 143, 154, 291, 397
    United Artists acquires, 127–8
White, Michael, 343, 344, 347, 384
Whitney, John "Jock" Hay, 283
Wilcox, Herbert, 240–1
Wilder, Audrey, 172, 356
Wilder, Billy, 4–5, 9, 31, 58, 64, 90, 107,
    123, 195, 202, 227, 295, 347, 387
    art collection of, 64
    Germany fled by, 31
    misogynistic fantasy of, 61
    SS marriage telegram of, 105
    on SS's financial dealings, 44
    SS's projects with, 67, 72, 265, 378
    SS's relationship with, 29, 60, 61, 72,
        227, 250, 342, 382
    as *We Were Strangers* script doctor, 114

Wilhelm, Hans, 120
Wilkerson, Billy, 114–15
William Morris Agency, 87, 131, 171, 183
Williams, Tennessee, 164, 180, 187
  substance abuse of, 219, 230
  Suddenly and, 218, 229–30
Williamson, Pat, 386
Willingham, Calder, 180
  Kwai screenplay and, 198–9
  Strange One and, 181, 183, 198
Wilson, Michael, 292
  Lawrence screenplay and, 237, 240, 242, 245–6, 273
  Kwai screenplay and, 199, 214
Winchell, Walter, 121, 267
Winters, Shelley, 89
With Lawrence in Arabia (Thomas), 241
Witness, The, 152
Wolfit, Donald, 245
Wood, Audrey, 218
Wood, Natalie, 103
Woodward, Joanne, 166, 222
Woolf, James, *African Queen* and, 130–1, 133, 134
Woolf, Sir John, *African Queen* and, 131, 133, 134, 140, 147
Woolfenden, John, 237
World War I:
  Austro-Hungarian Empire after, 9
  Galician pogroms after, 9–10
  Spiegel family in, 7–8
World War II, 52, 57, 70

Worth, Irene, 329
Worton Hall Studios, 143
Wyler, Catherine, 61, 82, 84
Wyler, Margaret "Talli," 59, 61, 82, 356, 377
Wyler, Melanie (Wyler's daughter), 60, 71, 82, 84, 343
Wyler, Melanie (Wyler's mother), 59
Wyler, Robert, 39
Wyler, William, 29, 107, 117, 133, 191, 265, 293, 300, 306
  SS's relationship with, 59, 60, 64, 71, 72, 82, 262–3, 305, 356
Wynter, Dana, 154

Yavne Umopseah (settlement), 14
Young, Freddie "F.A.," 236, 252, 254, 325
Young, Loretta, 91, 96, 97, 99
Youngstein, Max, 64, 68, 69, 70, 77, 99, 125, 144, 356

Zanuck, Darryl F., 64, 69, 70, 88, 158, 192
Zinnemann, Fred, 103, 191, 225, 276, 293, 305, 319
Zionists, Zionism, 5, 16, 383–4
  see also Hashomer Hatzair
Zipkin, Jerry, 189
Zola, Emile, 57
Zuckmayer, Carl, 25
Zukor, Adolph, 5

THE NEW BIOGRAPHICAL DICTIONARY OF FILM

David Thomson

The New Biographical Dictionary of Film is personal, opinionated, funny, daring, provocative and passionate – the definitive movie handbook for every filmmaker and film buff.

'An undisputed classic' Gaby Wood, *Observer*

'Essential reading . . . [Thomson] demonstrates epic erudition and an equally epic sense of mischief. He worships the cinema and simultaneously sees right through its artifice and its absurdities. This in turn makes him the best sort of true believer – passionate, often smitten, yet equipped with the most deadly bullshit detector imaginable . . . one of the great individual achievements in postwar criticism' Douglas Kennedy, *Independent*

'For film fans, there is no more transcendental book . . . Thomson concludes his entry on Robert Mitchum by calling him "untouchable". He ought to know' Christopher Bray, *Sunday Times*

'One of the great reference books of all time, never mind about film' Nicholas Lezard, *Evening Standard*

'Like Kenneth Tynan or Pauline Kael, Thomson acts as a goad as much as a guide, adapting a deeply personal sensibility to a thorough-going knowledge of his field . . . [a] trenchant, funny, inspirational book' Anthony Quinn, *Guardian*

'Still the only movie book you'd want on a desert island' Tom Charity, *Time Out*

0 316 72660 5

BENEATH MULHOLLAND
Thoughts on Hollywood and Its Ghosts
David Thomson

In this superbly eclectic collection of essays, from incisive critiques of James Stewart in *Vertigo* and Jack Nicholson in *Chinatown*, inspired takes on James Dean at 50 and Tony Manero's life beyond *Saturday Night Fever*, to Hollywood's preoccupation with money, sex, death and glory, David Thomson explores the twilight zone where the illusions of the American movie business becomes reality. Blending fact with fiction, criticism with speculation, Thomson immeasurably enlarges and enriches our already undying memories of, and pleasure in, the Hollywood movie.

'Movie writing as literature . . . Thomson's writing is elegant, quirky, personal, and packed with provocative, beguiling insights' Geoff Andrew, *Time Out*

'Consistently illuminated by Thomson's obvious love of cinema and by his ability to make us look at the familiar with a fresh eye . . . It is a long while since I read with such unalloyed enjoyment a book about my profession' Bryan Forbes, *Daily Telegraph*

'Nobody else has ever written about movie deaths, and our feelings about them, with such moral insight Nicholas Lezard, *Sunday Times*

'Thomas at the height of his powers: when he unleashes cauldons of bile upon modern Hollywood, it deserves every drop' *Esquire*

'The most obvious contender for the heavyweight title of best film critic in the world' *Independent*

0 349 11147 2

ADVENTURES IN THE SCREEN TRADE

A Personal View of Hollywood

William Goldman

As befits more than twenty years in Hollywood, Oscar-winning screenwriter William Goldman's sparkling memoir is as entertaining as many of the films he helped to create. From the writer of *Butch Cassidy and the Sundance Kid*, *All the President's Men* and *Marathon Man*, *Adventures in the Screen Trade* is an intimate view of movie-making, of acting greats such as Redford, Olivier, Newman and Hoffman, and the trials and rewards of working inside the most exciting business in the world.

'The most knowledgeable book ever about the irresistible spell of the cinema. Read it'
Sunday Telegraph

'Goldman's book is the best I have ever read on Hollywood'
Daily Mail

'Fast and witty ... A brave and very funny book'
Time Out

'This is real Hollywood'
Daily Telegraph

'Irreverent, vastly entertaining ... His text studded with insider's gossip, wild anecdotes and behind-the-scenes dramas, Goldman makes enough provocative statements in every chapter to keep any reader engrossed'
Publishers Weekly

0 349 10705 X

THE BAD AND THE BEAUTIFUL

A Chronicle of Hollywood in the Fifties

Sam Kashner and Jennifer MacNair

The Bad and the Beautiful is a vivid portrait of power, fame, and sex in 1950s Hollywood, from the rise of tabloid journalism to the making of legendary film icons.

In these tantalising stories of momentous events and legendary characters, Sam Kashner and Jennifer MacNair brilliantly recreate the drama and contradictions of Hollywood's most scandalous and dynamic decade. From colourful and humorous anecdotes about iconic figures such as Lana Turner, Rock Hudson, Kim Novak and Mae West to fascinating behind-the-scenes commentary on the making of classic films, *The Bad and the Beautiful* reveals the underground history of this turbulent decade in American film.

'A wonderful compendium of sleaze and gossip, *The Bad and the Beautiful* makes clear that many of the stars were far more interesting off screen than on screen'
J. G. Ballard, *New Statesman*

'What fun . . . Hollywood half a century ago may have been what this book's authors call "the world's cruellest company town", but compared with today's computerised-effects blockbuster factor, it sure was far more entertaining'
Gerald Kaufman, *Sunday Telegraph*

'For anyone wanting to fill a gap between Friedrich's *City of Nets* and Biskind's *Easy Riders, Raging Bulls*, this will do nicely'
Scotsman

0 7515 3084 0

JAMES DEAN

Paul Alexander

No more than a promising actor with a handful of films to his name when he died in 1955, James Dean has since been elevated to an iconic status surpassed only by Elvis Presley and Marilyn Monroe. And his image – a blend of '50s cool and tough-guy charm – has been vigorously marketed in the race to cash in on a legend that, forty years later, shows no sign of abating.

But until now, no serious biography has looked beyond the studio-manufactured clichés to the volatile polarities of this complex star. Was he bisexual or gay? A neorotic con-man or a lost boy trying to find himself? And to what extent did his sexuality fire his performances?

Drawing on many new and documented sources, and featuring previously unpublished photographs, Paul Alexander's revisionist and passionate biography will explode many people's myths about a rare acting genius.

'Sensational'
Daily Express

'Vivid and readable'
Sunday Telegraph

0 7515 1282 6

Other bestselling Time Warner Paperback titles available by mail: